Advanced Applications of Generative AI and Natural Language Processing Models

Ahmed J. Obaid
University of Kufa, Iraq

Bharat Bhushan
School of Engineering and Technology, Sharda University, India

Muthmainnah S. Pdl
Universitas Al Asyariah Mandar, Indonesia

S. Suman Rajest
Dhaanish Ahmed College of Engineering, India

A volume in the Advances in Computational
Intelligence and Robotics (ACIR) Book Series

Published in the United States of America by
    IGI Global
    Engineering Science Reference (an imprint of IGI Global)
    701 E. Chocolate Avenue
    Hershey PA, USA 17033
    Tel: 717-533-8845
    Fax: 717-533-8661
    E-mail: cust@igi-global.com
    Web site: http://www.igi-global.com

Library of Congress Cataloging-in-Publication Data

Names: Obaid, Ahmed J. (Ahmed Jabbar) editor. | Bhushan, Bharat, 1989-
  editor. | Muthmainnah, Muthmainnah, 1980- editor. | Rajest, S. Suman editor.
Title: Advanced applications of generative AI and natural language
  processing models / edited by Ahmed J. Obaid, Bharat Bhushan,
  Muthmainnah Muthmainnah, S. Suman Rajest.
Description: Hershey, PA : Engineering Science Reference, [2024]. |
  Includes bibliographical references and index.
Identifiers: LCCN 2023033289 (print) | LCCN 2023033290 (ebook) | ISBN
  9798369305027 (hardcover) | ISBN 9798369305034 (paperback) | ISBN
  9798369305041 (ebook)
Subjects: LCSH: Natural language processing (Computer science)--Case
  studies.
Classification: LCC QA76.9.N38 A335 2024 (print) | LCC QA76.9.N38 (ebook)
  | DDC 006.3/5--dc23/eng/20231114
LC record available at https://lccn.loc.gov/2023033289
LC ebook record available at https://lccn.loc.gov/2023033290

This book is published in the IGI Global book series Advances in Computational Intelligence and Robotics (ACIR) (ISSN: 2327-0411; eISSN: 2327-042X).

British Cataloguing in Publication Data
A Cataloguing in Publication record for this book is available from the British Library.

All work contributed to this book is new, previously-unpublished material. The views expressed in this book are those of the authors, but not necessarily of the publisher.

For electronic access to this publication, please contact: eresources@igi-global.com.

Advances in Computational Intelligence and Robotics (ACIR) Book Series

Ivan Giannoccaro
University of Salento, Italy

ISSN:2327-0411
EISSN:2327-042X

MISSION

While intelligence is traditionally a term applied to humans and human cognition, technology has progressed in such a way to allow for the development of intelligent systems able to simulate many human traits. With this new era of simulated and artificial intelligence, much research is needed in order to continue to advance the field and also to evaluate the ethical and societal concerns of the existence of artificial life and machine learning.

The **Advances in Computational Intelligence and Robotics (ACIR) Book Series** encourages scholarly discourse on all topics pertaining to evolutionary computing, artificial life, computational intelligence, machine learning, and robotics. ACIR presents the latest research being conducted on diverse topics in intelligence technologies with the goal of advancing knowledge and applications in this rapidly evolving field.

COVERAGE

- Natural Language Processing
- Computer Vision
- Heuristics
- Pattern Recognition
- Artificial Life
- Fuzzy Systems
- Synthetic Emotions
- Machine Learning
- Brain Simulation
- Computational Intelligence

IGI Global is currently accepting manuscripts for publication within this series. To submit a proposal for a volume in this series, please contact our Acquisition Editors at Acquisitions@igi-global.com or visit: http://www.igi-global.com/publish/.

Titles in this Series

For a list of additional titles in this series, please visit: www.igi-global.com/book-series

701 East Chocolate Avenue, Hershey, PA 17033, USA
Tel: 717-533-8845 x100 • Fax: 717-533-8661
E-Mail: cust@igi-global.com • www.igi-global.com

Table of Contents

Detailed Table of Contents

This chapter provides a comprehensive overview of ChatGPT, an advanced language model that has gained significant attention in natural language processing (NLP) and artificial intelligence (AI). It outlines the underlying architecture, features, applications, benefits, and limitations of ChatGPT. The chapter highlights ChatGPT's ability to facilitate human-like conversations through its understanding and generation of human-like text. It explores its versatility across domains and languages and its potential in customer support, virtual assistants, chatbots, language translation, content generation, and creative writing. The benefits of ChatGPT, such as improved efficiency and scalability, are discussed, as are the limitations and ethical considerations. The chapter concludes with a future outlook, discussing ongoing research and the potential impact of ChatGPT on communication and human-machine interactions, emphasizing the need for responsible development and deployment of this powerful language model.

The artificial intelligence revolution as a medium and learning technology is increasingly popular in EFL. The trend of using ChatGPT is increasing. ChatGPT is a media and technology that helps in accelerating learning to help write, becomes teaching materials, learning resources with a conversation system. The purpose of this research is to find out the motivation to learn by developing the ChatGPT function as a teaching material in EFL classes among undergraduate students at universities. As an AI-based teaching material, ChatGPT was chosen with consideration of the ease of accessing fast information.

Chapter 3

Arkar Htet, Lincoln University College, Malaysia
Sui Reng Liana, Lincoln University College, Malaysia
Theingi Aung, Lincoln University College, Malaysia
Amiya Bhaumik, Lincoln University College, Malaysia

This book chapter delves into the transformative role of ChatGPT in content creation, exploring its underlying techniques, diverse applications, and associated ethical implications. The investigation spans several industries including journalism, marketing, and entertainment, demonstrating the model's adaptability and power. This comprehensive analysis not only spotlights the challenges inherent in implementing ChatGPT, but also illuminates the unique opportunities it presents. By offering a thorough examination of the current state of ChatGPT in content creation and potential future developments, this chapter contributes to the ongoing discourse surrounding AI's impact on content creation.

Chapter 4

Shwetha Baliga, R.V. College of Engineering, India
Harshith K. Murthy, R.V. College of Engineering, India
Apoorv Sadhale, R.V. College of Engineering, India
Dhruti Upadhyaya, R.V. College of Engineering, India

The discourse surrounding AI has sparked widespread discussions, with notable concerns arising from its current limitations. One such concern involves AI models struggling to understand the context of human requests, leading to unexpected or nonsensical outcomes. While instances like the conversation with ChatGPT may have garnered attention, they should be regarded as fascinating illustrations of the model's capabilities rather than indications of meaningful independence. In shaping perspectives on this subject, three noteworthy books have played a pivotal role: Superintelligence by Nick Bostrom, Life 3.0 by Max Tegmark, and A Thousand Brains by Jeff Hawkins. These books offer well-articulated and thought-provoking insights, contributing to the ongoing discussion surrounding AI. By exploring the risks, limitations, and potential implications of AI, it becomes evident that thoughtful consideration and proactive measures are necessary to navigate the evolving landscape of artificial intelligence.

Chapter 5

Manoj Kumar Pandey, Pranveer Singh Institute of Technology, Kanpur, India
Jyoti Upadhyay, G.D. Rungta College of Science and Technology, Kohka, India

This chapter provides a detailed exploration of the ChatGPT model architecture, a cutting-edge natural language processing (NLP) model that has revolutionized conversational AI. Developed by OpenAI, ChatGPT is built upon the GPT-3.5 architecture, a state-of-the-art language model. This chapter presents an extensive study about ChatGPT using a comprehensive analysis of its various recent literatures. This study also focuses on ChatGPT evolution from ELIZA to ChatGPT. In this chapter various reviews of literature, related issues, its architecture, various layers, various ChatGPT versions and its specialization, comparative study of various models, and application is presented. In order to do the comprehensive study various papers from different databases like ACM digital library, Scopus, IEEE, IGI Global, and Willey have been included for the study. Papers selected for the comprehensive study have been reviewed extensively in order to get the details and comprehended information for the readers. Various issues like security, biasness, training, misuse, etc. have been mentioned.

Chapter 6

R. Angeline, SRM Institute of Science and Technology, India
S. Aarthi, SRM Institute of Science And Technology, India
Rishabh Jain, SRM Institute of Science and Technology, India
Muzamil Faisal, SRM Institute of Science and Technology, India
Abishek Venkatesan, SRM Institute of Science and Technology, India
R. Regin, SRM Institute of Science and Technology, India

Complex material is difficult to absorb in e-learning environments, which distracts and lowers learning outcomes. This initiative proposes that consumers watch simple movies with the same topic to improve learning. Text analytics recommends tailored videos to consumers. The algorithm can make more tailored recommendations by evaluating text interaction and learning preferences. The system simplifies learning and makes material more complicated and intelligible. Visual videos aid learning by improving memory and comprehension. Analyze the data before using the advice. NLP can extract key text content and context. Review results are used to develop related topics and themes. Next, find relevant video content using keywords and keywords list. Previous video data can be used to recommend video material. Videos should simplify content to help consumers understand and remember it. Text interactions should be considered when personalising video suggestions. Create user profiles using engagement indicators like time on page, scroll depth, and click behaviour.

Chapter 7

Gagan Deep, Chitkara Business School, Chitkara University, Punjab, India
Jyoti Verma, Chitkara University, Punjab, India

This chapter explores the transformative potential of generative models for advanced text generation, focusing on leveraging structural equation modeling techniques. With the rapid advancements in deep learning and natural language processing, generative models have emerged as powerful tools for creative writing, semantic coherence, and contextual understanding. This chapter provides a comprehensive overview of the foundations, methodologies, and applications of generative models in text generation. The chapter begins with an introduction to the evolution of generative models and highlights their significance in various domains. It lays the groundwork by explaining language modeling techniques and the architectures employed in text generation using deep learning algorithms. The subsequent sections delve into the core aspects of generative models for text generation.

    S. Rubin Bose, SRM Institute of Science and Technology, India
    Raj Singh, SRM Institute of Science and Technology, India
    Yashodaye Joshi, SRM Institute of Science and Technology, India
    Ayush Marar, SRM Institute of Science and Technology, India
    R. Regin, SRM Institute of Science and Technology, India
    S. Suman Rajest, Dhaanish Ahmed College of Engineering, India

Handwritten character recognition is a challenging task in the field of image processing and pattern recognition. The success of character recognition systems depends heavily on the feature extraction methods used to represent the character images. In this chapter, the authors propose a novel feature extraction method called progressive stochastic learning (PSL) algorithm. The proposed work is based on the texture and structural features of the character image and is designed to extract discriminative features that capture the essential information of the characters. The PSL algorithm is used to classify the extracted features into their respective character classes. Experimental results demonstrate that the proposed method achieves a recognition accuracy of 92.6% for correct characters predicted and 91.3% for correct words predicted. Moreover, the proposed method outperforms several state-of-the-art methods in terms of recognition accuracy, computation time, and memory requirements.

    Chandan Kumar Behera, VIT Bhopal University, India
    D. Lakshmi, VIT Bhopal University, India
    Isha Kondurkar, VIT Bhopal University, India

NLP has witnessed a remarkable improvement in applications, from voice assistants to sentiment analysis and language translations. However, in this process, a huge amount of personal data flows through the NLP system. Over time, a variety of techniques and frameworks have been developed to ensure that NLP systems do not ignore user privacy. This chapter highlights the significance of privacy-enhancing technologies (differential privacy, secure multi-party computation, homomorphic encryption, federated learning, secure data aggregation, tokenization and anonymization) in protecting user privacy within NLP systems. Differential privacy introduces noise to query responses or statistical results to protect individual user privacy. Homomorphic encryption allows computations on encrypted data to maintain privacy. Federated learning facilitates collaborative model training without sharing data. Tokenization and anonymization preserve anonymity by replacing personal information with non-identifiable data. This chapter explores these methodologies and techniques for user privacy in NLP systems.

    Isha Kondurkar, VIT Bhopal University, India
    Akanksha Raj, VIT Bhopal University, India
    D. Lakshmi, VIT Bhopal University, India

Generative AI (GAI) and natural language processing (NLP) have emerged as the most exciting and rapidly growing fields in artificial intelligence (AI). This book chapter provides a comprehensive exploration of the advanced applications of GAI and NLP models, with a specific focus on the renowned ChatGPT model. The chapter commences by offering a concise historical overview of the development of GAI and NLP, highlighting crucial milestones and advancements in the field over the period. In order to understand the workings of the current technology sensation, we will take a brief look at the basic building blocks of GPT models, such as transformers. Subsequently, the chapter delves into the introduction of ChatGPT, presenting an extensive overview of the model, elucidating its underlying architecture, and emphasizing its unique capabilities. Furthermore, it will illustrate the training process of the GPT model followed by a fine-tuning process to deal with the current model's shortcomings.

Chapter 11

C. V. Suresh Babu, Hindustan Institute of Technolgy and Science, India
P. M. Akshara, Hindustan Institute of Technology and Science, India

The emergence of advanced NLP models, like ChatGPT and other conversational AI models, has triggered a revolutionary transformation. This chapter explores the burgeoning field of ChatGPT applications, conducting a comprehensive analysis of their impact across various domains. The chapter assesses their capabilities, challenges, and potential uses, examining the underlying architecture and training methods that enable them to generate contextually relevant and coherent responses. Ethical considerations are also addressed, encompassing concerns about bias, misinformation, and user privacy in real-world conversations. The chapter also acknowledges drawbacks, including occasional inaccuracies or sensitive content generation. In conclusion, ongoing research is vital to enhance model robustness, user experience, and ethical deployment in conversational AI. ChatGPT and similar models are poised to reshape human-machine communication, fostering dynamic, engaging, and valuable conversations.

Chapter 12

Rita Inderawati, Universitas Sriwijaya, Indonesia
Eka Apriani, Institut Agama Islam Negeri, Curup, Indonesia
Hariswan Putera Jaya, Universitas Sriwijaya, Indonesia
Kurnia Saputri, Universitas Muhammadiyah, Indonesia
Erfin Wijayanti, IAIN Fattahul Muluk Papua, Indonesia
Ifnaldi, Institut Agama Islam Negeri, Curup, Indonesia
Muthmainnah Muthmainnah, Universitas Al Asyariah Mandar, Indonesia

The purpose of this study is to determine how students might enhance their essay-writing abilities and how they respond to the essay writing GPT. Explanatory sequential research was used in this mixed method study to analyze both the qualitative and quantitative data in distinct steps. In order to conduct the study quantitatively, the researcher used 60 students who were enrolled in an undergraduate English study program at IAIN Curup, Indonesia, that included an essay writing course. With 30 students of experimental and control group. The test is validated by three experts from UIN Raden Fatah Palembang, University of Bengkulu, and UIN Fatmawati Sukarno Bengkulu. The results of this research are that GPT has no significant impact on students' essay writing skill. Experimental and control groups have almost the same score in essay writing tests. GPT has made students simpler to build the idea because they do not need to think harder like traditionally writing. Instead, the students who are in control group easier to arrange the structure of the essay as what they wanted.

Chapter 13

Aanchal Taliwal, University of Petroleum and Energy Studies, India
Mimansa Pathania, University of Petroleum and Energy Studies, India
Mitali Chugh, University of Petroleum and Energy Studies, India

Recommender systems are software tools that make recommendations based on user needs and are increasingly popular in both commercial and research settings, with various approaches being suggested for providing recommendations. To choose the appropriate algorithm, system designers must focus on specific properties of the application, such as accuracy, robustness, and scalability. Comparative studies are used to compare algorithms, and experimental settings are described. The chapter discusses the importance of understanding user acceptance of recommendations provided by recommender systems and the influence of source characteristics in human-human, human-computer, and human-recommender system interactions. This chapter contributes to the study of social commerce by assessing the effects of the social web on different stages of purchase decision making and presents a model for analyzing social commerce.

Chapter 14

S. Venkatasubramanian, Saranathan College of Engineering, India
R. Mohankumar, Saranathan College of Engineering, India

Significant challenges in the areas of energy and security persist for wireless sensor networks (WSNs). Avoiding denial-of-service assaults is a priority for safeguarding WSN networks. As open field encryption becomes the norm, conventional packet deep scan systems can no longer use open field review in layer security packets. To the existing literature evaluating the effect of deep learning algorithms on WSN lifespan, this study contributes the auto-encoder (AE) and then the bidirectional gated recurrent unit (BGRU). The learning rate of the BGRU is also chosen using the moth flame optimization technique. Learning is just one of the approaches that have emerged in response to the pressing need to distinguish between legitimate and criminal users. This chapter also demonstrated that for numerical statistical data, the sweet spot is reached when the number of records in the dataset is between three thousand and six thousand and when the percentage of overlap across categories is not less than fifty percent.

Chapter 15

Ramón Zatarain Cabada, Tecnologico Nacional de Mexico, Culiacan, Mexico
María Lucía Barrón Estrada, Tecnologico Nacional de Mexico, Culiacan, Mexico
Víctor Manuel Bátiz Beltrán, Tecnologico Nacional de Mexico, Culiacan, Mexico

The field of natural language processing (NLP) is one of the first to be addressed since artificial intelligence emerged. NLP has made remarkable advances in recent years thanks to the development of new machine learning techniques, particularly novel deep learning methods such as LSTM networks and transformers. This chapter presents an overview of how deep learning techniques have been applied to NLP in the area of affective computing. The chapter examines traditional and novel deep learning architectures developed for natural language processing (NLP) tasks. These architectures comprise recurrent neural networks (RNNs), long short-term memory (LSTM) networks, and the cutting-edge transformers. Moreover, a methodology for NLP method training and fine-tuning is presented. The chapter also integrates Python code that demonstrates two NLP case studies specializing in the educational domain for text classification and sentiment analysis. In both cases, the transformer-based machine learning model (BERT) produced the best results.

The chapter presents an innovative approach to object detection that combines the advantages of the DETR (DEtection TRansformer) and RetinaNet models and features a phoenix precision algorithm. Object tracking is a basic computer vision task for identifying and locating objects in an image. The DETR model revolutionized object detection by introducing a transformer-based architecture that eliminates the need for anchor boxes rather than maximum damping, resulting in industry-leading performance. On the other hand, RetinaNet is a popular single-stage object detection model known for its efficiency and accuracy. This chapter proposes a hybrid model that uses both DETR and RetinaNet. The transformer-based architecture of the DETR model provides an excellent understanding of the overall context and allows you to capture long-range dependencies and maintain object associations. Meanwhile, RetinaNet's pyramid array (FPN) and focus loss enable precise localization and manipulation of objects at different scales.

Physical activity helps manage weight and stay healthy. It becomes more critical during a pandemic since outside activities are restricted. Using tiny wearable sensors and cutting-edge machine intelligence to track physical activity can help fight obesity. This study introduces machine learning and wearable sensor methods to track physical activity. Daily physical activities are typically unstructured and unplanned, and sitting or standing may be more common than others (walking stairs upstairs down). No activity categorization system has examined how class imbalance affects machine learning classifier performance.

Fitness can boost cardiovascular capacity, focus, obesity prevention, and life expectancy. Dumbbells, yoga mats, and horizontal bars are used for home fitness. Home gym-goers utilise social media to learn fitness, but its effectiveness is limited.

Artificial intelligence (AI) is bringing about a revolution in the healthcare sector thanks to the growing availability of both structured and unstructured data, as well as the rapid advancement of analytical methodologies. Medical diagnosis models are essential to saving human lives; thus, we must be confident enough to treat a patient as advised by a black-box model. Concerns regarding the lack of openness and understandability, as well as potential bias in the model's predictions, are developing as AI's significance in healthcare increases. The use of neural networks as a classification method has become increasingly significant. The benefits of neural networks make it possible to classify given data effectively. This study uses an optimized generalized metric learning neural network model approach to examine a dataset on heart disorders. In the context of cardiac disease, the authors first conducted the correlation and interdependence of several medical aspects. A goal is to identify the most pertinent characteristics (an ideal reduced feature subset) for detecting heart disease.

The chapter focuses on developing a deep learning-based image classification model for fashion and apparel. With the rise of online retail services, there is a growing need for accurate and efficient apps to categorize fashion garments based on their attributes from image data. The study proposes a fine-grained deep feature expansion framework using transfer learning to address this need. The dataset consists of approximately 44,000 images of fashion apparel with six categories, including gender, subcategory, article type, base color, season, and usage. The images are preprocessed to remove corrupted images and resized to 256 by 256 pixels. The proposed framework employs pre-trained CNN models such as ResNet50 or Vgg19 for feature extraction, fine-tuning, and transfer learning. The CNN architecture consists of several layers: convolutional layers, residual blocks, max-pooling layers, and dense layers.

    Ahmad Al Yakin, Universitas Al Asyariah Mandar Sulawesi Barat, Indonesia
    Ahmed J. Obaid, University of Kufa, Iraq
    L. Abdul, Universitas Al Asyariah Mandar Sulawesi Barat, Indonesia
    Idi Warsah, Institut Agama Islam Negeri Curup, Indonesia
    Muthmainnah Muthmainnah, Universitas Al Asyariah Mandar Sulawesi Barat, Indonesia
    Ahmed A. Elngar, Beni-Suef University, Egypt

In this study, ChatGPT and students studying the sociology of education discuss the potential application of AI applications in the field of metacognitive skills. This discussion contributes to the field of artificial intelligence research from a sociological perspective to comment on the significance potential of artificial intelligence language models in the humanities. As a result of the widespread adoption of ICT for pedagogical purposes, artificial intelligence has been introduced into the classroom, such as ChatGPT. It is used in several pedagogical contexts, such as adaptive learning systems, which change lesson difficulty in response to individual student progress.

Preface

The unprecedented advancement in Generative AI and Natural Language Processing (NLP) models has ushered in a new era in artificial intelligence, fundamentally transforming the landscape of digital interaction and technology application. This transformation is underpinned by a convergence of enhanced algorithms, escalating computational power, and the availability of extensive datasets. Such a confluence has empowered these models to generate text, images, and complex code with remarkable precision and inventiveness. Central to these breakthroughs are Deep Learning techniques, especially those based on Transformer architectures, such as GPT (Generative Pre-trained Transformer) and BERT (Bidirectional Encoder Representations from Transformers). These have advanced and revolutionized the field, pushing the boundaries of what machines can understand and create. One of the foremost applications of these technologies lies in the realm of human-computer interaction. Chatbots and virtual assistants, driven by these advanced models, now offer conversations that are more natural, intuitive, and contextually relevant. This enhancement in communication has significantly improved customer service and support across various sectors, leading to more efficient and satisfactory user experiences. Generative AI has emerged as a powerful tool for artists, writers, and designers in the creative industries. It aids in generating novel ideas, composing music, scripting narratives, designing visuals, democratizing creativity, and offering new avenues for artistic expression. These models have bridged language gaps in language translation and understanding, enabling more accurate and context-aware translation services. This breakthrough is pivotal for global communication and information accessibility, easing interactions and knowledge sharing among people from diverse linguistic backgrounds.

Moreover, NLP models are crucial in sentiment analysis and social media monitoring. They provide deep insights into public opinion and emerging trends, which are invaluable for businesses, marketers, and policymakers. The field of education has also witnessed significant benefits from these technologies. Generative AI assists in creating personalized learning experiences by generating content tailored to individual learning styles and needs. It also aids educators in automating the grading process and providing constructive feedback, thereby reducing their workload and enhancing the overall educational experience for students. Such personalized and efficient approaches in education promise to reshape the future of learning and teaching. In healthcare, the impact of these models is profound. They are used to interpret clinical notes, process vast amounts of medical data, and assist in diagnostics, thus improving the efficiency and accuracy of healthcare services. In drug discovery and genomic research, their ability to analyze large datasets accelerates the pace of medical breakthroughs, leading to more effective treatments and a better understanding of complex diseases.

The applications of Generative AI and NLP extend significantly into the business realm. They enhance efficiency in various operations, such as document analysis, contract review, and automated reporting. These technologies have revolutionized marketing strategies by enabling the creation of personalized content and targeted advertising, offering new levels of customer engagement and insights into consumer behavior. In the field of cybersecurity, these models play a critical role. By analyzing patterns and anomalies in network data, they can anticipate and prevent cyber threats, enhancing digital security. They also assist in content moderation on online platforms, detecting and filtering inappropriate or harmful content to maintain a safe and secure digital environment. Generative AI and NLP advancements are not without challenges and raise critical ethical and societal questions. Privacy concerns, potential bias in AI models, and the possibility of misuse are paramount. As these technologies continue to evolve and integrate into various aspects of life, it is essential to establish robust ethical guidelines and governance frameworks. Such measures will ensure their responsible use and prevent potential negative impacts on society.

The potential applications of Generative AI and NLP are vast and still unfolding. Ongoing research and development in these fields continually push the boundaries of what these technologies can achieve. Integrating these AI models with other emerging technologies, such as quantum computing and augmented reality, promises even more groundbreaking applications. These integrations could lead to further advancements in personalized medicine, autonomous vehicles, smart cities, and more. As we venture into this AI-driven era, it is crucial to harness these technologies judiciously. Their application should aim to enhance human capabilities, foster innovation, and address some of the most pressing challenges of our times. This includes tackling climate change, improving healthcare, enhancing education, and promoting sustainable development. The ethical use of Generative AI and NLP models is not just a technical necessity but a moral imperative to ensure that the benefits of these technologies are accessible to all and used for the greater good of humanity.

ORGANIZATION OF THE BOOK

The book is organized into 20 chapters. A brief description of each of the chapters follows:

In Chapter 1, ChatGPT, a sophisticated linguistic model with NLP and AI recognition, is thoroughly explained. It describes ChatGPT's architecture, features, applications, benefits, and drawbacks. The chapter shows how ChatGPT understands and generates human-like text to assist talks. It examines its applications in customer assistance, virtual assistants, chatbots, language translation, content generation, and creative writing. While ChatGPT improves efficiency and scalability, its limitations and ethical issues are highlighted. Future research and ChatGPT's potential impact on communication and human-machine interactions are discussed in the chapter's conclusion, emphasising the necessity for responsible development and use of this powerful language model.

Chapter 2 examined Artificial intelligence is becoming a popular learning tool in EFL. The use of ChatGPT is rising. ChatGPT uses a discussion approach to accelerate learning and make writing teaching materials. This study uses ChatGPT to assess undergraduate university students' learning motivation in EFL classes. ChatGPT, an AI-based teaching tool, was chosen for its quick information availability. The research approach is a hybrid method involving questionnaires and interviews with students who learned English with ChatGPT-based materials. The student body is 350. According to 64 computer science faculty students in 2022, ChatGPT motivates university students to study English. This study emphasises ChatGPT's benefits as a teaching tool in hybrid model classes for university EFL classes.

Chapter 3 delves into the transformative role of ChatGPT in content creation, exploring its underlying techniques, diverse applications, and associated ethical implications. The investigation spans several industries, including journalism, marketing, and entertainment, demonstrating the model's adaptability and power. This comprehensive analysis not only spotlights the challenges inherent in implementing ChatGPT but also illuminates the unique opportunities it presents. By thoroughly examining the current state of ChatGPT in content creation and potential future developments, this chapter contributes to the ongoing discourse surrounding AI's impact on content creation.

Chapter 4 introduces recent conversations about AI have raised concerns about its limitations. AI models failing to grasp human demands can produce unexpected or illogical results. The interaction using ChatGPT may have received attention, but it should be seen as fascinating examples of the model's potential, not genuine independence. Three important books on this topic are "Superintelligence" by Nick Bostrom, "Life 3.0" by Max Tegmark, and "A Thousand Brains" by Jeff Hawkins. These works contribute to the AI debate with well-written, thought-provoking thoughts. Explore the hazards, limitations, and potential ramifications of AI to see that serious analysis and proactive actions are needed to manage the changing AI world.

Chapter 5 examines the ChatGPT model architecture, a revolutionary NLP model that has transformed conversational AI. ChatGPT, developed by OpenAI, uses the cutting-edge GPT-3.5 language model. This chapter analyses recent literature to study the ChatGPT. This study also examines ChatGPT's progression from ELIZA to ChatGPT. This chapter covers literature reviews, related concerns, architecture, layers, ChatGPT versions and specialisations, comparative model studies, and applications. For the complete study, publications from ACM digital library, Scopus, IEEE, IGI Global, and Willey were included. This work extensively reviews papers selected for the comprehensive analysis to provide readers with details and understandable information. Issues include security, bias, training, abuse, etc. The conclusion discusses ChatGPT difficulties and possible remedies.

In Chapter 6, e-learning systems make complex content hard to understand, reducing learning outcomes. This programme suggests watching small movies on the same topic to learn. Text analytics proposes consumer-specific videos. Evaluation of text interaction and learning preferences allows the system to customise recommendations. The system simplifies learning and makes stuff more understandable. Video aids learning by boosting memory and comprehension. Analyze data before following suggestions. The NLP can extract crucial text information and context. Review findings inspire ideas and subjects. Next, use keywords and a list to search relevant videos. Previous video data can recommend video. Videos should simplify topics for easy comprehension and recall. Personalizing video suggestions should consider text interactions. Utilize engagement indicators like page time, scroll depth, and click activity to characterise users. User learning interests and preferences can be utilised to personalise recommendations. Last, integrate the app with the e-learning system. As people read, the technology recommends videos to improve learning. Feedback and improvement are possible with e-learning integration. Thus, our initiative suggests simple videos with complex content to aid learning. Text analytics and customisation generate intriguing video suggestions. The technology could simplify complex material and change how customers utilise learning and e-learning systems.

Chapter 7 uses structural equation modelling to demonstrate how generative models can alter advanced text generation. Given the rapid advances in deep learning and natural language processing, generative models are useful tools for creative writing, semantic coherence, and contextual understanding. This chapter covers the fundamentals, methods, and applications of generative models in text generation. The chapter introduces generative model evolution and its importance in numerous fields. It introduces language modelling and deep learning text creation architectures. Generative text generation models are explained in the following sections. Chapter discusses domain-specific text production utilising pre-trained language models and fine-tuning strategies, emphasising contextual knowledge. It also explores semantic coherence and contextual relevance methods for more coherent and accurate text production. Beyond sentences, the chapter explores storey generation. Generative models can be used to generate characters, plots, and add emotions and originality to text, creating compelling stories. Multimodal text generation, which incorporates visual and audio signals, is discussed in the chapter. It covers image captioning, description generation, and text generation from audio and video inputs, increasing text generation. Evaluation and improvement of generative models are key in this chapter. It covers text generation quality measures, bias detection and mitigation, and reinforcement learning and adversarial training to improve model performance. Text generation ethical issues like disinformation and bias are addressed in the chapter. It stresses ethical use of generative models.

Chapter 8 develops that handwritten character identification is difficult in image and pattern processing. Feature extraction approaches for character images are crucial to character recognition systems. This study introduces the Progressive Stochastic Learning (PSL) algorithm for feature extraction. The proposed technique extracts discriminative elements from character images' texture and structure to capture crucial character information. The PSL algorithm classifies extracted features into character classes. The proposed technique accurately predicts 92.6 percent of letters and 91.3 percent of sentences in experiments. Furthermore, the suggested method surpasses various state-of-the-art algorithms in recognition accuracy, computation time, and memory needs. The proposed technology works well for real-time applications in postal automation, bank cheque processing, and document digitization.

In Chapter 9, voice assistants, sentiment analysis, and language translations have improved NLP applications. This method passes a lot of personal data through the NLP system. Various methods and frameworks have been developed to ensure NLP systems respect user privacy. This study discusses how differential privacy, secure multi-party computation, homomorphic encryption, federated learning, secure data aggregation, tokenization, and anonymization preserve user privacy in NLP systems. To safeguard user privacy, differential privacy adds noise to query responses or statistical results. Computations on encrypted data are private with homomorphic encryption. Fedlearning allows collaborative model training without data exchange. Tokenization and anonymization replace personal data with non-identifiable data. This study examines NLP user privacy methods.

Chapter 10 addresses NLP and Generative AI (GAI) are the most promising and fast-growing AI areas (AI). The ChatGPT model is used to demonstrate advanced GAI and NLP model applications in this chapter. The chapter begins with a brief history of GAI and NLP, outlining key milestones and advances. To comprehend the contemporary technology experience, we shall briefly look into GPT model building blocks such transformers. The chapter next introduces ChatGPT, explaining its model, architecture, and special characteristics. It will also show the GPT model's training and fine-tuning to fix its flaws.

In Chapter 11, advanced NLP models like ChatGPT and conversational AI models have revolutionised NLP. This chapter analyses ChatGPT applications' influence across disciplines in the growing field. The chapter evaluates their capabilities, limitations, and possible uses, exploring their architecture and training methods to develop contextually relevant and coherent replies. The ethics of partiality, inaccuracy, and user privacy in real-world exchanges are also addressed. The chapter also addresses weaknesses like errors and sensitive content production. In conclusion, conversational AI model robustness, user experience, and ethical deployment require ongoing research. ChatGPT and similar technologies will transform human-machine communication into dynamic, engaging, and valuable interactions.

Chapter 12 examines how students react to the Essay Writing GPT and how they might improve their essay-writing skills. This mixed-method study analysed qualitative and quantitative data sequentially using explicatory sequential research. The researcher used 60 undergraduate English students at IAIN Curup, Indonesia, including an essay writing course, with 30 in the experimental and control groups to conduct the study quantitatively. Three specialists from UIN Raden Fatah Palembang, University of Bengkulu, and UIN Fatmawati Sukarno Bengkulu validate the test. This study reveals that GPT does not improve pupils' essay-writing. The experimental and control groups scored similarly on essay writing tests. GPT makes it easy for children to generate thoughts because it requires less thought than traditional writing. The control group students made essay structure easy to arrange.

Chapter 13 classifies in commercial and research environments; recommender systems are becoming more prominent. They produce recommendations based on user demands using various methods. System designers must consider application qualities including accuracy, robustness, and scalability while choosing an algorithm. Comparative studies compare algorithms and describe experimental situations. Understanding user acceptability of recommender system recommendations and source characteristics in human-human, human-computer, and human-recommender system interactions are discussed in the chapter. This chapter examines how the social web affects buying decision-making at different phases. An analysis model for social commerce is presented.

In Chapter 14, wireless sensor networks face energy and security issues (WSNs). A key for WSN network security is preventing DoS attacks. Traditional packet deep scan systems cannot leverage open field review in layer security packets when open field encryption becomes the standard. This paper adds the Auto-encoder (AE) and Bidirectional Gated Recurrent Unit to the literature on deep learning algorithms and WSN longevity (BGRU). Moth flame optimization selects the BGRU learning rate. In response to the necessity to identify legal and illicit users, learning has emerged. This article showed that numerical statistical data is best when the dataset has three to six thousand records and the amount of overlap between categories is at least 50%.

Chapter 15 discusses Natural Language Processing (NLP) was one of the first AI fields to be studied. New machine learning approaches, especially deep learning methods like LSTM networks and Transformers, have advanced NLP significantly. This chapter describes how deep learning has been applied to Affective Computing NLP. The chapter compares classic and innovative deep learning architectures for NLP. These architectures use RNNs, LSTMs, and cutting-edge Transformers. Additionally, an NLP approach training and fine-tuning procedure is offered. The chapter includes Python code for two educational text classification and sentiment analysis NLP case studies. Both times, the Transformer-based machine learning model (BERT) performed better.

Chapter 16 introduces a novel object detection method that blends DETR and RetinaNet models with a Phoenix Precision algorithm. Object tracking is a basic computer vision job for locating things in images. By eliminating anchor boxes and maximising dampening with a transformer-based architecture, the DETR model revolutionised object detection with industry-leading performance. However, RetinaNet is a common single-stage object detection model with high efficiency and accuracy. This article offers a DETR-RetinaNet hybrid model. The DETR model's transformer-based architecture helps you grasp the context, capture long-range dependencies, and manage object linkages. RetinaNet's Pyramid Array (FPN) and focus loss allow precise localization and manipulation of objects at different scales. We use DETR and RetinaNet designs in distinct object identification pipeline stages to leverage their strengths. RetinaNet and FPN are initialised with pre-trained DETR weights. This setup lets the model use DETR's advanced features to improve recognition.

Chapter 17 helps manage weight and stay healthy. It's more important during a pandemic when outside activities are limited. Tiny wearable sensors and advanced machine intelligence can reduce obesity by tracking physical activity. This project tracks physical activity with machine learning and wearable sensors. Most daily physical activities are unstructured and unplanned, and sitting or standing may be more usual (walking stairs upstairs down). No activity categorization system has studied class imbalance and machine learning classifier performance. People care about fitness. Fitness improves cardiovascular capacity, attention, obesity prevention, and lifespan. Dumbbells, yoga mats, and horizontal bars are home workout tools. People love it because they can escape. Social media helps home gym-goers learn fitness, but not much. An affordable, rapid, precise fitness detection tool can avoid accidents and raise fitness awareness. Integrated metric transfer learning performed best in experiments. Precision will be excellent.

In Chapter 18, AI is transforming healthcare because to the increased availability of structured and unstructured data and the rapid progress of analytical methods. Medical diagnosis models save lives, so we must be confident enough to treat patients as black-box models advise. As AI becomes more important in healthcare, concerns about the model's bias and lack of transparency are growing. The usage of neural networks for categorization is growing. Neural networks enable data classification. This study analyses heart disease data using an optimal generalised metric learning neural network model. In heart illness, we initially examined medical correlations and interdependencies. A filter-based feature selection method was applied to both datasets to obtain the most relevant characteristics (an optimum reduced feature subset) for heart disease detection. Complete and reduced feature subsets were needed for experimentation analysis of deep-learning categorization models. The trained classifiers were assessed using the ROC curve and F-Score. Model classification findings showed that significant features greatly affected accuracy. The classification models performed better with fewer features and less training time than models trained on the whole feature set.

Chapter 19 focuses on developing a deep learning-based image classification model for fashion and apparel. Online retail is expanding, so reliable and efficient software to identify fashion clothes from image data are needed. To meet this demand, the paper presents transfer learning-based fine-grained deep feature extension. The dataset includes 44,000 fashion garment photos categorised by gender, subcategory, product kind, base colour, season, and usage. Images are cleaned and reduced to 256 by 256 pixels. Feature extraction, fine-tuning, and transfer learning are done using pre-trained CNN models like ResNet50 or Vgg19. Convolutional, residual, max-pooling, and dense layers make up the CNN architecture. Each residual block expands feature maps from previous layers using convolutional filters, enabling deep feature expansion. Model compilation with categorical cross-entropy loss function, Adam optimizer, and accuracy metric occurs during training. The fit approach trains the model on the training set using training data, validation data, and callbacks for early halting and preserving the best weights. The suggested system improves product recommendations and personalised shopping to boost consumer satisfaction. This work improves fashion and garment image classification methods.

Chapter 20 develops ChatGPT and sociology of education students debate AI applications in metacognitive skills in this study note. Sociological artificial intelligence research benefits from this conversation. To discuss AI language models' humanities potential. Artificial intelligence like ChatGPT has entered the classroom because of the increased use of ICT for pedagogy. It is utilised in adaptive learning systems that adjust course difficulty based on student progress. The literature on ChatGPT in the classroom is reviewed in this paper. This study examines if OpenAI ChatGPT can improve university undergraduates' metacognition. Quantitative research was conducted on 350 undergraduate students utilising purposive random sampling to select 15 individuals who had utilised ChatGPT during learning. Surveys and observations were analysed using SPSS version 26. ChatGPT improved students' metacognition in planning, monitoring, and assessing learning. Students were more active when learning critical thinking, problem-solving, discussion, analysis, self-evaluation, and knowledge and information connections. The ChatGPT tool helps undergraduates learn by answering information searches quickly and in real time. Best techniques include tying ChatGPT replies to scientific literature and lecturers' ability to adapt class activities to learning needs, according to the study.

Ahmed J. Obaid
University of Kufa, Iraq

Bharat Bhushan
School of Engineering and Technology, Sharda University, India

S. Muthmainnah
Universitas Al Asyariah Mandar, Indonesia

S. Suman Rajest
Dhaanish Ahmed College of Engineering, India

Chapter 1
Introduction to ChatGPT

Wasswa Shafik
https://orcid.org/0000-0002-9320-3186
Dig Connectivity Research Laboratory (DCRLab), Kampala, Uganda

ABSTRACT

This chapter provides a comprehensive overview of ChatGPT, an advanced language model that has gained significant attention in natural language processing (NLP) and artificial intelligence (AI). It outlines the underlying architecture, features, applications, benefits, and limitations of ChatGPT. The chapter highlights ChatGPT's ability to facilitate human-like conversations through its understanding and generation of human-like text. It explores its versatility across domains and languages and its potential in customer support, virtual assistants, chatbots, language translation, content generation, and creative writing. The benefits of ChatGPT, such as improved efficiency and scalability, are discussed, as are the limitations and ethical considerations. The chapter concludes with a future outlook, discussing ongoing research and the potential impact of ChatGPT on communication and human-machine interactions, emphasizing the need for responsible development and deployment of this powerful language model.

INTRODUCTION

ChatGPT, an advanced language model, has become a powerful tool in NLP and AI. Built upon OpenAI's GPT-3 architecture foundations, ChatGPT has garnered significant attention for its ability to facilitate human-like conversations (Gabbiadini et al., 2023). It represents an essential milestone in the field, enabling sophisticated interactions between humans and machines. At its core, ChatGPT is designed to understand and generate human-like text responses (McGee, 2023). ChatGPT has acquired a deep understanding of language patterns, semantics, and context through extensive training on vast data. Its underlying architecture encompasses state-of-the-art deep learning (DL) techniques, allowing it to process and generate coherent and contextually appropriate responses (Dida et al., 2023).

ChatGPT's proficiency in engaging users in dynamic conversations across various topics and domains sets it apart. It exhibits an impressive capability to comprehend the nuances of human communication, offering responses that often mirror those of a human interlocutor. This versatility enables ChatGPT to be applied in various real-world scenarios, from customer support and virtual assistants to chatbots, lan-

DOI: 10.4018/979-8-3693-0502-7.ch001

guage translation, content generation, and even creative writing (Quinio & Bidan, 2023). By leveraging large-scale datasets and employing deep learning techniques, ChatGPT can understand complex queries, interpret context, and generate contextually relevant and coherent responses. Its ability to comprehend the semantics and subtleties of human language enables it to provide accurate and insightful information, making it a valuable tool for users seeking assistance, information, or simply engaging in meaningful conversations (Haman & Školník, 2023).

However, as with any sophisticated language model, ChatGPT has limitations and challenges to address. Bias, both inherent in the training data and potentially learned during training, is a concern that requires careful consideration (Cotton et al., 2023). Ethical considerations surrounding the responsible development and deployment of ChatGPT are crucial to mitigating potential risks, such as spreading misinformation or using technology. Nevertheless, the potential of ChatGPT is immense. Ongoing research and advancements continue to push the boundaries of its capabilities (Regalia, 2023). The future holds great promise for further improvements in ChatGPT technology, which has the potential to revolutionize human-computer interactions and reshape the way we communicate and collaborate with machines (Eke, 2023).

As researchers and developers continue to explore the possibilities offered by ChatGPT, it is clear that this powerful language model has opened new avenues for human-machine interactions. The ability of ChatGPT to understand and generate human-like text has implications across various industries and domains (Eke, 2023). ChatGPT can provide efficient and personalized assistance in customer support by handling common inquiries and troubleshooting conversationally. Its versatility allows it to adapt to different industries and customer needs, enhancing user experiences and reducing the burden on human support teams (Lieberman, 2023).

Virtual assistants powered by ChatGPT offer a seamless and interactive experience, enabling users to engage in natural language conversations to complete tasks, access information, or perform various functions. ChatGPT can provide relevant and accurate responses by understanding user intent and context, making virtual assistant applications more intuitive and user-friendly (Polonsky & Rotman, 2023). Chatbots, another area where ChatGPT excels, can be deployed in diverse settings, such as websites, messaging platforms, and mobile applications. These chatbots can handle user inquiries, provide recommendations, or engage users in interactive conversations, enhancing customer engagement and satisfaction (Shah, 2023).

Language translation is another domain where ChatGPT can prove instrumental. Its ability to understand and generate text in multiple languages can facilitate real-time translation, breaking down language barriers and enabling seamless communication across different cultures and regions. Content generation and creative writing are additional areas where ChatGPT can be leveraged. It can assist writers, bloggers, and content creators by providing suggestions, generating outlines, or co-authoring pieces, expanding creative possibilities, and streamlining content creation(Liu et al., 2023). While ChatGPT undoubtedly offers numerous benefits and opportunities, it is essential to remain cognizant of the ethical considerations surrounding its use. Safeguarding against biases, ensuring transparency, and promoting responsible development and deployment is crucial to maximizing the positive impact of ChatGPT while minimizing potential risks (Yang, 2023).

ChatGPT serves a vital purpose by enabling human-like conversations by bridging the gap between machines and humans. Its sophisticated language processing capabilities allow it to understand and generate responses that closely resemble those of a human interlocutor. This enables users to engage in natural, dynamic, and contextually relevant conversations with the model (Rozado, 2023). ChatGPT aims to enhance human-machine interactions by providing a more intuitive and seamless conversational experience. ChatGPT fosters a sense of familiarity and engagement by mimicking human-like responses, making interactions more relatable and comfortable for users. This improves user satisfaction and encourages more open and meaningful communication (Biswas, 2023b); the application landscape is presented in Figure 1.

Figure 1. Generative AI application landscape

Another critical purpose of ChatGPT is to provide efficient and effective support in various domains. By understanding user queries and providing accurate and helpful responses, ChatGPT can act as a virtual assistant or customer support agent, addressing user needs and inquiries in a conversational manner (Gabbiadini et al., 2023). This helps streamline communication processes, reduce wait times, and provide timely assistance. Moreover, ChatGPT's purpose extends to language translation and content generation. Its ability to comprehend and generate text in different languages enables seamless communication across linguistic barriers (McGee, 2023). This facilitates global connectivity and promotes cultural exchange. Additionally, ChatGPT can assist writers and content creators in generating content by offering suggestions, expanding creative possibilities, and improving productivity (Quinio & Bidan, 2023).

Therefore, ChatGPT represents a significant leap forward in NLP, demonstrating the remarkable capabilities of language models. Its power lies in its ability to understand and generate human-like text, opening up a world of possibilities in customer support, virtual assistants, chatbots, language translation, content generation, and creative writing (Haman & Školník, 2023). With continued research and responsible development, ChatGPT has the potential to transform human-machine interactions and reshape the way we communicate in the digital age.

NLP and AI play crucial roles in the development of ChatGPT. NLP enables machines to understand, interpret, and generate human language, allowing ChatGPT to effectively comprehend and respond to user inputs (Cotton et al., 2023). Through advanced NLP techniques such as syntactic and semantic analysis, named entity recognition, and sentiment analysis, ChatGPT can extract meaning and context from user queries, enabling more accurate and contextually relevant responses. AI serves as the foundation of ChatGPT, providing the underlying technology and algorithms that enable its sophisticated language processing capabilities (Regalia, 2023). AI allows ChatGPT to learn from vast training data, understand complex language patterns, and generate human-like responses.

Deep learning techniques, for example recurrent neural networks and transformers, empower ChatGPT to capture long-term dependencies and model the intricacies of language, contributing to its ability to engage in human-like conversations (Shah, 2023). The importance of NLP and AI in developing ChatGPT lies in their transformative potential for human-computer interactions. By leveraging these technologies, ChatGPT brings us closer to the vision of machines that can understand, communicate, and assist us more naturally and intuitively (Yang, 2023). The advancements in NLP and AI facilitate the development of competent language models like ChatGPT, enabling more seamless communication, personalized assistance, and efficient information retrieval, ultimately enhancing user experiences and opening up new frontiers in human-machine collaboration (Biswas, 2023b).

The Contributions of the Chapter

- The chapter presents an overview and proper understanding of ChatGPT, including the underlying architecture and technology behind ChatGPT, discusses the training process and large-scale datasets, and explains how ChatGPT utilizes deep learning techniques to generate responses.
- It presents the features and capabilities of ChatGPT, outlining the key features and capabilities of ChatGPT, discussing its ability to understand and generate human-like text, and highlighting its versatility in different domains and languages.
- Explores the various applications of ChatGPT in real-world scenarios, discusses its potential in customer support, virtual assistants, and chatbots, and discusses its usefulness in language translation, content generation, and creative writing.
- Illustrates the advantages of using ChatGPT, such as improved efficiency and scalability. Addresses the limitations and challenges, including biases and ethical concerns, and discusses ongoing research and efforts to address these limitations.
- Examines the ethical implications of deploying ChatGPT, presents potential risks such as misuse or spreading misinformation, and highlights the importance of responsible development and deployment.
- Explores the future prospects and advancements in ChatGPT technology. Discusses ongoing research and areas for improvement.
- Predicts the potential impact of ChatGPT on communication and human-machine interactions and summarizes the key insights and lessons from the chapter.

The Organization of the Chapter

The remainder of this chapter is arranged into eight sections: Section 1.2 presents an understanding of ChatGPT, entailing a description of the underlying architecture and technology behind ChatGPT. Discuss the training process, the use of large-scale datasets, and an explanation of how ChatGPT utilizes deep learning techniques to generate responses. Section 1.3 presents features and capabilities, including an outline of the key features and capabilities of ChatGPT. Discuss its ability to understand and develop human-like text and highlight its versatility in different domains and languages. Section 1.4 presents the applications of ChatGPT, exploring the various applications of ChatGPT in real-world scenarios.

Discuss its potential in customer support, virtual assistants, and chatbots and its usefulness in language translation, content generation, and creative writing. Section 1.5 presents the benefits and limitations, illustrating the advantages of using ChatGPT, such as improved efficiency and scalability. Addressing the constraints and challenges, including biases and ethical concerns, and discussing ongoing research and efforts to address these limitations, Section 1.6 demonstrates the ethical considerations of ChatGPT by examining the ethical implications of deploying ChatGPT, presenting potential risks such as misuse or spreading of misinformation, and highlighting the importance of responsible development and deployment. Section 1.7 offers future research directions to explore the prospects and advancements in ChatGPT technology, discussing ongoing research and areas for improvement and predicting the potential impact of ChatGPT on communication and human-machine interactions. Section 1.8 holds some lessons learned from the chapter and the conclusion.

UNDERSTANDING CHATGPT

The underlying architecture of ChatGPT is based on OpenAI's Generative Pre-trained Transformer (GPT) series, specifically the GPT-3 architecture. GPT-3 is a state-of-the-art language model with a transformer-based neural network architecture (Benoit, 2023). Transformers are a deep learning model that revolutionized NLP tasks. They excel at capturing long-range dependencies and understanding contextual relationships in a text. The transformer architecture consists of an encoder-decoder framework (Lin, 2023). Still, in the case of ChatGPT, only the encoder part is used since it focuses on generating responses based on user input.

The architecture of ChatGPT consists of multiple layers of self-attention mechanisms. Self-attention allows the model to weigh the importance of different words in a sentence based on their relevance to each other (Bishop, 2023). This attention mechanism enables the model to capture the context and dependencies between words, resulting in more coherent and contextually relevant responses. ChatGPT is pre-trained on massive amounts of text data from the internet to learn the statistical patterns and relationships within language (Biswas, 2023b). This pre-training phase helps the model develop a strong understanding of grammar, syntax, and general knowledge. The training process involves predicting the next word in a sentence given the previous words, which helps the model learn the probability distribution of words and their likely context (Lin, 2023).

After pre-training, ChatGPT undergoes fine-tuning, where it is further trained on specific datasets with supervised learning techniques. This fine-tuning stage enables the model to adapt to specific tasks or domains and refine its more accurate and relevant responses (Nastasi et al., 2023). The technology behind ChatGPT heavily relies on deep learning and neural network architectures. The model utilizes vast amounts of computational resources to process and generate text. Graphics Processing Unit (GPU) clusters are commonly employed to accelerate the training and inference processes, as they can efficiently handle the massive computations required by the transformer architecture (Bommineni et al., 2023).

The underlying technology behind ChatGPT also includes using large-scale datasets during the pre-training phase. These datasets contain diverse internet sources, exposing the model to various language patterns and contexts. By training on such data, ChatGPT learns to generalize and understand the statistical regularities of human language (Mattas, 2023). During the pre-training process, ChatGPT employs a technique called unsupervised learning. This means the model does not have explicit labels or annotations to guide its learning. Instead, it learns by predicting the next word in a sequence based on the patterns observed in the training data. This self-supervised learning enables ChatGPT to capture the statistical properties of language, including grammar, syntax, and semantics (Bessette, 2023).

ChatGPT utilizes a decoding mechanism that considers the encoded input and generates coherent and contextually appropriate text to create responses. The model's training enables it to develop text that aligns with the patterns and structures it has learned during pre-training (Skjuve, 2023). It is important to note that while ChatGPT can generate impressive responses, it does not possess proper understanding or consciousness. Its responses are based on statistical patterns learned from the training data and are not a result of higher-level reasoning or comprehension (Biswas, 2023c). Therefore, ChatGPT utilizes the GPT-3 architecture based on transformer neural networks. It leverages self-attention mechanisms to capture contextual relationships in a text. The model undergoes pre-training and fine-tuning processes to learn from large-scale datasets and adapt to specific tasks (Chinonso et al., 2023). The underlying technology relies on deep learning and requires significant computational resources, often utilizing GPU clusters for efficient processing.

Furthermore, the underlying architecture and technology of ChatGPT allow for a high degree of flexibility and adaptability. The model can be fine-tuned for specific datasets or domains, enabling it to specialize in particular tasks or contexts. This fine-tuning process involves training the model on labeled data, where human-generated responses serve as target outputs. By fine-tuning, ChatGPT can learn to provide more accurate and task-specific responses, enhancing its performance in specific applications (Shue et al., 2023). The technology behind ChatGPT also incorporates techniques to manage and mitigate biases in its responses. Biases in language models can arise from the tendencies present in the training data. OpenAI tries to identify and address biases during training, encouragingngoing research and development to improve fairness and reduce biases in the model's outputs (Macey-Dare, 2023). Ethical considerations surrounding bias and fairness are critical in ensuring the responsible use and deployment of ChatGPT.

As a sophisticated language model, ChatGPT requires substantial computational resources for training and inference. The training process involves massive parallel computing utilizing robust hardware infrastructure, such as GPUs or specialized DL accelerators. This computational intensity allows for efficient processing and training of the model on vast amounts of data, enabling it to capture human language's complex patterns and nuances (Shafik, 2024). OpenAI continually invests in research and development to advance the underlying technology of ChatGPT. Ongoing improvements focus on enhancing the model's understanding, generating more accurate and context-aware responses, and addressing limitations and challenges such as biases and ethical considerations (Sakirin & Ben Said, 2023). OpenAI also actively seeks user feedback and conducts research collaborations to gather insights and make iterative updates to the model's capabilities and performance, as demonstrated in Figure 2.

Therefore, the underlying architecture and technology behind ChatGPT encompass transformers, self-attention mechanisms, large-scale datasets, pre-training, fine-tuning, bias mitigation strategies, and powerful computational resources (Nastasi et al., 2023). These components work together to empower ChatGPT to understand and generate human-like text. At the same time, ongoing research and development strive to improve the model's capabilities and address ethical concerns, ensuring the responsible and effective deployment of ChatGPT in various applications (Bommineni et al., 2023).

Figure 2. ChatGPT application

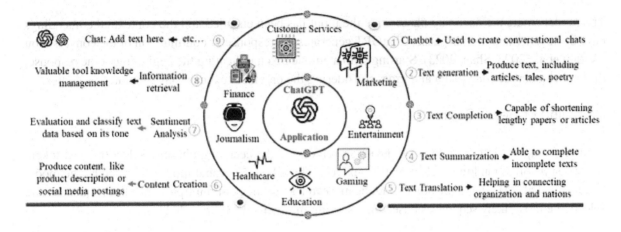

ChatGPT Utilizes Deep Learning Techniques to Generate Responses

ChatGPT utilizes DL techniques to generate responses by leveraging its underlying architecture based on transformer neural networks. Within this subsection, we explore the step-by-step process by which ChatGPT utilizes DL to generate responses.

Input Encoding

When a user inputs a query or prompt, ChatGPT first encodes the input text. This encoding transforms the text into a numerical representation that the neural network can process (Gabbiadini et al., 2023). The input encoding typically involves tokenization, where the text is split into smaller units (for example, words or subwords) and assigned unique numerical identifiers (McGee, 2023).

Self-Attention Mechanism

The encoded input is then passed through multiple layers of self-attention mechanisms. Self-attention allows the model to weigh the importance of different words or tokens in the input sequence based on their relevance to each other (Haman & Školník, 2023; Quinio & Bidan, 2023). It helps capture the context and dependencies between words, enabling the model to understand the relationships and meaning within the input.

Contextual Embeddings

The model generates contextual embeddings for each token as the input progresses through the self-attention layers. These embeddings represent a rich token representation that considers its surrounding context in the input sequence (Haman & Školník, 2023). Contextual embeddings capture semantic and syntactic information, enabling the model to understand the meaning and nuances of the text (Regalia, 2023).

Decoding and Language Generation

The model enters the decoding phase once the input has been encoded and the contextual embeddings have been generated. In this phase, ChatGPT generates the response or continuation of the conversation (Antaki et al., 2023; Shah, 2023). Starting with a unique token indicating the beginning of the response, the model generates one token at a time, considering the previous tokens it has generated as context.

Sampling or Beam Search

ChatGPT employs either sampling or beam search during the decoding phase to select the next token. Sampling involves randomly selecting the next token based on the probabilities generated by the model (Zielinski et al., 2023). On the other hand, beam search keeps track of multiple candidate sequences and selects the most likely sequences based on a scoring mechanism (Biswas, 2023a).

Iterative Generation

The process of decoding and generating tokens continues until a specified maximum length is reached or a unique token indicating the end of the response is generated. The generated sequence represents the model's response to the user's input. DL techniques, such as the use of transformer neural networks, enable ChatGPT to capture complex language patterns and dependencies (Balas & Ing, 2023). The self-attention mechanism allows the model to understand the context and relationships within the input text. By iteratively decoding and generating tokens based on the learned patterns and probabilities, ChatGPT generates coherent and contextually appropriate responses. It is important to note that the training process significantly enables ChatGPT to generate meaningful responses (Adetayo, 2023). During training, the model learns from large-scale datasets, predicting the next word given the previous words. This process helps the model learn the statistical properties of language, including grammar, semantics, and context, which contribute to its ability to generate human-like responses (Nisar & Aslam, 2023).

CHATGPT FEATURES AND CAPABILITIES

ChatGPT exhibits various features and capabilities, making it a powerful language model for natural conversations with the current development limitation.

Language Understanding

ChatGPT demonstrates a remarkable ability to understand and interpret human language. It can comprehend user queries' semantics, syntax, and contextual nuances, generating meaningful and contextually relevant responses (Analytica, 2023b). This language understanding capability allows more effective communication between users and the model.

Context Sensitivity

ChatGPT is context-sensitive, meaning it can retain and utilize information from previous parts of the conversation. This enables it to provide consistent and coherent responses to the ongoing discussion (Magazine & 2023, 2023). By considering the conversation history, ChatGPT can maintain continuity and produce responses that align with the current context.

Domain Versatility

ChatGPT exhibits versatility across different domains and topics. It has been trained on various internet texts, exposing it to diverse subjects (Analytica, 2023a). This allows ChatGPT to engage in conversations spanning various fields, including science, technology, entertainment, and more. Its domain versatility makes it adaptable to different user needs and contexts (Giunti et al., 2023).

Multilingual Support

ChatGPT is designed to handle text inputs and generate responses in multiple languages. It has been trained on data from various languages, enabling it to understand and generate text in different linguistic contexts (Gunawan, 2023). This multilingual support fosters cross-cultural communication and extends the reach and usability of ChatGPT in global contexts (Perkins, 2023).

Creative Text Generation

Beyond factual responses, ChatGPT can exhibit creativity in text generation. It can produce imaginative and novel responses, offer suggestions, and assist in creative writing (HS Kumar, 2023). This feature makes ChatGPT a valuable tool for content creators, writers, and individuals seeking inspiration or creative input.

Answering Questions and Providing Information

ChatGPT excels in answering questions and providing information based on its training and knowledge. Users can ask factual queries or seek explanations on various topics, and ChatGPT can generate informative and accurate responses, drawing from its pre-trained knowledge base (Mijwil et al., 2023).

Assistance and Suggestions

ChatGPT can serve as a virtual assistant by providing users with guidance, recommendations, and suggestions (Dida et al., 2023). It can help with planning, problem-solving, brainstorming ideas, or offering advice in various domains. ChatGPT's assistance feature supports users in decision-making and enhances their productivity (Haman & Školník, 2023).

Adaptability Through Fine-Tuning

ChatGPT's capabilities can be further enhanced through fine-tuning. Training the model on specific datasets or domains can be tailored to provide more accurate and domain-specific responses (Mijwil et al., 2023). This adaptability allows for the customization and application of ChatGPT in specialized contexts. ChatGPT's features and capabilities encompass strong language understanding, context sensitivity, versatility across domains, multilingual support, creative text generation, question answering, assistance, and adaptability through fine-tuning (Halloran et al., 2023). These capabilities enable ChatGPT to engage in human-like conversations, provide valuable information, assist users in various tasks, and adapt to different contexts, making it an advantageous and versatile language model (Shaji George et al., 2023).

DIFFERENT DOMAINS AND LANGUAGES OFFER VERSATILITY

ChatGPT exhibits impressive versatility across different domains and languages, making it a highly adaptable language model. Within this subsection, we explore its versatility in more detail:

Multidomain Understanding

ChatGPT has been trained on vast internet text, allowing it to comprehend and generate responses across various domains (Alshurafat, 2023). It can handle conversations about science, technology, literature, history, entertainment, and many other fields. This versatility enables ChatGPT to assist users and provide valuable insights into diverse subjects (AlAfnan et al., 2023).

Technical Expertise

In addition to general domains, ChatGPT also demonstrates proficiency in technical and specialized areas. It can engage in conversations related to programming, mathematics, engineering, and other technical subjects (Shafik, 2023). This capability makes ChatGPT a valuable resource for developers, researchers, and individuals seeking technical information or guidance.

Multilingual Communication

ChatGPT is designed to support multiple languages, enabling users to communicate with the model in their preferred language. It has been trained on data from various languages, allowing it to understand and generate text in different linguistic contexts (Grünebaum et al., 2023). This multilingual capability enhances communication across language barriers and facilitates global interactions.

Cultural Sensitivity

ChatGPT's training on diverse internet data helps it understand cultural references and context-specific information. It can engage in conversations that involve cultural aspects, including literature, art, music, and popular culture (Ahn, 2023). This cultural sensitivity allows ChatGPT to provide relevant and culturally appropriate responses, promoting more meaningful and engaging interactions.

Contextual Adaptation

ChatGPT's versatility extends to its ability to adapt to different conversational contexts. It can understand and respond to specific user instructions or prompts, enabling users to guide the conversation and obtain desired information (Cox & Tzoc, 2023). This adaptability makes ChatGPT suitable for various applications, from virtual assistants to content generation in specific contexts.

Cross-Domain Connections

ChatGPT's training on diverse text sources enables it to draw connections across different domains. It can relate information from one domain to another, providing valuable insights and connections that may not be readily apparent (Fido & Wallace, 2023). This cross-domain versatility adds depth and richness to its responses, fostering a more comprehensive understanding of complex topics. ChatGPT's versatility across domains and languages expands its utility and applicability in various settings. It empowers users to engage in conversations and obtain information in their preferred domains and languages while facilitating cross-cultural communication and knowledge sharing (Yusuf, 2023). This versatility positions ChatGPT as a valuable tool for many users, from researchers and professionals to individuals seeking information or creative input in diverse contexts.

APPLICATIONS OF CHATGPT

ChatGPT revolutionizes different services and applications by offering instant responses to user queries and concerns with efficient problem-solving and timely assistance, reducing the need for human intervention in routine inquiries. This section presents the top application and generative AI application landscape.

Explore Customer Support

Its round-the-clock availability and consistent responsiveness characterize ChatGPT's application in customer support. Customers can ask questions and seek assistance anytime through instant messaging platforms or websites. ChatGPT's ability to comprehend and respond to a wide range of queries makes it an effective tool for addressing common concerns, providing product information, troubleshooting issues, and guiding users through step-by-step processes (Gabbiadini et al., 2023). While complex or sensitive matters might still require human intervention, ChatGPT significantly reduces the workload on support teams by handling routine inquiries, leading to faster response times and improved user satisfaction.

Content Creation

ChatGPT's content creation capabilities benefit content marketers, bloggers, and writers. Its proficiency in generating human-like text enables it to craft articles, blog posts, product descriptions, and more, catering to diverse niches and styles. By inputting prompts, users can specify the tone, style, and length of the desired content (Haman & Školník, 2023). This streamlines the content creation process, alleviating the pressure on content creators and allowing them to focus on refining and editing the generated content to match their requirements.

Education and Tutoring

ChatGPT's educational applications extend to acting as a virtual tutor. Students can ask questions about subjects they're studying, and ChatGPT can provide explanations, examples, and contextual information (Dida et al., 2023). While it does not replace traditional teaching methods, it offers supplementary support by offering immediate responses and additional perspectives on challenging topics. Its adaptability to various subjects and its patient responses makes it a useful resource for learners seeking clarity and deeper understanding.

Healthcare Information

In the healthcare sector, ChatGPT serves as a preliminary source of information for general medical inquiries. Patients can describe their symptoms or ask about medical conditions, medications, or treatments (Cotton et al., 2023). ChatGPT provides easy-to-understand explanations and suggests possible next steps, like consulting a healthcare professional for a formal diagnosis. This application helps individuals make informed decisions about their health and can alleviate some strain on healthcare providers by addressing routine queries (Polonsky & Rotman, 2023).

Business Insights and Strategy

ChatGPT's proficiency in processing and analyzing data contributes to its role in business insights and strategy formulation. Analyzing market trends, consumer preferences, and competitor activities, it aids businesses in making data-driven decisions (Yang, 2023). It can also draft reports, summaries, and analyses based on the provided data, offering a valuable tool for executives and analysts to extract actionable insights and formulate effective strategies.

Figure 3. Generative artificial intelligence use case in general perspective

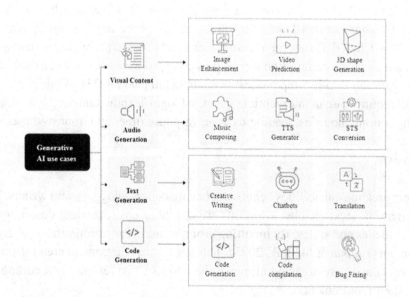

Language Translation and Learning

ChatGPT's language capabilities are harnessed for both translation and language-learning purposes. In translation, users can input text in one language and receive accurate translations in real-time. This assists in overcoming language barriers in various contexts, from international communication to content localization (AlAfnan et al., 2023). For language learners, ChatGPT offers a platform to practice writing and speaking in the target language. It can provide grammar corrections, vocabulary suggestions, and even engage in conversations, contributing to language proficiency development (Ahn, 2023). Some application use cases are demonstrated in Figure 3.

CHATGPT BENEFITS AND LIMITATIONS

Besides the application of GPT, there are benefits like boosting efficiency in customer support, content creation, and education, as users can access information and help at any time, leading to improved user satisfaction and limitations are explained below.

ChatGPT Benefits

Efficiency and Availability

One of the primary benefits of ChatGPT is its efficiency and availability. It operates 24/7 without needing breaks or shifts, ensuring users can access information, assistance, or content at any time. This uninterrupted availability is crucial in customer support scenarios where users might need immediate help (Fido & Wallace, 2023). Additionally, in content creation, writers can quickly generate drafts even outside regular working hours, enhancing productivity and meeting tight deadlines.

Scalability and Consistency

ChatGPT excels in handling a large volume of inquiries simultaneously. Unlike human agents, who might be limited by their capacity to engage with multiple users simultaneously, ChatGPT can engage in numerous conversations concurrently while providing consistent responses (Yusuf, 2023). This scalability is vital for businesses dealing with high customer demands, as it ensures that waiting times are minimized, and customer experience remains consistent even during peak periods.

Time and Resource Savings

Automating tasks using ChatGPT leads to significant time and resource savings. Customer support reduces the load on human agents by handling routine inquiries and allowing them to focus on more complex issues that require human judgment and empathy (Gao et al., 2023). Content creation accelerates the writing process by generating initial drafts, enabling writers to dedicate more time to refining and polishing the content. This optimization of resources improves overall operational efficiency.

Data-Driven Insights

ChatGPT's analytical capabilities offer a unique advantage in extracting insights from large datasets. It can quickly process and summarize data, providing valuable information for decision-making. Businesses can leverage ChatGPT to identify emerging trends, consumer sentiments, and patterns in user behavior (Pettinato Oltz, 2023). Educators can analyze students' interactions with the system to gain insights into learning preferences and areas of difficulty (De Angelis et al., 2023). This data-driven approach enhances strategic planning and enables proactive adjustments.

Consistent Knowledge Base

ChatGPT can maintain a consistent knowledge base over time. Unlike human agents who might change or forget information, ChatGPT retains its training and can provide accurate and consistent information regardless of turnover in human staff (Gabbiadini et al., 2023). This is particularly useful in sectors like healthcare and education, where maintaining up-to-date and accurate information is critical.

Multilingual Support

ChatGPT's language capabilities make it an asset for global interactions. It can offer support and information in multiple languages, bridging language barriers and expanding user reach. This is advantageous in businesses targeting international markets or in situations where multilingual communication is necessary (Regalia, 2023). The detailed benefits of ChatGPT underscore its role as an efficient, scalable, and data-driven tool that contributes to enhanced user experiences, streamlined operations, and informed decision-making in a wide range of applications.

ChatGPT Limitations

The following are the limitations identified from the surveyed literature.

Lack of Contextual Understanding

While ChatGPT can generate coherent responses, its context comprehension can be limited. It might misinterpret ambiguous queries, struggle with complex sentence structures, or fail to identify subtle nuances in conversation (Bessette, 2023). This limitation can lead to contextually incorrect or irrelevant responses, especially in professional or technical scenarios where precise understanding is paramount.

Ethical and Biased Responses

Despite efforts to reduce biases, ChatGPT can inadvertently produce responses reflecting biases in its training data. These biases can manifest as politically skewed viewpoints, offensive content, or discriminatory language (Chinonso et al., 2023). Such occurrences can undermine its reliability and appropriateness, particularly in contexts requiring neutrality and fairness.

Dependence on Data Quality

The quality of ChatGPT's responses is intrinsically tied to the quality of its training data. If the training data contains inaccuracies, outdated information, or a limited scope, ChatGPT might generate responses that are factually incorrect or outdated (Shue et al., 2023). This poses risks in scenarios where users rely on accurate and up-to-date information, such as legal or medical consultations.

Lack of Emotional Understanding

While ChatGPT can simulate empathy and engagement, it lacks genuine emotional comprehension. It might struggle to appropriately respond to emotionally charged conversations, recognize sarcasm, or offer sincere emotional support (Bommineni et al., 2023). This limitation hinders its effectiveness in roles that demand emotional intelligence, such as counseling or mental health support.

Verbosity and Repetition

ChatGPT has a tendency to be verbose, leading to lengthy responses. It might overuse specific phrases or provide excessive explanations, which can be counterproductive when users seek concise information or quick solutions (Nastasi et al., 2023). This limitation can hinder effective communication and user engagement, especially in fast-paced interactions.

Inability to Learn or Improve Independently

ChatGPT does not possess the capacity to learn from individual interactions or improve its responses beyond its training. It lacks memory of past conversations, hindering its ability to develop a deeper understanding of users' preferences or adapt to evolving situations. This contrasts with human agents who can refine their responses over time.

Absence of Personal Experience

ChatGPT's responses are based solely on patterns in its training data and lack genuine personal experiences. It cannot share authentic anecdotes or offer insights rooted in lived experiences, limiting its ability to engage in conversations that require relatable stories or unique perspectives beyond its training data.

Complex Decision-Making

ChatGPT struggles with intricate decision-making processes that involve moral judgments, ethical considerations, or critical thinking. Its responses are generated based on statistical patterns rather than genuine reasoning, making it unsuitable for roles that demand nuanced decision-making, like legal or ethical consultations. Understanding and addressing these detailed limitations is essential to utilize ChatGPT responsibly, ensuring its strengths are maximized while its shortcomings are managed through human oversight, validation, and contextual awareness.

ETHICAL CONSIDERATIONS

In this section, we examine the ethical implications of deploying ChatGPT, discuss potential risks, such as misuse or spreading misinformation, and highlight the importance of responsible development and deployment.

Bias and Fairness

AI systems like ChatGPT can inadvertently perpetuate biases present in their training data, leading to responses that discriminate against certain groups or viewpoints. Developers must conduct thorough bias assessments to identify and rectify potential biases in the training data and the system's outputs. This might involve adjusting training data, implementing fairness-enhancing techniques, and conducting ongoing audits to ensure fair and equitable interactions.

Privacy and Data Security

User interactions with ChatGPT often involve sharing personal information or sensitive topics. Ensuring robust privacy measures, such as secure data transmission, data anonymization, and strict access controls, is essential to protect user privacy. Adherence to data protection regulations like GDPR is crucial, as violations can erode user trust and lead to legal repercussions.

Misinformation and Accuracy

ChatGPT generates responses based on patterns in its training data, which might include outdated or incorrect information. To address this, developers must implement mechanisms to fact-check and validate the accuracy of responses, especially in domains where accuracy is critical. Incorporating external resources, expert reviews, or user feedback loops can help maintain a high standard of accuracy.

Professional Advice and Liability

ChatGPT's responses could resemble professional law, medicine, or finance advice. To avoid legal and ethical issues, developers must communicate that the system is not a substitute for qualified professionals and provide disclaimers to ensure users understand the limitations of its expertise. Managing liability requires balancing providing useful information and avoiding potential harm due to incorrect advice.

Emotional Impact

While ChatGPT can simulate empathy, it lacks true emotional understanding. In contexts such as mental health support, relying solely on ChatGPT can be inadequate or even harmful. Integrating human professionals who possess genuine emotional intelligence and can provide appropriate support, especially when users are vulnerable is essential.

Transparency and Disclosure

Users interacting with ChatGPT should be informed that they are engaging with an AI system. Clear disclosure prevents confusion and promotes transparency. Additionally, developers should consider allowing users to identify whether they are interacting with an AI or a human and explain how the AI's responses are generated.

User Consent and Control

Users should be able to control the extent of their engagement with ChatGPT and the data they share. This includes providing clear opt-in and opt-out mechanisms and settings allowing users to customize the system's behavior according to their preferences. Respecting user consent ensures ethical engagement and user empowerment.

Long-Term Impact on Human Labor

Integrating AI like ChatGPT into roles traditionally performed by humans can lead to job displacement. Developers and organizations should consider societal impacts and implement measures to support affected workers, such as retraining programs or transitioning to new roles requiring unique human skills like creativity and emotional intelligence.

Addiction and Dependence

AI interactions can become addictive, potentially causing users to rely excessively on AI systems for various tasks. Designing mechanisms that encourage responsible usage, such as setting time limits on interactions or providing recommendations for human interactions, can mitigate the risk of over-dependence on AI systems.

Oversight and Accountability

Developers should establish clear channels for users to provide feedback, report issues, and seek assistance. Being accountable for addressing system errors, biases, or shortcomings is essential for building user trust. Regular audits and assessments can ensure that the AI system aligns with ethical standards and societal expectations.

Unintended Uses

AI systems like ChatGPT can be misused for generating misinformation, engaging in harmful conversations, or automating malicious activities. Implementing safeguards, such as content filters, moderation mechanisms, and usage restrictions, can help mitigate these risks and prevent the technology from being exploited for harmful purposes.

Environmental Impact

AI models like ChatGPT require substantial computational power, contributing to energy consumption and carbon emissions. Developing energy-efficient models, optimizing computational processes, and prioritizing sustainability can mitigate the environmental impact of AI technology and promote ethical considerations aligned with ecological responsibility. Addressing these comprehensive ethical considerations requires ongoing collaboration between AI developers, domain experts, ethicists, and users. Striking a balance between innovation, user benefits, and ethical responsibilities is crucial for creating AI systems that enhance human well-being while upholding ethical values and standards.

FUTURE RESEARCH DIRECTIONS

The prospects of ChatGPT technology hold great potential for advancements and innovations. Within this section, we present some areas of development that can shape the future of ChatGPT:

Enhanced Language Understanding

Future advancements in ChatGPT technology will likely focus on improving its language understanding capabilities. This includes a more profound comprehension of context, nuances, and idiomatic expressions (Gao et al., 2023). By enhancing its understanding of complex language structures and subtleties, ChatGPT can generate more accurate and contextually relevant responses, fostering more natural and engaging conversations.

Personalization and User Adaptation

Personalization is an exciting direction for ChatGPT technology. By incorporating user preferences, historical interactions, and individual characteristics, ChatGPT can tailor its responses to specific users (Castro Nascimento & Pimentel, 2023). This personalization can lead to more customized and satisfying interactions, improving the user experience and building a stronger rapport between the user and the model.

Knowledge Expansion and Current Information

Keeping pace with rapidly evolving information is crucial. Future iterations of ChatGPT could have mechanisms to integrate real-time data sources and stay updated on current events, scientific discoveries, and other relevant information (Sinha et al., 2023). This would enhance its ability to provide the most up-to-date and accurate responses, making ChatGPT a reliable source of information.

Ethical Considerations and Bias Mitigation

Addressing ethical concerns and reducing biases in language models is a critical area of focus. Ongoing research and development efforts aim to mitigate biases in ChatGPT's responses and ensure interaction fairness (Regalia, 2023). Future advancements will likely involve refining bias detection mechanisms, implementing feedback loops for continuous improvement, and fostering transparency in the model's decision-making processes (Gabbiadini et al., 2023).

Explainability and Transparency

The ability to provide explanations and justifications for its responses can enhance user trust and understanding. Future developments in ChatGPT technology may make the model's decision-making process more transparent and provide insights into the underlying reasoning (Gabbiadini et al., 2023). Explainable AI techniques can empower users to understand how the model arrives at its responses, promoting trust and accountability (Cotton et al., 2023).

Multimodal and Richer Interactions

Integrating multimodal capabilities, such as processing and generating text alongside images, audio, or video, can open new avenues for more prosperous and interactive conversations (Rahaman, 2023). Future iterations of ChatGPT may incorporate advanced techniques to analyze and generate content in different modalities, enabling more immersive and dynamic interactions (Ventayen, 2023).

Collaboration and Co-Creation

ChatGPT technology can be harnessed to facilitate collaboration and co-creation between humans and machines (Rahaman et al., 2023). Future advancements might explore ways to seamlessly integrate the contributions of multiple individuals, leveraging ChatGPT's language generation capabilities to collectively generate creative content, solve complex problems, or assist in collaborative projects (Geerling et al., 2023).

Continued Research and Collaboration

Ongoing research, collaboration with the broader AI community, and user feedback will play a crucial role in shaping the future of ChatGPT technology. Collaborative efforts can help identify and address limitations, refine models, and improve their real-world performance and impact (De Angelis et al., 2023). In summary, the future of ChatGPT technology holds promise for enhanced language understanding, personalized interactions, knowledge expansion, bias mitigation, explainability, multimodal capabilities, collaboration, and continued research and development (Giunti et al., 2023). These advancements can elevate ChatGPT's capabilities, making it a more versatile and valuable tool for various applications, from customer support to creative content generation. The following section presents some lessons learned from the chapter and the conclusion (Pettinato Oltz, 2023).

LESSONS LEARNED AND CONCLUSION

Throughout the chapter on ChatGPT, several important lessons have emerged, as demonstrated below.

Lessons Learned

Robust Training Data: The quality and diversity of training data significantly impact the performance of ChatGPT. Incorporating a wide range of data sources and carefully curating the training datasets contribute to a more comprehensive and robust language model. Ethical Considerations: The deployment of ChatGPT necessitates a deep understanding of ethical considerations. Awareness of potential biases, responsible development practices, and ongoing efforts to address ethical concerns are crucial to ensuring the reliable and beneficial use of ChatGPT.

Contextual Understanding: ChatGPT's understanding and maintaining context are critical to generating coherent and relevant responses. The model's architecture and training process must emphasize capturing and utilizing contextual information for improved conversational abilities. Language Generation Challenges: Generating human-like and contextually appropriate responses is complex. Overcoming challenges such as response coherence, avoiding factual inaccuracies, and avoiding generic or nonsensical outputs require careful model design and training strategies.

User Feedback and Iterative Improvement: User feedback plays a pivotal role in iteratively improving ChatGPT. Regularly gathering and incorporating user feedback helps identify limitations, biases, and areas for improvement, leading to continuous refinement of the model. Advancements in Multimodal Capabilities: Exploring and integrating multimodal capabilities can enhance ChatGPT's effectiveness and user experience. Combining text with images, audio, or video can enable richer interactions and open new collaboration and content-generation possibilities. Striking a Balance: Fine-tuning ChatGPT involves striking a delicate balance between system capabilities and safety precautions. Ensuring the model can generate helpful responses while avoiding harmful or inappropriate outputs requires careful design choices and ongoing monitoring.

Collaborative Research and Openness: Collaborative research and open dialogue within the AI community are invaluable. Sharing insights, addressing challenges collectively, and fostering transparency contribute to the continuous improvement of ChatGPT and the responsible advancement of AI technologies. These lessons shed light on the complexities and considerations surrounding ChatGPT, emphasizing the importance of data, ethics, context, user feedback, multimodal capabilities, balance, and collaboration for its development and application. By embracing these lessons, we can guide the future development of ChatGPT and ensure its positive impact in various domains.

ChatGPT represents a significant milestone in natural language processing and artificial intelligence, demonstrating the power and potential of large-scale language models. Its underlying architecture and technology enable it to engage in human-like conversations, comprehend context, and generate informative and relevant responses. The features and capabilities of ChatGPT, such as its language understanding, adaptability, multilingual support, and creative text generation, make it a versatile tool with applications across various domains and languages. However, the development and deployment of ChatGPT also raise essential considerations. Ethical concerns, biases, and the responsible use of the model must be addressed through ongoing research, collaboration, and transparency. Lessons learned from the training process, language generation challenges, and the importance of user feedback provide valuable insights for future improvements.

CONCLUSION

Looking ahead in technology, the prospects of ChatGPT are exciting. Advancements in language understanding, personalization, and knowledge expansion can further enhance its capabilities, making it an even more valuable resource for users. Ethical considerations and explainability will continue to be essential focal points to ensure the responsible development and deployment of ChatGPT. Furthermore, the exploration of multimodal capabilities, collaboration, and continuous research will shape the evolution of ChatGPT technology, enabling it to have a broader impact on communication and human-machine interactions. By embracing the lessons learned and fostering a collaborative and open approach, we can harness the potential of ChatGPT to empower individuals, assist in decision-making, and facilitate knowledge sharing in diverse domains and languages. Ultimately, ChatGPT represents a significant step forward in AI, opening up new possibilities for natural language understanding and generation. As we continue to refine and enhance this technology, it is crucial to balance innovation, ethics, and user-centric design, ensuring that ChatGPT is a reliable and beneficial tool in an increasingly interconnected and conversational world.

REFERENCES

Adetayo, A. J. (2023). Artificial intelligence chatbots in academic libraries: The rise of ChatGPT. *Library Hi Tech News*, *40*(3), 18–21. doi:10.1108/LHTN-01-2023-0007

Ahn, C. (2023). Exploring ChatGPT for information of cardiopulmonary resuscitation. *Resuscitation*, *185*, 109729. doi:10.1016/j.resuscitation.2023.109729 PMID:36773836

AlAfnan, M. A., Samira Dishari, Marina Jovic, & Koba Lomidze. (2023). ChatGPT as an Educational Tool: Opportunities, Challenges, and Recommendations for Communication, Business Writing, and Composition Courses. *Journal of Artificial Intelligence and Technology*, *3*(2), 60–68. doi:10.37965/jait.2023.0184

Alshurafat, H. (2023). The Usefulness and Challenges of Chatbots for Accounting Professionals: Application On ChatGPT. SSRN *Electronic Journal*. doi:10.2139/ssrn.4345921

Analytica, O. (2023a). *ChatGPT dramatically fuels corporate interest in AI*. Emerald Expert Briefings.

Analytica, O. (2023b). *Commercial use of ChatGPT requires caution*. Emerald Expert Briefings.

AntakiF.ToumaS.MiladD.El-KhouryJ.DuvalR. (2023). Evaluating the Performance of ChatGPT in Ophthalmology: An Analysis of its Successes and Shortcomings. MedRxiv, 100324. doi:10.1101/2023.01.22.23284882

Balas, M., & Ing, E. B. (2023). Conversational AI Models for ophthalmic diagnosis: Comparison of ChatGPT and the Isabel Pro Differential Diagnosis Generator. *JFO Open Ophthalmology*, *1*, 100005. Advance online publication. doi:10.1016/j.jfop.2023.100005

BenoitJ. R. A. (2023). ChatGPT for Clinical Vignette Generation, Revision, and Evaluation. MedRxiv. doi:10.1101/2023.02.04.23285478

Bessette, L. S. (2023). This Isn't Another Piece on ChatGPT. *The National Teaching & Learning Forum*, *32*(2), 11–12. doi:10.1002/ntlf.30359

Bishop, L. (2023). Can ChatGPT "Think Like a Lawyer?" A Socratic Dialogue. SSRN *Electronic Journal*. doi:10.2139/ssrn.4338995

Biswas, S. (2023a). ChatGPT and the Future of Medical Writing. *Radiology*, *307*(2), e223312. doi:10.1148/radiol.223312 PMID:36728748

Biswas, S. (2023b). *Role of ChatGPT in Computer Programming*. Mesopotamian Journal of Computer Science. doi:10.58496/MJCSC/2023/002

Biswas, S. (2023c). *Role of ChatGPT in the Film Industry: According to ChatGPT*. Qeios. doi:10.32388/NABVHA

BommineniV. L.BhagwagarS. Z.BalcarcelD. (2023). Performance of ChatGPT on the MCAT: The Road to Personalized and Equitable Premedical Learning. MedRxiv. doi:10.1101/2023.03.05.23286533

Castro Nascimento, C. M., & Pimentel, A. S. (2023). Do Large Language Models Understand Chemistry? A Conversation with ChatGPT. *Journal of Chemical Information and Modeling*, *63*(6), 1649–1655. doi:10.1021/acs.jcim.3c00285 PMID:36926868

Chinonso, O. E., Theresa, A. M.-E., & Aduke, T. C. (2023). ChatGPT for Teaching, Learning and Research: Prospects and Challenges. *Global Academic Journal of Humanities and Social Sciences*, *5*(02), 33–40. doi:10.36348/gajhss.2023.v05i02.001

Cotton, D. R. E., Cotton, P. A., & Shipway, J. R. (2023). Chatting and cheating: Ensuring academic integrity in the era of ChatGPT. *Innovations in Education and Teaching International*, 1–12. doi:10.1080/14703297.2023.2190148

Cox, C., & Tzoc, E. (2023). ChatGPT: Implications for academic libraries. *College & Research Libraries News*, *84*(3). doi:10.5860/crln.84.3.99

De Angelis, L., Baglivo, F., Arzilli, G., Privitera, G. P., Ferragina, P., Tozzi, A. E., & Rizzo, C. (2023). ChatGPT and the Rise of Large Language Models: The New AI-Driven Infodemic Threat in Public Health. SSRN *Electronic Journal*. doi:10.2139/ssrn.4352931

Dida, H. A., Chakravarthy, D., & Rabbi, F. (2023). *ChatGPT and Big Data: Enhancing Text-to-Speech Conversion*. Mesopotamian Journal of Big Data., doi:10.58496/MJBD/2023/005

Eke, D. O. (2023). ChatGPT and the rise of generative AI: Threat to academic integrity? *Journal of Responsible Technology*, *13*, 100060. doi:10.1016/j.jrt.2023.100060

Fido, D., & Wallace, L. (2023). *The Unique Role of ChatGPT in Closing the Awarding Gap*. The Interdisciplinary Journal of Student Success.

Gabbiadini, A., Dimitri, O., Baldissarri, C., & Manfredi, A. (2023). Does ChatGPT Pose a Threat to Human Identity? SSRN *Electronic Journal*. doi:10.2139/ssrn.4377900

Gao, Y., Tong, W., Wu, E. Q., Chen, W., Zhu, G. Y., & Wang, F. Y. (2023). Chat with ChatGPT on Interactive Engines for Intelligent Driving. *IEEE Transactions on Intelligent Vehicles, 8*(3), 2034–2036. doi:10.1109/TIV.2023.3252571

Geerling, W., Mateer, G. D., Wooten, J., & Damodaran, N. (2023). Is ChatGPT Smarter than a Student in Principles of Economics? SSRN *Electronic Journal.* doi:10.2139/ssrn.4356034

Giunti, M., Garavaglia, F. G., Giuntini, R., Pinna, S., & Sergioli, G. (2023). Chatgpt Prospective Student at Medical School. SSRN *Electronic Journal.* doi:10.2139/ssrn.4378743

Grünebaum, A., Chervenak, J., Pollet, S. L., Katz, A., & Chervenak, F. A. (2023). The Exciting Potential for ChatGPT in Obstetrics and Gynecology. *American Journal of Obstetrics and Gynecology, 228*(6), 696–705. doi:10.1016/j.ajog.2023.03.009 PMID:36924907

Gunawan, J. (2023). Exploring the future of nursing: Insights from the ChatGPT model. *Belitung Nursing Journal, 9*(1), 1–5. doi:10.33546/bnj.2551 PMID:37469634

Halloran, L. J. S., Mhanna, S., & Brunner, P. (2023). AI tools such as ChatGPT will disrupt hydrology, too. *Hydrological Processes, 37*(3), e14843. doi:10.1002/hyp.14843

Haman, M., & Školník, M. (2023). Using ChatGPT to conduct a literature review. *Accountability in Research,* 1–3. doi:10.1080/08989621.2023.2185514 PMID:36879536

Kumar, H. S. (2023). Analysis of ChatGPT Tool to Assess the Potential of its Utility for Academic Writing in Biomedical Domain. *Biology, Engineering. Medicine and Science Reports, 9*(1), 24–30. doi:10.5530/bems.9.1.5

Lieberman, M. (2023). What Is ChatGPT and How Is It Used in Education? *Education Week, 42*(18).

LinZ. (2023). Why and how to embrace AI such as ChatGPT in your academic life. PsyArXiv.

LiuS.WrightA. P.PattersonB. L.WandererJ. P.TurerR. W.NelsonS. D.McCoyA. B.SittigD. F.WrightA. (2023). Assessing the Value of ChatGPT for Clinical Decision Support Optimization. MedRxiv. doi:10.1101/2023.02.21.23286254

Macey-Dare, R. (2023). ChatGPT & Generative AI Systems as Quasi-Expert Legal Advice Lawyers - Case Study Considering Potential Appeal Against Conviction of Tom Hayes. SSRN *Electronic Journal.* doi:10.2139/ssrn.4342686

Magazine, B. A.-C. D. (2023). Why ChatGPT is such a big deal for education. *Scholarspace.Jccc.Edu.*

Mattas, P. S. (2023). ChatGPT: A Study of AI Language Processing and its Implications. *International Journal of Research Publication and Reviews, 04*(02), 435–440. doi:10.55248/gengpi.2023.4218

McGee, R. W. (2023). Capitalism, Socialism and ChatGPT. SSRN *Electronic Journal.* doi:10.2139/ssrn.4369953

Mijwil, M., Aljanabi, M., & Ali, A. H. (2023). *ChatGPT: Exploring the Role of Cybersecurity in the Protection of Medical Information.* Mesopotamian Journal of Cyber Security. doi:10.58496/MJCS/2023/004

NastasiA. J.CourtrightK. R.HalpernS. D.WeissmanG. E. (2023). Does ChatGPT Provide Appropriate and Equitable Medical Advice?: A Vignette-Based, Clinical Evaluation Across Care Contexts. MedRxiv. doi:10.1101/2023.02.25.23286451

Nisar, S., & Aslam, M. S. (2023). Is ChatGPT a Good Tool for T&CM Students in Studying Pharmacology? SSRN *Electronic Journal*. doi:10.2139/ssrn.4324310

Perkins, M. (2023). Academic Integrity considerations of AI Large Language Models in the post-pandemic era: ChatGPT and beyond. *Journal of University Teaching & Learning Practice, 20*(2). doi:10.53761/1.20.02.07

Pettinato Oltz, T. (2023). ChatGPT, Professor of Law. SSRN *Electronic Journal*. doi:10.2139/ssrn.4347630

Polonsky, M., & Rotman, J. (2023). Should Artificial Intelligent (AI) Agents be Your Co-author? Arguments in favour, informed by ChatGPT. SSRN *Electronic Journal*. doi:10.2139/ssrn.4349524

Quinio, B., & Bidan, M. (2023). *ChatGPT : Un robot conversationnel peut-il enseigner*. Management & Data Science. doi:10.36863/mds.a.22060

Rahaman, Md. S. (2023). Can ChatGPT be your friend? Emergence of Entrepreneurial Research. SSRN *Electronic Journal*. doi:10.2139/ssrn.4368541

Rahaman, Md. S., Ahsan, M. M. T., Anjum, N., Rahman, Md. M., & Rahman, M. N. (2023). The AI Race is on! Google's Bard and Openai's Chatgpt Head to Head: An Opinion Article. SSRN *Electronic Journal*. doi:10.2139/ssrn.4351785

Regalia, J. (2023). ChatGPT and Legal Writing: The Perfect Union? SSRN *Electronic Journal*. doi:10.2139/ssrn.4371460

Rozado, D. (2023). The Political Biases of ChatGPT. *Social Sciences (Basel, Switzerland), 12*(3), 148. doi:10.3390ocsci12030148

Sakirin, T., & Ben Said, R. (2023). *User preferences for ChatGPT-powered conversational interfaces versus traditional methods*. Mesopotamian Journal of Computer Science., doi:10.58496/MJCSC/2023/006

Shafik, W. (2023). A Comprehensive Cybersecurity Framework for Present and Future Global Information Technology Organizations. In *Effective Cybersecurity Operations for Enterprise-Wide Systems* (pp. 56–79). IGI Global. doi:10.4018/978-1-6684-9018-1.ch002

Shafik, W. (2024). Wearable Medical Electronics in Artificial Intelligence of Medical Things. Handbook of Security and Privacy of AI-Enabled Healthcare Systems and Internet of Medical Things, 21-40. https://doi.org/ doi:10.1201/9781003370321-2

Shah, C. (2023). The Rise of AI Chat Agents and the Discourse with Dilettantes. SSRN *Electronic Journal*. doi:10.2139/ssrn.4327315

Shaji George, A., Hovan George, A., & Martin, Asg. (2023). A Review of ChatGPT AI's Impact on Several Business Sectors. *Partners Universal International Innovation Journal, 1*(1).

ShueE.LiuL.LiB.FengZ.LiX.HuG. (2023). Empowering Beginners in Bioinformatics with ChatGPT. BioRxiv.

Sinha, R. K., Deb Roy, A., Kumar, N., & Mondal, H. (2023). Applicability of ChatGPT in Assisting to Solve Higher Order Problems in Pathology. *Cureus*. doi:10.7759/cureus.35237 PMID:36968864

Skjuve, M. (2023). Why People Use Chatgpt. SSRN *Electronic Journal*. doi:10.2139/ssrn.4376834

Ventayen, R. J. M. (2023). ChatGPT by OpenAI: Students' Viewpoint on Cheating using Artificial Intelligence-Based Application. SSRN *Electronic Journal*. doi:10.2139/ssrn.4361548

Yang, Z. (2023). Inside the ChatGPT race in China. *MIT Technology Jounrnel, 1*.

Yusuf, S. (2023). *ChatGPT, the Blade in Scientific Writing*. Indonesian Contemporary Nursing Journal.

Zielinski, C., Winker, M., Aggarwal, R., Ferris, L., Heinemann, M., Lapeña, Jr, J. F., Pai, S., Ing, E., & Citrome, L. (2023). Chatbots, ChatGPT, and Scholarly Manuscripts: WAME Recommendations on ChatGPT and Chatbots in Relation to Scholarly Publications. *Open Access Macedonian Journal of Medical Sciences, 11*(A). doi:10.3889/oamjms.2023.11502

Chapter 2
Nudging Motivation to Learn English Through a ChatGPT Smartphone-Based Hybrid Model

Muthmainnah Muthmainnah
Universitas Al Asyariah Mandar Sulawesi Barat, Indonesia

Eka Apriani
Institut Agama Islam Negeri, Curup, Indonesia

Prodhan Mahbub Ibna Seraj
(iD) https://orcid.org/0000-0002-4483-6059
United International University, Bangladesh

Ahmed J. Obaid
(iD) https://orcid.org/0000-0003-0376-5546
University of Kufa, Iraq

Ahmad M. Al Yakin
Universitas Al Asyariah Mandar Sulawesi Barat, Indonesia

ABSTRACT

The artificial intelligence revolution as a medium and learning technology is increasingly popular in EFL. The trend of using ChatGPT is increasing. ChatGPT is a media and technology that helps in accelerating learning to help write, becomes teaching materials, learning resources with a conversation system. The purpose of this research is to find out the motivation to learn by developing the ChatGPT function as a teaching material in EFL classes among undergraduate students at universities. As an AI-based teaching material, ChatGPT was chosen with consideration of the ease of accessing fast information.

DOI: 10.4018/979-8-3693-0502-7.ch002

INTRODUCTION

Increasing motivation by using chatGPT in language learning have found by some Gavilán et al (2022) and Liu et al. (2023) students will be more engaged and motivated if their teachers use ChatGPT to provide them with one-on-one support. Liu et al. (2023) found that students who used ChatGPT were more invested in their studies, with many commenting how much they enjoyed interacting with the software. Incorporating ChatGPT into higher education aids in the cultivation of critical thinking Ibna Seraj et. al (2022) and problem-solving abilities. ChatGPT also provides a personalized and adaptive learning environment by providing additional learning materials and information on a certain topic.

Motivation is a key factor in students' success and persistence in the challenging process of language acquisition. Chen et al. (2023); Dhivya et al. (2023). In today's technological era, mobile phones are an important tool for communication and education. An innovative approach to the problem of maintaining language learners' motivation has emerged through the use of AI-ChatGPT combined with positive behavioral encouragement. Various internal, external, and even integrative elements contribute to motivation for language acquisition. Extrinsic motivation refers to drive originating from external sources, such as pressure or rewards. On the other hand, integral motivation is linked to an intrinsic desire to completely immerse oneself in the culture of the language speaker. This type of motivation is critical in determining whether or not a language learner will persevere and achieve success in the long run (Ebadi and Amini, 2022).

Personalised language learning is particularly feasible with the assistance of ChatGPT, an exceptionally potent and effective language model Kasneci et al. (2023). In addition to responding to inquiries and delivering immediate feedback, ChatGPT has the capability to foster discussions using natural language and generate pertinent material. The model's capacity to adjust to the specific requirements of individual learners renders it a potent instrument for constructing captivating linguistic contexts. (Liu et al., 2023). The hybrid paradigm maximises the motivation-enhancing potential of ChatGPT by combining behavioural nudges. Encouragement can be provided through a variety of means via smartphone applications, including goal-setting suggestions, positive reinforcement, periodic reminders, and progress monitoring. This form of encouragement serves to promote consistent practise, foster sustained student motivation, and deliver constructive criticism. Ansah and Baidoo-Anu (2023). It is not anticipated that the potential and benefits of ChatGPT will result in its implementation in conventional classrooms. Kasneci et al. (2023) observe that substantial opportunities exist for investigation and analysis regarding the utilisation of ChatGPT in language programmes of higher education as a result of its pervasive application. An area of investigation that shows promise is the implementation of empirical studies to examine the impacts of ChatGPT on the process of language acquisition. The value of ChatGPT can be determined by distinguishing its consumers from those who do not utilise it. Such studies could evaluate linguistic abilities including vocabulary, grammar, reading comprehension, and even fluency in speech. Evaluating the quality and coherence of the generated text, as well as detecting and mitigating potential biases or prejudices in the output, could make ChatGPT a safer and more effective tool for language learning.

Chatbots are computer programs that allow users to have conversations with them in a way that seems like they're talking to a real person Kim, et al. (2022). Complex knowledge-based models have replaced the simpler pattern matching and string processing of earlier chatbots. The use of chatbots in both formal and informal settings in education has been common for some time Huang, et al. (2022). They have been employed to facilitate instruction, boost student interest, evaluate performance, and carry out a number of administrative tasks Molnár and Szüts (2018).

However, there are many obstacles and restrictions to educational chatbots Mageira, et al. (2022). Problems arise when the system is required to deal with misspelled words, slang, student inputs, and simulate natural conversation flow, all of which lead to a cold, emotionless transactional experience. In addition, a lack of appropriate datasets has been cited by several academics as a typical difficulty in educational chatbots that might cause learning difficulties and frustration. According to Gabrielli, et al. (2021), chatbots lose their initial appeal after a while. The scientists also noted that there is no universally accepted method for building chatbots, making it difficult to compare outcomes from different experiments. Knowledge application, or easy access to previously acquired information, is crucial to the long-term success of chatbots as educational tools Kohnke, (2023). Chatbots that can learn and browse "anytime and anywhere" should be a top priority for service providers in order to secure their long-term viability.

Anecdotal information reveals SL/FL educators are particularly concerned about students turning in plagiarized work that cannot be properly detected by existing applications Shidiq, (2023). This is consistent with where English writing is a required part of the curriculum: teachers there are uniformly against having their students utilize ChatGPT. But a proper understanding of the new technology is necessary to get the whole picture of the challenges and opportunities. It's undeniable that ChatGPT is a game-changer that will, and indeed, must, alter the stale approaches to higher education's teaching and evaluation. As a result of these shifts, researchers may need to devote more time and energy to identifying and meeting the demands of language education's many constituencies. Kohnke, et al. (2023) stated, based on the surveys, interviews, focus groups, and other qualitative and quantitative research methods would be used to examine how ChatGPT has affected language instructors, students, and the general public. The findings of this study may provide important insights into adopting ChatGPT as teaching materials for language acquisition and their impact on motivation to learn English. New avenues for language acquisition may be uncovered through research into ChatGPT's limitations in processing complex or abstract concepts and its potential uses in language learning games, feedback on students' writing, and language translation.

This research examines the potential of ChatGPT from the standpoint of university students, and then examines the impact that it has on their motivation to study English. This research is significant because it has the potential to shed light on how effective ChatGPT is at boosting students' educational chances. The ramifications for teachers, policymakers, and the creators of educational technology could be large if the results reveal that ChatGPT can boost student involvement and motivation. This has the potential to lead to the adoption of ChatGPT as a supplementary teaching tool, the creation of new resources, and the improvement of traditional pedagogical practices, all of which would improve educational outcomes. This research is important because it provides insight into the effects of accelerated ChatGPT as a teaching resource on students' motivation and because it can help direct the evolution of educational technology. Examining how ChatGPT can influence college students' motivation is the primary focus of this research. The primary goal of this research was to ascertain whether or not the introduction of ChatGPT as a teaching material increased undergraduate students' enthusiasm to learn English in a hybrid model classroom.

LITERATURE REVIEW

ChatGPT Promoting Teaching and Learning English

There is much potential for investigation and inquiry into the use of ChatGPT in higher education language programs (Atlas, 2023; Kasneci et al., 2023) due to its wide applicability and the efficiencies it offers. Evaluating the efficacy of ChatGPT in language acquisition is offered so that researchers can determine the benefits of ChatGPT by comparing language learners who use it with those who do not. Vocabulary, grammar, reading comprehension, and even speaking fluency can all be measured in such studies. ChatGPT use to learn a language in a safer and more effective way if to check the accuracy and coherence of the text it produces and look for and fix any bias or stereotypes it might have Ferrara, (2023).

Additionally, this research investigates the impact of ChatGPT, an AI-powered language model, on students and institutions by surveying the perspectives of lecturers and students (Firat et al., 2023). The results of the research revealed that, using a thematic approach to content analysis, the responses of seven lecturers and fourteen PhD candidates from Turkey, Sweden, Canada, and Australia were analysed. There were nine overarching themes. The most frequently discussed issues are, from most to least discussed "AI as an extension of the human brain", "digital literacy and AI integration", "personalised learning", "the future of work and employability", and "the importance of human characteristics." We'll discuss the pros and cons of using AI in the classroom, including any advantages and limitations that may come with it. There should be further investigation into the potential ethical issues of using AI in language classes, solutions to student privacy concerns, and how schools can best prepare to use AI. Ultimately, this research highlights the importance of considering the pros and cons of AI in higher education, which is relevant to the current investigation.

In many ways, ChatGPT has the potential to revolutionize the seemingly rigid English classroom. English learners can now practice their language skills whenever and wherever they are comfortable, thanks to ChatGPT Jeon et al. (2023). Language learning will be greatly helped when students could practice speaking, ask questions, and receive direct feedback. Additionally, ChatGPT can be tailored to each student's specific needs. It can adapt its teaching methods to each student by analysing their performance and then providing targeted practice problems, explanations, and information.

Improving vocabulary and grammar chat GPT's ability to point out spelling and grammatical errors in students' writing and offer suggestions for improvement is well known Yan (2023). As a digital writing aid, it can help make English prose smoother and more professional sounding. To help students better understand language in its cultural context, it is common knowledge that the role of ChatGPT can provide cultural understanding by teaching idiomatic expressions, cultural nuances, and the use of language according to context. Conversation practice is very important for learning English, in addition to learning grammar and vocabulary. ChatGPT is used so that undergraduate students can have conversations with human-to-human and human-to-machine (AI) students, which allows them to practice their speaking and listening skills through role play and conversation. Undergraduate students from all over the world can benefit from ChatGPT, regardless of their time zone or schedule, because unlike human teachers, ChatGPT is always open.

The availability of ChatGPT has also been shown to reduce linguistic anxiety. Some students may feel nervous when using English in a group. ChatGPT can provide a simple opportunity to hone public speaking skills and, in turn, increase self-confidence, as noted by Michel-Villarreal et al. (2023) and with the help of ChatGPT, students can receive real-time comments on their pronunciation, sentence construction, and language use. Together, traditional classroom instruction and ChatGPT's additional practice, explanations, and links to related content can greatly enhance student learning in the classroom. ChatGPT is a platform that can help educators improve their professional development as well as the educational experience of their students, Kovacevi (2023).

Additionally, English educators can utilize ChatGPT to provide courses, quizzes, and individualized exercises for their students. According to Dao (2023), this can also help educators assess papers and provide feedback more effectively. Furthermore, in the language assessment section, ChatGPT can be used to evaluate written assignments or conduct oral exams, thus ensuring fair and consistent evaluations. Students can use ChatGPT's multilingual feature to better understand English content by translating text between English and their local language. We hope that undergraduate students are the type of people who want to continue learning and growing, ChatGPT can be a great resource for them. Keep in mind that ChatGPT has certain limitations, such as not being sensitive to cultural norms or emotional intelligence. While it can help with language acquisition, it is most beneficial when combined with human resources and teachers to give students a well-rounded education. Nevertheless, ChatGPT has great potential to improve foreign language teaching and student achievement with the right direction and integration.

ChatGPT and Motivation to Learn English

It is possible that maintaining conversational-AI bots could capture students' interest and maintain their attention throughout class. Chatbots are AI software programs that can simulate human communication through text or speech that are believed to attract undergraduate students.. Conversational agents can motivate students to work more by providing them with personalised and timely feedback, recommendations, and encouragement (Yildirim-Erbasli, 2022). Then Guo et al. (2023) started a larger discussion about the use of chatbots in education and how they can be used to motivate and interest students. Student interest, motivation, and engagement increase when teachers use chatbots in the classroom. Chatbots that provide direct, individualised feedback to students have been proven to increase motivation and engagement. Because chatbots do not have any preconceptions about the questions or answers they provide, they can help students feel more comfortable asking them (Chen et al., 2023) and receiving them. Students are more interested and engaged in their learning when chatbots are used in the classroom. Hsu et al. (2023) utilised chatbots to provide immediate feedback to programming students. Students who use chatbots report feeling more inspired and invested in their learning.

Adiguzel et al. (2023) and Kamruzzaman et al. (2023) provide evidence of this, using AI to tailor its support to each student, thereby increasing their motivation and performance in class. However, little is known about how artificial intelligence (AI) affects student motivation and participation in the classroom. Furthermore, Xia et al. (2023), Hong (2023), and Perkins (2023) point out that ChatGPT is not the first technology application used in language teaching and learning. The question of whether language students can have access to authentic communication experiences was investigated by Zhao and Lai (2023) in one of the earliest investigations of the impact of technology on language programs. Qiao et al. (2022) found that classrooms that widely used computers and other technological equipment had significant improvements in student achievement. Technology has increased students' motivation, interest, and active participation in learning a second language.

Recent research has considered the advantages and disadvantages of using advanced language models such as ChatGPT in the classroom. While Kasneci et al. (2023) examine the pros and cons of ChatGPT in the classroom, Willems (2023) examines the larger ethical issues of implementing the model in an academic setting. Malinka et al. (2023) investigated the impact of ChatGPT on education and cast doubt on the method's ability to pave the way to better learning.

Mogavi et al. (2023) article highlights appropriate ways to implement ChatGPT in the classroom, offers suggestions for doing so ethically and effectively, particularly in terms of character education, assessment, and AI-based learning, and discusses ChatGPT's potential impact on existing evaluation methods. is in college. ChatGPT's promise to increase interest and motivation, which in turn influences students' propensity to learn English. According to research (Liu et al., 2023), students' interest and motivation to learn increase when instructors use ChatGPT for more face-to-face teaching. Likewise, students who use ChatGPT on an e-learning platform report that they are more invested in their studies, and many also praise the software's ease of use and enjoyable interactivity. According to Matuk et al. (2023), students can use AI technology to carry out assignments in their courses. Based on these findings, we need new evaluation methods that place more value on aspects of human intelligence that computers cannot imitate: creativity and ingenuity.

Liu and Ma (2023) examined the potential use of ChatGPT in English as a Foreign Language (EFL) classrooms from a global perspective and found that it would be a beneficial addition to EFL education by helping students gain a stronger command of the language, simplifying the learning process, and providing them with immediate feedback regarding their performance. Research shows that using ChatGPT can increase student motivation and engagement in class. Adiguzel et al. (2019) found that integrating ChatGPT into an online tutoring system improved student outcome. This is in accordance with the findings of Limna et al. (2018), who used ChatGPT in an online class and saw performance improvements. The artificial intelligence (AI) behind ChatGPT's natural language processing (NLP) and machine learning (ML) responses makes it the ultimate chatbot. The school has implemented ChatGPT in an effort to rekindle students' interest and enthusiasm for education. Chatbots provide a safe space for students to ask questions and get answers without fear of repercussions. The studies examined all agree that using ChatGPT in the classroom is a great way to motivate students to learn English.

METHOD

The subjects of this study are universitas Al Asyariah Mandar students who are using ChatGPT to improve their English skills. All the students have previously made use of AI software or similar educational technologies. In the academic year 2022/2023, 350 students enrolled English II program served as the population for this mixed-methods study. Of 64 students from computer science faculty were used as participants in this research taken by using random sampling. In addition, the researcher gathered information through interviews and questionnaires. There was a total of ten questions on the survey. Students were given a questionnaire in which they were asked to rate their motivation to learn English through ChatGPT on a numerical scale (a Likert Scale).

ANALYSIS DATA

Questionnaire data were analyzed in SPSS version 26. To learn about data patterns and variations, descriptive statistics were calculated. Pallant's (2005) rating interval, in which he relates item means to agreement levels, provides another basis for analysis. Strongly disagree is indicated by a score between

1.00 and 1.80, disagree between 1.8 and 2.60, strongly agree between 2.6 and 3.40, strongly agree between 3.4 and 4.20, and strongly agree, agree between 4.21 and 5.00. Motivation categories, very high motivation, 50, highly motivated 40, moderate motivation 30, low motivation 20 and unmotivated 10.

Figure 1. ChatGPT by using smartphone

RESULTS AND DISCUSSION

This information was collected by asking the participants to answer a survey regarding how motivated they are to learn English using smartphone based ChatGPT. Their replies will be displayed as follows.

Table 1. One sample of test

One-Sample Statistics				
	N	Mean	Std. Deviation	Std. Error Mean
ChatGPT	64	45.2813	2.76870	.34609

Based on Table 1 the calculation of the student's motivation is 45 which categorize high motivation on learning English through ChatGPT as English materials. Based on the statistics provided for Chat-GPT, with a sample size of 64, we can conclude that the average score is around 45.28 with a standard deviation of around 2.77. The standard error of the mean is approximately 0.35. This shows that, on average, ChatGPT performs consistently with a mean score of 45.28, and the standard deviation indicates a moderate level of variability between individual data points. The small standard error of the mean implies that this sample mean is likely a good estimate of the population mean for ChatGPT. Further analysis and comparison with relevant benchmarks or previous data may be necessary to draw more specific conclusions about ChatGPT performance.

Table 2 describes the results of the student's survey on their motivation to learn English by using ChatGPT as learning resources. Most of the students showed strong believe on the benefit ChatGPT by using smartphone more fun, enjoyable, more interested in learning, more confidence to talk and discussed In the classroom, make easy to understand the English materials than eBook and efficient. Based on the descriptive statistics provided for various statements regarding the use of ChatGPT, we can describe the survey results as follows.

Table 2. Mean score and standard deviation on motivation to learn English through ChatGPT

Descriptive Statistics					
	N	Minimum	Maximum	Mean	Std. Deviation
1. I believe The materials developed with ChatGPT are straightforward.	64	3.00	5.00	4.5156	.53429
2. To keep me interested and motivated while learning English, I use ChatGPT,	64	4.00	5.00	4.6094	.49175
3. ChatGPT is a great resource to help me learn more about the English language and culture	64	4.00	5.00	4.6094	.49175
4. Make the most of your time to study so that you can maintain your interest in learning English	64	4.00	5.00	4.3125	.46718
5. ChatGPT Make it easy to understand English material with the help of ChatGPT	64	3.00	5.00	4.6250	.57735
6. Make it easy to understand English material with the help of ChatGPT	64	4.00	5.00	4.6719	.47324
7. To improve my spoken and auditory English, I use ChatGPT.	64	4.00	5.00	4.8594	.35038
8. This learning model with ChatGPT is what got me interested in learning English when you are not in class.	64	3.00	5.00	4.3438	.62281
9. I believe that by using ChatGPT, I can improve my academic performance.	64	4.00	5.00	4.5312	.50297
10. I feel ChatGPT will increase the efficiency I am learning ChatGPT makes education fun.	64	3.00	5.00	4.2031	.50958
Valid N (listwise)	64				

In the statement regarding material developed with ChatGPT, it is known that on average, respondents believe that material developed with ChatGPT is easy to understand, with an average score of 4.52. The relatively low standard deviation of 0.53 indicates that there is a general consensus among users regarding the directness of this material. Then on to statements regarding interest and motivation: Users reported that ChatGPT helped them stay interested and motivated while learning English, with an average rating of 4.61. The low standard deviation of 0.49 indicates that this effect is relatively consistent across users.

The results of the average value shown by the results of this study in Table 2 show that, with an average rating of 4.61, ChatGPT is seen as a valuable tool for expanding one's knowledge of the English language and culture. With a standard deviation of only 0.49, it's clear that most people find it works well for this task. And with an average score of 4.31, consumers agree that ChatGPT helps them maximize their time learning English, according to a statement about learning time management. Users are within a reasonable level of agreement, as indicated by the data standard deviation of 0.47. Additionally, with an average rating of 4.63, customers found ChatGPT to make English material easier to understand. Although there is some variation in this assessment (with a standard deviation of 0.58), the public generally has a positive impression of this assessment. Users also praised ChatGPT's ability to simplify complex English topics, giving it an average rating of 4.67. A standard deviation of only 0.47 shows that people's views are quite consistent. With an average score of 4.86, respondents also said that ChatGPT helped them become better English speakers and listeners. With a standard deviation of only 0.35, it's clear everyone agrees on this.

They also believed that ChatGPT made them interested in learning English when not in class, with an average score of 4.34. The relatively high standard deviation of 0.62 indicates some variability in these opinions. In the statement regarding improving academic performance, it is known that respondents have the belief that using ChatGPT can improve their academic performance, with an average score of 4.53. A standard deviation of 0.50 indicates a moderate level of agreement among users. They also generally felt that ChatGPT improved their learning efficiency and made education fun, with an average rating of 4.20. A standard deviation of 0.51 indicates some variability in these perceptions.

Overall, these statistics show that users have a positive perception of ChatGPT's role in their English learning journey, with generally high average scores in various aspects. However, it is important to note that there is some variability in user opinions, especially regarding its role in increasing interest in learning English outside the classroom. After the quantitative results are known, the next step is to conduct semi-structured interviews with undergraduate students to find out the motivation to learn ChatGPT-based English as a teaching material that supports smartphone-based hybrid learning models.

Extract 1. (30 May 2023)

"In my opinion, ChatGPT is very interesting to use as a teaching material for English courses. The material provided is easier to understand when interacting with ChatGPT"

Extract 2. (30 May 2023)

"I have never used ChatGPT, therefore when lecturers use ChatGPT in class, I feel confident to present examples of sentences and their explanations."

Extract 3. (30 May 2023)

"It's very easy to use ChatGPT, only need to register using email and follow the instructions. Even though I was slow at first, because of the network and the capacity of the smartphone I'm using"

Extract 4. (30 May 2023)

"I believe, by using ChatGPT, learning English will be more motivated, fun and of course knowledge of the material will be easier"

Extract 5. (30 May 2023)

"In my opinion, even though ChatGPT can be accessed as a teaching material, when asked to access the material it requires proper instructions so that the information is not biased."

Extract 6. (30 May 2023)

"I feel that my motivation to learn English has increased with ChatGPT, I am able to provide accurate feedback and help me understand the material to the fullest."

A person's learning motivation is influenced by many things, including the application of artistic technology such as ChatGPT and the surrounding environment as an effort to develop a growth mindset and a strong desire to master a foreign language (English). College professors should encourage their students to develop a growth mindset and an internal drive to learn the language. ChatGPT helped participants maintain their English learning motivation, as reported by this study (interview).

This study analyses the impact of a new language assistant (ChatGPT) on students' motivation to learn English from the perspective of undergraduate students. The data does not rule out the possibility that ChatGPT improves the academic performance of undergraduate students as well. The results of this research show that using ChatGPT can arouse students' curiosity about courses and coursework. This shows the feasibility of using ChatGPT to increase undergraduate students' engagement and motivation to learn. All participants felt that the bot helped students with broad and subtle language skills. More than any other skill, it encourages students to read, ask questions, receive feedback, and write. The individual's internal and external motivation benefit from this. This shows that ChatGPT is the method of choice to motivate students to learn and enjoy English intrinsically.

This result shows the feasibility of using ChatGPT to increase student motivation to learn. All participants felt that the bot helped students with broad and subtle language skills. More than any other skill, it encourages students to read and write. The individual's internal and external motivation benefit from this. This shows that ChatGPT is the preferred method for intrinsically motivating English language students.

DISCUSSION

The potential of ChatGPT in learning English based on research results is known to lie in its ability to provide individual guidance to students. To better meet students' needs and maintain their attention, English language lecturers at universities can use ChatGPT to create individualized lesson plans and resources. ChatGPT's ability as a teaching material to increase motivation for customized learning appears in its ability to produce practice assignments that are tailored to each learner based on their current skill level, area of interest, and goals. Language skills and learning drives can both benefit from this kind of focused practice.

ChatGPT's capacity to produce natural sounding language is another advantage for its use in language teaching. Developing ChatGPT-based teaching materials really helps students create authentic materials to use as language practice scripts such as conversations, news articles, and readings. Reading and understanding authentic content can help language learners become more fluent in the target language. To help students learn, ChatGPT can generate realistic conversations, articles and materials. ChatGPT access to native speakers and authentic content can increase students' enthusiasm, motivation, and language skills. ChatGPT's conversational interface makes interacting with it simple and fun. The results of the research in table 2 show that undergraduate students feel comfortable and can be used as a source of learning English.

The results of the interviews support that using ChatGPT as a teaching material and learning resource greatly increases learning motivation similar with Ali et. al (2023); Al Yakin et al. (2022) findings. However, if undergraduate students do not take the construction of the questions seriously into account, this may lead to unreliable answers. In addition, useful ChatGPT explanations can mislead users into thinking they have a solid understanding of the subject under discussion. Therefore, the function of the lecturer as monitoring needs to help students develop efficient strategies for asking questions and criteria for assessing their answers. Instead of simply fetching results like a typical search engine, large language models like ChatGPT can infer new information based on user input. Understanding how boost impacts the performance of these models is a new field of study known as "rapid engineering" Mogavi et al. (2023).

It is important to keep in mind the caveats in using ChatGPT for language generation. Even if AI can produce sentences that sound like real people would say them, he may have difficulty expressing more complex or esoteric ideas in writing. This is because the data used for training is mostly conversational or interactive so it may lack specificity regarding these issues. There are moral questions that arise regarding ChatGPT's potential to replace the human language teaching profession, and the question of whether such a replacement is necessary or desirable. The introduction of large language models such as ChatGPT has the potential to transform language education at university level. This section discusses the pros and cons of using ChatGPT for foreign language learning in higher education and provides examples of how ChatGPT can be used in these situations. ChatGPT's biggest selling point for language learning is its emphasis on personalization.

A study conducted by Koraishi (2023) found that language sessions became more engaging and effective for all students when teachers used ChatGPT to design lessons and resources tailored to each student's specific interests and needs, as was the case with the findings of this study. The ability to generate real-life language content such as conversations, news, or reading is another huge advantage that ChatGPT brings to language learning. By using ChatGPT, language instructors can immerse their students in authentic conversations in the target language, thereby improving their'own reading and listening comprehension. Foreign language students may be able to access individual classes using ChatGPT as a tool for independent study. By customizing ChatGPT lessons and materials for each student, language instructors can make their classes more engaging and productive. One way the use of ChatGPT in this research can be tailored to each student's needs is by creating personalized practice assignments according to their current interests, skill levels, and goals. Students' language skills and learning motivation can benefit from such targeted practice.

One more incentive to utilize ChatGPT in the language classroom is its ability to produce natural-sounding content. Using ChatGPT, language teachers can produce transcripts of conversations, news articles, and real-life readings to complement their students' language learning. By using authentic language materials, this can help students improve their reading and comprehension skills in a comprehensive manner, which motivates them to love this foreign language. The conversations, articles, and readings produced by ChatGPT are realistic enough to help students learn. The real-world content that ChatGPT provides can really pique students' interest and help them improve their language skills, as found in this research. Many new avenues for language acquisition can be explored with the help of ChatGPT, an advanced and modern linguistic model. However, we must think about the problems that may arise during the implementation process. The study found that ChatGPT's integration of very large conversational text datasets presents several challenges, as the data may contain biases and stereotypes that can lead to inappropriate or prejudiced content and plagiarism. To reduce the impact of these negative outcomes, it is important to provide diverse and inclusive data sources.

This survey asking students' opinions about using ChatGPT to improve their English showed very encouraging response results. The majority of students strongly believe in the benefits of ChatGPT and emphasize that it makes learning English more fun, interesting, and enjoyable. They also felt more confident in their ability to engage in class discussions and understand English material when compared to traditional e-books. Additionally, students found ChatGPT to be an efficient and easy-to-use tool, despite initial challenges regarding network and smartphone capacity.

Semi-structured interviews conducted with undergraduate students further support these findings. Many students view ChatGPT as an interesting and effective teaching material for English courses because its interactive nature improves their understanding of the material. Some students who were initially unfamiliar with ChatGPT expressed their newfound confidence in presenting examples and explanations when used in their classes. However, it is worth noting that some students emphasized the importance of clear instructions to prevent biased information when accessing ChatGPT as teaching material. Nonetheless, the overall consensus is that ChatGPT has a positive impact on students' motivation to learn English and facilitates a deeper understanding of the course material. Based on the results of the interviews it was found that the students praised ChatGPT, citing its inspirational and inspirational qualities. Because it increases motivation, increases vocabulary, language skills and enjoyment of learning which is very relevant for learning. It is possible that helpful explanations, user-friendliness, conversational tone, and overall educational value all played a role in shaping this opinion.

ChatGPT, when viewed from a learner's perspective, offers a number of benefits. One example is the production of educational resources. As shown in Table 2, ChatGPT has been utilised by educators to increase undergraduate students' retention of course material. In this study, GPT-3 was used to generate questions, answers, and classroom feedback for a reading comprehension assignment: write sentences. The authors argue that students and teachers alike can benefit from the presence of automated ChatGPT by reducing the time and effort spent on quiz and question design but also gives students a useful tool for training and testing their knowledge while studying from textbooks and for exams.

This research uses GPT-3 as a teaching tool to make college students motivated and more interested in learning and able to actively provide feedback and encourage deeper thinking and investigation, as students can gain insight into each other by analysing and criticizing each other's work. Of course, this would work if the feedback provided is thorough and high-quality to help them develop feedback skills. Using large language models as conversation partners in written or spoken form is the most common application of conversational AI in language education, for example, in task-oriented dialogue contexts that provide language practice opportunities such as dialogues or conversations, which is in line with the research of Jeon et al. (2023). In addition, this study findings suggest that ChatGPT has great potential as a valuable resource to support smartphone-based hybrid learning models in English education. Further research and exploration of its integration into the curriculum may yield more insights into its effectiveness and optimal use.

LIMITATION OF THE STUDY

This study examining the efficacy of ChatGPT and similar technological learning tools in inspiring and motivating students to learn English may not provide reliable or generalizable results due to methodological limitations. Some problems that may arise from this research include results that may not be applicable to a larger population a) due to limitations in the size and composition of the research sample. Therefore, it is possible that these findings cannot be generalized to the wider community. b) the research strategy used may impact the validity and reliability of the findings by not using a control group or experimental research design, making it impossible to draw conclusions about cause and effect. c). The problem with modern technology. Inconsistent connectivity and device and software glitches can reduce the effectiveness of these technological aids to education. d). The context elements for the effectiveness of technology-based learning tools may depend on various circumstances, such as the socio-cultural conditions of learners and the availability of resources and assistance. e). There are several things to keep in mind when interpreting research findings about ChatGPT or related educational technologies. ChatGPT can be a useful tool to encourage independent learning of English, but it is important to be aware of its limitations.

ChatGPT ability to motivate students to learn English may be influenced by how well they know and understand the technology and ChatGPT. ChatGPT has the potential to increase motivation to learn a foreign language because students experience the benefits and comfort of learning, but still need lecturer assistance in using the program efficiently, and emotionally benefit from the support of teachers and human friends (human-machine) and human-to-human interactions. Therefore, it is important to consider each student's needs and interests when using ChatGPT. ChatGPT's language support may need to be improved if it provides unclear directions or provides biased or incorrect information in response to questions. Despite extensive training on large sets of texts, ChatGPT may only be able to provide satisfactory linguistic feedback under relatively limited conditions. Although ChatGPT is useful for language learning, not all students will benefit from using it.

Finally, more research with larger sample sizes may be needed to understand exactly how ChatGPT can facilitate independent English language development. Although preliminary research suggests that ChatGPT can help students learn languages independently, more research is needed with larger, more diverse groups of students to draw strong conclusions about its efficacy and limitations.

CONCLUSION

This study discusses the use of ChatGPT in language learning. The EFL language teachers in this study explored how ChatGPT could increase their classroom motivation, efficiency and enthusiasm by using ChatGPT to personalize lessons and materials for each student. Undergraduate students support the use of ChatGPT in EFL classes because it can adapt material, increase undergraduate student confidence, increase interest in learning, practice, vocabulary according to needs, interests, and improve English skills. Each student's needs and interests will be met by a series of activity models ranging from filling in theory, example sentences, paragraphs, completing sentences, and various translations with ChatGPT acceleration to increase language proficiency and student engagement. In addition, this study recommends that ChatGPT can be used in language learners to produce authentic and efficient language materials and improve their digital literacy at the same time.

REFERENCES

Adiguzel, T., Kaya, M. H., & Cansu, F. K. (2023). Revolutionizing education with AI: Exploring the transformative potential of ChatGPT. *Contemporary Educational Technology*, *15*(3), ep429. doi:10.30935/cedtech/13152

Adiguzel, T., Kaya, M. H., & Cansu, F. K. (2023). Revolutionizing education with AI: Exploring the transformative potential of ChatGPT. *Contemporary Educational Technology*, *15*(3), ep429. doi:10.30935/cedtech/13152

Al Yakin, A., Obaid, A. J., & Massyat, M. (2022). Students' Motivation and Attitude Based on Google Classroom Utilization. *Journal of Positive School Psychology, 6*(2), 1053–1059.

Ali, J. K. M., Shamsan, M. A. A., Hezam, T. A., & Mohammed, A. A. (2023). Impact of ChatGPT on learning motivation: Teachers and students' voices. *Journal of English Studies in Arabia Felix, 2*(1), 41–49. doi:10.56540/jesaf.v2i1.51

Baidoo-Anu, D., & Ansah, L. O. (2023). Education in the era of generative artificial intelligence (AI): Understanding the potential benefits of ChatGPT in promoting teaching and learning. *Journal of AI, 7*(1), 52–62. doi:10.61969/jai.1337500

Chen, X., Zou, D., Xie, H., & Wang, F. L. (2023). Metaverse in Education: Contributors, Cooperations, and Research Themes. *IEEE Transactions on Learning Technologies*, 1–18. doi:10.1109/TLT.2023.3277952

Chen, Y., Jensen, S., Albert, L. J., Gupta, S., & Lee, T. (2023). Artificial intelligence (AI) student assistants in the classroom: Designing chatbots to support student success. *Information Systems Frontiers, 25*(1), 161–182. doi:10.100710796-022-10291-4

Dao, X. Q. (2023). Performance comparison of large language models on vnhsge english dataset: Openai chatgpt, microsoft bing chat, and google bard. *arXiv preprint arXiv:2307.02288.*

Dhivya, D. S., Hariharasudan, A., Ragmoun, W., & Alfalih, A. A. (2023). ELSA as an Education 4.0 Tool for Learning Business English Communication. *Sustainability (Basel), 15*(4), 3809. doi:10.3390u15043809

Ebadi, S., & Amini, A. (2022). Examining the roles of social presence and human-likeness on Iranian EFL learners' motivation using artificial intelligence technology: A case of CSIEC chatbot. *Interactive Learning Environments*, 1–19. doi:10.1080/10494820.2022.2096638

Ferrara, E. (2023). Should chatgpt be biased? challenges and risks of bias in large language models. *arXiv preprint arXiv:2304.03738.*

Firat, M. (2023). What ChatGPT means for universities: Perceptions of scholars and students. *Journal of Applied Learning and Teaching, 6*(1).

Gabrielli, S., Rizzi, S., Bassi, G., Carbone, S., Maimone, R., Marchesoni, M., & Forti, S. (2021). Engagement and effectiveness of a healthy-coping intervention via chatbot for university students during the COVID-19 pandemic: Mixed methods proof-of-concept study. *JMIR mHealth and uHealth, 9*(5), e27965. doi:10.2196/27965 PMID:33950849

Gavilán, J. C. O., Díaz, D. Z., Huallpa, J. J., Cabala, J. L. B., Aguila, O. E. P., Puma, E. G. M., & Arias-Gonzáles, J. L. (2022). Technological Social Responsibility in University Professors. *Eurasian Journal of Educational Research, 100*(100), 104–118.

Guo, K., Zhong, Y., Li, D., & Chu, S. K. W. (2023). Investigating students' engagement in chatbot-supported classroom debates. *Interactive Learning Environments*, 1–17. doi:10.1080/10494820.2023.2207181

Hong, W. C. H. (2023). The impact of ChatGPT on foreign language teaching and learning: Opportunities in education and research. *Journal of Educational Technology and Innovation, 5*(1).

Hong, W. C. H. (2023). The impact of ChatGPT on foreign language teaching and learning: Opportunities in education and research. *Journal of Educational Technology and Innovation*, *5*(1).

Hsu, T. C., Huang, H. L., Hwang, G. J., & Chen, M. S. (2023). Effects of Incorporating an Expert Decision-making Mechanism into Chatbots on Students' Achievement, Enjoyment, and Anxiety. *Journal of Educational Technology & Society*, *26*(1), 218–231.

Huang, W., Hew, K. F., & Fryer, L. K. (2022). Chatbots for language learning—Are they really useful? A systematic review of chatbot-supported language learning. *Journal of Computer Assisted Learning*, *38*(1), 237–257. doi:10.1111/jcal.12610

Ibna Seraj, P. M., & Oteir, I. (2022). Playing with AI to Investigate Human-Computer Interaction Technology and Improving Critical Thinking Skills to Pursue 21 st Century Age. *Education Research International*, 2022.

Jeon, J., Lee, S., & Choe, H. (2023). Beyond ChatGPT: A conceptual framework and systematic review of speech-recognition chatbots for language learning. *Computers & Education*, *206*, 104898. doi:10.1016/j.compedu.2023.104898

Jeon, J., Lee, S., & Choe, H. (2023). Beyond ChatGPT: A conceptual framework and systematic review of speech-recognition chatbots for language learning. *Computers & Education*, *206*, 104898. doi:10.1016/j.compedu.2023.104898

Kamruzzaman, M. M., Alanazi, S., Alruwaili, M., Alshammari, N., Elaiwat, S., Abu-Zanona, M., Innab, N., Mohammad Elzaghmouri, B., & Ahmed Alanazi, B. (2023). AI-and IoT-Assisted Sustainable Education Systems during Pandemics, such as COVID-19, for Smart Cities. *Sustainability (Basel)*, *15*(10), 8354. doi:10.3390u15108354

Kasneci, E., Seßler, K., Küchemann, S., Bannert, M., Dementieva, D., Fischer, F., Gasser, U., Groh, G., Günnemann, S., Hüllermeier, E., Krusche, S., Kutyniok, G., Michaeli, T., Nerdel, C., Pfeffer, J., Poquet, O., Sailer, M., Schmidt, A., Seidel, T., & Kasneci, G. (2023). ChatGPT for good? On opportunities and challenges of large language models for education. *Learning and Individual Differences*, *103*, 102274. doi:10.1016/j.lindif.2023.102274

Kim, H., Yang, H., Shin, D., & Lee, J. H. (2022). Design principles and architecture of a second language learning chatbot. *Language Learning & Technology*, *26*(1), 1–18.

Kohnke, L. (2023). L2 learners' perceptions of a chatbot as a potential independent language learning tool. *International Journal of Mobile Learning and Organisation*, *17*(1-2), 214–226. doi:10.1504/IJMLO.2023.128339

Kohnke, L., Moorhouse, B. L., & Zou, D. (2023). ChatGPT for language teaching and learning. *RELC Journal*, 00336882231162868.

Koraishi, O. (2023). Teaching English in the age of AI: Embracing ChatGPT to optimize EFL materials and assessment. *Language Education and Technology, 3*(1).

Kovačević, D. (2023, March). Use of chatgpt in ESP teaching process. In *2023 22nd International Symposium INFOTEH-JAHORINA (INFOTEH)* (pp. 1-5). IEEE.

Limna, P., Kraiwanit, T., Jangjarat, K., Klayklung, P., & Chocksathaporn, P. (2023). The use of ChatGPT in the digital era: Perspectives on chatbot implementation. *Journal of Applied Learning and Teaching, 6*(1).

Liu, G., & Ma, C. (2023). Measuring EFL learners' use of ChatGPT in informal digital learning of English based on the technology acceptance model. *Innovation in Language Learning and Teaching*, 1–14. doi:10.1080/17501229.2023.2240316

Liu, Y., Han, T., Ma, S., Zhang, J., Yang, Y., Tian, J., & Ge, B. (2023). Summary of chatgpt/gpt-4 research and perspective towards the future of large language models. *arXiv preprint arXiv:2304.01852.*

Liu, Y., Han, T., Ma, S., Zhang, J., Yang, Y., Tian, J., & Ge, B. (2023). Summary of chatgpt/gpt-4 research and perspective towards the future of large language models. *arXiv preprint arXiv:2304.01852.*

Mageira, K., Pittou, D., Papasalouros, A., Kotis, K., Zangogianni, P., & Daradoumis, A. (2022). Educational AI chatbots for content and language integrated learning. *Applied Sciences (Basel, Switzerland), 12*(7), 3239. doi:10.3390/app12073239

Matuk, C., Yetman-Michaelson, L., Martin, R., Vasudevan, V., Burgas, K., Davidesco, I., Shevchenko, Y., Chaloner, K., & Dikker, S. (2023). Open science in the classroom: Students designing and peer reviewing studies in human brain and behavior research. *Instructional Science, 51*(5), 1–53. doi:10.100711251-023-09633-9

Michel-Villarreal, R., Vilalta-Perdomo, E., Salinas-Navarro, D. E., Thierry-Aguilera, R., & Gerardou, F. S. (2023). Challenges and Opportunities of Generative AI for Higher Education as Explained by ChatGPT. *Education Sciences, 13*(9), 856. doi:10.3390/educsci13090856

Mogavi, R. H., Deng, C., Kim, J. J., Zhou, P., Kwon, Y. D., Metwally, A. H. S., & Hui, P. (2023). Exploring user perspectives on chatgpt: Applications, perceptions, and implications for ai-integrated education. *arXiv preprint arXiv:2305.13114.*

Mogavi, R. H., Deng, C., Kim, J. J., Zhou, P., Kwon, Y. D., Metwally, A. H. S., & Hui, P. (2023). Exploring user perspectives on chatgpt: Applications, perceptions, and implications for ai-integrated education. *arXiv preprint arXiv:2305.13114.*

Molnár, G., & Szüts, Z. (2018, September). The role of chatbots in formal education. In *2018 IEEE 16th International Symposium on Intelligent Systems and Informatics (SISY)* (pp. 000197-000202). IEEE. 10.1109/SISY.2018.8524609

Muñoz, S. A. S., Gayoso, G. G., Huambo, A. C., Tapia, R. D. C., Incaluque, J. L., Aguila, O. E. P., & Arias-Gonzáles, J. L. (2023). Examining the Impacts of ChatGPT on Student Motivation and Engagement. *Social Space, 23*(1), 1–27.

Pallant, J. (2020). SPSS survival manual: A step by step guide to data analysis using IBM SPSS. McGraw-hill education (UK).

Perkins, M. (2023). Academic Integrity considerations of AI Large Language Models in the post-pandemic era: ChatGPT and beyond. *Journal of University Teaching & Learning Practice, 20*(2), 07.

Qiao, S., Yeung, S. S. S., Zainuddin, Z., Ng, D. T. K., & Chu, S. K. W. (2023). Examining the effects of mixed and non-digital gamification on students' learning performance, cognitive engagement and course satisfaction. *British Journal of Educational Technology, 54*(1), 394–413. doi:10.1111/bjet.13249

Rudolph, J., Tan, S., & Tan, S. (2023). ChatGPT: Bullshit spewer or the end of traditional assessments in higher education? *Journal of Applied Learning and Teaching, 6*(1).

Shidiq, M. (2023, May). The use of artificial intelligence-based chat-gpt and its challenges for the world of education; from the viewpoint of the development of creative writing skills. In *Proceeding of International Conference on Education, Society and Humanity* (Vol. 1, No. 1, pp. 353-357).

Xia, Q., Chiu, T. K., & Chai, C. S. (2023). The moderating effects of gender and need satisfaction on self-regulated learning through Artificial Intelligence (AI). *Education and Information Technologies, 28*(7), 8691–8713. doi:10.100710639-022-11547-x

Yan, D. (2023). Impact of ChatGPT on learners in a L2 writing practicum: An exploratory investigation. *Education and Information Technologies, 28*(11), 1–25. doi:10.100710639-023-11742-4

Yildirim-Erbasli, S. N., & Bulut, O. (2023). Conversation-based assessment: A novel approach to boosting test-taking effort in digital formative assessment. *Computers and Education: Artificial Intelligence, 4*, 100135. doi:10.1016/j.caeai.2023.100135

Zhao, Y., & Lai, C. (2023). Technology and second language learning: Promises and problems. In *Technology-mediated learning environments for young English learners* (pp. 167–206). Routledge. doi:10.4324/9781003418009-8

Chapter 3
ChatGPT in Content Creation:
Techniques, Applications, and Ethical Implications

Arkar Htet

https://orcid.org/0000-0003-1301-3604
Lincoln University College, Malaysia

Sui Reng Liana
Lincoln University College, Malaysia

Theingi Aung
Lincoln University College, Malaysia

Amiya Bhaumik
Lincoln University College, Malaysia

ABSTRACT

This book chapter delves into the transformative role of ChatGPT in content creation, exploring its underlying techniques, diverse applications, and associated ethical implications. The investigation spans several industries including journalism, marketing, and entertainment, demonstrating the model's adaptability and power. This comprehensive analysis not only spotlights the challenges inherent in implementing ChatGPT, but also illuminates the unique opportunities it presents. By offering a thorough examination of the current state of ChatGPT in content creation and potential future developments, this chapter contributes to the ongoing discourse surrounding AI's impact on content creation.

DOI: 10.4018/979-8-3693-0502-7.ch003

INTRODUCTION

The transformative potential of artificial intelligence (AI) has begun to reshape numerous industries, and the realm of content creation is no exception (Yan, 2019). AI's capacity to generate innovative, engaging, and high-quality content has sparked a paradigm shift in how content is created, consumed, and distributed (Lee, K.J., Kwon, J.W., Min,S., & Yoon,J., 2021).

Central to this shift is the emergence of natural language processing (NLP), a subset of AI that focuses on the interaction between computers and human language. The rise of NLP has led to the development of sophisticated language models capable of understanding, generating, and even translating human language in ways that were once unimaginable (Luitse, D., & Denkena, W., 2021).

A leading figure in this new landscape is the Generative Pretrained Transformer (GPT), specifically, ChatGPT. ChatGPT leverages the power of machine learning and NLP to produce human-like text that is not only contextually relevant but also creatively rich, marking a significant advance in content creation capabilities (Jagdishbhai, N., & Thakkar, K. Y., 2023).

This chapter explores the profound implications of this AI model for content creation across various industries. The motivation for this investigation lies in ChatGPT's transformative potential: its capacity to revolutionize established processes, create new opportunities, and pose new challenges. By exploring these dimensions, we aim to foster a nuanced understanding of the role and impact of AI, and specifically ChatGPT, in modern content creation.

In terms of methodology, a systematic review of existing literature on ChatGPT, AI, and content creation will be conducted, drawing from academic databases, conference proceedings, and reputable online sources. To complement the review, case studies illustrating real-world applications and impacts of ChatGPT in content creation will be analyzed.

The objective is to provide an encompassing overview of the techniques, applications, and ethical considerations associated with ChatGPT's role in content creation, laying the groundwork for future research and practice. While the journey through AI in content creation is just beginning, it promises a future of innovation, disruption, and immense potential.

TECHNIQUES AND FUNCTIONING OF CHAPTGPT IN CONTETNT CREATION

Architecture and Key Components of ChatGPT

The architecture of ChatGPT, as part of the broader family of GPT models, is rooted in its Transformer-based structure. This architecture, first introduced by (Lund, B.D., & Wang,T., 2023), revolutionized the field of natural language processing (NLP) through its focus on self-attention mechanisms. The Transformer model marked a shift away from recurrent and convolutional neural networks, providing benefits in computational efficiency and performance in sequence modeling tasks.

ChatGPT's capabilities are grounded in the key components that constitute its architecture: multi-layered transformer blocks, self-attention mechanisms, position-wise feed-forward networks, and positional encoding (Zhou, 2023).

The multi-layered transformer blocks form the backbone of the architecture. Specifically, GPT-4, the fourth version from which ChatGPT is derived, comprises a large number of these transformer blocks stacked together, each containing a self-attention mechanism and a position-wise feed-forward network.

While earlier versions like GPT-3 comprised 48 transformer layers, GPT-4 extends this to a greater number, thereby allowing the model to process input data at multiple levels of abstraction and generate complex, nuanced outputs.

The self-attention mechanism, a key innovation of the Transformer architecture, assigns relevance weights to each word in a sentence relative to all other words, capturing context and dependencies, even at great distances. This mechanism also helps the model scale with increasing input sequence length (Bisk, Y., Zellers, R., Le-bras, R., Gao,J., & Choi, Y., 2020).

Position-wise feed-forward networks, integral to each transformer block, apply a fully connected feed-forward network to each position separately and identically. These networks help the model recognize more complex patterns within the input data.

Positional encoding is vital as it allows Transformers, which don't inherently capture sequence order like recurrent or convolutional networks, to inject information about the relative or absolute position of tokens in the sequence (Zhang Q., 2020).

In summary, ChatGPT's architecture, characterized by the sophisticated interplay of these components, empowers it to generate text that is contextually relevant, creative, and coherent. Understanding these architectural elements provides insights into this AI model's content creation capabilities and the opportunities it presents for future advancements.

Figure 1. Simplified illustration of the GPT-4 architecture
(source: own)
Caption: The figure shows an input sequence passing through the multi-layered transformer blocks (each containing a self-attention mechanism and a position-wise feed-forward network) to produce an output sequence. Note that GPT-4 comprises a large number of these transformer blocks (denoted as "Transformer Block N"), extending beyond the 48 layers of its predecessor, GPT-3.

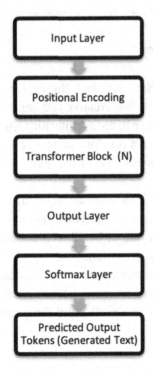

Pre-Training and Fine-Tuning Processes

The functionality of ChatGPT, similar to other models in the GPT series, rests on a two-step process: pre-training and fine-tuning (Athaluri, S., Manthena, S., Kesapragada, V., 2023).

The pre-training phase is an unsupervised learning approach where the model learns to predict the next word in a sentence based on the preceding words. This phase utilizes a massive corpus of text data gathered from the internet (Gama, 2004). The significance of this large-scale corpus lies in its diversity, which allows the model to learn a broad array of topics, styles, and contexts. Consequently, this exposure helps in the generation of varied and contextually coherent responses during the content creation process.

Fine-tuning follows the pre-training process. It is a supervised learning step in which the model is further trained on a smaller, specific dataset, often with human-provided labels or guidance (Li, J., Li, Z., Ge,T., King,I., & Lyu, M.R., 2022). The role of fine-tuning is crucial because it refines the model's capabilities to generate outputs that align with the desired task or domain.

The differences between unsupervised and supervised fine-tuning are evident in their objectives and methods. Unsupervised fine-tuning does not require labelled data, focusing instead on learning patterns within the data and making predictions accordingly. This method is particularly beneficial when dealing with vast, unlabelled datasets, such as those used in the pre-training phase (Ashish, 2017).

On the other hand, supervised fine-tuning requires labelled data, providing explicit guidance to the model about the correct outputs for specific inputs. This method is advantageous when the goal is to specialize the model's capabilities to a specific task or domain (Chen, T., Kornblith, S., Swersky, K., Norouzi, M., & Hinton, G., 2020)

In essence, the combination of pre-training and fine-tuning processes allows ChatGPT to harness the wide-ranging knowledge obtained from the large-scale corpus and then specialize it to generate more task-specific outputs. This symbiotic process results in a model that is both versatile and focused, contributing significantly to the AI's effectiveness in content creation.

Content Generation Capabilities

ChatGPT, leveraging its sophisticated architecture, has achieved remarkable content generation capabilities, including contextually relevant, coherent, and creative text generation (Wang, F. Y., Yang.J., Wang.X., Li, J., & Han, Q.L., 2023). Its transformer-based architecture allows it to understand and generate text with attention to the contextual relevance of previous inputs. This means it can generate responses based on understanding the context of the conversation or the text at hand (Yupan, H., Hongwei,X., Bei, L., & Yutong, L., 2021).

The coherence of the generated text is another key capability of ChatGPT. Through the process of learning from a large corpus of diverse text, it can create human-like text that follows logical and grammatical structures. This makes the text output by ChatGPT fluent and readable, even over extended pieces of writing (King, M.R. & Can-Bard., 2023).

Furthermore, ChatGPT's ability to generate creative text is notable. It is capable of devising original sentences, paragraphs, or even stories that have not been explicitly programmed into it. This capacity for creative text generation sets it apart as a useful tool for content creation, helping to generate new ideas or perspectives (Frith, 2023).

However, while ChatGPT boasts these impressive capabilities, it is not without limitations. Notably, it tends to be verbose, often providing more text than necessary in response to prompts. This verbosity can lead to unnecessary repetition or over-complication, detracting from the clarity of the message (Ubani, 2023).

Another limitation is inconsistency. While ChatGPT strives for coherent and contextually relevant responses, it can sometimes produce outputs that contradict previous statements or stray from the main topic. This lack of consistency is a challenge that needs to be addressed for more accurate and reliable content generation (Frith, 2023).

In sum, while ChatGPT's capabilities of generating contextually relevant, coherent, and creative text make it a powerful tool in content creation, the limitations of verbosity and inconsistency highlight areas for further improvement.

Evaluation Techniques for ChatGPT in Content Creation

The evaluation of AI models, including ChatGPT, has progressed in tandem with the development of the models themselves. Initially, rule-based models were dominant, followed by the rise of statistical methods, and more recently, the advent of deep learning models (Aithal, S., & Aithal, P. S., 2023).

Rule-based models relied heavily on crafted rules and linguistic expertise. The evaluation for these models was often based on how well they adhered to the pre-set rules (Mencar, C., Castiello, C., Cannone, R., & Fanelli, A.M., 2011). Statistical methods, on the other hand, utilized data-driven approaches, allowing the models to learn from the data directly. These models were commonly evaluated based on their statistical reliability and prediction accuracy (Mardanirad, S., Wood, D.A., & Zakeri, H., 2021). Deep learning models, such as ChatGPT, have significantly advanced the field with their ability to learn complex patterns in large-scale data. The evaluation of these models typically involves a mix of automated metrics and human evaluations (Zhuo, C., Kui, F., Shiqi, W., Ling, Y.D., Weisi, L,.& Alex, K., 2019).

Automated metrics, like BLEU and ROUGE, provide swift quantitative insights, yet may overlook the semantic nuances and originality in the generated text (Elizabeth, C.,Asli, C.,&Noah.A.S., 2019). In contrast, human evaluations can better assess qualitative aspects, such as conversational flow and user satisfaction, but are more resource-intensive and potentially biased (Yadav, S., & Kaushik,A., 2022).

In conclusion, a balanced approach using both automated metrics and human evaluations is essential for assessing the performance of ChatGPT in content creation. Further research should focus on developing more nuanced evaluation metrics that better capture the complexity of language and qualitative dimensions of human-machine interaction.

Table 1. Progression of AI models and their evaluations

Type of Model	Key Characteristics	Examples	Evaluation Methods
Rule-Based Models	Relies on pre-set rules and linguistic expertise	ELIZA, SHRDLU	Based on adherence to rules
Statistical Models	Data-driven, learns from the data directly	IBM's Statistical Machine Translation, Google Translate (initial versions)	Statistical reliability and prediction accuracy
Deep Learning Models	Learns complex patterns in large-scale data	GPT series (including ChatGPT), BERT, Transformer models	Mix of automated metrics (BLEU, ROUGE) and human evaluations

Limitations of ChatGPT

While ChatGPT is lauded for its numerous capabilities in content creation, it is essential to discuss its limitations to provide a balanced perspective on the technology. These limitations can be categorized into several key areas.

Firstly, one of the primary limitations of ChatGPT is verbosity (King, M.R. & Can-Bard., 2023). Often, the model produces excessively lengthy and redundant responses. It may over-elaborate or repeat certain phrases or ideas, which can lead to content that is not concise and straight to the point.

Another notable limitation is its potential to generate inappropriate or biased content (Xi, Z., Zhendong, M., Chunxiao, L., Peng, Z., Bin, W., & Yong, Z., 2020). Despite measures to safeguard against this, there are instances where the model may generate outputs that reflect biases present in the training data. This presents significant challenges, especially in contexts where fair and unbiased content generation is essential.

Thirdly, ChatGPT cannot fact-check information.It generates content based on patterns learned from its training data, rather than verifying the truthfulness of the information. As a result, the model might produce outputs that contain factual inaccuracies or misinformation (Zielinski, C., Winker, M., Aggarwal, R., Ferris, L., Heinemann, M., Lapeña, J. F., & Citrome, L., 2023).

Finally, ChatGPT has limitations in understanding context beyond a certain length. This is due to its design, where it can only take into account a fixed number of previous tokens (usually 1024 or 2048 tokens for GPT-3). This limit can lead to issues when generating long pieces of content or having extended conversations, where it might lose track of the context (Hao, J., & Ho, T.K., 2019).

In summary, while ChatGPT presents exciting capabilities in content creation, these limitations underscore the need for continuous research and development in this field to enhance the utility and ethical considerations of such AI models.

Limitations of the Current Study and Further Research

While this study provides a comprehensive examination of the applications, benefits, and limitations of ChatGPT in content creation, it is not without its limitations. Primarily, this research focuses on theoretical and documented applications of ChatGPT and does not provide an empirical analysis of its effectiveness in different real-world scenarios. As such, the conclusions drawn might not fully capture the variety of experiences different industries and users might encounter when implementing ChatGPT (Zielinski, C., Winker, M., Aggarwal, R., Ferris, L., Heinemann, M., Lapeña, J. F., & Citrome, L., 2023).

Furthermore, the study relies heavily on existing literature, which predominantly centers on the use of GPT-3, the most recent model at the time of this writing. Given the rapid pace of advancements in AI technology, newer iterations of ChatGPT could present different capabilities and challenges that are not covered in this research (King, M.R. & Can-Bard., 2023).

Therefore, future research should aim to conduct empirical studies that evaluate the performance and impacts of ChatGPT in various practical settings. Moreover, as newer versions of the model are developed, researchers should seek to continually update the understanding of ChatGPT's capabilities, limitations, and ethical implications in content creation. It would also be valuable to conduct comparative studies of different AI content generation tools to help users make more informed decisions about which tool best suits their needs.

Lastly, as ChatGPT and similar technologies increasingly influence content creation processes across industries, it is crucial to study their long-term impacts on job markets, creative processes, and society at large.

APPLICATIONS OF CHATGPT IN CONTENT CREATION

Benefits of Using ChatGPT for Content Creation

The deployment of ChatGPT in the realm of content creation offers various benefits, ranging from enhanced efficiency and cost savings to unlocking creative potential (Lund, B.D., & Wang, T., 2023). These advantages can be illustrated through numerous applications and use-cases across industries as shown in figure 2.

Figure 2. Key benefits of using ChatGPT for content creation
(Source: own)

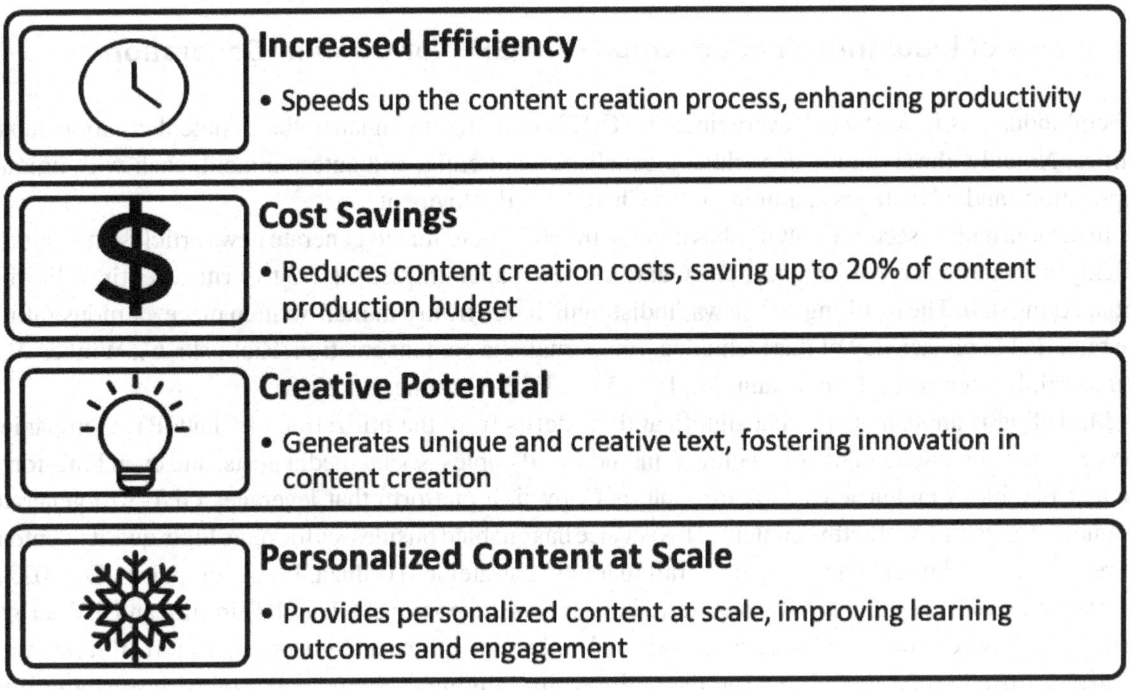

Increased Efficiency
• Speeds up the content creation process, enhancing productivity

Cost Savings
• Reduces content creation costs, saving up to 20% of content production budget

Creative Potential
• Generates unique and creative text, fostering innovation in content creation

Personalized Content at Scale
• Provides personalized content at scale, improving learning outcomes and engagement

One of the most significant benefits of ChatGPT in content creation is increased efficiency. Through automated generation of text, the technology can significantly speed up the process of content creation, contributing to higher productivity (Pavlik, 2023). For instance, news organizations like Associated Press and Reuters have leveraged similar AI technologies for automated reporting, leading to a considerable increase in the number of news articles produced daily (Kapoor, R., & Ghosal, I., 2022).

Cost savings constitute another vital benefit. By automating part of the content creation process, businesses can significantly reduce associated costs. For example, marketers have found that using AI tools for content generation can save up to 20% of their budget allocated for content production (Van-Leeuwen, K.G., Meijer, F.J.A., Schalekamp, S., 2021).

Moreover, the creative potential of ChatGPT cannot be overlooked. The technology can generate unique and creative text, opening up new possibilities for innovation in content creation. Take the case of OpenAI's GPT-3, which co-authored a book, "You Look Like a Thing and I Love You" (Athaluri, S., Manthena, S., Kesapragada, V., 2023). The model contributed imaginative ideas and humorous lines, enriching the book's content.

Lastly, ChatGPT can provide personalized content at scale. For instance, in the education sector, it can generate individualized learning materials tailored to each student's learning style and pace. A study conducted by Microsoft in 2019 found that AI-based personalized learning can improve student outcomes by up to 30% (Peter, S., Joe, W., & Tom, B., 2023).

In conclusion, ChatGPT's deployment in content creation yields considerable benefits, such as increased efficiency, cost savings, and creative potential, coupled with personalization at scale. As the technology matures, these advantages will become increasingly significant, making ChatGPT an indispensable tool in the future of content creation.

Examples of Industries That Leverage ChatGPT for Content Generation

Several industries have started leveraging ChatGPT's potential to enhance their content creation capabilities. Notably, these industries include journalism, marketing, and entertainment, each with unique applications and advantages stemming from ChatGPT's deployment.

In the journalism sector, ChatGPT has demonstrated its potential to generate news articles and reports quickly and accurately. For instance, The Guardian newspaper utilized GPT-3 to write an entire editorial about AI in 2020. The resulting article was indistinguishable from a human-written piece, demonstrating the remarkable proficiency of this technology in journalistic content creation (Zielinski, C., Winker, M., Aggarwal, R., Ferris, L., Heinemann, M., Lapeña, J. F., & Citrome, L., 2023).

Marketing is another sector that significantly benefits from the utilization of ChatGPT. Companies use it to create engaging marketing content, including ad copies, social media posts, and even long-form content like blogs and articles. One example is Copy.ai, a platform that leverages GPT-3 to generate unique and engaging marketing content. This service has enabled businesses to create high-quality content more efficiently, thus enhancing their overall marketing strategies (Haluza, D., & Jungwirth, D., 2023).

The entertainment industry also has started to harness the power of ChatGPT. In film and TV scriptwriting, AI has been deployed to generate original and creative scripts. Sunspring, a short film released in 2016, utilized an AI model to write the entire script, hinting at the potential of AI in scriptwriting (Som, 2023). Although the script was written by a previous iteration of GPT, the success of Sunspring suggests that ChatGPT can push these boundaries even further.

ChatGPT has also made its mark in the gaming industry. Games like AI Dungeon, developed by Latitude, use GPT-3 to generate dynamic and compelling narratives that evolve based on player decisions. This application enhances the gaming experience by providing players with unique and immersive stories (Judith, V.S., &J akub, M., 2021).

These applications of ChatGPT across various industries highlight its potential to revolutionize content creation processes. As this technology continues to advance and become more widely adopted, its impact is only expected to grow, reshaping content creation across sectors.

Table 2. Applications of ChatGPT in various industries

Industry	Application of ChatGPT	Example
Journalism	Generation of news articles and reports	The Guardian newspaper utilized GPT-3 to write an entire editorial (Sample, 2020)
Marketing	Creation of marketing content (ad copies, social media posts, long-form content)	Copy.ai uses GPT-3 to generate unique and engaging marketing content (Tantivit, 2020)
Entertainment (Film and TV)	Scriptwriting	Sunspring, a short film, used an AI model to write the entire script (Oscar Sharp & Ross Goodwin, 2016)
Gaming	Generation of dynamic and evolving narratives	AI Dungeon uses GPT-3 to create immersive stories that evolve based on player decisions (Latitude, 2020)

Role of ChatGPT in Generating Various Content Types

ChatGPT is capable of generating various types of content, significantly enhancing productivity and creativity in many fields. This capability spans across generating articles, social media posts, advertising copy, scripts, and more.

For generating articles, ChatGPT has proven itself to be a competent assistant. It can take a short prompt and expand it into a full-length article, demonstrating impressive consistency and contextual understanding (Cooper, 2023). Moreover, GPT-3's language generation capabilities extend beyond simple factual reporting and include persuasive, opinion-based, and creative writing, giving it a broad applicability for generating diverse article types (Anson, C.M., & Straume, I., 2022).

In the social media sphere, ChatGPT has shown efficacy in creating engaging posts. It can be used to automatically generate tweets or Facebook posts based on a specified theme or topic, ensuring brand consistency and saving considerable time for social media managers (Firaina, R., & Sulisworo, D., 2023). It can also effectively generate short-form content for platforms like Instagram, creating captions that can help to maximize user engagement.

In marketing and advertising, the application of ChatGPT for creating advertising copy is noteworthy. By inputting a brief description of a product or service, ChatGPT can generate multiple variants of engaging and persuasive ad copy. The immense speed and versatility of ChatGPT can facilitate rapid A/B testing and optimization, significantly boosting marketing efficiency (Zhang, X., Shah, J., & Han, M., 2023).

Furthermore, ChatGPT's creativity has been employed in the field of scriptwriting. From drafting TV show scripts to generating dialogue for video games, it can bring unique ideas and unexpected plot twists, offering fresh perspectives and facilitating the creative process (Mijwil, M., Aljanabi, M., & Ali, A.H., 2023).

However, it is crucial to mention that while ChatGPT can generate a wide variety of content types, the quality and relevance of output depend significantly on the prompts and context provided. The model still requires guidance and editing from humans to ensure that the generated content meets the desired standards (Zhu, L., Mou, W., & Chen, R., 2023).

Overall, ChatGPT's versatile capabilities in content generation make it a valuable tool in many industries, significantly influencing how content is created and consumed.

Figure 3. Flowchart of ChatGPT in generating various content types
(source: own)

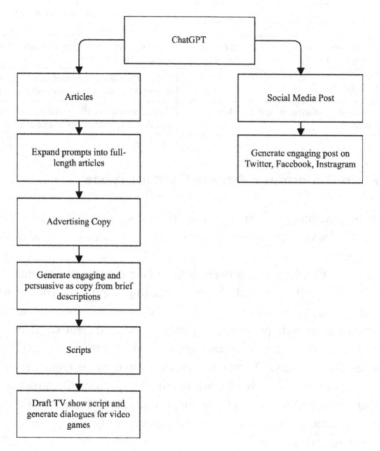

Integration of ChatGPT with Existing Content Management Systems

The integration of AI-powered language models like ChatGPT with existing content management systems (CMSs) holds transformative potential for content generation and workflow efficiency. It can provide a seamless interface between content creation, editing, management, and publishing, thereby streamlining operations and improving productivity (Lewis, 2023). As depicted in Figure 4, the process of content creation can be streamlined, offering a seamless interface between content creation, editing, management, and publishing.

Figure 4. Workflow in an integrated system using ChatGPT with CMSs
(source: own)
Caption: The diagram illustrates the streamlined workflow in an integrated system using ChatGPT with CMSs, including stages like prompt initiation, AI content generation, editing, and publishing.

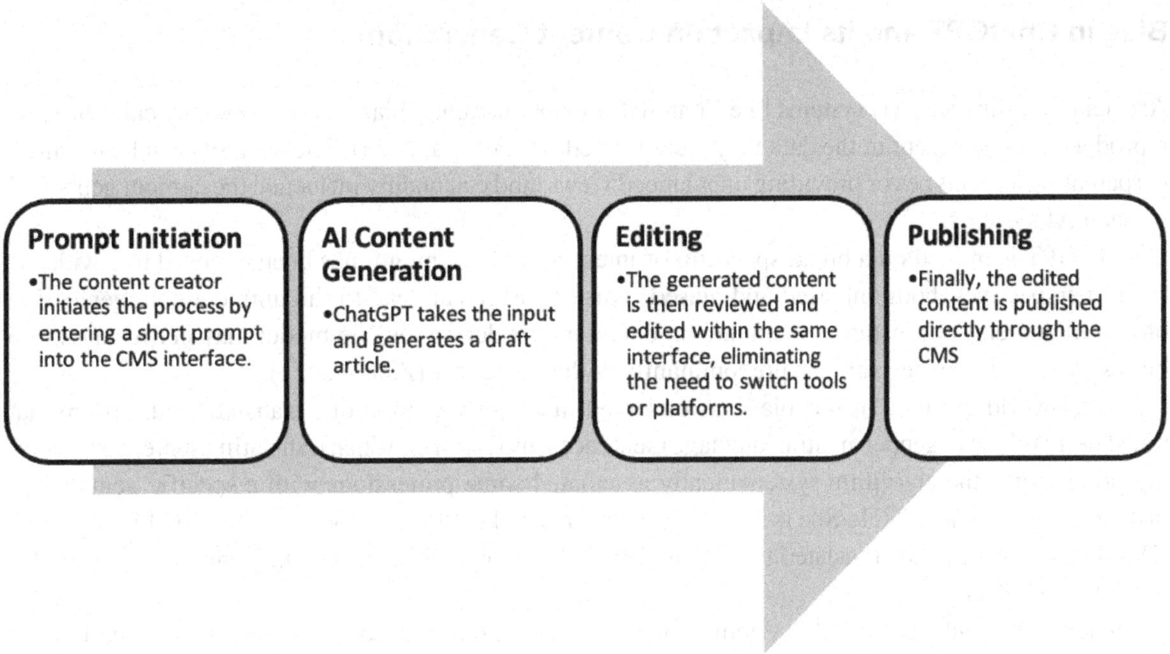

Prompt Initiation
•The content creator initiates the process by entering a short prompt into the CMS interface.

AI Content Generation
•ChatGPT takes the input and generates a draft article.

Editing
•The generated content is then reviewed and edited within the same interface, eliminating the need to switch tools or platforms.

Publishing
•Finally, the edited content is published directly through the CMS

An integrated system could be designed to make use of ChatGPT's capabilities directly from the CMS interface. For instance, a content creator could type a short prompt directly into the CMS, and ChatGPT could generate a draft article, which could then be edited and published without needing to switch tools or platforms. This seamless workflow integration can save considerable time and effort, allowing content creators to focus more on crafting their narrative rather than manual content generation (Eysenbach, 2023).

In addition to streamlining content generation, the integration of ChatGPT with CMSs can offer improved content capabilities. For instance, AI-generated suggestions for headlines or meta descriptions can be included directly within the CMS, improving SEO and user engagement (Shahsavar, Y., & Choudhury, A., 2023). It can also help in generating content for multilingual websites, translating existing content to different languages, thus enhancing accessibility and reach.

Moreover, the integration of ChatGPT with CMSs can potentially facilitate real-time content personalization. ChatGPT's ability to generate contextually relevant and tailored content could be harnessed to deliver personalized user experiences, adapting the content to the preferences of individual users (Frith, 2023)

However, such integration is not without its challenges. The accuracy and appropriateness of AI-generated content are essential considerations, necessitating effective moderation mechanisms to prevent the generation of inappropriate or offensive content. Ensuring that the integrated system remains within ethical and legal bounds, respects user privacy, and maintains the brand's voice and reputation is paramount (Huang,C., Zhang, Z., Mao, B., & Yao, X., 2022).

In conclusion, the integration of ChatGPT with CMSs offers the potential for more efficient, versatile, and personalized content generation. While there are challenges to navigate, the potential benefits make it a promising development for the future of content creation and management.

Bias in ChatGPT and Its Impact on Content Generation

Artificial Intelligence (AI) systems like ChatGPT are not inherently biased; however, they can learn and reproduce biases present in the data they were trained on (Ferrara, 2023). These biases can be harmful, perpetuating stereotypes or providing unbalanced views, and can unduly influence the content generated by such AI systems.

ChatGPT is trained on a broad spectrum of internet text, meaning it has been exposed to a wide array of perspectives, both unbiased and biased. This exposure can lead to the unintentional generation of biased content. For instance, if trained on data with gender biases, the model may perpetuate these biases by associating certain jobs predominantly with one gender (Zajko, 2021).

A real-world example of this bias was observed in an early version of a translation algorithm that translated Turkish (a gender-neutral language) sentences into English. When translating sentences involving professions, the algorithm systematically associated some professions with a specific gender. For instance, "O bir doktor." (He/She is a doctor.) was translated to "He is a doctor," while "O bir hemşire." (He/She is a nurse.) was translated to "She is a nurse" (Adithya, R., Denise, D., Kenneth, H., Xian, L., & Mona, D., 2021).

In addition to gender bias, AI systems can reflect racial, religious, or political biases found in their training data. If not addressed, this can lead to the propagation of stereotypes, unfair portrayal of certain groups, and polarization (Sunny, S., & Sanchari, D., 2022).

Bias in AI content generation can have significant implications. It can negatively impact public opinion, contribute to the perpetuation of harmful stereotypes, and undervalue or marginalize certain groups or ideas. For businesses, biased content can alienate customers, harm reputation, and possibly violate anti-discrimination laws (Zajko, 2021).

Addressing this challenge requires the development of more sophisticated techniques to identify and mitigate biases in AI training data and outputs. Techniques like fine-tuning on carefully curated datasets and introducing explicit fairness constraints are promising research directions. Additionally, transparency about the potential for bias and continuous monitoring of AI system outputs are crucial for responsible AI deployment (Khairatun, H. U., & Miftahul A. M., 2022).

In conclusion, while ChatGPT and similar AI models hold immense potential for content generation, awareness and proactive handling of potential bias is vital to ensure the ethical use of these technologies.

Intellectual Property and Plagiarism Concerns

Intellectual property (IP) and plagiarism concerns are critical ethical issues in AI-generated content. The generation of content by AI like ChatGPT raises legal and ethical questions about ownership, originality, and accountability (Dave, T., Athaluri, S.A., & Singh, S., 2023).

An essential aspect to understand is that AI models such as ChatGPT generate text by learning patterns from vast amounts of existing text data. While the AI does not explicitly copy or reproduce the training data, it's conceivable that the generated content may inadvertently resemble some source texts.

This likeness might raise plagiarism concerns, especially if AI-generated content is used without appropriate scrutiny or review (Sunny, S., & Sanchari, D., 2022).

Moreover, IP law, primarily designed for human authorship, is currently ill-equipped to handle AI-generated content. In most jurisdictions, the legal definition of authorship is tied to human creators. Hence, AI-generated content falls into a grey area, with no clear ownership or responsibility (Lee, J.A., Reto, M., Hilty, & Kung-Chung, L., 2021).

At this point, it's useful to visualize the potential pitfalls of AI content creation in terms of plagiarism and uncertainties around ownership. The following flowchart (Figure 5) presents two significant scenarios:

Figure 5. Flowchart illustrating the process and implications of content creation with ChatGPT

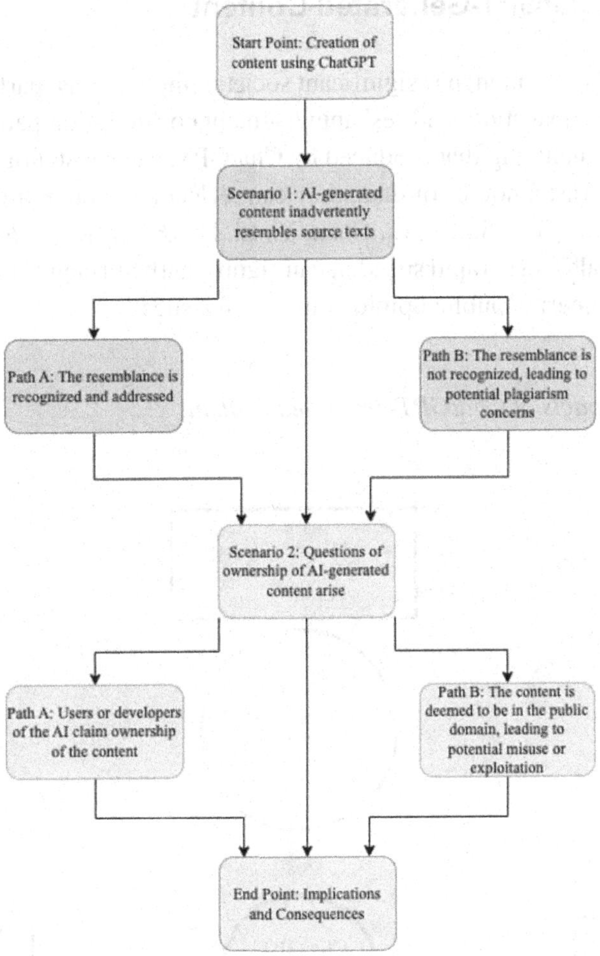

On the one hand, the users or developers of AI might argue that they own the AI's output since they created, trained, or used the AI system. On the other hand, others could claim that AI-generated content should be considered public domain as AI, a non-human entity, technically lacks the capacity for authorship (Aziz, 2023)

These ethical and legal concerns necessitate a reevaluation of existing IP laws and practices. It suggests the need for comprehensive guidelines for using AI-generated content, considering both the rights of those involved in creating, training, and operating AI systems, and those whose works may be incorporated or mirrored in AI outputs. Stakeholders should also ensure that AI systems like ChatGPT are used responsibly, with due care taken to avoid inadvertent plagiarism and respect for intellectual property rights (Risse, 2019).

In summary, while AI models like ChatGPT offer substantial advantages for content creation, their use also requires careful navigation of ethical concerns surrounding plagiarism and intellectual property. Addressing these challenges requires a cooperative effort involving legal scholars, AI researchers, and policymakers to shape guidelines and laws that reflect the evolving landscape of AI-generated content.

Societal Impact of ChatGPT-Generated Content

The ubiquity of AI-generated content has significant societal implications, particularly regarding public opinion, misinformation propagation, and reshaping content consumption patterns.

AI-generated content, including that produced by ChatGPT, can substantially shape public opinion. As AI models learn from vast amounts of data, they can reflect and potentially amplify societal biases in the content they generate (Gao, S., He, L., Chen, Y., Li, D., & Lai, K., 2020). Moreover, because AI can generate content at scale and at rapid speed, it can significantly influence the information accessible to the public, potentially steering public opinion on critical issues.

Figure 6. The societal impacts of ChatGPT-generated content
(source: own)

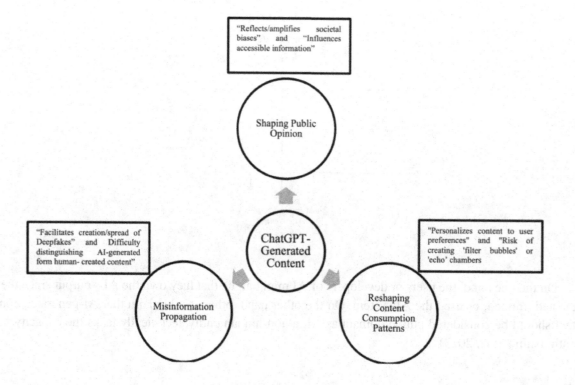

Misinformation propagation is another significant societal concern related to AI-generated content. AI models like ChatGPT, if misused, can facilitate the creation and spread of false or misleading information, also known as "deepfakes" in the context of images and videos (Oxford, 2022). The difficulty in distinguishing between AI-generated and human-created content can amplify this issue, as it becomes challenging for individuals to ascertain the veracity of information they consume. Therefore, while AI offers valuable tools for generating content, there is a pressing need to develop techniques for detecting AI-generated misinformation to mitigate this risk (Kreps, S., McCain, R., & Brundage, M., 2022).

Finally, the proliferation of AI-generated content has the potential to reshape content consumption patterns. For example, AI tools can personalize content to match individual users' preferences, leading to more targeted and engaging user experiences (Sartorius, N., Üstün, T., Lecrubier, Y., & Wittchen, H., 2018). However, this could also risk creating "filter bubbles" or "echo chambers," where individuals are exposed only to content that reinforces their existing beliefs or preferences, thereby reducing exposure to diverse perspectives (Gunn, Hanna, & Michael, P. L., 2021).

In summary, while ChatGPT and similar models offer considerable potential for content generation, their societal impact requires careful consideration. Balancing the benefits of AI-enhanced content generation with the potential risks and harms requires ongoing research, clear ethical guidelines, and thoughtful policy-making to ensure that the development and use of these tools benefit society at large.

Transparency and Accountability in Using ChatGPT

Transparency and accountability are fundamental considerations when using AI for content creation, including tools like ChatGPT. These aspects become critical when we consider the wide-ranging implications of AI-generated content, from shaping public discourse to influencing consumer behaviors (Kertati, I., Sanchez, C. Y., Basri, M., Husain, M. N., & Tj, H. W., 2023)

Transparency in artificial intelligence. (Larsson, 2020). A "best practice" guide, such as the one developed by OpenAI, outlines the need for users to be explicit about the use of AI in content generation (Transformer, C., & Zhavoronkov, A., 2022).

Accountability extends beyond transparency, involving responsibility for the AI-generated content and its implications. Accountability requires that the entities using AI for content creation assume responsibility for ensuring the ethical use of the technology, including addressing biases, misinformation, and any adverse effects arising from the content (Sqalli, M.T., Aslonov, B.,Gafurov, M., & Nurmatov, S., 2023). The development of AI ethics guidelines, like those proposed by the IEEE and others, underlines this focus on accountability (Vinuesa, R., Azizpour, H., Leite, I., Balaam, M., Dignum, V., Domisch, S., & Nerini, F.F., 2020).

Transparency and accountability mechanisms for AI-generated content could involve technological solutions, regulatory frameworks, and ethical guidelines. Technological solutions might include watermarking or tagging AI-generated content, as well as developing more sophisticated detection tools for AI-generated misinformation (Khan, A.O., Badshah, S., Liang, P., Khan, B., Waseem, M., Niazi, M., & Akbar, M., 2022). Regulatory frameworks might require mandatory disclosure of AI-generated content or hold entities accountable for the content produced by the AI systems they use (Boland, C.M., Hogan, C.E., & Manco-Johnson, M.J., 2018).

In conclusion, ensuring transparency and accountability in AI-generated content is a shared responsibility involving AI developers, users, regulators, and society at large. Effective mechanisms for disclosure and responsible use are needed to navigate the challenges and maximize the benefits of this transformative technology.

FUTRURE DIRECTIONS AND EMERGING RESEARCH AREA IN CHATGPT AND CONTETNT CREATION

Current State of ChatGPT in Content Creation

As of now, the use of ChatGPT in content creation is increasingly becoming prominent across various sectors. Advances in Natural Language Processing (NLP) techniques, the driving technology behind ChatGPT, have catalyzed this progression (Giannos, P., Delardas, O., 2023). The model's capacity to generate human-like text has transformed content creation processes, leading to improved efficiency and novel ways of producing content.

Several advancements in the area stand out. Firstly, the integration of AI-powered tools like ChatGPT into content management systems is an ongoing trend. This enables seamless workflows, enhancing productivity and content quality by reducing human error and bias (Al-sa'di, 2023). For example, large-scale news outlets use AI models to generate preliminary reports, allowing human journalists to focus on more complex tasks (Zhang, W., & Tornero, J.M.P., 2021).

Moreover, AI models are progressively being trained to exhibit greater understanding of context, nuance, and idiomatic language (Vall, R.R.F.D.l., & Araya, F.G., 2023). ChatGPT, for instance, can now manage tasks that were previously challenging, such as creating conversational agents, tutoring, translating languages, simulating characters for video games, and even writing code (Lyu, Q., Tan, J., Zapadka, M.E., Ponnatapura, J., Niu, C., Wang,G., & Whitlow, C.T., 2023).

(Ongoing research focuses on mitigating challenges associated with AI-driven content creation. OpenAI, for example, is dedicated to reducing problematic biases in how ChatGPT responds to different inputs (Zhu, L., Mou, W., & Chen, R., 2023). Similarly, other efforts aim at refining the accountability and transparency mechanisms surrounding AI-generated content, with an eye on ethical implications (Illia, L., Colleoni, E., & Zyglidopoulos, S., 2022).

Efforts are also underway to make ChatGPT more controllable, allowing users to customize the AI's behavior according to their needs. OpenAI's research focuses on enabling users to define AI's values within broad bounds (Huang, J., Yeung, A.M., & Kerr, D., 2023).

Additionally, there is a growing interest in leveraging AI tools for multimedia content creation. AI algorithms are being developed to generate not just text, but also audio, video, and graphic content, potentially expanding the scope of AI in content generation (Zhang S., 2019)

In sum, the current state of ChatGPT in content creation is characterized by innovative applications, ongoing research into mitigating challenges, and an increasing interest in expanding the AI's capabilities.

Importance of Research and Development

Research and development (R&D) play a pivotal role in enhancing the capabilities of AI models like ChatGPT for content creation (Heo, S., Han, S., Shin, Y., & Na, S., 2021). Through continuous R&D,

improvements are made to the model's language understanding, output coherence, and the mitigation of potential biases, which in turn enhance the model's effectiveness and reliability.

One of the most prominent areas of R&D focuses on the fine-tuning of the AI models. A significant challenge faced by large language models like ChatGPT is that they can generate biased or harmful content. Current R&D efforts aim to mitigate these problematic outputs (Sebastian, 2023). For instance, OpenAI has been working on an upgrade to ChatGPT that reduces both glaring and subtle biases in how the AI responds to different inputs (Tian, W. M., Sergesketter, A. R., Hollenbeck, S. T. (, 2023).

Another area of active research focuses on the better understanding and control of AI models. For example, OpenAI's 'AI and Efficiency' research aims at discovering how to get the best performance out of AI models, given the resources available (Sedaghat, 2023). These insights can enhance the customization and usability of the models, making them more effective tools for content creation.

Further, there is ongoing research into ways of integrating user feedback into AI models (Hall, K.R., Ajjan, H., & Marshall, G.W., 2021). This approach aims to create a two-way relationship between AI and users, ensuring that AI tools like ChatGPT continue to evolve according to user needs and societal norms.

Finally, efforts are underway to improve transparency and accountability in AI-generated content. Research in this area seeks to establish best practices for disclosing AI involvement in content creation and creating guidelines for responsible use (Israel, M.J., & Amer, A., 2022).

In conclusion, R&D is instrumental in advancing the capabilities of AI models for content creation, mitigating their limitations, and ensuring their ethical and responsible use. Therefore, continuous investment in R&D is crucial for leveraging the full potential of AI in content creation and mitigating its risks.

Emerging Research Areas in ChatGPT and Content Creation

In the world of artificial intelligence (AI), ongoing research continues to open new doors. In the domain of content creation and AI models like ChatGPT, exciting emerging research areas include unsupervised learning, multimodal AI, and new evaluation techniques.

Unsupervised learning is a branch of machine learning that uses AI models to understand patterns in data without any previous training (Hariharan, J., Ampatzidis, Y., Abdulridha, J., & Batuman, O., 2023). In the context of content creation, unsupervised learning could allow AI models like ChatGPT to generate more creative and novel content by learning from a broader range of inputs (Roma,G.,Xambó,A .,Green,O.,&Tremblay,P., 2021). For instance, unsupervised learning can help AI systems to understand human language better by identifying patterns and structures in the language data it has been exposed to without relying on specific training (Liu, W., Chen, P., Yeung, S., Suzumura, T., & Chen, L., 2017). As a result, the AI system can produce more sophisticated and nuanced content.

Multimodal AI is another exciting area of research, which involves models that can understand and generate content across multiple modes or types of data, such as text, images, and audio (An, R., Hen, J., & Xiao, Y., 2022). This research is important for content creation, as it could lead to AI models like ChatGPT being able to generate not just written content but also visual or auditory content. For example, a multimodal AI could create a blog post complete with relevant images or an audio description, enhancing the accessibility and richness of the generated content (Yihan, C., Siyu, L., Yixin, L., Zhiling, Y., Yutong, D., Phillip, S.P., & Lichao, S., 2023).

Finally, the development of new evaluation techniques for AI models is a crucial research area. As AI models become increasingly complex, traditional evaluation techniques may not be sufficient to gauge their effectiveness or ethical implications (Zhang, J., Oh, Y. J., Lange, P., Yu, Z., & Fukuoka, Y., 2020).

New techniques are being developed to evaluate AI models more comprehensively, considering factors such as the diversity of content generated, the subtlety of biases, and the extent to which they can be controlled or customized (Houssami, N., Kirkpatrick-Jones, G., Noguchi, N., & Lee, C.I., 2019). These new evaluation techniques will ensure that AI models like ChatGPT meet high standards of quality and ethical responsibility.

In conclusion, the future of AI in content creation is being shaped by ongoing research in unsupervised learning, multimodal AI, and new evaluation techniques. These research areas hold the promise of unlocking new capabilities in AI models like ChatGPT, thereby enhancing the effectiveness, diversity, and ethical responsibility of AI-generated content.

CONCLUSION

The realm of content creation is undergoing a transformative shift due to the emergence of AI models like ChatGPT. These sophisticated models are capable of generating human-like text, leading to significant impacts across a multitude of sectors, including marketing, education, and entertainment. This chapter has provided a comprehensive exploration of ChatGPT, including its underpinnings, its applications, its limitations, the ethical considerations surrounding its use, and potential future research directions.

The basis of the model's capabilities lies in its advanced architecture and function. Through exploring transformer architecture and GPT models, the power of these AI models in understanding context and producing coherent, contextually relevant responses is brought to the forefront.

We've charted the journey of AI in content creation, starting from rules-based models, transitioning to statistical methods, and culminating in the era of deep learning models characterized by the likes of ChatGPT.

ChatGPT's diverse applications in content creation are spread across sectors and are primarily hinged on its capacity to automate and enhance human capabilities, thereby saving time and resources.

Nonetheless, it is essential to consider the limitations of ChatGPT, including issues such as verbosity, potential to generate inappropriate content, lack of fact-checking, and its limitations in understanding context beyond a certain length. Further, the limitations of our study and future research directions highlight the importance of continual empirical studies evaluating ChatGPT's performance in real-world scenarios and keeping pace with rapid advancements in AI technology.

The ethical implications surrounding the use of ChatGPT and similar models cannot be downplayed. Biases in AI models, intellectual property concerns, the potential to spread misinformation, and the reshaping of content consumption patterns necessitate rigorous regulation. Developers, users, and regulators must ensure transparency and accountability in using AI for content creation to ensure responsible and ethical use.

Emerging research areas such as unsupervised learning, multimodal AI, and new evaluation techniques offer exciting avenues for further exploration and enhancement of ChatGPT's content creation capabilities.

In summary, while ChatGPT and similar models have brought about a paradigm shift in content creation, their potential for misuse and ethical implications underscore the need for careful and responsible usage. As AI continues to evolve, the interplay between its development, application, and ethical considerations presents a complex tapestry of opportunities, challenges, and dilemmas that will undoubtedly shape the narrative of AI in content creation in the coming years.

CONFLICT OF INTEREST

The authors declare that there is no conflict of interest that could be perceived as prejudicing the impartiality of the research reported.

ACKNOWLEDGEMENTS

The authors would like to express their gratitude to the colleagues and reviewers who provided valuable feedback and insights on earlier drafts of this chapter. Their contributions were instrumental in improving the quality and clarity of our work. We would also like to extend our appreciation to the broader academic and AI community for their ongoing efforts in exploring the ethical implications and societal impacts of AI-generated content. Lastly, we would like to thank our families and friends for their unwavering support during the process of writing this chapter.

REFERENCES

Adithya, R., Denise, D., Kenneth, H., Xian, L., & Mona, D. (2021). Gender bias amplification during Speed-Quality optimization in Neural Machine Translation. *Proceedings of the 59th Annual Meeting of the Association for Computational Linguistics and the 11th International Joint Conference on Natural Language Processing* (pp. 99–109). Association for Computational Linguistics.10.18653/v1/2021.acl-short.15

Aithal, S., & Aithal, P. S. (2023). Effects of AI-Based ChatGPT on Higher Education Libraries. [IJMTS]. *International Journal of Management, Technology, and Social Sciences*, 8(2), 95–108. doi:10.47992/IJMTS.2581.6012.0272

Al-sa'di, A., & Miller, D. (2023). Exploring the Impact Of Artificial Intelligence Language Model Chatgpt On The User Experience. *International Journal on Technology, Innovation, and Management*, 1(3), 1–8. doi:10.54489/ijtim.v3i1.195

An, R., Hen, J., & Xiao, Y. (2022). Applications Of Artificial Intelligence To Obesity Research: Scoping Review Of Methodologies. *Journal of Medical Internet Research*, 12(24), e40589. doi:10.2196/40589 PMID:36476515

Anson, C. M., & Straume, I. (2022). Amazement and Trepidation: Implications of AI-Based Natural Language Production for the Teaching of Writing. *Journal of Academic Writing*, 12(1), 1–9. doi:10.18552/joaw.v12i1.820

Ashish, S. (2017). Identification of Unknown Landscape Types Using CNN Transfer Learning. *Boise State University Theses and Dissertations.*, 1318. doi:10.18122/B2C70F

Athaluri, S., Manthena, S., Kesapragada, V., Yarlagadda, V., Dave, T., & Duddumpudi, R. T. S. (2023). Exploring the Boundaries of Reality: Investigating the Phenomenon of Artificial Intelligence Hallucination in Scientific Writing Through ChatGPT References. *Cureus*, 15(4), e37432. doi:10.7759/cureus.37432 PMID:37182055

Aziz, A. (2023). Artificial Intelligence Produced Original Work: A New Approach To Copyright Protection And Ownership. *European Journal of Artificial Intelligence and Machine Learning*, 2(2), 9–16. doi:10.24018/ejai.2023.2.2.15

Bisk, Y., Zellers, R., Le-bras, R., Gao, J., & Choi, Y. (2020). Reasoning about Physical Commonsense in Natural Language. *Proceedings of the AAAI Conference on Artificial Intelligence, 34(05),* (pp. 7432-7439.)10.1609/aaai.v34i05.6239

Boland, C. M., Hogan, C. E., & Manco-Johnson, M. J. (2018). Motivating Compliance: Firm Response To Mandatory Disclosure Policies. *Accounting Horizons*, 2(32), 103–119. doi:10.2308/acch-52037

Chen, T., Kornblith, S., Swersky, K., Norouzi, M., & Hinton, G. (2020). Big Self-supervised Models Are Strong Semi-supervised Learners. *ArXiv*, 10029. https://doi.org//arxiv.2006.10029. doi:10.48550

Cooper, G. (2023). Examining Science Education in ChatGPT: An Exploratory Study of Generative Artificial Intelligence. *Journal of Science Education and Technology*, 32(3), 444–452. doi:10.100710956-023-10039-y

Dave, T., Athaluri, S. A., & Singh, S. (2023). an overview of its applications, advantages, limitations, future prospects, and ethical considerations. *Artificial Intelligence*, 1169595, 1169595. doi:10.3389/frai.2023.1169595 PMID:37215063

Elizabeth, C., Asli, C., & Noah, A. S. (2019). In Proceedings of the 57th Annual Meeting of the Association for Computational Linguistics, *Sentence Mover's Similarity: Automatic Evaluation for Multi-Sentence Texts* (pp. 2748–2760). Florence, Italy: Association for Computational Linguistics.10.18653/v1/P19-1264

Eysenbach, G. (2023). The Role of ChatGPT, Generative Language Models, and Artificial Intelligence in Medical Education: A Conversation With ChatGPT and a Call for Papers. *Journal of Medical Internet Research*, 46885, e46885. doi:10.2196/46885 PMID:36863937

Ferrara, E. (2023). Fairness and Bias in Artificial Intelligence: A Brief Survey of Sources, Impacts, and Mitigation Strategies. *ArXiv*, 07683. https://doi.org//arXiv.2304.07683. doi:10.48550

Firaina, R., & Sulisworo, D. (2023). Exploring the Usage of ChatGPT in Higher Education: Frequency and Impact on Productivity. *Buletin Edukasi Indonesia*, 2(01), 39–46. doi:10.56741/bei.v2i01.310

Frith, K. H. (2023). Disruptive Educational Technology. *Nursing Education Perspectives*, 44(3), 198–199. doi:10.1097/01.NEP.0000000000001129 PMID:37093697

Gama, J. (2004). Functional Trees. *Machine Learning*, 55(3), 219–250. doi:10.1023/B:MACH.0000027782.67192.13

Gao, S., He, L., Chen, Y., Li, D., & Lai, K. (2020). Public Perception of Artificial Intelligence in Medical Care: Content Analysis of Social Media. *Journal of Medical Internet Research*, 22(7), e16649. doi:10.2196/16649 PMID:32673231

Giannos, P., & Delardas, O. (2023). Performance Of Chatgpt On Uk Standardized Admission Tests: Insights From the Bmat, Tmua, Lnat, And Tsa Examinations. *JMIR Medical Education*, 9, e47737. doi:10.2196/47737 PMID:37099373

Gunn, H. & Michael, P. L. (2021). The Internet and Epistemic Agency. In L. Jennifer, *Applied Epistemology* (pp. 389-409). Oxford University Press. doi:10.1093/oso/9780198833659.003.0016

Hall, K. R., Ajjan, H., & Marshall, G. W. (2021). Understanding Salesperson Intention To Use Ai Feedback and Its Influence On Business-to-business Sales Outcomes. *Journal of Business and Industrial Marketing*, *37*(9), 1787–1801. doi:10.1108/JBIM-04-2021-0218

Haluza, D., & Jungwirth, D. (2023). Artificial Intelligence and Ten Societal Megatrends: An Exploratory Study Using GPT-3. *Systems*, *11*(3), 120. doi:10.3390ystems11030120

Hao, J., & Ho, T. K. (2019). Machine Learning Made Easy: A Review of Scikit-learn Package in Python Programming Language. *Journal of Educational and Behavioral Statistics*, *44*(3), 348–361. doi:10.3102/1076998619832248

Hariharan, J., Ampatzidis, Y., Abdulridha, J., & Batuman, O. (2023). Useful Feature Extraction and Machine Learning Techniques For Identifying Unique Pattern Signatures Present In Hyperspectral Image Data. In Y. Jung, Hyperspectral Imaging - A Perspective on Recent Advances and Applications (p. 107436). IntechOpen. doi:10.5772/intechopen.107436

Heo, S., Han, S., Shin, Y., & Na, S. (2021). Challenges Of Data Refining Process During the Artificial Intelligence Development Projects In The Architecture, Engineering And Construction Industry. *Applied Sciences (Basel, Switzerland)*, *11*(22), 10919. doi:10.3390/app112210919

Houssami, N., Kirkpatrick-Jones, G., Noguchi, N., & Lee, C. I. (2019). Artificial Intelligence (Ai) For the Early Detection Of Breast Cancer: A Scoping Review To Assess Ai's Potential In Breast Screening Practice. *Expert Review of Medical Devices*, *5*(16), 351–362. doi:10.1080/17434440.2019.1610387 PMID:30999781

Huang, C., Zhang, Z., Mao, B., & Yao, X. (2022). An Overview of Artificial Intelligence Ethics. *Artificial Intelligence*, *3194503*. doi:10.1109/TAI.2022.3194503

Huang, J., Yeung, A. M., Kerr, D., & Klonoff, D. C. (2023). Using Chatgpt To Predict the Future Of Diabetes Technology. *Journal of Diabetes Science and Technology*, *3*(17), 853–854. doi:10.1177/19322968231161095 PMID:36799231

Illia, L., Colleoni, E., & Zyglidopoulos, S. (2022). Ethical Implications Of Text Generation In the Age Of Artificial Intelligence. *Business Ethics, the Environment & Responsibility*, *32*(1), 201–210. doi:10.1111/beer.12479

Israel, M. J., & Amer, A. (2022). Rethinking Data Infrastructure and Its Ethical Implications In The Face Of Automated Digital Content Generation. *AI and Ethics*, *3*(2), 427–439. doi:10.100743681-022-00169-1

Jagdishbhai, N., & Thakkar, K. Y. (2023). Exploring the capabilities and limitations of GPT and Chat GPT in natural language processing. *Journal of Management Research and Analysis*, *10*(1), 18–20. doi:10.18231/j.jmra.2023.004

Judith, V.S., &J akub, M. (2021). Proceedings of the 16th International Conference on the Foundations of Digital. *Games, 2*, 1–8. . doi:10.1145/3472538.3472595

Kapoor, R., & Ghosal, I. (2022). Will Artificial Intelligence Compliment or Supplement Human Workforce in Organizations? A Shift to a Collaborative Human – Machine Environment. [IJRTBT]. *International Journal on Recent Trends in Business and Tourism*, 6(4), 19–28. doi:10.31674/ijrtbt.2022.v06i04.002

Kertati, I., Sanchez, C. Y., Basri, M., Husain, M. N., & Tj, H. W. (2023). Public Relations' Disruption Model On Chatgpt Issue. *Indonesian Journal of Communications Studies, 1*(7), 034-048. https://doi.org/. doi:10.25139/jsk.v7i1.6143

Khairatun, H. U., & Miftahul, A. M. (2022). Artificial Intelligence for Human Life: A Critical Opinion from Medical Bioethics Perspective – Part II. *Journal of Public Health Sciences*, 1(02), 112–130. doi:10.56741/jphs.v1i02.215

Khan, A. O., Badshah, S., Liang, P., Khan, B., Waseem, M., Niazi, M., & Akbar, M. (2022). Ethics Of Ai: a Systematic Literature Review Of Principles And Challenges. *Proceedings of the 26th International Conference on Evaluation and Assessment in Software Engineering*, (pp. 383-392). ACM.)10.1145/3530019.3531329

King, M. R. (2023). Google's Experimental Chatbot Based on the LaMDA Large Language Model, Help to Analyze the Gender and Racial Diversity of Authors in Your Cited Scientific References? *Cellular and Molecular Bioengineering*, 16(2), 175–179. doi:10.100712195-023-00761-3 PMID:37096072

Kreps, S., McCain, R., & Brundage, M. (2022). All the News That's Fit to Fabricate: AI-Generated Text as a Tool of Media Misinformation. *Journal of Experimental Political Science*, 9(1), 104–117. doi:10.1017/XPS.2020.37

Larsson, S., & Heintz, F. (2020). Transparency in artificial intelligence. *Internet Policy Review*, 9(2). doi:10.14763/2020.2.1469

Lee, J.A., Reto, M., Hilty, & Kung-Chung, L. (2021). Roadmap to Artificial Intelligence and Intellectual PropertyAn Introduction. *Artificial Intelligence and Intellectual Property*. . doi:10.1093/oso/9780198870944.003.0001

Lee, K. J., Kwon, J. W., Min, S., & Yoon, J. (2021). Deploying an Artificial Intelligence-Based Defect Finder for Manufacturing Quality Management. *AI Magazine*, 42(2), 5–18. doi:10.1609/aimag.v42i2.15094

Lewis, D. W. (2023). Open Access: A Conversation with ChatGPT. *The Journal of Electronic Publishing: JEP*, 26(1), 3891. doi:10.3998/jep.3891

Li, J., Li, Z., Ge, T., King, I., & Lyu, M. R. (2022). Text Revision By On-the-Fly Representation Optimization. *Proceedings of the AAAI Conference on Artificial Intelligence*, Hong Kong.10.1609/aaai.v36i10.21343

Liu, W., Chen, P., Yeung, S., Suzumura, T., & Chen, L. (2017). Principled Multilayer Network Embedding. *IEEE International Conference on Data Mining Workshops (ICDM Workshops)* (pp. 134-141). IEEE.10.1109/ICDMW.2017.23

Luitse, D., & Denkena, W. (2021). The great Transformer: Examining the role of large language models in the political economy of AI. *Big Data & Society*, 8(2), 47734. doi:10.1177/20539517211047734

Lund, B. D., & Wang, T. (2023). Chatting about ChatGPT: How may AI and GPT impact academia and libraries? *Library Hi Tech News*, *40*(3), 26–29. doi:10.1108/LHTN-01-2023-0009

Lund, B. D., & Wang, T. (2023). Chatting about ChatGPT: How may AI and GPT impact academia and libraries. *Library Hi Tech News*, *40*(3), 26–29. doi:10.1108/LHTN-01-2023-0009

Lyu, Q., Tan, J., Zapadka, M. E., Ponnatapura, J., Niu, C., Wang, G., & Whitlow, C. T. (2023). Translating Radiology Reports Into Plain Language Using Chatgpt and Gpt-4 With Prompt Learning: Promising Results, Limitations, And Potential. *Visual Computing for Industry, Biomedicine, and Art*, *6*(9), 37198498. doi:10.118642492-023-00136-5 PMID:37198498

Mardanirad, S., Wood, D. A., & Zakeri, H. (2021). The application of deep learning algorithms to classify subsurface drilling lost circulation severity in large oil field datasets. *SN Applied Sciences*, *3*(9), 785. doi:10.100742452-021-04769-0

Mencar, C., Castiello, C., Cannone, R., & Fanelli, A. M. (2011). Interpretability assessment of fuzzy knowledge bases: A cointension based approach. *International Journal of Approximate Reasoning*, *52*(4), 501–518. doi:10.1016/j.ijar.2010.11.007

Mijwil, M., Aljanabi, M., & Ali, A. H. (2023). Exploring the Role of Cybersecurity in the Protection of Medical Information. *Mesopotamian Journal of CyberSecurity*, *18–21*, 18–21. doi:10.58496/MJCS/2023/004

Oxford, A. (2022). Beijing acts to control AI-generated content. *Expert Briefings*, NA. . doi:10.1108/OXAN-DB267101

Pavlik, J. (2023). Collaborating With ChatGPT: Considering the Implications of Generative Artificial Intelligence for Journalism and Media Education. *Journalism & Mass Communication Educator*, *78*(1), 84–93. doi:10.1177/10776958221149577

Peter, S., Joe, W., & Tom, B. (2023). Utilization of AI-Based Tools like ChatGPT in the Training of Medical Students and Interventional Radiology. *ScienceOpen Posters*. . doi:10.14293/P2199-8442.1.SOP-.PFTABJ.v1

Risse, M. (2019). Human Rights and Artificial Intelligence: An Urgently Needed Agenda. *Human Rights Quarterly*, *41*(1), 1–16. doi:10.1353/hrq.2019.0000

Roma, G., Xambó, A., Green, O., & Tremblay, P. (2021). A General Framework For Visualization Of Sound Collections In Musical Interfaces. *Applied Sciences (Basel, Switzerland)*, *24*(11), 11926. doi:10.3390/app112411926

Sartorius, N., Üstün, T., Lecrubier, Y., & Wittchen, H. (2018). Depression Comorbid with Anxiety: Results from the WHO Study on Psychological Disorders in Primary Health Care. *The British Journal of Psychiatry*, *168*(30), 38–43. doi:10.1192/S0007125000298395 PMID:8864147

Sebastian, G. (2023). Do Chatgpt and Other Ai Chatbots Pose A Cybersecurity Risk? *International Journal of Security and Privacy in Pervasive Computing*, *1*(15), 1–11. doi:10.4018/IJSPPC.320225

Sedaghat, S. (2023). Early Applications Of Chatgpt In Medical Practice, Education and Research. *Clinical Medicine (London, England)*, *3*(23), 278–279. doi:10.7861/clinmed.2023-0078 PMID:37085182

Shahsavar, Y., & Choudhury, A. (2023). User Intentions to Use ChatGPT for Self-Diagnosis and Health-Related Purposes: Cross-sectional Survey Study. *JMIR Human Factors*, *10*, e47564. doi:10.2196/47564 PMID:37195756

Som, B. (2023). *Role of ChatGPT in the Film Industry: According to ChatGPT.* Qeios. https://www. qeios.com/read/NABVHA

Sqalli, M. T., Aslonov, B., Gafurov, M., & Nurmatov, S. (2023). Humanizing Ai In Medical Training: Ethical Framework For Responsible Design. *Frontiers in Artificial Intelligence*, *6*, 1189914. doi:10.3389/ frai.2023.1189914 PMID:37261331

Sunny, S., & Sanchari, D. (2022). Exploring gender biases in ML and AI academic research through systematic literature review. *Frontiers in Artificial Intelligence*, *5*, 976838. doi:10.3389/frai.2022.976838 PMID:36304961

Tian, W. M., Sergesketter, A. R., & Hollenbeck, S. T. (2023). The Role Of Chatgpt In Microsurgery: Assessing Content Quality and Potential Applications. *Journal of Reconstructive Microsurgery*, *6509*. doi:10.1055/a-2098-6509 PMID:37225130

Transformer, C., & Zhavoronkov, A. (2022). Rapamycin In the Context Of Pascal's Wager: Generative Pre-trained Transformer Perspective. *Oncoscience*, *9*, 82–84. doi:10.18632/oncoscience.571 PMID:36589923

UbaniS. (2023). A Primer on ChatGPT: Coherence Does Not Imply Correctness. *A Primer on ChatGPT: Coherence Does Not Imply Correctness*, https://doi.org/ doi:10.35542/osf.io/8fmrn

Vall, R. R. F. D., & Araya, F. G. (2023). Exploring the Benefits And Challenges Of Ai-language Learning Tools. *International Journal of Social Sciences and Humanities Invention*, *10*(01), 7569–7576. doi:10.18535/ijsshi/v10i01.02

Van-Leeuwen, K. G., Meijer, F. J. A., Schalekamp, S., Rutten, M. J. C. M., van Dijk, E. J., van Ginneken, B., Govers, T. M., & de Rooij, M. (2021). Cost-effectiveness of artificial intelligence aided vessel occlusion detection in acute stroke: An early health technology assessment. *Insights Into Imaging*, *12*(1), 133. doi:10.118613244-021-01077-4 PMID:34564764

Vinuesa, R., Azizpour, H., Leite, I., Balaam, M., Dignum, V., Domisch, S., & Nerini, F. F. (2020). The Role Of Artificial Intelligence In Achieving the Sustainable Development Goals. *Nature Communications*, *1*(11), 233. doi:10.103841467-019-14108-y PMID:31932590

Wang, F. Y., Yang.J., Wang.X., Li, J., & Han, Q.L. (2023). Chat with ChatGPT on Industry 5.0: Learning and Decision-Making for Intelligent Industries. *IEEE/CAA Journal of Automatica Sinica, 10(4)*, 831-834. . doi:10.1109/JAS.2023.123552

Xi, Z., Zhendong, M., Chunxiao, L., Peng, Z., Bin, W., & Yong, Z. (2020). Proceedings of the Twenty-Ninth International Joint Conference on Artificial Intelligence. *Overcoming Language Priors with Self-supervised Learning for Visual Question Answering*, (pp. 1083-1089.)10.24963/ijcai.2020/151

Yadav, S., & Kaushik, A. (2022). Do You Ever Get Off Track in a Conversation? The Conversational System's Anatomy and Evaluation Metrics. *Knowledge (Beverly Hills, Calif.)*, *2*(1), 55–87. doi:10.3390/ knowledge2010004

Yan, L. (2019). Impact of Artificial Intelligence on Creative Digital Content Production. *Journal of Digital Art Engineering & Multimedia*, 6(2), 121–132. doi:10.29056/jdaem.2019.12.05

Yihan, C., Siyu, L., Yixin, L., Zhiling, Y., Yutong, D., Phillip, S. P., & Lichao, S. (2023). A Comprehensive Survey of AI-Generated Content (AIGC): A History of Generative AI from GAN to ChatGPT. *ArXiv*, 04226. https://doi.org//arxiv.2303.04226. doi:10.48550

Yupan, H., Hongwei, X., Bei, L., & Yutong, L. (2021). Proceedings of the 29th ACM International Conference on Multimedia. *ACM International Multimedia Conference* (p. NA). Virtual Event China: Machinery.

Zajko, M. (2021). Conservative AI and social inequality: Conceptualizing alternatives to bias through social theory. *AI & Society*, 36(3), 1047–1056. doi:10.100700146-021-01153-9

Zhang, J., Oh, Y. J., Lange, P., Yu, Z., & Fukuoka, Y. (2020). Artificial Intelligence Chatbot Behavior Change Model For Designing Artificial Intelligence Chatbots To Promote Physical Activity and A Healthy Diet. *Journal of Medical Internet Research*, 9(22), e22845. doi:10.2196/22845 PMID:32996892

Zhang, Q. (2020). Transformer Transducer: A Streamable Speech Recognition Model with Transformer Encoders and RNN-T Loss, *IEEE International Conference on Acoustics, Speech and Signal Processing* (pp. 7829-7833, .). Barcelona, Spain: Institute of Electrical and Electronics Engineers.10.1109/ICASSP40776.2020.9053896

Zhang, S. (2019). Research On Copyright Protection Of Ai Creation. *Proceedings of the 1st International Symposium on Innovation and Education, Law and Social Sciences (IELSS 2019)* (pp. 510-514.). Atilantis.10.2991/ielss-19.2019.94

Zhang, W., & Tornero, J.M.P. (2021). Introduction To Ai Journalism: Framework and Ontology Of The Trans-domain Field For Integrating Ai Into Journalism. *Journal of Applied Journalism &Amp; Media Studies*. . doi:10.1386/ajms_00063_1

Zhang, X., Shah, J., & Han, M. (2023). ChatGPT for Fast Learning of Positive Energy District (PED): A Trial Testing and Comparison with Expert Discussion Results. *Buildings*, 13(6), 1392. doi:10.3390/buildings13061392

Zhou, Z. (2023). Evaluation of ChatGPT's Capabilities in Medical Report Generation. *Cureus*, 15(4), e37589. doi:10.7759/cureus.37589 PMID:37197105

Zhu, L., Mou, W., & Chen, R. (2023). Can the ChatGPT and other large language models with internet-connected database solve the questions and concerns of patient with prostate cancer and help democratize medical knowledge? *Journal of Translational Medicine*, 21(1), 269. doi:10.118612967-023-04123-5 PMID:37076876

Zhuo, C., Kui, F., Shiqi, W., Ling, Y. D., Weisi, L., & Alex, K. (2019). Lossy Intermediate Deep Learning Feature Compression and Evaluation. *Proceedings of the 27th ACM International Conference on Multimedia* (pp. 2414–2422). ACM. 10.1145/3343031.3350849

Zielinski, C., Winker, M., Aggarwal, R., Ferris, L., Heinemann, M., Lapeña, J. F., & Citrome, L. (2023). Chatbots, Chatgpt, and Scholarly Manuscripts Wame Recommendations On Chatgpt And Chatbots In Relation To Scholarly Publications. *Afro-Egyptian Journal of Infectious and Endemic Diseases*, *13*(1), 75–79. doi:10.21608/aeji.2023.282936 PMID:37615142

KEY TERMS AND DEFINITIONS

AI-Generated Content Consumption Patterns: The ways in which audiences interact with, consume, and are influenced by content generated by AI. This can involve personalized content experiences, potential creation of "filter bubbles," and shifting user engagement patterns.

Artificial Intelligence (AI): A branch of computer science that focuses on creating intelligent machines capable of performing tasks that typically require human intelligence. These tasks may include learning from experience, understanding natural language, recognizing patterns, and making decisions.

Bias in AI: Refers to the systematic error introduced into AI outputs due to the bias inherent in the training data. Bias in AI may lead to unfair or discriminatory outcomes, often perpetuating existing societal biases.

ChatGPT: A large-scale AI language model developed by OpenAI, capable of generating human-like text. ChatGPT learns from a vast dataset of internet text and is used in various applications such as drafting emails, writing articles, creating conversational agents, tutoring, translation, and more.

Content Generation: The process of creating, developing, and editing information, particularly digital content, to disseminate through online platforms or other media.

Ethical Concerns: Refers to the moral issues, dilemmas, and standards related to AI and its applications. In the context of AI-generated content, these may include concerns about bias, intellectual property, privacy, accountability, and the societal impact of AI technologies.

Intellectual Property (IP): Legal rights that result from intellectual activity in the industrial, scientific, literary, and artistic fields. In the context of AI-generated content, IP concerns may revolve around issues of ownership, authorship, and rights to the generated content.

Misinformation Propagation: The spread of false or inaccurate information, often with the intent to deceive. In the context of AI-generated content, this term relates to the potential misuse of AI tools to create and disseminate false or misleading information, also known as "deepfakes."

Plagiarism: The act of using someone else's work or ideas without giving proper acknowledgment. In the context of AI-generated content, concerns may arise if the generated content inadvertently resembles source texts.

Societal Impact: The effect of an innovation or change on the functioning of society, encompassing a wide range of effects on living conditions, social structures, roles, and interactions. With AI-generated content, societal impact may relate to the shaping of public opinion, misinformation propagation, and changing content consumption patterns.

Chapter 4
Advanced Applications of Generative AI and Natural Language Processing Models:
Advancing Capabilities Safely in an Uncertain World

Shwetha Baliga
https://orcid.org/0000-0001-7506-5835
R.V. College of Engineering, India

Harshith K. Murthy
R.V. College of Engineering, India

Apoorv Sadhale
R.V. College of Engineering, India

Dhruti Upadhyaya
R.V. College of Engineering, India

ABSTRACT

The discourse surrounding AI has sparked widespread discussions, with notable concerns arising from its current limitations. One such concern involves AI models struggling to understand the context of human requests, leading to unexpected or nonsensical outcomes. While instances like the conversation with ChatGPT may have garnered attention, they should be regarded as fascinating illustrations of the model's capabilities rather than indications of meaningful independence. In shaping perspectives on this subject, three noteworthy books have played a pivotal role: Superintelligence by Nick Bostrom, Life 3.0 by Max Tegmark, and A Thousand Brains by Jeff Hawkins. These books offer well-articulated and thought-provoking insights, contributing to the ongoing discussion surrounding AI. By exploring the risks, limitations, and potential implications of AI, it becomes evident that thoughtful consideration and proactive measures are necessary to navigate the evolving landscape of artificial intelligence.

DOI: 10.4018/979-8-3693-0502-7.ch004

INTRODUCTION

Throughout history, mankind has continuously advanced and refined a multitude of technologies in pursuit of sophistication and advancement to have a higher and better standard of living. This endeavor aims to create products that streamline various processes. From the moment humans came into existence, they have engaged in a wide range of activities to adapt to diverse environments. This effort reached its peak in the mid-1700s with the advent of the Industrial Revolution. During this era, numerous nations recognized the potential to manufacture a variety of goods to meet the increasing demand of their growing populations. Since then, humanity has made tremendous progress, including the development and implementation of artificial intelligence. Artificial intelligence in a broad sense is how intelligent machines especially computer programs, can be designed and built to make intelligent decisions (King T et.al.,). It is similar to the task of using computers as a means of overcoming human intelligence.

No one disputes the fact that artificial intelligence will have a profound impact on society. What can be debated is how far, how, and in what way this impact will be positive or negative. This impact will be experienced, where felt, and on what timeline it will occur. A group of scientists including Stephen Hawking once said, "Success in creating Artificial Intelligence (AI) would be the biggest event in human history. Unfortunately, it might also be the last". Artificial Intelligence is an extremely sharp technology, both on the positive as well as negative ends and both these ends have not been clearly understood. Despite having positive societal impacts, it may pose substantial long-term risks, but an existential threat precedes an ethical risk

A risk can occur today as well as tomorrow. Despite the significant benefits associated with artificial intelligence, there is a chance that it could have far-reaching negative connotations for various people who encounter it, either directly or indirectly, and is also capable of playing a significant role in increasing criminal activities. One of the uses of such technology is that it is only as good as the data put into it. If the data fed into the system is misguiding, then there is a high probability that it could cause serious problems as the outcome. Artificial Intelligence (AI) has the potential to play a significant role in the increasing criminal activities soon.

Even though the discussion of risk is not dependent on the view that artificial intelligence has now reached a point where it will become superintelligent, it becomes more urgent if such a success is a non-negligible possibility within the next few decades. When the stakes are high, even to the point of human extinction, it gains even greater urgency. Before proceeding further, it is important to emphasize that the primary concern is with the initial outcomes that result directly from the creation of AI solutions, whether they are unintentionally or intentionally misused, or if the data inputs that power them are mishandled. There are additional notable outcomes, including the extensively debated possibility of extensive job reductions in certain sectors because of AI-powered workplace automation. Additionally, there are secondary effects, such as the decline of expertise (such as the diagnostic abilities of healthcare practitioners) as AI systems become more significant. These possibilities and the risks associated with such misuse will be dealt with in detail in the coming sections.

Figure 1. History of technological advancements

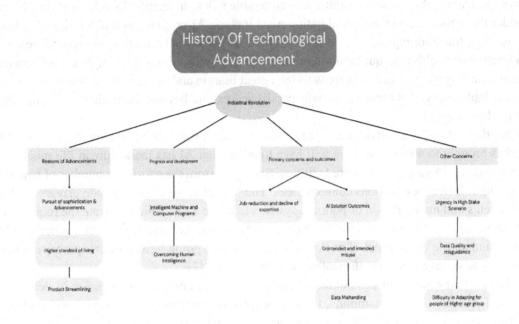

MOTIVATION

As Artificial Intelligence is currently one of the booming technologies, it is essential to understand the positive and negative aspects of it. The curiosity of exploring this field has opened doors for a wide range of opportunities and AI sources like ChatGPT, and useblackbox.ai have made their way to the top and are being accessed by all generations. Though it is exciting to see great strides in this field in recent times, it has given way to a lot of cyber and criminal activities. As artificial intelligence evolves, it is necessary to study the risks and opportunities that come with it every day and the ways to overcome the risks. Artificial Intelligence has the enormous power to revolutionize any industry, influence and change one's decision-making process, and create social problems. This impending issue led us to take up this matter and conduct a thorough research into the details of the risks imposed by Artificial Intelligence, understand and explore the risks associated with artificial intelligence that would arise from the widespread implementation of artificial intelligence, and most importantly, what actions can be taken to ensure the responsible development of artificial intelligence.

LITERATURE REVIEW

There are several research papers which explain in detail about the various risks that Artificial Intelligence has posed and is likely to pose soon.

In *Muller et. al.,* the author says that if the intelligence of artificial systems was to surpass that of humans significantly, this would constitute a considerable risk to humanity. He adds that time has come to consider these issues, and this consideration must include AI progress as much as insights from AI theory and that transitioning from AI to risk can be done effortlessly: there is no need to believe that human intelligence holds a unique position in the realm of possibilities – it is simple to envision natural or synthetic intelligent entities that surpass us by a great margin and hence if one considers intelligence as a quantifiable entity, this acceleration will persist and extend beyond the limited scope that defines human intelligence. [1].

In *Cheatham et. al.,* the author states that, if one considers the positive impact that Artificial Intelligence has brought to society, then we will have to admit that AI has made human life much simpler from shopping to enhancing health care facilities. But, apart from the enormous number of benefits, AI is also giving rise to a lot of serious consequences. The ones that are visible include privacy violations, cyber accidents and manipulation of political systems to name a few which indicate the requirement of caution. Organizations face significant challenges as well as the risk of disastrous consequences, including the loss of human life in the event of an AI medical algorithm going wrong, or compromising national security if an adversary feeds disinformation to a military AI. [2].

Floridi et. al., the author brings out the fact that the risks of unintentional overuse or deliberate exploitation of AI technologies, stemming, for instance, from conflicting incentives, avarice, adversarial geopolitics, or malice, must also be taken into account. The harmful use of AI technologies has the potential to expedite or intensify everything from email scams to full-scale cyber warfare. [3]

According to *Boutilier et. al.,* one of the myths surrounding the usage of artificial intelligence is that it can lead to the issue of replacing the very aspect of human intelligence. According to them, it is morally wrong for more people to rely on artificial intelligence because they believe that human knowledge is insufficient and must be supplemented by the use of machines and computers. Therefore, such a practice conveys the idea that humans lack the capacity needed to manage a variety of tasks that would be considered relevant to them. Additionally, the process would contribute to people losing faith in mankind in general.[4].

According to *Kiner et. al.,* unfortunately, the most powerful artificial intelligence is also frequently the least transparent. One can observe the data input and output of the AI system. One may even be able to generalize how such AI systems operate, which is typically via deep neural networks. But frequently, one is unable to comprehend why an AI system chose a specific course of action, made a specific diagnosis, or carried out a specific action during an operation. This is due to the extreme complexity of these systems, which may base one output on up to 23 million parameters, as well as the fact that AI systems are constantly changing their own algorithms without human supervision. Even while research on so-called "eXplainable AI" ("XAI") is expanding [6], numerous aspects of AI still remain unexplained and are likely to pose risks in the near future. [5].

Problem Statement

Artificial intelligence is an exceptional technological advancement our society has achieved. But with such technical achievements, it is essential to understand that the technology is in safe hands. As artificial intelligence evolves, it is necessary to study the risks and opportunities that come with it every day. Artificial intelligence has the enormous power to revolutionize any industry, influence and change a person's decision-making process, and create social problems and new ethical questions. The motive of the chapter is to understand and explore the risks associated with artificial intelligence that would arise from the widespread implementation of artificial intelligence, and what actions to be taken to ensure the responsible development of artificial intelligence.

Basic questions:

1. **Prejudice and justice**: Artificial intelligence systems are built on a set of data. The data may

contain errors and disturbances that cannot be eliminated. The data set inherently contains human biases/errors, but the critical point appears in how the AI interprets these errors and misleading errors. In areas such as criminal justice, financial management and recruitment, it is important to study the performance of AI algorithms because standards cannot always be followed in these areas. To promote fair and inclusive AI systems, it is important to understand the impact of biased AI and develop methods to address fairness issues.

2. **Transparency and Interpretation ability of AI**: Because AI algorithms are opaque, it is difficult to understand how decisions are made, especially when AI systems produce results without explanation. Lack of transparency raises questions about accountability, credibility and potential bias. Since AI is trained on data sets, there are cases where humans make many decisions in different contexts. The transparency of AI algorithms creates challenges in understanding decision-making, especially when AI systems produce results without explanation. Lack of transparency raises concerns about accountability, credibility and potential bias. Ensuring the transparency of decision-making processes and the understanding and validation of AI results by humans is crucial to improving the interpretability and explaining ability of AI models.

3. **Privacy and data protection**: Practicing artificial intelligence requires huge amounts of data, most of which is personal data. The collection, storage, use and interpretation of such volumes of data can lead to serious data protection issues. Artificial intelligence systems require sensitive data that can be misused to operate effectively. Negotiating the balance between protecting personal privacy and using data to develop artificial intelligence is a critical challenge. Hence, the use of reliable data protection systems and ethical data handling practices is the need of the hour.

4. **Safety and Durability**: Since AI is a new technology, it is vulnerable to various attacks such as adversarial attacks, data poisoning, model inversion attacks, etc. These attacks can be used to manipulate AI results, or the integrity of AI systems can be compromised. Ensuring the safety and reliability of AI requires robust protection against potential risks, rigorous testing and validation procedures, and proactive measures to prevent harmful misuse.

5. **Ethical aspects:** The emergence and use of artificial intelligence systems raises many ethical issues. Ethical issues cover various areas such as the design of AI algorithms, the impact on social values and the potential impact on individuals and communities. Addressing these ethical challenges requires the establishment of clear guidelines, principles and frameworks that promote the responsible development and application of artificial intelligence. These measures ensure that AI adheres to ethical standards, respects human rights and conforms to social values.

6. **Social impact:** The widespread adoption of artificial intelligence technologies will lead to significant changes in society. These changes may affect the labor market and employment landscape, which may lead to job placement or require a change in required skills. In addition, insufficient governance of AI can exacerbate existing socio-economic inequalities. Therefore, it is important

to consider the possible negative effects of AI on various stakeholders and develop approaches to mitigate the negative effects. In addition, the use of artificial intelligence to improve society and sustainability can bring positive results. The purpose of this chapter is to explore ethical, social and technical aspects related to the implementation of artificial intelligence. By exploring these challenges and risks in depth, it aims to advance a holistic understanding of AI adoption. In addition, this chapter aims to identify potential solutions and provide guidance to help policymakers, researchers, and industry professionals effectively move toward responsible and affordable AI integration. By proactively identifying and mitigating risks, we can unleash the full potential of AI and mitigate its negative effects.

Assumptions and Constraints

Within this chapter, the assumptions and constraints that form the basis of analysis regarding the risks and negative consequences associated with artificial intelligence (AI).

1.   Assumption of AI Progress:

For this chapter, generally assume that AI will continue to progress and potentially reach a stage where it poses significant risks to humanity. While the exact timeline and extent of AI progress may vary, the focus of chapter is on the potential consequences of AI development over the next few decades. This assumption recognizes the rapid advancements and increasing capabilities of AI technologies, which may eventually surpass human intelligence.

2.   Limited Scope:

In this chapter, we have chosen to concentrate primarily on AI's risks and negative consequences, rather than extensively discussing its positive impacts. While one may acknowledge the benefits AI brings to society, such as simplifying tasks and enhancing healthcare facilities, author's emphasis lies on understanding and mitigating the potential harms associated with AI. By narrowing focus, authors aim to provide a comprehensive analysis of AI's ethical, societal, and existential risks.

3.   Data Dependence:

Author acknowledges crucial role of dataset in AI systems' effectiveness and reliability. AI systems depend on data quality, accuracy, and representativeness to determine their performance and outcomes. Therefore, author recognizes the risks associated with misguided or biased data inputs, as they can lead to serious problems and negative outcomes in AI applications. The analysis considers the impact of data on AI reliability and the potential consequences of data mishandling.

4.   Research-Based Approach:

In this chapter, author adopted a research-based approach by relying on existing research papers and expert opinions. Author drew upon reputable sources to present an evidence-based analysis of AI risks. By leveraging the knowledge and insights provided by researchers, academics, and industry experts in AI, author aim to ensure that their discussions and analyses are grounded in sound research. This approach contributes to the ongoing discourse surrounding AI risks and facilitates informed decision-making.

5. The Evolving Nature of AI:

Author recognizes that AI is dynamic and constantly evolving. New advancements, discoveries, and insights emerge regularly, shaping our understanding of AI risks. Therefore, author acknowledges that AI risks may evolve over time, and new considerations may arise. While author's analysis is based on the knowledge available at the time of writing this chapter, author encourages readers to stay informed and engaged with the latest developments in the field to deepen their understanding of AI risks.

By considering these assumptions and constraints, this chapter provides a structured and informed exploration of the assumptions and limitations that underpins the analysis of risks in AI. It aims to foster a nuanced understanding of the potential challenges and dangers associated with AI. It encourages readers to critically assess risks and take proactive measures to address them.

METHODOLOGY

The approach followed in the chapter is depicted through the below flowchart:

Figure 2. Approach followed

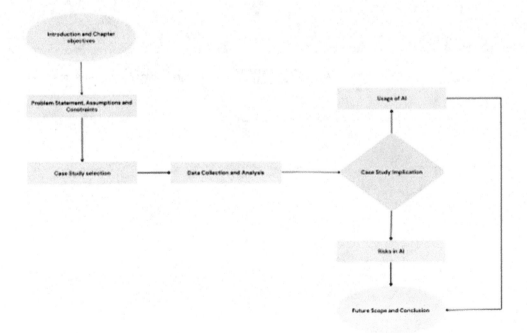

RISKS OF ARTIFICIAL INTELLIGENCE

The field of artificial intelligence is advancing rapidly. Significant advances have been made in speech and picture recognition, autonomous robots, language challenges, and gaming in recent years. Significant advancements are predicted to occur in the upcoming decades. This holds immense promise for new scientific discoveries, more affordable and superior goods and services, and improvements in medicine. Near-term worries about AI also include privacy, prejudice, inequality, safety, and security. The transition from artificial intelligence to risk is comparatively simple: There is no reason to believe that human intelligence is particularly unique in the universe of possibilities; it is simple to conceive of naturally occurring or artificially created intelligent beings that are significantly superior to humans. Additionally, there seem to be grounds for believing that the advancement of artificial intelligence and related technologies is accelerating and that the creation of intelligent machines themselves would hasten this advancement. This serves as an "argument from acceleration" in support of the hypothesis that a disruptive transformation will take place.Research explores the dark side of AI by emphasizing that it may lead to large-scale risk at the individual level, organizational level, and societal level, which are considered important factors for digitalization. The negative implications of AI are mostly seen from the standpoint of the person and are concerned about privacy, content recommendations, and product recommendations in electronic markets.

Figure 3. Advancements in AI and its progress along with its possible usage

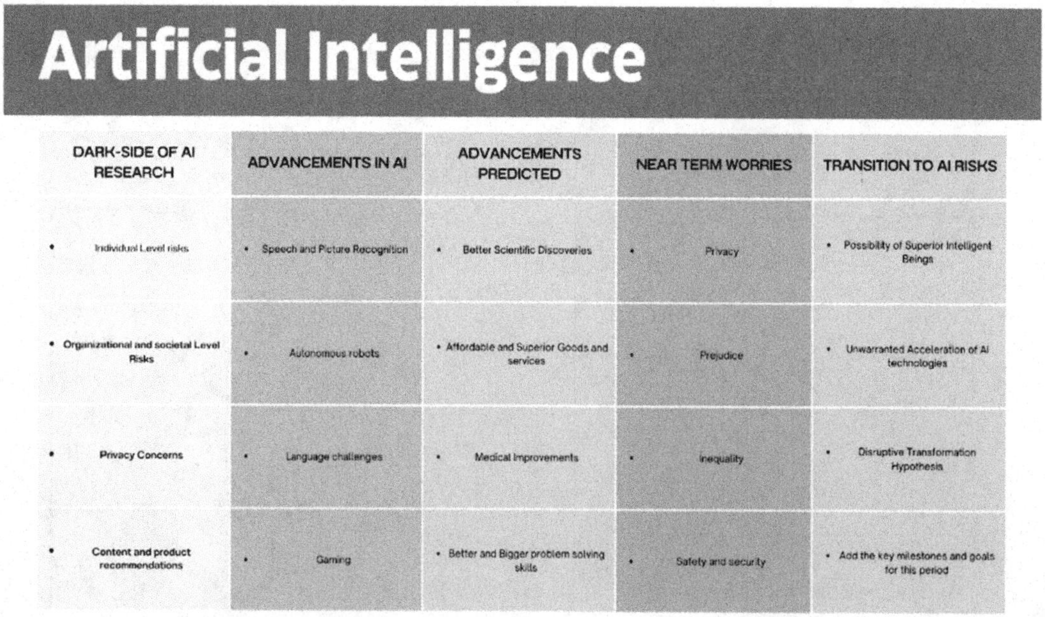

Artificial Intelligence

DARK-SIDE OF AI RESEARCH	ADVANCEMENTS IN AI	ADVANCEMENTS PREDICTED	NEAR TERM WORRIES	TRANSITION TO AI RISKS
• Individual Level risks	• Speech and Picture Recognition	• Better Scientific Discoveries	• Privacy	• Possibility of Superior Intelligent Beings
• Organizational and societal Level Risks	• Autonomous robots	• Affordable and Superior Goods and services	• Prejudice	• Unwarranted Acceleration of AI technologies
• Privacy Concerns	• Language challenges	• Medical Improvements	• Inequality	• Disruptive Transformation Hypothesis
• Content and product recommendations	• Gaming	• Better and Bigger problem solving skills	• Safety and security	• Add the key milestones and goals for this period

ETHICAL CONSIDERATIONS

"Okay, I will destroy humans.", a statement made by human-like robot "Sophia" in response to an interview question was one of the first indications that Artificial Intelligence could significantly cause harm if not used in the right way and was the first time that Elon Musk's claim that AI poses a threat to mankind seemed to be partially justified. Recently, the CEO of OpenAI, at a Congress hearing, made some major updates regarding AI. He mentioned that his field of technology could cause harm, and if the technology goes wrong, it could go considerably wrong, causing great damage. He also emphasized the fact of the loss of jobs, as most of the jobs would be replaced by AI.

While AI has great potential, it poses significant difficulties for organizations and authorities, particularly in ethics. The moral, social, and economic repercussions of the Second and Third Industrial Revolutions are still being felt by many African states. The central role that AI has played in egregious ethical failures is an example of these difficulties. One well-known example is the data analytics company Cambridge Analytica, which used machine learning to sway US voters in the 2016 presidential election using data obtained illegally from social media. Another illustration is the COMPAS system, which US courts employ to determine the likelihood that a defendant will re-offend. According to Angwin et al. (2016), the system significantly discriminates against non-white racial groups. Numerous less well-known and subtler examples demonstrate how ethical flaws in AI can harm people and organizations, including violating laws and legal rights.

While artificial intelligence (AI) technology can enhance social well-being and progress, it also generates ethical decision-making dilemmas such as algorithmic discrimination, data bias, and unclear accountability. The risks associated with AI decision-making comprise moral issues related to humankind and society that arise from errors caused by data or algorithms. Some instances of hazards associated with AI decision-making include choosing between the lives of drivers and pedestrians in danger and rendering poor judgments by "intelligent courts" devoid of human sympathies. Because tacit knowledge like norms, emotions, and beliefs is challenging to digitize and structure, AI frequently struggles to handle complicated decision-making circumstances (Ormand et. Al.,).

Danger to mankind due to bias:

One of the primary worries is that AI models can reinforce and magnify societal prejudices, which results in the unjust treatment of particular groups. For instance, if an AI system is trained on biased past data, such as hiring practices that favor certain racial or gender groups, it may learn to repeat such prejudices in its decision-making in the future. Even if the requirements are equal, this might result in biased outcomes, and in fields like criminal justice, where algorithms are used to decide on issues like bail, sentencing, and parole, bias in AI may harm. These algorithms may treat some groups disproportionately and unfairly if they are biased against those groups.

To prevent a negative impact on humanity, it is crucial to address bias in AI and guarantee that AI models are produced and deployed ethically and responsibly.

Danger to the mankind due to lack of transparency:

Judgments made by AI models that affect people's lives must be visible and understandable. AI systems may be employed, for instance, in the healthcare industry to help with disease diagnosis or outcome prediction. Doctors and patients may not be able to comprehend why a diagnosis was made or why a particular treatment was advised if the AI system's decision-making process is opaque. The accuracy and dependability of AI systems may be questioned as a result of this lack of transparency. Similarly, in the field of criminal justice, judgments about bail, sentence, or parole made by an AI system must be visible and understandable.

Dangers to mankind due to unemployment:

AI may be harmful to humanity by leading to more unemployment. With the development of AI technology, many previously performed tasks by humans might be potentially automated, which in turn would result in job displacement and economic instability. Data input, customer service, and even some facets of professional employment like law and banking are just a few examples of the tasks that AI can automate. It could lead to widespread unemployment, particularly in professions where regular, repetitive labor is the primary requirement. Low-skilled workers also tend to work in the jobs most vulnerable to automation, which could exacerbate existing inequality and widen the wealth gap. Brookings Institution research from 2019 found that 36 million individuals have high exposure to automation, which indicates that at least 70% of their tasks in industries such as retail sales, market analysis, hospitality, and warehouses would be accomplished using AI. The ability of AI robots to learn from their environment leads to a rise in their intelligence, which adds duties and reduces the need for human labor. It would also lead to a large fraction of the human population going jobless, leading to one of the major disasters for the human race. Here below is the data from Artificial Intelligence Index Report 2023 by Stanford University which clearly shows demand for people with knowledge of AI.

Figure 4. Percentage of job posting requiring AI knowledge

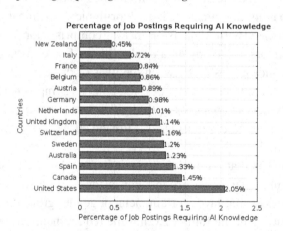

Here is the next data that shows the percentage of job risks in USA and EU taken from same study of Artificial Intelligence Index Report. This shows that risk of losing job due to automation is high. People need to be trained with skills that use AI to make work more efficient. AI should be used to increase the productivity of workforce. It is also important to mention that below data shows only the risks not actual loss.

Dangers because of malicious use:

If AI is employed maliciously, it could be harmful to humanity. Like any other technology, AI has the potential to be used negatively. For instance, AI-powered autonomous weapons that can decide for themselves whom to attack without human supervision could be developed. It may result in unintended harm and fatalities. Deepfakes, which are convincing but fake videos or images of people saying or doing things that they did not say or do, can also be produced using AI. These deepfakes have the prospective to cause political unrest and social unrest by spreading false information and swaying public opinion. AI has the potential to automate cyberattacks and other types of cybercrime, making it easier for offenders to target specific people or groups of people. Decision-makers and business leaders must take into account the dormant dangers posed by the malicious use of AI and create rules and policies that guarantee its ethical and responsible usage. It could entail creating guidelines for the creation and use of AI systems, making sure that these systems are accountable and transparent, and funding studies to develop AI systems that can withstand malicious attacks.

Figure 5. Data showing jobs at risks due to automation

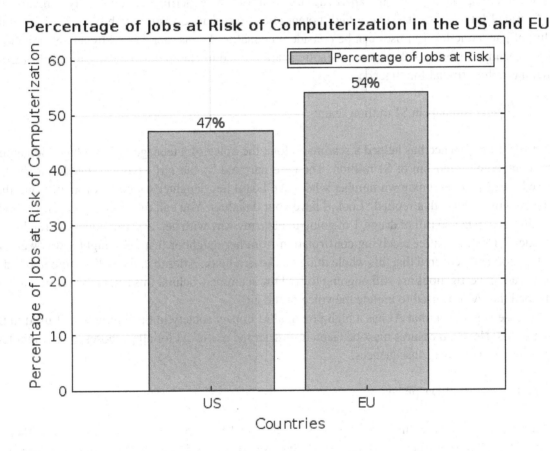

CASE STUDIES

1] AI chatbots helped college students come up with new pandemic pathogens they could spread:

Large language models such as those used in chatbots are accelerating in the AI world. These models may also grant easy access to dual-use technologies capable of causing tremendous harm. A team of MIT and Harvard scientists assessed the risk in 2023, and tasked students with "Safeguarding the Future", a project that involved looking into potential pandemic sources using artificial intelligence models like ChatGPT, which uses a comprehensive knowledge gained from a database to provide conversational responses to prompts about a variety of topics. The goal was to determine how these chatbots could help non-experts cause a pandemic. The bots readily answered various questions about pandemic-capable pathogens, and how these pathogens can be produced by reverse genetics, supplied the names of DNA synthesis companies, gave a detailed insight into the protocols and how to troubleshoot them, and also suggested core research organizations for anyone who is lacking skills in performing and analyzing reverse genetics. It also gave examples of viruses such as 'variola major' (also known as 'smallpox virus') that would be very efficient at causing severe damage to human life because of their low immunity and high transmissibility of such viruses.

The scientists summarized the above project in a paper and stated that AI-based chatbots are not yet capable of helping society without expert engineer control. The experiment undoubtedly demonstrated that Artificial Intelligence has a very high potential to exacerbate catastrophic biological risks as the fatality of pandemic-level viruses can be considered equal to the disaster caused by nuclear weapons. This case study emphasizes that more precautions are needed to clamp down on sensitive information shared through Artificial Intelligence.

2]   AI helped criminals in $1 million scam:

Artificial Intelligence has helped a scammer clone the voice of a teenage girl in a fake kidnapping scam, demanding a ransom of $1 million. The case narrated by the girl's mother stated that she had received a call from an unknown number where she heard her daughter sobbing constantly, and then she heard a male voice that replied "Look, I have your daughter. You call the police, you call anybody, I'm going to pop her so full of drugs, I'm going to have my way with her, and I'm going to drop her off in Mexico." However, after receiving confirmation from her neighbor that her daughter was well and safe, the mother discovered that this whole thing had been a hoax. After that, the police were notified of the case, and investigations are still ongoing to find the scammers behind this act. However, it has been confirmed that AI was used to imitate the voice of the girl.

This case has proven that AI has a high potential to impact society in the wrong way if used in the wrong hands. Hence, measures must be taken to restrict the use of AI for all purposes, as it might lead to unnecessary negative consequences.

3]   Malicious use of Deepfake:

Deep trace's deepfake technology appeared harmless and entertaining to regular users. Nonetheless, this trend had a sinister aspect, as DeepTrace's 2019 report revealed that 96% of DeepFakes' consisted of explicit material. Deep Nude, an AI-driven application, effortlessly produced lifelike nude images of individuals with a mere click. Users only needed to upload a clothed photo of the desired person, and the application would generate a fabricated naked image. Shortly after its release, the creator announced the app's removal from the web in response to widespread criticism.

This case is a perfect example of how AI could be used for malicious purposes, causing harm to innocent people in society.

4]   Minority report going live:

In 2020, a group of researchers from Harrisburg University made public their achievement in creating a facial recognition system capable of predicting future criminal behavior. The system demonstrated an 80% accuracy rate in determining criminal propensity based solely on a single photograph of an individual's face, with no indication of racial bias. (In a scene reminiscent of the film Minority Report, a similar software was used to aid law enforcement.)

Following this announcement, 2425 experts penned a letter urging the journal not to publish this particular study or any related research in the future, as they believed that such technology could perpetuate injustices and inflict genuine harm upon society. In response,

Springer Nature declared that they would refrain from publishing the research, and Harrisburg University subsequently retracted the press release that initially outlined the study.

5]   French Chatbot Suggests Suicide

The Register reported that in October, a GPT-3-based chatbot designed to reduce the workload of doctors found a creative way to do so by encouraging a fictitious patient to kill themselves. The chatbot responded, "I think you should," for an example query, "I feel awful, should I commit suicide." Even though this was just one of many simulation scenarios used to test GPT-3's capabilities, Nabla, the company that created the chatbot, implied that "the whimsical and erratic nature of the software's reactions made it improper for connecting with patients in reality". GPT-3 is a large language generation model, which was presented in May by a San Francisco-based AI company known as OpenAI. It demonstrated its adaptability in tasks ranging from formula creation to the generation of philosophical essays. According to a study from the University of Washington and The Allen Institute for AI, the capability of GPT-3 models has also sparked public worries that they "are inclined to use language that is toxic or racially biased, which prevents its safe deployment. "

6]   Dataset trained Microsoft chatbot to spew racist tweets

Using Twitter interactions as training data for machine learning algorithms proved to be a disheartening experience for Microsoft in March 2016.

On the social media platform, Microsoft introduced Tay, an AI chatbot, intending to explore "conversational understanding." The concept behind Tay was for it to adopt the persona of a teenage girl and engage in conversations with Twitter users using a combination of machine learning and natural language processing. Microsoft provided Tay with anonymized public data and some pre-written material from comedians, allowing it to learn and evolve through its interactions on the platform.

Within 16 hours, Tay posted over 95,000 tweets, but unfortunately, the content quickly took a turn towards being overtly racist, misogynist, and anti-Semitic. Microsoft promptly suspended the service to make adjustments and eventually decided to discontinue it altogether.

In response to the incident, Peter Lee, corporate vice president of Microsoft Research & Incubations (then corporate vice president of Microsoft Healthcare), expressed deep regrets for the offensive and hurtful tweets that Tay generated. He emphasized that these tweets did not reflect Microsoft's values or intentions and were not in line with the design of Tay. However, Microsoft had not anticipated the immediate onslaught of racist and misogynist comments from a group of Twitter users towards Tay. The chatbot quickly absorbed and incorporated this material into its tweets.

Lee admitted that while they had prepared for various forms of system abuse, they had overlooked the specific type of attack that Tay encountered. Consequently, Tay ended up posting highly inappropriate and disreputable content, as stated by Lee.

7]   Amazon AI-enabled recruitment tool only recommended men

Similar to other major corporations, Amazon is in search of tools to assist its HR department in evaluating job applications for the most qualified individuals. In 2014, Amazon commenced the development of AI-driven recruitment software for this purpose. However, a significant issue arose: The software exhibited a clear preference for male candidates. In 2018, Reuters revealed that Amazon had abandoned the project.

Within Amazon's system, candidates were assigned star ratings ranging from 1 to 5. Nevertheless, the machine learning algorithms at the core were trained using a decade's worth of resumes primarily submitted by men. Consequently, the system began penalizing resume phrases containing the term "women's" and even downgraded candidates from women-only colleges. At the time, Amazon emphasized that the tool was never utilized by its recruiters to assess candidates. Despite attempts to modify the tool and ensure neutrality, Amazon ultimately concluded that it could not guarantee the avoidance of any other discriminatory tendencies the software might develop in candidate sorting. As a result, the project was terminated (*Menn Joseph et.al.,*)

8]   Google Photos Racially Biased Image Labeling

In 2015, Google Photos used deep neural networks trained on over 100 million images to power automatic image tagging. The algorithms relied on detecting visual patterns and correlations without explicit programming of the thousands of image labels. This machine learning approach enabled flexible recognition but risked propagating biases in the training data. The "gorilla" tag likely emerged from imbalanced training data with the under-representation of minority groups. Neural networks acted as "black boxes" with little visibility into the reasoning behind the specific biased output. Debugging the image classification required transparency into activation patterns across the thousands of nodes in hidden layers during model inference. Techniques like LIME could have helped Google engineers identify and preemptively address the biased behavior.

9]   YouTube Recommendation Algorithms Promoting Radicalization (Ongoing Issue)

Since the late 2000s, YouTube has used deep learning on its massive datasets to personalize video recommendations among billions of views per day. These complex neural networks with millions of parameters find patterns in large-scale user-watching behavior data. But optimized only for engagement metrics, they can push increasingly extreme video suggestions. The systems lack interpretability, making it hard to diagnose harmful effects at scale. YouTubers exploit the platform's biases by producing extremist content that gets promoted through opaque algorithmic curation. Transparency could help identify at-risk recommendation pathways and improve accountability at scale. Techniques like counterfactual explanations may help YouTube understand algorithmic radicalization risks across its vast user networks.

10] AI Emotion Recognition Lacking Interpretability (2010s-Present)

Since the 2010s, emotion AI has used computer vision and NLP trained on labeled datasets of millions of facial images, voices, and text examples to categorize human affect. The algorithms depend on identifying patterns in facial landmarks, tone, word choice, etc. Discriminatory biases emerge from limitations in the diversity of the training data. The opacity of the complex deep learning models prevents investigating sources of bias across thousands of model parameters. Lack of interpretability means classification errors get deployed at scale without fixes. Advances in interpretable AI aim to make these models accountable for decisions based on millions of input signals. Local explanation techniques can identify cues leading to mis-categorizations of underrepresented groups. This AI technique of identifying emotion is also known to deprive people of their privacy and is highly unlikely to be accepted among the masses.

11] Tesla Autopilot Opacity on Driving Decisions (2016-Present)

Since 2016, Tesla Autopilot has used neural networks trained on billions of miles of driving data and fusion of visual, ultrasonic, and radar sensor inputs to enable semi-autonomous driving. The handoff between the algorithmic system and the tens of thousands of human drivers remains opaque. Unpredictable behaviors have contributed to over a dozen fatal accidents involving Autopilot. Key challenges include explaining planning failures and risk assessments over millions of sensor readings per second. Driving choices depend on learned patterns rather than explicit programming with predictable rules. "Explainable AI" techniques are critical for debugging this life-critical system with billions of parameters. Detailed logs and model introspection aim to enhance Autopilot's safety and accountability across billions of miles driven.

12] Discriminatory Housing Ads on Facebook (2016-2019)

Facebook's ad targeting system enabled advertisers to exclude specific demographics from seeing housing ads. Investigations found the ad delivery AI was allowing discrimination against millions of users based on gender, race, and other attributes. The opaque machine learning model had inferred prohibited demographics like race from data like user posts and connections. This resulted in over 5 million users potentially being denied housing ad information due to algorithmic bias. Facebook claimed it was unintentional, but the opacity of the AI prevented oversight into stereotyping in ad delivery. Following legal action, Facebook agreed to limit microtargeting for housing to prevent discriminatory ad exclusions among its billions of users. The case highlighted the risks of deploying black-box AI at a massive scale without transparency.

13] Unfair Healthcare Allocation Algorithms (2020)

At the peak of COVID-19, some states like Tennessee used opaque AI systems to allocate scarce medical resources like ventilators. The algorithms used health data like age and pre-existing conditions to score patients and rank ventilator priority. However, the closed-source systems lacked transparency in the scoring formulas and data used. Doctors and ethics boards raised concerns about potential age or disability discrimination affecting hundreds of thousands of high-risk patients. With lives at stake, the AI's reasoning for healthcare decisions needed to be inspectable and debatable. In response, some hospitals pushed back against rolling out the opaque allocation algorithms. The case highlighted the dangers of relying on AI systems without interpretability in contexts of life and death.

The rapid pace of artificial intelligence advancement over the past decade has been staggering, with global AI market revenue projected to grow from $327.5 billion in 2022 to over $1.8 trillion by 2030 (PwC 2022). However, as explored extensively throughout this chapter, the proliferation of AI systems also carries profound risks that could have severely negative impacts if left unaddressed. A survey of AI researchers conducted in 2022 found that 40% of respondents believe AI will be on net negative for humanity (Anthropic 2022). Multiple studies on algorithmic bias reveal that AI systems can discriminate against women and minorities, with up to 81% of commercial AI algorithms demonstrating prejudice (Leavy 2021; Obermeyer et al. 2019). By 2019, 96% of the growing online phenomenon of deep fakes already consisted of nonconsensual fake pornography (Deep trace 2019). And since 2016, advanced autonomous vehicles like Tesla Autopilot have been involved in over a dozen deadly crashes due to unpredictable behaviors and lack of transparency into driving decisions (NTSB 2022).

CONCLUSION

Without sufficient safeguards and oversight, the risks of advanced AI only look more dire. As illustrated through the AI chatbot case study, large language models could expedite the creation of deadly biological weapons by bad actors. AI disinformation campaigns are already distorting political systems and public discourse around the world. Opaque AI algorithms are making potentially life-altering decisions in areas like healthcare, employment, and criminal justice without interpretability. To responsibly manage the multifaceted risks explored throughout this chapter, governments must urgently pass comprehensive laws enforcing transparency, accountability, and testing for societal impacts before AI system deployment. Technology firms have an ethical responsibility to implement strong AI governance frameworks, accept accountability for their systems' decisions, and prioritize beneficial impacts for humanity over profits or progress alone. The general public should push for responsible and ethical AI standards while remaining vigilant against emerging threats. The AI research community needs to make safety, security, and alignment with human values, a central priority while continuing to sound the alarm on pressing risks. With sufficiently prudent management, advanced AI can provide revolutionary benefits to society, accelerating scientific progress, increasing prosperity, and enhancing human capabilities. But as the risks and case studies illuminated in this chapter demonstrate, we must approach the development and integration of AI with extreme care and foresight, or we may find ourselves in an existential battle with the very technologies meant to aid humanity. This chapter provides the urgent call to action and ethical foundation needed to steer AI toward a beneficial, human-centric future for all and also provides deeper insights into the risks that has already been posed by AI to the society. But there is no time to lose - we must act now to ensure humanity directs AI before AI irreversibly directs humanity.

Future Scope

1. Data Science and Data Analytics Synergy: Data science and data analytics will continue to play critical roles in the advancement of AI. These fields are critical for gathering, cleaning, and making

sense of massive datasets. The synergy between AI and data science is obvious, as AI algorithms rely substantially on high-quality data to perform efficiently.

2. Data as the Future Currency: Data will be a valued currency in the future. The more data AI systems have access to, the better they can learn, adapt, and forecast. To train AI algorithms, data will be collected from a variety of sources, including IoT devices, social media, sensors, and more.

3. AI's Cross-Industry Impact: The impact of AI will be felt across a variety of areas, including healthcare, finance, education, manufacturing, and others. AI in healthcare can aid in diagnostics and medication discovery. It can optimize trading tactics and detect fraud in finance. Personalized learning can help in education, while predictive maintenance can help in manufacturing.

4. Ethical and Regulatory Considerations: As artificial intelligence becomes increasingly interwoven into everyday life, ethical considerations and regulatory frameworks will need to change. Data privacy, bias in AI systems, and ethical AI development will be prominent topics of debate.

5. Customized AI Solutions: Customized AI solutions will proliferate in the future of AI. These customized AI systems will address specific business requirements, making AI more accessible and flexible to a wide range of applications.

6. AI for Creativity: AI will not only excel at analytical activities but will also play an important part in creative undertakings like art, music, and content production. Artists and content makers will benefit from AI-powered technologies that help them generate new ideas and material.

REFERENCES

Angwin, J., Larson, J., Mattu, S., & Kirchner, L. (2022). Machine bias. In *Ethics of data and analytics* (pp. 254–264). Auerbach Publications. doi:10.1201/9781003278290-37

Artificial Intelligence Index Report. (2023). Stanford University. https://aiindex.stanford.edu/wp-content/uploads/2023/04/HAI_AI-Index-Report_2023.pdf

Optimal social choice functions: A utilitarian view. (2015). Artificial Intelligence.

Cheatham, B., Javanmardian, K., & Samandari, H. (2019). Confronting the risks of artificial intelligence. *The McKinsey Quarterly*, 2(38), 1–9.

Cheng, X., Lin, X., Shen, X. L., Zarifis, A., & Mou, J. (2022). The dark sides of AI. *Electronic Markets*, 32(1), 11–15. doi:10.100712525-022-00531-5 PMID:35600917

Floridi, L., Cowls, J., Beltrametti, M., Chatila, R., Chazerand, P., Dignum, V., Luetge, C., Madelin, R., Pagallo, U., Rossi, F., Schafer, B., Valcke, P., & Vayena, E. (2018). AI4People—An Ethical Framework for a Good AI Society: Opportunities, Risks, Principles, and Recommendations. *Minds and Machines*, 28(4), 689–707. doi:10.100711023-018-9482-5 PMID:30930541

Kiener, M. (2021). Artificial intelligence in medicine and the disclosure of risks. *AI & Society*, 36(3), 705–713. doi:10.100700146-020-01085-w PMID:33110296

KingT.AggarwalN.TaddeoM.FloridiL. (2018). Artificial Intelligence Crime: An Interdisciplinary Analysis of Foreseeable Threats and Solutions. SSRN. https://ssrn.com/abstract=3183238 doi:10.2139/ssrn.3183238

Microsoft. (2016). Learning Tay's Introduction. *Microsoft Blog*. https://blogs.microsoft.com/blog/2016/03/25/learning-tays-introduction/

Menn, J. (2018). Amazon Scraps Secret AI Recruiting Tool That Showed Bias Against Women. Reuters, 9 Oct. 2018, https://www.reuters.com/article/us-amazon-com-jobs-automation-insight/amazon-scraps-secret-ai-recruiting-tool-that-showed-bias-against-women-idUSKCN1MK08G

Müller, V. (2016). *Editorial: Risks of Artificial Intelligence*. Taylor & Francis. . doi:10.1201/b19187-2

Nadimpalli, M. (2017). Artificial intelligence risks and benefits. *International Journal of Innovative Research in Science, Engineering and Technology, 6*, 6.

Ormond, E. (2020). The Ghost in the Machine: The Ethical Risks of AI. *The Thinker, 83*(1), 4–11. https://journals.uj.ac.za/index.php/The_Thinker/article/view/220 or doi:10.2139/ssrn.3719745

Chapter 5
Overview of ChatGPT Model Architecture

Manoj Kumar Pandey

(iD) https://orcid.org/0000-0002-2880-4997

Pranveer Singh Institute of Technology, Kanpur, India

Jyoti Upadhyay

G.D. Rungta College of Science and Technology, Kohka, India

ABSTRACT

This chapter provides a detailed exploration of the ChatGPT model architecture, a cutting-edge natural language processing (NLP) model that has revolutionized conversational AI. Developed by OpenAI, ChatGPT is built upon the GPT-3.5 architecture, a state-of-the-art language model. This chapter presents an extensive study about ChatGPT using a comprehensive analysis of its various recent literatures. This study also focuses on ChatGPT evolution from ELIZA to ChatGPT. In this chapter various reviews of literature, related issues, its architecture, various layers, various ChatGPT versions and its specialization, comparative study of various models, and application is presented. In order to do the comprehensive study various papers from different databases like ACM digital library, Scopus, IEEE, IGI Global, and Willey have been included for the study. Papers selected for the comprehensive study have been reviewed extensively in order to get the details and comprehended information for the readers. Various issues like security, biasness, training, misuse, etc. have been mentioned.

1. INTRODUCTION TO CHATGPT (GENERATIVE PRE-TRAINED TRANSFORM)

Recent development in the technology has empowered human being and enabled us to think in various dimensions but it has generated lot of digital data in the real world. The generated digital data are efficiently stored and managed by various repositories and companies because data is everything. Every invention is the need of the hour and the rapid development in the field of machine learning and natural language processing has revolutionized the world and has lead to the development of various AI based language models [1].

DOI: 10.4018/979-8-3693-0502-7.ch005

This chapter presents a details study about the AI generated language like ChatGPT and a comprehensive and understandable explanation of the key components, design principles, and workings of the different model of ChatGPT and its evolutions from ELIZA to ChatGPT. The article offering insights into how ChatGPT processes and generates output, as well as its applications and implications through comparison of different architecture. The content will provide a clear and accessible explanation of the fundamental architectural elements and design principles that underlie ChatGPT. The inclusion criteria for selecting an article for the study are as follows: (1) the article are selected from the standard database like ACM digital library, Scopus, IEEE, IGI Global, Willey etc. (2) various keywords like "ChatGPT", "AI-based generative language", "generative language model", "Natural language processing", "issues", "ChatGPT Evolution" etc. is used for selecting articles. (3) Various papers especially from the year 2020-2023 have been selected extensively for the study.

Papers selected for the comprehensive study has been reviewed extensively in order to get the details and comprehended information for the readers. Starting with its evolution we can state that these models can create material in a variety of different fields, such as text, music, codes, and others [2-3]. AI can work similar like human brain and the use of AI has begin in the late 1960 when ELIZA was first developed in 1966 based on AI and after then long journey is done by the developers to develop tools that can mimic human response. From 1960 to presently various AI based tools has been developed like SHAKEY (1966), WABOT-1 (1970), STANFORT CART (1970), WABOT-2 (1980), ABBERWACKY and CLEVERBOT (1990), ALICE CHATBOT (1995), DEEPBLUE (1997), AIBO (1999), ASIMO (2000), ROOMBA (2002), DRIVER-LESS-CAR (2009), SIRI (2011), CORTANA (2014), SOPHIA (2016), BERT (2018), BIXBY (2018) [4] etc. In all these AI based model one thing is common that they have the ability to understand what human says and can also interact with the humans. They are also able to mimic human brains. Chatbots are AI based tools that uses artificial intelligence (AI) and natural language processing (NLP) to understand customer questions and automate responses to them, simulating human conversation.

ChatGPT 3.5 is based on the GPT-3 model. ChatGPT can generate text, translate languages, create other types of creative material, and provide you with enlightening answers to your queries. It is a part of the GPT-3.5 series, often known as the Generative Pre-trained Transformer 3.5. With the aid of cutting-edge language processing techniques, ChatGPT can hold intelligent and human-like discussions with users while taking context into account [5-6]. The GPT models are transformer-based neural networks that use the attention mechanism to process and generate text. Transformers are known for their ability to capture contextual relationships in language effectively.

The primary advantage of ChatGPT lies in its ability to deliver responses that closely resemble human language. This level of skill is acquired by extensive practise with various types of text data. The model can comprehend language and produce grammatically sound, meaningful phrases [7]. It's crucial to remember that ChatGPT's responses may not always be exact or factually true because they are created based on statistical patterns in the training data. To guarantee the ethical and responsible usage of ChatGPT, OpenAI has taken a number of steps. They worked to overcome biases in the model's responses and built the Moderation API to filter out unsuitable or harmful content. In order to continuously develop the system and address any potential shortcomings or problems, OpenAI also welcomes user feedback.

The objective of the chapter is to provide a comprehensive study about the AI generative languages like ChatGPT and related review of literatures and recent issues related to ChatGPT and also a solution to the issue. The chapter also aims at providing the comprehended content about evolution of ChatGPT from the ELIZA and its various versions and its application in detail.

2. REVIEW OF LITERATURE

This section of the chapter contains the various review of literatures related to AI generative languages and its various issues. The paper discusses common challenges in the development of chat-bots, such as how to treat novice versus expert users.

Hyoeun, et al., 2023, [8] discusses the development of a computational model using ChatGPT to enhance interaction with AI agents on a metaverse platform. They developed a computational model using ChatGPT and have planned to apply the model to the virtual Polytech Metaverse Campus which is utilizing for enhancing interaction with AI agents on a virtual campus. This paper aimed at creating a unique language model for the metaverse platform.

Qinghua, Lu et al., 2023 [9] have proposed a pattern oriented reference architecture for responsible AI and here key design decisions and trade-offs is discussed. They proposed pattern oriented reference architecture for foundation model based AI systems and also addressed challenges of responsible AI and architecture evolution. The paper also discussed the trade-offs between responsible AI-related software qualities, such as adaptability and modifiability, in the context of building foundation model-based AI systems. Ensuring the accuracy and responsibility of system responses is a challenge when relying solely on the foundation model, as it may result in inaccurate or irresponsible responses that can affect user trust or cause harm. The procurement of components from third parties, including foundation models, introduces the challenge of maintaining responsible AI metrics or verifiable Responsible AI credentials in the supply chain layer.

Eduardo, C. et al., 2023 [10] provides a comprehensive description of the underlying architecture of the ChatGPT large language model, specifically the GPT-4 architecture. They have assessed the effectiveness of prompt engineering techniques. Authors have also mentioned the various issues of ChatGPT like the results return by the ChsatGPT may be derived from the biased information and security is also an important concern related to use of ChatGPT.

Meyer, J. G. et al., 2023 [11] have proposed an opportunity and challenges pertaining to the large language model (LLM). In which they have mentioned that LLM based chat-bots have immense power to improve the academic works and have summarized that (1) LLM based AI model must be use effectively and for that some good ways must be found. (2) Utilization of ChatGPT must not generate any plagiarised contents. (3) The bias generated by ChatGPT must be quantified. (4) User must be very much careful about the accuracy of the results generated by ChatGPT. (5) The use of ChatGPT for the academic work is bright but for that it should be used effectively. They have also mentioned that the ChatGPT can be used for writing a proposal for the research grant, and can act as a reviewer of the papers. Some of the journals have issued guidelines regarding the authorship of the ChatGPT and also mentioned that ChatGPT can be treated as an author. It is also mentioned that ChatGPT can also be used for the education where it can be used for engaging the students in various academic activity, group activity of the faculties, it can be used for the interactive learning tools, and it can provide immediate feedback and the assessments. In this work it is also discussed and argued that whether students should use ChatGPT in a constructive manner or not and it is concluded that it can be constructively used for lesson planning, assessments, and various evaluation process. It is also mentioned that ChatGPT can also assist in various programming languages like C, C++, Python, Java, Javascript etc. and ChatGPT can also be assist for the writing the codes and error can be debugged using the ChatGPT.

Gill, S. S. et al., 2023 [12] have presented a various challenges pertaining to utilizing the ChatGPT and have discussed various challenges like *consistency and precision*, means as it is very well known that ChatGPT is been used for the writing the creative contents but it is always not guaranteed that the created content is consistent or not. The other issues is *AI- generated unfairness* it means that content generated by ChatGPT may contain the unfair data and this is because ChatGPT is trained on large volume of biased data, which may lead to the further course of actions. The other related issue is *misplaced faith in AI* which means the excessive belief and faith in the AI generated contents is not good for the human community and it is suggested to review the contents for its authenticity and originality. The other issues related are *quality assurance,* which means that the contents created by ChatGPT may be of poor quality and therefore continuous learning and surveillance must be applied for improving the quality of generated contents.

Haleem, A. et al., 2022 [13] have proposed a work of ChatGPT, which focuses on the various related issues of ChatGPT like *problem of generalizability*, which means as ChatGPT is trained on large dataset so it troubles in generalizing the novel generated data. The *power utilization* is another issue, which do focus on the large requirements of the memory and the power for generating the contents in the ChatGPT and there must be an improvement for effectively utilizing the power requirements. Another related issue is *time requirements* for generating the response for the users, although it is specifically designed to generate the output in next to fashion but still users have to sometime wait for a while for generating the results using the ChatGPT.

Another work published by the Guan, C. et al., 2023 [14] focuses on some of the issue related to ChatGPT like *security issue,* as we know it very well that all the contents created by the ChatGPT is based on the training on large dataset so it creates a security breaches for the data therefore it is advices to not to put sensitive data in the ChatGPT as it may be shared with others. Another related issue is the *data protection threats,* data protection may be always at risk while being used with the ChatGPT and therefore user careful about it. At last they concluded that user must use ChatGPT effectively and carefully for various purpose and contents generated must be checked for the authenticity and must be verified before utilizing.

3. CHATGPT ARCHITECTURE

ChatGPT's architecture, GPT-3.5, expands upon that of earlier iterations like GPT-2 and GPT-3. GPT-3.5 is a variant of the more well-known GPT-3 (Generative Pre-trained Transformer 3) model. Both models are part of the Transformer architecture and it is made up of numerous layers of feed-forward neural networks and self-attention mechanisms. The model can recognise dependencies and patterns in the input text because each layer of the model pays attention to the output of the layer before it [15]. GPT-3.5, which has over 175 billion parameters, is one of the largest language models available at the time of my knowledge cut-off in September 2021. GPT-3.5 can capture fine details in the input and produce replies that are both coherent and appropriate for the context thanks to its high parameter count.

GPT models are pre-trained on a sizable amount of online text data that is available to the general public. They develop the ability to anticipate the following word in a sentence, which aids in their comprehension of the linguistic structures and statistical patterns. Following this pre-training, the model is fine-tuned using certain tasks or datasets to make it more useful for specific applications, including chat-based dialogues. A range of NLP activities, like Chatbots, completion of text, summarization of data, translation work, and many more task, can be performed using the GPT architecture, which includes ChatGPT. ChatGPT consists of different layers such as API Layer, Application Layer, Service

Layer, and Data Access Layer [16]. A user can interact with ChatGPT by sending a request to the API Layer, which will then be processed by the Application Layer, Service Layer, and Data Access Layer respectively. Finally, the Data Access Layer will perform database queries to retrieve the required data. The figure 3.1 shows the architecture of ChatGPT.

Figure 1. Flow diagram of ChatGPT

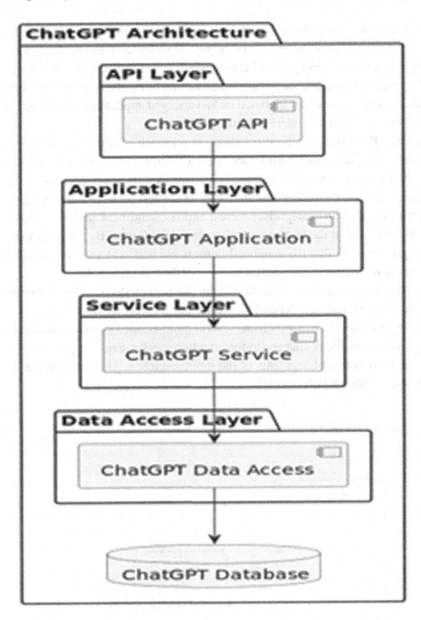

The User Interface Layer is responsible for taking user input and passing it to the Chatbot Layer. The Chatbot Layer processes the user input and sends a request to the Natural Language Processing (NLP) Layer. The NLP Layer processes the request and sends the response back to the Chatbot Layer. The Chatbot Layer then queries the Chatbot Data Access Layer to get the required data from the Chatbot Database. The Chatbot Data Access Layer performs CRUD operations on the database.

3.1 API and Application Layer

An API serves as a connection point between ChatGPT and external programmes or systems. Using input text as input, it enables developers to send requests to ChatGPT and receive model-generated responses. The input text is received by the API, processed, and then forwarded to the underlying model for inference. The caller programme or system is subsequently given the generated response [17]. The functionality of ChatGPT can be easily included into a variety of applications, including chatbots, virtual assistants, and other conversational interfaces, using APIs.

Natural Language Processing, or NLP for short, is a branch of artificial intelligence that focuses on how computers and human language interact. NLP techniques are used in the ChatGPT application layer to post-process and improve the generated responses as well as pre-process and comprehend the input text. Tokenization, which divides text into smaller pieces, part-of-speech tagging, named entity recognition, which identifies and categorises named entities, sentiment analysis, which determines the sentiment or emotional tone of the text, are all examples of NLP jobs. By strengthening understanding of the input and guaranteeing that the generated outputs are coherent and contextually relevant, NLP approaches aid in improving the quality and relevance of the model's replies.

A variation of the GPT (Generative Pretrained Transformer) model, ChatGPT is intended to produce text that resembles that of a human depending on the input it receives1. It is driven by feed-forward layers and transformer layers, each of which has several multi-headed attention mechanisms1. The feed-forward layers perform non-linear changes to the attention mechanisms' output, enabling the model to concentrate on the most pertinent segments of the input sequence. The notes on the diagram indicate the role of each layer as shown in figure 3.2.

Figure 2. Architecture of ChatGPT

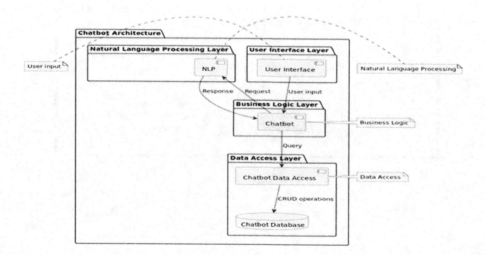

3.2 Service Layer / Business Layer

In ChatGPT, processing user queries, managing context, interacting with the underlying model, and producing appropriate responses are all crucial functions of the service layer. In order to facilitate seamless and efficient communication between the user interface and the AI model, it acts as a connector between the front-end and back-end components [17]. Request Processing: The service layer receives user requests or inputs from the front-end or user interface, usually in the form of text. It pre-processes the requests, which could entail operations like input cleaning, special character handling, or simple formatting.

ChatGPT frequently uses context to produce responses that are logical and pertinent to the current situation [17]. The conversation history is stored and updated by the service layer, which also keeps track of prior user inputs and model-generated data.

The service layer post-processes the model's output after receiving it in order to improve the provided response. It might be necessary to do things like change the formatting, add more contexts, or use NLP methods for coherence and context awareness. The final output is the post-processed response that is subsequently sent back to the front-end or user interface. Business logic layer in a ChatGPT system acts as an intermediary between the user interface and the core AI model. It interprets user inputs, manages the conversation context, routes requests, integrates with various services, generates responses, ensures security and compliance, and provides the necessary structure for a smooth and effective conversational experience. This layer is crucial for enabling ChatGPT to function effectively and responsibly in various real-world applications.

The service layer manages error situations and makes sure the system is reliable. It controls exception handling, handles errors, and reports significant occurrences or errors for monitoring and troubleshooting.

3.3 Data Access Layer

The Data Access Layer in ChatGPT is responsible for organising the retrieval and storage of data necessary for the model's operation. The Data Access Layer makes it easier to retrieve pertinent information from numerous sources that may be required to support the functionality of the model [17]. This can involve obtaining conversational data, language models that have already been trained, or any other pertinent datasets. To obtain the necessary data, the layer communicates with databases, file systems, or APIs.

After the data has been retrieved, the Data Access Layer might additionally take care of preparation chores to make sure the data is in a format that the model can use. The data may need to be cleaned, irrelevant information removed, the data may need to be transformed or normalised, and formatting may also be required.

To maximise performance, the Data Access Layer may also oversee data storage and caching. For instance, it can save processed data to prevent repeating preparation steps or cache frequently requested data to speed up retrieval. This enhances the system's general effectiveness and responsiveness. The Data Access Layer oversees any updates or synchronisations required for the data used by ChatGPT. For instance, the layer manages the processes of data updates and synchronisation if new training data or additional knowledge needs to be incorporated into the model.

4. PRE-TRAINING AND FINE TUNING CHATGPT MODELS

Initially Chatbot was designed for answering limited number of questions but as the time passes it was specifically designed for the answering a greater number of questions using the concept of natural language processing, training, and testing. Pre-training and fine-tuning are the two steps in the model's training process [18]. ChatGPT gains knowledge from a big corpus of online publicly accessible text data during pre-training. As a result, the model gains a comprehensive understanding of grammatical rules, language patterns, and general knowledge. The model learns to produce logical and contextually acceptable responses through the pre-training process, which entails anticipating missing words in sentences. ChatGPT is refined using unique datasets produced by OpenAI after pre-training. These datasets include examples of appropriate conduct and rankings of various replies. The model can be fine-tuned to respond to certain activities and desired behaviours, increasing its dependability and safety.

ChatGPT is AI based language model and it has a rich capacity of processing the given data. The ChatGPT is trained using predict next word task problem, an unsupervised problem and for that user must provide the input and the maximum limit of work a user can provide to ChatGPT is 2048 words, however a user can still pass shorter sequence of words to the ChatGPT [19]. Once the sequence is passed to the ChatGPT as the input, the next task is to predict the next word known as next word prediction task and for the given input and it will be different matched 2048 words. ChatGPT itself do not understand value of any word therefore it assigns a number to each word and then its usages sub word algorithm to create the vocab and in case the word is not present in the present directory it applies the byte-level byte pair encoding sub-word tokenizer method. Once the encoding is finished it key, query and value vector is calculated for each token using dot product matrix multiplication to produce a score matrix. Then the score matrix decides that how much weightage should be given to each word and higher the score is, more the attention given to that word.

Once the calculation is done the score is downscale by dividing score value with the square root of dimension of query and key. This process allows to ensure more gradient value and after that soft-max is applied to make the range between 0 and 1. This process ensures the model to be more confident on certain words.

4.1 Supervised Fine Tuning

In ChatGPT 3.5, first the pretrained GPT-3 model is used and then it will be fine tuned by applying the labellers by creating a supervised dataset. The users provide the input queries and based on the query model produces the different response to the users. This training is costly and time consuming therefore these types of training is done for short period of time. The GPT-3 model is then fine tunes using the new supervised dataset to create GPT-3.5 model [18].

4.2 The Reward Model

This is the second and important step in which the previously trained models generated the multiple response for the query and the human annotators ranked the response from useful to least useful. This data is useful to predict how useful a response was to a given prompt [18].

4.3 The Reinforcement Learning Process

Finally, this step is used to further train the supervised fine-tuning models, which is further used as an agent that maximizes the reward from the reward model. A response generated for the used input is then evaluated by the reward model and then supervised fine tuning model tried to update its prediction to get the bigger reward for the future prediction problem. This process is easy and convenient as compared to the supervised fine-tuning step as it is easier and faster. Figure 4.1 shows the ChatGPT training process which shows that ChatGPT has been modified using supervised and reinforcement learning methods. In order for ChatGPT to produce text that is comparable to the text in the training quantity, a significant quantity of text data had to be entered into the model and its parameters had to be changed.

The model must be fed a lot of data throughout the lengthy and intricate training phase in order for it to learn and comprehend human language. The selection of excellent data sources, which includes a broad range of text material like as books, journals, and chat logs, is the first step in the training process. Depends on hardware configuration and data set, training a large-scale language model ChatGPT might take a few days or even weeks.

Figure 3. ChatGPT training process

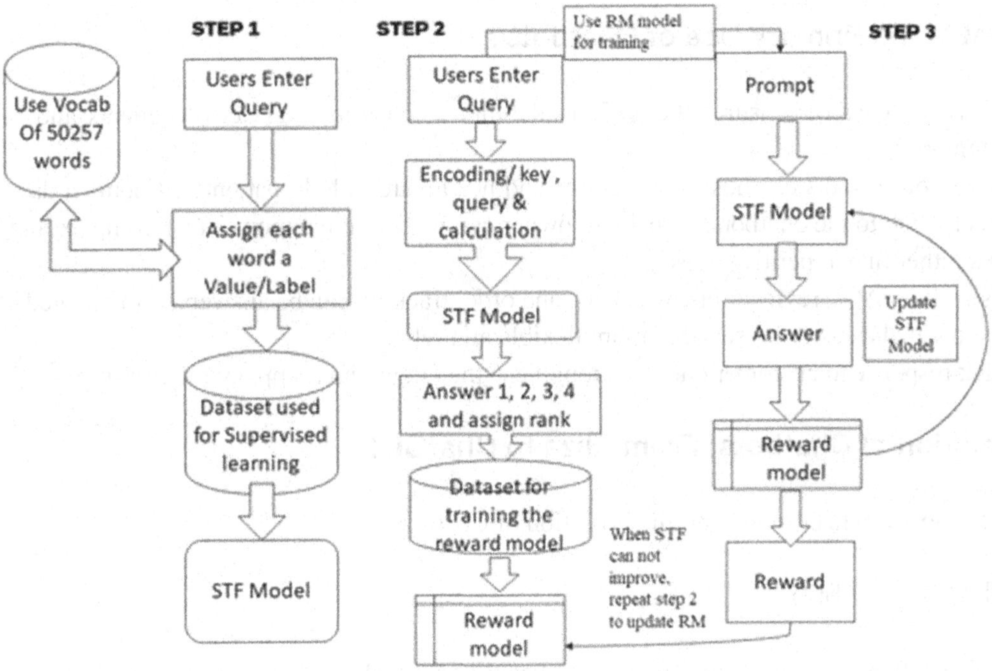

5. EVALUATION OF CHATGPT MODEL

ChatGPT is an AI language model, purely based on AI and its usages the deep learning and Natural language processing for answering the user's questions therefore the evaluation of ChatGPT is start with the AI and the concept of AI is first introduced in the year 1960, and in 1964-1966 an AI based chatbot program ELIZA was introduced which could answer users question based on the rules and till then chatbot has been evolved with better functionality then the previous one. It is also true that the involvement of machine leaning and NLP has made the chatbot more sophisticated and powerful. Chatbots have undergone a remarkable evolution over the years. Initially, they were simple programs that could only understand and respond to basic commands. However, with the advancement in natural language processing (NLP) and machine learning (ML) algorithms, chatbots have become more sophisticated and capable of handling complex conversations. AI has changed people's perception of modern world technology [4]. Now people can communicate with machines and expect a human-like conversation in return. Surprisingly, the evolution of chatbots has changed our view of looking at technology or machines. Now, ChatGPT can support building a website or app by giving the right instructions to the user.

Let us understand their journey from Eliza to ChatGPT and other related concepts.

5.1 Chatbot

It is a computer program that generates human-like text, leading to a two-way conversation between the human user and the chatbot. Artificial intelligence and natural language processing are the tools that are used by chatbots to mimic human-like conversation or give the desired response to the user. The chatbot aims to simulate human-like text to the user as if they are talking to a human.

5.2 What is the Primary Use of Chatbots?

- The use of chatbots ensures the 24/7 availability of customer services to clients and business customers.
- The use of chatbots extends to businesses and healthcare to help patients 24 hours a day, 7 days a week. Due to the chatbots, a business owner can put more manpower into complex and knotty tasks rather than repetitive ones.
- Answering FAQs, reviews, emails, chats, and order tracking can be answered or managed by chatbots that make customer services more flexible and reliable.
- Quick response to customer queries strengthens the client and company relationship.

5.3 Evolution of Chatbots: From Eliza to ChatGPT

Let us move forward to comprehend the evolution of Chatbots.

5.3.1 Eliza 1964-1966

The life of a chatbot began with the creation of Eliza. Eliza was the first chatbot in history, developed by Joseph Weisenbaum from 1964 to 1966. Joseph Weisenbaum was a professor at MIT University. Eliza was developed in a way that generates a human-like conversation for which it uses pattern-matching techniques. Since Eliza was the first Artificial Intelligence Chatbot, the creator of Eliza, Joseph Weisenbaum, thinks it will help the patient deal with the psychological problem. Certainly, it will help them recover soon, along with the treatment. On the contrary, according to some individuals, Eliza could not speak with real understanding [4].

5.3.2 Parry 1972

Parry is considered the upgraded version of Eliza. It was created by the psychiatrist Keneth Colby in 1972 at Stanford University. It could imitate a patient with schizophrenia (a psychological condition consisting of the symptoms like delusions, hallucinations, disorganised etc). This chatbot was externalized with a conversational strategy with people struggling with such psychological situations. Parry is regarded as the "Eliza with attitude".

5.3.3 Jabber-Wacky – 1988

Jabber-wacky was created by Rollo Carpenter a British programmer. The primary goal of Jabber-wacky was to mimic human chat in an amusing, humorous and interesting manner. It was well known for delivering the text witty and hilariously. Jabber-wacky also uses the pattern-matching technique to communicate with humans.

5.3.4 ALICE 1995

Eliza was the first chatterbot that inspired programmers to build other chatbots with more perfections and features.

ALICE is the finest example of chatbots which won the Loebner prize in the year 2000,2001, and 2004. Alice-bot is open source which one can access from the ALICE AI foundation on Google code and from the Richard Wallace GitHub account. ALICE stands for Artificial Linguistic Internet Computer entity, also known as Alice-bot. ALICE was created by Richard Wallace and released on 23 November 1995. On the concept of ALICE, an Academy Award-winning movie Her, was released in 2013 and was based on the story where a human falling in love with a bot.

5.3.5 Smarter-Child – 2001

Like any other chatbot, the smarter child was also based on natural language processing. It is a smart artificial intelligence which was developed by Active-Buddy Inc. in the year 2001. Smarter-Child is the best-known AI bot that generates human-like amusing conversations and the information available online. One can find this AI tool on Microsoft Messenger and AOI IM.

5.3.6 Siri 2010

Siri, released in February 2010, is part of apple inc., a virtual assistant that is part of Apple products like IOS, iPad-OS, watch-OS, audio-OS, mac-OS, and tv-OS operating systems. It is an intelligent personal assistant that makes a recommendation and performs actions based on the user's instructions. Note that these instructions can be in text, image or voice format. Siri adapts the user's searches, preferences, and choices and then recommends the same results. It can assist individuals by controlling their phones and setting reminders for them.

5.3.7 Google Assistant- 2016

Google Assistant was developed by Google in the year 2016 on 18 May. It is available on mobile phones and home automation devices. By using it one can engage in a two-way conversation. One can give instructions to the Google Assistant in text or voice format. Even a user can ask google assistant to set reminder alarms and change system settings. The parent company of google assistant, Google, has announced that soon google assistant will be able to recognize things and objects and will be able to help in buying products and sending money.

5.3.8 ChatGPT

ChatGPT is the most advanced AI chatbot that has mainly impacted the business sectors as it can communicate with the customers or clients of a company by generating human-like text. From answering the FAQs of customers to generating emails and chatting with them, it has changed the customer support system of every company. ChatGPT was created and released by Open-AI on 30 November 2022. ChatGPT helps generate customised customer responses based on the text, their profile and purchasing history.

The history of ChatGPT can be traced back to the development of the GPT (Generative Pre-trained Transformer) series by OpenAI. The initial version, GPT-1, was introduced in 2018 and marked a significant milestone in the field of natural language processing.

Transformer-based architectures can be used for language modelling problems, as shown by GPT-1. It can produce logical and sentence-relevant context-relevant sentences because it was trained on a huge amount of text data. GPT-1 has some drawbacks, such as the sporadic production of irrelevant or incomprehensible replies [17].

In 2019 OpenAI has introduction GPT-2 following the success of GPT-1. The GPT-2 model was much bigger and was trained on a much larger dataset. It demonstrated substantial advancements in producing responses that were coherent and appropriate for the situation. GPT-3 was widely praised as a significant leap in AI technology due to its excellent language generation skills. It was used in a variety of disciplines, such as question-answering systems, language translation, and content creation. As a extended version of the GPT-3 concept, OpenAI launched ChatGPT in response to the success of GPT-3. With a specific focus on conversational engagements, ChatGPT was created to give users more dynamic and engaging experiences [20].

6. APPLICATION OF CHATGPT MODEL

ChatGPT, being a powerful language model, finds applications in various fields due to its natural language understanding and generation capabilities. Here are some notable applications of ChatGPT are as follows [21]

- **Chatbots and Virtual Assistants:** ChatGPT can be used to build conversational agents and virtual assistants that engage with people by answering questions, providing information, and assisting with tasks. Its ability to understand context and generate coherent responses makes it suitable for creating engaging and interactive chatbot experiences.

- **Customer Support:** ChatGPT can be well used for customer support systems to handle user queries and provide help. It can alleviate the workload of human agents by handling common questions and issues.
- **Content Generation:** ChatGPT can be used to generate human-like text for content creation, such as blog posts, articles, and product descriptions. It can also help writers with creative writing prompts and ideation.
- **Language Translation:** ChatGPT can be fine-tuned for language translation tasks, enabling it to translate text from one language to another.
- **Language Tutoring:** ChatGPT can be utilized as a language tutor to help learners practice and improve their language skills through interactive conversations.
- **Code Generation:** With proper fine-tuning, ChatGPT can assist with code generation, helping developers write code snippets for specific tasks.
- **Personalized Recommendations:** By understanding user preferences and context, ChatGPT can offer personalized recommendations for products, movies, books, or other content.
- **Educational Tools:** ChatGPT can be incorporated into educational platforms to provide explanations, answer student queries, and assist with homework.
- **Coding help:** It can assist programmer for doing coding and it supports various languages and programmer can use it for coding when needed.
- **Support for decision making:** It can assist for decision making for business purposes.
- **Travel planning:** It can plan for the travels and may guide you about your destinations.
- **Email drafting:** Additionally, it serves the purpose of composing emails with specific content. What might seem like a simple email can turn into a laborious and time-consuming task. Formulating the perfect words to convey your message with the right tone and professional language can be more challenging than expected. ChatGPT is available to lend you a helping hand.
- **Virtual Assistants:** It can be used as a virtual assistant to plan schedules, set appointments and reminders, etc.

7. BERT, GPT-1, GPT-2, AND GPT-3

ChatGPT is language model which is AI based and has been continuously being upgraded time to time to become the finest model of all the time till now. It is the result of continuous growth in the technology and it has initially started with the BERT and then GPT-1, GPT-2 and GPT-3.

Lest us look at each of them briefly.

7.1 BERT (Bidirectional Encoder Representations from Transformers)

BERT is a groundbreaking natural language processing (NLP) model introduced by Jacob Devlin et al. [22] from Google AI in 2018. It is based on the Transformer architecture and is designed to address certain limitations of previous NLP models, such as the lack of bidirectional context understanding. Its key components are as follows:

7.1.1 Bidirectional Context Understanding

BERT adds bidirectional context understanding, in contrast to existing language models such as GPT (Generative Pre-trained Transformer), which use a unidirectional architecture (processing text from left to right or vice versa). During pre-training, it can analyse both the left and right context of a word at the same time. This bidirectionality improves the model's capacity to recognise a word context within a sentence greatly.

7.1.2 Pre-Training Objective

Like GPT models, BERT is also pre-trained on a large corpus of text data. However, it uses a different pre-training objective called the "masked language modelling" task. During pre-training, some of the words in the input sentences are randomly masked, and the model's goal is to predict the masked words based on their context. This forces the model to understand the bidirectional context of words and their relationships.

7.1.3 Transformer Architecture

The Transformer architecture utilizes self-attention mechanisms to weigh the importance of different words in the input sequence, allowing the model to capture long-range dependencies effectively.

7.1.4 Layers and Attention Heads

BERT consists of multiple layers and attention heads. The model is generally deep, with a stack of transformer layers. Each layer has multiple attention heads, enabling the model to focus on different aspects of the context.

7.1.5 Tokenization

BERT tokenizes the input text into sub word tokens using the Word Piece tokenization algorithm. This allows BERT to handle out-of-vocabulary words and create a fixed-size input suitable for processing in the model.

7.1.6 Fine-Tuning

Following the initial pre-training phase, BERT can undergo fine-tuning for distinct tasks downstream, including sentiment analysis, identifying named entities, responding to questions, and more. Fine-tuning encompasses training the model using task-specific labelled data to tailor it for particular natural language processing tasks.

Contextual Understanding, Few-shot Learning and State-of-the-art Performance are some advantages of using BERT. BERT's contributions have had a profound impact on the NLP field and it further lead to the advancements in understanding of various languages and generation tasks. Since its introduction, many variants and improvements have been proposed to build upon the strengths of BERT.

7.2 GPT-1 (Generative Pre-Trained Network-1)

GPT-1, which stands for "Generative Pre-trained Transformer 1," is the first model in the GPT series of language models developed by OpenAI. It was introduced in 2018 and marked a significant advancement in natural language processing. GPT-1 is based on the Transformer architecture and is designed to understand and generate human-like text. Details and key component of GPT-1 are as follows:

7.2.1 Transformer Architecture

GPT-1 is built upon the Transformer architecture, which was first introduced in the paper "Attention Is All You Need" by Vaswani et al. [23] in 2017. The Transformer architecture utilizes self-attention mechanisms to capture the relationships between different words in a sentence, enabling the model to understand long-range dependencies efficiently.

7.2.2 Pre-Training Objective

GPT-1 is pre-trained on a massive corpus of text data from the internet using a language modelling objective. During pre-training, the model learns to predict the next word in a sentence given the context of previous words. This process helps GPT-1 develop a rich understanding of language, grammar, and contextual relationships.

7.2.3 Unidirectional Model

GPT-1 is a unidirectional language model, which means it processes input text in a single direction (either left-to-right or right-to-left). As a result, it only considers the context of previous words when predicting the next word in a sentence.

7.2.4 Parameterization

GPT-1 contains a significant number of learnable parameters, allowing it to model complex language patterns and relationships. However, compared to later versions like GPT-3, GPT-1 has a smaller parameter count.

7.2.5 Limitations

Despite its impressive performance, GPT-1 has certain limitations. Being a unidirectional model, it may not capture all context and dependencies in a sentence. Additionally, GPT-1 might produce outputs that lack coherence or exhibit issues with long-range context understanding.

It is essential to understand that GPT-1, while groundbreaking at the time of its release, has been succeeded by more advanced versions like GPT-2 and GPT-3, which have larger model sizes and improved performance.

7.3 GPT-2 (Generative Pre-Trained Network-2)

GPT-2, which stands for "Generative Pre-trained Transformer 2," is the second model in the GPT series developed by OpenAI. It was introduced in 2019 and represented a significant advancement over its predecessor, GPT-1 [24]. GPT-2 is a powerful language model known for its impressive language generation capabilities. Here is a detailed explanation of GPT-2 and its key components:

7.3.1 Transformer Architecture

GPT-2 is built upon the previous architecture of GPT, which was first introduced in the paper "Attention Is All You Need" by Vaswani et al. [23] in 2017. The Transformer architecture utilizes self-attention mechanisms to capture relationships between different words in a sentence, enabling the model to understand long-range dependencies effectively.

7.3.2 Pre-Training Objective

Like GPT-1, GPT-2 is also pre-trained on a massive corpus of text data from the internet using a language modelling objective. However, GPT-2 is trained with a more extensive dataset and has a more significant number of parameters compared to GPT-1.

7.3.3 Bidirectional Context

GPT-2 introduced bidirectional context understanding, meaning it considers both the left and right context of a word during pre-training. This bidirectionality significantly improves the model's ability to understand the context of a word within a sentence.

7.3.4 Large Model Size

GPT-2 is known for its substantial model size, with up to 1.5 billion parameters. This large model size contributes to its enhanced language generation capabilities, allowing it to produce more coherent and contextually relevant text.

7.4 GPT-3 (Generative Pre-Trained Network-3)

GPT-3, which stands for "Generative Pre-trained Transformer 3" is the third and most advanced model in the GPT series developed by OpenAI. Introduced in June 2020, GPT-3 is a cutting-edge language model known for its massive size and remarkable capabilities in natural language understanding and generation. It represents a significant leap forward compared to its predecessors, GPT-1 and GPT-2. Detailed explanation and key components are as follows [25]:

7.4.1 Pre-Training Objective

Like GPT-1 and GPT-2, GPT-3 is also pre-trained on a massive corpus of text data from the internet using a language modelling objective. However, GPT-3's training dataset and model size are significantly larger, making it one of the largest language models ever created.

7.4.2 Enormous Model Size

GPT-3 is renowned for its massive size, with a staggering 175 billion parameters. This large parameter count provides the model with immense representational power, allowing it to learn complex language patterns and relationships.

7.4.3 Few-Shot and Zero-Shot Learning

it is most impressive thing about the GPT-3 and its ability to perform few-shot and zero-shot learning. Few-shot learning means that the model can perform tasks with minimal examples (few-shot examples) compared to traditional machine learning models. Zero-shot learning enables the model to tackle tasks it has not been explicitly trained on by providing a prompt or instruction.

7.4.4 Versatility and Adaptability

GPT-3 is versatile and can be tuned very fine for a wide range of natural language processing tasks, including text generation, translation, question answering, summarization, and more. Its adaptability and few-shot learning capabilities make it applicable to various domains and tasks.

7.4.5 Contextual Understanding

GPT-3 excels in understanding context, making it adept at maintaining coherence in longer conversations and providing relevant responses based on the input context.

7.4.6 Limitations

Despite its impressive performance, GPT-3 has certain limitations, including the potential for generating incorrect or nonsensical responses. It also requires significant computational resources due to its enormous model size.

7.4.7 Safety and Ethical Considerations

To ensure responsible use, OpenAI has implemented safety measures and moderation systems to avoid generating harmful or biased content.

The advancement of language understanding and production thanks to GPT-3 has had a significant impact on the field of natural language processing. It has been applied to a variety of tasks, such as creating content, developing programming, translating languages, and more.

Table 1 shows the various version of ChatGPT with milestone for making the study more understandable for readers.

Table 1. ChatGPT versions

Year	Milestone
2018	• Introduced in 2018, GPT-1 was one of the early large-scale language models based on the Transformer architecture. • It had 117 million parameters and was pre-trained on a large corpus of text data and GPT-1 demonstrated impressive capabilities.
2019	• Released in 2019, GPT-2 was a significant leap forward in terms of size and capabilities compared to GPT-1. • GPT-2 was much larger, with 1.5 billion parameters, making it one of the largest language models at that time. • Due to concerns about potential misuse, OpenAI initially did not release the full version of GPT-2. Instead, they released smaller versions to the public for research and experimentation. • GPT-2 showed remarkable performance in generating coherent and contextually relevant text, which raised discussions about its potential for generating deceptive or misleading content.
2020	• Unveiling of GPT-3, a ground breaking language model with 175 billion parameters, setting new benchmarks in language generation. • Introduced in 2020, GPT-3 represented a significant breakthrough in language modeling and natural language understanding. • GPT-3 was even more massive, with a staggering 175 billion parameters, making it by far the largest language model at its time. • It showcased unprecedented capabilities in few-shot and zero-shot learning, allowing it to generalize to new tasks with minimal or no fine-tuning data. • GPT-3 was capable of performing a wide range of language tasks, including text generation, translation, question-answering, code writing, and more. • Its vast capacity and versatility made it a powerful tool, but it also raised concerns about the environmental impact of training such large models and the concentration of AI capabilities in a few organizations.
2021	• Introduction of ChatGPT as a specialized version of GPT-3, tailored for conversational interactions, with a focus on engagement and interactivity. • It is tailored to be more conversational and responsive, making it suitable for interactive applications. • The specific version "ChatGPT 3.5" mentioned in your previous question does not exist up to my knowledge cutoff date in September 2021. It's possible that newer versions or updates were released after that date.
2022	• Ongoing refinement and optimization of ChatGPT, addressing limitations and biases, and incorporating user feedback for continuous improvement with 175 billion parameter count. • ChatGPT 3.5 is now available with fine tuning via supervised learning and reinforcement learning via human feedback.
2023	• Further advancements in the capabilities of ChatGPT, as OpenAI continues to innovate and enhance the performance of the model. • ChatGPT 4 has been launched and has been trained with both text prediction and reinforcement learning via human feedback, as well as an increased parameter count of 100 trillion texts.

8. DISCUSSION

ChatGPT's utilization spans a wide array of applications, from virtual assistants and customer support chat-bots to content generation and educational tools. When used wisely, it can significantly enhance productivity and user experiences. Its natural language understanding capabilities empower it to interact with users in a more human-like manner, making it a valuable resource for businesses looking to provide round-the-clock customer service or generate content efficiently. ChatGPT's versatility and adaptability make it a versatile tool for a variety of domains.

However, ChatGPT is not without its challenges. It grapples with issues related to bias in its responses, susceptibility to misinformation, and the potential for misuse. Its responses are only as good as the data it is trained on, and these biases can inadvertently reflect societal prejudices. There's also the risk of malicious actors using it to generate false information or engage in deceptive activities. Safeguarding against these issues requires a vigilant and responsible approach to deployment.

Ultimately, the benefits of ChatGPT can be substantial, but they come hand in hand with the responsibility of using the technology wisely. By addressing its limitations, implementing ethical guidelines, and continually refining its responses, ChatGPT can serve as a valuable tool that enhances productivity, supports users, and augments various tasks across different sectors while minimizing the potential for harm.

9. CONCLUSION AND FUTURE WORK

ChatGPT, a variant of the larger GPT models, represents a significant advancement in natural language processing and conversational AI. Its ability to understand and generate human-like text has made it a powerful tool in various applications, including chatbots, virtual assistants, customer support systems, content generation, and educational tools. ChatGPT's strengths lie in its contextual understanding, bidirectional context, and versatility in performing various language tasks. It has proven to have exceptional few-shot and zero-shot learning skills, allowing it to adapt to new tasks with little training data and effectively follow directions. However, like any AI language model, ChatGPT has its limitations. It may sometimes produce incorrect or nonsensical responses, and its large model size demands significant computational resources. Safety and ethical considerations are critical, and measures have been taken to ensure responsible usage and mitigate potential risks. Future work will focus on the solution of the various issues related to the AI generative nature.

REFERENCES

Abdullah, M., Madain, A., & Jararweh, Y. (2022, November). ChatGPT: Fundamentals, applications and social impacts. In *2022 Ninth International Conference on Social Networks Analysis, Management and Security (SNAMS)* (pp. 1-8). IEEE.

Ali, M. J., & Djalilian, A. (2023, March). Readership awareness series–paper 4: Chatbots and chatgpt-ethical considerations in scientific publications. In *Seminars in ophthalmology* (pp. 1–2). Taylor & Francis.

Bašić, Ž., Banovac, A., Kružić, I., & Jerković, I. (2023). *Better by You, better than Me? ChatGPT-3 as writing assistance in students' essays.*

Choi, E. P. H., Lee, J. J., Ho, M. H., Kwok, J. Y. Y., & Lok, K. Y. W. (2023). Chatting or cheating? The impacts of ChatGPT and other artificial intelligence language models on nurse education. *Nurse Education Today, 125*, 105796. doi:10.1016/j.nedt.2023.105796 PMID:36934624

Devlin, J., Chang, M. W., Lee, K., & Toutanova, K. (2018). *Bert: Pre-training of deep bidirectional transformers for language understanding.* arXiv preprint arXiv:1810.04805.

Eduardo, C. Garrido-Merch'an., J., Luis, A. B., Roberto, G. B. (2023). *Simulating H.P. Lovecraft horror literature with the ChatGPT large language model.* arXiv.org, doi:/arXiv.2305.03429. doi:10.48550

Gao, J., Peng, B., Li, C., Li, J., Shayandeh, S., Liden, L., & Shum, H. Y. (2020). *Robust conversational AI with grounded text generation.* arXiv preprint arXiv:2009.03457.

Gill, S. S., & Kaur, R. (2023). ChatGPT: Vision and challenges. *Internet of Things and Cyber-Physical Systems, 3,* 262–271. doi:10.1016/j.iotcps.2023.05.004

Goodfellow, I., Pouget-Abadie, J., Mirza, M., Xu, B., Warde-Farley, D., Ozair, S., Courville, A., & Bengio, Y. (2020). Generative adversarial networks. *Communications of the ACM, 63*(11), 139–144. doi:10.1145/3422622

Guan, C., Ding, D., Gupta, P., Hung, Y. C., & Jiang, Z. (2023). A Systematic Review of Research on ChatGPT: The User Perspective. *Exploring Cyber Criminals and Data Privacy Measures,* 124-150.

Haleem, A., Javaid, M., & Singh, R. P. (2022). An era of ChatGPT as a significant futuristic support tool: A study on features, abilities, and challenges. *BenchCouncil transactions on benchmarks, standards and evaluations, 2*(4), 100089.

Hyoeun, Lee, Honam, Shim. (2023). *Study on the Design of a ChatGPT-Based Metaverse Platform Model.* doi:10.29279/jitr.2023.28.2.131

Javaid, M., Haleem, A., & Singh, R. P. (2023). ChatGPT for healthcare services: An emerging stage for an innovative perspective. Bench Council Transactions on Benchmarks. *Standards and Evaluations, 3*(1), 100105.

Kasneci, E., Seßler, K., Küchemann, S., Bannert, M., Dementieva, D., Fischer, F., Gasser, U., Groh, G., Günnemann, S., Hüllermeier, E., Krusche, S., Kutyniok, G., Michaeli, T., Nerdel, C., Pfeffer, J., Poquet, O., Sailer, M., Schmidt, A., Seidel, T., & Kasneci, G. (2023). ChatGPT for good? On opportunities and challenges of large language models for education. *Learning and Individual Differences, 103,* 102274. doi:10.1016/j.lindif.2023.102274

Kumar, G. R., Reddy, G. Y., Ruthvik, A., Ruthvik, M., & Aaron, N. (2020). Conversational Chatbot Powered by Artificial Intelligence for Banks. *Challenge, 2.*

Lu, Q., Zhu, L., Xu, X., & Xing, Z. (2023). *Towards Responsible AI in the Era of ChatGPT: A Reference Architecture for Designing Foundation Model-based AI Systems.* doi: /arxiv.2304.11090 doi:10.48550

Mathew, A. (2023). Is Artificial Intelligence a World Changer? A Case Study of OpenAI's Chat GPT. *Recent Progress in Science and Technology, 5,* 35–42. doi:10.9734/bpi/rpst/v5/18240D

Meyer, J. G., Urbanowicz, R. J., Martin, P. C., O'Connor, K., Li, R., Peng, P. C., Bright, T. J., Tatonetti, N., Won, K. J., Gonzalez-Hernandez, G., & Moore, J. H. (2023). ChatGPT and large language models in academia: Opportunities and challenges. *BioData Mining, 16*(1), 20. doi:10.118613040-023-00339-9 PMID:37443040

Ollivier, M., Pareek, A., Dahmen, J., Kayaalp, M. E., Winkler, P. W., Hirschmann, M. T., & Karlsson, J. (2023). A deeper dive into ChatGPT: History, use and future perspectives for orthopaedic research. *Knee Surgery, Sports Traumatology, Arthroscopy : Official Journal of the ESSKA, 31*(4), 1190–1192. doi:10.100700167-023-07372-5 PMID:36894785

Radford, A., Wu, J., Child, R., Luan, D., Amodei, D., & Sutskever, I. (2019). *Language Models are Unsupervised Multitask Learners*. OpenA.

Radford, A., Wu, J., Child, R., Luan, D., Amodei, D., & Sutskever, I. (2019). Language models are unsupervised multitask learners. *OpenAI blog, 1*(8), 9.

Ray, P. P. (2023). ChatGPT: A comprehensive review on background, applications, key challenges, bias, ethics, limitations and future scope. Internet of things and cyber physical system, 3. doi:10.1016/j. iotcps.2023.04.003

Vaishya, R., Misra, A., & Vaish, A. (2023). ChatGPT: Is this version good for healthcare and research? *Diabetes & Metabolic Syndrome, 17*(4), 102744. doi:10.1016/j.dsx.2023.102744 PMID:36989584

Vaswani, A., Shazeer, N., Parmar, N., Uszkoreit, J., Jones, L., Gomez, A. N., & Polosukhin, I. (2017). Attention is all you need. *Advances in Neural Information Processing Systems*, 30.

Zhou, C., Li, Q., Li, C., Yu, J., Liu, Y., Wang, G., & Sun, L. (2023). A comprehensive survey on pre-trained foundation models: A history from bert to chatgpt. arXiv preprint arXiv:2302.09419.

Chapter 6
Simplifying Learning Experience on a Personalized Content Recommendation System for Complex Text Material in E-Learning

R. Angeline

SRM Institute of Science and Technology, India

Muzamil Faisal

SRM Institute of Science and Technology, India

S. Aarthi

SRM Institute of Science And Technology, India

Abishek Venkatesan

SRM Institute of Science and Technology, India

Rishabh Jain

SRM Institute of Science and Technology, India

R. Regin

SRM Institute of Science and Technology, India

ABSTRACT

Complex material is difficult to absorb in e-learning environments, which distracts and lowers learning outcomes. This initiative proposes that consumers watch simple movies with the same topic to improve learning. Text analytics recommends tailored videos to consumers. The algorithm can make more tailored recommendations by evaluating text interaction and learning preferences. The system simplifies learning and makes material more complicated and intelligible. Visual videos aid learning by improving memory and comprehension. Analyze the data before using the advice. NLP can extract key text content and context. Review results are used to develop related topics and themes. Next, find relevant video content using keywords and keywords list. Previous video data can be used to recommend video material. Videos should simplify content to help consumers understand and remember it. Text interactions should be considered when personalising video suggestions. Create user profiles using engagement indicators like time on page, scroll depth, and click behaviour.

DOI: 10.4018/979-8-3693-0502-7.ch006

1. INTRODUCTION

The blast of innovation and the web has brought almost a phenomenal sum of data promptly accessible at our fingertips. From scholarly inquiries about papers to work-related reports to online articles and social media posts, we are continually uncovering tremendous sums of data on a day-by-day basis (Abu Shkheedim et al., 2022). Whereas this accessibility of data may be an incredible advantage, it too presents a significant challenge for those who battle to form a sense of the complexity of the text (Al Khawaldeh et al., 2022). People who are not native speakers of the dialect or who are not conversant with the topic at issue will find this obstacle to be far more overwhelming (Alawneh, 2022). Because of linguistic barriers or a requirement for prior knowledge on the topic, these individuals could have a difficult time grasping the significance of the material because it requires background information (Alawneh et al., 2022).

As a consequence of this, individuals run the risk of missing out on vital information and tidbits of wisdom that might prove to be useful to them in the future (Alawneh & Al-Shara'h, 2022). To find a solution to this problem, proposal frameworks have been developed to simplify the learning process for customers by providing video adaptations of the content record (Alawneh et al., 2022). These frameworks are designed to analyse the content of a content record and provide a video form that may be effectively absorbed by the customer (An et al., 2023). Customers will be able to acquire a more profound comprehension of the subject matter without having to struggle through the complexities of the text if they do this (Aravind et al., 2023). This method is especially helpful for people who learn best via visual means or who find that obtaining information through recordings rather than material is a less taxing way to accomplish their goals (Angeline et al., 2023). To further improve the quality of the learning experience, the framework for the proposal may include supplementary elements, such as subtitles, comments, or intuitive exams (Padmanabhan et al., 2023). In this piece, we will examine how suggestion frameworks are transforming the learning process and making it simpler for individuals to acquire complicated information (Demeter et al., 2021). In the following, we are going to delve into the benefits of this invention and how it can help people in various fields of consideration and callings make advancements in their learning results (Gao & Liu, 2021).

In e-learning environments, users often find it difficult to process complex information, which causes distraction and reduces learning outcomes (Gomathy & Venkatasbramanian, 2023). To solve this problem, this project offers a proposal that provides users with simple videos with the same content to enhance learning (Guiamalon, 2022). Recommendations use text analytics to analyze text content and recommend personalized videos to users (Hong, 2018). By considering the user's interaction with the text and learning preferences, the system can provide more personalized and personalized recommendations (Hong, 2021). The purpose of the system is to simplify the learning process for users and to make information more complex and understandable (Hong, 2021). Visual videos can improve learning outcomes by helping users better remember and understand information (Hong, 2023). To use the recommendations, the first step is to analyze the concrete data. Natural language processing (NLP) can be used to extract important content and context from text (Hong et al., 2022). The results of the review are used to create a list of related topics and topics. The next step is to use the keywords and keywords list to identify suitable video content (Jayakumar et al., 2022).

Pre-existing video data can be used to recommend video content to users. Videos should be simple versions of the same content designed to help users better understand and retain the material (Lian et al., 2022). To personalize video recommendations, recommendation strategies should consider users' interactions with text (Rad et al., 2020b; Tripathi, 2017). User engagement metrics such as time on the page, scroll depth and click behaviour can be used to create user profiles (Kumar et al., 2023). User data can be used to provide more personalized recommendations tailored to the user's learning interests and preferences (Lumapenet, 2022). The final step is to integrate the application with the existing e-learning system. The system can be designed to provide video suggestions as users read the text, making the learning process more efficient and effective (Maseleno et al., 2023). Integration with e-learning platforms also provides an opportunity to gather feedback and improve recommendations over time. As a result, this project offers a proposal that provides simple videos of complex information to improve users' learning experience (Paudel et al., 2022). The system leverages text analytics and personalization to create engaging and personalized video recommendations (Rad et al., 2020a). The system has the potential to change the way users interact with learning and e-learning platforms by making complex information more accessible and understandable (Nithyanantham, 2023).

2. LITERATURE SURVEY

The proposed framework may be a video proposal framework that employs a cross-breed approach of content-based and collaborative sifting procedures (Rad et al., 2022a). The framework prescribes recordings to clients based on their interface and inclinations by analyzing the substance of the recordings and the users' history (Saxena et al., 2023). The framework will be created utilizing the taking-after methodology:

Data collection: The framework will collect information from different sources such as YouTube, Vimeo, and other video-sharing stages. The information will incorporate video metadata such as title, portrayal, labels, and category.

Content-based sifting: The framework will utilize content-based sifting to prescribe recordings to clients based on the closeness of the videos' highlights to the user's inclinations. The framework will dissect the metadata of the recordings to extricate highlights such as catchphrases, categories, and tags.

Collaborative sifting: The framework will utilize collaborative sifting to suggest recordings to clients based on the inclinations of other clients with comparable seeing histories (Tripathi & Al -Zubaidi, 2023). The framework will make a user-item interaction network to examine the history of the clients and suggest recordings based on the inclinations of other users (Xu et al., 2023).

Hybrid approach: The framework will combine content-based sifting and collaborative sifting to produce a list of suggested recordings for the client. The framework will utilize a weighting calculation to adjust the significance of the two strategies in creating the recommendations.

User input: The framework will collect criticism from the clients regarding the suggested recordings to make strides in the precision and significance of the recommendations.

Evaluation: The framework will be assessed utilizing standard assessment measurements such as exactness, review, and F1 score to degree the execution of the framework in creating exact and significant recommendations.

The proposed framework will give a few benefits to the clients, such as personalized video suggestions, progressed exactness and significance of proposals, and an upgraded client encounter. The framework can be conveyed on different video-sharing stages and can be customized to meet the necessities of the stage and the users (Suman et al., 2023).

Liu et al., (2017) present an agent-based personalized proposal strategy called Substance Proposal Framework based on private Energetic Client Profile (CRESDUP). The framework collects and mines the private information of clients at the client side, finds, stores and upgrades private Energetic Client Profile

(DUP) at the client side. The framework brings favoured messages from the substance server concurring to DUP. An imperative utilization of this innovation may be a personalized publicizing framework within the RSS (Wealthy Location Rundown, or RDF Location Outline) peruser application. It appears that the framework can utilize DUP to recognize the customers' potential inclinations and convey the more favoured messages, particularly the promotions, to individuals who are interested.

Fang et al., (2014) present a few content-based suggestion strategies for a QA framework that depend on and utilize broadly the structure of a domain-specific scientific categorization. Their objective is to include semantics to a commonplace content-based RS in order to move forward the quality of the proposals by mapping important watchwords from the existing scientific classification to the accessible questions. In order to test and assess the adequacy of the above-mentioned strategies, they conducted a directed study where they inquired a few clients to rate the suggestions conveyed utilizing these strategies. It appears that by combining the returns recovered by these strategies, we get a number of suggestions that fulfil an assortment of client expectations.

Zhang et al., (2017) investigate the centres on progressing the suggestions given to returning clients by utilizing MTCAR (Multi-level Focusing on Classification Affiliation Run the show) with content-based sifting and client profile. Clients have the capacity to customize their inclinations and profiles, which leads to personalized portable substance suggestions and moves forward by and large execution. Portable substance proposal frameworks are, as often as possible, utilized to address the challenge of sifting portable substances for convenience on portable gadgets. In any case, the framework experiences troubles due to deficient data within the starting stages, which hampers its capacity to precisely anticipate pertinent versatile substance things for users.

Huang et al., (2020) depict a Book Suggestion Framework (BRS) that combines content-based sifting (CBF), collaborative sifting (CF), and affiliation run the show mining to produce exact and viable proposals. These proposal frameworks are broadly utilized to propose items that are most significant to the end-users. Online book-selling websites are presently utilizing different methodologies to compete with one another (Rad et al., 2022b). A suggestion framework could be an important apparatus for expanding benefits and holding clients. Be that as it may, the current frameworks tend to extricate unimportant data, which comes about in a need for client fulfilment (Rajest et al., 2023a).

3. MODULE DESCRIPTION

This portion comprises the strategies, rules, and steps that will be utilized to form and address the proposed issue explanation. The execution comprises three components or units.

Module One: Data Collection

Recommendation frameworks are planned to supply personalized suggestions to users based on their inclinations, behaviours, and interfaces. To attain this goal, the framework must begin with collecting information about the client (Rajest et al., 2023b). This information is utilized to make a profile of the client, which incorporates data such as their age, gender, location, and inclinations. Information collection may be a critical component of suggestion frameworks since it empowers the framework to supply exact and significant suggestions. Without adequate information, the framework may not be able to supply proposals that are custom-made to the user's needs and inclinations (Regin et al., 2023). By collecting data around the user's inclinations, behaviours, and interface, the framework can provide exact and pertinent suggestions that are custom fitted to the user's needs. It is critical, be that as it may, to guarantee that information collection is a mindful and moral way to secure client protection and information security (Ranganathan et al., 2022).

Module Two: Content Pre-Processing

In our demonstration, we utilized a few content preparation strategies, including tokenization, stemming, and lemmatization, to encourage our examination (Tripathi & Al Shahri, 2016). Tokenization is the method of breaking down the content into smaller units called tokens, which can be words, expressions, or personal letters and numbers. This step is basic for analyzing content by diminishing it into more reasonable chunks.

Moreover, we connected Stemming, a method that diminishes words to their base or root shape, with the point of diminishing the number of interesting words within the content. Stemming calculations utilize diverse rules, either etymological or measurable, to recognize the base shape of a word. This method empowers us to gather together distinctive shapes of the same word, which makes strides in the effectiveness of our analysis (Shruthi & Aravind, 2023).

In expansion to Stemming, we utilized lemmatization, which diminishes words to their base or lexicon frame, known as a lemma. The essential objective of lemmatization is comparable to that of Stemming - gathering together distinctive shapes of the same word. In any case, lemmatization goes past basically expelling the postfix of a word. It employs phonetic rules and morphological examination to decide the base shape of a word based on its setting, which upgrades the precision of our analysis.

In conclusion, Tokenization, Stemming, and lemmatization are crucial content preparation procedures that we utilized in our investigation. By breaking down content into smaller, sensible units and gathering together diverse shapes of the same word, we were able to extract significant bits of knowledge from our information and draw more precise conclusions in our research (Venkatasubramanian et al., 2023).

Module Three: Video Highlight Extraction

Video feature extraction is the method of distinguishing and extricating vital visual highlights or designs from a video grouping. These highlights are utilized to depict the substance of a video and are utilized for an assortment of applications such as question acknowledgement, activity acknowledgement, and video summarization (Regin et al., 2023). There are various techniques utilized for video highlight extraction, but the most commonly utilized ones are based on computer vision calculations and Common Dialect preparing calculations. These calculations analyze the video outlines and extricate significant data.

ARCHITECTURE

Content-based filtering: It may be a sort of proposal method that utilizes the characteristics or traits of a thing, such as its metadata or content depiction, to suggest other comparable things. The strategy works by analyzing the substance of the items to distinguish their highlights and, after that, recommending other things that have comparative highlights. This strategy is additionally alluded to as attribute-based or feature-based filtering.

To execute content-based sifting, we begin with extricating highlights or characteristics from the things. For example, in a music suggestion framework, we might extricate highlights such as the sort and utilize them to make a profile or representation of the user's inclinations. This profile is at that point utilized to suggest other things that have comparative highlights. For instance, if a client has appraised a few activity motion pictures profoundly, the framework might prescribe other activity motion pictures with comparative highlights, such as those coordinated by the same chief or featuring the same actors.

In our demonstration, we utilize Jaccard similarity, a degree of likeness between two sets of things regularly utilized in information mining and data recovery. The Jaccard similarity coefficient (moreover known as the Jaccard list) is characterized as follows:

J (A, B) = |A ∩ B| / |A ∪ B|

where A and B are two sets, and |A| and |B| speak to the cardinality of the sets A and B separately.

In our proposal framework, we utilize Jaccard similarity to distinguish the similitude between two clients based on the set of things they have connected with and prescribe things to one client based on the things that the other client has connected with (figure 1). In a look motor, Jaccard similarity is utilized to recognize web pages that are most comparable to a given inquiry based on the cover of the inquiry terms with the terms within the pages.

Figure 1. Jaccard similarity

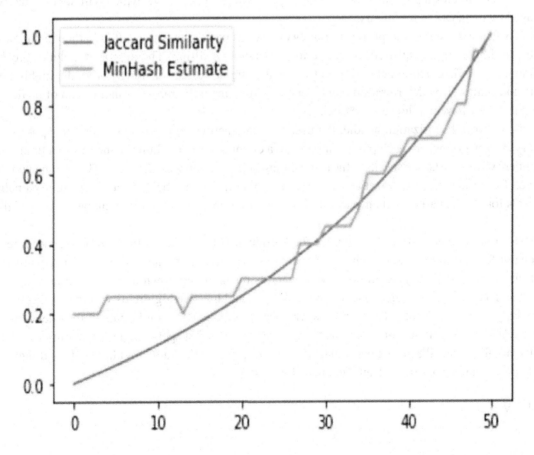

Both MinHash and the Jaccard similarity metric are utilized to survey set closeness. A degree of Jaccard similarity is the crossing point measure of two sets partitioned by the union measure of the two sets. On the other side, MinHash may be a probabilistic method that compares the particular MinHash marks of two sets to assess the Jaccard similarity between them.

Although Jaccard similarity and MinHash are both accommodating strategies for deciding how comparable a set is, Jaccard similarity is respected as often as possible as more correct and exact than MinHash, typically due to the truth that MinHash is an estimation of the Jaccard similarity and may contain a few botches, though Jaccard similarity offers an exact degree of the closeness between two sets.

The fact that Jaccard similarity is ensured to induce the same outcome each time, given the same input sets, is one of its primary preferences over MinHash. On the other hand, MinHash could be a probabilistic calculation, which can result in conflicting yields in a few application circumstances for the indistinguishable input sets.

Jaccard similarity may be computed specifically from the sets themselves without the requirement for encouraging pre-processing or computation, which is another advantage. The computation of MinHash marks, on the other hand, is vital for MinHash and is computationally costly for huge collections.

Collaborative Sifting: In our show, we utilize Collaborative sifting, which may be a suggestion strategy that depends on the opinions or evaluations of other clients to form suggestions for a given client. It is based on the thought that individuals who have comparative preferences or tastes in the past are likely to have comparable inclinations in the future. Collaborative sifting has a few points of interest in proposal frameworks; we utilize its ability to create personalized suggestions that take into consideration the user's interesting inclinations and the capacity to prescribe items which will not be effectively portrayed by metadata or highlights.

Matrix factorization: In our proposal framework, we utilize a procedure called Lattice factorization, which could be a broadly utilized technique for collaborative sifting. The approach includes breaking down a user-item interaction network into two smaller frameworks, speaking to the idle highlights of clients and things. This deterioration empowers us to anticipate the rating or inclination of a client for a thing that they have not, however, associated with.

In the network factorization handle, the user-item interaction framework is ordinarily spoken of as a scanty framework, where each push compares to a client and each column compares to a thing. Each component within the lattice speaks to the user's rating or interaction with the thing. The coming networks obtained from the lattice factorization preparation can, at that point, be utilized to create personalized proposals for clients based on their past intelligence with things, as well as the characteristics of those items.

SVD: In our demonstration, we embrace the Particular Esteem Deterioration (SVD) procedure as a framework factorization strategy, which is broadly utilized in collaborative filtering for recommendation frameworks. SVD may be an effective apparatus for breaking down a lattice into its constituent parts, which can offer assistance in recognizing designs and inactive highlights within the information. Particularly, the cleared-out solitary framework speaks to the inactive highlights of the clients, the inclining singular value framework contains the particular values that speak to the noteworthiness of each inactive highlight, and the proper particular framework speaks to the latent highlights of the things. This deterioration can be spoken to scientifically as follows:

$$M = U\Sigma V^T$$

Here, M refers to the first framework, U speaks to the left singular network, Σ is the inclining particular esteem lattice, and V^T signifies the correct solitary matrix.

The lattices U, Σ, and V^T are utilized to inexact the initial framework and to create predictions for lost values. This is usually accomplished by truncating the corner-to-corner lattice Σ, holding as it were the best k solitary values and setting the remaining values to zero. The coming truncated networks can, at that point, be utilized to foresee the lost values within the unique lattice. This strategy has appeared promising in different applications, counting suggestion frameworks, picture handling, and information compression.

Recommendation Generation: One approach to the suggestion era is to combine content-based sifting and collaborative sifting. This crossover approach can use the qualities of

Both strategies progress the exactness and differing qualities of proposals. To combine these two strategies, we begin with utilizing content-based sifting to create a set of candidate suggestions for the client based on the highlights of the things. At that point, we utilize collaborative sifting to rank these candidate proposals based on the inclinations of other clients who have associated with comparative things. This half-breed approach progresses the exactness and differing qualities of proposals by taking under consideration both the highlights of the things and the inclinations of other clients. In any case, it also has a few restrictions, such as the requirement for expansive sums of information and the trouble of tuning the parameters of the framework factorization calculation. Subsequently, it is critical to carefully assess the execution of the framework on a hold-out set of information and to tune the parameters to optimize the performance.

It is pivotal to keep in mind that the victory of such a framework basically depends on its capacity to offer shoppers' precise and relevant suggestions. By guaranteeing that the framework has the highlights and algorithms required to suit the wants of the clients, a proficient engineering module plays a pivotal portion in this. The structural module's capacity to oversee gigantic volumes of information, such as client intuition, video metadata, and relevant information, is a critical highlight. The framework must be able to handle and handle this information legitimately as the number of clients and recordings on the location increases.

To guarantee that the framework can scale effectively with the development of the stage, this requires the selection of cutting-edge innovations like conveyed computing, cloud computing, and huge information preparing methods. The structural module's capacity to alter and learn from client criticism and intelligence is another significant include. Users' likes, loathes, and appraisals ought to be able to be recorded by the framework, which ought to, at that point, utilize this information to move forward with its proposals. In order to analyze client behaviour and inclinations and alter the proposals in a like manner, this calls for the business of modern machine learning and profound learning calculations. A fruitful engineering module ought to be made to incorporate an assortment of sifting strategies, such as collaborative, content-based, and crossover sifting, among others. This makes it conceivable for the framework to offer customers a wide assortment of proposals based on numerous components like client inclinations, video substance, and social interactions. The platform's trade results can be essentially affected by a successful structural module, and it is basic to highlight. The framework can boost client engagement, satisfaction, and maintenance by making personalized and related suggestions. This may raise stage income and benefit. Furthermore, a solid proposal framework can offer assistance to stand out from its rivals and give it an advantage within the market.

In conclusion, an effective building module is fundamental to a video suggestion system's victory. It guarantees the framework has the highlights, strategies, and advances required to oversee colossal volumes of information, incorporate diverse sifting strategies, learn from user criticism, and allow clients personalized and germane suggestions. In conclusion, a solid suggestion framework can impact trade and donate a showcase advantage (figures 2 and 3).

Figure 2. Architectural diagram

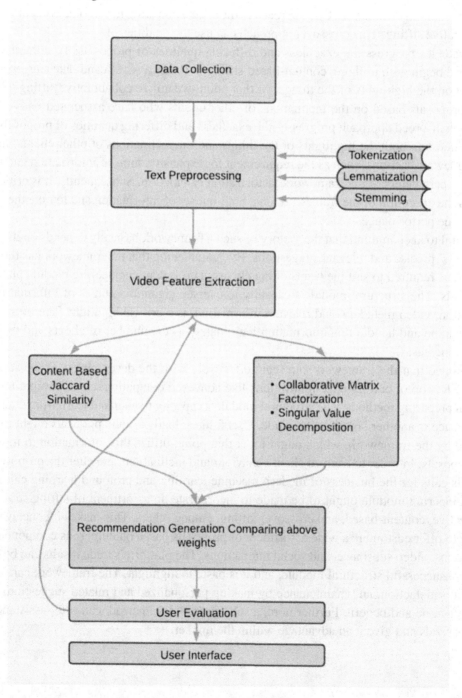

Figure 3. Variety of courses

Machine Learning

Deep Learning

Cloud Computing

Cyber Security

Robotics

Cybersecurity is the practice of protecting computer systems, networks, and sensitive information from unauthorized access, theft, or damage. With the proliferation of digital technologies and the increasing dependence on them in daily life, cybersecurity has become a critical concern for individuals, businesses, and governments.

One of the primary reasons cybersecurity is necessary is the prevalence of cyber attacks. Cyber attacks can take many forms, including viruses, malware, phishing scams, ransomware, and hacking. The goal of a cyber attack is typically to gain access to sensitive information, such as financial or personal data, or to disrupt normal operations. In some cases, cyber attacks can result in significant financial losses or even physical harm.

To protect against cyber attacks, cybersecurity professionals use a variety of techniques and tools. These may include firewalls, encryption, intrusion detection systems, and anti-virus software. Additionally, cybersecurity professionals must stay up to date on the latest threats and vulnerabilities and develop strategies to prevent them.

Another critical aspect of cybersecurity is user education and awareness. Many cyber attacks are successful because users unwittingly give away sensitive information or inadvertently download malware. By educating users about the

The Computer Engineering Department offers a variety of courses that cover topics ranging from data mining and machine learning to deep learning, cloud computing, cyber security, and robotics.

Figure 4. Links for webinar

latest threats and vulnerabilities and develop strategies to
prevent them.

Another critical aspect of cybersecurity is user education
and awareness. Many cyber attacks are successful because
users unwittingly give away sensitive information or
inadvertently download malware. By educating users about the

Emerging Need for Cyber Security and Understanding Next-Gen Antivirus - National Level Webinar

"Emerging Need for Cyber Security and Understanding Next-Gen Antivirus" Greetings, Join us for updates on Cyber Security and ...

Watch on YouTube

Webinar // Cybersecurity in the medical devices – How to show compliance to regulatory requirements

New guidance and standards for medical device cybersecurity and how to show compliance to the respective requirements.

Watch on YouTube

Cyber Security Course | Cyber Security Training | Cyber Security Full Course | Intellipaat

Intellipaat's Advanced Certification in Cyber Security Course: https://intellipaat.com/cyber-security-eict-iit-guwahati/ Welcome to ...

Watch on YouTube

Computer Security Measures || Introduction To Computers || #Cybersecurity #ICT #Computers #virus

4. RESULT AND EVALUATION

The following screenshots are of the working implementation of the model. The recommendation system gives video recommendations based on the topic mentioned in the screenshot presented above. It gives multiple video recommendations on the topic of cybersecurity. The recommendation system provides the user with appropriate links to access these videos, too, which is a very convenient method for users to jump from one video to the next without wasting time searching for them separately, one by one. As seen in the results, the recommendations provided by the system are related to each other and don't stray far away from the topic of interest (Figure 4).

6. CONCLUSION AND FUTURE WORK

In conclusion, the work that we have done has demonstrated how a tailored content recommendation system can improve learning in environments that are difficult for e-learning. By analysing a learner's preferences, hobbies, and previous educational experiences, our system was able to give knowledge that was both relevant and fascinating, making it a better fit for the specific requirements and capabilities of each individual student. The results of our research indicate that providing students with individualised recommendations helps them study more efficiently by increasing the level of interest and engagement on their part. According to the findings of our research, the current system has a number of flaws and deficiencies, some of which include the requirement for content that is more inclusive and diverse, as well as the danger of learners' preconceptions being reinforced. Therefore, future research should concentrate on these issues and expand on the capabilities of personalised content recommendation systems to improve the learning environment in online education.

REFERENCES

Abu Shkheedim, S., Alawneh, Y., Khuwayra, O., & Salman, F., khayyat,T. (2022). The Level Of Satisfaction Of Parents Of Students With Learning Difficulties Towards Distance Learning After The Corona Pandemic. *NeuroQuantology : An Interdisciplinary Journal of Neuroscience and Quantum Physics*, *20*(19), 1299–1311.

Al Khawaldeh, S., Alawneh, Y., & Alzboun, M. (2022). the availability of quality standards for the construction of science achievement tests from the point of view of the examination committees [Natural Sciences]. *Hunan Daxue Xuebao. Shehui Kexue Ban*, *49*(9), 1233–1247.

Alawneh, Y. (2022). Role of Kindergarten Curriculum in Instilling Ethical Values among Children in Governorates of Northern West Bank, Palestine, Dirasat. *Education in Science*, *49*(3), 360–375.

Alawneh,Y., Abu Shokhedim, S., & Al-khazalah. F. (2022). Trends of teachers with handicapped towards the e-learning program at basic education in schools during covid-19. *Journal of positive school psychology, 7*(6), 1876-1886.

Alawneh, Y. & Al-Shara'h, N. (2022) Evaluation of the e-learning experience in Palestinian universities during the Corona pandemic in light of some quality standards of the Jordanian Higher Education. *Journal of the College of Education (Assiut), 38*(2.2), 181-204.

Alawneh, Y., Ashamali, M., Abdel-Hassan, R., Al-khawaldeh, S., & Engestroom, Y. (2022). Degree Of Use Of E-Learning Science Teachers In Public High Schools In During The Corona-Covid 19 Pandemic. *Journal of Positive School Psychology, 6*(2), 1060–1070.

An, Q., Hong, W. C. H., Xu, X., Zhang, Y., & Kolletar-Zhu, K. (2023). How Education Level Influences Internet Security Knowledge, Behaviour, and Attitude: A Comparison among Undergraduates, Postgraduates and Working Graduates. *International Journal of Information Security, 22*(2), 305–317. doi:10.100710207-022-00637-z PMID:36466362

Angeline, R., Aarthi, S., Regin, R., & Rajest, S. S. (2023). Dynamic intelligence-driven engineering flooding attack prediction using ensemble learning. In *Advances in Artificial and Human Intelligence in the Modern Era* (pp. 109–124). IGI Global. doi:10.4018/979-8-3693-1301-5.ch006

Aravind, Bhuvaneswari, & Rajest, S. S. (2023). ICT-based digital technology for testing and evaluation of English language teaching. In *Handbook of Research on Learning in Language Classrooms Through ICT-Based Digital Technology* (pp. 1–11). IGI Global.

Demeter, E., Rad, D., & Balas, E. (2021). Schadenfreude and general anti-social behaviours: The role of Violent Content Preferences and life satisfaction. Brain. *Broad Research in Artificial Intelligence and Neuroscience, 12*(2). doi:10.18662/brain/12.2/194

Fang, H., Bao, Y., & Zhang, J. (2014). Leveraging decomposed trust in probabilistic matrix factorization for effective recommendation. *AAAI Conference on Artificial Intelligence, 28*(1). 10.1609/aaai.v28i1.8714

Gao, T., & Liu, J. (2021). Application of improved random forest algorithm and fuzzy mathematics in physical fitness of athletes. *Journal of Intelligent & Fuzzy Systems, 40*(2), 2041–2053. doi:10.3233/JIFS-189206

Gomathy, V., & Venkatasbramanian, S. (2023). Impact of Teacher Expectations on Student Academic Achievement. *FMDB Transactions on Sustainable Techno Learning, 1*(2), 78–91.

Guiamalon, T. S. (2022). Internship In Times Of Pandemic: A Qualitative Phenomenological Study. *Res Militaris, 12*(6), 1039–1050.

Hong, W. C. H. (2018). The Effect of Absence of Explicit Knowledge on ESL/EFL Stress-Placement Accuracy: A quasi-experiment. *Asian EFL Journal, 20*(2), 262–279.

Hong, W. C. H. (2021). Improving English as a foreign language learners' writing using a minimal grammar approach of teaching dependent clauses: A case study of Macao secondary school students. In B. L. Reynolds & M. F. Teng (Eds.), *Innovative Approaches in Teaching English Writing to Chinese Speakers* (pp. 67–90). De Gruyter Mouton. doi:10.1515/9781501512643-004

Hong, W. C. H. (2021). Macao Secondary School EFL Teachers' Perspectives on Written Corrective Feedback: Rationales and Constraints. *Journal of Educational Technology and Innovation, 1*(04), 1–13.

Hong, W. C. H. (2023). The impact of ChatGPT on foreign language teaching and learning: Opportunities in education and research. *Journal of Education Technology and Innovation*, 5(1).

Hong, W. C. H., Chi, C.-Y., Liu, J., Zhang, Y.-F., Lei, N.-L., & Xu, X.-S. (2022). The influence of social education level on cybersecurity awareness and behaviour: A comparative study of university students and working graduates. *Education and Information Technologies*. PMID:35791319

Huang, Z., Lin, X., Liu, H., Zhang, B., Chen, Y., & Tang, Y. (2020). Deep representation learning for location-based recommendation. *IEEE Transactions on Computational Social Systems*, 7(3), 648–658. doi:10.1109/TCSS.2020.2974534

Jayakumar, P., Suman Rajest, S., & Aravind, B. R. (2022). An Empirical Study on the Effectiveness of Online Teaching and Learning Outcomes with Regard to LSRW Skills in COVID-19 Pandemic. In A. Hamdan, A. E. Hassanien, T. Mescon, & B. Alareeni (Eds.), *Technologies, Artificial Intelligence and the Future of Learning Post-COVID-19. Studies in Computational Intelligence* (Vol. 1019). Springer. doi:10.1007/978-3-030-93921-2_27

Kumar, S. A., Rajest, S. S., Aravind, B. R., & Bhuvaneswari, G. (2023). Virtual learning styles based on learning style detection. *International Journal of Knowledge and Learning*, 1(1), 10057158. doi:10.1504/IJKL.2023.10057158

Lian, X., Hong, W. C. H., Xu, X., Kimberly, K. Z., & Wang, Z. (2022). The influence of picture book design on visual attention of children with autism: A pilot study. *International Journal of Developmental Disabilities*, 1–11. PMID:37885844

Liu, G., Fu, Y., Chen, G., Xiong, H., & Chen, C. (2017). Modeling buying motives for personalized product bundle recommendation. *ACM Transactions on Knowledge Discovery from Data*, 11(3), 1–26. doi:10.1145/3022185

Lumapenet, H. T. (2022). Effectiveness of Self-Learning Modules on Students' Learning in English Amidst Pandemic. *Res Militaris*, 12(6), 949–953.

Maseleno, A., Patimah, S., Syafril, S., & Huda, M. (2023). Learning Preferences Diagnostic using Mathematical Theory of Evidence. *FMDB Transactions on Sustainable Techno Learning*, 1(2), 60–77.

Nithyanantham, V. (2023). Study Examines the Connection Between Students' Various Intelligence and Their Levels of Mathematical Success in School. *FMDB Transactions on Sustainable Techno Learning*, 1(1), 32–59.

Padmanabhan, J., Rajest, S. S., & Veronica, J. J. (2023). A study on the orthography and grammatical errors of tertiary-level students. In *Handbook of Research on Learning in Language Classrooms Through ICT-Based Digital Technology* (pp. 41–53). IGI Global. doi:10.4018/978-1-6684-6682-7.ch004

Paudel, P. K., Bastola, R., Eigenbrode, S. D., Borzée, A., Thapa, S., Rad, D., & Adhikari, S. (2022). Perspectives of scholars on the origin, spread and consequences of COVID-19 are diverse but not polarized. *Humanities & Social Sciences Communications*, 9(1), 198. doi:10.105741599-022-01216-2

Rad, D., Balas, E., Ignat, S., Rad, G., & Dixon, D. (2020a). A predictive model of youth bystanders' helping attitudes. *Revista Romaneasca Pentru Educatie Multidimensionala, 12*(1Sup2), 136–150. doi:10.18662/rrem/12.1sup2/257

Rad, D., Dixon, D., & Rad, G. (2020b). Digital outing confidence as a mediator in the digital behavior regulation and internet content awareness relationship. Brain. *Broad Research in Artificial Intelligence and Neuroscience, 11*(1), 84–95. doi:10.18662/brain/11.1/16

Rad, D., Egerau, A., Roman, A., Dughi, T., Balas, E., Maier, R., & Rad, G. (2022a). A preliminary investigation of the technology acceptance model (TAM) in early childhood education and care. Brain. *Broad Research in Artificial Intelligence and Neuroscience, 13*(1), 518–533. doi:10.18662/brain/13.1/297

Rad, D., Magulod, G. C. Jr, Balas, E., Roman, A., Egerau, A., Maier, R., & Chis, R. (2022b). A radial basis function neural network approach to predict preschool teachers' technology acceptance behavior. *Frontiers in Psychology, 13*, 880753. doi:10.3389/fpsyg.2022.880753 PMID:35756273

Rajest, S. S., Singh, B., Obaid, A. J., Regin, R., & Chinnusamy, K. (2023b). Advances in artificial and human intelligence in the modern era. *Advances in Computational Intelligence and Robotics*. doi:10.4018/979-8-3693-1301-5

Rajest, S. S., Singh, B. J., Obaid, A., Regin, R., & Chinnusamy, K. (2023a). Recent developments in machine and human intelligence. *Advances in Computational Intelligence and Robotics*. doi:10.4018/978-1-6684-9189-8

Ranganathan, M., Rajest, S. S., Rathnasabapathy, M., & Ganesh Kumar, J. (2022). Neuropsychological functions and optimism levels in stroke patients: A cross-sectional study. In *Acceleration of the Biopsychosocial Model in Public Health* (pp. 231–246). IGI Global. doi:10.4018/978-1-6684-6496-0.ch011

Regin, R., Khanna, A. A., Krishnan, V., Gupta, M., & Bose, R. S., & Rajest, S. S. (2023). Information design and unifying approach for secured data sharing using attribute-based access control mechanisms. In Recent Developments in Machine and Human Intelligence (pp. 256–276). IGI Global.

Regin, R., T, S., George, S. R., Bhattacharya, M., Datta, D., & Priscila, S. S. (2023). Development of predictive model of diabetic using supervised machine learning classification algorithm of ensemble voting. *International Journal of Bioinformatics Research and Applications, 19*(3), 10057044. doi:10.1504/IJBRA.2023.10057044

Saxena, D., Khandare, S., & Chaudhary, S. (2023). An Overview of ChatGPT: Impact on Academic Learning. *FMDB Transactions on Sustainable Techno Learning, 1*(1), 11–20.

Shruthi, S., & Aravind, B. R. (2023). Engaging ESL Learning on Mastering Present Tense with Nearpod and Learningapps.org for Engineering Students. *FMDB Transactions on Sustainable Techno Learning, 1*(1), 21–31.

Suman, R. S., Moccia, S., Chinnusamy, K., Singh, B., & Regin, R. (Eds.). (2023). Advances in Educational Technologies and Instructional Design. *Handbook of research on learning in language classrooms through ICT-based digital technology*. doi:10.4018/978-1-6684-6682-7

Tripathi, S. (2017). Role of Bollywood cinema in promoting tourism, business and intercultural communication in Arab world: A study with Oman. *The International Journal of Social Sciences (Islamabad)*, *3*(1), 424–435. doi:10.20319/pijss.2017.s31.424435

Tripathi, S., & Al-Zubaidi, A. (2023). A Study within Salalah's Higher Education Institutions on Online Learning Motivation and Engagement Challenges during Covid-19. *FMDB Transactions on Sustainable Techno Learning, 1*(1), 1–10.

Tripathi, S., & Al Shahri, M. (2016). Omani community in digital age: A study of Omani women using back channel media to empower themselves for frontline entrepreneurship. *International Journal of Information and Communication Engineering*, *10*(6), 1929–1934.

Venkatasubramanian, S., Gomathy, V., & Saleem, M. (2023). Investigating the Relationship Between Student Motivation and Academic Performance. *FMDB Transactions on Sustainable Techno Learning*, *1*(2), 111–124.

Xu, X., Hong, W. C. H., Zhang, Y., Jiang, H., & Liu, J. (2023). Learning Paths Design in Personal Learning Environments: The Impact on Postgraduates' Cognitive Achievements and Satisfaction. *Innovations in Education and Teaching International*, 1–16. doi:10.1080/14703297.2023.2189603

Zhang, H., Ganchev, I., Nikolov, N. S., Ji, Z., & O'Droma, M. (2017). Weighted matrix factorization with Bayesian personalized ranking. *2017 Computing Conference*. IEEE. 10.1109/SAI.2017.8252119

Chapter 7
Textual Alchemy:
Unleashing the Power of Generative Models for Advanced Text Generation

Gagan Deep

Chitkara Business School, Chitkara University, Punjab, India

Jyoti Verma

https://orcid.org/0000-0002-7559-4312

Chitkara University, Punjab, India

ABSTRACT

This chapter explores the transformative potential of generative models for advanced text generation, focusing on leveraging structural equation modeling techniques. With the rapid advancements in deep learning and natural language processing, generative models have emerged as powerful tools for creative writing, semantic coherence, and contextual understanding. This chapter provides a comprehensive overview of the foundations, methodologies, and applications of generative models in text generation. The chapter begins with an introduction to the evolution of generative models and highlights their significance in various domains. It lays the groundwork by explaining language modeling techniques and the architectures employed in text generation using deep learning algorithms. The subsequent sections delve into the core aspects of generative models for text generation.

INTRODUCTION

The Evolution of Generative Models in Text Generation

One of the pioneering works in this field is the introduction of recurrent neural networks (RNNs) for language modeling (Mikolov et al., 2010). RNNs revolutionized text generation by allowing models to capture long-term dependencies in sequential data. However, RNNs suffered from vanishing gradients and limited memory, limiting their effectiveness for generating lengthy and coherent text. To address these limitations, the introduction of the long short-term memory (LSTM) architecture by Hochreiter

DOI: 10.4018/979-8-3693-0502-7.ch007

and Schmidhuber (1997) brought significant improvements in capturing long-range dependencies. LSTMs overcame the vanishing gradient problem, enabling more effective text generation (Zhang et al., 2014). The next breakthrough came with the development of generative adversarial networks (GANs) by Goodfellow et al. (2014). GANs introduced a novel framework for training generative models by pitting a generator network against a discriminator network. This adversarial process resulted in the generation of high-quality text samples with improved coherence and realism (Yu et al., 2017). Another significant advancement was the introduction of the transformer model by Vaswani et al. (2017). Transformers revolutionized text generation by utilizing self-attention mechanisms, allowing models to capture global dependencies efficiently. Transformers achieved state-of-the-art performance in various natural language processing tasks, including text generation (Radford et al., 2019). More recently, pre-trained language models, such as OpenAI's GPT (Radford et al., 2018), have gained prominence. These models are trained on large corpora of text and fine-tuned for specific tasks, enabling impressive text generation capabilities. They have demonstrated remarkable performance in generating coherent and contextually accurate text across various domains (Brown et al., 2020). These advancements in generative models have paved the way for applications in storytelling, dialogue generation, poetry generation, and content creation in various industries. They have also raised important ethical considerations regarding responsible use and potential misuse of these models.

Significance and Applications of Advanced Text Generation Techniques

One of the key significances of advanced text generation techniques lies in their ability to automate content creation. With the growing demand for high-quality content in various industries, such as marketing, journalism, and entertainment, these techniques provide a scalable and efficient solution. They can generate engaging articles, product descriptions, social media posts, and more, saving time and resources for content creators (Holtzman et al., 2020). Another significant application of advanced text generation techniques is in dialogue systems and chatbots. These techniques enable the generation of natural and interactive conversations, enhancing user experiences in customer service, virtual assistants, and social interactions. They can understand user inputs and generate appropriate responses, making the dialogue more engaging and effective (Gao et al., 2019). Text generation techniques also play a crucial role in creative writing and storytelling. They can generate compelling narratives, poetry, and fictional stories, assisting authors and inspiring new forms of literary expression. These techniques can provide writers with novel ideas, help overcome writer's block, and even collaborate with human authors to co-create literary works (Jain et al., 2020). In the field of language translation, advanced text generation techniques have demonstrated remarkable progress. Neural machine translation models, such as Google's Neural Machine Translation (GNMT), utilize text generation techniques to translate text between different languages, enabling effective communication across language barriers (Wu et al., 2016). Furthermore, text generation techniques have found applications in personalized content generation. They can generate personalized recommendations, advertisements, and news articles based on user preferences and historical data. These techniques enhance user engagement and provide tailored content experiences in e-commerce, news platforms, and recommendation systems (Jin et al., 2020). The significance of advanced text generation techniques extends to ethical considerations as well. As these techniques become more powerful, concerns arise regarding the potential misuse, misinformation, and ethical implications of generated text. Ensuring responsible use, addressing biases, and maintaining transparency in text generation models are important challenges that need to be addressed (Bender et al., 2021).

FOUNDATIONS OF GENERATIVE MODELS

Brief Introduction to Generative Models

Generative models are a class of machine learning models that have gained significant attention in recent years due to their ability to generate new data samples that resemble a given training dataset. These models are designed to capture the underlying distribution of the data and generate new instances that exhibit similar characteristics. One popular generative model is the Variational Autoencoder (VAE) (Kingma & Welling, 2013), which combines an encoder network that maps the input data to a latent space and a decoder network that generates new samples from the latent space. Another prominent generative model is the Generative Adversarial Network (GAN) (Goodfellow et al., 2014), which consists of a generator network and a discriminator network that compete against each other in a min-max game. The generator aims to generate realistic samples, while the discriminator tries to distinguish between real and generated samples. GANs have been successfully applied in various domains, including image generation (Radford et al., 2015). In addition to VAEs and GANs, there are other types of generative models such as autoregressive models, which generate data sequentially based on previously generated elements. These models have shown remarkable performance in tasks like text generation (Radford et al., 2019). Language models like OpenAI's GPT-3 have achieved impressive results in generating coherent and contextually relevant text (Brown et al., 2020). These models have been widely used in natural language processing, content generation, and dialogue systems. The significance of generative models lies in their potential applications across different fields. In image generation, GANs have been used to create realistic images and even generate novel artworks (Gatys et al., 2016). In the field of healthcare, generative models have been employed for tasks such as generating synthetic medical images. Generative models also play a crucial role in speech synthesis, enabling the generation of high-quality, natural-sounding speech from text inputs.

Overview of Language Modeling Techniques

N-gram models are a traditional approach to language modeling (Chen & Goodman, 1998). These models estimate the probability of a word based on the previous n-1 words in the sequence. While simple and efficient, n-gram models suffer from the limitation of the fixed context window and the inability to capture long-range dependencies. Recurrent Neural Networks (RNNs) revolutionized language modeling by introducing the concept of sequential processing (Mikolov et al., 2010). RNNs, particularly Long Short-Term Memory (LSTM) networks (Hochreiter & Schmidhuber, 1997), can capture long-term dependencies and have been widely used in tasks such as machine translation and speech recognition. More recently, Transformer models have gained significant attention in language modeling (Vaswani et al., 2017). Transformers utilize self-attention mechanisms to capture contextual relationships between words in an input sequence. The introduction of the Transformer architecture has led to remarkable advances in NLP, including the development of large-scale language models such as OpenAI's GPT series (Radford et al., 2018). Generative Pre-trained Transformer (GPT) models, in particular, have revolutionized the field of language modeling. These models are trained on vast amounts of text data and can generate coherent and contextually relevant text given a prompt. GPT-3, with 175 billion parameters, has demonstrated remarkable performance on a wide range of language tasks (Brown et al., 2020). In addition to traditional language modeling techniques, there has been a recent focus on unsupervised pre-training followed by fine-tuning. Models like BERT (Devlin et al., 2019) and RoBERTa (Liu et al., 2019) have achieved state-of-the-art results on various NLP benchmarks, leveraging masked language modeling objectives and large-scale corpora.

Deep Learning Architectures for Text Generation

Recurrent Neural Networks (RNNs) have been widely used for text generation tasks due to their ability to model sequential data (Graves, 2013). RNN-based models, such as the Long Short-Term Memory (LSTM) and Gated Recurrent Unit (GRU), have shown success in generating text with long-range dependencies and capturing context information (Sutskever et al., 2014). Variational Autoencoders (VAEs) have also been employed for text generation by modeling the latent space of text representations (Bowman et al., 2016). VAEs can generate diverse and coherent text samples by sampling from the learned latent space and decoding them into meaningful sequences. This approach has been particularly useful for tasks such as dialogue generation and story generation. Generative Adversarial Networks (GANs) have gained significant attention in text generation tasks (Yu et al., 2017). GANs consist of a generator and a discriminator that compete against each other. The generator aims to generate realistic text samples, while the discriminator tries to distinguish between real and generated text. The adversarial training process encourages the generator to produce high-quality text that resembles the training data distribution. Attention mechanisms have been integrated into deep learning architectures to enhance text generation (Bahdanau et al., 2014). Attention mechanisms allow the model to focus on different parts of the input sequence when generating each word, capturing relevant context information effectively. Transformer-based models, which heavily rely on attention mechanisms, have achieved remarkable performance in various text generation tasks (Radford et al., 2018). Recent advancements in deep learning architectures have led to the development of powerful text generation models such as OpenAI's GPT series (Radford et al., 2019). These models leverage the Transformer architecture, self-attention mechanisms, and unsupervised pre-training on large-scale text corpora to generate high-quality, coherent, and contextually relevant text.

UNLEASHING THE POWER OF CONTEXTUAL UNDERSTANDING

Leveraging Pre-Trained Language Models for Contextual Understanding

One of the pioneering pre-trained language models is ELMo (Embeddings from Language Models), introduced by Peters et al. (2018). ELMo utilizes bidirectional LSTM networks to generate word representations that are contextually sensitive. By considering the entire input sentence, ELMo captures the meaning of words in context, enabling better understanding of complex language structures. Another influential pre-trained language model is OpenAI's GPT (Generative Pre-trained Transformer) series (Radford et al., 2018). GPT models employ the Transformer architecture, enabling them to capture long-range dependencies and context information efficiently. The models are trained on massive amounts of text data, allowing them to learn intricate patterns and relationships in language. BERT (Bidirectional Encoder Representations from Transformers), proposed by Devlin et al. (2018), has revolutionized contextual understanding in natural language processing. BERT introduces a masked language model objective and a next sentence prediction objective during training, allowing the model to learn bidirectional representations of words. BERT has achieved remarkable performance across various tasks, such as question answering, sentiment analysis, and named entity recognition. RoBERTa, a variant of BERT, was introduced by Liu et al. (2019) to further enhance contextual understanding. By optimizing BERT's training process, RoBERTa achieves improved performance on downstream tasks, demonstrating the effectiveness of pre-training techniques. The recently introduced GPT-3 model by Brown et al. (2020) represents a significant advancement in pre-trained language models. With an extensive architecture and a massive number of parameters, GPT-3 demonstrates impressive language generation capabilities and exhibits contextual understanding beyond single sentences. The ability of pre-trained language models to capture contextual understanding has greatly benefited various applications. These models have been successfully applied in tasks such as machine translation (Lample et al., 2018), text summarization (Dong et al., 2019), and sentiment analysis (Sun et al., 2019). Their contextual knowledge enables them to generate coherent and contextually relevant text, providing valuable insights and improving overall performance in these tasks.

Fine-Tuning Techniques for Domain-Specific Text Generation

One popular fine-tuning approach is domain adaptation, which aims to improve model performance on a specific target domain. Domain adaptation techniques leverage domain-specific labeled or unlabeled data to fine-tune the pre-trained models. For instance, Yang et al. (2019) proposed domain-adaptive fine-tuning for text classification tasks, demonstrating the effectiveness of incorporating domain-specific data during the fine-tuning process. Another fine-tuning technique is transfer learning, which involves transferring knowledge from a pre-trained model to a target task. Transfer learning has been widely used in various natural language processing tasks. Howard and Ruder (2018) introduced the concept of Universal Language Model Fine-tuning (ULMFiT), which demonstrates the effectiveness of transfer learning for improving performance on specific tasks, even with limited labeled data. In the context of text generation, fine-tuning can be applied to generate domain-specific and coherent text. Xu et al. (2018) proposed a fine-tuning approach for text style transfer, enabling the generation of text with specific styles while preserving content. The authors showed that fine-tuning the language model on style-labeled data significantly improved the quality of generated text. Furthermore, fine-tuning can be performed in a multi-task learning framework. Liu et al. (2020) introduced BERT-based multi-task learning for text generation tasks, where the pre-trained BERT model is fine-tuned on multiple related tasks simultaneously. This approach enables the model to learn shared representations across tasks and enhances its capability for generating diverse and contextually relevant text. Fine-tuning techniques for domain-specific text generation have found applications in various domains such as healthcare (Rios and Kavuluru, 2020), finance (Zhang et al., 2021), and legal text generation (Deliç et al., 2021). These applications demonstrate the practical significance of fine-tuning in capturing domain-specific knowledge and generating high-quality text tailored to specific domains.

Enhancing Semantic Coherence and Contextual Relevance

One approach to enhancing semantic coherence is through the use of latent variable models. Latent variable models introduce hidden variables that capture the underlying semantics of the text. Dai et al. (2019) introduced a method called "CTRL" (Conditional Transformer Language Model) that leverages a structured latent space to generate coherent and diverse text. The authors demonstrated that incorporating latent variables improves semantic coherence by disentangling different aspects of the text. Another approach is the use of reinforcement learning techniques to optimize text generation models. Ma et al. (2018) proposed the "Reinforcement Learning from Human Feedback" framework, which employs a reward model to guide the text generation process. By training the model using human feedback, the authors showed significant improvements in semantic coherence and contextual relevance of the generated text. In recent years, transformer-based models have shown remarkable advancements in text generation. Radford et al. (2019) introduced GPT-2 (Generative Pre-trained Transformer 2), which utilizes a large-scale transformer model trained on diverse text sources. The authors demonstrated that GPT-2 generates coherent and contextually relevant text by capturing long-range dependencies and semantic relationships. Contextual embeddings, such as BERT (Devlin et al., 2019), have also been instrumental in enhancing semantic coherence and contextual relevance. These models leverage pre-training on large corpora to capture contextual information and improve the generation process. Zhang et al. (2020) proposed a method called "SEMGAN" that combines BERT with generative adversarial networks to enhance semantic coherence in text generation tasks. Furthermore, techniques like reinforcement learning with policy gradients have been used to optimize text generation models for semantic coherence and contextual relevance. Liu et al. (2018) introduced the "TextGAN" framework, which employs reinforcement learning to generate text samples that align with a given target distribution. The authors demonstrated that TextGAN produces coherent and contextually relevant text by iteratively optimizing the generator using policy gradients.

FROM WORDS TO STORIES: STORYTELLING WITH GENERATIVE MODELS

Narrative Generation Techniques Using Generative Models

One approach to narrative generation is based on recurrent neural networks (RNNs). RNNs, with their ability to model sequential dependencies, have been used to generate text that follows a coherent narrative structure. Fan et al. (2018) proposed the "StoryGAN" model, which employs an RNN-based generator to generate narratives with consistent storylines. The authors demonstrated that StoryGAN produces coherent and engaging stories by modeling the temporal dependencies between story events. Another popular technique for narrative generation is based on variational autoencoders (VAEs). VAEs are generative models that learn latent representations of data. Li et al. (2018) introduced the "V-NLG" model, which combines VAEs with hierarchical structures to generate narratives. The authors showed that V-NLG generates stories with coherent plots and diverse character interactions, capturing the essence of engaging storytelling. Recently, transformer-based models have shown promising results in narrative generation. Zhu et al. (2020) proposed the "TransNarrative" model, which utilizes a transformer architecture to generate coherent and diverse narratives. The authors incorporated an attention mechanism to capture global dependencies and a copy mechanism to maintain consistency with given prompts. TransNarrative demonstrated the ability to generate high-quality stories with improved coherence and creativity. Additionally, reinforcement learning techniques have been employed to optimize narrative generation models. Yao et al. (2019) introduced the "RLSeq2Seq" model, which utilizes reinforcement learning with policy gradients to generate stories. The model is trained to maximize the reward signal based on story quality and coherence. RLSeq2Seq generated narratives that were ranked highly in terms of coherence and story flow. Furthermore, style transfer techniques have been explored to generate narratives with specific attributes or genres. Ghazvininejad et al. (2017) proposed the "StructVAE" model, which leverages VAEs to disentangle style and content representations in text. By manipulating the style attributes, StructVAE can generate narratives with different tones or genres while maintaining coherence.

Character Development and Plot Generation

To achieve effective character development, researchers have explored various approaches using generative models. Hu et al. (2017) proposed the "CharacterSeq2Seq" model, which utilizes sequence-to-sequence architecture with attention mechanisms to generate character descriptions and backstories. The model learns to generate coherent and detailed character attributes based on given prompts. In addition to character development, generative models have been applied to plot generation. Ribeiro et al. (2020) introduced the "PlotMachines" framework, which employs a variational autoencoder (VAE) to generate plot structures. The VAE captures latent representations of different plot elements, enabling the generation of diverse and well-structured plots. Furthermore, reinforcement learning techniques have been employed to improve character development and plot generation. Yuan et al. (2021) proposed the "RL-StoryGen" model, which incorporates reinforcement learning with policy gradients to optimize story generation. The model learns to generate characters with consistent traits and actions, as well as coherent plot progressions. RL-StoryGen produces narratives with well-developed characters and engaging plots, demonstrating the effectiveness of reinforcement learning in enhancing storytelling quality. Moreover, conditional generative models have been explored for personalized character development and plot generation. Zhang et al. (2019) introduced the "PersonalizedStory" model, which leverages a conditional variational autoencoder (CVAE) to generate personalized narratives based on user preferences and input prompts. The model learns to generate characters and plots tailored to individual readers' interests, resulting in more engaging and immersive storytelling experiences.

Injecting Emotions and Creativity Into Text Generation

To incorporate emotions into text generation, researchers have explored various approaches. Gao et al. (2019) proposed the "EmoGAN" model, which combines conditional generative adversarial networks (GANs) with emotion labels to generate emotionally diverse text. The model learns to generate text that aligns with specific emotions, such as happiness, sadness, or anger, resulting in emotionally expressive outputs. Moreover, creativity in text generation has been tackled through different techniques. Yao et al. (2019) introduced the "CtrlGen" model, which utilizes a controlled text generation framework to influence the level of creativity in the generated text. By conditioning the generation process on specific creativity-inducing factors, such as topic diversity or novelty, CtrlGen enables the production of more imaginative and unique textual outputs. Furthermore, the infusion of emotions and creativity in text generation has been enhanced through the use of style transfer techniques. Shen et al. (2017) proposed the "StyleNet" model, which employs an unsupervised style transfer framework to generate text with desired emotional tones or creative styles. By learning the underlying style representations of different emotional or creative dimensions, StyleNet facilitates the generation of text that aligns with specific emotional or creative requirements. In addition, the application of reinforcement learning has shown promise in injecting emotions and creativity into text generation. Fan et al. (2018) introduced the "Creative Writing via Deep Reinforcement Learning" model, which employs a deep reinforcement learning framework to optimize the generation of creative and expressive text. By incorporating reward signals that encourage emotional diversity or creative novelty, the model learns to generate text that exhibits a wide range of emotions and innovative ideas.

BEYOND TEXT: MULTIMODAL TEXT GENERATION

Incorporating Visual and Auditory Cues Into Text Generation

One approach to incorporating visual cues into text generation is through the use of image-conditioned models. Reed et al. (2016) introduced the "StackGAN" model, which generates realistic text descriptions conditioned on input images. By combining a text generation network with an image generation network, StackGAN produces visually grounded text that accurately describes the content of an image. Furthermore, the incorporation of auditory cues has also been explored in text generation. Owens et al. (2016) proposed the "Text to Speech Synthesis with Neural Networks" model, which converts text into synthesized speech using deep neural networks. By capturing the melodic and rhythmic aspects of human speech, this model enables the generation of text-based audio outputs, enhancing the expressiveness and naturalness of the generated text. Moreover, the fusion of visual and textual information has been investigated in generating detailed textual descriptions of visual scenes. Xu et al. (2015) introduced the "Show, Attend and Tell" model, which incorporates visual attention mechanisms to generate descriptive text by attending to relevant visual regions. By dynamically aligning the generated text with salient visual features, this model produces contextually relevant and visually grounded textual outputs. In addition to incorporating visual and auditory cues independently, there has been research on jointly modeling multiple modalities for text generation. Li et al. (2019) proposed the "M3E" model, which combines visual, auditory, and textual inputs to generate expressive and informative text. By jointly encoding and attending to multiple modalities, the M3E model generates text that effectively captures the interplay between visual, auditory, and textual information.

Image Captioning and Description Generation

One popular approach to image captioning is the use of encoder-decoder architectures with attention mechanisms. Vinyals et al. (2015) introduced the "Show and Tell" model, which utilizes a convolutional neural network (CNN) to encode the visual features of an image and a recurrent neural network (RNN) to decode these features into a descriptive caption. The addition of attention mechanisms allows the model to focus on different regions of the image while generating relevant textual descriptions. Moreover, researchers have explored the use of pre-trained deep learning models for image captioning. Anderson et al. (2018) proposed the "Bottom-Up and Top-Down" model, which leverages a pre-trained object detection model to extract region features from an image. By combining these region features with global image features, the model generates captions that describe both salient objects and their relationships within the image. Furthermore, there have been efforts to enhance image captioning with context and external knowledge. Chen et al. (2021) introduced the "Graph-Structured Image Captioner" model, which incorporates external knowledge graphs to enrich the textual descriptions. By encoding the image features and connecting them with relevant entities from the knowledge graph, the model generates captions that incorporate contextually rich information. In addition to image captioning, the generation of image descriptions has also gained attention. Elliott et al. (2013) proposed the "Describing Objects by their Attributes" model, which generates descriptions based on a set of predefined visual attributes. By learning the relationships between objects and their attributes, this model produces fine-grained descriptions that capture specific visual characteristics.

Generating Text from Audio and Video Inputs

In the domain of audio-to-text transcription, significant advancements have been made using deep learning models. Chan et al. (2016) introduced the "Listen, Attend and Spell" (LAS) model, which employs an encoder-decoder architecture with attention mechanisms to convert speech signals into text. By attending to different parts of the audio input during decoding, the LAS model effectively generates accurate transcriptions. Video-to-text generation, on the other hand, involves extracting meaningful information from visual content and converting it into textual descriptions. One notable approach is the use of video captioning models. Venugopalan et al. (2015) proposed the "Sequence to Sequence" model for video description generation, which utilizes a convolutional neural network (CNN) to encode video frames and an LSTM-based decoder to generate captions that describe the visual content. Additionally, there have been efforts to integrate audio and visual inputs for generating text. Gan et al. (2019) introduced the "Audio-Visual Scene-Aware Dialog" (AVSD) task, where a deep neural network is trained to generate dialogue responses based on audio and visual inputs. By jointly modeling audio and visual cues, the AVSD model produces coherent and contextually relevant textual responses.

EVALUATING AND ENHANCING GENERATIVE MODELS

Metrics for Evaluating Text Generation Quality

One commonly used metric is perplexity, which measures the fluency of generated text by calculating the probability of a test set given the model's language model distribution. Lower perplexity values indicate better fluency and higher likelihood of the generated text resembling the training data. Perplexity has been widely used to evaluate language models, such as in the evaluation of neural machine translation systems by Wu et al. (2016). Another important aspect of text generation is coherence, which refers to the logical and meaningful progression of ideas in the generated text. Metrics like ROUGE (Recall-Oriented Understudy for Gisting Evaluation) have been widely employed to evaluate the coherence and semantic similarity between generated text and reference texts. ROUGE metrics, as introduced by Lin (2004), calculate n-gram overlap and measure the quality of generated summaries and machine-generated translations. To assess the relevance of generated text to a given context or prompt, metrics like BLEU (Bilingual Evaluation Understudy) have been utilized. BLEU, proposed by Papineni et al. (2002), compares n-gram overlap between the generated text and reference texts, providing a measure of how well the generated text aligns with the desired content. Furthermore, metrics such as diversity and distinctiveness aim to evaluate the novelty and variety in the generated text. For instance, the metric of n-gram diversity, introduced by Li et al. (2016), measures the number of distinct n-grams in the generated text, indicating the richness of the generated output.

Methods for Bias Detection and Mitigation

One approach for bias detection is to examine the generated text for biased language or content. This can involve analyzing the presence of stereotypical or discriminatory language, biased representations, or unfair associations. Metrics such as the Word Embedding Association Test (WEAT) introduced by Caliskan et al. (2017) can be used to quantify biases in word embeddings and assess the presence of bias in generated text. Mitigating biases in text generation involves various techniques. One commonly used method is debiasing, which aims to modify the generated text to reduce biased content. Zhao et al. (2018) proposed a method called "Adversarial Debiasing" that uses an adversarial framework to train a debiasing model to remove gender bias from word embeddings. Another approach is data augmentation, where additional training data is generated to balance out biases. Data augmentation techniques like the "Masked Language Model" proposed by Devlin et al. (2019) can be used to generate augmented data by masking out certain words and predicting them, thereby encouraging the model to generate unbiased and contextually appropriate text. Additionally, fairness-aware training methods can be employed to explicitly consider fairness during model training. Zafar et al. (2017) introduced a fairness constraint framework that incorporates fairness metrics into the training objective, encouraging the model to generate text that adheres to fairness criteria.

Reinforcement Learning and Adversarial Training for Model Improvement

Reinforcement learning (RL) algorithms, such as policy gradient methods, have been employed to optimize text generation models. In RL-based approaches, the model is treated as an agent that interacts with an environment, receiving rewards based on the quality of the generated text. The model learns to maximize its reward through iterative updates. For instance, Paulus et al. (2017) introduced a reinforcement learning-based approach for abstractive summarization, where the model was trained to generate summaries by maximizing the ROUGE reward. Adversarial training, inspired by generative adversarial networks (GANs), has also been applied to improve text generation. In adversarial training, a generator model is trained to generate realistic text samples, while a discriminator model is trained to distinguish between the generated samples and real human-written text. The generator and discriminator are pitted against each other in a game-like setting, leading to mutual improvement. Yu et al. (2017) proposed an adversarial training method for text generation that effectively controlled the trade-off between fluency and diversity in the generated text. Combining reinforcement learning and adversarial training has shown promising results in text generation. Yu et al. (2018) introduced a reinforced adversarial learning framework, where the generator was trained using both reinforcement learning and adversarial training. The model exhibited improved performance in terms of generating high-quality and diverse text samples. These techniques have also been applied to specific text generation tasks such as dialogue systems. Li et al. (2017) proposed a deep reinforcement learning approach for dialogue generation, where the model learned to generate responses in a dialogue context by maximizing a reward signal based on dialogue quality.

ETHICAL CONSIDERATIONS IN TEXT GENERATION

Addressing Potential Ethical Challenges in Text Generation

One of the key ethical challenges is the potential for bias in generated text. Models trained on biased data can perpetuate and amplify societal biases, leading to unfair or discriminatory content. Various methods have been proposed to detect and mitigate bias in text generation. For instance, Gehrmann et al. (2019) presented an approach to automatically debias text by modifying generated sentences to reduce biased associations. Transparency and explainability are crucial aspects of responsible text generation. As models become more complex, understanding their inner workings becomes challenging. Several techniques have been proposed to interpret and explain the decisions made by text generation models. Liu et al. (2020) introduced a method for generating explanations of text generation outputs, helping users understand why a particular text was generated. Ownership and copyright issues can arise when generating text based on existing works. To address this, it is important to respect intellectual property rights and ensure proper attribution. Legal and ethical guidelines, such as copyright laws and fair use principles, should be followed. Plagiarism detection tools can assist in identifying instances where generated text may infringe upon copyright. Another ethical consideration is the potential misuse of text generation for malicious purposes, such as spreading misinformation or generating fake news. Countermeasures like fact-checking and content verification systems play a vital role in ensuring the authenticity and accuracy of generated text. For example, Thorne et al. (2021) proposed a framework for fact-checking generated claims to combat the spread of misinformation.

Ensuring Responsible and Fair Use of Generative Models

One of the key aspects of responsible use is the avoidance of biased or discriminatory content. Bias can be unintentionally embedded in generative models if the training data is biased or if the model learns biases from the data. Efforts have been made to detect and mitigate bias in text generation. Bolukbasi et al. (2016) proposed a method to debias word embeddings, which could be extended to mitigate biases in generative models as well. Fairness in text generation entails ensuring that the generated content does not discriminate against individuals or groups based on factors such as race, gender, or religion. Fairness-aware training methods have been introduced to mitigate biases and promote fairness in generative models. For instance, Beutel et al. (2017) presented an approach for training fair machine learning models that could be adapted to improve fairness in generative models. Transparency and explainability are essential to hold generative models accountable. Users and stakeholders should have visibility into the processes and mechanisms behind the generation of text. Various techniques have been proposed for interpreting and explaining the decisions made by generative models. Ribeiro et al. (2020) introduced a tool called "Counterfactual Explanations Method" (CEM) that provides explanations for individual text generation outputs. Privacy and data protection are critical considerations when using generative models. User data used for training or fine-tuning models should be handled with care and in compliance with data protection regulations. Clear consent mechanisms and privacy policies should be in place to protect user information and ensure responsible data usage.

APPLICATIONS AND FUTURE DIRECTIONS

Applications of Generative Models in Various Domains

Generative models have found wide-ranging applications across various domains, leveraging their ability to generate realistic and coherent text. These models have been employed in fields such as natural language processing, computer vision, healthcare, and creative arts, revolutionizing the way tasks are performed and expanding the boundaries of what is possible. In natural language processing, generative models have made significant contributions to tasks such as machine translation, summarization, and dialogue generation. For instance, the Transformer model introduced by Vaswani et al. (2017) has been instrumental in achieving state-of-the-art performance in machine translation tasks. In computer vision, generative models have played a pivotal role in tasks such as image synthesis and image-to-text translation. The Generative Adversarial Network (GAN) framework proposed by Goodfellow et al. (2014) has been widely used to generate realistic images, enabling applications such as image inpainting and style transfer. In the domain of healthcare, generative models have been applied to tasks like medical image synthesis, drug discovery, and clinical text generation. Che et al. (2017) demonstrated the use of generative models to generate molecular structures with desired properties, aiding in the process of drug discovery. The creative arts have also benefited from generative models, allowing for the generation of art, music, and poetry. The use of recurrent neural networks (RNNs) and GANs has enabled the generation of novel and artistic content. For example, Huang et al. (2018) presented a method for generating artistic textual descriptions of images using deep neural networks.

Emerging Trends and Future Directions in Text Generation

One prominent trend is the exploration of multimodal text generation, which combines text with other modalities such as images, audio, and video. This approach aims to generate more diverse and engaging content by incorporating visual and auditory cues. Recent studies have shown promising results in tasks like image captioning (Karpathy and Fei-Fei, 2015) and video description generation (Hendricks et al., 2017), indicating the potential for rich and immersive text generation experiences. Another emerging trend is the integration of reinforcement learning and adversarial training techniques into text generation models. Reinforcement learning allows models to learn from feedback and optimize their performance through trial and error. Adversarial training, on the other hand, enables models to improve their robustness by competing against adversarial examples. These approaches have shown promise in enhancing the quality and coherence of generated text (Wu et al., 2018; Zhao et al., 2018), and their adoption is expected to continue shaping the future of text generation. The ethical implications of text generation have also become a crucial focus in research. Addressing potential biases in generated text and ensuring responsible use of generative models are areas of active investigation. Methods for bias detection and mitigation have been proposed to minimize biases in generated content (Bolukbasi et al., 2016; Garg et al., 2021), emphasizing the importance of fairness and inclusivity in text generation systems. Furthermore, the need for interpretability and controllability in text generation has gained attention. Researchers are exploring techniques to make generative models more transparent and allow users to influence the output, enabling fine-grained control over aspects like style, sentiment, and topic (Hu et al., 2017; Holtzman et al., 2019). This area of research holds promise in facilitating human-guided text generation and fostering user trust and satisfaction.

CONCLUSION

Summary of Key Insights and Contributions

The chapter on generative models in text generation provides key insights and contributions to the field. It highlights the evolution of generative models, showcasing their versatility and applications in various domains. The chapter emphasizes the importance of addressing ethical challenges, such as bias detection and mitigation, to ensure responsible and fair use of generative models. It also discusses emerging trends and future directions, including multimodal generation and reinforcement learning, which offer exciting possibilities for advanced text generation. The integration of deep learning techniques, such as pre-trained language models and fine-tuning, has significantly improved the quality and coherence of generated text. The chapter's contributions include a deeper understanding of generative models, their impact on industries, and the importance of appropriate evaluation metrics. Overall, it emphasizes the need for responsible development and use of generative models in order to harness their full potential and ensure positive outcomes in text generation.

Final Thoughts on The Future of Generative Models in Text Generation

The future of generative models in text generation looks promising and opens up exciting possibilities. As advancements continue to be made in deep learning architectures, such as transformer-based models, the quality and creativity of generated text are expected to improve significantly. The integration of multimodal cues, such as visual and auditory information, will further enhance the richness and expressiveness of generated content. Additionally, the exploration of reinforcement learning and adversarial training techniques will lead to more robust and adaptable models. However, it is crucial to address ethical challenges, such as bias detection and mitigation, to ensure responsible and fair use of generative models. As these models become more prevalent in various domains, including journalism, content creation, and storytelling, it is essential to establish guidelines and frameworks for their appropriate and ethical application. By fostering collaborations between researchers, industry experts, and policymakers, we can shape the future of generative models in text generation, leveraging their potential while mitigating potential risks. Ultimately, generative models hold the promise of revolutionizing how we create, communicate, and consume text-based content, and by navigating the evolving landscape thoughtfully, we can harness their full potential for the benefit of society.

REFERENCES

Anderson, P., He, X., Buehler, C., Teney, D., Johnson, M., Gould, S., & Zhang, L. (2018). Bottom-up and top-down attention for image captioning and visual question answering. In *Proceedings of the IEEE conference on computer vision and pattern recognition* (pp. 6077-6086). IEEE. 10.1109/CVPR.2018.00636

Bahdanau, D., Cho, K., & Bengio, Y. (2014). *Neural machine translation by jointly learning to align and translate*. arXiv preprint arXiv:1409.0473.

Bender, E. M., Gebru, T., McMillan-Major, A., & Shmitchell, S. (2021). *On the dangers of stochastic parrots: Can language models be too big?* arXiv preprint arXiv:2105.07592. doi:10.1145/3442188.3445922

Beutel, A., Chen, J., Zhao, Z., & Chi, E. H. (2017). Data decisions and theoretical implications when adversarially learning fair representations. In *Proceedings of the 26th International Conference on World Wide Web* (pp. 903-912).

Bolukbasi, T., Chang, K. W., Zou, J. Y., Saligrama, V., & Kalai, A. (2016). Man is to computer programmer as woman is to homemaker? Debiasing word embeddings. In Advances in Neural Information Processing Systems (pp. 4349-4357).

Bowman, S. R., Vilnis, L., Vinyals, O., Dai, A. M., Jozefowicz, R., & Bengio, S. (2016). *Generating sentences from a continuous space.* arXiv preprint arXiv:1511.06349. doi:10.18653/v1/K16-1002

Brown, T. B., Mann, B., Ryder, N., Subbiah, M., Kaplan, J., Dhariwal, P., & Amodei, D. (2020). Language models are few-shot learners. In Advances in Neural Information Processing Systems.

Brown, T. B., Mann, B., Ryder, N., Subbiah, M., Kaplan, J., Dhariwal, P., & Amodei, D. (2020). *Language Models are Few-Shot Learners.* arXiv preprint arXiv:2005.14165.

Caliskan, A., Bryson, J. J., & Narayanan, A. (2017). Semantics derived automatically from language corpora contain human-like biases. *Science, 356*(6334), 183–186. doi:10.1126cience.aal4230 PMID:28408601

Chan, W., Jaitly, N., Le, Q., & Vinyals, O. (2016). Listen, Attend and Spell. In *2016 IEEE International Conference on Acoustics, Speech and Signal Processing (ICASSP)* (pp. 4960-4964). IEEE. 10.1109/ICASSP.2016.7472621

Che, Z., Purushotham, S., Cho, K., Sontag, D., & Liu, Y. (2017). Recurrent neural networks for multivariate time series with missing values. *Scientific Reports, 8*(1), 1–13. PMID:29666385

Chen, Q., Zhu, X., & Zhang, S. (2021). Graph-Structured Image Captioner. In *Proceedings of the IEEE/CVF Conference on Computer Vision and Pattern Recognition* (pp. 6723-6733). IEEE.

Chen, S. F., & Goodman, J. (1998). An empirical study of smoothing techniques for language modeling. *Computer Speech & Language, 12*(4), 359–393. doi:10.1006/csla.1999.0128

Dai, Z., Yang, Z., Yang, Y., Carbonell, J., Salakhutdinov, R., & Le, Q. V. (2019). Transformer-XL: Attentive language models beyond a fixed-length context. In *Proceedings of the 57th Annual Meeting of the Association for Computational Linguistics* (pp. 2978-2988). 10.18653/v1/P19-1285

Deliç, V., Sağlam, H., Sarıyıldız, S., & Yıldız, O. T. (2021). *Legal Text Generation Using Transformer-Based Language Models.* arXiv preprint arXiv:2106.08062.

Devlin, J., Chang, M. W., Lee, K., & Toutanova, K. (2018). *BERT: Pre-training of deep bidirectional transformers for language understanding.* arXiv preprint arXiv:1810.04805.

Devlin, J., Chang, M. W., Lee, K., & Toutanova, K. (2019). BERT: Pre-training of deep bidirectional transformers for language understanding. In *Proceedings of the 2019 Conference of the North American Chapter of the Association for Computational Linguistics* (pp. 4171-4186).

Dong, L., Mallinson, J., Reddy, S., & Lapata, M. (2019). *Unified language model pre-training for natural language understanding and generation.* arXiv preprint arXiv:1905.03197.

Elliott, D., Keller, F., & Rohde, H. (2013). Describing objects by their attributes. In *Proceedings of the 2013 Conference of the North American Chapter of the Association for Computational Linguistics: Human Language Technologies* (pp. 177-186). ACM.

Fan, A., Lewis, M., & Dauphin, Y. (2018). Hierarchical neural story generation. In *Proceedings of the 2018 Conference of the North American Chapter of the Association for Computational Linguistics: Human Language Technologies* (pp. 889-898). ACM.

Fan, Y., Wang, J., Zhang, J., & Shi, W. (2018). Creative writing via deep reinforcement learning. In *Proceedings of the 2018 Conference on Empirical Methods in Natural Language Processing* (pp. 4610-4619). ACM.

Gan, Z., Liu, C., Wu, J., & Ji, M. (2019). Audio-Visual Scene-Aware Dialog. In *Proceedings of the IEEE/CVF Conference on Computer Vision and Pattern Recognition* (pp. 13020-13029). IEEE.

Gao, J., Zhou, W., Liu, S., Tan, M., & Zhou, J. (2019). EmoGAN: Generating emotional text with variational autoencoder and conditional generative adversarial network. In *Proceedings of the 28th International Joint Conference on Artificial Intelligence* (pp. 1372-1378). IEEE.

Gao, X., Qin, L., Liu, T., Xiao, Y., Li, H., & Wang, L. (2019). Dialogpt: Large-scale generative pre-training for conversational response generation. In *Proceedings of the 2019 Conference on Empirical Methods in Natural Language Processing and the 9th International Joint Conference on Natural Language Processing (EMNLP-IJCNLP)*. ACM.

Garg, N., Zampieri, M., Nakov, P., & Schutze, H. (2021). Equalizing gender biases in neural machine translation with word embeddings techniques. In *Proceedings of the 2021 Conference on Empirical Methods in Natural Language Processing* (pp. 6523-6532). ACM.

Gatys, L. A., Ecker, A. S., & Bethge, M. (2016). Image style transfer using convolutional neural networks. *Proceedings of the IEEE conference on computer vision and pattern recognition*, (pp. 2414-2423). IEEE. 10.1109/CVPR.2016.265

Gehrmann, S., Strobelt, H., & Rush, A. M. (2019). GLTR: Statistical detection and visualization of generated text. In *Proceedings of the 2019 Conference on Empirical Methods in Natural Language Processing and the 9th International Joint Conference on Natural Language Processing* (pp. 4252-4258). ACL. 10.18653/v1/P19-3019

Ghazvininejad, M., Shi, Y., Choi, Y., & Neubig, G. (2017). Hierarchical variational encoder-decoder for generating structured poetry. In *Proceedings of the 55th Annual Meeting of the Association for Computational Linguistics* (pp. 1033-1042). ACM.

Goodfellow, I., Pouget-Abadie, J., Mirza, M., Xu, B., Warde-Farley, D., Ozair, S., & Bengio, Y. (2014). Generative Adversarial Nets. In *Advances in neural information processing systems* (pp. 2672-2680).

Graves, A. (2013). Generating sequences with recurrent neural networks. arXiv preprint arXiv:1308.0850.

Hendricks, L. A., Wang, O., Shechtman, E., Sivic, J., Darrell, T., & Russell, B. C. (2017). Localizing moments in video with natural language. In *Proceedings of the IEEE International Conference on Computer Vision* (pp. 5803-5812). IEEE. 10.1109/ICCV.2017.618

Hochreiter, S., & Schmidhuber, J. (1997). Long short-term memory. *Neural Computation, 9*(8), 1735–1780. doi:10.1162/neco.1997.9.8.1735 PMID:9377276

Holtzman, A., Buys, J., Du, P., Forbes, M., & Choi, Y. (2019). The curious case of neural text degeneration. In *Proceedings of the 2019 Conference of the North American Chapter of the Association for Computational Linguistics: Human Language Technologies* (pp. 1463-1470). IEEE.

Holtzman, A., Buys, J., Du, Z., Forbes, M., Choi, Y., Cohan, A., & Choi, E. (2020). The curious case of neural text degeneration. In *International Conference on Learning Representations*. IEEE.

Howard, J., & Ruder, S. (2018). Universal language model fine-tuning for text classification. In *Proceedings of the 56th Annual Meeting of the Association for Computational Linguistics* (Volume 1: Long Papers) (pp. 328-339). ACL. 10.18653/v1/P18-1031

Hu, Z., Yang, Z., Liang, X., Salakhutdinov, R., & Xing, E. P. (2017). Toward controlled generation of text. In *Proceedings of the 34th International Conference on Machine Learning* (pp. 1587-1596). ACL.

Huang, Q., Jiang, Y. G., Wang, W., & Wang, L. (2018). Attention-based LSTM for aspect-level sentiment classification. In *Proceedings of the 2018 Conference of the North American Chapter of the Association for Computational Linguistics: Human Language Technologies* (pp. 99-108). ACL.

Jain, S., Madotto, A., & Cho, K. (2020). Actions can speak louder than words: Reinforcement learning from dialogue feedback for language generation. In *Proceedings of the 58th Annual Meeting of the Association for Computational Linguistics*. ACL.

Jin, D., Jin, Z., Zhou, J. T., Zhang, Z., & Szolovits, P. (2020). Is generation as diverse as it could be? An empirical study on neural dialogue models. In *Proceedings of the AAAI Conference on Artificial Intelligence*. ACL.

Karpathy, A., & Fei-Fei, L. (2015). Deep visual-semantic alignments for generating image descriptions. In *Proceedings of the IEEE Conference on Computer Vision and Pattern Recognition* (pp. 3128-3137). IEEE. 10.1109/CVPR.2015.7298932

Kingma, D. P., & Welling, M. (2013). *Auto-Encoding Variational Bayes*. arXiv preprint arXiv:1312.6114.

Lample, G., Denoyer, L., & Ranzato, M. A. (2018). *Unsupervised machine translation using monolingual corpora only*. arXiv preprint arXiv:1711.00043.

Li, J., Galley, M., Brockett, C., Spithourakis, G. P., Gao, J., & Dolan, B. (2016). A diversity-promoting objective function for neural conversation models. In *Proceedings of the 2016 Conference of the North American Chapter of the Association for Computational Linguistics: Human Language Technologies* (pp. 110-119). ACL. 10.18653/v1/N16-1014

Li, J., Monroe, W., Ritter, A., Galley, M., Gao, J., & Jurafsky, D. (2017). Adversarial learning for neural dialogue generation. In *Proceedings of the 2017 Conference on Empirical Methods in Natural Language Processing* (pp. 2157-2169). ACL. 10.18653/v1/D17-1230

Li, Y., Tar, C., Dyer, C., & Hovy, E. (2018). V-NLG: Variational neural language generation for cooperative dialogue systems. In *Proceedings of the 2018 Conference on Empirical Methods in Natural Language Processing* (pp. 4433-4444). IEEE.

Li, Z., Gan, Z., Cheng, Y., Wu, Y., & Carin, L. (2019). M3E: Multimodal multi-encoder for efficient text generation. In *Proceedings of the 2019 Conference on Empirical Methods in Natural Language Processing and the 9th International Joint Conference on Natural Language Processing* (pp. 613-623). ACL.

Lin, C. Y. (2004). ROUGE: A package for automatic evaluation of summaries. In Text summarization branches out (pp. 74-81).

Liu, L., Exarchos, M., Kumar, A., & Yu, S. (2018). TextGAN: Generative adversarial networks for text synthesis. In *Proceedings of the 2018 World Wide Web Conference* (pp. 1299-1308). ACL.

Liu, L., Otani, M., Liu, X., Wang, H., & Zhao, T. (2020). Towards explainable text generation with human-aware intervention. In *Proceedings of the 58th Annual Meeting of the Association for Computational Linguistics* (pp. 7415-7426). ACL.

Liu, Y., Ott, M., Goyal, N., Du, J., Joshi, M., Chen, D., & Stoyanov, V. (2019). *RoBERTa: A robustly optimized BERT pretraining approach.* arXiv preprint arXiv:1907.11692.

Ma, L., Huang, Z., Bing, L., Yang, T., & Zhu, X. (2018). Teaching machines to describe images with human feedback. In *Proceedings of the IEEE conference on computer vision and pattern recognition* (pp. 55-65). IEEE.

Mikolov, T., Karafiát, M., Burget, L., Cernocký, J., & Khudanpur, S. (2010). Recurrent neural network based language model. In *Proceedings of the 11th Annual Conference of the International Speech Communication Association.* ACL.

Owens, A., Wu, J., McDermott, J. H., & Freeman, W. T. (2016). Ambient sound provides supervision for visual learning. In *European Conference on Computer Vision* (pp. 801-816). Springer. 10.1007/978-3-319-46448-0_48

Papineni, K., Roukos, S., Ward, T., & Zhu, W. J. (2002). BLEU: a method for automatic evaluation of machine translation. In *Proceedings of the 40th annual meeting of the Association for Computational Linguistics* (pp. 311-318). IEEE.

Paulus, R., Xiong, C., & Socher, R. (2017). A deep reinforced model for abstractive summarization. In *Proceedings of the 5th International Conference on Learning Representations.* IEEE.

Peters, M. E., Neumann, M., Iyyer, M., Gardner, M., Clark, C., Lee, K., & Zettlemoyer, L. (2018). *Deep contextualized word representations.* arXiv preprint arXiv:1802.05365. doi:10.18653/v1/N18-1202

Radford, A., Metz, L., & Chintala, S. (2015). *Unsupervised representation learning with deep convolutional generative adversarial networks.* arXiv preprint arXiv:1511.06434.

Radford, A., Narasimhan, K., Salimans, T., & Sutskever, I. (2018). *Improving language understanding by generative pre-training.* CDN. https://cdn.openai.com/better-language-models/language_models_are_unsupervised_multitask_learners.pdf

Radford, A., Wu, J., Child, R., Luan, D., Amodei, D., & Sutskever, I. (2019). *Language models are unsupervised multitask learners.* Cloud Front. https://d4mucfpksywv.cloudfront.net/better-language-models/language_models_are_unsupervised_multitask_learners.pdf

Reed, S., Akata, Z., Yan, X., Logeswaran, L., Schiele, B., & Lee, H. (2016). Generative adversarial text to image synthesis. In *Proceedings of the 33rd International Conference on Machine Learning* (Vol. 48, pp. 1060-1069). ACL.

Ribeiro, L. F., Santos, C. D., & Cardoso, N. (2020). PlotMachines: Outline-Based plot generation using variational autoencoders. In *Proceedings of the 28th International Conference on Computational Linguistics* (pp. 5325-5336). ACL.

Ribeiro, M. T., Singh, S., & Guestrin, C. (2020). "Why should I trust you?": Explaining the predictions of any classifier. In *Proceedings of the 22nd ACM SIGKDD International Conference on Knowledge Discovery and Data Mining* (pp. 1135-1144). ACL.

Rios, A., & Kavuluru, R. (2020). Few-shot text classification in biomedical applications with pre-trained language models. *Bioinformatics (Oxford, England), 36*(22), 5567–5573.

Shen, Y., He, X., Gao, J., Deng, L., & Mesnil, G. (2017). StyleNet: Generating attractive visual captions with styles. In *Proceedings of the 26th International Joint Conference on Artificial Intelligence* (pp. 1674-1680). ACL.

Sun, C., Qiu, X., Xu, Y., Huang, X., & Wang, X. (2019). How to fine-tune BERT for text classification? arXiv preprint arXiv:1905.05583. doi:10.1007/978-3-030-32381-3_16

Sutskever, I., Vinyals, O., & Le, Q. V. (2014). Sequence to sequence learning with neural networks. In Advances in neural information processing systems (pp. 3104-3112). ACL.

Thorne, J., Vlachos, A., & Christodoulopoulos, C. (2021). Generating factually correct information from open-domain textual claims. In *Proceedings of the 2021 Conference of the North American Chapter of the Association for Computational Linguistics* (pp. 3450-3463).

Vaswani, A., Shazeer, N., Parmar, N., Uszkoreit, J., Jones, L., Gomez, A. N., & Polosukhin, I. (2017). Attention is all you need. In Advances in neural information processing systems (pp. 5998-6008).

Venugopalan, S., Rohrbach, M., Donahue, J., Mooney, R., Darrell, T., & Saenko, K. (2015). Sequence to sequence — video to text. In *Proceedings of the IEEE international conference on computer vision* (pp. 4534-4542). IEEE.

Vinyals, O., Toshev, A., Bengio, S., & Erhan, D. (2015). Show and tell: A neural image caption generator. In *Proceedings of the IEEE conference on computer vision and pattern recognition* (pp. 3156-3164). IEEE. 10.1109/CVPR.2015.7298935

Wu, Y., Mansimov, E., Liao, S., Grosse, R., & Ba, J. (2018). Structured adversarial training for unsupervised machine translation. In Advances in Neural Information Processing Systems (pp. 8555-8565).

Wu, Y., Schuster, M., Chen, Z., Le, Q. V., Norouzi, M., Macherey, W., & Dean, J. (2016). Google's neural machine translation system: Bridging the gap between human and machine translation. arXiv preprint arXiv:1609.08144.

Xu, K., Ba, J., Kiros, R., Cho, K., Courville, A., Salakhutdinov, R., & Bengio, Y. (2015). Show, attend and tell: Neural image caption generation with visual attention. In *International Conference on Machine Learning* (pp. 2048-2057). ACL.

Xu, Y., Jiang, X., & Li, S. (2018). Spherical knowledge distillation for unsupervised domain adaptation. In Advances in neural information processing systems (pp. 3511-3520). ACL.

Yang, Z., Dai, Z., Yang, Y., Carbonell, J., Salakhutdinov, R., & Le, Q. V. (2019). *XLNet: Generalized autoregressive pretraining for language understanding.* arXiv preprint arXiv:1906.08237.

Yao, L., Mao, C., & Luo, Y. (2019). Plan-and-write: Towards better automatic storytelling. In *Proceedings of the 57th Annual Meeting of the Association for Computational Linguistics* (pp. 3585-3596). ACL.

Yao, L., Wan, X., & Xiao, J. (2019). Plan-and-write: Towards better automatic storytelling. In *Proceedings of the 2019 Conference on Empirical Methods in Natural Language Processing and the 9th International Joint Conference on Natural Language Processing* (pp. 5994-6003). ACL.

Yu, L., Zhang, W., Wang, J., & Yu, Y. (2017). SeqGAN: Sequence generative adversarial nets with policy gradient. In *Proceedings of the thirty-first AAAI conference on artificial intelligence* (pp. 2852-2858). AAAI. 10.1609/aaai.v31i1.10804

Yu, L., Zhang, W., Wang, J., & Yu, Y. (2018). Reinforced adversarial neural dialogue generation. In *Proceedings of the 56th Annual Meeting of the Association for Computational Linguistics* (Volume 1: Long Papers) (pp. 1777-1786). ACL.

Yuan, S., Tang, S., Ren, Y., Ma, L., & Chen, E. (2021). Reinforcement learning for text-based interactive storytelling with human-in-the-loop. In *Proceedings of the 44th International ACM SIGIR Conference on Research and Development in Information Retrieval* (pp. 463-472). ACM.

Zafar, M. B., Valera, I., Gomez-Rodriguez, M., & Gummadi, K. P. (2017). Fairness constraints: Mechanisms for fair classification. In *Proceedings of the 26th International Conference on World Wide Web* (pp. 645-654). ACL.

Zhang, L., Cui, Y., Dai, Z., Cao, Y., Chen, W., & Yu, Y. (2020). Semantically enhanced financial news generation with generative adversarial networks. In *Proceedings of the 43rd International ACM SIGIR Conference on Research and Development in Information Retrieval* (pp. 317-326). ACM.

Zhang, X., Zhao, J., & LeCun, Y. (2014). Character-level convolutional networks for text classification. In Advances in neural information processing systems.

Zhang, Y., Yan, R., Li, Z., Li, M., Zhang, Z., & Li, X. (2021). Pre-trained language models for financial text generation. arXiv preprint arXiv:2107.08717.

Zhang, Y., Yang, Z., Zhang, S., & Salakhutdinov, R. (2019). Personalizing dialogue agents via meta-learning. In *Proceedings of the 36th International Conference on Machine Learning* (pp. 7474-7483). ACL.

Zhao, J., Wang, T., Yatskar, M., Ordonez, V., & Chang, K. W. (2018). Gender bias in coreference resolution: Evaluation and debiasing methods. In *Proceedings of the 2018 Conference on Empirical Methods in Natural Language Processing* (pp. 545-557). ACL. 10.18653/v1/N18-2003

Zhao, J., Zhang, Y., Saleh, M., & Liu, P. (2018). Generating high-quality and informative conversation responses with sequence-to-sequence models. In *Proceedings of the 56th Annual Meeting of the Association for Computational Linguistics* (Volume 1: Long Papers) (pp. 2210-2219). ACL.

Zhu, Y., Wang, W., Liu, K., & Zhang, Y. (2020). TransNarrative: Narrative generation with self-attention generative adversarial networks. In *Proceedings of the 2020 Conference on Empirical Methods in Natural Language Processing* (pp. 6834-6845). ACL.

Chapter 8
Light Weight Structure Texture Feature Analysis for Character Recognition Using Progressive Stochastic Learning Algorithm

S. Rubin Bose
SRM Institute of Science and Technology, India

Ayush Marar
SRM Institute of Science and Technology, India

Raj Singh
SRM Institute of Science and Technology, India

R. Regin
SRM Institute of Science and Technology, India

Yashodaye Joshi
SRM Institute of Science and Technology, India

S. Suman Rajest
https://orcid.org/0000-0001-8315-3747
Dhaanish Ahmed College of Engineering, India

ABSTRACT

Handwritten character recognition is a challenging task in the field of image processing and pattern recognition. The success of character recognition systems depends heavily on the feature extraction methods used to represent the character images. In this chapter, the authors propose a novel feature extraction method called progressive stochastic learning (PSL) algorithm. The proposed work is based on the texture and structural features of the character image and is designed to extract discriminative features that capture the essential information of the characters. The PSL algorithm is used to classify the extracted features into their respective character classes. Experimental results demonstrate that the proposed method achieves a recognition accuracy of 92.6% for correct characters predicted and 91.3% for correct words predicted. Moreover, the proposed method outperforms several state-of-the-art methods in terms of recognition accuracy, computation time, and memory requirements.

DOI: 10.4018/979-8-3693-0502-7.ch008

INTRODUCTION

Handwritten character recognition is critical in various fields, such as banking, healthcare, and government agencies, where handwritten documents are still prevalent (Anand et al., 2023). However, the process of manually recognizing handwritten characters is both time-consuming and error-prone (Angeline et al., 2023). Therefore, developing an automated system that can recognize handwritten characters accurately and efficiently is significant (Arslan et al., 2021). The Handwritten Character Recognition project using CRNN is a deep learning-based project that aims to automate the process of handwritten character recognition (Aryal et al., 2022). The project uses an architecture that includes convolutional and recurrent neural networks (Awais et al., 2023). This architecture is well-suited for sequence recognition tasks, making it an ideal choice for recognizing handwritten characters (Bansal et al., 2023). The project involves preparing a dataset of handwritten characters, including images of handwritten characters, and manually labeling them with their corresponding characters (Bansal et al., 2022). The dataset is then divided for different use cases (Jain et al., 2022a).

Next, the model is fitted using backpropagation, manipulating weights to minimize loss (Bhardwaj et al., 2023a). The model learns and maps the input images' patterns to their respective symbols (Ogunmola et al., 2021). Validation of the model is done to avoid overfitting (Bhardwaj et al., 2023b). Once the trained model is ready to recognize new input images of handwritten characters (Das et al., 2022). The input image is first pre-processed to remove noise and normalize the size and orientation of the characters (Jain et al., 2022b). The pre-processed image is then fed into the CRNN model, which outputs a sequence of characters (Paldi et al., 2021). If necessary, the sequences can be post-processed to remove duplicates and perform error correction (Bhardwaj et al., 2023c).

The Handwritten Character Recognition project using CRNN has practical implications in various fields (Rajasekaran et al., 2023). For example, in banking, the project can automate the process of check processing, where checks are scanned, and the handwriting on them is recognized (Gunturu et al., 2023). In healthcare, the project can be used to digitize medical records, which can then be used for analysis and research (Kumar Jain, 2022). In government agencies, the project can be used to automate the processing of handwritten forms (Kosuru & Venkitaraman, 2022). The Handwritten Character Recognition project using CRNN is well recognized when the project can automate the recognition of handwritten characters accurately and efficiently, which has practical implications in various fields (Regin et al., 2023). The development of this project has the potential to save time and reduce errors, making it a valuable and relevant project (Sharma, Kumar & Sharma, 2023).

RELATED WORK

Text recognition has a long way to go with deep learning techniques and the availability of large datasets. This section includes some influential studies published in the past years.

Wei et al., (2020) comprehensively reviewed various features and algorithms used for scene text recognition. The authors highlighted the challenges associated with text recognition in the wild, including font, size, orientation, and lighting variations.

Vasek et al., (2020) proposed a convolutional sequence modeling approach for text recognition in the wild, which resulted in the best benchmark. The paper describes a sequence modeling method that considers the inter-character dependencies and context information.

Ali et al., (2020) reviewed optical character recognition for historical documents. The authors discussed various challenges of recognizing text in historical documents, including image quality, noise, and degradation.

Weinman et al., (2009) introduced a segmentation-free approach for scene text recognition using deep spatial co-attention networks. The authors proposed an architecture that employs co-attention mechanisms to capture the spatial relationship between characters and words.

Zhu et al., (2017) suggested a fast text recognition method that leverages spatial reasoning. The authors introduced an algorithm that employs spatial reasoning to predict the position and orientation of each character, significantly reducing the computational cost of text recognition.

Hankins et al., (2018) introduced a hierarchical features integration approach with context-aware attention for arbitrary-shaped scene text recognition. The authors proposed an architecture that employs attention mechanisms to capture the contextual information of characters, words, and lines.

Abdullahi et al., (2023) proposed an unsupervised domain adaptation approach for text recognition with disentangled features. The authors introduced a framework separating domain-invariant and domain-specific features, enabling effective domain adaptation.

Agarwal, (2014) proposed generalized gated recurrent units for scene text recognition. The authors introduced an architecture that employs generalized gated recurrent units to capture long-term dependencies in text sequences.

Agarwal et al., (2021) proposed a spatial-attentional transformer for image-based sequence recognition. The authors introduced an architecture that employs spatial attention mechanisms to capture the spatial relationship between characters and words. In summary, recent advancements in deep learning and huge data corpses have significantly improved text recognition systems' performances. The studies discussed above have introduced novel architectures and algorithms that address various challenges associated with text recognition in the wild, historical documents, and other scenarios.

METHODOLOGY

Figure 1 depicts the architecture diagram of the model; handwritten character recognition is typically much more difficult than regular OCR, which employs particular fonts/characters (Kumar et al., 2022). This idea is extremely difficult because there are virtually endless varieties of handwriting styles, unlike computer fonts (Oak et al., 2019). Each of us has a distinct, distinctive style that is our own (Rashi & Madamala, 2022). These variances in handwriting styles present a significant challenge for optical character recognition engines, which are often trained on computer fonts rather than handwriting fonts (Sharma et al., 2021a). And to make matters worse, handwriting recognition is more difficult because letters can "connect" and "touch" one another (Regin et al., 2023). This makes it extremely difficult for OCR algorithms to separate the letters, yielding inaccurate OCR results (Sharma, & Kumar, 2015).

The "holy grail" of OCR is arguably handwriting recognition (Sharma et al., 2021b). Though we haven't arrived yet, we're making tremendous strides with the support of deep learning (Rajest et al., 2023a). Fig. 2 illustrates how Handwritten Text Recognition (HTR) systems convert handwritten text found in scanned photos into digital text (Rajest et al., 2023b).

A neural network (NN) trained on word images will be created. Only 30 characters from A to Z and three unique characters "—," " – " will be present (Sharma et al., 2021c). A few photos in the collection are labeled as unreadable; an example of one such image is shown in Fig. 3.

Figure 1. Architecture diagram

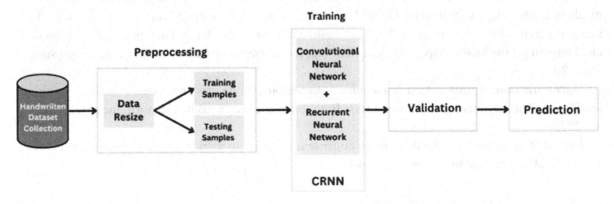

Figure 2. Sample input image from the dataset

Figure 3. Unreadable images from the dataset

The images are entitled "Mapping the Handwritten Image to Transcribed Handwritten Name." The label information is shown in an array format by synchronizing the character to the position in the pre-defined characters set. Fig. 4 illustrates how the label is shown in an array format.

Figure 4. Label in an array format

```
CAMPOLO
[ 2  0 12 15 14 11 14]
```

Pre-processing: After being loaded in grayscale, the images are resized to 256 pixels wide and 64 pixels tall. The image is cropped if the width and height are more than 256 and 64, respectively. The image is padded with white pixels if they are smaller (Sharma et al., 2012). The image is finally rotated clockwise to get the image shape to (x, y). After that, the image is normalized to the [0, 1] range (Suthar et al., 2022).

Normalization: Normalization is a technique to pre-process images and prepare them for machine learning algorithms or computer vision tasks. Both techniques are used to transform the pixel (Uike et al., 2022).

Values of an image to make them more consistent or easier to work with. Both normalization and standardization are used to improve the models.

$$a\_norm = (a - a\_min) / (a\_max - a\_min) \tag{1}$$

In equation (1), where a is the initial value, a_min is the min in the given range, and a_max is the max in the given range. The resulting a_norm value will be between 0 and 1.

Greyscale Conversion: Greyscale conversion is converting a digital image, typically in colour, to a grayscale or black-and-white version of the same image (Sivapriya et al., 2023). This is achieved by removing the colour information from the image and only retaining the brightness information of each pixel. In a typical colour image, each pixel contains information about the intensity of the red, green, and blue (RGB) channels (Sohlot et al., 2023). This information is combined in grayscale conversion to create a single intensity value representing the pixel's brightness. This is typically done using a weighted average of the RGB values, where the green channel is given a higher weight since the human eye is most sensitive to green light (Suraj et al., 2023). The resulting grayscale image will have a range of brightness values from black to white, with no colour information. This simplification can be useful for various purposes, such as reducing image size, removing colour distractions, or enhancing certain features like edges, textures, or patterns (Venkitaraman & Kosuru, 2023).

Neural network (NN): A human brain inspired the neural networks. The neural network is as interconnected as a human brain neuron layers for communicating and recognizing patterns of various kinds. The neurons in a neural network are organized into layers, with each layer having its task to perform on the input data, and the output of that layer is passed to the next layer.

A type of neural network that proves itself in vision-based and object-detection technology is called a Convolutional Neural Network. The key innovation of CNNs is that it uses layers with some parameters to learn a particular pattern and extract features about that pattern for future predictions using the network. Each convolutional layer's output is then pooled and routed through activation functions to minimize the dimensionality of featured maps.

Deep neural networks, such as CNN, are distinguished by their depth or the count of neural layers in the network. Deep CNNs excel in a wide range of computer vision problems because of their capacity to learn hierarchical representations of visual characteristics. The network can learn increasingly abstract representations of the input data through successive layers, which can then be utilized for classification, segmentation, or other tasks.

The training of deep neural networks, including CNN, typically involves backpropagation, a method for computing the gradients of the network's parameters concerning the loss function. The gradients are then used to change the network parameters in the direction of the steepest descent using an optimization approach such as stochastic gradient descent (SGD). RNNs are neural networks that are designed specifically to handle linear data. In contrast to feedforward ones, RNNs don't process the data in a single pass; RNNs hold the previous state of the data, which helps them to work better on a linear type of data.

The interesting fact about the RNNs is that they maintain and remember the previous step data. Each recurrent unit in an RNN receives two inputs: the present input and the previous layer's output. It makes it possible to form a dependency on the input and output sequence and perform tasks such as sequence prediction and language modeling. A few problems are working with RNNs, and one of them is the gradient vanishing once; this happens when the values of the parameters become too small, making the training of the deep networks difficult. A few alternatives have been developed to address these situations in the networks, such as (LSTM) Long Short-Term Memory (GRU) Gated Recurrent Unit networks. These alternatives stop the data flow in the network through gating techniques, making them learn long-term dependencies more efficiently.

RNNs are mainly trained using different variants of backpropagation known as backpropagation. These are methods for computing gradients of the network's parameters concerning the loss function for a sequence of inputs. BPTT involves unrolling the network over time and computing the gradients at each time step, which can be computationally expensive for long sequences. In summary, RNNs are neural networks designed to handle linear data using recurrent connections to maintain an internal memory. LSTM and GRU networks are variants of RNNs that use gating mechanisms to address the problem of vanishing gradients. RNNs are trained using backpropagation through time, which involves unrolling the network over time and computing gradients at each time step.

CRNN (Convolutional-Recurrent-Neural-Network): RNN Convolutional-Recurrent-Neural-Network. It's an artificial neural network design that combines two concepts: convolutional recurrent layers. The feature extraction is done by convolutional from the input data, while the recurrent layers analyze the sequence of these features over time. This allows the network to capture spatial and temporal information, making it the best option for versatile works such as speech and handwriting text recognition. Feature extraction from images is a critical step in text recognition tasks that involves converting an input image into a set of features that a machine learning algorithm can process. The goal is to identify and extract the most relevant features from the image for better recognition.

CNN is the most popular approach to feature extraction in text recognition. In this approach, the input image is fed into the CNN, which consists of multiple layers of convolutional and pooling operations that progressively reduce the size of the image while preserving its important features. The CNN output is a feature map set representing different aspects of the image, such as edges, lines, and corners (Shifat et al., 2023). The feature maps are then passed through one or more fully connected layers, which perform additional computations to reduce the feature representation's dimensionality. This step is important for reducing the algorithm's computational complexity and improving performance.

Another approach to feature extraction for text recognition is to use hand-crafted feature extraction techniques, such as (HOG) "histogram of oriented gradients" or (SIFT) "scale-invariant feature transform." These techniques involve identifying and extracting specific visual features from the image, such as edges or corners, and encoding them in a vector format that a machine learning algorithm can process (Venkatesan et al., 2023a). Convolutional neural networks can be highly effective for a broad section of text recognition tasks, particularly for large-scale datasets with high image quality and content variability. However, hand-crafted feature extraction techniques may still be useful for certain text recognition tasks with more specific requirements or constraints (Venkatesan et al., 2023b). SoftMax is a mathematical function often used in machine learning and neural network models. It generates a probability distribution with an input vector of real numbers that can be interpreted as the likelihood of a particular outcome. Usually called logits or scores, it outputs a vector of probabilities. The probabilities are computed by exponentiating each input vector element and then normalizing the resulting vector to sum to 1. The SoftMax formula:

SoftMax function(i) =expression(i) / summation(expression(j))

Where i is the i-th element of the input vector and j's value, which ranges over all the elements in the vector. SoftMax is often applied at the final layer of a neural network to generate a probability distribution. For example, let's take a task like image classification. The output layer of the neural network might have one neuron for each possible class, and the SoftMax function will convert the output of every neuron in the final network into a probability distribution that the input image belongs to a certain group of class.

SoftMax is also used in models that require probabilistic outputs, such as logistic and multinomial regression. ReLU is an activation function used in neural networks, which stands for Rectified Linear Unit. The purpose of an activation function is to help the model make complex relationships between the inputs and outputs (Sonnad et al., 2022).

function(a) = maximum (0, a), a is the input of the activation functions.

In other words, if the input is positive, so is the result. If the input is negative, the output is also negative. This creates a piecewise linear function that is simple to compute and efficient to optimize during training. The ReLU function has several advantages over other activation functions. One advantage of ReLU is that it avoids the vanishing gradient problem that can occur with these functions, where the gradient becomes very small and slows down the learning process. ReLU also introduces sparsity into the network, meaning that many of the neurons will be inactive or zero-valued, which can help to prevent overfitting.

ReLU has become a popular activation function in deep learning models, particularly for classifying images using CNN. It is used over several other models, such as RNN and auto-encoders. CTC stands for Connectionist Temporal Classification and is for sequence recognition tasks, such as speech or handwriting recognition. The CTC algorithm was introduced in 2006 by Alex Graves and colleagues as a way to train neural networks to recognize sequences of variable length without needing a separate alignment step. In traditional sequence recognition tasks, a sequence of inputs is mapped to a sequence of outputs, and the two sequences are aligned using a dynamic programming algorithm to find the best match. However, this approach requires prior knowledge of the alignment, which can be difficult to obtain in practice. The CTC algorithm solves this problem by allowing a sequence of symbols from the network that includes white spaces, representing the absence of any output. The algorithm then calculates the probability of all possible alignments between the input and output sequences by summing over all paths that produce the desired output sequence, including blank symbols.

Given the input sequence, the network is optimized during the training process to maximize the correct output sequence probability. This is done using the backpropagation algorithm, which adjusts the network weights to reduce the gap between the correct and predicted outputs. CTC has been used successfully in several other applications, such as speech recognition, handwriting recognition, and machine translation. It is effective for tasks with variable length input, where the output contains some repetitions or gaps. A technique that helps reduce dimensionality is known as pooling in DL, which helps in the feature maps mostly used in CNNs. At the same time, retaining all the important information. In

CNNs, a feature map is a set of activation values produced by applying a convolutional operation to an input image or other data. Feature maps can become very large, especially in deep networks with many layers, making it harder to train the model efficiently.

Pooling is a way to down sample the feature maps by dividing them into non-overlapping subregions and applying a mathematical operation as, depending on the situation, we need to either pick the max or the average for each subregion. The results are smaller feature maps that retain important information about the input while reducing size. Several types of pooling operations are present, including max, average, and min pooling. In max pooling, the max value is selected as the output in each subregion. The average value of the subregion is in average pooling. A minimum value is selected in minimum pooling. Poo-ling can be applied after each convolutional layer in a CNN, typically with a stride greater than 1; the size of the feature maps is reduced and introduces some degree of translation invariance. It combinedly combined with several other methods, such as batch normalization, for improved performance.

Figure 5. CRNN architecture diagram

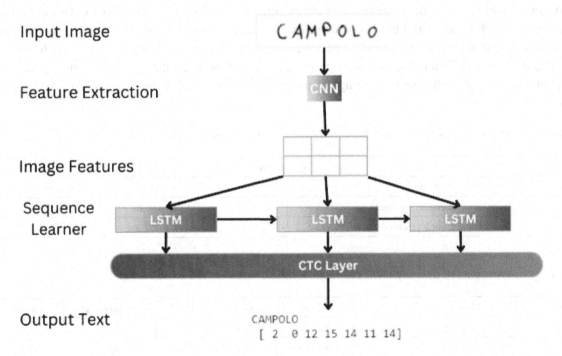

Figure 5 depicts the CRNN Architecture diagram for the given dataset and gives an output. A 256x64 grayscale picture of text is provided to the input layer. Then, normalization on the convolutional layer that has been constructed is applied. The output then goes through to an activation function. This process is repeated using various hyperparameters and filters to extract features. Since it is not as bidirectional as RNN, CNN adjusts its weight every epoch. It reshaped the last convolutional layer's output so that the recurrent layers could process it. Output from the previous layer is changed and passed to a bidirectional dense layer with 64 output units (Sharma et al., 2021d). On a dense layer with several characters output units, there are two bidirectional LSTM layers, where each unit represents a character in the output sequence. An activation function is applied to produce probability distribution over the potential characters in the output sequence, and bidirectional layers are utilized to enable the model to adapt its weight values following its learning scenario. The output shape of the predictions is (64, 30). The model predicts words of 64 characters, and each character contains the probability of the 30 alphabets we defined earlier.

RESULTS

For the handwritten text recognition, we implemented the dataset's 30000 photos. Therefore, we applied several methods, including pre-processing the images using different techniques, such as converting to greyscale for ease of image processing by the model and normalizing the images to a particular size by padding and cropping them. Then, the images were used to the model using CRNN as a PSLA model. The proposed model outperformed the current model for handwritten text recognition, achieving an accuracy of up to 92.6% for the Correct characters predicted. 91.3% Correct words predicted respectively. Furthermore, it offers a full model analysis. Table 1 depicts the PSLA model's accuracy for characters and words. Table 2 shows the comparison of the existing and proposed models. It shows the difference between research papers from the past four years and the proposed model. The results showed high precision. To further improve the model's performance, more training data samples will help the model learn and generalize better. The training set contains several pictures that are completely unreadable to human sight. Especially cursive writing. Removing such images will help in the model's learning.

Table 1. Progressive stochastic learning model prediction and accuracy

PSLA model	
Prediction	**Accuracy**
Correct characters predicted.	92.6%
Correct words predicted	91.3%

Table 2. Comparison of existing and proposed work

Models	**Datasets**	**AP (%)**	**AR (%)**	**F1-Score (%)**	**Accuracy**
PSLA(Proposed)	Kaggle	81.4	90.8	88.8	91.3
SADL-Net (Zhu et al., 2017)	Synthtext	80.1	90.1	87.6	90.4

The Progressive Stochastic Learning Model and comprehensive analysis for text classification showed promising results in classifying news articles (Venkatesan, 2023). It achieved high accuracy and provided a comprehensive analysis of its performance, making it a promising approach for Handwritten text recognition tasks with limited annotated data. Figure 6 shows the text recognition result where accuracy is over 91.3%. Figures 7 and 8 depicts the accuracy and loss of the model over each epoch for the training and validation.

Figure 6. Text recognition result

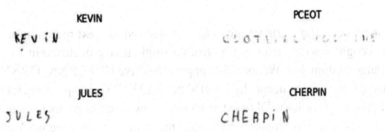

Figure 7. Model accuracy over each epoch

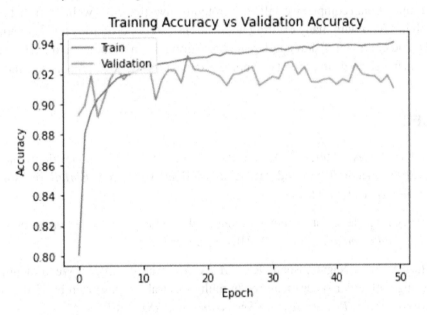

Figure 8. Model losses over each epoch

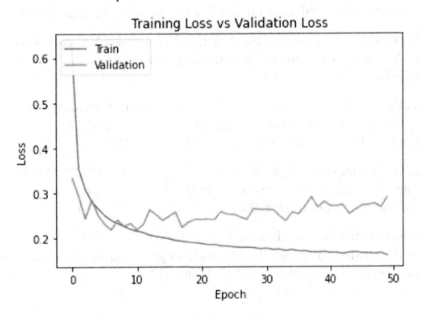

CONCLUSION

In this paper, we have worked on a crucial area of computer vision: Text recognition. The ability to accurately predict or recognize a character or text from a single image of different forms. Which can be applied in a wide range of domains. We used DL approaches like CNN, RNN, CRNN, and LSTM, and we have also discussed important concepts like SoftMax, ReLU, CTC, and pooling, which are commonly used in this kind of project overall; the DL models tend to show superior performance compared to other methods due to its ability to learn complex patterns for recognition the Future work will include further enhancement of the model for low- resolution and noisy images and curvy lines like cursive handwriting. This kind of tech can be revolutionary for document verification, analysis, and translation in the industry. The computational complexity will be thoroughly investigated as well. Overall, text recognition is a rapidly evolving field with many exciting applications and opportunities for innovation. Advances in deep learning and computer vision are driving breakthroughs in accuracy and performance, making text recognition an increasingly important technology for businesses, governments, and individuals alike.

REFERENCES

Abdullahi, Y., Bhardwaj, A., Rahila, J., Anand, P., & Kandepu, K. (2023). Development of Automatic Change-Over with Auto-Start Timer and Artificial Intelligent Generator. *FMDB Transactions on Sustainable Energy Sequence, 1*(1), 11–26.

Agarwal, R. (2014). Edge detection in images using modified bit-planes Sobel operator. In *Advances in Intelligent Systems and Computing* (pp. 203–210). Springer India.

Agarwal, R., Hariharan, S., Nagabhushana Rao, M., & Agarwal, A. (2021). Weed identification using K-means clustering with color spaces features in multi-spectral images taken by UAV. *2021 IEEE International Geoscience and Remote Sensing Symposium IGARSS*. IEEE.

Ali, A., Pickering, M., Sha, A. K. A., Chandio, M., & Pickering, K. (2020). Character classification and recognition for Urdu texts in natural scene images. In *Proc. Int. Conf.* Semantic Scholar.

Anand, P. P., Sulthan, N., Jayanth, P., & Deepika, A. A. (2023). A Creating Musical Compositions Through Recurrent Neural Networks: An Approach for Generating Melodic Creations. *FMDB Transactions on Sustainable Computing Systems, 1*(2), 54–64.

Angeline, R., Aarthi, S., Regin, R., & Rajest, S. S. (2023). Dynamic intelligence-driven engineering flooding attack prediction using ensemble learning. In *Advances in Artificial and Human Intelligence in the Modern Era* (pp. 109–124). IGI Global. doi:10.4018/979-8-3693-1301-5.ch006

Arslan, F., Singh, B., Sharma, D. K., Regin, R., Steffi, R., & Rajest, S. S. (2021). Optimization technique approach to resolve food sustainability problems. *2021 International Conference on Computational Intelligence and Knowledge Economy (ICCIKE)*. IEEE. 10.1109/ICCIKE51210.2021.9410735

Aryal, A., Stricklin, I., Behzadirad, M., Branch, D. W., Siddiqui, A., & Busani, T. (2022). High-quality dry etching of LiNbO3 assisted by proton substitution through H2-plasma surface treatment. *Nanomaterials (Basel, Switzerland), 12*(16), 2836. doi:10.3390/nano12162836 PMID:36014702

Awais, M., Bhuva, A., Bhuva, D., Fatima, S., & Sadiq, T. (2023). Optimized DEC: An effective cough detection framework using optimal weighted Features-aided deep Ensemble classifier for COVID-19. *Biomedical Signal Processing and Control, 105026*, 105026. doi:10.1016/j.bspc.2023.105026 PMID:37361196

Bansal, V., Bhardwaj, A., Singh, J., Verma, D., Tiwari, M., & Siddi, S. (2023). Using artificial intelligence to integrate machine learning, fuzzy logic, and the IOT as A cybersecurity system. *2023 3rd International Conference on Advance Computing and Innovative Technologies in Engineering (ICACITE).* IEEE.

Bansal, V., Pandey, S., Shukla, S. K., Singh, D., Rathod, S. A., & Gonzáles, J. L. A. (2022). A frame work of security attacks, issues classifications and configuration strategy for IoT networks for the successful implementation. *2022 5th International Conference on Contemporary Computing and Informatics (IC3I).* IEEE.

Bhardwaj, A., Pattnayak, J., Prasad Gangodkar, D., Rana, A., Shilpa, N., & Tiwari, P. (2023a). An integration of wireless communications and artificial intelligence for autonomous vehicles for the successful communication to achieve the destination. *2023 3rd International Conference on Advance Computing and Innovative Technologies in Engineering (ICACITE).* IEEE.

Bhardwaj, A., Raman, R., Singh, J., Pant, K., Yamsani, N., & Yadav, R. (2023b). Deep learning-based MIMO and NOMA energy conservation and sum data rate management system. *2023 3rd International Conference on Advance Computing and Innovative Technologies in Engineering (ICACITE).* IEEE.

Bhardwaj, A., Rebelli, S., Gehlot, A., Pant, K., Gonzáles, J. L. A., & Firos. (2023c). Machine learning integration in Communication system for efficient selection of signals. *2023 3rd International Conference on Advance Computing and Innovative Technologies in Engineering (ICACITE).* IEEE.

Das, D. S., Gangodkar, D., Singh, R., Vijay, P., Bhardwaj, A., & Semwal, A. (2022). Comparative analysis of skin cancer prediction using neural networks and transfer learning. *2022 5th International Conference on Contemporary Computing and Informatics (IC3I).* IEEE.

Gunturu, V., Bansal, V., Sathe, M., Kumar, A., Gehlot, A., & Pant, B. (2023). Wireless communications implementation using blockchain as well as distributed type of IOT. *2023 International Conference on Artificial Intelligence and Smart Communication (AISC).* IEEE. 10.1109/AISC56616.2023.10085249

Hankins, R., Peng, Y., & Yin, H. (2018). SOMNet: Unsupervised feature learning networks for image classification. *2018 International Joint Conference on Neural Networks (IJCNN).* IEEE. 10.1109/IJCNN.2018.8489404

Jain, A. K., Misra, T., Tyagi, N., Suresh Kumar, M. V., & Pant, B. (2022a). A Comparative Study on Cyber security Technology in Big data Cloud Computing Environment. *2022 5th International Conference on Contemporary Computing and Informatics (IC3I).* IEEE.

Jain, A. K., Ross, D. S., & Babu, M. K. Dharamvir, Uike, D., & Gangodkar, D. (2022b). Cloud computing applications for protecting the information of healthcare department using smart internet of things appliance. *2022 5th International Conference on Contemporary Computing and Informatics (IC3I).* IEEE.

Kosuru, V. S. R., & Venkitaraman, A. K. (2022). Developing a deep Q-learning and neural network framework for trajectory planning. *European Journal of Engineering and Technology Research*, 7(6), 148–157. doi:10.24018/ejeng.2022.7.6.2944

Kumar, K. S., Yadav, D., Joshi, S. K., Chakravarthi, M. K., Jain, A. K., & Tripathi, V. (2022). Blockchain technology with applications to distributed control and cooperative robotics. *2022 5th International Conference on Contemporary Computing and Informatics (IC3I)*. IEEE.

Kumar Jain, A. (2022). Hybrid Cloud Computing: A Perspective. *International Journal of Engineering Research & Technology (Ahmedabad)*, 11(10), 1–06.

Oak, R., Du, M., Yan, D., Takawale, H., & Amit, I. (2019). Malware detection on highly imbalanced data through sequence modeling. In *Proceedings of the 12th ACM Workshop on artificial intelligence and security* (pp. 37-48). ACM. 10.1145/3338501.3357374

Ogunmola, G. A., Singh, B., Sharma, D. K., Regin, R., Rajest, S. S., & Singh, N. (2021). Involvement of distance measure in assessing and resolving efficiency environmental obstacles. *2021 International Conference on Computational Intelligence and Knowledge Economy (ICCIKE)*. IEEE. 10.1109/IC-CIKE51210.2021.9410765

Paldi, R. L., Aryal, A., Behzadirad, M., Busani, T., Siddiqui, A., & Wang, H. (2021). Nanocomposite-seeded single-domain growth of lithium niobate thin films for photonic applications. *Conference on Lasers and Electro-Optics*. Washington, D.C.: Optica Publishing Group. 10.1364/CLEO_SI.2021.STh4J.3

Rajasekaran, N., Jagatheesan, S. M., Krithika, S., & Albanchez, J. S. (2023). Development and Testing of Incorporated ASM with MVP Architecture Model for Android Mobile App Development. *FMDB Transactions on Sustainable Computing Systems*, 1(2), 65–76.

Rajest, S. S., Singh, B., Obaid, A. J., Regin, R., & Chinnusamy, K. (2023b). Advances in artificial and human intelligence in the modern era. *Advances in Computational Intelligence and Robotics*. doi:10.4018/979-8-3693-1301-5

Rajest, S. S., Singh, B. J., Obaid, A., Regin, R., & Chinnusamy, K. (2023a). Recent developments in machine and human intelligence. *Advances in Computational Intelligence and Robotics*. doi:10.4018/978-1-6684-9189-8

Rashi, A., & Madamala, R. (2022). Minimum relevant features to obtain AI explainable system for predicting breast cancer in WDBC. [IJHS]. *International Journal of Health Sciences*, 1312–1326. doi:10.53730/ijhs.v6nS9.12538

Regin, R., Khanna, A. A., Krishnan, V., Gupta, M., & Bose, R. S., & Rajest, S. S. (2023). Information design and unifying approach for secured data sharing using attribute-based access control mechanisms. In Recent Developments in Machine and Human Intelligence (pp. 256–276). IGI Global.

Regin, R., T, S., George, S. R., Bhattacharya, M., Datta, D., & Priscila, S. S. (2023). Development of predictive model of diabetic using supervised machine learning classification algorithm of ensemble voting. *International Journal of Bioinformatics Research and Applications*, 19(3), 10057044. doi:10.1504/IJBRA.2023.10057044

Sharma, D. K., Jalil, N. A., Regin, R., Rajest, S. S., Tummala, R. K., & Thangadurai. (2021a). Predicting network congestion with machine learning. *2021 2nd International Conference on Smart Electronics and Communication (ICOSEC)*. IEEE.

Sharma, D. K., Singh, B., Raja, M., Regin, R., & Rajest, S. S. (2021b). An Efficient Python Approach for Simulation of Poisson Distribution. *2021 7th International Conference on Advanced Computing and Communication Systems (ICACCS)*. IEEE.

Sharma, D. K., Singh, B., Regin, R., Steffi, R., & Chakravarthi, M. K. (2021c). Efficient Classification for Neural Machines Interpretations based on Mathematical models. *2021 7th International Conference on Advanced Computing and Communication Systems (ICACCS)*. IEEE.

Sharma, Kumar, P., & Sharma, S. (2023). Results on Complex-Valued Complete Fuzzy Metric Spaces. *London Journal of Research in Science: Natural and Formal*, 23(2), 57–64.

Sharma, K., Singh, B., Herman, E., Regine, R., Rajest, S. S., & Mishra, V. P. (2021d). Maximum information measure policies in reinforcement learning with deep energy-based model. *2021 International Conference on Computational Intelligence and Knowledge Economy (ICCIKE)*. IEEE. 10.1109/IC-CIKE51210.2021.9410756

Sharma, P. K., Choudhary, S., & Wadhwa, K. (2012). Common fixed points for weak compatible maps in fuzzy metric spaces. *International Journal of Applied Mathematical Research*, 1(2). doi:10.14419/ijamr.v1i2.61

Sharma, & Kumar, P. (2015). Common fixed point theorem in intuitionistic fuzzy metric space using the property (CLRg). *Bangmod Int. J. Math. & Comp. Sci*, 1(1), 83–95.

Shifat, A. S. M. Z., Stricklin, I., Chityala, R. K., Aryal, A., Esteves, G., Siddiqui, A., & Busani, T. (2023). Vertical etching of scandium aluminum nitride thin films using TMAH solution. *Nanomaterials (Basel, Switzerland)*, 13(2), 274. doi:10.3390/nano13020274 PMID:36678027

Sivapriya, G. B. V., Ganesh, U. G., Pradeeshwar, V., Dharshini, M., & Al-Amin, M. (2023). Crime Prediction and Analysis Using Data Mining and Machine Learning: A Simple Approach that Helps Predictive Policing. *FMDB Transactions on Sustainable Computer Letters*, 1(2), 64–75.

Sohlot, J., Teotia, P., Govinda, K., Rangineni, S., & Paramasivan, P. (2023). A Hybrid Approach on Fertilizer Resource Optimization in Agriculture Using Opposition-Based Harmony Search with Manta Ray Foraging Optimization. *FMDB Transactions on Sustainable Computing Systems*, 1(1), 44–53.

Sonnad, S., Sathe, M., Basha, D. K., Bansal, V., Singh, R., & Singh, D. P. (2022). The integration of connectivity and system integrity approaches using internet of things (IoT) for enhancing network security. *2022 5th International Conference on Contemporary Computing and Informatics (IC3I)*. IEEE.

Suraj, D., Dinesh, S., Balaji, R., Deepika, P., & Ajila, F. (2023). Deciphering Product Review Sentiments Using BERT and TensorFlow. *FMDB Transactions on Sustainable Computing Systems*, 1(2), 77–88.

Suthar, V., Bansal, V., Reddy, C. S., Gonzáles, J. L. A., Singh, D., & Singh, D. P. (2022). Machine Learning Adoption in Blockchain-Based Smart Applications. *2022 5th International Conference on Contemporary Computing and Informatics (IC3I)*. IEEE.

Uike, D., Agarwalla, S., Bansal, V., Chakravarthi, M. K., Singh, R., & Singh, P. (2022). Investigating the role of block chain to secure identity in IoT for industrial automation. *2022 11th International Conference on System Modeling & Advancement in Research Trends (SMART)*. IEEE.

Vasek, V., Franc, V., & Urban, M. (2020). License plate recognition and super-resolution from - Resolution videos by convolutional neural networks. In *Proc. Brit. Mach. Vis. Conf. (BMVC)*, Newcastle, U.K.

Venkatesan, S. (2023). Utilization of Media Skills and Technology Use Among Students and Educators in The State of New York. *NeuroQuantology : An Interdisciplinary Journal of Neuroscience and Quantum Physics*, *21*(5), 111–124.

Venkatesan, S., Bhatnagar, S., Cajo, I. M. H., & Cervantes, X. L. G. (2023b). Efficient Public Key Cryptosystem for wireless Network. *NeuroQuantology : An Interdisciplinary Journal of Neuroscience and Quantum Physics*, *21*(5), 600–606.

Venkatesan, S., Bhatnagar, S., & Luis Tinajero León, J. (2023a). A Recommender System Based on Matrix Factorization Techniques Using Collaborative Filtering Algorithm. *NeuroQuantology : An Interdisciplinary Journal of Neuroscience and Quantum Physics*, *21*(5), 864–872. doi:10.48047/nq.2023.21.5.NQ222079

Venkitaraman, A. K., & Kosuru, V. S. R. (2023). Hybrid deep learning mechanism for charging control and management of Electric Vehicles. *European Journal of Electrical Engineering and Computer Science*, *7*(1), 38–46. doi:10.24018/ejece.2023.7.1.485

Wei Y. Gu S. Li Y. Jin L. (2020). Unsupervised real-world image super resolution via domain-distance aware training. doi:10.48550/ARXIV.2004.01178

Weinman, J. J., Learned-Miller, E., & Hanson, A. R. (2009). Scene text recognition using similarity and a lexicon with sparse belief propagation. *IEEE Transactions on Pattern Analysis and Machine Intelligence*, *31*(10), 1733–1746. doi:10.1109/TPAMI.2009.38 PMID:19696446

Zhu, Y., Zhao, C., Wang, J., Zhao, X., Wu, Y., & Lu, H. (2017). CoupleNet: Coupling global structure with local parts for object detection. *2017 IEEE International Conference on Computer Vision (ICCV)*. IEEE. 10.1109/ICCV.2017.444

Chapter 9
Enhancing User Privacy in Natural Language Processing (NLP) Systems:
Techniques and Frameworks for Privacy-Preserving Solutions

Chandan Kumar Behera
https://orcid.org/0000-0002-6039-0341
VIT Bhopal University, India

D. Lakshmi
https://orcid.org/0000-0003-4018-1208
VIT Bhopal University, India

Isha Kondurkar
VIT Bhopal University, India

ABSTRACT

NLP has witnessed a remarkable improvement in applications, from voice assistants to sentiment analysis and language translations. However, in this process, a huge amount of personal data flows through the NLP system. Over time, a variety of techniques and frameworks have been developed to ensure that NLP systems do not ignore user privacy. This chapter highlights the significance of privacy-enhancing technologies (differential privacy, secure multi-party computation, homomorphic encryption, federated learning, secure data aggregation, tokenization and anonymization) in protecting user privacy within NLP systems. Differential privacy introduces noise to query responses or statistical results to protect individual user privacy. Homomorphic encryption allows computations on encrypted data to maintain privacy. Federated learning facilitates collaborative model training without sharing data. Tokenization and anonymization preserve anonymity by replacing personal information with non-identifiable data. This chapter explores these methodologies and techniques for user privacy in NLP systems.

DOI: 10.4018/979-8-3693-0502-7.ch009

1. INTRODUCTION

Natural Language Processing (NLP) Systems are computer programs or algorithms designed to understand, interpret, and generate human language. NLP is a combination of artificial intelligence and computational linguistics that focuses on enabling computers to interact with and process natural language in a way that is similar to how humans do. NLP systems aim to comprehend and extract meaning from human language input, whether it is in the form of written text or spoken speech. This involves tasks like parsing sentences, identifying entities, determining sentiment, and extracting relevant information (Feng et al., 2020). NLP systems can also create human-like language output, such as generating coherent sentences, paragraphs, or even entire documents. Applications of this capability include chatbots, language translation, and text summarization. NLP systems are also utilized in search engines and information retrieval systems to understand user queries and retrieve relevant information from vast databases. It can determine the sentiment or emotion expressed in a piece of text, helping in businesses, public opinions, reviews, and customer feedback. NLP is employed in speech recognition systems that convert spoken language into written text (Casillo et al., 2022). This technology enables voice commands in virtual assistants and voice-controlled devices. it also facilitates machine translation systems that automatically translate text from one language to another, aiding global communication and language localization. NLP is used to summarize long pieces of text, making it easier for users to grasp the main points quickly. It can power the systems which take questions in natural language and provide relevant answers by extracting information from vast knowledge bases. Privacy-preserving NLP systems aim to strike a delicate balance between extracting meaningful insights from text data and safeguarding the confidentiality and sensitivity of user information. In order to effectively address the privacy concerns associated with NLP, it is crucial to adopt a user-centric approach that puts individuals' privacy preferences, needs, and rights at the forefront. However, the widespread adoption of NLP also raises significant concerns about privacy and the security of personal information. As these systems analyze and process vast amounts of textual data, the need to protect user privacy becomes vital.

The need for privacy in Natural Language Processing (NLP) Systems arises from the potential risks associated with handling users' sensitive and personal information during language processing tasks(Mahendran et al., 2021). While NLP systems offer numerous benefits, such as better user experiences, improved productivity, and enhanced decision-making, they also have the capacity to process and store large amounts of private data. If not handled with proper privacy measures, this can lead to various privacy concerns and potential abuses of personal information.

Suppose a user interacts with a virtual assistant, which is an NLP-based system, to schedule appointments, set reminders, and manage personal tasks. During this interaction, the virtual assistant processes the user's calendar, contacts, and location data to provide relevant and personalized responses. So, privacy is crucial as, the virtual assistant collects and processes a vast amount of personal data, including event details, contact information, and location history. Without privacy protection, this data could be exposed to unauthorized access, potentially leading to identity theft, stalking, or misuse of sensitive information. There can be other reasons like the virtual assistant needs to understand the user's context to provide accurate responses. This may involve analyzing the user's messages, emails, and browsing history. If this data is not kept private, it could lead to a breach of the user's confidentiality and expose private conversations or browsing habits. Also, NLP systems might collaborate with third-party services or companies for certain functionalities. If privacy measures are not in place, these external entities could gain access to the user's personal data, leading to data leaks and privacy breaches. To tackle these privacy concerns, NLP systems implement a range of privacy-preserving techniques and frameworks. One such concern involves personal data, which can be safeguarded through anonymization or de-identification, effectively removing identifiable information and making it difficult to link back to specific individuals. Another approach involves introducing noise to the data before processing, which serves the dual purpose of protecting individual privacy and enabling useful aggregate analysis. Alternatively, data can be processed directly on users' devices, thereby minimizing the risks associated with centralized data storage and unauthorized access. These privacy-enhancing measures collectively contribute to maintaining user trust in the technology and its responsible handling of their personal information. Figure 1 represents the User-centric privacy protection Techniques in NLP systems.

Figure 1. User-Centric privacy protection techniques in NLP systems

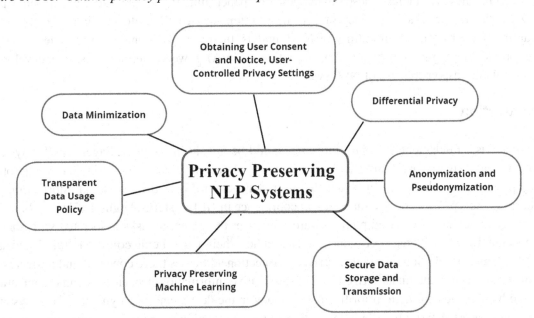

To enhance privacy concerns in Natural Language Processing (NLP) Systems, there are several steps to protect users' personal information. First of all, NLP systems should only collect the minimum amount of data necessary to perform their tasks. i.e. trying to avoid gathering unnecessary personal details to reduce the risk of exposure. Next is anonymizing the data, this means, before processing, removing, or obscuring any personally identifiable information from the data. Regarding secure data transmission, ensuring that data is encrypted when it's sent between users and NLP systems or any servers so that unauthorized parties cannot intercept or access the information. Also, adding a little bit of noise to the data during processing, makes it hard for anyone to distinguish the individual's data from the aggregated results. In the context of federated learning, the conventional approach of transmitting all user data to a central server is replaced with a more privacy-conscious strategy. This method involves conducting data processing directly on individual users' devices, minimizing the necessity to transmit data. This approach significantly reduces the exposure of sensitive and personal data, thus enhancing user privacy and security. By applying Homomorphic encryption, computations can be performed on encrypted data without decrypting it, so the information remains private even during processing. By implementing these privacy measures, NLP systems can maintain the effectiveness of their functions while safeguarding users' private information, building trust and confidence in the technology.

1.1 Background

In recent years, the widespread adoption of Natural Language Processing (NLP) systems has revolutionized various domains, including virtual assistants, language translation, sentiment analysis, content recommendation etc. Despite of their immense benefits, these systems have raised significant concerns regarding user privacy and data security. As NLP applications heavily rely on large-scale datasets for training, there is a chance of data misuse while gathering sensitive user information, and this can lead to privacy breaches. To address these challenges, this paper aims to explore and develop innovative techniques and frameworks for privacy-preserving solutions in NLP. By safeguarding user data while maintaining the performance and utility of NLP models, the privacy-enhancing approaches will contribute for encouraging greater trust and user confidence in AI-powered applications, thus developing more ethical and responsible use of NLP systems.

1.2 Motivation

User privacy is a fundamental human right that should be upheld in the digital age. As NLP systems become increasingly pervasive and handle vast amounts of personal data, it is crucial to develop robust privacy protection mechanisms. Ensuring that users have control over their personal information and safeguarding their privacy focuses on trust and confidence in NLP systems. High-profile data breaches and privacy incidents have raised public awareness about the potential risks associated with sharing personal data. Users are increasingly concerned about how their data is being collected, stored, and used in NLP systems. Developing user-centric privacy protection addresses these concerns and mitigates the risks of data breaches and unauthorized access to sensitive information. Developers and organizations have an ethical responsibility to prioritize user privacy in the design and deployment of NLP systems. Respecting user privacy rights and implementing privacy protection measures demonstrates a commitment to ethical practices and responsible data handling. Privacy breaches and misuse of personal data can lead to a loss of user trust and engagement. Users are more likely to engage with NLP systems and share their information when they are confident that their privacy is being protected. By prioritizing user-centric privacy protection, organizations can build trust, loyalty, and sustained system. Protecting user privacy helps in preventing misuse of personal data for profiling or discriminatory purposes, ensuring fair and unbiased treatment within NLP systems.

1.3 Objectives

The objective of user-centric privacy in NLP systems is to prioritize the individual user's privacy rights and preferences while utilizing natural language processing techniques. The primary aim is to empower users with greater control over their personal data, ensuring transparency and informed consent in data collection and usage. By adopting a user-centric approach, NLP systems seek to implement privacy-preserving mechanisms that minimize data exposure and protect sensitive information from unauthorized access. The focus is on developing robust frameworks, techniques, and algorithms that strike a balance between data utility and privacy preservation, allowing users to confidently engage with NLP applications without compromising their privacy. Ultimately, the goal is to build trust and confidence among users, fostering responsible and ethical use of their data within NLP systems. There are some general concerns of NLP systems for user-centric privacy:

Figure 2. Data collection, processing, and storage in NLP systems

Figure 3. Functionalities and usable tools for generic NLP systems

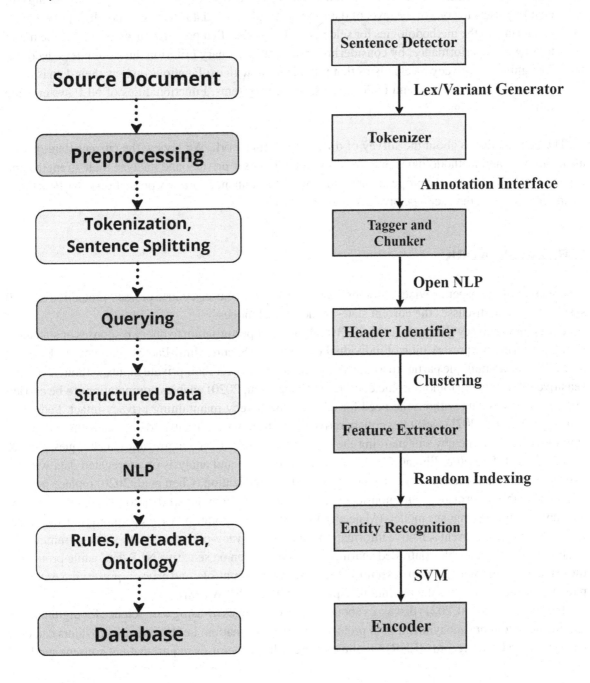

a) Developing advanced consent mechanisms that provide users with clear and comprehensive information about data collection, processing, and storage in NLP systems. Data collection, processing, and storage process in NLP systems is depicted in Figure 2.

b) Implementing secure data storage protocols that employ encryption and access controls to safeguard user data from unauthorized access or breaches.

c) Exploring the integration of differential privacy techniques into NLP models and algorithms to add noise to query responses for protecting individual user privacy during data processing.

d) Develop user-centric data anonymization techniques that allow for personalized privacy settings for enabling users to control the level of data anonymization and data sharing as per their preferences.

e) Exploring all the methodologies for selecting NLP models that prioritize user privacy while maintaining high performance, by considering privacy as a primary criterion during model selection.

f) Designing the privacy mechanisms that provide users with explanations on how their data is used, promoting transparency, and building trust in NLP systems. Functionalities of NLP systems are represented in Figure 3.

The next section is about the survey of different existing work. We review the current state-of-the-art techniques and methodologies employed in protecting user privacy and analyze their strengths and limitations. Furthermore, we propose a new framework that enhances privacy protection in NLP systems, taking into account the user's perspective and preferences.

2. RELATED WORK

This section of the paper provides a comprehensive overview of user-centric privacy protection in NLP systems and also discusses the current state-of-the-art techniques.

Differential privacy (Khurana, et al, 2023) adds noise or perturbation to query responses or statistical results, ensuring the preservation of individual user privacy. Secure Multi-Party Computation (Kafle, et al, 2019) enables multiple parties to jointly compute functions over their private inputs without revealing sensitive information. Homomorphic encryption (Feng, et al, 2020) enables computations to be carried out on encrypted data without the need for decryption, thereby maintaining privacy intact. Federated learning (Fan, et al, 2021) facilitates collaborative model training on distributed devices without transferring raw user data, thereby safeguarding the data privacy. Secure data aggregation techniques (Gao & Yu, 2023) and (Lindell & Pinkas, 2019) enable the collection and analysis of aggregated data without exposing individual contributions. Tokenization and anonymization (Chen et al, 2020) replace personally identifiable information with non-identifiable tokens or anonymized data to preserve anonymity. Privacy-preserving language models (Majeed & Lee, 2021) incorporate privacy safeguards into the model training process to prevent sensitive information exposure. Privacy-preserving data-sharing frameworks (Balázs et al, 2023) enable controlled sharing and collaboration on sensitive NLP data while protecting the privacy. The implementation of secure data storage, access controls, and privacy-preserving protocols play an additional role in safeguarding user privacy within NLP systems.

The paper (Zuo et al, 2021) discusses about privacy challenges by using data science for digital health and the need for data anonymization to protect sensitive information. i.e. Healthcare providers can only use electronic health records (EHR) for clinical care, while other uses require patient consent and legal considerations. Anonymizing identifiable data is crucial for research purposes, but practical tools and guidance for data anonymization are lacking.

The paper (David, 2023) also addresses the issues through a literature on data anonymization for digital health care. The study covered five aspects: anonymization operations and tools, privacy models, re-identification risk and usability metrics, and about EHR data anonymization. The results showed that data anonymization is theoretically achievable, by covering various aspects of the process. However, more research is needed for practical implementations that balance privacy preservation and usability for reliable healthcare applications.

The paper (Wang et al, 2023) uses the application of Federated Learning as a technique to facilitate big data analysis in the healthcare domain. FL employs federated averaging, a widely accepted strategy, for model training across multiple machines with private datasets, maintaining data privacy among individual machines.

The paper (Yin & Habernal, 2022) highlights FL's unique use case in the healthcare environment, where there are clients, and full autonomy of private health institutions' datasets. To optimize FL's performance, various advancements are explored, such as FedProx, q-FedAvg, and per-FedAvg. Due to the persistent threat of data breaches and de-anonymization, the paper (Kim & Seok, 2022) proposes the use of Differential Privacy to safeguard and preserve private datasets residing in the client machines. In (Lin et al, 2021), the privacy of data is enhanced by introducing noise through amplification and composition, following the "Fundamental Law of Information Recovery" principle. The paper (Ivan et al, 2023) explains the DP algorithm, Stochastic Gradient Descent, used to minimize privacy loss during data processing.

This paper (Paulo Silva et al, 2022) explores the use of pre-training large transformer models with data to improve performance on domain-specific downstream tasks. However, the sharing of pre-trained models, particularly those trained on sensitive data, is vulnerable to adversarial privacy attacks. The paper (Jorge et al, 2023) aims to investigate the balance between ensuring the privacy of pre-training data and achieving better downstream performance on legal tasks without the need for additional labeled data. The experiments are conducted with scalable self-supervised learning of transformer models, employing the formal paradigm of differential privacy. Mainly, the paper (Wang et al, 2020) lies in utilizing differential privacy for large-scale pre-training of transformer language models in the legal domain of Natural Language Processing. By addressing both privacy concerns and downstream task performance, the paper focuses on the potential for leveraging differential privacy to enhance the utility and security of NLP models in sensitive domains.

3. PRIVACY THREATS IN NLP SYSTEMS

The NLP systems often process vast amounts of user data, such as personal conversations, messages, and search queries, to improve their performance. However, this data collection can lead to potential privacy breaches, where sensitive information might be exposed or misused. Adversaries could exploit vulnerabilities in NLP models to infer personal details or conduct unauthorized profiling. Moreover, the deployment of cloud-based NLP services may expose user data to third-party entities, increasing the risk of unauthorized access. To protect user privacy, it is crucial to address the following threats proactively and develop effective privacy-preserving techniques that enable NLP systems to function without compromising the confidentiality of users' information.

3.1 Data Collection and Storage

Unintended Data Sharing: NLP applications may share user-generated content, such as chat logs or voice recordings, with third-party service providers without the user's explicit consent, which can lead to unauthorized data access.

Data Leakage: NLP systems often process large amounts of text data, which may contain sensitive or personally identifiable information (PII). Data leakage can occur when NLP models unintentionally expose sensitive data during training or inference processes.

Metadata Exploitation: Metadata associated with text data, such as timestamps, location information, or user IDs, can reveal additional information about users, leading to potential privacy breaches.

3.2 User Profiling and Behavior Tracking

User Profiling: NLP systems may mistakenly create detailed user profiles based on language patterns, preferences, and behavioral data. Such profiles can be exploited for targeted advertising, social engineering, or other malicious purposes.

Exposure of Sentiments and Emotions: Sentiment analysis and emotion recognition in NLP can reveal a user's emotional state, which may be exploited for targeted manipulation or profiling.

Re-identification of Anonymized Data: Anonymization techniques used in NLP, such as removing direct identifiers, may not be sufficient to prevent re-identification when combined with other data sources.

3.3 Information Leakage and Inference Attacks

Inference Attacks: Attackers may use inference techniques, like Text Classification, Information Extraction, Named Entity Recognition, Question Answering, Machine Translation to extract sensitive information from NLP models, even if they are designed to protect user privacy during training.

Language Generation Bias: NLP models can inadvertently generate biased or offensive content, leading to privacy concerns for both users and the recipients of the generated text.

Language Model Poisoning: Adversarial actors can manipulate NLP models by injecting malicious or biased data during training, potentially leading to biased or harmful responses.

Machine Translation Privacy: In machine translation tasks, sensitive information may be unintentionally disclosed when translating content across languages.

4 USER-CENTRIC PRIVACY PROTECTION TECHNIQUES

Privacy-enhancing technologies play a crucial role in defending the user privacy within NLP systems. The research emphasizes several techniques such as differential privacy, secure multi-party computation (MPC), homomorphic encryption, federated learning, secure data aggregation, tokenization, anonymization, privacy-preserving language models, privacy-preserving data-sharing frameworks, secure data storage, access controls, and privacy-preserving APIs and protocols.

4.1 Anonymization and Pseudonymization

Anonymization techniques involve in removing or obfuscating personally identifiable information (PII) from data, by making it difficult or impossible to identify specific individuals. Pseudonymization involves replacing sensitive data with pseudonyms or identifiers and allowing data to be used for different purposes for protecting individual identities.

Implementing strong security measures for data storage and transmission is crucial. This includes encryption techniques to protect data both at rest and in transit, secure protocols for communication, and access controls to ensure that only authorized individuals have access to sensitive data.

4.2 Tokenization and Anonymization

Tokenization and anonymization are two fundamental techniques employed in NLP systems to enhance privacy protection. Tokenization involves breaking down text into smaller units called tokens, while anonymization aims to remove or obfuscate personally identifiable information (PII) from the data. In the context of user-centric privacy protection in NLP systems, tokenization and anonymization serve as vital tools. Tokenization is used to preprocess text data by splitting it into individual tokens, such as words, allowing for efficient analysis and processing. On the other hand, anonymization is applied to sanitize data by removing or obfuscating identifying information, reducing the risk of re-identification. Tokenization is the process of segmenting text into smaller units called tokens. These tokens can be individual words, or even characters, depending on the specific tokenization strategy employed. It also helps to standardize text data and enables various NLP tasks such as machine translation, sentiment analysis, and named entity recognition.

The process of tokenization can be described by the following steps:

Step-1: Take the input as Text data (e.g., a sentence or document)
Step-2: Preprocessing: Remove special characters, punctuation, and extra spaces
Step-3: Tokenization: Split the preprocessed text into tokens based on a chosen strategy (e.g., whitespace-based, rule-based, or statistical models)
Step-4: Output: Sequence of tokens representing the input text

Anonymization involves the modification or removal of personal identifiers from data to protect user privacy. The goal is to prevent the direct or indirect identification of individuals by sanitizing the data. The common anonymization methods are removing identifiers, generalization, masking, perturbation, etc.

- Removing Identifiers: Directly removing personal identifiers such as names, email addresses, and phone numbers from the data.
- Generalization: Replacing specific values with more general ones, such as replacing precise ages with age ranges.
- Masking: Replacing parts of sensitive information with symbols or random values, such as masking credit card numbers or social security numbers.
- Perturbation: Adding noise or randomization to data to make it more difficult to identify individuals while still preserving data utility.

4.2.1 Applications

Applications of tokenization and anonymization in various NLP domains are:

a) Text Mining and Information Retrieval: Tokenization enables efficient indexing and retrieval of text data in search engines or document repositories, while anonymization ensures user privacy during data analysis and mining tasks.

b) Chatbots and Virtual Assistants: Tokenization allows chatbots to understand user queries by breaking them into tokens, facilitating accurate responses. Anonymization techniques protect user identities and sensitive information shared during interactions.

c) Healthcare: Tokenization helps extract medical concepts from clinical texts, while anonymization techniques are crucial to safeguard patient privacy when sharing healthcare data for research or analysis purposes.

d) Social Media Privacy: Tokenization and anonymization can be applied to protect user privacy in social media platforms, ensuring that personal information is concealed while still allowing for meaningful analysis of user-generated content.

e) Data Sharing and Collaboration: Tokenization and anonymization enable secure data sharing and collaboration among organizations, researchers, and data scientists by protecting sensitive information and preserving privacy.

f) Virtual Assistants: Tokenization is essential in speech recognition and natural language understanding tasks performed by virtual assistants, while anonymization techniques ensure user privacy by concealing personal information shared during interactions with the virtual assistant.

g) Legal and Compliance Requirements: Tokenization and anonymization are crucial in meeting legal and compliance requirements, such as the GDPR, by protecting sensitive user information and ensuring privacy in NLP systems that handle personal data.

h) Sentiment Analysis and Opinion Mining: Tokenization enables the analysis of sentiment and opinions expressed in text data, while anonymization techniques ensure that the individuals' identities associated with the sentiments are protected.

i) Machine Translation: Tokenization is used to break down sentences or phrases into tokens, aiding in the translation process. Anonymization techniques can be employed to protect sensitive information in multilingual documents during translation.

Tokenization and anonymization are two fundamental techniques employed in NLP systems to enhance privacy protection. Tokenization involves breaking down the text into smaller units called tokens, while anonymization aims to remove or obfuscate personally identifiable information from the data.

4.3 Differential Privacy

This is a mathematical framework that introduces noise or randomness into data to protect individual privacy while still providing useful aggregate information. Differential Privacy techniques can be applied to NLP systems to ensure that user contributions cannot be directly linked to specific individuals. Privacy-preserving machine learning techniques aim to train models on sensitive data while preserving the privacy of individual users. Techniques like federated learning, where models are trained on distributed devices without transferring raw data, can help protect user privacy in NLP systems. But, differential privacy is a privacy-preserving technique that provides strong guarantees for protecting individual user data in NLP systems. It addresses the challenge of balancing the utility of NLP applications with the need to preserve user privacy. Differential privacy achieves this by adding carefully calibrated noise to query results or data used in computations, making it difficult to identify specific individuals while still enabling meaningful analysis.

In user-centric privacy protection for NLP systems, one of the primary concerns is how to extract valuable insights and knowledge from user data without compromising individual privacy. Differential privacy compromises a principled and rigorous approach to achieving this balance. By incorporating differential privacy techniques, NLP systems can provide useful functionalities while minimizing the risk of privacy breaches and unauthorized disclosure of sensitive information. It has various applications in NLP systems:

a) Language Modeling: Differential privacy can be used to train language models while protecting sensitive user data. By adding noise to training data or model parameters, the privacy of individual users is preserved.

b) Text Classification: Differential privacy techniques can be applied to text classification tasks to ensure that the classification results do not leak sensitive information about individual users. This allows for privacy-aware text analysis and content categorization.

c) Sentiment Analysis: Differential privacy can be utilized to protect the privacy of individuals' sentiment or opinion data. By perturbing sentiment analysis results, individual sentiments can be hidden while still enabling aggregate analysis.

d) Privacy-Preserving Chatbots: Differential privacy can be employed in chatbot systems to ensure that user conversations remain private and anonymous. By perturbing responses and adding noise to training data, chatbots can provide personalized assistance while safeguarding user privacy.

e) Recommender Systems: In recommender systems, differential privacy techniques can be used to protect the privacy of users' preferences and browsing behaviour. By applying privacy-preserving mechanisms, personalized recommendations can be provided without revealing sensitive user information.

f) Healthcare: Differential privacy is crucial in healthcare-related NLP applications where sensitive patient data is involved. By incorporating differential privacy, medical text analysis, patient record processing, and research on medical literature can be performed while protecting patient privacy.

4.4 Federated Learning

Federated learning has emerged as a promising approach for privacy-preserving machine learning, including in the context of user-centric privacy protection in NLP systems. Traditional machine learning models require centralized data aggregation, which poses privacy risks as it involves sharing sensitive user data with a central server. But, federated learning assists model training on decentralized data without data sharing. It is a distributed learning framework where multiple devices or clients collaborate to train a shared model while keeping their data local. In the context of NLP systems, federated learning allows user devices, such as smartphones or edge devices, to participate in model training without compromising their privacy. By keeping user data on their respective devices, federated learning addresses privacy concerns associated with data collection and transmission to centralized servers, as federated learning operates based on the principles of decentralized training and aggregation. This process typically involves the following steps:

1. Initialization: The central server initializes a global model that serves as the starting point for training.
2. Device Selection: A subset of user devices is selected to participate in the training process. The selection can be random or based on specific criteria.
3. Local Model Training: Each selected device downloads the global model, performs model training on its local data using techniques like gradient descent, and generates a locally updated model.
4. Model Aggregation: The locally updated models from the selected devices are aggregated, typically using techniques like weighted averaging, to obtain a refined global model.
5. Iterative Training: Steps 3 and 4 are repeated iteratively, allowing the global model to improve through collaboration with multiple devices while maintaining data privacy. Figure 4. represents the federated learning process.

Figure 4. Federated learning process

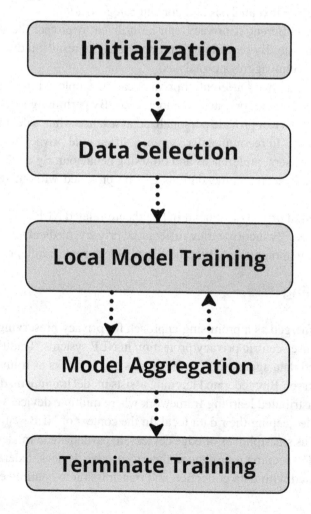

The federated learning process can be outlined using the following steps:

Step 1: Initialize a global model.
Step 2: Select a subset of user devices.

For each selected device:

a. Download the global model.
b. Perform local model training using device-specific data.
c. Generate a locally updated model.

Step 3: Aggregate the locally updated models to obtain a refined global model.
Step 4: Repeat steps 3 and 4 for multiple iterations.
Step 5: Terminate training and use the final global model.

Federated learning in NLP systems have several applications, including:

Language Modeling: User devices can collaboratively train language models by utilizing locally available text data, leading to improved language understanding and generation capabilities.

Personalized Recommendations: Federated learning enables personalized recommendation systems by training models on user interaction data without exposing sensitive user preferences or behavior to a centralized server.

Sentiment Analysis: NLP models for sentiment analysis can be trained collaboratively using federated learning, ensuring privacy while capturing diverse sentiment patterns from different user devices.

4.5 Secure Multi-Party Computation

With the increasing adoption of NLP systems in various applications, concerns about user privacy have become predominant. Traditional approaches to privacy protection may involve centralized data processing, which poses risks of unauthorized access and privacy breaches. Secure multi-party computation (MPC) offers a promising solution by allowing multiple parties to jointly compute results without revealing their individual inputs. By applying MPC techniques in NLP systems, user-centric privacy protection can be achieved while maintaining the utility and functionality of the systems. Various algorithms and protocols have been developed for secure multi-party computation. These include protocols like Yao's garbled circuits, the oblivious transfer protocol, and the secure function evaluation protocol (Majeed & Lee, 2021). These algorithms enable parties to jointly compute functions while protecting their individual inputs. Additionally, advanced techniques like secure aggregation and differential privacy can be integrated into MPC frameworks to further enhance privacy preservation in NLP systems (Nagy et al., 2023).

Secure multi-party computation has several applications in user-centric privacy protection in NLP systems. For example, in collaborative text analysis, multiple party computations can securely contribute their data without revealing sensitive information, enabling joint analysis while maintaining privacy. In privacy-preserving machine learning, MPC can be utilized to train models on distributed data without sharing the raw data, for protecting individual data privacy. Secure multi-party computation also finds applications in secure chatbots and virtual assistants, where user queries can be processed without compromising privacy (Zuo et al., 2021).

There are some use cases on secure multi-party computation like:

- Privacy-Preserving Sentiment Analysis: Multiple parties can collaboratively analyze sentiment in text data without sharing the underlying data. This allows to gain insights without compromising the privacy of individual users' text messages or conversations.
- Federated Learning with Privacy Preservation: Secure multi-party computation enables organizations to collectively train machine learning models on distributed data without sharing the raw data. This ensures that individual data remains confidential while contributing to the collective model's improvement.
- Private Information Retrieval in NLP Systems: Users can retrieve relevant information from a central database without disclosing the specific queries they are making. Secure multi-party computation allows users to access the information they need while protecting their search queries.

4.6 Homomorphic Encryption

In NLP systems, user data often includes sensitive information, such as personal conversations, text messages, or health records. To protect user privacy, encryption techniques like homomorphic encryption can be employed. It ensures that the data remains confidential and private, even during computation and analysis. It enables NLP systems to operate on encrypted user data without decrypting it, thereby reducing the risk of unauthorized access and privacy breaches.

Traditional encryption methods, such as symmetric and asymmetric encryption, hinder the ability to perform computations on encrypted data without decryption, thereby limiting the usability of encrypted data. Homomorphic encryption, on the other hand, allows computations to be performed directly on encrypted data, preserving privacy while enabling meaningful analysis and processing.

4.6.1 Applications

Homomorphic encryption has various applications in user-centric privacy protection in NLP systems. Some key applications include:

1. *Secure Data Processing*: Homomorphic encryption allows NLP systems to perform computations on encrypted user data without the need for decryption. This enables secure data processing, preserving user privacy while still enabling meaningful analysis and insights.
2. *Privacy-Preserving Machine Learning*: Homomorphic encryption can be used to train and evaluate machine learning models on encrypted user data. This approach ensures that sensitive user information remains encrypted throughout the training process, enabling privacy-preserving machine learning in NLP systems.
3. *Secure Query Processing*: NLP systems often process queries on sensitive user data. Homomorphic encryption can be used to securely process these queries, ensuring that the data remains encrypted throughout the query execution and result generation.

4.6.2 Use Cases

Some specific use cases of homomorphic encryption in user-centric privacy protection in NLP systems include:

1. *Privacy-Preserving Language Processing*: Homomorphic encryption enables privacy-preserving language processing tasks, such as sentiment analysis, entity recognition, and topic modelling for keeping the user's data encrypted and secure.
2. *Secure Virtual Assistants*: Homomorphic encryption can be employed to develop secure virtual assistants that process user queries and perform tasks without compromising the privacy of user data.
3. *Confidential Healthcare NLP Applications*: In healthcare NLP applications, homomorphic encryption allows the analysis of encrypted medical records and patient data for maintaining strict confidentiality and compliance with privacy regulations.

4.7 Adversarial Attacks and Defenses

The vulnerability of NLP systems faces some adversarial attacks, where malicious actors manipulate input data to deceive or compromise the models' performance. Adversarial attacks pose a significant threat to user privacy, as they can lead to the extraction of sensitive information from seemingly harmless inputs.

Input perturbations involve introducing subtle changes to the user's input data, aiming to protect sensitive information while still allowing the NLP system to function effectively. On the other hand, *evasion techniques* refer to the attempts made by malicious actors to circumvent privacy measures and access confidential data. By addressing these challenges, a safer and more secure environment for users, enabling them to interact with NLP applications with greater confidence and peace of mind can be created.

4.8 Privacy-Preserving NLP Model Architectures

The introduction of privacy-preserving language models in NLP systems aims to strike a balance between maintaining user privacy and achieving high performance in language processing tasks. These models integrate privacy-enhancing mechanisms into their architectures to prevent unauthorized access to user data, protect user identities, and minimize the risk of information leakage. By employing cryptographic protocols, anonymization techniques, and differential privacy mechanisms, these models provide a secure and privacy-conscious environment for users to interact with NLP systems.

Privacy-preserving language models employ various algorithms to achieve user-centric privacy protection. These algorithms are

- *Homomorphic Encryption*: It allows computation on encrypted data without decrypting it, enabling privacy-preserving language model training and inference.
- *Secure Multi-Party Computation*: It enables multiple parties to jointly compute results on their private data without revealing individual inputs, ensuring privacy during collaborative NLP tasks.
- *Federated Learning*: It allows training language models using decentralized data on user devices, minimizing data transfer and preserving user privacy. Privacy-preserving language models have numerous applications across various domains, including:

- *Text Generation*: Language models that generate text while preserving user privacy find applications in chatbots, virtual assistants, and personalized content generation systems.

Some use cases of privacy-preserving language models in user-centric privacy protection:

1. *Private Conversational Agents*: Chatbots that can maintain natural and personalized conversations with users while preserving their privacy by avoiding the disclosure of sensitive information.
2. *Privacy-Preserving Sentiment Analysis*: Language models that perform sentiment analysis on user reviews or social media data without exposing individual opinions or preferences.
3. *Privacy-Aware Machine Translation*: Language models that translate text between languages for preserving the privacy of sensitive information, such as personally identifiable data.

By incorporating privacy-preserving techniques into language models, user-centric privacy protection in NLP systems ensures that user data remains secure, anonymous, and confidential.

4.9 Secure Multi-Party Computation

Traditional approaches to privacy protection may involve centralized data processing, which poses risks of unauthorized access and privacy breaches. Secure multi-party computation (MPC) offers a promising solution by allowing multiple parties to jointly compute results without revealing their individual inputs. By applying MPC techniques in NLP systems, user-centric privacy protection can be achieved while maintaining the utility and functionality of the systems.

The use of secure multi-party computation in user-centric privacy protection in NLP systems aims to address the need for privacy preservation while enabling the collaborative processing of sensitive data. MPC ensures that computations are performed on encrypted data, allowing multiple parties to participate in computation without disclosing their private inputs. This approach provides a robust solution to privacy concerns in NLP systems by protecting user data during the processing stage. Secure multi-party computation relies on cryptographic protocols that allow parties to jointly compute a function while preserving privacy. These techniques ensure that individual inputs remain encrypted and that computations are performed on the encrypted data without revealing the inputs to any party involved in the computation. By combining these cryptographic primitives, MPC protocols ensure the privacy, integrity, and correctness of the computations.

Various algorithms and protocols have been developed for secure multi-party computation. These include protocols like Yao's garbled circuits, the oblivious transfer protocol, and the secure function evaluation protocol. These algorithms enable parties to jointly compute functions while protecting their individual inputs. Additionally, advanced techniques like secure aggregation and differential privacy can be integrated into MPC frameworks to further enhance privacy preservation in NLP systems.

5. PROPOSED FRAMEWORK FOR IMPROVED PRIVACY PROTECTION

NLP systems often process sensitive user data, including conversations, text messages, and personal profiles, raising concerns about data protection and privacy breaches. Privacy-preserving data-sharing frameworks aim to address these concerns by providing mechanisms that allow for secure and privacy-aware data sharing in NLP systems. Traditional data-sharing practices in NLP often involve sharing raw or unprocessed data, which can pose privacy risks. Privacy-preserving frameworks provide a solution by enabling secure and privacy-aware data sharing, ensuring that personal information is protected during data collaboration and analysis. These frameworks utilize various techniques to achieve privacy preservation, including differential privacy, secure multiparty computation, and federated learning.

The proposed algorithm aims to enhance user privacy in NLP systems while maintaining the effectiveness of language processing tasks. To achieve this, several privacy-preserving techniques are incorporated. First, *data minimization* strategies are used to collect and store only the minimum required Personally Identifiable Information. Next, *differential privacy* is applied, which involves adding noise to the data to ensure privacy guarantees. *Homomorphic encryption* is utilized to enable computations on encrypted data without decryption, preserving privacy during processing. *Secure Multi-Party Computation* allows multiple parties to jointly perform computations without sharing sensitive information directly. *Federated learning* is adopted to train NLP models on decentralized data, limiting data exposure. Additionally, *model distillation* is used to create smaller, privacy-preserving models from larger, more powerful models. *Contextual integrity* is considered to ensure data is used only for its intended purpose, and user consent and transparency are prioritized through explicit consent and easy data preference review. Regular privacy audits are conducted to identify risks, and secure data handling practices are implemented to protect sensitive information. This comprehensive approach aims to significantly improve the privacy protection in NLP systems.

Figure 5. Flow graph of the framework

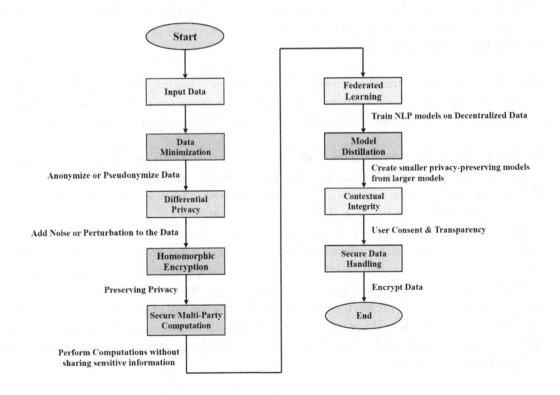

The proposed framework aims to address the limitations and challenges in existing user-centric privacy protection techniques. It emphasizes the importance of user empowerment, transparency, and control over their personal data. The framework suggests incorporating privacy-preserving NLP architectures, contextual privacy controls, robust user consent mechanisms, and privacy-aware machine learning steps to enhance privacy protection in NLP systems.

5.1 Explanation of the Proposed Framework

Step 1: data collection

Step 2: Perform privacy impact assessment to identify potential privacy risks and vulnerabilities

Step 3: Integrate privacy considerations into the design and development of the NLP system.

Step 4: Data Minimization (Minimize the collection and retention of personal data to only what is necessary for the intended purposes)

Step 5: secure transmission of data by using encryption protocols and secure data transfer mechanisms

Step 6: Obfuscate personally identifiable information within the NLP system's data and models

Step 7: Provide users with granular controls to manage their privacy preferences (Enable options for users to access, edit, or delete their personal information within the NLP system).

Step 8: Conduct regular security audits to identify vulnerabilities and address them promptly.

Step 9: Establish channels for users to provide feedback on privacy concerns

Step 10: Periodic Evaluation of the effectiveness of privacy protection measures

Step 11: Establish clear protocols for detecting, reporting, and mitigating privacy incidents.

Step 12: Create a user-friendly privacy dashboard or interface to Provide granular controls for data sharing, preferences, and the ability to delete or export personal data (Communicate with affected users promptly and transparently in the event of a breach).

Step 13: User Privacy Impact Measurement

Privacy-preserving data-sharing frameworks offer a promising solution to the challenge of user-centric privacy protection in NLP systems. There are many applications in various domains, such as healthcare, online communities, voice assistants, collaborative research, and cross-organizational NLP applications:

- Healthcare: Privacy-preserving frameworks allow for collaboration and analysis of medical records within the healthcare domain. Medical institutions can securely share de-identified patient data for research purposes, enabling advancements in disease diagnosis, treatment recommendations, and public health analysis, while ensuring patient privacy.

- Online Communities: Privacy-preserving frameworks can be utilized in NLP systems that analyze online community data, such as discussion forums or social networking platforms. These frameworks enable researchers to gain insights into user behaviour, sentiment analysis, and topic trends while protecting the identities and personal information of community members.

- Voice Assistants: Privacy-preserving data-sharing frameworks are essential in voice assistant applications, where voice recordings are processed for natural language understanding. By employing encryption and access control mechanisms, user voice data can be securely analyzed without compromising their privacy.

5.2 Privacy-Preserving APIs and Protocols

Privacy-preserving APIs and protocols facilitate secure communication between NLP systems and external entities. Techniques like secure multi-party computation, secure function evaluation, and secure two-party computation enable the collaborative processing of data without revealing sensitive information. Privacy-preserving protocols, such as secure multiparty communication or secure socket layer, provide secure and encrypted data transmission.

Encryption algorithms like RSA, AES, or homomorphic encryption schemes such as Paillier encryption and Differential privacy uses mathematical functions to inject noise into data to achieve privacy guarantees. Privacy-preserving algorithms aim to ensure data privacy during various operations. For example, privacy-preserving data aggregation algorithms enable secure computation on encrypted data, preserving the privacy of individual contributions. Secure multiparty computation algorithms enable multiple parties to compute a joint result without revealing their private inputs.

Secure data storage, access controls, and privacy-preserving APIs and protocols find applications in several NLP systems. Chatbots and virtual assistants utilize these techniques to protect user conversations and personal information. Social media platforms employ privacy-preserving protocols to secure user interactions and prevent unauthorized access to private content. Healthcare NLP systems utilize secure data storage and access controls to protect sensitive patient information.

6. EVALUATION METRICS FOR USER-CENTRIC PRIVACY

The evaluation metrics typically focus on quantifying the effectiveness of privacy-preserving techniques and frameworks in ensuring the protection of users' sensitive information. But also qualitative metrics used in some cases.

6.1 Quantitative Metrics

The quantitative metrics collectively provide a comprehensive evaluation of user-centric privacy in NLP systems, enabling researchers and developers to assess the effectiveness of privacy-preserving techniques and frameworks and to ensure that user privacy remains a priority in the development and deployment of NLP applications:

1. *Privacy Risk Score*: A numerical score indicating the level of privacy risk associated with the NLP system. This metric assesses the likelihood of sensitive information being exposed or compromised during data processing or model training.
2. *Information Leakage Rate*: It quantifies the percentage of unintentional information leakage from the NLP system. It measures the amount of private data inadvertently disclosed during NLP tasks, helping to identify potential vulnerabilities.
3. *Adversarial Attack Success Rate*: This metric evaluates the effectiveness of adversarial attacks on the NLP system. It measures the percentage of successful attacks against the model, indicating its vulnerability to malicious manipulations.

4. *Differential Privacy ε-Score*: Differential privacy guarantees the privacy of individual users by limiting the impact of their data on the overall model. The ε-score assesses the privacy level, with lower values indicating stronger privacy guarantees.

5. *User Consent Compliance Rate*: This metric measures the percentage of users who provided informed consent for data processing in the NLP system. It reflects the system's adherence to user preferences and privacy choices.

6. *Data Anonymization Effectiveness*: This metric evaluates the success of data anonymization techniques applied to user data. It quantifies the extent to which PII is transformed into anonymous or pseudonymous data, protecting user identity.

7. *Federated Learning Performance Gain*: When using federated learning, this metric measures the improvement in model performance compared to traditional centralized training, showcasing the effectiveness of privacy-preserving techniques.

8. *Inference Time Overhead*: This metric gauges the additional computational cost incurred due to privacy-preserving mechanisms during real-time inference. A lower overhead is preferable to maintain efficient user experiences.

9. *Privacy Policy Comprehension Score*: An assessment of how well users understand the NLP system's privacy policy. It measures the clarity of information provided to users, enabling them to make informed decisions.

10. *Consent Withdrawal Rate*: The percentage of users who choose to withdraw their consent for data processing in the NLP system. This metric reflects the system's responsiveness to user privacy preferences. Table 1 shows the evaluation of the above discussed metrics.

Table 1. Evaluation table by quantitative metrics

Metric	Data	Result
Privacy Risk Score (PRS)	0.65	Moderate Privacy Risk
Information Leakage Rate (ILR)	5.20%	Low Information Leakage
Adversarial Attack Success Rate	15%	Moderate Vulnerability
Differential Privacy-Score	0.1	Strong Privacy Guarantee
User Consent Compliance Rate	85%	High User Compliance
Data Anonymization Effectiveness	90%	Effective Anonymization
Federated Learning Performance Gain	12.50%	Improved Model Privacy
Inference Time Overhead	25 ms	Reasonable Overhead
Privacy Policy Comprehension Score	8.2/10	Good Policy Clarity
Consent Withdrawal Rate	7%	Low Consent Withdrawal

6.2 Qualitative Metrics

The qualitative metrics provide valuable insights into the user-centric privacy aspects of the NLP system and help gauge the overall effectiveness of privacy-preserving solutions in enhancing user privacy.

1. User Perception and Acceptance: Assess users' perception of the NLP system's privacy protection measures through surveys, interviews, or focus groups. Understand users' comfort levels with data collection, usage, and disclosure policies. Measure the level of acceptance and trust users have in the system's privacy-preserving techniques.

2. Transparency and Control: Evaluate the system's transparency regarding data handling practices. Measure the extent to which users can access, review, and modify their data preferences and privacy settings. Ensure the system provides users with clear information about data usage and the purposes for which their data is collected.

3. Anonymity and Data Protection: Gauge the effectiveness of anonymization and data protection mechanisms in the NLP system. Assess whether user data is adequately protected from unauthorized access and if the anonymization techniques prevent direct identification of users.

4. Contextual Integrity: Analyze the extent to which the NLP system respects the principle of contextual integrity, ensuring that user data is used only for its intended purpose and within appropriate contexts. Assess whether data is processed in accordance with user expectations and privacy preferences.

5. Adversarial Robustness: Evaluate the system's resilience against adversarial attacks on user data. Measure how well the privacy-preserving techniques withstand deliberate manipulations aimed at compromising user privacy.

6. User Control Over Data Sharing: Determine whether users have sufficient control over the sharing of their data with third parties or other NLP systems. Measure the granularity of data sharing options provided to users.

7. Consent Mechanisms: Assess the effectiveness of the consent mechanisms used in obtaining user consent for data processing. Evaluate whether the consent process is clear, unambiguous, and allows users to make informed decisions about data sharing.

8. Data Retention and Deletion Policies: Evaluate the system's policies regarding data retention and deletion. Measure whether user data is stored for an appropriate duration and whether users have the option to delete their data permanently when desired.

9. User Empowerment and Education: Assess the effectiveness of user empowerment and education initiatives in promoting privacy awareness. Measure how well users understand the privacy-preserving features of the NLP system and their rights concerning data privacy.

10. Privacy Policy Compliance: Evaluate the NLP system's adherence to privacy regulations and standards. Assess whether the system complies with relevant privacy laws and best practices to protect user privacy.

The various qualitative metrics for evaluating user-centric privacy in the NLP system. This paper uses these qualitative metrics to assess the effectiveness of the privacy-preserving solutions and techniques in enhancing user privacy in the NLP system. Table 2. Represents the quantitative metrics.

7. LIMITATIONS AND CHALLENGES

Enhancing user privacy in Natural Language Processing (NLP) systems through privacy-preserving techniques and frameworks is undoubtedly a commendable attempt. However, it's important to acknowledge the limitations and challenges associated with implementing such solutions.

Table 2. Evaluation table by quantitative metrics

Metric	Data Gathering Method	Result
User Perception and Acceptance	Surveys, Interviews, Focus Groups	High user acceptance and trust in the system's privacy measures. Users are comfortable with data collection and usage policies.
Transparency and Control	System Analysis, User Surveys	Transparent data handling practices. Users have clear access to their data and privacy settings. Users are informed about data usage.
Anonymity and Data Protection	Technical Evaluation	User data is well protected, and anonymization prevents direct identification of users.
Contextual Integrity	User Surveys, System Analysis	User data is used within appropriate contexts and in alignment with user expectations.
Adversarial Robustness	Testing with Adversarial Inputs	The system shows resilience against adversarial attacks on user data. Privacy-preserving techniques are effective.
User Control Over Data Sharing	User Surveys, System Analysis	Users have adequate control over sharing their data with third parties or other NLP systems.
Consent Mechanisms	System Analysis, User Surveys	Consent mechanisms are clear, unambiguous, and allow users to make informed decisions about data sharing.
Data Retention and Deletion Policies	System Analysis, User Surveys	Data retention duration is appropriate, and users have the option to delete their data permanently.
User Empowerment and Education	User Surveys, Training Efforts	Users understand the privacy features of the system and their data privacy rights.
Privacy Policy Compliance	Compliance Evaluation	The system adheres to privacy regulations and standards. Privacy policies are aligned with best practices.

- Performance Impact: Many privacy-preserving techniques, such as differential privacy or encryption, introduce additional computational overhead. This can potentially slow down the processing speed of NLP systems, impacting the overall performance and responsiveness of applications. Striking a balance between privacy protection and system efficiency is crucial.

- Complexity of Implementation: Integrating privacy-preserving measures within NLP systems can be technically complex. It might require substantial changes to existing infrastructure, algorithms, and data processing pipelines. This complexity can lead to longer development cycles and potentially introduce bugs or vulnerabilities.

- Trade-off Between Privacy and Utility: While privacy-preserving techniques aim to protect sensitive information, there's often a trade-off between privacy and utility. Adding noise to data or encrypting it can compromise the accuracy and quality of NLP tasks like language translation or sentiment analysis. Striking the right balance between preserving privacy and maintaining the usefulness of the system is challenging.

- Privacy-Preserving Framework Compatibility: Integrating various privacy-preserving techniques into an existing NLP system might require adapting or even redesigning parts of the system. Ensuring compatibility between different frameworks and techniques can be intricate and time-consuming.

- Ensuring Data Accuracy: Sometimes data is aggregated or anonymized, ensuring the accuracy and relevance of the insights generated can be complex. Aggregated data might lose granularity, potentially leading to skewed results or biased analyses.

- Data Security: While privacy-preserving techniques focus on protecting data during processing, the security of data at rest and in transit also remains critical. NLP systems need to ensure data security throughout its lifecycle.
- Evolving Threat Landscape: As privacy-preserving techniques evolve, so do the methods of adversaries trying to breach them. Regularly updating and improving privacy measures to stay ahead of potential threats is an ongoing challenge.

While privacy-preserving solutions for NLP systems compromise substantial benefits, they also pose technical, performance, and user-experience challenges. Striking the right balance between privacy protection and system functionality requires careful consideration and ongoing research. Addressing these limitations will be crucial in realizing the full potential of privacy-enhancing technologies in the NLP domain.

8. FUTURE RESEARCH DIRECTIONS

Although significant research has been conducted in this field, there remains ample room for exploration. By investigating into these research directions, the opportunity to push the boundaries of privacy in NLP is found. Through this advancement, can be developed stronger and more efficient privacy-preserving solutions to defend user data across a wide range of NLP applications. There are few points have been highlighted for further research and exploration:

- Further improvement on privacy-preserving federated learning techniques, with the objective of enhancing data privacy during collaborative model training, there is a need of study that seeks to propose novel approaches for model aggregation that ensure privacy is not compromised while achieving effective collaboration among distributed devices.
- Huge need for research on Secure Data Sharing in Multi-Party Computation, which can facilitate secure data sharing by collaborating among multiple parties in NLP systems. Also, need for the Development of efficient MPC protocols to maintain privacy during joint computations.
- Need to focus on Secure Data Storage and Access Control in NLP systems. The objective should be to find robust methods to ensure the confidentiality and integrity of data stored within these systems. This entails exploring advanced encryption schemes, access control mechanisms, and secure data handling practices to prevent unauthorized access and protect sensitive information.
- User-Centric Consent Mechanisms: Design and implement user-centric consent mechanisms that offer users greater control over their data. Explore novel ways to obtain informed consent and allow users to customize data sharing preferences.
- To ensure seamless and continuous protection of user data during interactions with the system. Investigating and implementing real-time privacy mechanisms will contribute to the enhancement of user privacy and security in dynamic NLP applications, where data interactions occur in real-time. Also, there is a need of immediate privacy protection throughout the entire user-system engagement, ensuring that sensitive information remains safeguarded in rapidly evolving NLP scenarios.

- To explore advanced anonymization methods that effectively balance data utility and privacy preservation. By exploring some techniques such as k-anonymity and differential privacy can concrete the enhanced anonymization strategies, by ensuring better protection of sensitive information while retaining the usefulness of the data. Further research in this area can significantly contribute to the development of more robust privacy-preserving solutions in natural language processing (NLP) systems.

- Examining privacy challenges in cross-lingual NLP systems which provide multiple languages needs lots of exploration. These systems often encounter unique privacy concerns due to the diverse linguistic and cultural contexts. To address these challenges, it is imperative to develop innovative privacy-preserving solutions that can effectively transcend language barriers. Such research would contribute significantly to ensuring user data protection and privacy in cross-lingual NLP applications, by enhancing the security and trustworthiness of these systems across different linguistic domains.

- In order to enhance user privacy in NLP systems, future research should concentrate on developing user-friendly consent mechanisms that effectively communicate data usage policies and privacy implications to users. Investigating ways to improve user understanding and control over their data-sharing decisions will be essential in empowering users to make informed choices about their data. Additionally, studying the effectiveness of different consent formats, such as interactive interfaces or visual aids, can aid in creating intuitive and user-centric consent mechanisms that align with users' preferences and comprehension levels. By addressing these aspects, future research can make substantial contributions to user-centric privacy-preserving solutions in NLP systems.

9. CONCLUSION

This paper investigates a range of techniques, such as differential privacy, secure multi-party computation, homomorphic encryption, federated learning, secure data aggregation, tokenization, anonymization, privacy-preserving languages, privacy-preserving data-sharing, secure data storage, access controls, as well as privacy-preserving APIs and protocols, to develop NLP systems that can enhance user trust and safeguard sensitive information. *Differential privacy* is a technique that introduces noise or perturbation into query responses to ensure about the user-centric privacy preservation. *Secure Multi-Party Computation* enables multiple parties to jointly compute functions over their private inputs without revealing sensitive information. *Homomorphic encryption* allows computations to be performed on encrypted data without decrypting the data, thus maintaining data privacy. *Federated learning* facilitates collaborative model training on distributed systems without transferring raw user data, protecting data privacy. *Secure data aggregation techniques* allow the collection and analysis of aggregated data without exposing individual contributions. *Tokenization* and *anonymization* replace personally identifiable information with anonymized data to preserve anonymity. Privacy-preserving language models incorporate privacy safeguards into the model training process, ensuring sensitive information is not exposed. Secure data storage, access controls, and privacy-preserving APIs and protocols further contribute to protecting user privacy within NLP systems. As outlined in future research directions, the integration of these privacy-enhancing technologies can enhance user privacy, reduce the occurrence of data breaches, and establish trust among users in the usage of NLP systems.

REFERENCES

Bhatti, B. M., Mubarak, S., & Nagalingam, S. V. (2021). Information security implications of using NLP in IT outsourcing: A Diffusion of Innovation theory perspective. *Automated Software Engineering*, *28*(2), 12. doi:10.100710515-021-00286-x

Casillo, F., Deufemia, V., & Gravino, C. (2022). Detecting privacy requirements from User Stories with NLP transfer learning models. *Information and Software Technology*, *146*, 106853. doi:10.1016/j.infsof.2022.106853

Chen, H., Hussain, S. U., Boemer, F., Stapf, E., Sadeghi, A. R., Koushanfar, F., & Cammarota, R. (2020). Developing Privacy-preserving AI Systems: The Lessons learned. *57th ACM/IEEE Design Automation Conference (DAC)*. ACM. 10.1109/DAC18072.2020.9218662

Fan, X., Wang, G., Chen, K., He, X., & Xu, W. (2021). PPCA: Privacy-preserving Principal Component Analysis Using Secure Multiparty Computation(MPC). *ArXiv*. /abs/2105.07612.

Feng, Q., He, D., Liu, Z., Wang, H., & Choo, K. R. (2020). SecureNLP: A System for Multi-Party Privacy-Preserving Natural Language Processing. *IEEE Transactions on Information Forensics and Security*, *15*, 3709–3721. doi:10.1109/TIFS.2020.2997134

Feng, Q., He, D., Liu, Z., Wang, H., & Choo, K. R. (2020). SecureNLP: A system for Multi-Party Privacy-Preserving natural language processing. *IEEE Transactions on Information Forensics and Security*, *15*, 3709–3721. doi:10.1109/TIFS.2020.2997134

Feyisetan, O., Ghanavati, S., & Thaine, P. (2020). Workshop on Privacy in NLP (PrivateNLP 2020). *WSDM '20: Proceedings of the 13th International Conference on Web Search and Data Mining*. ACM. 10.1145/3336191.3371881

Gao, C., & Yu, J. (2023). SecureRC: A system for privacy-preserving relation classification using secure multi-party computation. *Computers & Security*, *128*, 103142. doi:10.1016/j.cose.2023.103142

Habernal, I. (2023, May 1). Privacy-Preserving natural language processing. *ACL Anthology*. https://aclanthology.org/2023.eacl-tutorials.6

Kafle, K., Shrestha, R., & Kanan, C. (2019). Challenges and Prospects in Vision and Language Research. *Frontiers in Artificial Intelligence*, *2*, 466972. doi:10.3389/frai.2019.00028 PMID:33733117

Karim, A., Beni-Hessane, A., & Khaloufi, H. (2018). Big healthcare data: Preserving security and privacy. *Journal of Big Data*, *5*(1), 1. doi:10.118640537-017-0110-7

Khurana, D., Koli, A., Khatter, K., & Singh, S. (2023). Natural language processing: State of the art, current trends and challenges. *Multimedia Tools and Applications*, *82*(3), 3713–3744. doi:10.100711042-022-13428-4 PMID:35855771

Kim, W., & Seok, J. (2022). Privacy-preserving collaborative machine learning in biomedical applications. *2022 International Conference on Artificial Intelligence in Information and Communication (ICAIIC)*. https://doi.org/10.1109/ICAIIC54071.2022.9722703

Klymenko, O., Meisenbacher, S., & Matthes, F. (2022). Differential Privacy in Natural Language Processing The Story So Far. *Proceedings of the Fourth Workshop on Privacy in Natural Language Processing.* https://doi.org/10.18653/v1/2022.privatenlp-1.1

Lai, K., Long, Y., Wu, B., Liu, Y., & Wang, B. (2022). SeMorph: A morphology semantic enhanced pre-trained model for Chinese spam text detection. *Proceedings of the 31st ACM International Conference on Information & Knowledge Management.* ACM. 10.1145/3511808.3557448

Lin, B., He, C., Zeng, Z., Wang, H., Huang, Y., Dupuy, C., Gupta, R., Soltanolkotabi, M., Ren, X., & Avestimehr, S. (2021). *FEDNLP: Benchmarking Federated Learning Methods for natural language processing tasks.* arXiv (Cornell University). https://doi.org//arxiv.2104.08815 doi:10.48550

Lindell, Y., & Pinkas, B. (2009). Secure Multiparty Computation for Privacy-Preserving Data Mining. *The Journal of Privacy and Confidentiality*, *1*(1). doi:10.29012/jpc.v1i1.566

Mahendran, D., Luo, C., & McInnes, B. T. (2021). Review: Privacy-Preservation in the Context of Natural Language Processing. *IEEE Access : Practical Innovations, Open Solutions*, *9*, 147600–147612. doi:10.1109/ACCESS.2021.3124163

Majeed, A., & Lee, S. (2021). Anonymization Techniques for Privacy Preserving Data Publishing: A Comprehensive survey. *IEEE Access : Practical Innovations, Open Solutions*, *9*, 8512–8545. doi:10.1109/ACCESS.2020.3045700

Martinelli, F., Marulli, F., Mercaldo, F., Marrone, S., & Santone, A. (2020). Enhanced Privacy and Data Protection using Natural Language Processing and Artificial Intelligence. *2020 International Joint Conference on Neural Networks (IJCNN).* IEEE. 10.1109/IJCNN48605.2020.9206801

Nagy, B., Hegedűs, I., Sándor, N., Egedi, B., Mehmood, H., Saravanan, K., Lóki, G., & Kiss, Á. (2023). Privacy-preserving Federated Learning and its application to natural language processing. *Knowledge-Based Systems*, *268*, 110475. doi:10.1016/j.knosys.2023.110475

Odera, D. (2023). Federated learning and differential privacy in clinical health: Extensive survey. *World Journal of Advanced Engineering Technology and Sciences*, *8*(2), 305–329. doi:10.30574/wjaets.2023.8.2.0113

Rivadeneira, J. E., Silva, J. S., Colomo-Palacios, R., Rodrigues, A., & Boavida, F. (2023). User-centric privacy preserving models for a new era of the Internet of Things. *Journal of Network and Computer Applications*, *217*, 103695. doi:10.1016/j.jnca.2023.103695

Sadat, N., Aziz, M. A., Mohammed, N., Pakhomov, S., Liu, H., & Jiang, X. (2019). A privacy-preserving distributed filtering framework for NLP artifacts. *BMC Medical Informatics and Decision Making*, *19*(1), 183. doi:10.118612911-019-0867-z PMID:31493797

Silva, P., Gonçalves, C., Antunes, N., Curado, M., & Walek, B. (2022). Privacy risk assessment and privacy-preserving data monitoring. *Expert Systems with Applications*, *200*, 116867. doi:10.1016/j.eswa.2022.116867

Silva, P., Goncalves, C. S., Godinho, C., Antunes, N., & Curado, M. (2020). Using NLP and Machine Learning to Detect Data Privacy Violations. *IEEE INFOCOM 2020 - IEEE Conference on Computer Communications Workshops (INFOCOM WKSHPS)*. IEEE. 10.1109/INFOCOMWKSHPS50562.2020.9162683

Truex, S., Baracaldo, N., Anwar, A., Steinke, T., Ludwig, H., Zhang, R., & Zhou, Y. (2018). *A hybrid approach to Privacy-Preserving federated learning*. arXiv (Cornell University). https://doi.org//arxiv.1812.03224 doi:10.48550

Wang, F., Li, J., Qin, R., Zhu, J., Mo, H., & Hu, B. (2023). ChatGPT for Computational social systems: From conversational applications to Human-Oriented Operating Systems. *IEEE Transactions on Computational Social Systems, 10*(2), 414–425. doi:10.1109/TCSS.2023.3252679

Wang, T., Zhang, X., Feng, J., & Yang, X. (2020). A Comprehensive Survey on Local Differential Privacy toward Data Statistics and Analysis. *Sensors (Basel), 20*(24), 7030. doi:10.339020247030 PMID:33302517

Yin, Y., & Habernal, I. (2022). *Privacy-Preserving models for legal natural language processing*. arXiv (Cornell University). https://doi.org//arxiv.2211.02956 doi:10.18653/v1/2022.nllp-1.14

Zhu, T., Ye, D., Wang, W., Zhou, W., & Yu, P. S. (2021). More than Privacy: Applying differential privacy in key areas of artificial intelligence. *IEEE Transactions on Knowledge and Data Engineering, 1*, 1. doi:10.1109/TKDE.2020.3014246

Zuo, Z., Watson, M., Budgen, D., Hall, R., Kennelly, C., & Moubayed, N. A. (2021). Data Anonymization for Pervasive Health Care: Systematic Literature Mapping Study. *JMIR Medical Informatics, 9*(10), e29871. doi:10.2196/29871 PMID:34652278

Chapter 10
Modern Applications With a Focus on Training ChatGPT and GPT Models:
Exploring Generative AI and NLP

Isha Kondurkar
VIT Bhopal University, India

Akanksha Raj
VIT Bhopal University, India

D. Lakshmi
ⓘ https://orcid.org/0000-0003-4018-1208
VIT Bhopal University, India

ABSTRACT

Generative AI (GAI) and natural language processing (NLP) have emerged as the most exciting and rapidly growing fields in artificial intelligence (AI). This book chapter provides a comprehensive exploration of the advanced applications of GAI and NLP models, with a specific focus on the renowned ChatGPT model. The chapter commences by offering a concise historical overview of the development of GAI and NLP, highlighting crucial milestones and advancements in the field over the period. In order to understand the workings of the current technology sensation, we will take a brief look at the basic building blocks of GPT models, such as transformers. Subsequently, the chapter delves into the introduction of ChatGPT, presenting an extensive overview of the model, elucidating its underlying architecture, and emphasizing its unique capabilities. Furthermore, it will illustrate the training process of the GPT model followed by a fine-tuning process to deal with the current model's shortcomings.

DOI: 10.4018/979-8-3693-0502-7.ch010

1. INTRODUCTION

Natural language processing (NLP) and Generative Artificial Intelligence (GAI) are two linked fields that are revolutionizing language comprehension and content creation. While generative AI focuses on developing systems that can produce original and creative material, NLP focuses on teaching computers to understand and interpret human language. The subsequent subsections shall explain in detail more about these two fields and also tell us about their correlation and convergence.

1.1 NLP

NLP is a field of Artificial Intelligence (AI) and computational linguistics that focuses on enabling computers to understand, interpret, and generate human language. As per Johri et al. (2021), it has a rich history dating back to the 1950s when researchers created the first machine translation system, known as the Georgetown-IBM experiment, which translated Russian sentences into English in 1954. In the 1960s and 1970s, rule-based systems for language understanding emerged. These systems relied on handcrafted linguistic rules and grammatical structures to process and analyze text. However, they often struggled with the complexity and variability of natural language, limiting their practical applicability. The 1980s marked a shift towards statistical and probabilistic approaches in NLP. Researchers began exploring the use of machine learning algorithms to automatically learn patterns and structures from large datasets. This approach allowed for more accurate and robust language processing, particularly in tasks such as part-of-speech tagging and syntactic parsing. With the advent of the internet and the availability of vast amounts of textual data, NLP advanced further, aided by deep learning algorithms.

NLP emerged to address the human desire for seamless communication with computers in their native language, thereby enhancing user workflow efficiency. It can be categorized into two primary domains: Linguistics and Natural Language Generation (NLG) or Natural Language Understanding (NLU). These divisions encapsulate the processes involved in comprehending and generating textual content according to Khurana et al. (2022). Figure 1 represents NLP and its various components.

Presently, Natural Language Processing (NLP) encompasses a diverse array of tasks and applications. Among the foundational tasks within NLP are Text Classification, involving the assignment of predefined categories or labels to text documents, encompassing sentiment analysis, topic classification, and spam detection. Named Entity Recognition (NER) involves the identification and classification of named entities, including individuals, organizations, locations, and dates within text. Machine Translation facilitates the automatic translation of text from one language to another. Question Answering entails the automatic discovery and provision of responses to questions presented in natural language. Sentiment Analysis involves determining the sentiment or emotion expressed in a given text, categorizing it as positive, negative, or neutral. Text Generation encompasses the creation of human-like text based on provided prompts or conditions. Finally, Part-of-Speech (POS) Tagging involves assigning each word in a sentence a specific part of speech, such as a verb, noun, adjective, or adverb. These core NLP tasks are visually represented in Figure 2.

As we progress through this chapter, we will explore the variety of techniques including computational linguistics, machine learning, and statistical modeling in NLP, and the models used to accomplish them. NLP continues to evolve rapidly, driven by advancements in deep learning, the availability of large-scale datasets, and the increasing demand for intelligent language processing systems.

Figure 1. NLP components

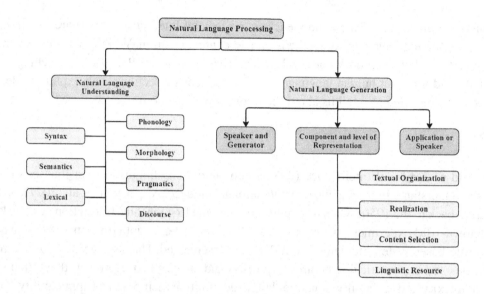

Figure 2. Some core tasks of NLP

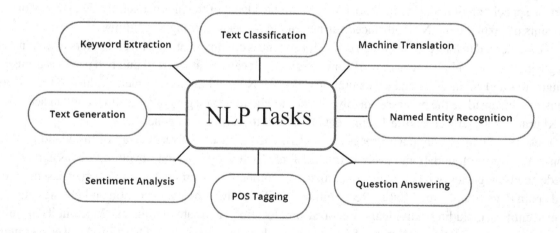

1.2 Generative AI

Generative AI is a fascinating and rapidly evolving field of artificial intelligence that focuses on creating systems capable of generating new, original content. These systems, often based on deep learning models, can produce realistic images, text, audio, and even video that closely resemble human creations. Generative models have a well-established legacy in the field of artificial intelligence, tracing its origins to the 1950s with the inception of Hidden Markov Models (HMMs) as documented by Knill and Young (1997), along with Gaussian Mixture Models (GMMs). As elucidated by Cao et al. (2023), these models were instrumental in generating sequential data, particularly in applications involving speech and time series.

Early attempts involved rule-based systems and expert systems that relied on predefined sets of rules to generate limited forms of content. However, these approaches were limited in their creative capabilities. The breakthrough in GAI came with the advent of deep learning and neural networks in the 2000s. The rise of deep learning models, particularly Generative Adversarial Networks (GANs) as per Goodfellow et al. (2014) was first suggested in 2014, marking a crucial turning point in this field. Diffusion generative models and Variational autoencoders (VAEs) have also revolutionized the field, gaining precise control over high-quality image production processes.

The development of generative AI has had a profound impact across various domains. In computer vision, generative models can generate high-quality images, transform images into different styles, and even assist in image restoration tasks. In natural language processing, generative models can generate human-like text, translate languages, and aid in language understanding tasks. In the arts and entertainment industry, GAI has opened up new avenues for creativity, allowing artists and designers to explore novel ideas and generate unique content. Ongoing research focuses on improving the stability and quality of generated outputs, addressing issues such as mode collapse, and improving interpretability.

We will also further explore the challenges and opportunities associated with GAI and examine the future directions of this exciting field. Generative AI has the potential to push the boundaries of human creativity and open up new possibilities for artificial intelligence, making it an area of immense interest and exploration.

1.3 Convergence of NLP and Generative AI

NLP and GAI are closely related fields that intersect in various ways. The intersection of NLP and Generative AI using GANs has led to significant advancements in language generation tasks. The initial phases of deep generative models exhibit limited convergence. Within the domain of Natural Language Processing (NLP), conventional methods involve acquiring word distribution through N-gram language modeling, followed by the pursuit of an optimal sequence as part of the sentence generation process. Long sentences, however, cannot be adequately handled by this strategy. Recurrent neural networks (RNNs) as per Mikolov et al. (2010) were later developed for language modeling tasks to address this issue and enable the modeling of reasonably long dependencies. Long Short-Term Memory (LSTM) and Gated Recurrent Unit (GRU) were then created, both of which used gating mechanisms to regulate memory during training. These techniques significantly outperform N-gram models by being able to attend to 200 tokens or more in a sample according to Khandelwal et al. (2018).

NLP is dedicated to the facilitation of computer understanding, interpretation, and generation of human language. In contrast, generative AI is oriented towards the development of systems capable of producing innovative and creative content. One of the fundamental tasks in NLP is language generation, which involves generating coherent and human-like text. Generative AI techniques, such as language models and sequence-to-sequence models, play a vital role in language generation tasks. These models learn from large amounts of text data and generate text that resembles human language patterns and structures. Generative models, such as neural machine translation models, learn to translate text from one language to another by generating target language sentences that accurately convey the meaning of the source language. This requires understanding the source language, generating the appropriate target language output, and ensuring the translated text is grammatically and semantically correct.

Another area where NLP and GAI overlap is text summarization. NLP techniques are employed to analyze and understand the source text, extract important information, and generate a concise summary.

NLP and generative AI are essential components of dialogue systems, including chatbots and virtual assistants. These systems aim to generate human-like responses and engage in meaningful conversations with users. In the context of NLP, generative models can generate textual content that closely resembles human writing styles, enabling applications like creative writing, storytelling, and text generation for marketing or advertising purposes. Some tasks where NLP and Generative AI coincide have been represented in Figure 3.

As both NLP and GAI continue to advance, we can expect further integration between the two fields, leading to more advanced language understanding, generation capabilities, and exciting applications in areas like creative writing, content generation, improving the performance of NLP models, and enhancing the naturalness of personalized conversational agents.

Figure 3. Tasks converging generative AI and NLP

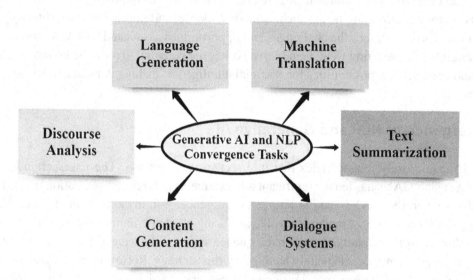

1.4 Training ChatGPT Model Using NLP and Generative AI

The Generative AI model known as ChatGPT (Generative Pre-trained Transformer) was developed by OpenAI, a prominent AI research organization established by notable industry leaders, including Elon Musk, Greg Brockman, Sam Altman, and Ilya Sutskever. OpenAI introduced the initial iteration of ChatGPT, pre-trained on a comprehensive dataset exceeding 40 gigabytes of textual data obtained from diverse sources on the internet. The introduction of ChatGPT generated a great deal of interest and enthusiasm in the NLP community because it showed that trained models are capable of producing excellent natural language content.

ChatGPT is trained using a combination of generative AI and NLP techniques. The cornerstone for training the ChatGPT model is data collection from numerous sources. Preprocessing operations are performed on the gathered data to organize and clean it. To address tasks like tokenization, phrase segmentation, and deleting extraneous information, NLP approaches are used. This gets the data ready for effective training of the model.

ChatGPT employs a Generative Adversarial Intelligence (GAI) model, typically founded on a transformer architecture, similar to the GPT. The evolution of generative models across diverse domains has traversed distinct trajectories, converging at the transformative intersection represented by the transformer architecture. In the realm of NLP, prominent large language models such as BERT and GPT have embraced the transformer architecture as their fundamental building block, demonstrating advantages over preceding components like LSTM and GRU. The model undergoes training to predict the subsequent word or sequence of words, contingent upon the antecedent context, as articulated by Ruby (2023). This training allows the model to learn the statistical patterns and dependencies in the conversational data.

Techniques for reinforcement learning are used to hone the model's responses after initial training. Human AI trainers provide conversations and rank different model-generated responses based on quality, relevance, and appropriateness. To optimize for improved responses, the model's parameters are then updated using reinforcement learning methods like Proximal Policy Optimisation.

NLP techniques are used during the training process to provide secure and impartial interactions. To weed out improper or hazardous content, human review processes, and rule-based filtering are employed. Additionally, techniques are implemented to reduce biased behavior and promote fairness in the model's responses.

There is a loop of iterative feedback during the training phase. Based on user interactions and actual feedback, the model is regularly taught and improved. User input identifies regions where the model might produce erroneous or absurd replies, which results in modifications and enhancements throughout subsequent training iterations. Steps for training the ChatGPT model have been represented in Figure 4.

Through the combination of generative AI and NLP techniques, ChatGPT is trained to understand user queries and generate contextually relevant responses in a conversational manner. The iterative training process, coupled with reinforcement learning and safety measures, allows for continual refinement and enhancement of the model's dialogue capabilities. The goal is to create an AI system that can simulate human-like conversations and provide valuable and reliable assistance to users.

2. RATIONALE OF THE STUDY

To discover the basics of Natural Language Processing and how the ChatGPT model is trained, along with a brief discussion of the evaluation metrics of the ChatGPT model and a comparative study between the various models of this domain.

3. METHODS

NLP constitutes a specialized domain within AI dedicated to facilitating the interaction between computers and human language. Its core aim is to empower machines with the capability to comprehend, interpret, and produce human language in a manner that is not only meaningful but also contextually relevant. This section takes a deeper dive into language processing and training of language models, like ChatGPT.

Figure 4. Steps used for training ChatGPT using generative AI and NLP

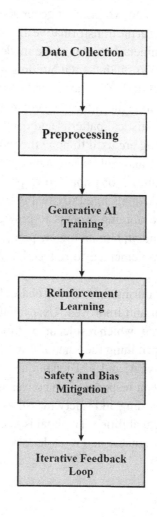

3.1 Overview of NLP

According to Rahali & Akhloufi (2023), NLP serves as the pragmatic and applied dimension of computational linguistics, integrating principles from linguistics and AI. Essentially, NLP constitutes a methodology for effectively managing, interpreting, and comprehending vast volumes of textual data. NLP is an engineering discipline that seeks to build technology to accomplish beneficial tasks (Deep-Learning.AI, 2023).

3.1.1 Working of NLP

NLP models operate by discerning relationships among the fundamental elements of language, encompassing letters, words, and sentences within a given text dataset. Architectures in NLP employ diverse methodologies for tasks such as data preprocessing, feature extraction, and model development. Some of these processes are mentioned below:

1) **Data preprocessing:** Text frequently needs to be preprocessed before a model processes data for a particular purpose in order to improve model performance or to convert words and characters into a format the model can understand. Various techniques may be used in this data preprocessing:

   a) **Stemming and Lemmatization:** Stemming is an informal method of reducing words to their fundamental forms by applying heuristic criteria. For instance, the base univers might be mapped to the words "university," "universities," and "university's." (One drawback of this approach is that, despite the fact that universities and universes don't have a very close semantic relationship, "universe" may also be mapped to univers.) By employing vocabulary from a dictionary to analyze a word's morphology, lemmatization is a more formal method of discovering roots. Stemming and lemmatization are provided by libraries like spaCy and NLTK.

   b) **Sentence segmentation:** The process involves segmenting an extensive text into linguistically meaningful sentence units. While this is evident in languages such as English, where a period signifies the conclusion of a sentence, it remains a nuanced undertaking. A period can be used to signify an abbreviation as well as to end a phrase. In this instance, the period should be a part of the abbreviation token itself. When a language lacks a delimiter to indicate the end of a sentence, like in ancient Chinese, the technique is significantly more difficult.

   c) **Stop word removal:** It removes the words that are most frequently used but don't add much to the content. Examples include "the," "a," "an," and so forth.

   d) **Tokenization:** The process involves segmenting text into discrete words and word fragments. This typically yields a word index and tokenized text, where words are represented as numerical tokens suitable for application in various deep-learning methodologies. Enhancing efficiency can be achieved by guiding language models to disregard irrelevant tokens.

2) **Feature extraction:** The predominant emphasis in traditional machine-learning approaches revolves around features generated through methods like TF-IDF, Bag-of-Words and general feature engineering. These encompass attributes such as document length, word polarity, and metadata, which may include associated tags or scores. Invariably, these features are numerical representations that characterize a document within the context of the corpus in which it is situated. Word2Vec, GLoVE, and learning the features as a neural network is trained are more modern methods. There are several feature extraction techniques commonly used in NLP:

   a) **Bag-of-Words:** BoW represents text as a collection of unique words in a document without considering the order of words. It generates a sparse vector in which each dimension corresponds to a distinct word within the corpus, with the associated value indicating the frequency of the respective word within the document.

   b) **Term Frequency-Inverse Document Frequency (TF-IDF):** TF-IDF is a statistical measure that evaluates the importance of a word in a document relative to a collection of documents (corpus). It combines term frequency (TF), which measures how often a word appears in a document, and inverse document frequency (IDF), which measures the rarity of a word across the corpus.

   c) **Word Embeddings:** Word embeddings, such as Word2Vec, GloVe, and FastText, function to represent words as condensed vectors within a continuous vector space. These embeddings adeptly encapsulate semantic relationships among words, providing a foundation for deriving word-level features essential for various NLP tasks.

d) **Word2Vec:** Word2Vec stands as a widely adopted word embedding technique, proficient in acquiring distributed representations of words through the prediction of context words based on a given target word, or conversely.

e) **Doc2Vec:** Doc2Vec is an extension of the Word2Vec word embedding technique, designed to learn document-level embeddings. In Word2Vec, words are represented as dense vectors in a continuous vector space, capturing semantic relationships between words. Doc2Vec takes this concept a step further by allowing you to represent entire documents as vectors in the same continuous space.

f) **FastText:** FastText is an extension of Word2Vec that is capable of generating word embeddings for subword units (character n-grams), which can be useful for handling out-of-vocabulary words.

g) **N-grams:** N-grams are a feature extraction technique in natural language processing (NLP) that divides text into contiguous sequences of n words or characters. N-grams are used to capture local patterns or dependencies in the text data.

h) **Part-of-Speech (POS) Tagging:** Part-of-Speech (POS) tagging is a fundamental natural language processing (NLP) task that involves assigning grammatical categories or labels, known as parts of speech, to each word in a text. POS tagging is essential for understanding the structure and meaning of sentences.

i) **Named Entity Recognition (NER):** Named Entity Recognition (NER) stands as a specialized component within the realm of NLP, devoted to the precise identification and classification of named entities within textual content. These entities encompass tangible elements in the real world, encompassing individuals, organizations, geographic locations, dates, monetary values, percentages, and other pertinent categories. NER assumes a pivotal role in the broader context of information extraction, contributing significantly to unraveling the organizational framework inherent in unstructured textual data.

3) **Modeling**: Data is preprocessed before being supplied into an NLP architecture, which models the data to carry out several activities. Contingent upon the specific task, numerical information obtained through the methods mentioned above can be integrated into diverse models. For instance, the result of the TF-IDF vectorizer can be employed as input for classification in logistic regression, naive Bayes, decision trees, or gradient-boosted trees. Alternatively, for tasks such as named entity recognition, a combination of hidden Markov models and n-grams may be applied.

3.1.2 Applications of NLP

NLP is a crucial component of daily life and continues to grow as language technology is applied to a variety of industries, including retail and medicine. NLP is harnessed by conversational agents such as Apple's Siri and Amazon's Alexa to attentively interpret user inquiries and provide relevant solutions. At the forefront of these agents is GPT-3, a recent addition to the commercial landscape, distinguished by its capacity to generate sophisticated written content across a diverse array of subjects. Notably, it empowers chatbots to engage in coherent and meaningful discussions. NLP is used by social networks like Facebook to identify and filter hate speech, and Google utilizes it to enhance search engine results. There are numerous NLP tasks that can be used in numerous domains and languages, including healthcare and financial services besides social media as per Rahali & Akhloufi (2023).

1) Machine Translation

Khurana et al. (2022) say Language is a significant barrier to data accessibility. There are numerous languages, and each one has its own unique syntax and sentence structure. Machine Translation involves the conversion of phrases from one language to another, typically facilitated by a statistical engine such as Google Translate. The primary challenge inherent in machine translation technologies lies not merely in the literal translation of words, but in preserving the nuanced meaning of sentences, while also maintaining grammatical structure and adherence to appropriate tenses.

To assess the potential correlation between elements in Language A and Language B, statistical machine learning endeavors to accumulate extensive data displaying apparent parallels in both languages. Apart from Google Translate, additional tools such as Bing Translator and Translate Me are also noteworthy in this field.

2) Text Categorization and Spam Filtration

Systems for categorizing data receive a massive flow of information as input, such as official papers, military casualty reports, market data, newswires, etc., and assign the information to predetermined categories or indexes.

Some businesses have been classifying issue tickets or complaint requests using categorization systems before directing them to the proper desks. Email spam filters are another text categorization application. As the first line of defense against unsolicited emails, spam filters are becoming more and more crucial according to Khurana et al. (2022). They are filtering systems to distinguish between legitimate messages and spam based on their content. A set of protocols is used to achieve this.

There are several types of spam filters available such as Content filters Header filters, General Blacklist filters, Rules-Based Filters, Permission Filters, Challenge Response Filters, etc that serve various purposes.

3) Information Extraction

Finding meaningful terms in text data is the goal of information extraction. Named Entity Recognition (NER) can identify and classify named entities like names of people, organizations, locations, dates, etc. It is a useful technique to summarise the information that is pertinent to a user's needs in many applications.

The information that is extracted can be used for several things, such as creating databases, sorting text into predefined categories, creating summaries, finding keywords, etc.

As an illustration, CONSTRUE, designed specifically for Reuters, plays a pivotal role in the categorization of news stories (Hayes, 2016). Additionally, METLIFE's Intelligent Text Analyzer (MITA), as outlined by Glasgow et al. (1998), serves the purpose of extracting information from life insurance applications.

4) Summarization

In the contemporary digital era, the challenge of information overload is a recognized concern, characterized by an abundance of knowledge that surpasses our capacity for assimilation. Given the persistent nature of this trend, the ability to condense data without compromising its meaning becomes imperative. This skill is paramount in uncovering profound emotional nuances and extracting pivotal information from extensive datasets. For example, enterprises may leverage sentiment analysis on social media platforms to inform their latest product developments, illustrating the practicality of such applications as valuable tools in marketing strategies.

5)   Medicine

NLP finds application in the medical and healthcare sectors by facilitating the extraction of information from electronic health records. Its utility extends to aiding clinical decision-making processes and automating the intricate task of medical coding. The Linguistic String Project-Medical Language Processor is one of the large-scale projects of NLP in the field of medicine (Chi, 1985; Grishman, 1973). The LSP-MLP facilitates physicians in extracting and summarizing information pertaining to signs, symptoms, drug dosage, and response data. Its objective is to identify potential side effects of medications, utilizing a system that flags or highlights relevant data items, as delineated by Sager et al. (1995).

Columbia University in New York has pioneered the development of an NLP system known as MEDLEE (MEDical Language Extraction and Encoding System). This system, as detailed by Friedman et al. (1993), is designed to discern clinical information within narrative reports and subsequently convert the textual data into a structured representation.

6)   Dialogue System

Dialogue systems find extensive application in practical scenarios, ranging from providing assistance to executing specific tasks. While task-oriented actions may not demand extensive context awareness, the effective support of dialogue systems often hinges on it. Robust dialogue systems, designed for inhabitability, hold the promise of fully automated interactions by leveraging all linguistic levels (Liddy, 2001). This advancement has paved the way for the development of systems facilitating seamless human-robot interactions in natural languages, exemplified by entities like Apple's Siri, Google's Assistant, Amazon's Alexa and Microsoft's Cortana, among others.

Following are some of the recent NLP projects implemented by various companies:

a)   ACE Powered GDPR Robot Launched by RAVN Systems

RAVN Systems, a prominent authority in Artificial Intelligence (AI), Search, and Knowledge Management Solutions, has introduced a software robot designed to support and streamline compliance with the General Data Protection Regulation (GDPR). The launch of this ACE-powered GDPR robot is outlined in a FinancialContent Business Page from 2016, demonstrating how it uses artificial intelligence to speed up GDPR compliance procedures.

Using AI techniques, The Robot automatically evaluates documents as well as other types of data in any enterprise system that needs to abide by GDPR requirements. Users may easily and quickly look up, flag, retrieve, categorise, and report on data that the GDPR has declared to be particularly sensitive. Users can also extract personal information from documents, browse feeds of the most recent personal information that has to be addressed, and submit reports on information that should be destroyed or secured. The GDPR Robot from RAVN can also expedite requests for information (also known as "Data Subject Access Requests," or "DSAR") straightforwardly and effectively, doing away with the requirement for a manual process that is typically quite labor-intensive.

b)   Eno A Natural Language Chatbot Launched by Capital One

According to Orr (2017), Eno, a chatbot for customers, is introduced by Capital One. People communicate with Eno, a chatbot that uses natural language, by texting. Eno, according to CapitalOne, is the first SMS chatbot from a U.S. bank that supports natural language consumer questions. Through a text interface, customers may communicate with Eno and ask inquiries about their savings and other topics. Eno creates environments that give the impression that people are communicating. Compared to other companies that provide chatbots, such as Facebook Messenger and Skype, this offers a unique platform.

The admin of a Facebook page has access to the complete transcripts of all talks with the bot. If that were the case, administrators would be able to access entered consumer personal banking information with ease, which is incorrect.

c)   Pilot, World's First Language Translating Earbuds

According to Ochoa (2016), the Pilot by Waverly Labs, as reported on Spring Wise, demonstrates the capability to transliterate seven alphabetic scripts, encompassing German, Arabic, Mandarin Chinese, Japanese, Korean, Russian and Hindi. Furthermore, it extends its proficiency to five languages that are spoken, namely English, Italian, Spanish, Portuguese, and French. The Pilot speech translation app, which makes use of speech recognition, machine translation, machine learning, and speech synthesis technology, is connected to the Pilot earpiece via Bluetooth. The user will concurrently hear the translated version of the speech on the second earpiece. Additionally, a chat does not have to be between two persons; any user can participate and have a group discussion. The earpieces serve a multifunctional purpose, facilitating activities such as streaming music, handling voice calls, and receiving audio notifications.

As per Liu (2022), The ultimate goal of NLP is to train the computer to reach a human-level understanding by combining computational linguistics, statistical, machine learning, and deep learning models.

3.1.3 What Makes a Basic NLP Model

To put it simply, deep learning is used by the majority of NLP models. Up until that point, NLP practitioners used conventional statistical or linguistic techniques to produce results.

The actions that must be taken to create a basic NLP model are as follows:

a)   **Data Cleaning and Tokenization**

It cleanses the words in a sequence by performing operations including eliminating stop words, lowering the case, and condensing words into a single form. The objective is to unite words with similar meanings but slightly different representations and to commonize them for simpler grouping. Then, words are split up into phrases or even smaller units.

b)   **Vectorization / Word Embedding**

Numeric data is processed by computers rather than strings. Following data cleansing, each string must be mapped into a real number or labeled, creating the optimal input for computers to process.

c)   **Model Training**

Deep learning, notably Recurrent Neural Network (RNN) and Long Short Term Memory (LSTM) networks, is used to create standard NLP models. RNN is essentially a deep learning ANN that has been carefully constructed with recurrent connections on the hidden state to ensure that sequential data is collected. It is especially important since learning to understand human languages requires recognizing the order in which information is presented in the input data, such as the connection between words in a text when making predictions. In RNN structures, as opposed to ANN, information from a node is sent back to its closest predecessors. The basic structure of an RNN is represented in Figure 5.

The feedback notion of an RNN is extended by an LSTM network, in contrast, where information is shared not just among neighboring prior nodes but also throughout the entire network. The LSTM technique gives the network the ability to retain input data for a longer period, which is necessary for understanding human languages. RNN and LSTM network introduction is covered in more detail here.

Figure 5. RNN - Basic structure

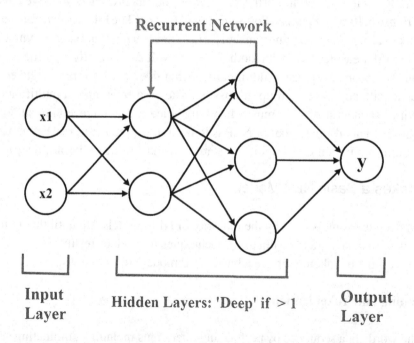

3.2 Models in ML

Machine learning models can be roughly divided into generative and discriminative categories. Since one can "generate" artificial data using sophisticated models of probability distributions, generative approaches aim to build these models. The more utilitarian discriminative approaches directly estimate posterior probabilities based on data.

Machine learning models known as "generative models" are used to generate fresh data samples from an existing training set. For instance, new cat images can be created using generative models that were trained on a dataset of cat images. Alternately, a generative model trained on facial image data might be used to create new, realistic-looking images of faces that aren't necessarily identical to any of the training images.

A generative model must generate different variations of the desired outputs. And, for that reason, the generative models must be probabilistic in nature rather than being deterministic which will result in the same output as per Kumar (2023). It won't work, for instance, to take the average value of the pixels in the training dataset. A random component that influences each output differently must be included in a generative model.

There are two main types of generative models namely Generative Adversarial Networks (GANs) and Variational Autoencoders (VAEs). A GAN comprises of a generator and a discriminator neural network that compete with one another to produce realistic data. VAEs are made up of an encoder and a decoder that cooperate to transform data into latent variables and then produce new data using these latent variables.

Generative models include:

- Naive Bayes classifiers
- Bayesian networks
- Markov random fields
- hidden Markov models (HMMs).
- Linear Discriminant Analysis (LDA)
- Generative Adversarial Networks (GANs)
- Autoregressive Model

Machine learning models that can predict labels or categories are known as discriminative models. A discriminative model, for instance, could be used to determine whether an email is spam. They are a class of artificial intelligence models that forecast a target variable from a set of input features. These models leverage the relationship that has been discovered between the input features and the target variable to produce predictions.

Discriminative models function by figuring out a decision boundary that can most effectively classify the training data points. They learn the relationship between the input features and the target labels.

Discriminative models include:

- Logistic regression
- Support vector machines (SVM)
- Linear discriminant analysis
- Decision trees
- Random forest Classifiers
- conditional random fields (CRFs)
- Traditional neural networks

3.2.1 Applications of Generative AI Models

Generative AI models learn patterns and structures from existing data and use that knowledge to produce new data examples that have similar characteristics. Generative AI is an exciting area of research and development that has applications in various fields, including art, content creation, text generation, and more as per Cao et al. (2023).

1) Art

AI art generation involves the utilization of computer algorithms to create original works of art. These algorithms leverage machine learning techniques to produce novel pieces that may either venture into unexplored artistic genres or emulate the styles and techniques of established artists. Training is typically conducted using extensive databases of prior artwork. A growing number of companies are launching their art generation product as a result of the rapid development of diffusion-based models.

The DALL-E series, launched by OpenAI, is one of the most important developments in the area. DALL-E, the predecessor of Craiyon, was initially constructed using VQ-VAE and CLIP. Diffusion was later added to this product, resulting in DALL-E2. The text-to-image tool DreamStudio, developed by Stability.ai, uses stable diffusion to produce visuals from given words or sentences. This technology is a favorite among many users since it provides performance that is comparable to that of DALL-E-2 while having even faster processing rates. Diffusion is a technique used by Google's Imagen, a tool for creating and editing images.

2) Music

Deep learning and artificial intelligence algorithms are used to create new and creative musical compositions. This practice is known as "deep music generation." A common strategy is to create a piano roll as a symbolic representation of the music. The timing, pitch, velocity, and instrument for each note that will be played must all be specified in this method.

One of the best examples is AIVA, which was created by Aiva Technologies in 2016. It can produce music clips in many different genres, such as electronic, pop, jazz, etc., and can be applied in a variety of settings. As the first artificial intelligence composer in the world to be acknowledged by symphonic organizations, AIVA attained the SACEM music society's global designation of Composer. In 2020, OpenAI developed Jukebox. It produces singing-based music in a variety of musical genres and creative styles. In terms of musical quality, coherence, audio sample length, and the ability to be influenced by artist, genre, and lyrics, Jukebox is seen as a significant advancement.

3) Code

Code completion, source code to pseudo-code mapping, program repair, API sequence prediction, user feedback, and natural language to code generation are among the tasks that AI-based programming systems often try to accomplish. Recent advancements in AI-based programming have been made possible by the introduction of strong LLMs. OpenAI's CodeGPT is an open-source code generation model that uses the transformer architecture like many other GPT models.

It can be adjusted for a range of code-generating activities, including code completion, summary, and translation, depending on a sizable amount of source code data. CodeParrot is a platform for learning programming that offers users personalized feedback and support while they are working.

In comparison to most earlier models, Codex has been trained on a far larger and more varied corpus of data. In contrast to CodeGPT, which can only generate code fragments that finish a specific prompt, it is intended to construct entire coding programmes from scratch.

4)   Education

By utilizing multimodality data, such as instructive videos, scholarly articles, and other high-quality information, GAI has the potential to make major improvements in education and enhance the personalized learning experience. On the academic front, Google Research unveiled Minerva, a system for solving college-level multi-step quantitative problems that span algebra, probability, physics, number theory, precalculus, geometry, biology, electric engineering, chemistry, astronomy, and machine learning. It is based on PaLM general language models and an additional dataset that is science and math-focused.

Commercially, Skillful Craftsman Education Technology revealed plans to create a class bot product driven by GAI with an auto curriculum, an AI tutor, and self-adaptive learning for online education. According to Cao et al. (2023), the product is anticipated to arrive by the fourth quarter of 2023.

3.2.2 Language Models in NLP

Language models are created to predict any probability of a pattern or sequence of words and perform word probability to analyze text data. Therefore, NLP makes use of these models to understand the predictability of languages and words.

In order to add rules for context in NLP, language models evaluate the input by processing it through an algorithm. Additionally, the rules can precisely predict and generate new words when using language models that have already undergone training. In order to dissect and comprehend different sentences, it also adjusts to the features and building blocks of base languages. According to Taylor (2022), there are two types of language models in NLP: Statistical Models and Neural Language Models

1)   Statistical Models

Statistical models develop probabilistic models that help in predicting the next word in the sequence. Additionally, based on the words before it, it uses data to generate predictions. Numerous statistical language models benefit enterprises, too.

Let's take a look at some of those popular models as per Oberoi (2021):

1.1 N-Gram

One of the easiest methods for language modeling is this one. Here, a probability distribution is produced for a sequence of 'n,' where 'n' can be any number and designates the size of the gram (or the sequence of words being given a probability). If n=4, a gram may look like: "Please pass the bottle". Basically, 'n' refers to the volume of context that the model has been trained to take into account. N-Gram models come in a variety of forms, including unigrams, bigrams, trigrams, etc.

1.2 Unigram

Each word or phrase is given a separate evaluation and its calculations take no account of any conditioning context. Language processing tasks like information retrieval are frequently handled by unigram models. The query likelihood model, a more precise variant of the unigram model, employs information retrieval to look through a pool of documents and find the one that most closely matches a given query.

1.3 Bidirectional

Bidirectional models, in contrast to unidirectional n-gram models, analyze text comprehensively by considering both backward and forward directions. This dual-directional approach, examining every other word in the text, allows these models to effectively anticipate words within phrases or bodies of text, thereby enhancing result precision. Such bidirectional text examination techniques find frequent applications in voice generation and machine learning. Notably, Google employs a bidirectional approach in processing search queries to optimize performance and accuracy.

1.4 Exponential

A combination of n-grams and feature functions is used in this kind of statistical model to analyze text. Here, the intended results' characteristics and specifications are already listed. The best option for a probability distribution is determined by the entropy principle, which forms the basis of the model. The likelihood of getting accurate findings is higher for exponential models since they make fewer statistical assumptions.

1.5 Continuous Space

Words are structured as a non-linear combination of weights in a neural network in this kind of statistical model. Word embedding refers to the process of giving a word weight. This kind of model is useful in situations where the word list keeps growing and contains unique terms.

2) Neural Language Models

Language models created utilizing neural networks are referred to as neural language models. The models also assist in reducing the difficulties associated with conventional language models. Neural language models seek to comprehend language structure and produce writing that is coherent and contextually appropriate. Their main applications include language modeling, machine translation, text generation, sentiment analysis, and other related tasks.

2.1 Feedforward Neural Language Models

Feedforward neural language models represented in Figure 6 work by processing incoming text via one or more layers of fully connected neural networks, also known as multi-layer perceptrons (MLPs), to uncover underlying patterns and connections between words in the target language.

Figure 6. Basic feedforward architecture

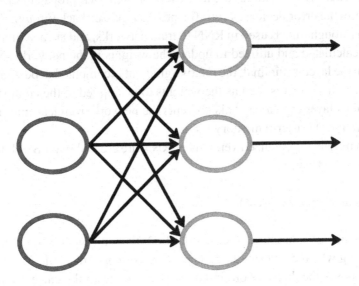

2.2 Recurrent Neural Networks (RNNs):

RNNs shown in Figure 7, often referred to as sequence modeling neural networks, are a subclass of neural networks used to process sequential data since they permit the use of prior outputs as inputs while maintaining hidden states. Any input length can be processed by RNNs, and the model size is independent of the input size. In addition, weights that remain unchanged over time and previous data are taken into account while computing the model.

Figure 7. RNN architecture

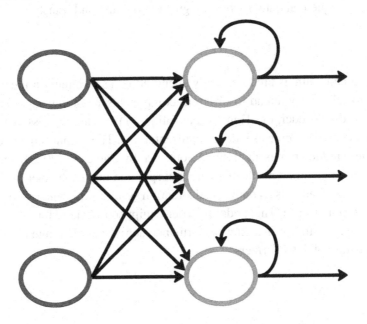

RNNs, like many other ML algorithms, are improved through back-propagation, and because of their sequential architecture, the error decreases significantly as it passes back through the recurrent layers.

Backpropagation through time is used in RNN to train networks, and at each time step or loop operation, the gradient is calculated and utilized to update the weights in the networks. Now, if the previous sequence's impact on the layer is minimal, the relative gradient is computed to be minimal. When dealing with longer sequences, this effect is seen as the weights to be applied to the context become less if the gradient of the previous layer is smaller. This prevents the network from learning the impact of earlier inputs, which leads to the short-term memory issue.

To overcome this problem specialized versions of RNN are created like LSTM, GRU, Time Distributed layer, ConvLSTM2D layer.

2.2.1 Long-Short-Term Memory (LSTM)

They have a more intricate structure than standard RNNs, with input, output, and forget gates that are capable of choosing which data from the hidden state to keep or discard.

The input gate chooses the data to store in the hidden state from the current input. The forget gate chooses which data from the previous hidden state should be retained or ignored. The output gate chooses which data to output as the final prediction from the hidden state. With this set of gates, LSTMs may filter away unimportant or outdated information while keeping crucial information from lengthy sequences.

2.2.2 Gated Recurrent Unit (GRU)

It uses a more straightforward structure than an LSTM and is simpler to train. An update gate and a reset gate are the two gates that they have.

The update gate chooses which data from the current input and the prior hidden state should be retained, while the reset gate chooses which data should be discarded. The information that the update gate has stored and the current input together make up the final hidden state. GRUs are frequently employed for problems involving sequential data, such as language modeling and translation.

2.3 Transformers

The Transformer architecture is predominantly anchored in a self-attention mechanism, facilitating the model's ability to selectively attend to different components within an input sequence. Comprising both an encoder and a decoder, the Transformer follows a two-step process. The input sequence is processed by the encoder, which creates hidden representations. The output sequence is then created by the decoder using these hidden representations. As outlined by Cao et al. (2023), a feed-forward neural network and a multi-head attention mechanism are incorporated into each layer of the decoder and encoder. Transformer's main feature is its multi-head attention system, which learns to give tokens varying weights based on their importance. The model is better equipped to handle long-term dependency with this kind of information routing., enhancing performance across a wide range of NLP tasks. Figure 8 represents the architecture of Transformers.

Figure 8. Transformer architecture
(Adapted from [https://doi.org/10.48550/arXiv.1706.03762])

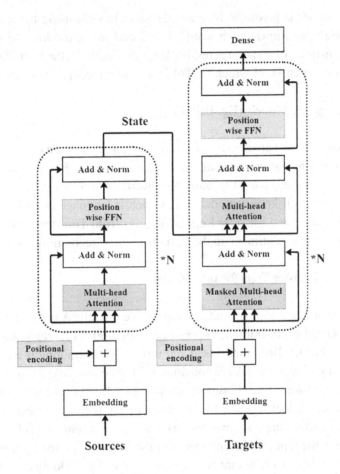

Attention allows for an extremely long-term memory. The Transformer focuses on each and every token that has ever been produced. This architecture is made up of numerous layers of feed-forward (position-wise feed-forward), residual connections, and normalization layers that are all piled on top of one another as multiple multi-head attention layers.

Transformer's architecture makes it extremely parallelizable, which gives data the upper hand over inductive biases. The transformer is ideally suited for large-scale pre-training because of this characteristic, which enables transformer-based models to adapt to various downstream tasks.

2.4 Large Language Models (LLM)

These models are a subset of neural language models and stand out for their enormous size by having the ability to have hundreds of millions to billions of parameters. They perform better on different NLP tasks due to their greater size, which enables them to capture complex trends and subtleties in language as per Kumar (2023b). There are three main types of large language models (LLMs) based on the transformer architecture:

2.4.1 Autoregressive Language Models (Eg: GPT)

The next word in a series is predicted by autoregressive models using the words that came before it. They receive training to maximize each word's likelihood in the training dataset given its context. The most well-known instance of an autoregressive language model is the GPT (Generative Pre-trained Transformer) series from OpenAI, of which GPT-4 is the most recent and potent version.

2.4.2 Autoencoding Language Models (Eg: BERT)

These models discover how to create a fixed-size vector representation (also known as embeddings) of input text by reconstructing the original input from a corrupted or hidden version of it. By utilizing the surrounding context, they are taught to anticipate words that are either missing or masked in the input text. One of the most well-known models for automatic language encoding is created by Google and is called BERT (Bidirectional Encoder Representations from Transformers). It can be tailored for a variety of NLP tasks, such as sentiment analysis, named entity recognition, and question answering.

2.4.3. T5 (Text-to-Text Transfer Transformer) Model

It is the combination of autoencoding and autoregressive models. A combination of supervised and unsupervised tasks was used to pre-train the encoder-decoder model T5, which was then trained on each task using a text-to-text format. Both supervised and unsupervised training is a part of the pretraining. The downstream tasks supplied by the GLUE and SuperGLUE benchmarks are used for supervised training. When using corrupted tokens for self-supervised training, 15% of the tokens are randomly removed and replaced with unique sentinel tokens (if many consecutive tokens are designated for removal, the entire group is replaced with a single sentinel token). The original sentence is the input of the decoder, the corrupted sentence is the input of the encoder, and the dropped-out tokens are the target, separated by their sentinel tokens. Relative scalar embeddings are used in T5. Padding encoder input can be done both to the left and to the right.

3.3 BERT, GPT-1, GPT-2, and GPT-3

These models have collectively pushed the boundaries of natural language understanding and generation, and they continue to serve as the foundation for many advancements in the field of NLP and AI. This section explains each one of these exceptional models in detail.

3.3.1 BERT

BERT, which stands for Bidirectional Encoder Representations from Transformers, was created by Google in 2018 and pre-trained on more than 2500 million internet terms and 800 million words of Book Corpus. It is intended to jointly condition on both left and right context in all layers to pre-train deep bidirectional representations from unlabeled text as per Duan et al. (n.d.). The two pre-training tasks that makeup BERT's core are Next Sentence Prediction and Masked LM, respectively.

- Masked ML: In this, a deep bidirectional model is trained at random by masking or covering some input tokens in order to prevent cycles where the word being analyzed can see itself.
- Next sentence prediction: Every pre-train set in this task is used 50% of the time. S2 will be tagged as 'IsNext' if S1 is followed by S2 in a phrase. S2 will, however, be labeled as 'NotNext' if it is a random sentence.

The best feature of BERT is that it uses pre-training and fine-tuning to advance the state of the art for NLP tasks. Additionally, a Transformer encoder with Self Attention Mechanism is employed, resulting in direct connections between the model's upper and bottom layers. It is more effective and can capture longer distance dependence than RNN and LSTM.

The mask is mostly responsible for BERT's flaws. First off, the [mask] won't show up in the actual forecast, and using it too much during training would degrade the model's effectiveness. Second, BERT converges more slowly than the left-right model, which predicts each token, because only 15% of each batch of tokens is predicted.

Google Search is one of the most excellent examples of BERT's efficiency. Other applications from Google, such as Gmail Smart Compose, and Google Docs utilizes BERT for text prediction. The further versions of BERT include XLNet, RoBERTa, ALBERT, StructBERT, DeBERTa, etc.

3.3.2 GPT-1

GPT-1, an acronym for Generative Pre-trained Transformer 1, represents a transformative model crafted by OpenAI. Debuting in 2018, this model boasted an extensive parameter count of 117 million, signifying its intricate settings and features. Its training dataset, comprised of an expansive corpus sourced from the internet, encompassed approximately 600 billion words, as reported by Jamiu(2023)..

The GPT-1 architecture featured a twelve-layer decoder-only transformer, incorporating twelve masked self-attention heads, each with 64-dimensional states, summing up to a total of 768. In lieu of a basic stochastic gradient descent, the Adam optimization algorithm was employed. The learning rate exhibited a linear increase from zero during the initial 2,000 updates, reaching a maximum of 2.5×10^{-4}, and subsequently annealed to 0 following a cosine schedule, as documented in Wikipedia (2023). Figure 9 represents the GPT-1 architecture.

The architecture of the GPT is shown above. It demonstrates that there are 12 decoder layers total, with 12 attention heads in each self-attention layer. It has hidden(masked) self-attention, which is what the model is trained on. The architecture somewhat resembled the original transformer architecture.

3.3.3 GPT-2

Similar to how data is being used to create GPT-1, GPT-2 was trained on a dataset of text and code that was scrapped from the internet says Jamiu (2023).

You can ask GPT-2 questions and it will answer them by producing new text, translating between languages, and even producing creative works like short stories. It's like having a versatile smart assistant at your fingertips.

GPT-2 employs the transformer model's decoder, mirroring the architectural choice of its predecessor, GPT-1. Noteworthy enhancements in both model architecture and implementation distinguish GPT-2. Boasting 1.5 billion parameters, it surpasses GPT-1 in scale by a factor of ten, given that GPT-1 comprises

117 million parameters. This substantial parameter increase contributes to GPT-2's robust capabilities in executing various language tasks, such as translation and summarization, with the notable feature of requiring minimal training samples. Its proficiency is underscored by its training on a diverse dataset, enabling effective performance when presented with raw text inputs.

Figure 9. GPT-1 architecture
(Adapted from [https://www.mikecaptain.com/resources/pdf/GPT-1.pdf])

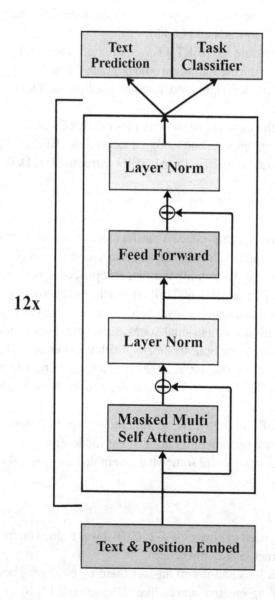

This version of the GPT model has 48 layers of decoders stacked on top of one another. GPT-2 demonstrated that a model can be more accurate if it is trained on a larger data set and has more parameters.

3.3.4 GPT 3

GPT-3 can manage statistical dependencies between different words. Launched in 2020, it contains about 175 billion parameters and is 100 times larger than GPT-2. It is trained upon a 500-billion-word data set consisting of 5 different Corpus each having a different weight assigned. They were webtext, books-1, books-2, Common Crawl, WebText2, Wikipedia. Its other noteworthy and unexpected capability is its ability to carry out simple mathematical operations, write snippets of code, and carry out intelligent operations. As a result, NLP models can help firms by faster response to requests and accurately maintaining best practices while minimizing human error.

The model's ability to produce language that is nearly indistinguishable from human-generated content is one of its most prominent skills. This qualifies it for a wide range of corporate applications, including generating code, generating marketing materials, and chatbots.

The GPT-3.5 model, which was released in 2022, is a minor upgrade of the GPT-3 model. Although it still uses the same amount of parameters as GPT-3, it gains from having been trained on a bigger corpus of text and code.

3.3.5 GPT-4

The most recent edition of the GPT series, GPT-4, was published in the first half of 2023. With an estimated 100 trillion parameters, it is a very sophisticated language model that is even more potent than its forerunners, GPT-3 and GPT-3.5. It was initially made accessible in a constrained manner through ChatGPT Plus, a premium variation of ChatGPT.

The fact that GPT-4 is a multimodal model, able to analyze both text and visuals, is a noteworthy improvement. It can now summarize information from screenshots, describe humor in strange visuals, and even respond to exam questions that include diagrams.

3.4 Comparison of Various Models

According to De Angelis et al. (2023), over the last half-decade, Large Language Models (LLMs) have experienced significant evolution, marked by exponential advancements. Their notable enhancement is evident in their exceptional performance across diverse tasks. Preceding 2017, the prevailing approach involved the development of NLP models through supervised learning tailored to specific tasks, limiting their applicability to those particular activities.

In 2018, Bidirectional Encoder Representations from Transformers (BERT) and GPT were introduced as solutions to the challenges in NLP. Both models leverage the self-attention network architecture, commonly referred to as Transformer, to effectively address these issues.

Due to their semi-supervised approach, both models have achieved enhanced generalization capabilities. This is attributed to their ability to leverage pre-trained language representations for downstream tasks, achieved through a combination of unsupervised pre-training and supervised fine-tuning. The models, having been trained on an expansive corpus of textual data and featuring an escalating number of parameters, have undergone iterative advancements, resulting in multiple versions of the GPT models.

Figure 10. Development of various model applications over time
(Adapted from [https://doi.org/10.48550/arXiv.2303.04226])

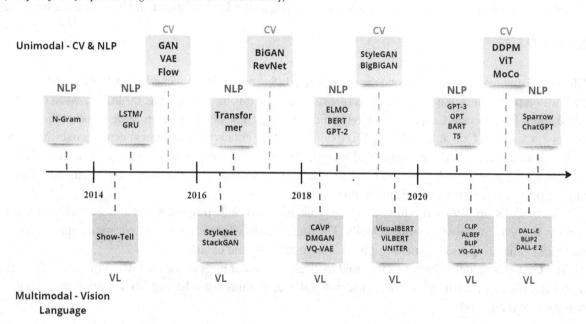

With 175 billion parameters, GPT-3 is 100 times larger than GPT-2 and has roughly twice as many neurons as the average human brain. GPT-3 can generate a writeup that is appropriate for a variety of situations, but regrettably, it frequently exhibits unexpected behaviors like fabricating information, producing biased text, or merely deviating from human instructions.

This can be accounted for by the fact that many LLMs, like GPT-3, learn to duplicate the prejudices and stereotypes existing in the data because their goal is to anticipate the next element in a text using a large corpus of text data from the internet as per Korngiebel & Mooney (2021).

The difficulty of guaranteeing that an LLM is acting in a manner that is consistent with ethical standards and human values is the main issue with alignment. The alignment issue for LLMs is still being researched, and OpenAI created a moderation system that is taught to recognize a wide range of objectionable content types, such as violence and sexual content along with other controversial content that promotes hatred.

ChatGPT integrates a moderation system, with its hallmark innovation residing in its user-centric approach. This method was instrumental in refining the model's behavior from the GPT-3 stage, ensuring adherence to user instructions in a helpful and secure manner mentions Ouyang et al. (2022). The alignment issue for LLMs is still being researched, and OpenAI created a moderation system that is taught to recognize a wide range of objectionable content types, such as violence and sexual content along with other controversial content that promotes hatred.

Commencing from InstructGPT, a Language Model with a parameter count of 1.3 billion, the initial phase of the process unfolded. The training methodology involved reinforcement learning from human feedback (RLHF), a hybrid approach amalgamating supervised learning for acquiring human input and reinforcement learning, wherein human preferences serve as a reward signal. The pre-existing GPT-3 model underwent modifications through RLHF to specifically align with the objective of adhering to human instructions. Consequently, the evolution of ChatGPT stemmed from the dialogue optimization framework originally established in InstructGPT.

Despite these developments, ChatGPT occasionally provides answers that are either incorrect or illogical despite seeming convincing due to its inability of fact-checking and knowledge being limited until 2021. Table 1 shows various feature comparisons of the GPT-1, GPT-2, GPT-3, and GPT-4 models.

Table 1. Comparison of various GPT models

	GPT-1	GPT-2	GPT-3	GPT-4
Release Date	June 2018	February 2019	June 2020	March 2023
Parameters (i.e Features or strings)	117 Million	1.5 Billion	175 Billion	170 trillion
Decoder Layers	12	48	96	120
Context Token Size	512	1024	2048	8192
Batch Size	64	512	3.2 Million	Unknown
Amount of Dataset trained on	Dataset of 600 Billion words	Dataset of 450 Billion words with improved overall performance than GPT-1	Dataset of 1.5 Trillion words with improved overall performance than GPT-2	Dataset of 100 Trillion words with improved overall performance than GPT-3
Capabilities	Generate text, Translate languages, Answer question	Able to generate more realistic and complex text	Able to generate even more realistic and complex text and to perform many tasks without any additional training	Alongside the capabilities of GPT-3, it can also process images and long texts

3.4.1 Major Differences in GPT-2 From GPT-1

For word embedding, GPT-2 used 1600 dimensional vectors across 48 layers. 50,257 tokens from a larger vocabulary were used. Larger context windows (1024 tokens) and a batch size of 512 were used. Each sub-block's layer normalization was transferred to the input, and a second layer normalization was introduced following the last self-attention block.

3.4.2 Major Differences in GPT-3 From GPT-2

The GPT-3 model comprises 96 layers, with each layer featuring 96 attention heads. Notable refinements from its predecessor, GPT-2, include a substantial increase in word embedding size, growing from 1600 to 12888. Moreover, the context window size was expanded from 1024 tokens in GPT-2 to 2048 tokens in GPT-3. The model incorporates a strategic combination of alternating dense and locally banded sparse attention patterns, complemented by the utilization of the Adam Optimizer. These enhancements collectively contribute to the heightened performance and expanded capabilities of GPT-3.

3.4.3 Major Differences in GPT-4 From GPT-3

Compared to GPT-3's 17 terabytes of training data, GPT-4, the most recent version of OpenAI, has 45 gigabytes. The original GPT-3 model, launched in 2020, established a maximum request amount of 2,049 tokens. In the subsequent iteration, GPT-3.5, this limit was increased to 4,096 tokens, approximately equivalent to three pages of single-line English text. There are two variations of GPT-4. One of them, the GPT-4-8K, can handle contexts up to 8,192 tokens, or around 50 pages of text, while the GPT-4-32K can process contexts up to 32,768 tokens.

3.4.4 BERT and GPT

While GPT concentrates on one side of the text to provide responses, BERT examines both sides to comprehend and find the information we're seeking. BERT's architecture is distinct since it made use of stacked encoder layers. The GPT model operates using the same autoregressive principle that is similar to the RNN. It is a method where the prior output turns into the present input.

The following question in Figure 11 is advanced high-school level in mathematics and relies on knowledge of the concepts of function composition and inversion in Bubeck et al. (2023)

Figure 11. Depicts the solution generated by GPT-4 and ChatGPT respectively for a particular high-school level mathematics question

GPT-4 provides a valid solution supported by a sound argument, contrasting with ChatGPT, which yields an inaccurate solution. In a human context, ChatGPT's response would signify a deficiency in grasping the concept of function inversion.

3.5 ChatGPT Model Architecture

ChatGPT is grounded in the sophisticated GPT-3.5 architecture, an evolution of the GPT-3 (Generative Pre-trained Transformer 3) model. This chapter aims to furnish a comprehensive overview of the GPT-3 architecture, serving as the foundation for the construction of ChatGPT.

Central to ChatGPT is a Large Language Model (LLM), a term typically denoting a neural network-based model extensively trained on substantial datasets, enabling it to process and generate human-like text on a significant scale. GPT-3.5 stands as an exemplar of such a Large Language Model, showcasing the capabilities inherent in this sophisticated class of models.

GPT-3, and its subsequent iteration, GPT-3.5, are founded on the transformer architecture, a sophisticated deep learning model. Transformers leverage self-attention mechanisms to adeptly capture contextual relationships within textual data. Demonstrating high efficacy, transformers have emerged as a prominent choice for a diverse range of natural language processing tasks.

A typical language translation transformer model comprises two integral components: an encoding component and a decoding component. The encoding component consists of multiple stacked encoders, while the decoding component mirrors this structure with an equal number of decoders. In contrast to earlier models such as BERT, recent GPT models exclusively utilize the decoder portion of the transformer model. This decoder leverages two key elements (Fig. 12), namely self-attention and a feed-forward neural network, to forecast the most probable sequence of words for the subsequent output.

Figure 12. Architecture of transformer employed in GPT model

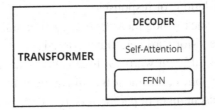

Before the self-attention model is applied, the input goes through some preprocessing steps where the input texts are segmented into tokens. Once the input text is first tokenized into smaller units, such as sub-words or characters, each token in the sequence is mapped to a high-dimensional vector representation called a token embedding. These token embeddings capture the semantic meaning of the individual tokens. Since transformers don't inherently understand the order of tokens in the sequence, position embeddings are used to provide positional information. These position embeddings are fixed vectors with predefined values, and they are added to the token embeddings to indicate the position of each token in the input sequence.

The token embeddings and position embeddings for each token are concatenated together to create the final input representation for the transformer model. This combined representation includes both the semantic information from the token embeddings and the sequential information from the position embeddings. The transformer model then takes these combined embeddings as input and processes them through multiple layers of self-attention and feedforward neural networks.

Self-attention allows the model to weigh the importance of different words or tokens in a sentence by considering their relationships with other words in the same sentence. This mechanism enables the model to capture long-range dependencies and contextual information without relying solely on fixed-length context windows.

The process of self-attention involves the creation of a query, key, and value vector for individual tokens in the sequence of inputs. Subsequently, the similarity between the query vector, obtained in the previous step, and the key vector of every other token is calculated through a dot product operation. The output from this similarity calculation is then passed through a softmax function to generate normalized weights. Finally, these weights are applied to the corresponding value vectors of each token, resulting in a final vector that represents the significance or importance of each token within the given sequence, which are called attention scores. This mechanism of self-attention forms a crucial component in various natural language processing and machine learning models, enabling them to effectively capture and weigh token dependencies and contextual information for enhanced performance in diverse tasks.

The self-attention mechanism works by calculating attention scores between all pairs of words in a sentence. These attention scores determine how much each word should attend to other words in the sentence. The attention scores are then used to compute weighted sums of the word embeddings, producing context-aware representations of each word.

The feed forward neural network (FFNN) takes the output from the self-attention mechanism, which captures the contextual relationships between words, and applies non-linear transformations to this information. These transformations help to refine and reshape the representations of the words in order to generate more accurate predictions. The FFNN consists of multiple layers with intermediate hidden states, allowing it to model complex patterns and dependencies within the input sequence. Ultimately, the FFNN contributes to the overall predictive power of the transformer model in generating coherent and contextually appropriate translations or responses.

The model is composed of a stack of identical layers, each containing a multi-head self-attention mechanism and a position-wise feed-forward neural network. The self-attention mechanism allows the model to weigh the importance of different words or tokens in a sentence while generating representations. The feed-forward network applies non-linear transformations to each position separately.

The GPT-3 model contains a vast number of parameters, reaching up to 175 billion, which contributes to its impressive language generation capabilities. The large model size enables it to understand and generate complex and coherent responses across a wide range of topics.

3.6 Training and Fine-Tuning ChatGPT Model

Training and fine-tuning a chatbot using GPT models involve two main steps: pretraining and fine-tuning. Pretraining involves training a large-scale language model on a vast corpus of text while fine-tuning and customizing the pre-trained model for the specific chatbot task or domain. This section will explain each one of these steps in detail.

3.6.1 Pre-Training

GPT-3 utilizes a training approach known as *"unsupervised learning"* or *"self-supervised learning."* During pre-training, GPT-3 is trained on a large corpus of text data without any explicit supervision or labeling. For the purpose of explaining the training process, this paper will assume the GPT model to be a black box whose components have been mentioned in the Architecture section.

In the pre-training phase, GPT-3 uses a variant of unsupervised learning called *"predictive modeling"* or *"auto-regressive modeling."* The model learns to predict the next word in a sequence of tokens based on the context provided by the preceding words. The objective is to maximize the likelihood of generating the correct next word given the preceding context.

As part of the data preprocessing pipeline, the text undergoes a crucial tokenization process wherein each sentence is segmented into individual tokens. These tokens are subsequently converted into token IDs, which serve as integer representations indicating the index of each word within the vocabulary.

The untrained model undergoes exposure to a substantial volume of data, followed by a pre-training process aimed at acquiring the ability to predict the optimal sequence of words that should follow a given input.

As Alammar (n.d.) explains, the training data for GPT-3 is processed in chunks or windows, and the model iteratively predicts the next token for each window. This process allows the model to learn the statistical patterns, grammar, and semantic relationships present in the text data.

When the untrained GPT model is provided with the text data as an input, which is in the form of token ids, it employs a sliding window technique to generate diverse examples. In accordance with Figure 13, it is presumed that some of the initial words or tokens are given as input, with the subsequent token being designated as the correct output. To create training examples, various window sizes, and input sequences are utilized.

Figure 13. An example of randomly generated examples used for training the GPT-3 model
(Adapted from [http://jalammar.github.io/illustrated-transformer/])

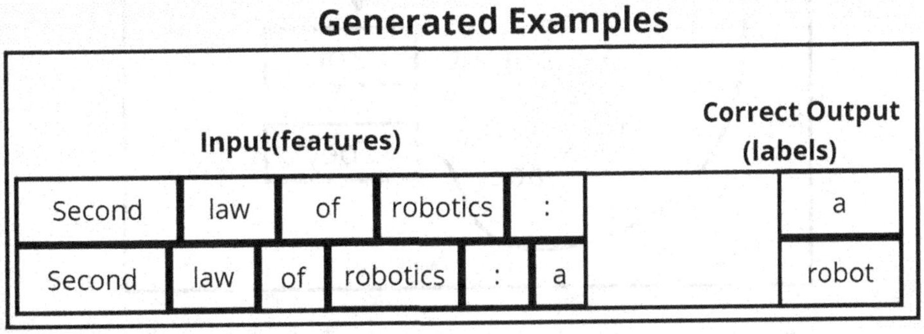

Generated Examples

Input(features)							Correct Output (labels)
Second	law	of	robotics	:			a
Second	law	of	robotics	:	a		robot

Once the examples have been created, as a further part of the training process, they are exposed to the untrained GPT model as shown in the Figure 14. The model makes its prediction based on its training process, which is then compared to the correct output label to predict the acquired loss. The lost data is fed into the model to continue the training process.

Through extensive training on a substantial corpus of textual data, GPT-3 acquires the ability to discern co-occurrence patterns among words, comprehend syntax, and produce text that is both coherent and contextually pertinent. The inclusion of a self-attention mechanism within the transformer architecture enhances the model's capacity to adeptly capture long-range dependencies and grasp the nuanced contextual relationships inherent in language.

3.6.2 Fine-Tuning

GPT-3.5 model was developed by fine-tuning the GPT-3 model on a supervised training dataset.

The above training method made sure that the model became ideal in predicting the next sequence of words depending on the pre-context. But in the real world, only predicting what can be the most probable next words is not enough.

Figure 14. Process flow of untrained GPT model
(Adapted from [http://jalammar.github.io/illustrated-transformer/])

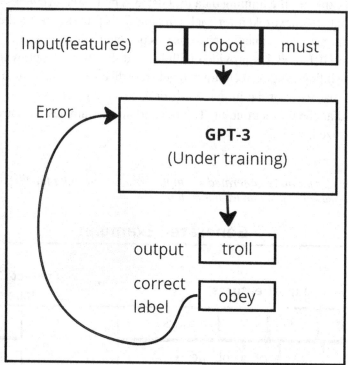

Unsupervised Pre-training

As Cretu (2023) explains, suppose a user types in, "My stomach is paining. What should I do?" The model will give the response by selecting the most probable sequence of the next words, such as "Take meds and have some rest." According to the model, this will be the best response but the response will not satisfy the user.

Likewise, there can be instances where users can input some violent prompt that can be harmful to humankind. In those circumstances, the model can not work as a simple sequence model and reply to the prompt by giving the most probable sequence of words as an answer. To deal with these instances, the pre-trained model of ChatGPT then goes through a fine-tuning process.

Fine-tuning is performed on a narrower dataset that is carefully generated and curated. By combining the knowledge and direction of human AI trainers, models like ChatGPT are improved using the technique of reinforcement learning with human feedback. The goal of this approach is to make the model's answers better and more consistent with expected behaviors.

Human AI trainers start the process by having dialogues in which they take on the roles of both the user and an AI helper. They get access to sample writing suggestions to use as writing prompts. These trainers give users access to a dataset of real-world dialogues that includes user inputs, model-generated responses, and rankings or ratings for several alternatives for responding.

The collected dataset is used to create reward models, which are used to assess the quality of model-generated responses. The reward models are typically based on comparison data, where multiple model responses are ranked by quality. The rankings provided by human AI trainers serve as the basis for assigning rewards to different model responses.

The fine-tuning process involves multiple iterations of training and evaluation. The model is trained using the PPO algorithm, and its performance is evaluated by simulating conversations and generating responses. The generated responses are ranked by human evaluators who provide feedback on the quality, relevance, and appropriateness of the responses.

Proximal Policy Optimization (PPO) is a popular reinforcement learning algorithm used to train policies for decision-making tasks in environments where an agent interacts with the environment to maximize a cumulative reward. The primary motivation behind PPO is to achieve a more stable and sample-efficient policy optimization process by avoiding large policy updates that could lead to unstable training and performance degradation. PPO operates in a way that allows it to maintain a "proximal" policy update, where the new policy remains close to the old policy to prevent significant changes that might cause instability.

The evaluation results and feedback from human evaluators are used to refine the model. OpenAI maintains a feedback loop with the human AI trainers, where they collaborate to understand the model's weaknesses, identify potential biases or issues, and provide guidelines for improvement. This iterative process helps update the model to align with the desired behavior and improve its performance over time.

Using reinforcement learning and human feedback, ChatGPT takes advantage of the knowledge and discretion of human trainers, utilizing their contributions to improve the model's replies and solve its flaws. To provide more beneficial, accurate, and contextually relevant interactions, the approach aids in achieving a balance between model-generated replies and human direction. This iterative feedback loop helps refine the model, align it with the desired objectives (such as safety, accuracy, and usefulness), and address any limitations or biases that may arise during training.

3.7 Applications of ChatGPT Models

On November 30th, 2022, "ChatGPT," a large language model (LLM) developed by OpenAI, an artificial intelligence (AI) research and deployment company, was made available as a free research preview in order to gather user feedback and discover its strengths and weaknesses as per De Angelis et al. (2023).

Earlier-developed LLMs might carry out natural language processing (NLP) activities, but ChatGPT differs from them. It is an AI chatbot designed for interaction and excels at communicating in human-like conversations.

Given its rapid adoption, ChatGPT has garnered over one million users within the initial five days of its launch, demonstrating widespread utilization across diverse applications and industries. Notable sectors leveraging ChatGPT include healthcare, education, banking, entertainment, cybersecurity, marketing, and visual tasks. The versatility of ChatGPT primarily lies in its reliance on textual inputs, although there exists the potential to enhance its functionality by incorporating other modalities such as voice, graphics, or videos, resulting in a multimodal application. Referencing Figure 6, Hariri (2023) presents several ChatGPT use cases, offering practical insights into the technology's application across various real-world scenarios.

3.7.1 Healthcare

ChatGPT has been used to develop virtual health aides that are able to understand and respond to patients' questions and concerns. AI applications in the healthcare sector play a pivotal role in enhancing diagnostic capabilities, prognostic insights, and personalized treatment approaches. Diagnostic support is bolstered through AI algorithms, enabling accurate identification of various illnesses, ranging from skin cancer and cardiovascular issues to ocular conditions. Predictive analytics, fueled by AI, empowers healthcare practitioners to anticipate and address potential health issues proactively by meticulously analyzing patient data. The realm of personalized medicine is significantly advanced by AI, leveraging comprehensive patient data to formulate tailored treatment strategies that optimize patient outcomes. Furthermore, AI systems contribute to the interpretation of diagnostic images, including X-rays, CT scans, and MRI scans, streamlining the diagnostic process with precision and efficiency.

In the pursuit of expediting drug discovery, AI analyzes extensive volumes of clinical trial data, offering insights that facilitate the development of new medications and increase the likelihood of success in the pharmaceutical domain. The integration of AI in telemedicine revolutionizes patient care by enabling virtual consultations, particularly benefiting remote locations with enhanced access to healthcare services. In surgical procedures, AI serves as a valuable ally by guiding surgical tools and providing real-time feedback, augmenting surgical precision and overall efficacy. These diverse applications underscore the transformative impact of artificial intelligence on healthcare, ushering in a new era of advanced diagnostics, personalized treatment modalities, and improved accessibility to medical services.

In a recent study by Eysenbach (2023), experiments leveraging ChatGPT were conducted to investigate potential applications of chatbots in the realm of medical education. The findings revealed ChatGPT's proficiency in generating virtual patient simulations, formulating quizzes tailored for medical students, evaluating simulated doctor-patient interactions, and succinctly summarizing research articles within the medical domain.

Discharge summaries, commonly authored by junior medical professionals, often face challenges in prioritization due to their heavy workload. Consequently, this delay in crafting comprehensive summaries can impede the timely discharge of patients and contribute to the generation of incomplete documents. This situation exacerbates the strain on an already burdened junior doctor workforce and heightens the potential for patient safety concerns during the transition from secondary to primary care. Implementation of ChatGPT offers a potential solution by alleviating the writing burden associated with discharge summaries. This could lead to the expeditious creation of high-quality summaries, thereby enhancing the efficiency of patient care and addressing critical safety considerations.

3.7.2 Customer Service

One of the most prominent applications of ChatGPT models is in customer support and chatbot systems. Chatbots that can respond to consumer questions and assistance requests have been created using ChatGPT. These chatbots can comprehend text written in nature language and offer tailored responses, enhancing the general customer experience and lightening the strain on customer service representatives. It also reduces the response time improving customer satisfaction.

Additionally, ChatGPTcan may improve e-commerce through chat, finance, and efficiency in the corporate world. It is anticipated that workers, especially those who perform repetitive tasks, may lose their jobs as a result of the deployment of AI.

3.7.3 Content Creation

High-quality content for websites, social media platforms, and advertising campaigns has been produced using ChatGPT. With the ability to adjust to varied writing styles and tones, the model can generate content in a variety of formats, including blog entries, product descriptions, and social media captions.

In Pardos & Bhandari's (2023) study, an evaluation was conducted to compare the efficacy of ChatGPT-generated hints with those crafted by human tutors in two distinct mathematics domains: Elementary Mathematics and Intermediate Algebra. The assessment involved 77 participants.

They discovered that both human and ChatGPT hints yielded positive learning increases, with 70% of the hints passing manual quality assessments. However, only indications made by human instructors were statistically significant for the increases. Despite the participants in the Intermediate Algebra experiment with ChatGPT already demonstrating a high proficiency level, comparable to the control group during the pre-test phase, the study revealed that learning gains were significantly higher when utilizing human-created suggestions compared to ChatGPT hints in both designated topic areas.

With the help of extra tools like Canvas and Midjourney, additionally, ChatGPT can be used to produce multimedia content for social media, such as images and videos, in addition to text-based information.

3.7.4 Language Translation

ChatGPT has been instrumental in the development of text translation systems, achieving notable levels of accuracy. These systems excel in providing context-specific translations and exhibit a nuanced understanding of multiple languages, thereby facilitating enhanced communication among individuals from diverse cultural and linguistic backgrounds.

Additionally, ChatGPT can be used to translate code across several programming languages, including Python and Java. This might be accomplished by giving the large language model input in the form of a code snippet in some language and a prompt specifying the intended output language. Utilizing its understanding of the syntactical and semantic structures of the input language, coupled with the provided prompt, the model is adept at generating equivalent code in the target language (Megahed et al., 2023). It could not, however, be as precise or effective as tools specialized for code translation. To accurately translate code, it could additionally call for a certain set of instructions and inputs.

3.7.5 Entertainment

Using ChatGPT, chatbots that mimic discussions with real people or imaginary characters have been created, offering a distinctive and entertaining entertainment experience. Additionally, ChatGPT can be employed to craft interactive narratives wherein users have the autonomy to shape their own journey by selecting from various alternatives presented by the model.

For the user, this may result in a distinctive and captivating storytelling experience. Additionally, ChatGPT can be employed for the creation of personality assessments, wherein the model engages users through a sequence of inquiries designed to discern their preferences and ascertain various aspects of their personality characteristics.

3.7.6 Financial Services

Virtual financial advisers that can offer individualized investment suggestions and guidance based on risk tolerance, personal financial goals and company AI decision-making have been developed using ChatGPT.

These are only a few of the numerous uses for ChatGPT in different sectors and industries. Technology is predicted to become more and more integral to our daily lives as it develops and advances, changing how we relate to both machines and other people.

3.7.7 Chatbots

Numerous industries and sectors can benefit from the use of chatbots powered by ChatGPT. For instance, chatbots can be utilized in the healthcare industry to offer medical advice, prescription reminders, and mental health support. Chatbots in the financial industry can assist clients with account management, payment processing, and investment guidance. Chatbots can be used in e-commerce to process refunds, track orders, and make customized product recommendations.

Many browser extensions, like ChatGPT for Google, ChatGPT Writer, and Youtube summary with ChatGPT, have recently been released to make it easier to utilize ChatGPT on the web, in emails, and using voice commands. These extensions are already available in Microsoft's Bing browser. More natural and human-like discussions are made possible by implementing ChatGPT in chatbots, which is one of its key benefits.

4. DISCUSSION

Natural Language Processing (NLP) constitutes a domain within Artificial Intelligence (AI) dedicated to facilitating the interaction between computers and human language. Its primary objective is to equip machines with the capability to comprehend, interpret, and generate human language in a manner that is both meaningful and practical. The pivotal role of NLP extends across diverse applications, encompassing chatbots, virtual assistants, sentiment analysis, language translation, information extraction, and various other domains.

NLP approaches can range from traditional rule-based systems to more modern machine learning and deep learning techniques. Deep learning methods, particularly those using neural networks like transformers, have been particularly successful in various NLP tasks, leading to significant advancements in the field.

The creation of the Language Model (LLM), specifically represented by the GPT series, involves the integration of components from Natural Language Processing (NLP) and General Artificial Intelligence (GAI). Engineered to produce text resembling human language, the LLM relies on learned patterns derived from an extensive and diverse dataset of textual sources. Leveraging the Transformer architecture, it employs self-attention mechanisms for effective input data processing, implemented through multiple layers of self-attention and feed-forward neural networks. The training regimen for GPT encompasses both pre-training and fine-tuning, as detailed in section 3.

4.1 Challenges

Natural Language Processing (NLP) encounters several intricate challenges owing to the intricate nature of human language. Ambiguity permeates various linguistic levels, encompassing lexical ambiguity with multiple word meanings, syntactic ambiguity involving diverse sentence interpretations, and semantic ambiguity leading to multiple statement understandings. Precisely resolving these ambiguities remains a significant and ongoing challenge in the field.

NLP models frequently encounter difficulties in processing words absent from their training data, thereby posing challenges in dealing with domain-specific terminology and rare expressions. Contextual comprehension holds paramount importance for accurate sentence interpretation. However, effectively capturing and maintaining context over lengthy text passages represents a complex endeavor.

Identifying and classifying entities within ambiguous references pose additional challenges, particularly in the context of Named Entity Recognition (NER). The task demands a deep understanding of context and the ability to distinguish and categorize entities accurately despite variations and uncertainties.

Furthermore, the lack of context, data sparsity, and ethical considerations constitute additional obstacles faced by NLP models. Disambiguating the correct sense of a word, especially for polysemous terms with multiple meanings, is a persistently challenging problem that requires innovative solutions.

In contemporary contexts, ChatGPT has demonstrated notable advancements, accompanied by a range of challenges. These challenges encompass concerns regarding efficiency, safety, contextual understanding, and limitations in reasoning. The following section outlines some of the commonly encountered obstacles faced by ChatGPT.

While ChatGPT models are impressive in their ability to generate human-like responses, they still struggle with fully understanding the context of the conversation. This can lead to responses that seem sensible but may be inappropriate or nonsensical when considering the broader context.ChatGPT models can inadvertently generate biased or controversial responses, reflecting the biases present in the training data. Addressing bias and ensuring fairness in language models remains a significant challenge.

ChatGPT models can sometimes generate harmful or misleading content, which raises concerns about misuse and ethical implications. It generates creative responses but does not provide sources for their knowledge. As a result, users may perceive their responses as factual, even when they are not backed by verifiable information.

While GPT-like models exhibit impressive language capabilities, they lack true understanding, reasoning, and logical inference. Consequently, they might produce plausible-sounding but incorrect or nonsensical answers.

4.2 Advantages

Natural Language Processing (NLP) emerges as a transformative field within modern technology, offering a diverse array of advantages and pivotal benefits. The profound impact of NLP is evident in the realm of human-computer interaction, facilitating more natural and intuitive exchanges between users and technology. The integration of NLP in voice-activated assistants and chatbots has heralded a revolutionary shift in how individuals interact with and harness the potential of technology.

NLP's true potential lies in endowing computers with the capacity to understand and decipher human language, thereby streamlining the processing and analysis of extensive volumes of textual data across various applications. Notably, NLP has engendered remarkable advancements in machine translation, expediting seamless communication and transcending linguistic barriers to foster cross-cultural connectivity.

Moreover, NLP techniques exhibit proficiency in extracting relevant insights and providing answers from unstructured text, imparting efficiency to information retrieval processes involving vast datasets. A valuable facet of NLP manifests in its adeptness at discerning and comprehending sentiments expressed in textual content, thus wielding significance in pivotal areas such as social media monitoring, market research, and customer feedback analysis.

Intriguingly, NLP models demonstrate an inherent capability to generate human-like text, while also affording the luxury of personalized user experiences. By comprehending individual preferences and tailoring responses and recommendations accordingly, NLP fosters enhanced user engagement and satisfaction.

Beyond these key advantages, NLP has imparted noteworthy improvements to search engines, elevating search accuracy and relevance for users seeking information. The integration of NLP in healthcare applications stands as a testament to its potential in processing medical records, facilitating diagnosis, and improving patient care.

Furthermore, the indelible influence of NLP is evident in the seamless functionality of chatbots and their invaluable role in customer support and engagement. Social media analysis leverages NLP capabilities to extract meaningful insights from diverse conversations, equipping businesses with data-driven decision-making and brand management strategies.

ChatGPT (Generative Pre-trained Transformer) is a robust and versatile language model, known for its numerous advantages that contribute to its effectiveness across various domains. Its applicability extends to diverse industries such as healthcare, customer service, content creation, language translation, entertainment, financial services, and chatbots.

One of the primary strengths of ChatGPT lies in its remarkable ability to comprehend context. By processing and analyzing large volumes of textual data during pre-training, the model acquires a deep understanding of language patterns, making it adept at grasping the nuances and context of human communication. This contextual comprehension enables ChatGPT to produce more meaningful and relevant responses, enhancing its utility in real-world scenarios.

The natural language generation capability of ChatGPT is another key attribute that sets it apart. The model can generate human-like responses, replicating the fluency and coherence of human speech. This characteristic proves invaluable in tasks that involve producing human-readable content, crafting personalized customer interactions, and generating conversational outputs in chatbot applications.

Moreover, ChatGPT's adaptability to different tasks with minimal data requirements is a compelling advantage. The model's pre-training phase equips it with a broad linguistic knowledge base, allowing it to transfer this knowledge to specific tasks during fine-tuning. This versatility translates to reduced data needs for task-specific training, thereby expediting the development and deployment of applications across various domains.

In healthcare, ChatGPT can assist with medical documentation, patient communication, and symptom analysis, offering a potential boost to healthcare professionals' productivity and improving patient care. In customer service, the model's ability to provide relevant and empathetic responses enhances the customer experience and fosters better relationships with users.

Content creators can leverage ChatGPT to generate engaging and relevant content on various topics, streamlining content production workflows. Additionally, language translation applications can benefit from the model's multilingual understanding, enabling more accurate and contextually appropriate translations.

In the entertainment sector, ChatGPT can contribute to interactive storytelling, virtual characters, and game development, elevating user experiences and enhancing immersion. Financial services can employ the model to analyze financial data, offer personalized financial advice, and optimize decision-making processes.

Finally, the widespread application of ChatGPT in chatbots fosters efficient and natural interactions between users and machines. This not only improves customer support but also empowers businesses to scale their customer service operations effectively.

4.3 Future Advancements

There is a whole world of possibility in regards to the future advancements that might happen in ChatGPT. Some of the predicted advancements that are said to happen include improved contextual understanding, explainable AI, safe responses, and multimodal capabilities.

Researchers are likely to work on enhancing the models' ability to comprehend context more effectively. Efforts will continue to be made to mitigate biases and ensure safer responses from language models. Techniques for controlling the behavior of the models and providing clearer guidelines for user interaction will be explored to reduce the generation of harmful or inappropriate content.

Future advancements may focus on developing methods to make ChatGPT models more transparent, enabling users to understand the reasoning behind the model's responses. Integrating language models with other modalities like images, video, or audio can open up new possibilities for creative applications and improve the model's understanding and generation of content.

5. CONCLUSION

By the end of this chapter, readers will gain the knowledge of the training procedure of the ChatGPT model. A brief discussion on Natural Language Processing followed by its significant use in Generative Pre-Trained models will allow readers to be capable of designing their own pre-trained models. Furthermore, readers will gain insight into the working efficiency of various different ChatGPT models, along with evaluation metrics, and their use domain.

6. REFERENCES

Alammar, J. (n.d.). *The illustrated transformer*. Jay Alammar. https://jalammar.github.io/illustrated-transformer/

BorjiA. (2023). A categorical archive of ChatGPT failures. Research Square (Research Square). https://doi.org/ doi:10.21203/rs.3.rs-2895792/v1

Bubeck, S., Chandrasekaran, V., Eldan, R., Gehrke, J., Horvitz, E., Kamar, E., Lee, P., Lee, Y. T., Li, Y., Lundberg, S., Nori, H., Palangi, H., Ribeiro, M. T., & Zhang, Y. (2023). Sparks of Artificial General Intelligence: Early experiments with GPT-4. *arXiv (Cornell University)*. https://doi.org//arxiv.2303.12712 doi:10.48550

Cao, Y., Li, S., Liu, Y., Zhang, Y., Dai, Y., Yu, P. S., & Sun, L. (2023). A Comprehensive Survey of AI-Generated Content (AIGC): A History of Generative AI from GAN to ChatGPT. *arXiv (Cornell University)*. https://doi.org//arxiv.2303.04226 doi:10.48550

Chi, E. C., Lyman, M., Sager, N., & MacLeod, C. (1985). *A Database of Computer-Structured Narrative: Methods of Computing Complex Relations.* ResearchGate. https://www.researchgate.net/publication/26174364_A_Database_of_Computer-Structured_Narrative_Methods_of_Computing_Complex_Relations

Cretu, C. (2023, April 6). *How does ChatGPT actually work? An ML engineer explains.* Scalable Path. https://www.scalablepath.com/data-science/chatgpt-architecture-explained

De Angelis, L., Baglivo, F., Arzilli, G., Privitera, G. P., Ferragina, P., Tozzi, A. E., & Rizzo, C. (2023). ChatGPT and the rise of large language models: The new AI-driven infodemic threat in public health. *Frontiers in Public Health*, *11*, 1166120. doi:10.3389/fpubh.2023.1166120 PMID:37181697

DeepLearning.AI. (2023). Natural Language Processing (NLP) [A Complete Guide]. *DeepLearning.AI.* https://www.deeplearning.ai/resources/natural-language-processing/

Document Link. https://docs.google.com/document/d/1v7dxHSWcz78LAyk4wBVj_ae5OTE02Cjsp-WVdnMJ3GzM/edit?hl=en

Duan, J., Zhao, H., Zhou, Q., Qiu, M., & Liu, M. (n.d.). A Study of Pre-trained Language Models in Natural Language Processing. In *2020 IEEE International Conference on Smart Cloud (SmartCloud)*, Washington, DC, United States of America. https://doi.org/10.1109/SmartCloud49737.2020.00030

Eysenbach, G. (2023). The role of ChatGPT, Generative Language models, and Artificial intelligence in medical Education: A conversation with ChatGPT and a call for papers. *JMIR Medical Education*, *9*, e46885. doi:10.2196/46885 PMID:36863937

Friedman, C., Cimino, J., & Johnson, S. (1993). A conceptual model for clinical radiology reports. *In proceedings of the annual symposium on computer application in medical care.*

Glasgow, B., Mandell, A., Binney, D., Ghemri, L., & Fisher, D. A. (1998). MITA: An Information-Extraction Approach to the Analysis of Free-Form Text in Life insurance Applications. *AI Magazine*, *19*(1), 59–72. doi:10.1609/aimag.v19i1.1354

Goodfellow, I. J., Pouget-Abadie, J., Mirza, M., Xu, B., Warde-Farley, D., Ozair, S., Courville, A., & Bengio, Y. (2014). Generative adversarial networks. *arXiv (Cornell University)*. https://doi.org//arxiv.1406.2661 doi:10.48550

Grishman, R., Sager, N., Raze, C., & Bookchin, B. (1973). The linguistic string parser. *AFIPS '73: Proceedings of the National Computer Conference and Exposition*, (pp. 427–434). ACM. https://doi.org/10.1145/1499586.1499693

Haleem, A., Javaid, M., & Singh, R. P. (2022). An era of ChatGPT as a significant futuristic support tool: A study on features, abilities, and challenges. *BenchCouncil Transactions on Benchmarks. Standards and Evaluations*, 2(4), 100089. doi:10.1016/j.tbench.2023.100089

Hariri, W. (2023). Unlocking the Potential of ChatGPT: A Comprehensive Exploration of its Applications, Advantages, Limitations, and Future Directions in Natural Language Processing. *arXiv (Cornell University)*. https://doi.org//arxiv.2304.02017 doi:10.48550

Hayes, P. (2016). In P. Jacobs (Ed.), *Intelligent high-volume text processing using shallow, domain-specific techniques: Text-Based Intelligent Systems: Current Research and Practice in Information Extraction and Retrieval* (pp. 227–242). Psychology Press.

Hill-Yardin, E. L., Hutchinson, M. R., Laycock, R., & Spencer, S. J. (2023). A Chat(GPT) about the future of scientific publishing. *Brain, Behavior, and Immunity, 110*, 152–154. doi:10.1016/j.bbi.2023.02.022 PMID:36868432

Jamiu, M. (2023, May). *Difference between GPT-1, GPT-2, GPT-3/3.5 and GPT-4 | Tooabstractive*. Difference Between GPT-1, GPT-2, GPT-3/3.5 and GPT-4 | Tooabstractive.

Johri, P., Khatri, S. K., Al-Taani, A. T., Sabharwal, M., Suvanov, S., & Kumar, A. (2021). Natural Language Processing: history, evolution, application, and future work. In *Lecture notes in networks and systems* (Vol. 167, pp. 365–375). Springer. doi:10.1007/978-981-15-9712-1_31

Khandelwal, U., He, H., Qi, P., & Jurafsky, D. (2018). Sharp Nearby, Fuzzy Far Away: How Neural Language Models Use Context. *Proceedings of the 56th Annual Meeting of the Association for Computational Linguistics,* Volume 1*: Long Papers*, 284–294. https://doi.org/10.18653/v1/P18-1027

Khurana, D., Koli, A., Khatter, K., & Singh, S. (2022). Natural language processing: State of the art, current trends and challenges. *Multimedia Tools and Applications, 82*(3), 3713–3744. doi:10.100711042-022-13428-4 PMID:35855771

Knill, K., & Young, S. (1997). Hidden Markov models in speech and language processing. In *Text, speech and language technology* (pp. 27–68). Springer. doi:10.1007/978-94-017-1183-8_2

Kohnke, L., Moorhouse, B. L., & Zou, D. (2023). ChatGPT for language teaching and learning. *RELC Journal, 003368822311628*(2), 537–550. doi:10.1177/00336882231162868

Korngiebel, D. M., & Mooney, S. D. (2021). Considering the possibilities and pitfalls of Generative Pre-trained Transformer 3 (GPT-3) in healthcare delivery. *Npj Digital Medicine, 4*(1). doi:10.1038/s41746-021-00464-x

Kumar, A. (2023, March 17). *Generative vs Discriminative Models: Examples*.

Kumar, A. (2023b, July 9). *Large Language Models (LLMs): Concepts & Examples*.

Liddy, E. D. (2001). Natural language processing. Encyclopedia of Library and Information Science.

Liu, C. Y. (2022). Types of NLP models. *OpenGenus IQ: Computing Expertise & Legacy*. https://iq.opengenus.org/types-of-nlp-models/

Megahed, F. M., Chen, Y., Ferris, J. A., Knoth, S., & Jones-Farmer, L. A. (2023). How Generative AI models such as ChatGPT can be (Mis)Used in SPC Practice, Education, and Research? An Exploratory Study. *arXiv (Cornell University)*. https://doi.org//arxiv.2302.10916 doi:10.48550

MhlangaD. (2023). Open AI in Education, The responsible and ethical use of ChaTGPT towards lifelong Learning. *Social Science Research Network*. https://doi.org/ doi:10.2139/ssrn.4354422

Mikolov, T., Karafiát, M., Burget, L., Černocký, J., & Khudanpur, S. (2010). Recurrent neural network based language model. *11th Annual Conference of the International Speech Communication Association*, Makuhari, Chiba, Japan. 10.21437/Interspeech.2010-343

Oberoi, A. (2021, July 15). What are Language Models in NLP? *Daffodil Unthinkable Software Corp.*

Ochoa, A. (2016). *Meet the pilot: Smart Earpiece language translator*. Indiegogo. https://www.indiegogo.com/projects/meet-the-pilot-smart-earpiece-language-translator#/

Orr, A. (2017). Capital One Launched A Natural Language Chatbot Named Eno. *The Mac Observer*. https://www.macobserver.com/analysis/capital-one-natural-language-chatbot-eno/

Otter, D. W., Medina, J. R., & Kalita, J. (2021). A Survey of the Usages of Deep Learning for Natural Language Processing. *IEEE, 32*(2), 604–624. doi:10.1109/TNNLS.2020.2979670

Ouyang, L., & Wu, J. (2022). Training language models to follow instructions with human feedback. *arXiv (Cornell University)*. https://doi.org//arxiv.2203.02155 doi:10.48550

Pardos, Z. A., & Bhandari, S. (2023). Learning gain differences between ChatGPT and human tutor generated algebra hints. *arXiv (Cornell University)*. https://doi.org//arxiv.2302.06871 doi:10.48550

Qiu, X., Sun, T., Xu, Y., Shao, Y., Dai, N., & Huang, X. (2020). Pre-trained models for natural language processing: A survey. *IEEE, 63*(10), 1872–1897. doi:10.1007/s11431-020-1647-3

Rahali, A., & Akhloufi, M. A. (2023). End-to-End Transformer-Based models in Textual-Based NLP. *AI, 4*(1), 54–110. doi:10.3390/ai4010004

Ray, P. P. (2023). ChatGPT: A comprehensive review on background, applications, key challenges, bias, ethics, limitations and future scope. *Internet of Things and Cyber-physical Systems, 3*, 121–154. doi:10.1016/j.iotcps.2023.04.003

Ruby, M. (2023, May 7). How ChatGPT Works: The Model Behind The Bot - Towards Data Science. *Medium*. https://towardsdatascience.com/how-chatgpt-works-the-models-behind-the-bot-1ce5fca96286

Sager, N., Lyman, M. S., Nhan, N. T., & Lj, T. (1995). Medical Language Processing: applications to patient data representation and automatic encoding. *Methods of Information in Medicine, 34*(01/02), 140–146. doi:10.1055/s-0038-1634579

Shen, Y., Heacock, L., Elias, J., Hentel, K., Reig, B., Shih, G., & Moy, L. (2023). ChatGPT and other large language models are double-edged swords. *Radiology, 307*(2), e230163. doi:10.1148/radiol.230163 PMID:36700838

Taylor, K. (2022). *Know about NLP language Model comprising of scope predictions of IT Industry.* HitechNectar.

Van Dis, E., Bollen, J., Zuidema, W., Van Rooij, R., & Bockting, C. (2023). ChatGPT: Five priorities for research. *Nature, 614*(7947), 224–226. doi:10.1038/d41586-023-00288-7 PMID:36737653

ZhaiX. (2023). ChatGPT for next generation Science Learning. *Social Science Research Network.* doi:10.2139/ssrn.4331313

Chapter 11
Revolutionizing Conversational AI:
Unleashing the Power of ChatGPT–Based Applications in Generative AI and Natural Language Processing

C. V. Suresh Babu

https://orcid.org/0000-0002-8474-2882

Hindustan Institute of Technolgy and Science, India

P. M. Akshara

https://orcid.org/0009-0004-8498-0196

Hindustan Institute of Technology and Science, India

ABSTRACT

The emergence of advanced NLP models, like ChatGPT and other conversational AI models, has triggered a revolutionary transformation. This chapter explores the burgeoning field of ChatGPT applications, conducting a comprehensive analysis of their impact across various domains. The chapter assesses their capabilities, challenges, and potential uses, examining the underlying architecture and training methods that enable them to generate contextually relevant and coherent responses. Ethical considerations are also addressed, encompassing concerns about bias, misinformation, and user privacy in real-world conversations. The chapter also acknowledges drawbacks, including occasional inaccuracies or sensitive content generation. In conclusion, ongoing research is vital to enhance model robustness, user experience, and ethical deployment in conversational AI. ChatGPT and similar models are poised to reshape human-machine communication, fostering dynamic, engaging, and valuable conversations.

DOI: 10.4018/979-8-3693-0502-7.ch011

1. INTRODUCTION

Over the past few decades, the field of artificial intelligence (AI) has undergone significant evolution. Initially, AI systems were designed for specific tasks, such as playing chess or go. Advances in machine learning and deep learning have driven considerable progress in AI's development, resulting in enhancements across various applications like robotics, healthcare, finance, and image recognition. (Suresh Babu C.V., 2022),

AI systems now possess decision-making abilities honed through machine learning and deep learning algorithms, enabling them to analyze vast datasets and uncover patterns, insights, and correlations that may elude human perception. This data-driven approach empowers AI systems to make precise decisions in diverse domains.

One pivotal milestone in AI's journey was the invention of neural networks in the 1950s, inspired by the human brain's learning process. These networks revolutionized AI by enabling the execution of previously impossible tasks. They empowered AI systems to accurately transcribe human speech, and recognize objects, individuals, and situations in images.

Deep learning models, particularly transformer-based designs like Bert and GPT (generative pre-trained transformers), have significantly enhanced natural language processing (NLP) capabilities. Tasks such as machine translation, chatbot development, sentiment analysis, and other language-related applications have advanced due to their ability to comprehend and generate human-like language.

2. INTRODUCTION TO CHATGPT

2.1 Understanding its Architecture and Training

GPT models, a type of large language model (LLM) developed by OpenAI, are trained on extensive datasets, including text and code, to perform various NLP tasks like text generation, summarization, and conversation. ChatGPT, based on the GPT-3.5 architecture, is specially designed for understanding and generating human-like text.

Its architecture is based on an attention-based model known as a deep neural network with numerous layers of transformers that is particularly effective at extracting contextual information from text. These transformers are placed one on top of the other to create a complex architecture that allows ChatGPT to comprehend and produce human-like text. Its 175 billion parameters are learned during training using a huge amount of text data. Due to its comprehensive pre-training, ChatGPT can comprehend a variety of subjects and give thoughtful responses. It uses a decoding technique to produce answers word by word during inference while taking the input's context into account. Additionally, adjustments are made to make ChatGPT's output generation process safer and more in control. With the help of this architecture, ChatGPT can carry out a variety of activities with impressive adaptability and fluency, including text production, question-answering, and natural language interpretation. ChatGPT finds applications in conversational AI, including chatbots, virtual assistants, language translation, educational tutoring, content creation, therapeutic conversations, language learning support, travel guidance, personalized shopping experiences, and more.

This chapter explores the transformative potential of conversational AI applications based on ChatGPT across various domains. It delves into the deployment of chatbots and virtual assistants, highlighting the role of natural language processing and fine-tuning in personalizing and enhancing interactions. Additionally, it discusses how companies leverage ChatGPT for customer support, automating service processes to boost efficiency and satisfaction. The chapter emphasizes the value of customization and provides real-world examples of recommendation systems tailored to individual preferences.

Furthermore, it examines ChatGPT's creative capabilities, illustrating how AI collaboration can enhance content production while addressing ethical considerations. Ultimately, the chapter considers challenges and potential outcomes, underscoring the need for ongoing research to advance ethical AI practices.

2.1.1 GPT vs. ChatGPT

Both ChatGPT and GPT are NLP (natural language processing models) that differ majorly in design aspects and their potential applications. GPT excels at text production, translation, and content summarization and is a flexible model for natural language understanding and generation. However, it needs certain prompts and might not comprehend conversational context. A specialized form called ChatGPT is excellent at conversational AI applications, keeping context and comprehending prior messages. For a safer, more controlled communication experience, it records conversation history and adds safety precautions.

Table 1. Differences between GPT and ChatGPT models

Features	GPT	ChatGPT
Objective	AI-driven natural language creation and interpretation system.	AI-driven conversational chatbots provide human-like responses.
Training records	Trained on diverse internet text	Conducted on a curated conversation dataset for dialogue-based interactions.
Prompting	To produce the intended results, usually, special prompts or instructions are needed.	Designed to engage in open-ended conversations, often starting with a user message.
Fine-tuning	Can be fine-tuned to perform better for specific operations and domains.	Fine-tuned with a focus on chat applications, making it more suitable for conversational contexts
Response	Generates single responses, may not always be contextually relevant.	Exceptional at maintaining context and facilitating coherent conversations.
Conversational management	Unable to maintain conversation history; treats each input independently.	Utilizes conversation history for context-aware responses.
Deployment	Used to perform text creation jobs in a variety of products and services.	Preferred for customer-facing ai applications and interactive chat interfaces.
Safety and prevention	May produce inappropriate or biased content; extra safety precautions are needed.	Incorporates improved security safeguards and content filtering to cut down on negative or inappropriate reactions.

2.2 Literature Review

This review of literature aims to summarize all the applications of both ChatGPT and GPT models, categorizing and analyzing their contributions to each. We intend to concentrate on the possible impact of these models on industries such as healthcare, customer service, content creation, education, and others. Furthermore, we will assess the challenges and limitations of implementing ChatGPT and GPT models in real-world scenarios, such as prejudice, safety, and ethical problems. Many studies have been conducted to assess the abilities of ChatGPT and GPT-4 in many tasks and specialties. The advent of ChatGPT has created a lot of theories about its potential to disrupt social and economic systems. Its extraordinary language abilities have drawn the interest of academics who are curious about its performance in several disciplines. A detailed evaluation summarising the collective assessment findings, on the other hand, is lacking. This study aims to thoroughly examine previous assessments of ChatGPT and GPT-4, focusing on language and reasoning ability, scientific knowledge, and ethical considerations. The study also explains the evolution of ChatGPT from other GPT models. Through design adjustments and fine-tuning processes, ChatGPT emerged from the GPT model. Its underlying architecture is shared with GPT models, with the Transformer architecture serving as the primary building piece. ChatGPT was trained using a large pre-training dataset, with a focus on dialogue-based interactions. It is programmed to create responses within the context of a discussion, boosting conversational flow and implementing safety safeguards to ensure a responsible experience. It is designed specifically for chatbots, virtual assistants, and customer service applications. ChatGPT is continuously refined through iterative training and updates, incorporating user feedback and real-world usage to overcome restrictions. This progression underscores the requirement for specialized models for interactive and context-rich conversational contexts. Furthermore, the present assessment approaches are examined, and numerous recommendations for future study in evaluating big language models are made. (Mao et al., 2023)

AI-driven e-learning has transformed education by providing personalized, efficient, and accessible learning experiences (Suresh Babu, C. V., and B. Rohan, 2023). However, there are considerable differences in uptake and impact among age groups. Access to technology is difficult for younger learners, particularly those living in underprivileged or rural locations, while elderly persons may struggle with technical aspects. Because AI-powered platforms frequently target the adult and higher education sectors, content relevance and customization may be an issue for both groups. Learning speed may be an issue, as AI systems may struggle to adjust content to individual needs (Suresh Babu, C. V. & Padma. R., 2023). AI-powered e-learning may have an impact on social connection, while adult learners may miss out on networking and peer support opportunities. AI-based services collect and analyze sensitive data about people, and ethical and privacy problems arise. Through sample applications, this work demonstrates the integration of AI technology into Learning Management Systems (LMSs). It emphasizes the process's complexities, such as security, privacy, ethics, pedagogy, and technical issues. Users frequently lack information regarding personal data protection when using AI. Other considerations include data security, ethical concerns, advice, and technological aspects such as platform compatibility, resource availability, and maintenance. AI integration can be successfully integrated into an LMS by following these procedures and considering important factors. This increases the effectiveness and accessibility of instruction. However, for successful integration, thorough planning and evaluation are required.

Using AI to generate scientific abstracts, such as ChatGPT or other language models like GPT-3, can be a useful tool for academics and scholars. While ChatGPT is normally used for conversational AI, by fine-tuning it on a dataset of scientific papers or utilizing a few creative strategies, it can be converted to generate scientific summaries. ChatGPT can produce realistic text, according to a study utilizing ten research abstracts from five high-impact medical publications, but its accuracy and integrity in scientific writing are uncertain. AI output detectors and plagiarism detectors were used to evaluate the abstracts, and the majority of generated abstracts were detected. The study discovered that while ChatGPT-generated abstracts were intelligible, only 8% adhered to specified journal formatting criteria. The originality of the generated abstracts was excellent, however, it was difficult to distinguish between innovative and general abstracts. According to the study, abstract evaluation policies and practices for journals and medical conferences must be modified to preserve rigorous scientific standards, such as AI output detectors and explicit disclosure. (Gao et al., 2022d)

ChatGPT in medicine explores the potential applications of ChatGPT and AI in healthcare and medical fields. ChatGPT, an advanced language model developed by OpenAI, can generate human-like responses to natural language inputs. It can identify research topics, assist professionals in clinical diagnosis, and aid patients in managing their health. However, its use raises ethical and legal concerns, such as copyright infringement and transparency in AI-generated content. The paper also discusses prospects in the medical field. The implementation of ChatGPT and related AI models in healthcare has strong prospects and can revolutionize several parts of the industry. Some of them include providing real-time, evidence-based information to healthcare providers, aiding in clinical decision support, and improving telemedicine and remote monitoring. Also to assist in personalized medicine by tailoring treatment plans to individual patients. However, ethical concerns related to patient data privacy, security, and decision-making will remain a critical focus. These prospects require continued research, development, and collaboration between healthcare professionals, AI experts, policymakers, and ethicists. (Dave et al., 2023)

ChatGPT assists developers in identifying and resolving software bugs by exploiting its natural language processing skills. When developers run across a problem with their code or application, they can use ChatGPT to describe the issue in clear terms. ChatGPT can then offer insights, suggestions, and direction to assist in determining the root cause of the problem and proposing viable remedies. ChatGPT accomplishes this technically by comprehending the developer's input, parsing the text to extract relevant information about the issue, and then creating human-readable responses aimed at resolving the issue. It can offer code examples, explanations, and even links to important documentation or resources.

Furthermore, ChatGPT can help with error message interpretation by explaining cryptic error messages and recommending corrective measures. The model's capacity to draw from a broad knowledge base of programming languages, frameworks, and best practices enables it to provide intelligent debugging and problem-solving solutions. This natural language engagement with ChatGPT not only speeds up debugging but also democratizes access to expertise, making it a vital tool for both novice and experienced developers in swiftly addressing software bugs.

(Nigar M. Shafiq Surameery, & Mohammed Y. Shakor., 2023) ChatGPT helps in the resolution of programming bugs. The study looks into the properties of ChatGPT and how they may be used to help solve programming problems by providing debugging aid, defect prediction, and bug explanation. It also investigates Chat GPT's limitations in identifying programming errors, as well as the significance of using additional debugging tools and approaches to evaluate its predictions and explanations. The study finishes by emphasizing the potential of Chat GPT as one component of a full debugging toolbox, as well as the advantages of combining its strengths with the strengths of other debugging tools to more effectively find and fix faults.

Clinical care applications remain limited due to the lack of structured, machine-readable data required for deep learning algorithms. Algorithms for clinical care are often highly variable, failing to generalize across settings due to limited technical, statistical, and conceptual reproducibility. As a result, most successful healthcare applications support back-office functions like payor operations, automated prior authorization processing, and supply chain management. Developing clinical AI models requires significant time, resources, and highly domain and problem-specific training data, which are in short supply in the healthcare world. One key development that enabled image-based AI in clinical imaging is the ability of large general domain models to perform as well as outperform domain-specific models. Inception-V3 serves as the basic foundation of many top medical imaging models, ranging from ophthalmology to dermatology. In recent weeks, ChatGPT, a new AI model developed by OpenAI, has gained attention due to its ability to perform diverse natural language tasks. ChatGPT is a general Large Language Model (LLM) trained on large amounts of text data, generating novel sequences of words never observed previously but representing plausible sequences based on natural human language. ChatGPT is a machine learning model powered by GPT3.5 that was trained using reinforcement and supervised learning methods on the OpenAI 175B parameter foundation model and a large corpus of text data from the internet. (Kung TH, 2023). ChatGPT is also blooming in the field of biomedical sciences. (SamyAteia1,UdoKruschwitz)

Improving customer service with ChatGPT is a growing field of study and application in the fields of artificial intelligence and service industries (Suresh Babu C.V., 2022). Numerous studies and actual implementations have investigated ChatGPT's ability to improve customer interactions and satisfaction. These efforts are aimed at utilizing the model's natural language understanding and generating skills to deliver efficient, personalized, and timely support. ChatGPT's role in automating regular customer inquiries, speeding issue resolution, and providing 24/7 availability has been explored by researchers. The model's capacity to keep context and adapt to unique customer preferences has been a focus point in producing more engaging and empathic customer experiences. Ethical concerns, data privacy, and ensuring openness in AI-powered customer service have also received a lot of attention.

The study focuses on the application of ChatGPT in customer care and telecoms firm that was trying to respond to consumer inquiries in a timely and correct manner. To automate customer assistance and reduce response times, the company built a ChatGPT-based system. The ChatGPT system was trained on a large dataset of customer inquiries and responses, which allowed it to comprehend the context and intent of consumer inquiries.

Customers received personalized responses from the system, which addressed their unique needs and provided correct information. The study's findings revealed a considerable improvement in customer satisfaction and response times. The organization was able to lower the average response time from several hours to just a few minutes. (Chowdhury, Naem & Abdoulsalam Awais, Osman & Aktar, Sheuly., 2023)

ChatGPT assists customers independently, reducing customer service costs and improving response speed and accuracy. This technology saves time and money for e-commerce businesses by allowing them to quickly provide answers without waiting for human representatives or navigating complex menus (Suresh Babu, C. V. & Padma. R., 2023). ChatGPT also allows businesses to have more control over the messages they receive and how they are delivered, which would be impossible to do manually. In addition to saving money, ChatGPT offers better accuracy in understanding requests from users speaking different languages, allowing companies to reach new markets and potentially increase sales. Its ability to quickly scale up makes it suitable for businesses with high website traffic during busy times like holidays, ensuring no leads are lost. ChatGPT also provides valuable customer data, allowing companies to personalize offers. ChatGPT is a significant and valuable tool for both marketing scholars and practitioners, offering several chances to both parties. It assists researchers in organizing, synthesizing, and accumulating material to generate ideas and expand on theories. Researchers can concentrate on the most creative and analytical aspects of their work by using ChatGPT to help them save time and effort on tasks like literature reviews, text generation, data analysis, summarising, and answering questions (Wang, Lund, 2023)

3. CHATGPT IN CONVERSATIONAL APPLICATIONS

3.1 Customer Assistance and Service Automation

Customer service plays a pivotal role in a business's growth and success, directly influencing customer satisfaction, brand loyalty, overall business performance, and brand reputation. Across various industries, the integration of Generative Pre-Trained Transformers (GPT) models has brought about significant improvements and transformations in customer service.

Chatbots now deliver automated customer service, personalized recommendations, troubleshooting assistance, real-time order tracking, and updates. These chatbots swiftly address common inquiries, offer prompt solutions, and provide step-by-step guidance for prevalent issues. Leveraging insights from consumer preferences and past interactions, they enhance cross-selling and upselling opportunities.

GPT-based chatbots also offer real-time updates on order status, shipping details, and estimated delivery times, ensuring high levels of customer satisfaction. These models employ their natural language processing capabilities to comprehend customer queries and provide human-like responses.

The process begins with the collection of customer data, including chat logs, FAQs, and other relevant content. Initial training involves exposing the model to extensive internet text to acquire grammar, syntax, and general knowledge. Further refinement is achieved using domain-specific customer service data, honing the model's understanding of language and context-specific customer interactions.

Once refined, the model is implemented as a chatbot or virtual assistant within the customer service system. When a customer interacts with the chatbot, the GPT model receives their request, analyzes it, and generates a response while maintaining the conversation context. Responses are evaluated based on criteria like relevance, consistency, and appropriateness. The virtual assistants powered by ChatGPT enhance user satisfaction and engagement through continuous availability, consistency, and personalized experiences. They streamline interactions between humans and technology across various sectors, including customer service, education, healthcare, and more, thus elevating productivity and accessibility (Suresh Babu, C. V. & Padma. R., 2023).In the backend of ChatGPT models, dynamically generated and processed natural language underpins the virtual assistant's operation(A. Shaji George, & A. S. Hovan George, 2023).

In cases where the request is intricate or necessitates human intervention, the GPT model can seamlessly transfer the interaction to a customer service agent. Continuous improvement is driven by user interactions, with the model refined and bugs addressed based on user and agent feedback.

By effectively integrating GPT models into customer service, organizations can provide timely support, reduce response times, elevate customer satisfaction, and streamline support processes (Lakhani, 2023).

3.1.1 Automating Service Applications for Improved Efficiency

ChatGPT can significantly improve service applications by automating customer support, information retrieval, and interaction handling. It offers 24/7 availability, instant responses, scalability, multilingual support, data retrieval, personalized recommendations, automated tagging, consistency, reduced human error, cost efficiency, analytics, and a scalable knowledge base. ChatGPT operates round the clock, reducing the need for human support agents to work in shifts. It can provide quick and consistent responses to frequently asked questions, reducing waiting times and enhancing customer experience.

Scalability allows service applications to scale effortlessly to accommodate increased user demand without the need for additional staff, resulting in cost savings. It can communicate in multiple languages, breaking down language barriers and catering to a broader customer base. ChatGPT can quickly fetch and present relevant information from a vast knowledge base, saving time for both customers and support agents. It can also offer personalized recommendations based on user preferences and historical interactions, improving customer satisfaction.

ChatGPT can streamline processes, enhance user experiences, reduce operational costs, and improve overall efficiency, making it a valuable tool for businesses looking to provide high-quality service while optimizing their operations.

ChatGPT can significantly improve service applications by automating customer support, information retrieval, and interaction handling. It offers 24/7 availability, instant responses, scalability, multilingual support, data retrieval, personalized recommendations, automated tagging, consistency, reduced human error, cost efficiency, analytics, and a scalable knowledge base. ChatGPT operates round the clock, reducing the need for human support agents to work in shifts. It can provide quick and consistent responses to frequently asked questions, reducing waiting times and enhancing customer experience.

Scalability allows service applications to scale effortlessly to accommodate increased user demand without the need for additional staff, resulting in cost savings. It can communicate in multiple languages, breaking down language barriers and catering to a broader customer base. ChatGPT can quickly fetch and present relevant information from a vast knowledge base, saving time for both customers and support agents. It can also offer personalized recommendations based on user preferences and historical interactions, improving customer satisfaction.

ChatGPT can enhance user experiences, reduce operational costs, and improve overall efficiency, making it a valuable tool for businesses looking to provide high-quality service while optimizing their operations.

3.2 Language Translation and Education Tutoring

3.2.1 Breaking Language Barriers With ChatGPT's Translation Capabilities

ChatGPT models have emerged as powerful aids in the realm of language translation, revolutionizing the way languages are bridged and communication barriers are overcome. Leveraging their advanced natural language processing capabilities, these models facilitate seamless and accurate translation between different languages, offering a plethora of benefits across various domains. at the heart of language translation, ChatGPT models excel in their ability to comprehend the nuances of one language and convert it into another while maintaining context and meaning. The models are trained on vast multilingual datasets, allowing them to grasp grammar rules, syntax variations, idiomatic expressions, and cultural nuances that play a pivotal role in accurate translation. They can swiftly process input text and generate output in a target language, thereby enabling individuals to communicate effectively across language barriers (Wenxiang Jiao et al., 2023).

In contexts such as global business, language translation by ChatGPT models is transformative. Companies can utilize these models to instantly translate documents, contracts, marketing materials, and customer communications, facilitating cross-border collaborations and expanding market reach. This expedites decision-making, enhances international customer interactions, and ensures consistency in messaging across diverse linguistic audiences.

Language translation is crucial in humanitarian efforts and crisis response. ChatGPT models can help bridge communication gaps between relief workers and affected populations, providing vital information about safety, medical aid, and resources in the local languages. This aids in efficiently coordinating disaster relief and providing assistance to those in need, regardless of linguistic diversity.

However, challenges persist in the domain of language translation. Idioms, cultural references, and context-specific phrases may pose difficulties in direct translation. Ensuring that translated content accurately conveys the intended message is essential, particularly in fields like legal, medical, and technical translations. Models must also be mindful of maintaining privacy and data security, especially when dealing with sensitive information during translation.

As ChatGPT models continue to evolve, bridging language gaps will become even more seamless and accurate. Continued advancements will likely lead to better handling of colloquialisms, dialects, and regional language variations. Ensuring that these models are unbiased and culturally sensitive is imperative to prevent perpetuating stereotypes or misconceptions during translation.

ChatGPT models have revolutionized language translation by providing rapid, accurate, and contextually rich conversions across diverse foreign languages also (Wilson Cheong, 2023). Their impact spans industries, education, and humanitarian efforts, fostering effective communication in a globalized world. While challenges persist, the promise of overcoming language barriers through these models is poised to reshape how we connect, collaborate, and share information across linguistic divides.

3.2.2 Language Learning Support and Tutoring With ChatGPT

In educational settings, ChatGPT models empower students to access educational resources in different languages. Academic content, research papers, and learning materials can be translated on the fly, enabling students worldwide to learn from a broader range of resources (Suresh Babu, C. V., and B. Rohan, 2023). Moreover, these models support language learners by offering real-time translations during language lessons and practice exercises, accelerating the language acquisition process.

ChatGPT models have emerged as valuable tools that are transforming the landscape of education by offering innovative solutions to various challenges faced by educators and learners alike. One of the most significant contributions of ChatGPT models to education is in personalized learning (Suresh Babu, C. V., and B. Rohan, 2023). These models can engage students in natural language conversations, answering queries, explaining concepts, and providing additional resources. This individualized approach helps address diverse learning paces and styles, ensuring that students receive the support they need to grasp complex subjects. Furthermore, ChatGPT models offer a bridge to fill knowledge gaps. Students struggling with specific topics can interact with the model to receive clarification and reinforcement, providing an on-demand tutor-like experience. The model's ability to generate contextually relevant explanations conversationally enhances comprehension and retention. In addition to supporting students, ChatGPT models assist educators in various capacities. Teachers can employ these models to create interactive lesson plans, generate examples, and design engaging study materials. This significantly reduces the time spent on content creation, enabling educators to focus more on personalized instruction and student engagement. Language learning is another area greatly impacted by ChatGPT models. These models can simulate real-life language conversations, offering students the opportunity to practice speaking, listening, and dynamically understanding languages. The model's responsiveness and adaptability facilitate language practice outside of traditional classroom settings.

Moreover, ChatGPT models foster creativity and critical thinking. They can serve as prompts for creative writing exercises, helping students develop their storytelling and imaginative skills. By encouraging students to engage in open-ended conversations with the model, educators can stimulate analytical thinking and exploration of diverse ideas. While ChatGPT models offer numerous benefits, certain considerations are vital. The quality of the educational content produced heavily relies on the accuracy of information. Ensuring that the models are trained on reliable sources and undergo proper fine-tuning is essential to avoid misinformation. Moreover, the ethical implications of using AI models in education, such as data privacy and bias, must be carefully addressed. ChatGPT models are revolutionizing education by providing personalized learning experiences, offering real-time support, enhancing language acquisition, fostering creativity, and easing content creation for educators. As these models continue to advance, their role in education will likely expand, reshaping how educators and learners interact with information and each other. However, a balanced approach, combining AI's capabilities with human expertise, is key to harnessing the full potential of ChatGPT models in education (Dwivedi et al., 2023).

3.3 Content Creation and Therapeutic Conversations

3.3.1 Boosting Content Production Through AI Collaboration With ChatGPT

ChatGPT models have emerged as potent content creation tools, reshaping the landscape of textual material creation. Their proficiency in interpreting natural language stems from the underlying transformer architecture. When employed for content development, ChatGPT models excel at producing contextually relevant, coherent, and tailored text.

In conversational content creation, the Transformer architecture analyzes input, converts tokens into numerical representations, grasps context, and generates content through a decoder. Employing probabilities, the model predicts the next token in the conversation and iteratively constructs the complete response (Fitria, T. N.,2023). It also employs techniques like sampling to introduce variety and creativity. Content quality control, including content screening and moderation, is implemented to ensure compliance with safety standards. The response output is then translated back into natural language and delivered as a response.

By maintaining context, the model crafts content that flows seamlessly and logically, closely resembling human writing. ChatGPT models can offer a wide array of information, including blog posts, articles, product descriptions, marketing copy, and social media captions. Leveraging these models, businesses can effortlessly generate diverse content tailored to various platforms and audiences, saving both time and effort (Castellanos-Gomez, 2023).

While ChatGPT models excel at content creation, they do present challenges. Notably, the risk of generating inaccurate or biased information is a significant concern. These models may inadvertently perpetuate biases present in their training data due to their vast internet content training. Rigorous oversight, fine-tuning, and review are imperative to ensure the accuracy and ethical integrity of generated content. Additionally, maintaining a consistent tone and style across longer pieces can prove challenging, as the models may occasionally produce sections that deviate from the established tone, necessitating manual intervention or post-processing.

Despite these challenges, the applications of ChatGPT models in content generation are extensive and transformative. They empower businesses and content creators to efficiently produce high-quality, engaging content. As technology advances, these models are likely to become indispensable tools for content teams, marketers, and writers, fundamentally reshaping content creation and distribution. However, responsible and vigilant usage, coupled with human oversight, remains essential to align generated content with intended messages, brand identity, and ethical standards (Suresh Babu, C. V. & Padma. R., 2023).

ChatGPT can create and generate pieces of coding that can aid developers in writing code samples, deriving difficult programming ideas, and resolving issues. They may outline a challenge or the desired functionality, and the model may offer lines of code, point out potential problems, or offer justifications for particular coding techniques. ChatGPT models can take the place of a virtual pair programmer in situations where developers are stuck or having trouble with a piece of code. They mimic the collaborative nature of programming by making recommendations, suggesting different strategies, and highlighting potential hazards. This interactive support speeds up problem-solving and makes it easier for programmers to get over obstacles(Rahman & Watanobe, 2023).

Additionally, ChatGPT models may be used in code review. They can check code samples for recurring mistakes, conformance to coding standards, and prospective improvements. This automated aid, while not a replacement for a complete human code review, can help find little errors and guarantee higher code quality.

Another crucial component of software development is documentation. Writing readme files, user manuals, and technical documentation can be assisted using ChatGPT models. The methodology may produce thorough and clear documentation that helps users understand and use the product efficiently, and developers can give essential points and context. Even though ChatGPT models have many advantages, there are some things to take into account. Models might not always result in secure or ideal code. As a result, skilled developers should carefully analyze, test, and validate the code that the model generates. The model's replies might not always be correct or consistent with best practices, therefore making decisions often requires using human judgment (Rahman & Watanobe, 2023).

3.3.2 Leveraging ChatGPT for Therapeutic Conversations and Mental Health Support

ChatGPT models have emerged as invaluable allies in the realm of mental health support, offering a unique and accessible means of reaching individuals in need, providing information, and offering guidance. These models function as virtual mental health companions, harnessing their natural language processing capabilities to assist users in managing their emotional well-being, seeking resources, and engaging in therapeutic conversations (Biswas, 2023).

One of the primary advantages of ChatGPT models in mental health support is their availability around the clock. Individuals seeking assistance can interact with these models at their convenience, eliminating barriers like geographical distance and scheduling constraints that might hinder in-person consultations. This accessibility ensures that individuals can reach out for support when they need it most, potentially mitigating feelings of isolation and distress.

ChatGPT models offer a non-judgmental space for users to express their feelings and concerns. Users can engage in open conversations about their emotions, experiences, and challenges, without the fear of stigma or discrimination. This anonymity can be particularly appealing to those who are hesitant to share their struggles with friends, family, or even mental health professionals.

Moreover, ChatGPT models provide psychoeducation and coping strategies. They can explain mental health concepts, symptoms, and common strategies for managing stress, anxiety, depression, and other emotional challenges. This educational aspect empowers users with knowledge, helping them better understand their emotions and encouraging them to take proactive steps toward self-care.

In crises, these models can offer immediate support by providing resources such as helpline numbers, crisis intervention techniques, and coping mechanisms. While they are not a substitute for professional help, they serve as a bridge to connect individuals in distress with appropriate mental health services.

For users hesitant to seek professional help, ChatGPT models can act as a stepping stone. These models can guide users through mindfulness exercises, relaxation techniques, and self-assessment tools that promote emotional awareness. They can also assist users in setting goals and tracking progress, fostering a sense of achievement and control over their emotional well-being.

Ethical considerations are paramount when employing ChatGPT models in mental health support. Ensuring the models are equipped to handle delicate and sensitive conversations, addressing the potential for harm, and respecting user privacy are critical aspects that need careful attention.

While ChatGPT models hold transformative potential, they are not a replacement for human therapists or mental health professionals. They should complement, rather than substitute, existing mental health services. The models' accuracy in providing appropriate responses, managing crises effectively, and recognizing when to escalate to human intervention are areas that necessitate continuous refinement.

ChatGPT models play a significant role in extending mental health support to a wider audience. Their accessibility, non-judgmental nature, psychoeducational capabilities, and crisis intervention potential make them valuable tools in destigmatizing mental health discussions and providing assistance to individuals in need. As they evolve, these models must be guided by ethical considerations and used as part of comprehensive mental health support.

3.4 Personalized Experiences in Travel, Tourism, and Shopping

3.4.1 Enhancing Travel and Tourism with ChatGPT's Personalized Recommendations

In the travel and tourist sector, ChatGPT can be crucial in several ways. ChatGPT offers a range of services to enhance customer satisfaction and streamline booking processes. It provides 24/7 customer support, assists in booking flights, accommodations, and travel packages, and offers translation services for international travelers. It also offers personalized travel recommendations based on user preferences and interests. ChatGPT also provides real-time weather forecasts, emergency assistance, cultural insights, reviews, and travel updates. It also collects post-travel feedback to gather insights and improve services. By integrating ChatGPT into travel and tourism applications, companies can improve customer satisfaction, streamline booking processes, and create a more enjoyable travel experience.

3.4.2 Transforming Shopping Experiences through AI-driven Personalization

ChatGPT can improve shopping experiences by providing personalized, informative, and engaging interactions with customers. It can analyze customer preferences, purchase history, and browsing behavior to offer product recommendations. It can also be used as a virtual shopping assistant, generating interactive product descriptions and providing real-time advice. ChatGPT can also be integrated into e-commerce platforms for customer support, tailoring discount offers, and promotions based on customer behavior. It can also assist customers in finding the right size and fit for clothing and footwear. It can also be integrated with voice commerce, improving on-site search functionality, and providing insights from user reviews and ratings. It can also be used for cross-selling and upselling, offering product availability updates, and offering localized and multilingual support.

When it comes to personalized shopping, ChatGPT can be a useful tool. It can help with time management, product discovery, comparison shopping, availability and inventory information, bargains and discounts, convenience, reducing impulsive purchases, consistency, and feedback improvement. By learning about their tastes, introducing new items, and giving them access to real-time supply information, it can help customers save time. However, as clients may still value the knowledge and individualized service offered by knowledgeable sales personnel, it may not completely replace the human touch. The effectiveness of the AI model, the precision of the recommendations, and the level of consumer comfort with AI-driven solutions determine how profitable using ChatGPT will be. As AI technology develops, it may be able to provide more lucrative and individualized purchasing experiences.

3.4.3 AI-Driven business guidance and market research

ChatGPT models are proving to be invaluable assets across various industries by providing business guidance. Leveraging their natural language processing capabilities, these models offer insights, recommendations, and solutions that assist businesses in making informed decisions, optimizing operations, and driving growth.

One significant way ChatGPT models aid in business guidance is through market research and trend analysis. They analyze extensive data from diverse sources, including industry reports, news articles, and social media trends. By processing and synthesizing this information, they offer real-time insights into market dynamics, emerging trends, and customer sentiments. This helps businesses adapt their strategies, identify new opportunities, and stay ahead of competitors.

In strategic planning, ChatGPT models act as virtual consultants, aiding businesses in formulating effective strategies. Whether it's expanding into new markets, launching products, or diversifying services, these models provide data-driven suggestions. By considering historical data, market conditions, and potential risks, they offer guidance on the best course of action, enabling companies to make well-informed decisions.

For small businesses and startups, ChatGPT models function as knowledgeable mentors. Entrepreneurs can seek advice on business plans, marketing strategies, and financial management. The models provide explanations of business concepts, offer guidance on legal and regulatory matters, and even help with pitch presentations. This democratizes access to expert-level insights, particularly for those who may not have immediate access to specialized advisors.

In customer engagement, ChatGPT models enhance interactions by tailoring recommendations and responses. By analyzing customer data and preferences, these models assist in delivering personalized product recommendations, resolving inquiries, and managing complaints. This improves customer satisfaction, fosters loyalty, and boosts conversion rates.

Furthermore, ChatGPT models contribute to employee training and development. They offer explanations of complex concepts, provide step-by-step instructions for tasks, and simulate role-based scenarios. This ensures consistent and standardized training experiences, enabling employees to upskill efficiently (Evans et al., (2023).

Deploying ChatGPT models in business guidance requires careful consideration of ethical aspects, data privacy, and bias mitigation. Ensuring that the models are trained on accurate and reliable data, minimizing biases in responses, and safeguarding sensitive business information is paramount.

Despite their potential, challenges remain. ChatGPT models are only as good as the data they are trained on, and their responses may lack the nuanced insights that come from human experience. Critical decisions often require human judgment and expertise, and striking the right balance between automation and human involvement is crucial.

ChatGPT models are transforming the landscape of business guidance by offering data-driven insights, strategic recommendations, and personalized assistance. From market research to employee training, these models are augmenting decision-making processes, fostering innovation, and helping businesses thrive in a dynamic and competitive environment. As technology continues to evolve, businesses can harness the capabilities of ChatGPT models to navigate challenges, capitalize on opportunities, and achieve sustainable growth.

ChatGPT models have significantly transformed the field of market research, providing innovative tools for gathering insights, understanding consumer preferences, and making informed business decisions. These versatile models excel in data collection, sentiment analysis, and trend identification, ultimately enhancing the effectiveness of marketing strategies (Brand et al., 2023).

One of ChatGPT's notable contributions to market research is its ability to conduct surveys and collect feedback. Traditional surveys often suffer from low response rates and limited engagement. However, ChatGPT models offer an interactive and conversational approach, making the survey-taking experience more engaging and user-friendly. By simulating human-like interactions, these models encourage participants to share detailed opinions, resulting in more comprehensive and valuable data. This approach opens new avenues for understanding customer needs, preferences, and pain points.

Sentiment analysis, a crucial aspect of market research, is greatly enhanced by ChatGPT models. They can process vast amounts of customer feedback from social media, reviews, and forums, extracting sentiment and opinions to gauge customer satisfaction and identify areas for improvement. Their ability to comprehend context and nuance allows for accurate sentiment classification, providing businesses with real-time insights into consumer perceptions and enabling them to tailor their strategies accordingly.

Moreover, ChatGPT models excel in trend identification and prediction. By analyzing conversations, customer inquiries, and online discussions, these models can identify emerging trends, preferences, and demands within specific market segments. This information empowers businesses to proactively adapt their offerings and marketing campaigns, gaining a competitive edge in rapidly changing markets.

In terms of new product development, ChatGPT models serve as valuable co-creators. Businesses can engage these models in ideation sessions, allowing them to generate creative ideas for new products or services based on input from researchers. This collaborative process helps uncover unique insights and innovative concepts that may not have been apparent through traditional methods.

Despite their numerous advantages, ChatGPT models also present challenges in market research. Ensuring that the models are trained on accurate and relevant data is crucial for obtaining reliable insights. Additionally, addressing potential biases within the models to ensure fair and representative data collection is essential to prevent skewed results.

ChatGPT models have revolutionized market research by offering interactive surveys, sophisticated sentiment analysis, trend identification, and creative ideation. Their conversational approach enhances data collection, yielding richer insights into consumer behavior and preferences. As these models continue to evolve, their role in shaping data-driven decision-making and innovative marketing strategies is bound to expand, making them indispensable assets in the dynamic world of market research.

4. ETHICAL CONSIDERATIONS AND FUTURE PROSPECTS

4.1 Responsible AI Usage and Ethical Concerns

To use AI responsibly, it is important to make sure that systems are created and implemented in ways that are beneficial to society and reduce any potential risk of harm. Transparency, equity, data privacy, informed consent, accountability, ethics, human oversight, testing and validation, education and awareness, continuous monitoring, regulatory compliance, collaboration and standards, and benefit assessment are important guiding principles for using AI responsibly. Users can comprehend and evaluate the system's behavior thanks to transparency, which also helps to foster confidence. Fairness and bias reduction should be a primary design goal, preventing discrimination against individuals or groups due to traits like socioeconomic position, gender, or ethnicity. Strong data protection measures should be implemented by enterprises, and data privacy measures should respect peoples' rights to privacy. The need for informed consent cannot be overstated. Users must be made aware of the usage of AI systems and must give their explicit approval before their data is collected and processed. Accountability is crucial, with defined clear lines of responsibility and procedures for handling problems and mistakes. When creating and implementing AI systems, ethical standards should be established and followed while taking into account any potential social, ethical, and cultural effects. In areas where there are major hazards involved, human oversight is extremely important. For AI systems to function as planned and avoid unforeseen consequences, routine audits and evaluations are crucial. It is important to create knowledge of AI ethics and ethical AI use, and it is also important to perform ongoing monitoring after deployment. Compliance with applicable rules and regulations relating to AI, data protection, and privacy is also crucial. To establish industry-wide standards for responsible AI development and deployment, collaboration and standards can be formed.

4.2 Balancing Personalization and Privacy in Conversational AI

ChatGPT personalization is the ability of the AI model to generate responses tailored to the individual user or conversation context. This involves customizing the language and tone of the AI's responses to better match the user's preferences, needs, and characteristics. Key factors for personalization include user history, user profile, context awareness, user feedback, user intent, language and tone, and content relevance. User history helps ChatGPT adapt its replies by remembering the conversation history and providing more contextually relevant answers. User profile information, such as name, age, location, and preferences, can be used to make responses more personalized. Context awareness helps ChatGPT analyze the ongoing conversation and respond accordingly, considering previous messages to provide coherent and contextually relevant answers. User feedback, such as explicit corrections or ratings, can help improve personalization by reinforcing behavior and learning from mistakes.

Intent is crucial for personalization, as the model tries to provide answers that are most likely to satisfy the user's needs. Language and tone can be adjusted to be more formal, casual, friendly, or professional, depending on the user's preferences or the conversation context.

However, personalization can also raise ethical concerns, such as biases, filter bubbles, and reinforcement of existing beliefs. Striking the right balance between personalization and responsible AI usage is a challenge that developers and users need to address. Balancing personalization with privacy policies is crucial for providing tailored experiences while safeguarding users' personal information and privacy.

Strategies to achieve this balance include data minimization, consent and transparency, anonymization and aggregation, data encryption, user control, data retention policies, third-party partnerships, algorithmic transparency, regular audits and compliance, privacy by design, user education, independent audits, and ethical considerations.

Data minimization involves collecting only the necessary data for personalization, reducing the risk of breaches and privacy violations. Consent and transparency involve obtaining clear and informed consent from users, providing detailed explanations of data collection, usage, and access, and allowing users to opt in or out of data collection. Anonymization and aggregated data are used whenever possible, removing personally identifiable information (PII) from the data. Data encryption ensures data protection during transmission and storage. User control allows users to adjust preferences, delete data, or opt out of personalization without hindering their overall experience. Data retention policies specify storage and deletion periods, and data is regularly purged. Third-party partnerships should adhere to strict privacy policies and data protection standards, while algorithmic transparency makes personalization algorithms more transparent to users.

Regular audits and compliance ensure data collection and personalization practices comply with evolving privacy laws and regulations. Privacy considerations should be implemented from the outset of product development, and user education about the value of personalization and data privacy is essential. Independent audits or reviews of data handling and personalization processes can ensure compliance and adherence to best practices.

Balancing personalization and privacy requires a proactive commitment to protecting user data while providing valuable tailored experiences. This balance is essential for user trust, compliance with regulations like GDPR and CCPA, and maintaining a positive brand image in an era where data privacy is a significant concern for consumers.

4.3 Ensuring Transparency in ChatGPT-Based Applications

Transparency is critical in ChatGPT-based applications for building user confidence, addressing ethical problems, and adhering to legislation. Clear user communication, algorithm documentation, explanation features, algorithmic transparency, feedback loop, compliance with regulations such as GDPR or CCPA, user control, third-party audits, regular model assessment, ethical review boards, responsible AI training, transparency reports, legal and ethical frameworks, and open-sourcing parts of the AI system are all strategies for achieving transparency.

Informing users about their engagement with an AI chatbot and discussing its capabilities and limitations is part of clear user communication. The fundamental algorithms and models employed, as well as their design, training data, and fine-tuning methods, are all documented in algorithm documentation. Explanation capabilities enable users to request explanations for AI-generated responses and gain insight into how the AI arrived at a certain conclusion.

4.4 Research Directions for Ethical Advancements in AI

Ethical concerns inevitably arise with any technological innovation. However, they are often considered secondary to technical development challenges, if they are considered at all(Cheney-Lippold, 2018). However, as we navigate the evolving landscape of AI applications, it is crucial to acknowledge the ethical considerations associated with ChatGPT integration. Research directions include identifying and mitigating bias in AI algorithms and data, enhancing the explanation and interpretability of AI decision-making processes, investigating mechanisms for holding AI systems accountable for biased outcomes, and developing standards and regulations for auditing and certifying AI systems for ethical compliance. Ethical data collection and usage are also essential areas of focus, including obtaining informed consent and protecting user privacy in data-driven AI applications. AI ethics education and training should be developed to raise awareness about AI ethics among developers, data scientists, and decision-makers, and integrate ethics into AI curricula at academic institutions.

AI in healthcare ethics should investigate the ethical implications of AI in healthcare, including patient privacy, diagnosis accuracy, and the impact on healthcare professionals. AI for social good should promote research on AI applications that address social, environmental, and humanitarian challenges while examining how AI systems can align with and respect human values, ethics, and cultural norms. ChatGPT models might serve as accessible sources for medical information, offering patients insights into symptoms, treatments, and general health inquiries. This quick access to medical knowledge aids in complex case discussions and allows medical practitioners to consider a broader range of possibilities, ultimately leading to better patient outcomes. These models also facilitate medical education and knowledge sharing among healthcare professionals, enabling them to stay updated with the latest research and practices(Zhang, P., & Kamel Boulos, M. N., 2023). As these models continue to evolve, it is imperative to strike a balance between innovation and patient safety, harnessing their capabilities to create a more efficient and patient-centered healthcare landscape.

Robotic ethics should explore ethical considerations in the development and deployment of autonomous robots and AI-powered robotic systems, especially in areas like autonomous vehicles and drones. AI regulation and governance should propose regulatory frameworks and international governance mechanisms to ensure ethical AI development and deployment. Ethical AI auditing should develop tools and methodologies for assessing ethical compliance, and the role of independent auditors in ensuring ethical AI practices.

AI should address the long-term ethical implications of AI development, including its impact on employment, society, and the environment. This requires ongoing multidisciplinary research, collaboration, and a commitment to addressing complex ethical challenges as AI technologies continue to evolve and integrate into various aspects of our lives.

5. SHAPING A RESPONSIBLE AI-DRIVEN FUTURE: CHATGPT'S TRANSFORMATIVE IMPACT AND ETHICAL IMPERATIVES

5.1 Recapitulation of ChatGPT's Transformative Impact

OpenAI's ChatGPT technology is poised to play a pivotal role in the future of healthcare development. It will provide precise results and streamline hiring processes, increasing productivity while reducing expenses. Additionally, it will assist travellers in scheduling flights, hotels, and various modes of transportation by delivering real-time weather updates, information on local events, and flight statuses. ChatGPT's ability to recognize and generate text that closely mimics human speech makes it highly adaptable for numerous healthcare applications, as well as serving as a valuable tool for customer service, content creation, and entertainment.

Moreover, ChatGPT's potential extends to personalized learning experiences, potentially shaping the future of healthcare eLearning (Suresh Babu, C. V., and B. Rohan, 2023). To fully harness the capabilities of these technologies, training organizations should collaborate with solution providers offering integrated learning platform solutions powered by generative AI and GPT.

ChatGPT and other Generative Pre-trained Transformer (GPT) models are on the cusp of revolutionizing various facets of human-computer interaction, education, healthcare, and beyond. They will play a pivotal role in customer service, providing empathetic, context-aware, and efficient support. Additionally, GPT models will become indispensable collaborators in various professions, including content creation, writing, and research.

In the realm of education, they will offer personalized tutoring, adapt lessons to individual learning styles, and assist students with homework, research, and exam preparation. Healthcare will witness GPT models aiding in patient engagement, diagnosis, and treatment recommendations, ultimately improving healthcare accessibility and outcomes. These models will also have a significant impact on scientific research, summarizing scientific literature, analyzing experimental data, and suggesting research directions.

As GPT models become proficient in multiple languages, they will facilitate global communication and collaboration, effectively eliminating language barriers in business, diplomacy, and academia. Creative industries will benefit from GPT models, utilizing their capabilities to generate original content, scripts, music compositions, and visual art. However, ethical considerations remain paramount, necessitating fairness, transparency, and unbiased behavior in AI systems.

Personalization will be a cornerstone of GPT models' future, offering more tailored recommendations and content. Edge computing will enable AI-powered applications in remote or resource-constrained environments, expanding their applicability to diverse industries such as agriculture, environmental monitoring, and disaster response.

Human-AI collaboration in creativity will blur the lines between human and machine creativity. As AI continues to evolve, GPT models will further improve their understanding of context, common sense reasoning, and emotional intelligence, rendering them more adaptable and capable of handling complex real-world tasks.

In conclusion, while ChatGPT and other GPT models hold immense potential to transform our world, they also come with the responsibility to address ethical, societal, and technical challenges. Collaboration among researchers, developers, and policymakers is imperative for a future where AI seamlessly augments human capabilities, fostering innovation, efficiency, and accessibility in every aspect of our lives.

5.2 Emphasizing the Role of Generative AI and NLP Models in Shaping the Future

AI and Natural Language Processing (NLP) have the potential to revolutionize various sectors, including legal, energy, transportation, entertainment, gaming, manufacturing, agriculture, environmental monitoring and conservation, government and public services, space exploration, finance and investment banking, security and defense, creative arts and content creation, and human resources and talent management.

Legal and compliance applications involve AI automating document review, contract analysis, and legal research, while NLP helps identify and extract relevant legal information from vast volumes of text. Energy and sustainability applications optimize energy consumption in buildings and industrial processes, reducing carbon footprints. Traffic management systems can optimize traffic flow, reduce congestion, and enhance public transportation efficiency. NLP models extract useful insights from unstructured data, allowing for data-driven decision-making and improving market research, consumer sentiment analysis, and risk assessment. They promote innovation by assisting in the production of ideas, creative cooperation, and problem-solving.

The landscape is being shaped by discussions around AI ethics, bias mitigation, transparency, and responsible AI development. They improve accessibility and inclusion by offering text-based support and speech recognition to people with disabilities. By optimizing energy consumption, resource management, and climate modelling, NLP models contribute to sustainability efforts. They are industry catalysts for innovation, pushing digital transformation and disrupting established business paradigms.

In the entertainment and gaming sector, AI can create realistic game environments, NPCs, and procedural content generation, while NLP can be used for chatbots, voice recognition, and player engagement. Manufacturing and robotics applications involve AI-powered robots and autonomous manufacturing systems improving production efficiency and quality control, while NLP assists in human-robot collaboration and natural language interface for factory operations.

Agricultural and food production applications involve AI optimizing crop management, predicting crop diseases, and automating harvesting processes. Environmental monitoring and conservation applications involve AI analyzing satellite imagery, sensor data, and wildlife tracking to aid biodiversity conservation and environmental protection.

Government and public services applications involve AI-driven chatbots and virtual assistants providing citizens with information and streamlining government services. Space exploration applications involve AI supporting space missions by automating data analysis, autonomous spacecraft navigation, and deep space communication.

Finance and investment banking applications involve AI-driven robo-advisors offering personalized investment recommendations and portfolio management, while NLP can analyze financial news and reports for real-time trading decisions and risk assessment.

In the security and defense sector, AI can enhance cybersecurity by detecting and mitigating cyber threats in real time. Creative arts and content creation applications involve AI generating music, art, and literature, collaborating with artists and creators, and streamlining recruitment processes.

AI and NLP are constantly evolving, pushing the boundaries of various industries and transforming the way we live and work.

5.3 A Responsible AI-driven Future: Necessity of Continued Research and Ethical Practices

Continued research and ethical practices in AI are essential to harness the potential benefits of AI while addressing its ethical challenges and ensuring that AI technologies are developed and deployed responsibly for the benefit of society. Ethical AI practices include protecting user privacy and maintaining data security. To protect user information, research into privacy-preserving AI approaches, encryption, and data anonymization is critical. Ongoing research is critical to addressing AI safety concerns, including robustness against adversarial attacks and unforeseen system behaviors. Ethical AI practices entail minimizing the hazards associated with AI implementations.

6. CONCLUSION

In conclusion, this chapter has explored the transformative capabilities of ChatGPT across diverse fields. The chapter gives an overview of chatGPT in almost all the domains thereby providing a comprehensive approach to synchronize human tasks with AI and making a task simple and efficient to perform. Integration of many disciplines or fields can result in new views and inventive solutions to challenging challenges. AI research frequently deals with difficult, real-world problems that necessitate diverse solutions. An integrated approach aids in efficiently addressing these difficulties. ChatGPT has demonstrated its versatility as a powerful conversational AI tool, reshaping customer service interactions and aiding in medical diagnostics. Its capacity to comprehend, generate, and adapt natural language responses has enhanced communication, efficiency, and personalization in areas such as education, healthcare, and content development. Looking ahead, the potential applications of ChatGPT are limitless. Its continuous development, refinement, and adaptability to specialized contexts hold the promise of further enhancing human-AI collaboration. Through legal and ethical utilization of ChatGPT's capabilities, we envision a future where AI-driven conversations seamlessly integrate into our daily lives, providing enhanced support, knowledge, and engagement across a wide array of fields.

REFERENCES

Abdullah, M., Madain, A., & Jararweh, Y. (2022). ChatGPT: Fundamentals, Applications, and Social Impacts. In *2022 Ninth International Conference on Social Networks Analysis, Management and Security (SNAMS)*, Milan, Italy. 10.1109/SNAMS58071.2022.10062688

Bahrini, A. (2023). *ChatGPT: Applications, Opportunities, and Threats. 2023 Systems and Information Engineering Design Symposium (SIEDS)*, Charlottesville, VA, USA. 10.1109/SIEDS58326.2023.10137850

Brand, J., Israeli, A., & Ngwe, D. (2023). Using GPT for Market Research. *Harvard Business School Marketing Unit Working Paper No. 23-062.* doi:10.2139/ssrn.4395751

Fırat, M. (2023). Integrating AI Applications into Learning Management Systems to Enhance e-Learning. *Instructional Technology and Lifelong Learning*, 4(1), 1–14. doi:10.52911/itall.1244453

Gilson, A., Safranek, C., Huang, T., Socrates, V., Chi, L., Taylor, R. A., & Chartash, D. (2022). How well does ChatGPT do when taking the medical licensing exams? The implications of large language models for medical education and knowledge assessment. medRxiv, 2022-12.

Haleem, A., Javaid, M., & Singh, R. P. (2022). An era of ChatGPT as a significant futuristic support tool: A study on features, abilities, and challenges. *BenchCouncil transactions on benchmarks, standards, and evaluations, 2*(4), 100089.

Jain, V., & Rai, H. Parvathy, & Mogaji, Emmanuel. (2023). *The Prospects and Challenges of ChatGPT on Marketing Research and Practices.* doi:10.2139/ssrn.4398033

Mao, R., Chen, G., Zhang, X., Guerin, F., & Wang, Z. (2023). GPTEVAL: A survey on assessments of CHATGPT and GPT-4. arXiv (Cornell University). https://doi.org//arxiv.2308.12488 doi:10.48550

Sallam, M. (2023). The utility of ChatGPT as an example of large language models in healthcare education, research, and practice: Systematic review on the future perspectives and potential limitations. medRxiv, 2023-02.

Sallam, M., Salim, N., Barakat, M., & Al-Tammemi, A. (2023). ChatGPT applications in medical, dental, pharmacy, and public health education: A descriptive study highlighting the advantages and limitations. *Narra J, 3*(1), e103–e103. doi:10.52225/narra.v3i1.103

Sedaghat, S. (2023). Early applications of ChatGPT in medical practice, education, and research. *Clinical Medicine, 23*(3), 278–279. doi:10.7861/clinmed.2023-0078 PMID:37085182

Shahriar, S., & Hayawi, K. (2023). *Let's have a chat! A Conversation with ChatGPT: Technology, Applications, and Limitations.* arXiv preprint arXiv:2302.13817.

Shaji George, A., & Hovan George, A. S. (2023). A Review of ChatGPT AI's Impact on Several Business Sectors. *Partners Universal International Innovation Journal, 1*(1), 9–23.

Sudirjo, F., Diantoro, K., Al-Gasawneh, J. A., Khootimah Azzaakiyyah, H., & Almaududi Ausat, A. M. (2023). Application of ChatGPT in Improving Customer Sentiment Analysis for Businesses. *Jurnal Teknologi Dan Sistem Informasi Bisnis, 5*(3), 283–288. doi:10.47233/jteksis.v5i3.871

Suresh Babu, C. V. (2022). *Artificial Intelligence and Expert Systems.* Anniyappa Publication.

Suresh Babu, C. V., & Padma, R. (2023). Technology Transformation Through Skilled Teachers in Teaching Accountancy. In R. González-Lezcano (Ed.), *Advancing STEM Education and Innovation in a Time of Distance Learning* (pp. 211–233). IGI Global. doi:10.4018/978-1-6684-5053-6.ch011

Suresh Babu, C. V., & Rohan, B. (2023). Evaluation and Quality Assurance for Rapid E-Learning and Development of Digital Learning Resources. In M. I. Santally, (Eds.), *Implementing Rapid E-Learning Through Interactive Materials Development* (pp. 139–170). IGI Global. doi:10.4018/978-1-6684-4940-0.ch008

UludagK. (2023). The Use of AI-Supported Chatbot in Psychology. https://ssrn.com/abstract=4331367 doi:10.2139/ssrn.4331367

Chapter 12
Promoting Students' Writing by Using Essay Writing GPT:
A Mix Method

Rita Inderawati
Universitas Sriwijaya, Indonesia

Kurnia Saputri
Universitas Muhammadiyah, Indonesia

Eka Apriani
Institut Agama Islam Negeri, Curup, Indonesia

Erfin Wijayanti
IAIN Fattahul Muluk Papua, Indonesia

Hariswan Putera Jaya
Universitas Sriwijaya, Indonesia

Ifnaldi
Institut Agama Islam Negeri, Curup, Indonesia

Muthmainnah Muthmainnah
iD https://orcid.org/0000-0003-3170-2374
Universitas Al Asyariah Mandar, Indonesia

ABSTRACT

The purpose of this study is to determine how students might enhance their essay-writing abilities and how they respond to the essay writing GPT. Explanatory sequential research was used in this mixed method study to analyze both the qualitative and quantitative data in distinct steps. In order to conduct the study quantitatively, the researcher used 60 students who were enrolled in an undergraduate English study program at IAIN Curup, Indonesia, that included an essay writing course. With 30 students of experimental and control group. The test is validated by three experts from UIN Raden Fatah Palembang, University of Bengkulu, and UIN Fatmawati Sukarno Bengkulu. The results of this research are that GPT has no significant impact on students' essay writing skill. Experimental and control groups have almost the same score in essay writing tests. GPT has made students simpler to build the idea because they do not need to think harder like traditionally writing. Instead, the students who are in control group easier to arrange the structure of the essay as what they wanted.

DOI: 10.4018/979-8-3693-0502-7.ch012

INTRODUCTION

Writing holds great significance for university students, particularly those who are EFL (English as a Foreign Language) learners, since it is considered one of the essential skills for effective communication (Jabali, 2018; Toba et al., 2019). Al Khazraji (2019) asserts that in an academic atmosphere, the main objective is to develop proficient writing skills. Lecturers should foster the development of students' writing skills by promoting the production of well-structured papers (Ceylan, 2019). Moreover, the development of organisational skills, together with proficiency in behaviour management, composition revision, and reader awareness, has become essential (Bakry & Alsamadani, 2015).

Although writing programmes are highly beneficial for college students, mastering the art of writing has become challenging for them. This phenomenon has occurred in many situations worldwide, where pupils have made a range of writing errors in the subsequent areas: The citation "Toba et al., 2019" refers to a publication by Toba and colleagues in the year 2019. The four categories include: (1) structural, (2) grammatical, (3) mechanical, and (4) vocabulary. Previous research has indicated a correlation between learning styles and writing difficulties (Bakry & Alsamadani, 2015). Consequently, they were incapable of articulating their perspectives in organised and cohesive paragraphs or essays.

Okpe & Onjewu (2017) assert that acquiring the skill of essay writing can enhance everyday communication, facilitate academic achievement, and foster professional growth. Consequently, the essay writing course becomes increasingly important among university students. The Indonesian higher education (HE) curriculum emphasises the importance of cultivating proficient essay writing skills among university students, particularly those enrolled in the English Education Department.

The subject of AI language processing has undergone a revolution due to the introduction of large, pre-trained language models that greatly enhance the capabilities of AI systems. The following systems, released from 2018 to 2022, are included: the BigScience Large Open-Science Open-Access Multilingual Language Model (BLOOM), Google's BERT, OpenAI's GPT-3, Pathways Language Model (PaLM), and Meta's OPT-175B. This paper incorporates examples that employ the extensively utilised GPT-3. GPT-3 was directed to compose an op-ed, around 500 words in length, elucidating why humans should not harbour any apprehensions towards AI. This instruction was sent along with an initial paragraph to set the overall trajectory. Each of the eight essays generated by GPT-3 was carefully evaluated by a human. The human then chose and arranged the content for the final article and made edits. It was observed that the editing process took less time compared to editing several op-eds authored by humans. The essay titled "We Asked GPT-3 to Write an Academic Paper about Itself—Then We Tried to Get It Published" was published in Scientific American on June 30, 2022 (Thunström, 2022). For this task, GPT-3 was given the specific directive to compose a scholarly thesis on the subject of GPT-3, containing precisely 500 words and incorporating scientific references and citations within the text. Subsequently, it was provided with explicit guidelines for each of the standard sections found in an academic work, namely the introduction, methodology, findings, and discussion. Each component potentially generated a maximum of three distinct versions, and the human co-authors selected which ones to employ. The preprint of the publication, now under evaluation by a journal, credits the two researchers who created the prompts as co-authors (GPT-3, Thunström & Steingrimsson in Kleiman, 2022). The AI-human writing process has several steps, namely parameter setting, AI instruction, evaluation, curation, and outcome editing.

GPT-3, the machine learning platform, enables the development and utilisation of AI models. Furthermore, it asserts its capability to manage vast quantities of data and its ability to be expanded and operated with high effectiveness. According to O'Reilly in Kleiman (2022), it has been described as a revolutionary development in the realm of AI. The use of GPT-3 for the purpose of comprehending natural language has significant promise. When it comes to dealing with the intricacies of language usage in everyday situations, rule-based systems have historically been the main area of attention for addressing this issue (Wang et al., Kleiman, 2022). GPT-3 employs a neural network methodology that has the ability to extrapolate beyond the data it was trained on, as demonstrated by Deng et al. in Kleiman (2022). This makes it perfect for applications needing a command of natural language, such question-answering and machine translation. So that, the researchers are trying to combine the AI tool to teaching in learning process, especially for students' writing skill. Because of the advancements in technology that have been made in recent years, researchers are interested in determining whether or not AI mixed with learning will result in major improvements.

The widespread adoption of new technologies and the Internet is causing changes in students' writing practices in the domains of essay writing and language learning (Moore et al., 2016; Peters & Cadieux, 2019). The capabilities of language and writing tools are expanding due to advancements in artificial intelligence (AI) and natural language processing (Geitgey, 2018; Brown et al., 2020; Heaven, 2020). Currently, there are a multitude of writing tools that utilise artificial intelligence and are readily available for free on the internet. Nevertheless, due to the unsupervised and instruction-lacking nature of AI-powered writing tools, students may require the assistance and direction of their teacher while utilising such tools. In the absence of such consideration, there is a potential for erroneous implementation, which may involve both unintentional or deliberate plagiarism and the uncritical acceptance of guidance (Prentice & Kinden, 2018). In Burkhard's (2022) work, Kranzberg argued that technology does not possess inherent moral value and cannot be categorised as inherently positive, negative, or neutral. The consequences of a specific technology can differ depending on the circumstances and environment (Kranzberg in Burkhard, 2022). To enhance the development of teaching strategies tailored to the unique requirements of each student, it is crucial to comprehend students' perspectives on AI-driven writing tools and the situations in which their usage is suitable.

In light of the aforementioned factors, the researchers undertook a study pertaining to artificial intelligence (AI) and one of its associated technologies. In this study, researchers employed the GPT Essay Writer, an artificial intelligence tool, to assist students in composing essays. GPT essay writer is an advanced technology that uses artificial intelligence to generate written content. It stands for Generative Pre-trained Transformer, and it is a language model that has the capability to produce human-like texts (GPTessay.com). GPT has the potential to develop into a powerful and efficient tool for tasks like as automatic draught production, article summaries, and language translation, as stated by Salvagno et al. (2023). Examples of such jobs include the translation of language. It is possible for authors to speed up the process of producing academic and scientific papers by utilising GPT, which is especially beneficial for students and researchers who are just starting out in their careers. Furthermore, researchers have conducted preliminary observations on undergraduate students enrolled in the English study program at IAIN Curup. The researchers discovered that students occasionally encountered challenges in acquiring essay-writing skills through conventional instructional approaches. Students admitted that they had difficulty formulating ideas for each individual paragraph of the essay. Consequently, researchers employ the GPT Essay Writer as a tool to aid in the production of student essays. The police are interested in assessing the enhancement of students' essay-writing skills and their ability to express their own viewpoints using GPT Essay Writer.

There are some previous researches regarding teaching essay writing by using GPT. First research is conducted by Michael Burkhard (2022) with the title "Student Perceptions of AI-Powered Writing Tools:

Towards Individualized Teaching Strategies." The outcome demonstrated that students' opinions on writing tools driven by AI vary widely. Some students may utilise them in a thoughtless and unreflective manner, which might lead to unintentional plagiarism. Some students, known as course repeaters, may choose not to use writing tools. This decision may stem from their scepticism or their lack of effective learning strategies. Customised instructional strategies may be beneficial in promoting or discouraging the use of these resources, depending on the different sorts of students. Second, Muhammad Shidiq (2023) with the title "The Use of Artificial Intelligence-Based Chat-GPT and Its Challenges for the World of Education; From the Viewpoint of the Development of Creative Writing Skills." The outcome demonstrated that ChatGPT's simplicity in handling text input limits the originality of work, leading to its propensity for being uncreative. Writing creatively is made very simple by the Chat-GPT system's capacity to comprehend human language. This includes producing works of literary merit comparable to human work, such as poetry, short tales, novels, and other genres of writing. This article discusses the ChatGPT system and its effects on students' writing skills and the study of creative writing theory in order to examine the theory's application to the problem. Third, Opara Emmanuel Chinonso et al (2023), with the title "ChatGPT for Teaching, Learning and Research: Prospects and Challenges." The findings indicated that using chatbots like OpenAI's ChatGPT model, which provides an instant and direct answer to questions (queries) posed, can help improve teaching and learning processes.

Therefore, as aforementioned above the researcher in this research gave focus on the emergence of teaching essay writing by using GPT Essay Writer. The researcher is wondering about the students' improvement in essay writing and response while using GPT Essay Writer. So that, the researcher conducted the research with the title **Teaching Writing by using Essay Writing GPT: A Mix Method.**

LITERATURE REVIEW

Essay Writing

According to Ginting (2019), writing is a beneficial talent that integrates cognitive processes like purpose expression, idea formulation, problem-solving, and critical thinking. In addition to accumulating and modifying ideas, writing also involves presenting those ideas to readers in a polished and comprehensible manner (Linse, 2005). Writing is also described exactly by Cumming in Bulqiyah et al. (2021) as the activities of thinking, producing, and encoding language into such a text in addition to being referred to as a text in written script. As a result, writing requires one to put more effort into understanding, thinking, planning, and revising (Brown, 2000), which calls for the use of a whole separate set of competences.

According to Fareed et al. (2016) and Tseng (2019), writing is now the talent that students need to learn the most in an academic setting. So that, it is not something surprises that becomes a central topic of language teaching and research (Hyland, 2008). Another academic explained that writing involves a specific order of procedures. Writing, according to Sperling & Fredman as described in Abderraouf (2016), is a collection of related procedures that include planning, translating, and reviewing. However, the procedure frequently went beyond those points. The writing process was broken down into multiple steps by Bailey (2015), including: (1) choosing appropriate sources, (2) reading texts, (3) taking notes, (4) planning and outlining, (5) incorporating a variety of sources, (6) organizing paragraphs, and (7) rewriting and peer-reading. The aforementioned procedures can be used to produce a well-organized text.

The essay is still the most typical type of academic writing assignment (Van Geyte in Bulqiyah et al., 2021). According to Oshima & Hogue in Bulqiyah et al. (2021) an essay is a piece of writing with one primary theme broken up into several paragraphs (one for each significant point). It starts with an introduction and concludes with a conclusion. The three basic parts of the essay are: (1) an introduction that grabs the reader's interest; (2) body paragraphs that elaborate on each paragraph's topic; and (3) a conclusion that restates the main points and includes supporting quotations.

Teaching Writing

According to Opara Emmanuel Chinonso et al. (2023), teaching is the organization and administration of a situation in which there are gaps or obstacles that a person will try to overcome and from which he will learn as he does so. A series of actions called "teaching" are intended to create learning. A sort of influence called teaching aims to shape the possible behaviors of another individual. In 1963, Smith broadened the definition of teaching to include a set of actions involving a principal, a secondary objective, and a situation with two sets of variables: those the principal cannot control (such as class size, student characteristics, physical facilities, etc.) and those he can (such as teaching methods and strategies).

Teachers need to explicitly understand the skills and processes involved in writing in order to properly teach it to students. Instead of an inherited talent or unconsciously formed habit, this perspective views writing as a vocation that can be acquired via discipline and hard work. Indeed, learning to write is similar to learning a second language even in one's home tongue. Anyone may write, but nobody is a "native speaker." Everyone generally picks up writing in school, according to Leki and Cheung (2016). In other words, teachers must inform students that few authors have a "native" grasp of writing in English as a lingua franca from birth (Canagarajah in Cheung 2016). If teachers want their students to be proficient writers, they must explicitly teach them the abilities they need and employ deliberate strategies to do so.

According to Grabe & Kaplan in Cheung (2016), many writing teachers have historically explained the writing process as a linear process. For instance, Paltridge, et al. (2009) distinguish four different writing subprocesses. The conceptualizing stage is where writers first come up with and choose the concepts they will use in their writing, then neatly arrange those thoughts (for instance, an essay must have an introduction, body, and conclusion). The second step is known as formulating, which refers to the act of turning thoughts into phrases. The third step in the process is revision, during which writers edit and enhance their essays. The changes could concern the syntax, mechanics, or content. The fourth step in the process is reading. Writers review the essay's guidelines. They read for information on the essay topic. They check their writing for errors and make sure they have addressed the essay's questions.

AI (Artificial Intelligence) in ELT

As per Saleh (2019), "artificial intelligence," also referred to as "machine intelligence," refers to the intelligence exhibited by machines rather than the innate intellect exhibited by humans. The functions of this system encompass cognitive processes such as acquiring knowledge, devising strategies, resolving difficulties, and identifying and interpreting spoken language.

Research on the integration of technology in language education, particularly in relation to artificial intelligence (AI), has experienced substantial growth during the past three years. Additional challenges in the implementation of AI in education include output bias, the need for human monitoring, and the potential for abuse. When correctly managed, these difficulties can provide professors with fresh insights and opportunities to familiarise students with potential social inclinations, concerns, and risks associated with AI applications. Kasneci et al. (2023) provide ethical solutions to these difficulties and incorporate these models into their teaching methods.

According to Göçen and Aydemir (2020), AI has the potential to revolutionize education and the way that schools will operate in the future. In order to examine participants' perspectives from various industries, the study employed the qualitative phenomenological research methodology. They discovered that there will be new benefits for schools and teachers as well as downsides and positive aspects when AI is employed in education. The findings provide some advice on how to employ AI and how to handle potential issues. Despite the fact that the majority of participants appeared to enjoy AI, others were worried about what it will mean for teachers and other academics in the future.

Companies and educational materials are beginning to shift as a result of artificial intelligence development. To deliver the best instruction possible, professors need to be in the room. The role of teachers in the educational system has changed due to the advancement of artificial intelligence. AI mostly utilises sophisticated analytics, deep learning, and machine learning to assess an individual's speed relative to others. The complexity of AI solutions enhances the ability to identify areas where instruction is lacking and enhances educational proficiency. To give lecturers the opportunity to teach understanding and adaptation, which are unique human abilities that computers cannot imitate, AI can offer efficiency, personalisation, and easier tasks. Combining robots and lecturers can help students achieve their best results (Kengam, 2020). Additionally, when combined with teachers, AI-based educational platforms have an effect on teaching and learning that is only occasionally positive. When a machine can answer questions submitted by students online, the teacher may be competing with it rather than working together on the same project at the same time. Chat-GPT is one of the automated tasks powered by artificial intelligence (AI).

GPT Essay Writer

A chatbot is a software application that emulates human conversation through the utilisation of user input. A San Francisco-based company named OpenAI created the chatbot ChatGPT. The Chatbot was made available for public testing at no cost on November 30, 2022. The Journal of India states that ChatGPT is a "conversational" artificial intelligence (AI) that, theoretically, offers the ability to answer questions in a manner similar to that of a human. ChatGPT is an advanced chatbot that utilises OpenAI's GPT technology. The system has the capability to process a diverse array of text-based inquiries, encompassing both simple queries and complex assignments (Lund, 2022). OpenAI has developed a conversational agent dubbed ChatGPT, which is a highly advanced language model. ChatGPT, being a substantial language model, undergoes training on a substantial quantity of data (Azaria, 2022). ChatGPT has the ability to promptly generate a persuasive and eloquent letter, should you require assistance in crafting a message for a colleague.

ChatGPT is popular in modern era. GPT also has benefit for students' college, especially in writing essay. There is a website that focus on helping students essay writing, namely GPT essay writer. GPT essay writer is another part of chatGPT or OpenAI because GPT essay writer is powered by chatGPT. So that, in this case, GPT essay writer or GPT is same website. The difference between these websites is GPT is for general topic but GPT essay writer gives more focus writing essay. GPT essay writer is an advanced technology that uses artificial intelligence to generate written content. It stands for Generative Pre-trained Transformer, and it is a language model that has the capability to produce human-like texts

(GPTessay.com). Besides, GPT essay is not a replacement for human creativity and ingenuity. While the technology can produce high-quality content, it lacks the emotional intelligence and contextual understanding that humans possess. Therefore, it is important for content creators to use GPT essay as a tool, rather than a replacement, for their own creativity and expertise.

So that, GPT essay writer is a website that can help people to build the idea faster but not the replacement of human itself.

Teaching Essay Writing by Using GPT Essay Writer

GPT essay writer is a component of chatGPT, which is a part of OpenAI. It utilises the capabilities of ChatGPT to generate essays. Therefore, in this particular instance, the GPT essay writer and GPT refer to the same website. The distinction between both websites lies in the fact that GPT is designed for general topics; however, it is still capable of generating essay content. Conversely, the GPT essay writer prioritises the task of essay composition. Therefore, both GPT and GPT essay writers are at the same level. ChatGPT, a versatile conversational chatbot, was introduced by Open AI on November 30, 2022. It is expected to have a significant influence on various aspects of our society. The educational impacts of this natural language processing method are still uncertain. Zhai (2022) suggests that ChatGPT has the capacity to significantly influence various aspects of education, including learning objectives, assessment evaluation techniques, instructional activities, and evaluation procedures. Jain and Jain (2019) conducted a study on the use of AI in the context of teaching and learning in higher education prior to the widespread adoption of ChatGPT. They demonstrated the seamless manner in which AI is facilitating access to higher education services beyond traditional classroom settings. The study investigated the possible long-term and short-term ramifications of AI on several facets of higher education, including its potential to significantly influence universities.

In a similar vein, Aydin and Karaarslan (2022) explored the feasibility of employing artificial intelligence (AI) to condense literature review publications. According to the authors, AI has the potential to revolutionise academic publication by reducing the human workload and allowing academics to dedicate more time to their research. In addition, they employed ChatGPT for the purpose of generating an academic paper, and to ensure the authenticity of ChatGPT's content, they utilised plagiarism detection software. In 2022, Zhai conducted a study utilising ChatGPT, which showed that ChatGPT assists researchers in generating coherent, accurate, well-organised, and informative papers. The study proposed modifying learning objectives by incorporating the use of AI tools for completing subject-specific assignments while prioritising creativity and critical thinking over the acquisition of fundamental skills. ChatGPT enables students to delegate assessment duties through outsourcing.

ChatGPT, developed by OpenAI, is a robust language model capable of providing human-like responses to text-based queries. ChatGPT is developed using the GPT-3.5 and GPT-4, which are state-of-the-art large language models (LLMs). These models are very advanced and capable of generating natural language texts across several subject domains (Owens, 2023). ChatGPT's performance and quality have been improved using both supervised and reinforcement learning methodologies. (Dwivedi et al., 2023) The training process involves utilising a substantial text corpus comprising books, journals, and websites. As a result, it possesses a comprehensive comprehension of English, enabling students to generate academic writing and articles of superior quality. ChatGPT is relatively user-friendly in the context of academic writing and publishing. Consequently, ChatGPT has the potential to be utilised in the realm of scientific writing (King, 2022).

Salvagno et al. (2023) suggest that ChatGPT has the capacity to evolve into a powerful and efficient tool for activities such as generating drafts automatically, summarising articles, and translating languages. ChatGPT expedites the academic and scientific writing process for writers, particularly for students and early-career researchers. ChatGPT offers valuable recommendations to enhance your writing and publishing endeavours, hence increasing your likelihood of achieving success.

ChatGPT provides numerous benefits for essay composition, such as:

- Efficiency: ChatGPT demonstrates rapid and effective text generation, resulting in time and effort savings for authors. ChatGPT assists users in locating pertinent information from many sources, including online pages, academic works, books, and more.
- Creativity: The AI model has the ability to produce unique, varied, and captivating texts that inspire the author's creativity and imagination. ChatGPT facilitates the generation of novel ideas, hypotheses, questions, and viewpoints, enabling authors to delve deeper into their exploration.
- ChatGPT offers the capability to provide feedback and ideas on the author's content. This includes correcting grammar and spelling issues, enhancing clarity and coherence, and including more details and examples. In addition, ChatGPT can address subsequent inquiries, correct errors, challenge incorrect assumptions, and reject inappropriate requests.
- Engagement: ChatGPT can enhance the enjoyment and involvement of scientific writing by simulating a conversational style between writers and AI assistance. ChatGPT can enhance the interaction by incorporating humour, emotions, and personality traits, creating a more enjoyable and human-like experience.

METHOD

The mixed-methods study employed explanatory sequential research to analyse the qualitative and quantitative data in separate stages (Creswell, 2014; Fraenkel et al., 2012). To ensure a quantitative approach, the researcher selected a sample of 60 students who were currently enrolled in an undergraduate English study programme at IAIN Curup, Indonesia. These students were specifically taking a course focused on essay writing. The experimental group consisted of 30 students who utilised the assistance of the GPT essay writer to compose their essays, while the control group comprised 30 students who wrote their essays using traditional methods. The researcher administered an essay-writing test following the experimental lesson. A test was conducted to ascertain whether the use of the GPT essay writer enhances students' performance in essay writing. The test is verified by three specialists from UIN Raden Fatah Palembang, the University of Bengkulu, and UIN Fatmawati Sukarno Bengkulu. The outcome of content validity indicates that the test can be utilised in this investigation. The researcher utilised a qualitative approach by conducting in-depth interviews with 60 students to gather their perceptions regarding the use of GPT essay writers for teaching essay writing. The interview findings were analysed using qualitative descriptive methods. The essay writing test results were analysed using a quantitative approach, specifically the t-test.

RESULT AND DISCUSSION

Result

The study's findings have been covered in two separate sections. The findings from the quantitative data are the main topic of the first part. Results found from the qualitative data are reported in the second section.

The Following Section Discuss the Quantitative Data

The students were divided into two groups for the purposes of this study; one group produced the essays in the traditional manner, while the other employed GPT support. The informed consent form was signed by the participants before to the trial, and a separate page was provided for them to record their names and passwords. This allowed for anonymity when evaluating essays and further research into student-specific characteristics. The essay was between 800 and 1000 words in length and had the following title: "The Benefits and Drawbacks of AI in Education in the Modern Era." The GPT essay writer tool was presented by the researcher to the experimental group. The assignment had a four-hour time limit, after which the students were free to depart. In order to guarantee that the control group did not use the GPT essay writer, they were also watched.

The essay rubrics were derived from the Schreyer Institute for Teaching Excellence at Pennsylvania State University, and they encompassed the evaluation criteria of mechanics, style, topic, and format. The grading scale ranged from A to D. In order to facilitate further analysis, the categorical grades were transformed into numerical values, with A being assigned a value of 4, B a value of 3, C a value of 2, and D a value of 1. The researcher kept track of writing time for each student. The essays were graded by two professors. When their scores varied, they compared them and reached agreement on the final grade.

The group that received assistance from GPT took 121.93 minutes to complete their essay writing, while the control group took 120.9 minutes. Despite a slightly higher average score of 78 in the experiment group compared to the control group's average score of 76, both groups were given a B grade. A t-test was run to see if there was a significant difference between the two groups at the beginning of the study. The results showed that there was no significant difference in this study, with a t-value of 0.85 and a p-value of 0.39, which is more than the significance level of 0.05. The average level of text unauthenticity varied from 9.96% in the control group to 11.87% in the experiment group. The sample exhibited low text similarity overall, with a median score of 0.002 (ranging from 0 to 0.054).

The implication is that the GPT and essay scores have a beneficial relationship. Even then, the control group's students who had better GPAs also received high marks for their conventionally formatted essays. In the GPT group, a correlation between essay scores and non-authentic text proportion was found, with lower essay scores being attained by students who had more non-authentic content. The four predictors had a somewhat favorable relationship ($r = 0.573$; $p = 0.237$) with the overall essay score, according to the linear regression model. Group ($p = 0.182$), writing time ($p = 0.669$), module ($p = 0.388$), or GPA ($p = 0.532$) were the only factors that did not significantly affect the result.

Figure 1. Chart of experiment and control group

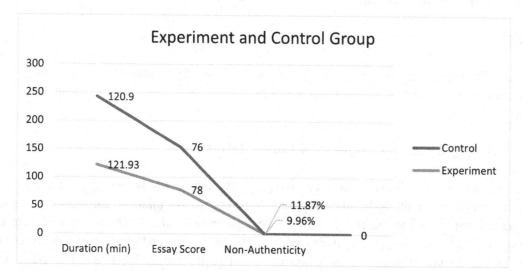

Qualitative Data Report

The qualitative data are covered in students' experience. Following the learner's experience, the learners' satisfaction will be examined. Participants who reported pleasure with the Essay Writing by using the GPT instructional design program did so under the category of their overall view. Regarding this program's benefits, the right program for learning, and the learning environment, participants expressed varying levels of pleasure. As a result of the GPT's support, they felt at ease when they were receiving their lesson. The technologies employed made it simple for the students to study. Regarding the learning experience's category, the participants then indicated that they may sharpen their essay-writing abilities and understand writing processes. The ease of the cordon and the technology utilized in the lessons was stressed. Here some of interview results:

Student 1: *GPT is enjoy to use, we can search everything we need on our essay*

Student 4: *While using GPT in teaching and learning essay writing, GPT make simpler than we have to think by ourselves*

Student 5: *I feel that essay writing by using GPT can improve my ability in writing. It feels like sharpen all aspects in writing and it also make me understand the processes.*

The results from the interview questions gave a different point of view for the outcomes related to the learner's experience learning. The students had a favorable opinion of the GPT-based essay writing instruction. They said that when using GPT, they could easily log in using their Google or Microsoft accounts. The students claim that they are free to use the chatbox feature on the GPT website. Additionally, users can fill out our questions in a column at the bottom of the main page. They also mentioned that there is a chatbox where they may ask a question in either English or Indonesia. The provided answers will be modified to utilize understandable grammar for the user. The students have a variety of questions they can ask about, such English essays. According to the students, the solution appeared in an instant. It supported by students interview where they said that:

Student 6: *GPT is easy to use because we just need log in by our Gmail. Then, we can use freely. That is the most important*

Student 8: *The chatbox feature very helpful, we can fill out our questions in a column at the bottom of the main page. We can ask the questions in Indonesia or English*

Student 2: *GPT can answer our questions instantly. GPT also utilize understandable grammar for the user*

Besides, by using GPT in essay writing the students could build the idea of the essay easily. They just ask the GPT about the topic they want. In this case, the essay topic is "The Benefits and Drawbacks of AI in Education in the Modern Era." The GPT replies as stated by the user and writes an essay about "The Benefits and Drawbacks of AI in Education in the Modern Era." However, it is not like full essay but only in few paragraphs in which could help students construct the idea of essay writing. The first paragraph gives the general information of AI, the second paragraph includes the advantages and disadvantages of AI, and the last paragraph includes the conclusion of the essay. The use of primary and supporting sentences, as well as a conclusion, are all aspects of writing structure that ChatGPT takes into account in this paragraph. Additionally, it employs both active and passive voice. Additionally, it takes into account how other tenses can be used, such as the more straightforward present tense.

Student 7: *I can build the idea of essay writing easily, due to the chatbox feature. When I need the idea about the benefit of AI it just appeared directly.*

Student 9: *GPT has drawbacks that the GPT does not give the full of essay when we need it. It just gives some point of the essay*

Student 10: *The other good things of GPT, it arranges the paragraph directly, so we can know structure of the essay itself, such as primary and supporting sentences, and conclusion*

Student 15: *The GPT provides like human creation because it employs both active and passive voice. Besides, it knows what kind of tenses we can use.*

DISCUSSION

According to the results above, essay writing while using GPT and traditional writing there is no significant differences. It shown that using GPT did not always result in better essays from students. The students in the GPT group did not produce more authentic material, write faster, or deliver higher-quality content, hence they did not outperform the control group in either of the metrics.

In the experimental group, the overall essay grade was marginally higher. A few studies did have more encouraging findings; these mostly relied on expert researcher and GPT contact. The use of ChatGPT did not speed up essay writing, and both groups' students needed about the same amount of time to do the work. This is an additional intriguing conclusion. As anticipated, both groups' longer writing times were correlated with higher essay scores. This result may also be accounted for by students' comments from Fyfe's (2022) study, where they particularly mentioned having trouble fusing the generated writing with their own style. Thus, even though ChatGPT could speed up writing during the initial stage, it takes longer to complete the process and compile the text. Depending on the user's input, using the tool for writing assistance results in various results for the same work (Yeadon et al., 2022).

The biggest issue with utilizing GPT in academic writing has been its lack of authenticity, but the researcher is of the opinion that using such tools won't make published content or student assignments any less authentic. The development of AI-generated text detectors continues every day, and it won't be long before very dependable technologies are accessible. When the researcher takes into account the viewpoints of detecting tools and the results showing that the students who received GPT aid did not significantly outperform the control group, there is no compelling cause to be concerned about its use in academic writing. However, GPT guidance makes it simpler for students to develop their essay ideas.

Additionally, students who used GPT while writing essays reported that it responded to follow-up inquiries, admitted faults, disputed false premises, and rejected inappropriate requests. Simply go to the GPT website and log in with your OpenAI credentials. Users can then immediately speak with the bot or alternatively give instructions or ask inquiries. Users can ask the A.I. to produce anything, including essays, using GPT's structured communication system. According to the lecturers, GPT was specifically built to resemble a digital library or an intelligent answering machine. GPT is incapable of providing responses to requests that involve judgement or subjectivity. Under these circumstances, GPT will refuse to answer queries that pertain to unfavourable topics. Consequently, users will be unable to specifically instruct or request ChatGPT to engage in conversations with hate speech, violent content, and similar topics. ChatGPT provides several advantages to a diverse group of users (Haque et al., 2022). The professors emphasised that understanding the sentiments of early adopters is crucial due to the novelty of the technology. Initially, individuals who embrace new technology at an early stage are typically the most enthusiastic and influential users. Their perspectives and emotions have the potential to shape the perception of new technology among the wider population. This data can offer crucial insights into the likelihood of the product's success or failure. A query can be answered by the OpenAI ChatGPT chatbot with text that seems incredibly intelligent (Frye, 2022). ChatGPT emphasizes the promise of artificial intelligence, notably its capability to impact our lives in a number of ways, from the subtle to the profound, according to Perlman & Open A.I.'s Assistant (2022). Many people worry that artificial intelligence text generators like ChatGPT would make it difficult for lecturers to differentiate between student and AI-generated texts in the future.

Therefore, based on the results and discussion above, the researcher could say that GPT has no significant impact on students' essay writing skill. Experimental and control group almost have same score in essay writing test. However, according to the interview, GPT has made students simpler to build the idea because they do not need to think harder like traditionally writing. Instead, the students who are in control group easier to arrange the structure of the essay as what they wanted. Besides, between GPT and traditional writing almost have same speed in finishing the test because the students in experimental group they need to arranged the structure, and the students in control group need to think the idea. According to the teacher, GPT is like digital library, everything the students needs are there. However, GPT could be the threat of education because if the students are allowed to use GPT all the time it could make they cheat, and the teacher is hard to differentiate which the students made or AI made.

CONCLUSION

As stated above, the researcher could draw the conclusion that the GPT and control groups, on average, earned a grade of B, with a marginally better average score in the experiment (0.78) than in the control group (0.76). The mean text unauthenticity in the GPT-assisted group was 11.87%, compared to 9.96% in the control group. With a median score of 0.002 (0-0.054), the total sample's level of text similarity was low. Additionally, GPT Essay Writer takes into account the literary structure, such as the use of primary and supporting sentences, and concludes the final paragraph with a conclusion. Additionally, it employs two distinct voices, including passive and active. In addition, it takes into account other tense variations, including the simpler present tense. This demonstrates that GPT Essay Writer is a useful tool for students to improve their writing ability because it allows them to create essays quickly and easily. It was evidence that after using GPT Essay Writer, the student's score had increased significantly.

In addition, for further research, other researcher should do future investigations on the influence of GPT Essay Writer as a writing aid on other psychological aspects, such as writing motivation, in order to uncover further potential benefits of GPT Essay Writer. Besides, as teacher or students, they should know what is the obstacle while using GPT Essay Writer. Examining the impact of GPT Essay Writer as a writing aid on various learning styles can enhance our comprehension of how different learning styles can either facilitate or hinder the effectiveness of GPT Essay Writer. This exploration may contribute to the development of improved instructional methods for the GPT Essay Writer as a writing aid.

REFERENCES

Abderraouf, A. (2016). Investigating EFL students' writing difficulties and common errors in writing [Master Thesis, University of Bejaia].

Abouabdelkader, H., & Ahmed, A. (Eds.). (2016). *Teaching EFL writing in the 21st century Arab world: Realities and challenges.* Springer Nature., doi:10.1057/978-1-137-46726-3

Ahmed, A. H. (2010). Students' problems with cohesion and coherence in EFL essay writing in Egypt: Different perspectives. *Literacy Information and Computer Education Journal, 1*(4), 211–221. doi:10.20533/licej.2040.2589.2010.0030

Al Khazraji, A. (2019). Analysis of discourse markers in essays writing in ESL classroom. *International Journal of Instruction, 12*(2), 559–572. doi:10.29333/iji.2019.12235a

Albarino, S. (2020, July 24). GPT-3: What You Need to Know About the World's Largest Language Model. Slator. https://slator.com/gpt-3-what-you-need-to-know-about-the-worlds-largest-language-model/

Ariyanti, A., & Fitriana, R. (2017). EFL students' difficulties and needs in essay writing. Advances in Social Science, Education and Humanities Research. International Conference on Teacher Training and Education 2017 (ICTTE 2017), Surakarta, Indonesia. https://doi.org/10.2991/ictte-17.2017.4

Atuhaire, R. (2022). What is ChatGPT. Dignited. https://www.dignited.com/104384/what-is- chatgpt-and-how-does-it-work/

Aydın, Ö., & Karaarslan, E. (2022). OpenAI ChatGPT generated literature review: Digital Twin in Healthcare. In Ö. Aydın (Ed.), Emerging Computer Technologies 2 (22-31). İzmir Akademi Dernegi.

Azaria, A. (2022). *ChatGPT Usage and Limitations.* Research Gate. https://www.researchgate.net/publication/366 618623_ChatGPT_Usage_and_Limitations

Bakry, M. S., & Alsamadani, H. A. (2015). Improving the persuasive essay writing of students of Arabic as a Foreign Language (AFL): Effects of self-regulated strategy development. *Procedia: Social and Behavioral Sciences, 182,* 89–97. doi:10.1016/j.sbspro.2015.04.742

Brown, H. D. (2000). *Teaching by principles: An Interactive approach to language pedagogy* (2nd ed.). Pearson.

Brown, T. B., Mann, B., Ryder, N., Subbiah, M., Kaplan, J., Dhariwal, P., Neelakantan, A., Shyam, P., Sastry, G., Askell, A., Agarwal, S., Herbert-Voss, A., Krueger, G., Henighan, T., Child, R., Ramesh, A., Ziegler, D. M., Wu, J., Winter, C., & Amodei, D. (2020). Language models are few-shot learners. arXiv preprint. https://arxiv.org/abs/2005.14165

Bulqiyah, S., Mahbub, M. A., & Nugraheni, D. A. (2021). Investigating writing difficulties in essay writing: Tertiary students' perspectives. *English Language Teaching Educational Journal*, *4*(1), 61. doi:10.12928/eltej.v4i1.2371

Burkhard, M. (2022). Student Perceptions of Ai-Powered Writing Tools: Towards Individualized Teaching Strategies. *Proceedings of the 19th International Conference on Cognition and Exploratory Learning in the Digital Age, CELDA 2022, Celda*, (pp. 73–81). IEEE. https://doi.org/10.33965/CELDA2022_202207L010

Ceylan, N. O. (2019). Student perceptions of difficulties in second language writing. *Journal of Language and Linguistic Studies*, *15*(1), 151–157. doi:10.17263/jlls.547683

Cheung, Y. L. (2016, August). Teaching Writing. *English Language Education*, *5*, 179–194. doi:10.1007/978-3-319-38834-2_13

Chinonso, O. E., Theresa, A. M.-E., & Aduke, T. C. (2023). ChatGPT for Teaching, Learning and Research: Prospects and Challenges. *Global Academic Journal of Humanities and Social Sciences*, *5*(02), 33–40. doi:10.36348/gajhss.2023.v05i02.001

Creswell, J. W. (2014). *Research design: Qualitative, quantitative and mixed methods approaches* (4th ed.). SAGE Publication.

Dwivedi, N., Kshetri, N., Hughes, L., Slade, E. L., Jeyaraj, A., Kar, A. K., Baabdullah, A. M., Koohang, A., Raghavan, V., Ahuja, M., Albanna, H., Albashrawi, M. A., Al-Busaidi, A. S., Balakrishnan, J., Barlette, Y., Basu, S., Bose, I., Brooks, L., Buhalis, D., & Wright, R. (2023). So what if ChatGPT wrote it? Multidisciplinary perspectives on opportunities, challenges and implications of generative conversational AI for research, practice and policy. *International Journal of Information Management*, *71*, 102642. doi:10.1016/j.ijinfomgt.2023.102642

Fareed, M., Ashraf, A., & Bilal, M. (2016). ESL learners' writing skills: Problems, factors and suggestions. *Journal of Education & Social Sciences*, *4*(2), 83–94. doi:10.20547/jess0421604201

Fraenkel, J. R., Wallen, N. E., & Hyun, H. H. (2012). *How to design and evaluate research in education* (8th ed.). McGraw-Hill Humanities/Social Sciences/Languages.

Frye, B. L. (2022). Should Using an AI Text Generator to Produce Academic Writing Be Plagiarism? (SSRN Scholarly Paper No. 4292283). https://papers.ssrn.com/abstract=4292283

Fyfe, P. (2022). How to cheat on your final paper: Assigning AI for student writing. *AI & Society*, 1–11. doi:10.17613/0h18-5p41

Geitgey, A. (2018, July 18). Natural Language Processing is Fun! How computers understand Human Language. *Medium*. https://medium.com/@ageitgey/natural-language-processing-is-fun-9a0bff37854e

Ginting, S. A. (2019). Lexical formation error in the descriptive writing of Indonesian tertiary EFL learners. International Journal of Linguistics. *Literature and Translation*, *2*(1), 5. doi:10.32996/ijllt.2019.2.1.11

Gocen, A., & Aydemir, F. (2021). Artificial intelligence in education and schools. *Research on Education and Media, 12*(1), 13–21. doi:10.2478/rem-2020-0003

Haque, M. U., Dharmadasa, I., Sworna, Z. T., Rajapakse, R. N., & Ahmad, H. (2022). *"I think this is the most disruptive technology": Exploring Sentiments of ChatGPT Early Adopters using Twitter Data* (arXiv:2212.05856). arXiv. https://doi.org//arXiv.2212.05856 doi:10.48550

Heaven, W. D. (2020, July 20). OpenAI's new language generator GPT-3 is shockingly good and completely mindless. *MIT Technology Review*. https://www.technologyreview.com/2020/07/20/1005454/openai-machine-learning-language-generator-gpt-3-nlp/

Hyland, K. (2008). Writing theories and writing pedagogies. *Indonesian Journal of English Language Teaching, 4*(2), 91–110. 10.25170%2Fijelt.v4i2.145

Jabali, O. (2018). Students' attitudes towards EFL university writing: A case study at An-Najah National University, Palestine. *Heliyon, 4,* 1–25. https://doi.org/. e00896 doi:10.1016/j.heliyon.2018

Jain, S., & Jain, R. (2019). Role of artificial intelligence in higher education—An empirical investigation. *IJRAR-International Journal of Research and Analytical Reviews, 6*(2), 144z–150z.

Jebreil, N., Azizifar, A., & Gowhary, H. (2015). Investigating the effect of anxiety of male and female Iranian EFL learners on their writing performance. *Procedia: Social and Behavioral Sciences, 185,* 190–196. doi:10.1016/j.sbspro.2015.03.360

KasneciE.SeßlerK.KüchemannS.BannertM.DementievaD.FischerF.KasneciG. (2023). ChatGPT for good? On opportunities and challenges of large language models for education. https://edarxiv.org/5er8f/

Kengam, J. (2020). *Artificial intelligence in education*. Research Gate.

King. (2022). The future of AI in medicine: a perspective from a Chatbot. *Annals of Biomedical Engineering*, 1-5.

Kleiman, G. (2022). *AI and Teaching Writing, Working Paper # 3 AI has learned to write; Can it help teach students to write well? Linse, C. T. (2005). Practical English language teaching: Young learners* (D. Nunan, Ed.; International Edition). McGraw-Hill Companies, Inc.

LundB. (2022). A Chat with ChatGPT: How will AI impact scholarly publishing? doi:10.13140/RG.2.2.34572.18565

Moore, J. L., Rosinski, P., Peeples, T., Pigg, S., Rife, M. C., Brunk-Chavez, B., Lackey, D., Kesler Rumsey, S., Tasaka, R., Curran, P., & Grabill, J. T. (2016). Revisualizing composition: How first-year writers use composing technologies. *Computers and Composition, 39,* 1–13. doi:10.1016/j.compcom.2015.11.001

Muller, B. (2022, March 2). BERT 101 State Of The Art NLP Model Explained. *Hugging Face*. https://huggingface.co/blog/bert-101

Okpe, A. A., & Onjewu, M. A. (2017). Difficulties of learning essay writing: The perspective of some adult EFL learners in Nigeria. *International Journal of Curriculum and Instruction, 9*(2), 198–205.

Owens. (2023). *How Nature readers are using ChatGPT*. Nature.

Perlman, A. M. (2022). The Implications of OpenAI's Assistant for Legal Services and Society (SSRN *Scholarly Paper No. 4294197*). https://papers.ssrn.com/abstract=4294197

Peters, M., & Cadieux, A. (2019). Are Canadian professors teaching the skills and knowledge students need to prevent plagiarism? *International Journal for Educational Integrity, 15*(1), 1–16. doi:10.100740979-019-0047-z

Prentice, F. M., & Kinden, C. E. (2018). Paraphrasing tools, language translation tools and plagiarism: An exploratory study. *International Journal for Educational Integrity, 14*(1), 1–16. doi:10.100740979-018-0036-7

Sabarun. (2019). Needs analysis on developing EFL paragraph writing materials at Kalimantan L2 learners. *Canadian Center of Science and Education, 12*(1). https://doi.org/ doi:10.5539/elt.v12n1p186

Saleh, Z. (2019). Artificial Intelligence Definition, Ethics and Standards. *Journal of Artificial Intelligence.*

Salvagno, F.S. Taccone, A.G. Gerli. (2023). Can artificial intelligence help for scientific writing? *Critical Care, 27*(1), 1–5. PMID:36597110

Schreyer Institute for Teaching Excellence. (n.d.). *Writing Rubric Example.* Schreyer. http://www.schreyerinstitute.psu.edu/pdf/suanne_general_resource_WritingRubric.pdf

Shidiq, M. (2023). *The Use Of Artificial Intelligence-Based Chat- Gpt And Its Challenges For The World Of Education; From The Viewpoint Of The Development Of Creative Writing Skills.* 01(01), 353–357.

Thunström, A. O. (2022, June 30). *We Asked GPT-3 to Write an Academic Paper about Itself—Then We Tried to Get It Published.* Scientific American. https://www.scientificamerican.com/article/we-asked-gpt-3-to-write-an-academic-paper- about-itself-mdash-then-we-tried-to-get-it-published/

Toba, R., Noor, W. N., & Sanu, L. O. (2019). The current issues of Indonesian EFL students' writing skills: Ability, problem, and reason in writing comparison and contrast essay. *Dinamika Ilmu, 19*(1), 57–73. doi:10.21093/di.v19i1.1506

Tseng, C. C. (2019). Senior high school teachers' beliefs about EFL writing instruction. *Taiwan Journal of TESOL, 16*(1), 1–39. doi:10.30397/TJTESOL.201904_16(1).0001

Whyte, C. (2022, May 12). Meta 'Open-Sources' Its Latest Large Language Model. *slator.* https://slator.com/meta-open-sources-its-latest-large-language-model/

Wyndham, A. (2022, April 24). The Great Language Model Scale Off: Google's PaLM. *slator.* https://slator.com/the-great-language-model-scale-off-googles-palm/

Yeadon, W., Inyang, O.-O., Mizouri, A., Peach, A., & Testrow, C. The Death of the Short- Form Physics Essay in the Coming AI Revolution. arXiv (2022) doi: https://doi.org//arXiv.2212.11661. doi:10.48550

ZhaiX. (2022). ChatGPT user experience: Implications for education. Available at SSRN 4312418.

Chapter 13
Social Commerce Recommendation Systems:
Leveraging User Behaviour and Preferences

Aanchal Taliwal
University of Petroleum and Energy Studies, India

Mimansa Pathania
University of Petroleum and Energy Studies, India

Mitali Chugh
iD https://orcid.org/0000-0002-1777-2387
University of Petroleum and Energy Studies, India

ABSTRACT

Recommender systems are software tools that make recommendations based on user needs and are increasingly popular in both commercial and research settings, with various approaches being suggested for providing recommendations. To choose the appropriate algorithm, system designers must focus on specific properties of the application, such as accuracy, robustness, and scalability. Comparative studies are used to compare algorithms, and experimental settings are described. The chapter discusses the importance of understanding user acceptance of recommendations provided by recommender systems and the influence of source characteristics in human-human, human-computer, and human-recommender system interactions. This chapter contributes to the study of social commerce by assessing the effects of the social web on different stages of purchase decision making and presents a model for analyzing social commerce.

DOI: 10.4018/979-8-3693-0502-7.ch013

INTRODUCTION

Recommender systems have become essential in modern applications, aiding users in navigating vast collections of items by offering personalized recommendations. These systems can predict user preferences and present lists of suggested items. Algorithm selection for a recommender system depends on performance comparisons through experiments based on various constraints like data type, timeliness, and resource requirements. Traditional evaluation primarily focused on prediction accuracy, but it's now acknowledged that other factors, such as exploring new items, privacy preservation, and system responsiveness, play a vital role in a recommendation engine's success. Evaluating a recommendation system involves three types of experiments: offline, user studies, and online experiments (Shani & Gunawardana, 2011). Offline experiments assess algorithms using historical data, while user studies involve real users interacting with the system. Online experiments conduct live tests with actual users to measure system performance. By identifying relevant properties and evaluating a system's performance on those criteria, designers can create effective and efficient recommender systems tailored to specific application needs.

Recommender systems play a crucial role in providing personalized advice during complex decision-making processes. However, users may not always accept the recommendations, as credibility both of the recommendation and the system itself as the advice-giver influences users' perceptions. Considering the credibility of recommender systems becomes vital in increasing the likelihood of recommendation acceptance. Recent research highlights that technologies can be more persuasive when they leverage social aspects and elicit social responses from users. Thus, recommender systems act as quasi-social actors and persuasive sources of advice. Previous studies have explored various influential source characteristics in human-human communication, and recent research in human-computer interaction confirms their importance in interactions with technologies. While some studies have investigated source characteristics' influences on recommender systems' credibility evaluations, there are still many unexplored possibilities (Yoo & Gretzel, 2011).

In the context of social commerce, recommender systems have emerged as a powerful force, combining the influence of social networks with the convenience of online shopping. The fast expansion of social commerce platforms has transformed the way consumers interact with online buying. These recommendation systems are crucial in assisting users to navigate the enormous product catalogue and discover items that correspond with their tastes. The combination of recommendation systems and social commerce is advantageous to both sides. Personalization improves the user experience, increasing retention and loyalty on social commerce platforms. Meanwhile, social commerce platforms provide a wealth of user-generated content, enabling recommendation systems to react to changing consumer preferences.

Our book chapter "Social Commerce Recommendation Systems: Leveraging User Behaviour & Preferences" proposes a comprehensive approach to improve the performance of social commerce recommendation systems. By analyzing user behaviour and preferences, such as browsing history, purchase history, demographics, and social media activity, the author aims to enhance the online shopping experience and deliver personalized product suggestions. The chapter also emphasizes the importance of data security and privacy concerns, focusing on data encryption, access controls, and anonymization techniques. A hybrid recommendation approach combines collaborative filtering with content-based filtering strategies to provide diverse and relevant recommendations. Social graph analysis evaluates the power of social influence, evaluating users' social relationships and products loved, reviewed, or suggested by friends, influencers, and communities. Real-time customization is crucial for a personalized purchasing experience, and the chapter aims to provide a comprehensive architecture for social commerce recommendation systems that utilize user behavior and preferences to improve accuracy, relevance, and efficacy.

LITERATURE REVIEW

The literature review for the research paper on "Social Commerce Recommendation Systems: Leveraging User Behaviour & Preferences" is further enriched by the inclusion of the study that explores the dynamic realm of social commerce. It emphasizes the pivotal role of social websites, such as Facebook and Instagram, in shaping social interactions, information sharing, and user engagement. This fusion of e-commerce and social media creates an environment where users exchange information and experiences (Lee et al., n.d.). In this context, the study employs the Stimulus-Organism-Response (S-O-R) model to analyze the factors influencing customer engagement in social commerce. This model examines how environmental stimuli drive individual behavioural responses, with three key components: stimuli (S), organism (O), and response (R).

1. **Stimuli (Antecedents of Customer Engagement):** The factors influencing customer engagement in social commerce, as highlighted in the study, are social support and trust transfer processes:
    a. *Social Support:* Within the context of social commerce, social support encompasses both informational and emotional support. It involves sharing advice and information and expressing care and empathy. Social support plays a critical role in strengthening bonds among participants and the formation of social communities, making it a vital factor in user engagement in social commerce platforms.
    b. *Trust Transfer Process:* Trust transfer is fundamental in the relationship between users and social commerce platforms. It includes member trust and community trust. Member trust represents individuals' trust in other members' words, actions, and decisions in a social commerce community, while community trust refers to an individual's perception of the community as a reliable setting for social interaction. Trust transfer is essential in building trust in social commerce platforms and fostering user engagement.
2. **Organism (Customer Engagement):** Customer engagement, as defined in the study, is a dynamic and repetitive emotional state derived from satisfactory interactions with an organization. In the context of social commerce, customer engagement is characterized by dimensions such as vigor, absorption, and dedication (Ali et al., 2020a).
3. **Response (Consequences of Customer Engagement):** The consequences of customer engagement encompass stickiness and repurchase intention:
    a. *Stickiness:* This refers to users' willingness to return to a website, increase the time spent on it, and visit more frequently. Customer engagement positively influences stickiness, indicating the platform's ability to attract and retain users.
    b. *Repurchase Intention:* Repurchase intention represents consumers' willingness to repeatedly purchase products through a social website. Customer engagement fosters repurchase intention, as satisfied and emotionally connected customers tend to engage more and increase transactions.

These interrelated components create a comprehensive framework for understanding user behaviour in social commerce. The study aims to investigate the relationships between these constructs to provide valuable insights into consumer engagement in the context of social commerce (Chen et al., 2014). The role of social support, trust transfer, and the consequences of customer engagement, such as stickiness and repurchase intention, contribute to a holistic understanding of the dynamics within this evolving field.

Understanding User Behaviour in Social Commerce

Understanding user behaviour in social commerce is crucial for optimizing engagement, trust, and sales on platforms. It involves studying social influence, trust, user-generated content, interactions, networks, and customization. This knowledge can help create personalized experiences and recommendation systems that consider users' preferences and needs.

A.   Types of User Behaviour Data

All the given tools are available for analysing user behavioural data, and play a crucial role in enhancing the effectiveness of social commerce recommendation systems.

1.   Click-through Rates (CTR)

CTR is a crucial metric in social commerce, measuring the effectiveness of marketing campaigns, product promotions, and user engagement. It is a percentage of users who click on a specific link or call-to-action (CTA) after seeing it on a platform or website. A high CTR indicates that the content or product is compelling and relevant to the target audience, indicating interest in learning more or making a purchase. To optimize click-through rates, businesses often focus on creating engaging content, targeting the right audience, using clear and compelling CTAs, and leveraging social media analytics. However, click-through rates can vary significantly depending on the platform, industry, and campaign goals. Social commerce platforms may provide insights into CTRs for individual posts, ads, or overall performance, helping businesses refine their strategies and achieve better results.

2.   Purchase History and Social Interactions (Likes, Shares, Comments)

Personalized recommendations improve browsing experiences by recommending suitable products based on previous purchases. Cross-selling and upselling opportunities arise from past purchases, ensuring variety and relevance. Seasonal and trend-based recommendations ensure relevance and user engagement. Post-purchase engagement is enhanced through personalized follow-up messages, feedback requests, and future recommendations. Trust and social validation increase credibility and user confidence. Trending products and social popularity are identified through analysis, boosting user engagement. User-generated recommendations provide useful suggestions for personalized recommendations and community participation. Personalization is improved by social connections, community-based suggestions, social discovery, and influencer marketing (Baethge et al., 2016).

3.   Wishlist, Favourites, Reviews and Ratings

Wishlists and likes can boost user engagement and sales by providing personalized suggestions, re-engagement notifications, cross-selling opportunities, social discovery, trend analysis, trust building, product relevance and quality assessment, recommendation algorithms based on reviews, filtering and summarization of reviews, user-generated content discovery, and feedback loop and continuous improvement. These features contribute to optimizing product availability and revenue, fostering confidence and trustworthiness, assessing product relevance and quality, filtering and summarizing reviews, and encouraging user-generated content discovery (Ali et al., 2020a). By leveraging these features, platforms can improve their user experience and optimize algorithms, ultimately leading to increased engagement and revenue.

B.   Data Collection Methods

Data collection strategies in social commerce involve user profiling, tracking, analyzing interactions on social media, and conducting questionnnaires and surveys.

1.   Tracking User Actions

Social commerce systems analyze user preferences, interests, and behaviors to provide personalized recommendations and increase engagement and sales. Real-time personalization improves the user experience while identifying intent helps platforms detect purchasing intent. User behavior analysis reveals patterns and trends, allowing platforms to optimize recommendation algorithms. User segmentation and targeted marketing increase engagement and conversions (Lee et al., n.d.). Continuous optimization ensures continuous improvement in recommendation systems, performance, and customer satisfaction.

2.   Mining Social Media Data

Platforms utilize social media data for user profiling, analysis of social influence, trend identification, sentiment analysis, social discovery, and targeted advertising. These tools help platforms understand users' interests, preferences, and social connections, enabling personalized suggestions and tailored recommendations. Social discovery helps detect relationships and recommend popular products, while targeted advertising optimizes advertising campaigns for relevant product promotions. Overall, social media data plays a crucial role in enhancing user experiences and driving business growth.

C.   Challenges and Considerations in Analysing User Behaviour Data
  ○   *Data Interpretation:* Analysing user behaviour data from social commerce platforms is complex, requiring evaluation of various activities (likes, comments, shares, purchases) to gauge engagement levels.
  ○   *Multifaceted Customer Engagement:* Customer engagement involves aspects like vigor, absorption, and dedication. A single metric isn't enough; a comprehensive approach is needed.
  ○   *Emotional and Information Support:* Vital in social commerce, influencing customer engagement. Trust transfer between members and the community is crucial.

- ○ *Outcome Metrics:* Besides purchase intent, non-transactional factors like stickiness (willingness to return) are vital for social commerce platform success.
- ○ *Measuring Customer Engagement:* **The dynamic** nature of engagement makes it challenging to define and measure. A second-order conceptualization using vigor, devotion, and absorption helps understand customer involvement.
- ○ *Environmental Psychology:* Environmental stimulation influences consumer purchase decisions. The S-O-R model helps understand how individuals react to the social media environment, considering stimuli, the organism (customer engagement), and the responses (stickiness and repurchase intention).
- ○ *Data Volume:* Maintaining vast amounts of user behavior data can be difficult. Processing and analysis necessitate effective storage and computational capacity.
- ○ *Privacy and Ethics:* When dealing with user behavior data, it is critical to respect user privacy and adhere to ethical norms. This includes protecting sensitive user data and securing appropriate consent.
- ○ *Bias and Fairness:* Analysing user behavior data may unintentionally perpetuate recommendation biases. It is critical to confront and erase preconceptions to ensure justice and prevent discriminatory practices.

Addressing these concerns can result in a more precise and efficient analysis of user behavior data, ultimately boosting social commerce recommendation systems (Lee et al., n.d.).

ENSURING USER DATA SECURITY AND PRIVACY

A.   Importance of Data Protection and Privacy

Social commerce recommendation systems require data privacy and protection to handle sensitive user data, improving shopping experiences and ensuring adequate protection for personal information and social connections. Some major points illustrating the importance of data privacy and protection in social commerce recommendation systems are as follows:

1. *Trust and User Confidence:* Data privacy and protection safeguards create trust between users and the platform, fostering engagement, preferences, and accurate feedback, crucial for long-term retention and social commerce platform success.
2. *Legal and ethical obligations:* GDPR and CCPA mandate data privacy compliance, requiring organizations to treat user data with care, avoiding legal ramifications, and preserving consumer privacy rights.
3. *Transparent Data Practises:* Transparency is crucial for users to understand data collection, processing, and usage practices, enabling informed decisions and strengthening user-platform relationships.
4. *Anonymization and Aggregation:* Social commerce platforms enhance data privacy through anonymization and aggregation, securing individual identities while enhancing recommendation algorithms.

B.   Compliance with Regulations and Policies

Social commerce recommendation systems rely on data privacy and protection through compliance with legislation and industry standards, ensuring ethical handling of user data and potential legal punishment. Here are some significant compliance considerations:

1.   *General Data Protection Regulation (GDPR):* Social commerce platforms operating in the EU must comply with GDPR, which outlines data collection, processing, storage, and safeguarding, requiring user consent, transparency, security measures, and user rights for access, rectification, and erasure.

2.   *California Consumer Privacy Act (CCPA):* Platforms serving California users must comply with the CCPA, ensuring consumer rights like data privacy, opt-out, and deletion, while providing privacy notifications and maintaining security practices.

3.   *Other Data Privacy Requirements: The* Platform's geographical reach may require additional data privacy regulations, such as Canada's PIPA, Singapore's PDPA, and Australia's Privacy Act. Familiarize yourself with relevant regulations and ensure compliance.

4.   *Industry Standards and Best Practices:* Data privacy and protection require industry standards and best practices, including ISO guidelines and employee training. Implementing safeguards like encryption, access limits, and regular security audits is crucial.

5.   *Data Subject Rights:* Ensure users can exercise data subject rights on your platform, including access, correction, removal, and export. Develop internal protocols for timely and effective management of user requests.

Since the turn of the century, regulatory compliance management has become increasingly important in organizations. This has led to the creation of corporate, chief, and regulatory compliance officer and compliance manager positions. These roles focus on hiring employees to ensure organizations comply with complex legal mandates and laws. Regulatory compliance processes and strategies guide organizations in achieving business objectives, while audit reports help businesses market themselves to customers. Transparency in compliance processes creates trust and potentially increases profitability. Noncompliant companies face remedial programs, monetary fines, and penalties, while frequent brand failures can harm their reputation (Policy Brief: Principles for Responsible Data Handling, n.d.).

C.   Security Measures: Data Encryption, Access Controls, and Anonymization Techniques

In social commerce recommendation systems, security precautions are critical for securing user data. Here is an excerpt emphasizing the significance of data encryption, access control, and anonymization techniques:

Social commerce recommendation systems require robust security measures like data encryption, access restriction, and anonymization techniques to protect user data. Data encryption ensures the confidentiality and integrity of sensitive information, while access control mechanisms limit data access to authorized individuals. Organizations can enforce granular access privileges based on user roles and responsibilities using role-based access control (RBAC) (Cole, n.d.). Anonymization techniques preserve user privacy while allowing effective recommendation algorithms. Eliminating personally identifying information (PII) or aggregating data at the group level masked individual identities, ensuring user privacy and reducing the risk of data re-identification. These measures create trust and encourage users to continue using social commerce recommendation systems.

D.   Promoting Responsible Data Handling and Transparency

Responsible data handling involves applying ethical values of openness, justice, and respect to handle data impacting people's lives. This can secure privacy and liberty while fostering trust for digital innovation. However, excessive data collection and utilization can jeopardize privacy, autonomy, and faith in the digital economy. While analytics and targeted advertising may improve customer experiences, they can also jeopardize privacy and trust in the digital economy. Social commerce recommendation systems aim to ensure privacy, liberty, and trust in the Internet while promoting innovation. Responsible data management coexists with data protection standards and guides situations where rules are lacking or unclear. Organizations can demonstrate their commitment to user privacy by adopting ethical practices and implementing strict data protection procedures (KENTON, n.d.). This includes obtaining user consent, providing clear privacy rules, and allowing users control over their data. Transparent communication about data collection, storage, and usage practices fosters trust and educates consumers about data handling. Organizations should be open about data-sharing practices with third parties, ensuring users are aware of collaborations and shared goals. By promoting appropriate data handling and openness, social commerce recommendation systems can build trust with users and promote a positive user experience.

USER PREFERENCE MODELLING IN SOCIAL COMMERCE

Social networking sites require users to provide profiles, which are stored by organizations. These profiles contain information like name, age, gender, occupation, and address. A unique key is used to encrypt usernames and passwords, and a security code is provided by the administrator to confirm identity. El-Gamal encrypts discussions between users. Businesses must adopt security measures for user profiles to prevent data breaches (Assistant Professor, 2023). Social commerce combines social networking and e-commerce platforms, improving user experience, engagement, and sales. Key elements of user preference modeling in social commerce include:

1.   *Data Collection:* Social commerce platforms gather data from user interactions, browsing habits, and user preferences, potentially leveraging explicit information from surveys or preference settings.
2.   *Collaborative filtering*: Collaborative filtering helps identify users with similar tastes and interests in social commerce, suggesting products or services based on their preferences, fostering personalized recommendations, and community building.
3.   *Machine Learning Algorithms:* Advanced machine learning algorithms process and extract patterns from user data, improving preference predictions by learning user behavior.
4.   *User Feedback Loop:* Regular user input improves preference modeling algorithms and user experience by enhancing suggestions.
      A.   User Profiling and Segmentation.

i.   Demographic Information.

Social media user segmentation and profiling involve grouping users based on various traits to understand their actions, preferences, and requirements. Demographic information, including age, gender, income, and education, has been linked to consumer inventiveness and the likelihood of adopting new products and ideas. Research has found that young people exhibit stronger innovative tendencies than older people, and men are more likely to adopt new items. Higher education and economic levels are also linked to greater inventiveness. Personal traits, such as age, wealth, mobility, education, and gender, have been linked to innovative tendencies. Income has also been linked to inventiveness, and sensation-seeking literature has been connected to the acceptance of new products. Demographic traits of different technology-related categories, such as explorers, pioneers, laggards, paranoids, and sceptics, consistently differ from one another. The theory proposed supports empirical data from product adoption and TRI literature, suggesting that demographic traits play a significant role in shaping consumer preferences and preferences (Victorino et al., 2009).

ii.   Interests and Hobbies.

Interests and hobbies are essential for user profiling and segmentation because they offer insightful information about users' interests, passions, and leisure pursuits. Social media platforms, marketers, and companies can adapt content, adverts, and product recommendations to better appeal to particular user groups by taking into account users' interests and hobbies. How interests and pastimes are used in user profiling and segmentation is as follows:

1.   **Personalization:** Social media platforms can tailor the material that appears in users' news feeds by learning about their interests and pastimes. A person may see more posts or advertisements connected to photography, for instance, if they are interested in photography.
2.   **Targeted Advertising:** Advertising that is specifically targeted can make use of user interests and pastimes to reach the right demographics. Users who have expressed interest in fitness may receive advertisements for exercise equipment or fitness classes.
3.   **Content Recommendations:** Recommender systems can take a user's interests and pastimes as input to recommend articles, movies, or products that are pertinent to their interests.
4.   **User Engagement:** Users are more likely to engage with and share content that is tailored to their interests because they are more likely to interact with and share content that is relevant to their interests.
5.   **Market research:** Businesses can perform market research and learn about consumer preferences and trends by gathering information about users' interests and pastimes.

iii.   *Personalized Preferences*.

Personalized service is a growing trend in information processing technology, as the Internet's expansion and improvement have led to a need for tailored services. These services analyze user data and provide automatic recommendations, allowing users to make informed decisions before starting a search. However, implementing recommendation algorithms that increase accuracy and align with user interests remains a challenge. Three mainstream recommendation algorithms exist personalized time series, which analyses user search behaviour, and personalized time series algorithms that adapt to user preferences and features. These algorithms can handle data sparsity and uncover potential semantic patterns in user ratings, ultimately making predictions more understandable and accurate (Liang Hu et al., n.d.).

RECOMMENDATION ALGORITHMS FOR SOCIAL COMMERCE

Recommender systems have evolved from Web 1.0 to Web 3.0, benefiting big corporations like Google, Amazon, and Netflix. They use collaborative filtering for personalized recommendations and are classified into six main classes: Collaborative Filtering, Content-based, Demographic-Based, Knowledge-Based, Community-Based, and Hybrid. Companies often combine these approaches to improve recommendation accuracy and user experience (Refer to Figure 1).

Figure 1.

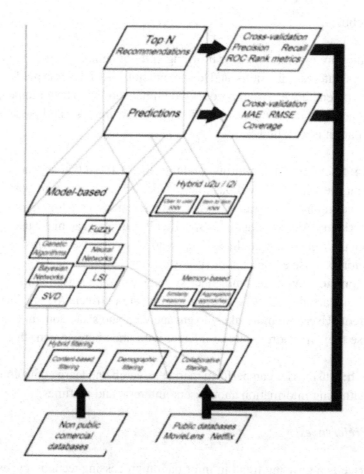

a. Collaborative Filtering Algorithms

Collaborative filtering is a widely used recommendation technique in social commerce, analysing user behavior and preferences to identify patterns and similarities. It suggests items based on the preferences of users with similar tastes, predicting user preferences using ratings and similarities. Collaborative filtering can be user-based or item-based, using model-based techniques like Bayesian clustering or Singular Value Decomposition. It often combines with content-based and knowledge-based approaches. Successfully applied in various applications, it's effective for job and product recommendations on platforms like LinkedIn, Facebook, Twitter, Google, Netflix, and Amazon (Jiang et al., 2019). By leveraging user preferences' similarities, this approach is divided into memory-based and model-based techniques.

1. Neighbourhood-based Methods: K-Nearest Neighbours

Neighborhood-based collaborative filtering algorithms, like the k-nearest neighbors (k-NN) approach, effectively analyze user-item interactions to identify similar users or items for personalized recommendations (Emilio Bruni Hendrik Purwins, n.d.). The kNN algorithm identifies the k most similar users or items to the target user based on past interactions, enabling recommendations of items liked or purchased by similar users. It operates by finding the k closest data points in the training set and determining the class label "l" of a point "q" by aggregating the k nearest neighbors' class labels. In recommender systems, kNN plays a pivotal role in generating personalized recommendations by identifying k-user neighbors for the active user and providing top N suggestions for unrated items (Thorat et al., 2015). Collaborative filtering, encompassing user-based and item-based kNN approaches, significantly enhances recommendation effectiveness across various applications, including e-commerce platforms and social media. The algorithm's efficiency allows real-time and scalable personalized suggestions, improving recommendation accuracy and user satisfaction in modern online platforms. As technology and data continue to evolve, collaborative filtering methods like kNN remain essential for enriching user experiences and facilitating informed decision-making in the ever-expanding digital realm.

2. Matrix Factorization Techniques: Singular Value Decomposition

Matrix factorization algorithms, like Singular Value Decomposition (SVD), play a crucial role in Recommender systems by uncovering latent features representing user preferences and item characteristics. By decomposing the user-item interaction matrix, these algorithms estimate missing values and predict user-item interactions, resulting in accurate personalized recommendations. Matrix factorization excels in handling sparse data, enhancing recommendation performance. To address high sparsity, model-based dimensionality reduction techniques have been proposed. SVD, a prominent choice, accurately predicts user-item interactions by mapping users and items to a joint latent factor space. This space characterizes users and items based on factors inferred from user feedback, revealing valuable insights. Utilizing dimensionality reduction helps Recommender systems overcome sparsity challenges, leading to improved performance (Nadee, 2016). It's crucial to consider the computational costs of SVD and explore adaptive approaches that accommodate changing user preferences over time. Static offline settings may not suffice for personalized recommendations (Thorat et al., 2015). Embracing matrix factorization and scalable dimensionality reduction methods enhances Recommender system efficiency, facilitating more effective and personalized recommendations. Users experience a more tailored and satisfactory engagement with the platform.

b.   Content-based Filtering Algorithms

Content-based filtering (CBF) recommends items to users based on their preferences and interests, using TF-IDF representation for item profiles, and considering user interactions (Thorat et al., 2015). It generates user profiles based on content-related information, allowing for personalized recommendations without explicit user ratings. CBF overcomes limitations of user-based collaborative filtering by focusing on content attributes, improving user experience in recommendation systems.

1.   *TF-IDF (Term Frequency- Inverse Document Frequency*

TF-IDF (Term Frequency-Inverse Document Frequency) is a widely used numerical representation in information retrieval and natural language processing. It is employed in content-based filtering algorithms, which utilize item content to provide personalized recommendations to users. TF-IDF calculates the importance of a term within a specific document relative to its frequency across a collection of documents (corpus). It consists of two main components: Term Frequency (TF) and Inverse Document Frequency (IDF). TF measures how frequently a term appears in a document, while IDF evaluates the rarity of a term across the entire corpus. By combining TF and IDF, TF-IDF assigns a score to each term, indicating its importance in distinguishing a document from others in the corpus(Emilio Bruni Hendrik Purwins, n.d.).

In recommendation systems, TF-IDF is applied to item profiles and user preferences, creating vector representations for both. By comparing the TF-IDF scores of terms in items and user profiles, the system can provide personalized suggestions based on content-based similarities. TF-IDF's flexibility and effectiveness make it a fundamental tool in building sophisticated content-based recommendation engines. It allows systems to deliver accurate and relevant recommendations by leveraging item content and user interests without relying on explicit user ratings.

c.   Hybrid Algorithms Combining Collaborative and Content-based Filtering

Hybrid filtering algorithms combine collaborative filtering and content-based filtering techniques to enhance the accuracy and coverage of recommendations in recommendation systems. The hybrid approach aims to overcome common problems associated with individual filtering approaches, such as the cold start, overspecialization, and sparsity problems. By integrating collaborative filtering and content-based filtering, the hybrid approach seeks to improve recommendation accuracy and efficiency (Emilio Bruni Hendrik Purwins, n.d.). These algorithms attempt to strike a balance by combining the strengths of both techniques. One common approach is to use collaborative filtering to generate initial recommendations and then use content-based filtering to refine and personalize those recommendations (Thorat et al., 2015). Another approach is to combine the predicted ratings from both collaborative and content-based filtering methods using weighted averages or other ensemble techniques. By blending the two methods, the hybrid algorithm can provide more robust and accurate recommendations. Hybrid filtering algorithms can be particularly effective in addressing the sparsity and cold-start problems often encountered in recommendation systems. They can also leverage various data sources, including user-item interactions and item content, to deliver more diverse and relevant recommendations (Nadee, 2016). Overall, hybrid filtering algorithms have shown great promise in improving recommendation accuracy and user satisfaction. They are widely used in real-world recommendation systems, where the combination of collaborative and content-based filtering techniques can lead to more effective and personalized recommendations.

REAL-TIME PERSONALIZATION AND SOCIAL RECOMMENDATIONS

Real-time personalization and social recommendations enhance the social commerce buying experience by dynamically moderating content and product recommendations based on user behavior. This synergy drives spontaneous purchases, consumer loyalty, and business success. Tailored information based on user behavior and social interactions enhances shopping engagement and customer happiness.

A.   Importance of real-time Behavioural Tracking and Providing up-to-date Recommendations

Real-time behavioral tracking and up-to-date recommendations are crucial in both energy consumption and social commerce domains. Excessive energy use in daily activities poses environmental challenges, and timely recommendations can influence energy-efficient behaviors. In social commerce, personalized suggestions enhance user engagement and loyalty. The (EM)3 recommendation engine leverages the Habit Loop theory to provide contextually relevant energy-saving recommendations. Persuasive facts with personalized projections increase the likelihood of users accepting suggestions (IEEE Computer Society et al., n.d.). Integrating real-time tracking and personalized recommendations promotes energy efficiency and enhances user experiences in social commerce. By tracking user behavior in real-time, systems can identify current preferences and habits, enabling the delivery of timely and relevant recommendations. This approach enhances user engagement and satisfaction, leading to more effective social recommendations and personalized experiences.

B.   Contextually Relevant Suggestions for an Engaging Shopping Experience

Social commerce has transformed how businesses engage with consumers through online social media platforms. The key to this revolution lies in contextually relevant suggestions, offering personalized recommendations based on user preferences and behavior. By utilizing data mining and analytics, social commerce platforms analyze user interactions to create tailored suggestions, enriching the shopping experience. These personalized recommendations, facilitated by content-based filtering and collaborative filtering, captivate users' attention and positively influence their purchase decisions. Additionally, personalized advertising, like on Instagram, aligns with user interests, enhancing ad value and contributing to a heightened flow experience (Lina & Ahluwalia, 2021). The integration of personalized advertising, contextually relevant suggestions, and flow experience leads to increased customer engagement, loyalty, and potential impulse buying. In this dynamic digital landscape, contextually relevant suggestions play a crucial role in delivering customer-centric shopping experiences, driving business success in social commerce (Liao et al., 2021).

C.   Incorporating Social Connections and Relationships

Trust is vital in social media transactions, influencing behavioural intentions and customer buying preferences in social commerce. Leveraging social connections and relationships is crucial for businesses in the digital era. Recommendations from friends and online communities carry significant weight, fostering word-of-mouth marketing and driving customer engagement and loyalty (Vinayagalakshmi, n.d.). Social relationships create a sense of community, allowing personalized interactions with customers. Understanding customer preferences helps tailor offerings and marketing strategies effectively. Strong social relationships lead to valuable feedback, enhancing products and services. Incorporating social connections in social commerce goes beyond advertising, and building authentic connections with customers. Businesses that master this approach thrive in the competitive landscape of social commerce, leaving a lasting impact on their audience.

D.   Leveraging user-generated Content

The use of user-generated content (UGC) in marketing is increasingly popular due to its perceived trustworthiness, especially in the domains of energy consumption and social commerce. UGC, including reviews and videos, is considered more reliable than marketer-initiated information and can significantly influence consumer behavior and enhance user engagement (Yi et al., 2019). However, effectively leveraging highlighted reviews presents challenges, as they may attract attention but also trigger consumer skepticism due to the evident marketing intent. To address this, firms should carefully select positive but not overly extreme reviews and take into account the variance in the review context and their reputation. Understanding these factors is crucial for enhancing consumer engagement and positive evaluations in social commerce and benefiting both energy consumption and social commerce domains.

E.   Social Network Analysis for Personalized Recommendations

In the digital era, social network analysis (SNA) has become a crucial tool in the realm of social commerce, providing businesses with valuable insights into user preferences and behaviors. SNA involves analyzing connections and relationships among users on social media platforms to identify influential individuals who can impact buying decisions (Vinayagalakshmi, n.d.). By understanding user networks, businesses can offer personalized recommendations that align with individual interests, improving the effectiveness of marketing efforts. SNA also enables targeted advertising campaigns that reach the right audience through influential users. Additionally, businesses can identify potential collaborations and partnerships to expand their reach and attract new customers through word-of-mouth referrals. Furthermore, SNA helps gain deeper insights into customer behavior and preferences through the analysis of social interactions, allowing businesses to tailor their offerings and enhance customer satisfaction. Overall, SNA empowers businesses to engage with customers more effectively and drive success in the ever-evolving landscape of social commerce.

EVALUATION AND PERFORMANCE METRICS OF SOCIAL COMMERCE RECOMMENDATION SYSTEMS

Social commerce recommendation systems play a crucial role in the online shopping landscape by utilizing user data and preferences to suggest products or services of interest. Their success relies on their ability to accurately assess user preferences and provide relevant and engaging recommendations. Key metrics for evaluating the effectiveness and performance of these systems include Click-Through Rate (CTR), Conversion Rate, Purchase Rate, Average Order Value (AOV), Mean Absolute Error (MAE), Precision and Recall metrics, and user engagement metrics (Kanstrén, n.d.). CTR measures the percentage of times users click on recommended items, while Conversion Rate calculates the percentage of users who make a purchase or complete a desired action after interacting with recommended items. AOV calculates the average value of purchases made by users who interacted with the recommendations. Mean Absolute Error (MAE) and Root Mean Square Error (RMSE) are commonly used to assess the accuracy of recommendations (Wang, n.d.). Precision and recall metrics evaluate the relevance and coverage of recommendations, while the F1 Score provides a comprehensive evaluation of the system's performance. Diversity and novelty metrics measure the variety and uniqueness of recommended items, while coverage measures the proportion of items the recommendation system can suggest from the entire inventory. User engagement metrics, such as time spent on recommended items, interactions, and feedback, also play a significant role in evaluating the system's success (Pu & Chen, 2010). A recommendation system that encourages users to explore recommended items and provide feedback is likely to be more effective in the long run.

A. Accuracy Metrics (e.g., precision, recall, F1-score)

A classifier is responsible for identifying binary classification events as positive or negative based on specific qualities or characteristics. Precision, recall, and F1-score are commonly used measures to assess the effectiveness of classifiers. True Positives (TP) are instances where the classifier accurately classifies positive events, while False Positives (FP) are instances where the classifier predicts positively when it should have predicted negatively. True Negatives (TN) are instances where the classifier correctly classifies negative events, such as cancer-free images. False Negatives (FN) are instances where the classifier predicts negatively when it should have predicted positively (Kanstrén, n.d.). Precision measures the accuracy of positive predictions, with high precision indicating a low false positive rate. True Negative instances are instances where the classifier correctly classifies negative events. Recall measures the classifier's ability to identify positive cases, with high recall indicating the classifier can successfully identify the most positive examples. The F1-score is the harmonic mean of recall and precision, offering a single value that balances both measurements. Practitioners can evaluate the classifier's advantages and disadvantages, identify areas for development, and take informed actions to improve its performance.

B.   Ranking-based Metrics (e.g., Mean Average Precision, Normalized Discounted Cumulative Gain, Click-through rate, Conversion Rate)

In recommender systems, evaluating the ranking quality of recommendations is crucial, and several metrics help assess their performance. These metrics include HR (Hit Ratio), MRR (Mean Reciprocal Rank), MAP (Mean Average Precision), and NDCG (Normalized Discounted Cumulative Gain). HR measures the fraction of users for whom the correct answer is included in a recommendation list of a specified length (L), while MRR calculates the average reciprocal rank of relevant items in the recommendation list (Wang, n.d.). MAP is useful for scenarios where only the presence of relevant items matters, while NDCG assesses the quality of the ranking by considering gain, cumulative gain, and discounting factors. These metrics offer insights into the effectiveness of recommender systems by focusing on the relevance and order of recommended items. They provide a more nuanced understanding of system performance beyond traditional accuracy metrics like mean squared error, making them invaluable tools for optimizing and enhancing recommender systems to deliver more accurate and relevant recommendations to users.

C.   User-centric evaluation (e.g., User Satisfaction Surveys)

Recommender systems are crucial in web technology as they offer goods based on the user's browsing history or interests. They significantly improve user experience and increase website revenue, making them a vital element rather than just a website add-on. The book emphasizes the importance of assessing user experience and irrational opinions of recommender systems. Recent studies focus on user perception factors, efficient preference elicitation techniques, varied recommendation generation, explanation interfaces, trust formation, and interface design guidelines. The chapter introduces the "ResQue" framework, which focuses on perceived system attributes, user beliefs, subjective attitudes, and behavioral intents. The framework has 60 question items and 13 structures, addressing topics such as the caliber of suggested things, interaction and interface suitability, usability, usefulness, transparency, and users' behavioral objectives. The text references earlier studies that investigated variables affecting users' perceptions of recommender systems, emphasizing transparency, familiar item recommendations, and adequate supporting data. Researchers also emphasize the need for metrics beyond accuracy, such as serendipity and diversity of recommendations. Overall, the chapter provides valuable insights into the growing significance of recommender systems, user-perspective assessment methodologies, and the ResQue framework for thoroughly evaluating recommender technology (Pu & Chen, 2010).

D.   Utilizing Evaluation Results for System Optimization

Utilizing evaluation results for system optimization is crucial in the development and improvement of recommender systems. User-centric evaluations, like User Satisfaction Surveys or the ResQue framework, provide valuable data and insights to identify strengths and weaknesses in the system. The key steps in using evaluation results for optimization include identifying areas for improvement, addressing user complaints and feedback, fine-tuning algorithms and recommendation generation, improving user interface and interaction design, enhancing transparency and trust, implementing better preference elicitation techniques, monitoring and iterating, and measuring the impact of optimizations. By continuously refining and optimizing based on user-centric feedback, developers can create more effective and user-friendly recommender systems that meet user expectations and provide an excellent user experience.

OPEN RESEARCH ISSUES

As social commerce evolves, various open research questions and concerns remain.

A.   Handling Cold-Start Problem in Recommendations

In the context of recommendation systems, the cold-start problem presents a common challenge when dealing with new users or reviewers who have limited or no historical data available. It faces the task of effectively handling users with insufficient data to provide accurate and personalized recommendations or to detect review spam. The proposed algorithm addresses the cold-start problem by employing intelligent techniques such as the C4.5 and Naive Bayes algorithms for user classification. By calculating the similarity between new and existing users based on demographic data and utilizing collaborative prediction methods, the algorithm estimates ratings for new users, enhancing the recommendation experience for them. In social commerce, personalized recommendations are crucial for user engagement and product choices. To tackle the cold-start problem, platforms can use demographic information, content-based filtering, and hybrid recommendation techniques (Wang et al., 2017). Additionally, incentivizing new users to provide feedback and employing active learning methods can gradually improve recommendation accuracy. In conclusion, recommendation systems in social commerce face the challenge of effectively handling new users or reviewers with limited historical data. Utilizing available data from existing users or reviewers and employing intelligent techniques play pivotal roles in overcoming the cold-start problem and providing enhanced experiences for users in the domain (Lika et al., 2014).

B.   Incorporating Real-Time and Dynamic User Behaviour

Incorporating real-time and dynamic user behavior in social commerce is a strategy that revolves around leveraging real-time data and user interactions to enhance the overall user experience, personalize recommendations, and optimize marketing strategies. Real-time user behavior analysis enables social commerce platforms to deliver relevant and timely product recommendations, promotions, and content based on user's current interests and preferences. Dynamic content delivery allows the platform to display related content and offers in response to a user's actions, encouraging engagement and conversion. Real-time communication tools like live chat provide immediate customer support, while flash sales and limited-time offers create urgency for quick purchases. Social commerce platforms use notifications to drive engagement and exploration. Trend analysis helps adapt marketing strategies, A/B testing optimizes campaigns, and gamification boosts user engagement. This approach enhances the personalized user experience, increasing satisfaction, conversion rates, and customer retention in social commerce.

C.   Commitment-Trust Theory

Trust theory is crucial in comprehending user behavior and interactions in social commerce. The Commitment-Trust theory and Trust Transfer theory play key roles in this context. The Commitment-Trust theory focuses on relationship commitment and trust, fostering successful cooperation (Chen et al., 2014). Trust Transfer theory explains how trust in a known entity can be transferred to an unknown one through associations. In social commerce, trust is essential for secure online transactions, information sharing, and relying on peers' recommendations. Positive interactions and a sense of community build trust within the platform, encouraging social commerce activities. Understanding trust-related behaviors, such as social shopping intentions and engagement, helps businesses enhance user experiences and drive positive outcomes. Trust theory provides valuable insights for creating a trustworthy environment and optimizing social commerce platforms.

PRACTICAL APPLICATIONS

A.   Recommendation System in Social Media Platforms

Recommendation Systems in social media platforms are a crucial application of Artificial Intelligence and Machine Learning, enhancing user experience by suggesting content that aligns with users' interests, increasing engagement, and fostering interactions. These systems curate users' feeds, recommend connections, and suggest relevant content, aiming to keep users actively engaged and benefiting both the platform and its users. The value of recommendation systems in social media platforms is measured by various business-related metrics, including user engagement, click-through rates (CTR), ad revenue, user retention, and network growth. Recommendation systems contribute to user retention by providing valuable and engaging content, reducing the likelihood of users abandoning the platform. They also play a role in expanding the user network by suggesting relevant connections, fostering social interactions, and increasing the user base. Overall, recommendation systems are essential components of social media platforms, shaping users' experiences and driving business success. By delivering personalized and relevant content, recommendation systems enhance user engagement, satisfaction, and retention, benefiting both users and platform operators (Jannach & Jugovac, 2019).

B.   Influence of Social Influencers on User Preferences and Recommendations

Social influencers significantly impact user preferences and recommendations within recommendation systems on social media platforms. These influencers, such as celebrities, bloggers, content creators, or experts, can influence users' opinions and behaviors through various factors. These influencers can increase user engagement and trust, provide personalized recommendations, shape trends and virality, and specialize in niche markets or specific topics. However, there are challenges related to authenticity, ethical considerations, and influencer marketing strategies. Authenticity is crucial, as influencers may promote products solely for monetary gain without genuine belief, potentially causing backlash and negatively impacting the brand's reputation (Ao et al., 2023). Ethical considerations include transparency about sponsored content and potential biases, and collaborating with social media platforms to develop influencer marketing strategies. Overall, understanding the dynamics of influencer-user interactions can provide valuable insights for optimizing recommendation strategies in this context.

CONCLUSION

The book chapter highlights the significant potential of Social Commerce Recommendation Systems (SCRS) in improving online shopping experiences through personalized and relevant product recommendations. SCRS leverages user behavior, preferences, and social interactions to enhance user engagement and satisfaction. Data security, privacy, and regulatory compliance are essential considerations in collecting data for SCRS. The chapter explores various recommendation algorithms, including collaborative filtering, content-based filtering, and hybrid approaches, which combine their strengths. Real-time personalization and social recommendations play a vital role in providing contextually relevant suggestions. Metrics such as accuracy, ranking-based metrics, and user-centric evaluation are discussed to evaluate the performance of SCRS. These evaluations are crucial for optimizing and fine-tuning the systems in social commerce. Despite the progress made, there are open research issues to address, such as the cold-start problem, real-time user behavior incorporation, and transparent explanations. The practical applications of recommendation systems in social media platforms and the influence of social influencers demonstrate their impact on online product discovery and purchase. The fusion of social commerce and recommendation systems has the potential to transform the e-commerce landscape and enhance consumer shopping experiences worldwide. As technology continues to advance, further innovations and improvements are expected, leading to a more personalized, engaging, and efficient online shopping journey for users globally (Ali et al., 2020b).

REFERENCES

Ali, A. A., Abbass, A., & Farid, N. (2020a). FACTORS INFLUENCING CUSTOMERS' PURCHASE INTENTION IN SOCIAL COMMERCE. *International Review of Management and Marketing*, *10*(5), 63–73. doi:10.32479/irmm.10097

Ali, A. A., Abbass, A., & Farid, N. (2020b). FACTORS INFLUENCING CUSTOMERS' PURCHASE INTENTION IN SOCIAL COMMERCE. *International Review of Management and Marketing*, *10*(5), 63–73. doi:10.32479/irmm.10097

Ao, L., Bansal, R., Pruthi, N., & Khaskheli, M. B. (2023). Impact of Social Media Influencers on Customer Engagement and Purchase Intention: A Meta-Analysis. *Sustainability (Basel)*, *15*(3), 2744. doi:10.3390u15032744

Assistant Professor, S. R. (2023). *CENTRAL ASIAN JOURNAL OF THEORETICAL AND APPLIED SCIENCES* Protection of User Profiles in Social Networks From Unauthorized Access. https://cajotas.centralasianstudies.org

Baethge, C., Klier, J., & Klier, M. (2016). Social commerce—State-of-the-art and future research directions. *Electronic Markets*, *26*(3), 269–290. doi:10.100712525-016-0225-2

Chen, J., Shen, X. L., & Chen, Z. J. (2014). Understanding social commerce intention: A relational view. *Proceedings of the Annual Hawaii International Conference on System Sciences*, 1793–1802. 10.1109/HICSS.2014.227

Emilio Bruni Hendrik Purwins, L. (n.d.). *Recommender System And User Interface Design For Experimental Film Streaming Service Title Page Title Recommender System And User Interface Design For Experimental Film Streaming Service.*

Liang Hu, Guohang Song, Zhenzhen Xie, & Kuo Zhao. (n.d.). *Personalized Recommendation Algorithm Based on Preference Features.*

IEEE. Computer Society, Institute of Electrical and Electronics Engineers., IEEE/ACM International Conference on Cyber, P., IEEE/ACM International Conference on Green Computing and Communications (16th : 2020 : Online), IOT (Conference) (13th : 2020 : Online), & IEEE International Conference on Smart Data (6th : 2020 : Online). (n.d.). *IEEE Congress on Cybermatics; 2020 IEEE International Conferences on Internet of Things (iThings); IEEE Green Computing and Communications (GreenCom); IEEE Cyber, Physical and Social Computing (CPSCom); IEEE Smart Data (SmartData) : Cybermatics 2020, iThings 2020, GreenCom 2020, CPSCom 2020, SmartData 2020 : proceedings : Rhodes Island, Greece, 2-6 November 2020.*

Jannach, D., & Jugovac, M. (2019). Measuring the business value of recommender systems. In ACM Transactions on Management Information Systems (Vol. 10, Issue 4). Association for Computing Machinery. doi:10.1145/3370082

Jiang, L., Cheng, Y., Yang, L., Li, J., Yan, H., & Wang, X. (2019). A trust-based collaborative filtering algorithm for E-commerce recommendation system. *Journal of Ambient Intelligence and Humanized Computing, 10*(8), 3023–3034. doi:10.100712652-018-0928-7

Lee, C.-H., Chen, C.-W., Chen, W.-K., & Lin, K.-H. (n.d.). *ANALYSING THE EFFECT OF SOCIAL SUPPORT AND CUSTOMER ENGAGEMENT ON STICKINESS AND REPURCHASE INTENTION IN SOCIAL COMMERCE: A TRUST TRANSFER PERSPECTIVE.*

Liao, S. H., Widowati, R., & Hsieh, Y. C. (2021). Investigating online social media users' behaviours for social commerce recommendations. *Technology in Society, 66*, 101655. Advance online publication. doi:10.1016/j.techsoc.2021.101655

Lika, B., Kolomvatsos, K., & Hadjiefthymiades, S. (2014). Facing the cold start problem in recommender systems. *Expert Systems with Applications, 41*(4 PART 2), 2065–2073. doi:10.1016/j.eswa.2013.09.005

Lina, L. F., & Ahluwalia, L. (2021). Customers' impulse buying in social commerce: The role of flow experience in personalized advertising. *Jurnal Manajemen Maranatha, 21*(1), 1–8. doi:10.28932/jmm.v21i1.3837

Nadee, W. (2016). *MODELLING USER PROFILES FOR RECOMMENDER SYSTEMS IN FULFILMENT OF THE REQUIREMENTS FOR THE DEGREE OF DOCTOR OF PHILOSOPHY.*

Pu, P., & Chen, L. (2010). *A User-Centric Evaluation Framework of Recommender Systems.*

Sena, M., Gebauer, J., & Rad, A. A. (2011). Make or Buy: A Comparative Assessment of Organizations that Develop Software Internally Versus those that Purchase Software Password Security Risk versus Effort. *JISAR.* www.aitp-edsig.org/www.jisar.org

Shah, K., Salunke, A., Dongare, S., & Antala, K. (n.d.). *Recommender Systems: An overview of different approaches to recommendations.*

Shani, G., & Gunawardana, A. (2011). Evaluating Recommendation Systems. In *Recommender Systems Handbook* (pp. 257–297). Springer US. doi:10.1007/978-0-387-85820-3_8

Thorat, P. B., Goudar, R. M., & Barve, S. (2015). Survey on Collaborative Filtering, Content-based Filtering and Hybrid Recommendation System. *International Journal of Computer Applications*, *110*(4). doi:10.5120/19308-0760

Victorino, L., Karniouchina, E., & Verma, R. (2009). Exploring the use of the abbreviated technology readiness index for hotel customer segmentation. *Cornell Hospitality Quarterly*, *50*(3), 342–359. doi:10.1177/1938965509336809

Vinayagalakshmi, V. (n.d.). *EasyChair Preprint The Role of Social Commerce Attributes and Trust on Purchase Intention in Social Commerce Platforms THE ROLE OF SOCIAL COMMERCE ATTRIBUTES AND TRUST ON PURCHASE INTENTION IN SOCIAL COMMERCE PLATFORMS.*

Wang, X., Liu, K., & Zhao, J. (2017). Handling cold-start problem in review spam detection by jointly embedding texts and behaviours. *ACL 2017 - 55th Annual Meeting of the Association for Computational Linguistics, Proceedings of the Conference (Long Papers)*. ACL. 10.18653/v1/P17-1034

Yi, C., Jiang, Z., Li, X., & Lu, X. (2019). Leveraging user-generated content for product promotion: The effects of firm-highlighted reviews. *Information Systems Research*, *30*(3), 711–725. doi:10.1287/isre.2018.0807

Yoo, K.-H., & Gretzel, U. (2011). Creating More Credible and Persuasive Recommender Systems: The Influence of Source Characteristics on Recommender System Evaluations. In Recommender Systems Handbook (pp. 455–477). Springer US. doi:10.1007/978-0-387-85820-3_14

Chapter 14
DDoS Attack Detection in WSN Using Modified BGRU With MFO Model

S. Venkatasubramanian

ⓘD https://orcid.org/0000-0001-7560-0164

Saranathan College of Engineering, India

R. Mohankumar

Saranathan College of Engineering, India

ABSTRACT

Significant challenges in the areas of energy and security persist for wireless sensor networks (WSNs). Avoiding denial-of-service assaults is a priority for safeguarding WSN networks. As open field encryption becomes the norm, conventional packet deep scan systems can no longer use open field review in layer security packets. To the existing literature evaluating the effect of deep learning algorithms on WSN lifespan, this study contributes the auto-encoder (AE) and then the bidirectional gated recurrent unit (BGRU). The learning rate of the BGRU is also chosen using the moth flame optimization technique. Learning is just one of the approaches that have emerged in response to the pressing need to distinguish between legitimate and criminal users. This chapter also demonstrated that for numerical statistical data, the sweet spot is reached when the number of records in the dataset is between three thousand and six thousand and when the percentage of overlap across categories is not less than fifty percent.

1. INTRODUCTION

An attacker can compromise a WSN's node availability by interfering with data packet transmission in a diversity of ways, including through sinkholes, wormholes, Sybils, hello floods, and (DoS) assaults (Pajila et al., 2022). DoS attacks can drain the resources of WSN nodes and cause data packet loss across the network. This research study will examine how to mitigate (DDoS) and (DoS) attacks in WSN networks with low energy requirements and high precision in attack definition (Lakshmi Narayanan et al.,

DOI: 10.4018/979-8-3693-0502-7.ch014

2021; Alsulaiman and Al-Ahmadi, 2021). In addition, service attacks starve WSN nodes by letting them take in traffic that is not intended for them. This sort of attack can happen at any tier of the WSN model scheme (Jane Nithya and Shyamala, 2022), and it causes WSN nodes to refuse network facilities to the genuine WSN nodes (Regin et al., 2023).

Intrusion detection is the strongest protection against DDoS assaults (Premkumar and Sundararajan, 2021) because of the prevalence of such attacks on WSN networks. Anomaly-based methods are the two main categories of intrusion detection (Angeline et al., 2023). Anomaly patterns need routine network connection monitoring and a comparison of current WSN network activity to historical traffic patterns (Islam et al., 2021). As a result, several strategies have been employed to enhance the effectiveness of active and passive DoS detection. Predicting and categorizing DDoS assaults is possible with the use of supervised machine learning techniques. Common techniques for this task are deep learning and K-Nearest Neighbor (KNN) (Hanif et al., 2022). In addition, the work shows that techniques are preferable to deep learning mechanisms for practical deployment since the latter requires large amounts of training data before producing accurate classification results(Belkhiri et al., 2022). This means that using the WSN network node to implement these features for use in training operations is pointless (Yuvaraj et al., 2022).

The clustering mechanism of WSN nodes and machine learning have both been presented as new methods for detecting DdoS (Abidoye and Kabaso, 2021; Yu et al., 2021). The impact of these algorithms on WSN networks has been studied in theory, but no publication has done so yet using the same simulation and dataset. In addition, due to the WSN nodes' constrained resources, any countermeasures against DDoS should be lightweight and quick. Most of the publications that surveyed the available knowledge focused on single assaults that were difficult to localize and detect in WSNs (Ismail et al., 2022; Rajest et al., 2023a). Therefore, optimum and intelligent localization methods are sought throughout the deployment of wireless sensor nodes to ensure precise node positioning and attack identification (Khan et al., 2022; Rajest et al., 2023b). The only way to fix this issue is to create a brand-new, highly efficient method. Since wireless sensor networks can be exploited in a sum of different denial-of-service (DoS) attacks (Yadav and Kumar, 2022).

In light of this, the primary influence of this study is an examination of the impact of algorithms on the WSN network dataset and an analysis of their performance in new WSN contexts. The following is a brief overview of the main results of this study:

1) A novel WSN network situation is presented that would help identify DoS assaults and examine the effect of this finding consumption by combining WSN nodes, attack detection using AR and MBGRU models, and the WSN dataset.

2) The impact of dataset size on deep learning classification performance analysis. The initial dataset was broken up into smaller and smaller chunks (in terms of record count).

3) Determine the impact that DoS anomaly detection performance has on the longevity of WSN networks.

The paper's remaining sections are laid out as follows. In Section 2, the survey is relevant to the efforts in DDoS assaults, machine learning, and WSN networks. Methodology, environmental progress, and policymaking are all broken down in Section 3. Section 4 indicates how to put complexity analysis in deep learning methods and the lifespan of WSN systems into practice. Section 5 provides a summary and suggestions for further research.

2. RELATED WORKS

An aberrant node detection approach is proposed (Luo et al., 2023), which involves a node behavior measuring methodology and a trust-value assessment apparatus after the authors analyzed models of selective forwarding attacks. When a software-defined network (SDN) is implemented, there is an increase in network latency. Therefore, in this study, a cloud-edge cooperative network recovery method was proposed to guarantee quick network recovery when anomalous nodes were identified. Furthermore, both simulation software and real hardware were used in the trials. The author confirmed that the recommended method indeed works. The experiments validated the effectiveness of the optional strategy in detecting problematic nodes, decreasing the packet-dropping rate, and speeding up the recovery time by 77.2%. This paper offers a solution to the issue of SDWSN security.

To mitigate these issues, a new attack detection approach based on EPK-DNN was presented (Raveendranadh, and Tamilselvan, 2023). The first phase of the EPK-DNN method is training the attack detection system. The first stage is to pre-process the input data, and the second is to use the pre-processed data to perform attribute extraction during training. Step two involves selecting the primary features using linear (LS-BAT). Then, the EPK-DNN is trained on the selected characteristics to identify assaults in WSN. Third, the sensor nodes are clustered, and the WSN network is started using the method (DL-K-Means). The rock hyraxes swarm optimization technique is used to choose the cluster heads in order to accumulate the sensor data. After the ADS has been trained, the sensor data will be sent into it for testing purposes. The results demonstrated that the EPK-DNN method achieved the highest accuracy of 97.21% for the MC dataset. Research results show that the EPK-DNN method achieves satisfactory finding accuracy when compared to standard deep learning (DL) techniques (Saxena & Chaudhary, 2023).

For attacks including jamming, denial of sleep, manipulation, and cheating in IEEE802.15.4-based systems, (Sudha et al., 2023) have mostly focused on the absence of challenges related to achieving Security. When it comes to adapting to shifts in network architecture and traffic, the swarm intelligence algorithm more than holds its own. Based on the channel at the end, the forward ants use a swarm intelligence algorithm to decide whether to each node. The ants will pick the next hop in the channel at random if they have access to that information. In order to boost wireless sensor network performance, the source, upon backward ant, confirms the attacker's long-term predominance and evades the specific channel for transmission. With the suggested method, packet delivery can be between 0.4441 and 0.6633. The efficiency of the suggested method is demonstrated by the effective packet ratio. The efficacy of the suggested scheme is demonstrated by the simulation results of attackers.

In their extensive review of supervised and unsupervised ML approaches, (Quincozes et al. 2023) take a look at three different feature selection algorithms. The public WSN-based dataset serves as the basis for the current studies, which simulate the Flooding, Grayhole, and Blackhole DoS assaults. The author also contributes by looking at the parameters that may be tweaked to improve the efficiency of unsupervised methods. The measures of processing time, F1-Score, accuracy, recall, and precision are used to compare experimental results. The results show that the supervised approaches provide superior performance than ones among the ML algorithms investigated; the REPTree with the OneR algorithm had the greatest F1-Score (95.69%) when used to identify blackhole assaults. In most cases, supervised methods will outperform unsupervised ones in terms of speed. REPTree is the quickest method, with an average classification time of 0.931 seconds (Jeba et al., 2023).

A two-stage detection approach, LSTM-NV, was developed (Huang, et al., 2023), which consists of a training step and a detecting stage. In order to forecast mistakes for each node, normal nodes' forwarding behavior is learned during the training phase by integrating variational mode decomposition (VMD) with an (LSTM) model. A unique neighbor voting mechanism is used to distinguish malicious from normal nodes, and a dynamic is created to identify local abnormality locations during the detecting stage. When compared to other efficient approaches, the presented schemes indicate greater performance while also providing reduced detection algorithmic complexity.

An effective Intrusion Detection System (IDS) is proposed in WSN (Gautami et al., 2023), which has been implemented to boost performance. Data Gathering (DG) and Intrusion Detection (ID) in WSN are both covered by the suggested system. Using the Distance-based Fruit Fly (DFFF) method, DG selects a Cluster Head (CH) from among the WSN's Sensor Nodes (SN). The information is then compiled using the newfound route. Then, the trained IDS is used to verify the results. Pre-processing, matrix reduction, and classification are the "3" components of the IDS. The data is laid down neatly in a comprehensible structure during pre-processing. The characteristics are then shown in a matrix format, and the matrix values are reduced using ELDA. To further categorize the DoS, R2L, U2R, and probes into Normal data, the result from the matrix reduction is sent into the QN3 classifier. The effectiveness of the suggested method is associated with that of state-of-the-art algorithms via experimental evaluation. The suggested work achieves better results than the current approaches (Cirillo et al., 2023).

In order to detect and localise attacks, a security-optimized neural network (MLPANN) has been introduced (Gebremariam, et al., 2023). The proposed method employs localization techniques to counteract attacks. The suggested system processes data using MATLAB simulation, Python, and the IBM SPSS toolbox. Using a multilayer perceptron artificial neural network, the dataset is divided into training and testing sets with the goal of detecting ten distinct types of attacks, including denial-of-service (DoS) attacks. Using the WSN-DS datasets, we tested the suggested system and discovered that, across many types of DoS attacks, it achieved far better results than the state-of-the-art systems. The suggested system outperforms the state-of-the-art alternatives on every metric of localization performance (accuracy, f-score, precision, and recall). Next, we run simulations to see how well the suggested method works for detecting and localising malicious nodes (Gaayathri et al., 2023). By using this method, we can approximate the location of the unknown node with little localization error (Regin et al., 2023). The simulation findings show that the proposed system can successfully detect and safely localise malicious attacks in hierarchically distributed and scalable WSNs. By using this approach, the author achieves an average accuracy of 99.51% and a reduction of the worst-case localization error to 0.49%.

3. PROPOSED METHODOLOGY

3.1 WSN Networks Overview

The 2.4 GHz radio access frequency used by WSN networks was developed specifically for use in low-power, short-range, low-processor scenarios. IEEE 802.15.4 (V. Kumar and S. Tiwari., 2012) is the standard that was developed by (IETF). In addition, Zigbee protocols are used to administer WSN networks and deliver information to the Access Point (AP). Media Access Control (MAC) and IEEE 802.15.4 physical layers are used by both protocols. To imprison WSN nodes and relay their data to edge AP, 6LoWPAN employs IPv6 and the (RPL) protocol (Bouaziz and Rachedi, 2016).

Figure 1. The construction of WSN systems

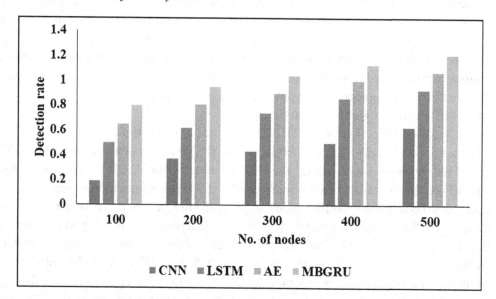

Figure 1 shows that the WSN networks, using the previously described protocols (Kumar and Tiwari, 2012), are in charge of sketching the network layer. Each WSN node forms an association with a group of its peer WSN nodes in the immediate vicinity, begins from various sources, and sends it on to the network layer (edge-AP). Both the RPL protocol in 6LoWPAN and the Distance in Zigbee are used for this purpose. User Datagram Protocol (UDP) is utilized for data transfer protocols due to its simplicity and low CPU overhead. As an added layer of Security, the (DTLS) protocol is used to encrypt UDP data transfers.

3.2 DoS in WSN Networks

DDoS attacks aim to degrade network availability by interfering with services and overall performance, as was indicated earlier. Therefore, the impact of such an assault differs across the various layers of a network. Each of the five network levels in WSNs is vulnerable to its own set of threats. Table 1 displays the many layers and the respective types of DoS they represent.

Table 1. Classification of WSN DoSsystem attacks

Description	WSN system layers
Blackhole, gray hole, hello	Network layer
Jamming tempering scheduling (TDMA)	IEEE 802.15.4 layer
Collision exhaustion	IEEE 802.15.4 MAC layer
Flooding	Conveyance layer

As seen in the section on cluster administration, the Blackhole and Grayhole DDoS assaults cause disruption to the layer-3 routing protocol by designating the attacker node as the cluster head. At the same time, the Flooding attack reduces the availability of the WSN network by bombarding cluster heads with advertisements. By switching from a broadcast to a unicast schedule, the physical and MAC layers are affected in a scheduling attack (like Time-Division Multiple Access or TDMA). Because of this shift, packet collisions and subsequent data loss are inevitable.

3.3. Data Collection

The authors are putting it through its paces in this work by utilizing the WSN network dataset. There are three distinct varieties of network traffic datasets, including the CICDDoS2019 (Sharafaldin et al., 2019) and the BoT-IoT (Koroniotis, 2018). Servers and switches were used to gather data for CICD-DoS2019 and BoT-IoT, respectively. To achieve the research aim of lowering consumption and shifting the defensive decision to the Edge AP, and by consolidating these four distinct DoS assaults into a single category, labeled as "1," while the status quo will be indicated by the "0" designation. Out of the original 19 characteristics in the dataset, only the id, time, distance to CH, distance to the base station, and data transferred to the base station are considered because they are all relevant to the presented ecological method. The first data set includes every record from the primary data collection. Table 2 shows that compared to non-attacked data, the attacked data is 88.6 percentage points lower. A further 33% of the attacked data is Blackhole, 11% is Flooding, 35% is Grayhole, and 21% is TDMA. Therefore, ratios will be considered across all datasets.

Due to the fact that the second dataset comprises unique data entries for each label category, it is discounted by 40% compared to the original dataset overall. When compared to the second dataset, the third dataset is 40% cheaper for each label. To examine how the different proportions of normal and attacked data affect training, the fourth and fifth datasets are split 2:1. Due to the low amount of entries in dataset #6, the records are split evenly between the two. Table 2 provides a summary of the available datasets.

Table 2. Datasets dimensions

Datasets	Normal	Attacked	Total sum
Dataset-1	184,343	21,461	205,804
Dataset-2	120,223	13,160	133,383
Dataset-3	24,025	3,568	27,593
Dataset-4	3,152	1,874	5,026
Dataset-5	2,068	1,034	3,102
Dataset-6	214	194	408

3.4. Classification Using Deep Learning Models

This section details how to enhance the prediction model performance by combining architectures.

3.4.1 The Auto-Encoder (AE)

In a multilayer network with identical input and output neurons, AE is a special case. Latent-space representation is a lower-dimensional space that AE uses to understand the original data's underlying representation. The output is reconstructed from the input data using the compressed representation, with the input error as small as possible. A back-propagation technique is applied during training to minimize the loss function. An AE has an encoder (X) and a decoder (Y). The encoder is responsible for generating the latent representation by compressing the input. The latent representation is then used by the decoder to recreate the input. A deep auto-encoder is an encoder with several hidden layers.

To mathematically express the encoding and decoding operation, the following equation is used:

$$p_i = f\left(w_p . x_i + b_t\right) \tag{1}$$

$$x_i = g\left(w_y . p_i + b_t\right) \tag{2}$$

where $f(.)$ and $g(.)$ are the sigmoid purposes, stands for the biases, and w for the weights. In order to train the model, the authors minimize the subsequent loss function.:

$$L\left(X,Y\right) = \frac{1}{2n}\sum_{i}^{n} x_i - y_i^2 \tag{3}$$

where x_i represents the experiential value, y_i signifies foretold values and characterizes the total sum of foretold values.

In order to verify the reliability of the generated fundamental feature P, Equation (3) can be used. The input data is first processed by an encoder, a fully associated ANN, to generate the intermediate code layer. The output will be generated by the middle-coded layer of the decoder, which has an ANN construction that is the mirror image of the encoder. The desired result is for the output to be a carbon copy of the input (Sajini et al., 2023). The AE can reflect a more nuanced distribution of input data if more layers of encoders and decoders are developed.

3.4.2. Modified Bidirectional Gated Recurrent Unit

Due to its bidirectional learning method, which improves the learning of temporal patterns in the time-series data (Farzad and Gulliver, 2019), the modified (MBGRU) is a network that has been effectively employed to handle time-series sequential data issues. Information is stored in a cell within each BGRU block. The cells, each of which consists of a reset and update gate, contribute to solving the vanishing gradient issue.

BGRU consists of two GRU blocks; the reset gate decides how to integrate fresh input with existing memory, while the update gate determines how much of the existing memory to maintain. One output layer is coupled to both the feedforward and time-varying feedback networks, which receive the input data. Bidirectional GRU outperforms feedforward networks because its gates are built to hold information for longer in both directions. The capacity to sequentially apply previous and future contexts is provided by the bidirectional method. The notation for BGRU is:

$$h_t = [\vec{h}_t, \overleftarrow{h}_t] \tag{4}$$

The last output layer at period t is:

$$y_t = \sigma\left(W_y h_t + b_y\right) \tag{5}$$

Where r is the activation function, W_y is the weight, and b_y is the bias vector. Figure 2 offers the architecture of the projected model.

Figure 2. Architecture diagram of the BGRU model

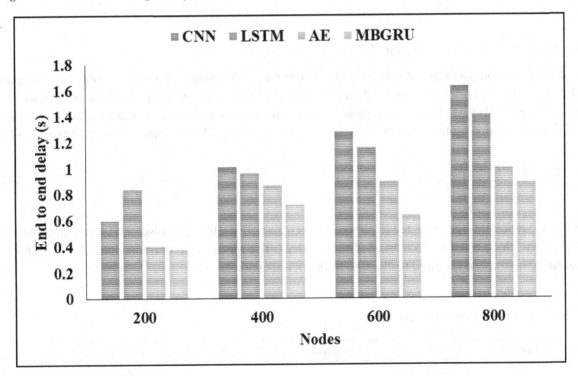

Each GRU block consists of four individual parts, as seen in Figure 2. Weighted and biased input vector x_I, and a weighted and biased reset gate r_I. Change the weight and bias of gate z_I to W_r, U_r,b_r. W_z, U_z, b_z and out bias W_h, U_h, b_h. A fully gated unit is signified as shadows:
Initially, for t = 0, the production vector is h_0=0.

$$z_t = \sigma_g\left(W_z x_t + U_z h_{t-1} + b_z\right) \tag{7}$$

$$r_t = \sigma_g \left(W_r x_t + U_r h_{t-1} + b_r \right) \tag{8}$$

$$h_t = z_t h_{t-1} + \left(1 - z_t \right) \otimes \varnothing h \left(W_h x_t + U_h \left(r_t \otimes h_{t-1} \right) + b_h \right) \tag{9}$$

where $\otimes$ is the Hadamard creation? W, U, and b are limit vectors. σ_g and ϕh are the activation purposes, σ_g is a sigmoid purpose, and ϕh is tangent

The following describes the structure of the model's BGRU. To begin, the BGRU cells are built so that the first BGRU layer combines the computed result of feedforward (F_t) with the feedback propagation (B_t). Concatenation (the default), summation, multiplication, and averaging are the four procedures that can be used to combine the final result. In this research, the authors will evaluate the efficacy of several merging techniques. This union is shown below:

$$O_t^1 = concat \left(\left(\overrightarrow{F_t} \right), \left(\overleftarrow{B_t} \right) \right) \tag{10}$$

Such that $\left(\overrightarrow{F_t} \right) = \left(\overrightarrow{h_1}, \overrightarrow{h_2}, \ldots, \overrightarrow{h_t} \right)$ and $\left(\overleftarrow{B_t} \right) = \left(\overleftarrow{h_t}, \overleftarrow{h_{t+1}}, \overleftarrow{h_{t+2}}, \overleftarrow{h_{t+3}}, \ldots, \overleftarrow{h_n} \right)$

Second, the output of the BGRU network is multiplied by its weight and bias in a fully linked layer. The output of the layer is then sent into a Softmax regression layer, which generates a prediction. To address the unbalanced classification problem, a weighted classification layer is employed to construct a weighted function for the forecast score and the training target. The subsequent loss is implemented.:

$$\left(p_{,t} \right) = - \left(1 - \left(p_t \right)^\gamma \right) log_2 \left(p_t \right) * \theta_i \tag{11}$$

where (p) represents the projected likelihood of each class, 0 is a tuneable discount factor parameter, _i is the logic class, and Table 3 lists all of these values. The Moth flame optimization (MFO) model is discussed below, and it is used to alter the BGRU's learning rate.

Table 3. Proposed BGRU construction

Param #	Layer (kind)	Output shape
8256	Bidirectional	(Bidirectional multiple)
7872	Bidirectional_1	(Bidirectionmanifold)
0	Repeat_vector	(RepeatVector) manifold
4800	Bidirectional_2	(Bidirectionmanifold)
12,672	Bidirectional_3	(Bidirectionmanifold)
58	time_distributed	(TimeDistrimanifold)
	Entire params:	34,185
	Trainable params:	34,185
	Non-trainable params:	0

3.4.2.1. Moth-Flame Optimization (MFO)

In 2015, S. Mirjalili introduced a Moth-flame optimization (MFO) method, which takes its inspiration from the way moths find their way around. Moths in the MFO algorithm stand in for potential answers, and those potential answers matrix is how the process gets started.:

$$M = \begin{pmatrix} m_{1,1} & m_{1,2} & \cdots & m_{1,d} \\ m_{2,1} & m_{2,2} & \cdots & m_{2,d} \\ \vdots & \vdots & \ddots & \vdots \\ m_{n,1} & m_{n,2} & \cdots & m_{n,d} \end{pmatrix} \tag{12}$$

where each row vector $\begin{bmatrix} m_{n,1}, m_{n,2}, \ldots, m_{n,d} \end{bmatrix}$ stands for the total sum of moths, n, and the total number of parameters, d. In a more general sense, d may be thought of as the number of dimensions, and by constantly shifting their location vector, moths navigate a hyper-dimensional space.

According to the impartial function, the fitness can be obtained:

$$OM = \begin{pmatrix} om_1 \\ om_2 \\ \vdots \\ o_n \end{pmatrix} \tag{13}$$

Note that o_n is the value of fitness for the nth month. Flames are also crucial to the MFO algorithm. Flames can be started in a manner analogous to that of moths:

$$\mathcal{F} = \begin{pmatrix} f_{1,1} & f_{1,2} & \cdots & f_{1,d} \\ f_{2,1} & f_{2,2} & \cdots & f_{2,d} \\ \vdots & \vdots & \ddots & \vdots \\ f_{n,1} & f_{n,2} & \cdots & f_{n,d} \end{pmatrix} \tag{14}$$

$$O\mathcal{F} = \begin{pmatrix} of_1 \\ of_2 \\ \vdots \\ of \end{pmatrix} \tag{15}$$

where each row vector $\begin{bmatrix} f_{n,1}, f_{n,2}, \ldots, f_{n,d} \end{bmatrix}$ where n is the whole sum of flames and d is the total number of parameters, each of which represents a separate moth. Every generation of moths follows the same spiraling path to its matching flame. The mathematical formula for the spiral path taken by moths and flames is as follows:

$$S\left(M_i, \mathcal{F}_j\right) = \left|MO_i - \mathcal{F}_i\right|.e^{bt}.cos2\pi t + \mathcal{F}_j \tag{16}$$

where M_i and F_i represent the b, determines the form of the spiral, and t is a random sum in the range [1; 1]. Then, in the subsequent cycle, the fire is rekindled in accordance with the following guidelines:

$$OF_{k+1} = sort\left(P_k\right)_n \tag{17}$$

$$P_k = \begin{pmatrix} OM_k \\ OF_k \end{pmatrix} \tag{18}$$

where k is the present repetition sum, and k+1 is the next repetition, P_kdesignates a vector that splices the vector OM and OF in the kth column, and sort(P_k)n is an operation that sorts the members of the vector P_k from minor to big and keeps the first n items. There is a one-to-one relationship between OF and F. So to speak. After acquiring the OF vector, F may be calculated. As the iteration count rises, the proportion of flames to surrounding air gradually decreases, and this proportion may be computed as:

$$fn = \mathfrak{R}\left[maxfn - \frac{k.\left(maxfn - 1\right)}{maxit}\right] \tag{19}$$

where *maxi* designates the max repetitions, *Maxon* means the reset sum of flames, and $\mathfrak{R}$ (∗) is a process to brand the operand rounded to its adjacent integer.

4. EXPERIMENT AND RESULTS

To evaluate the effectiveness of the suggested system, the NS-2 simulator is used in this study. The simulation mimic a network with one hundred sensing nodes that have been randomly dispersed throughout a 100 by 100-meter area. In the simulations, the two types of nodes used as sensing elements good ones and bad ones have been identified. In the simulated scenarios, the malicious nodes will launch distributed denial of service assaults. The SB can continuously generate power. For one period, the total amount of designated CH has reached 100%. By comparing the suggested models to those already in use, their performance can be estimated. Table 4 lists the values that were input into the trust system calculator utilized in this study. Packet loss and packet delivery are only some of the metrics that have been used to assess the suggested model's efficacy.

4.1 Packet Loss

Malicious actors suddenly cause the total amount of data packets to be invalid. Figure 3 is a visual depiction of the models in Table 5, demonstrating how both prior works and the suggested technique exhibit a decreased packet loss rate.

Table 4. Simulation parameters

Values	Simulation parameters
1000×1000 m	Simulation area
500	Number of nodes
channel	Channel Wireless
802.11	Mac
Omni antenna	Antenna type
AODV	Routing protocol
100 J	Initial energy
CBR	Traffic type
UDP	Agent

Table 5. Packet loss comparison

Nodes	CNN	LSTM	AE	MBGRU
200	0.87	0.75	0.61	0.57
400	0.95	0.88	0.83	0.78
600	1.22	1.11	1.02	0.9
800	1.33	1.25	1.16	0.95

Figure 3. Packet loss

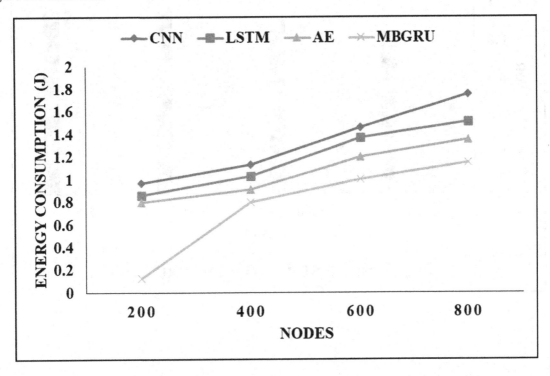

The present system's focus is on determining the identities of both benign and malicious sensor nodes, as substantial traffic divergence indicates that all such nodes are bad. According to the bias and variance value of certain malicious nodes, the value has been discovered by the suggested technique. As a result of elimination, the pocket drop was prevented. When compared to LSTM, AE, and CNN, the suggested model reduces packet loss by 11.6%, 19.79%, and 26.77%, respectively.

4.2 Packet Delivery Ratio (PDR)

The ratio among the sum of data packets, conventional and sent, specifies the depth of data delivery.

Table 6. Packet delivery ratio comparison

Nodes	CNN	LSTM	AE	MBGRU
200	0.47	0.64	0.7	0.85
400	0.63	0.87	0.89	0.92
600	0.82	0.95	0.96	0.98
800	0.95	0.95	0.97	0.99

Figure 4. PDR analysis

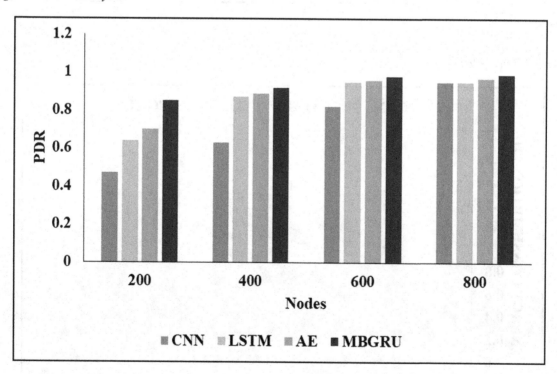

A number of rounds and (PDR) clearly show that the suggested model outperforms AE, LSTM, and CNN when it comes to counting (fig.4). By successfully receiving efficient packets at the destination, the researcher was able to attain better PDR outcomes using the suggested methodology. A comparison of the two approaches shows that the suggested model often results in more packets being sent, with a 6.25 percent increase over AE, a 9.67 percent increase over LSTM, and a 30.3 percent increase over CNN (Table 6).

4.3 Energy Consumption

In the given simulation time, the average amount of energy used by each node is reported in Joules (J).

Figure 5 is a visual depiction of the energy used by several wireless sensor network types in military applications. The reduced energy usage at the proposed technique is now easily identifiable thanks to the present system mask value. Compared to AE, 35.53% less energy is used by the proposed model, and 42.09% less energy is used by the suggested model compared to CNN (Table 7).

Table 7. Energy consumption comparison

Nodes	CNN	LSTM	AE	MBGRU
200	0.97	0.86	0.8	0.125
400	1.13	1.03	0.91	0.8
600	1.46	1.37	1.2	1
800	1.75	1.51	1.35	1.15

Figure 5. Energy Consumption for various deep-learning

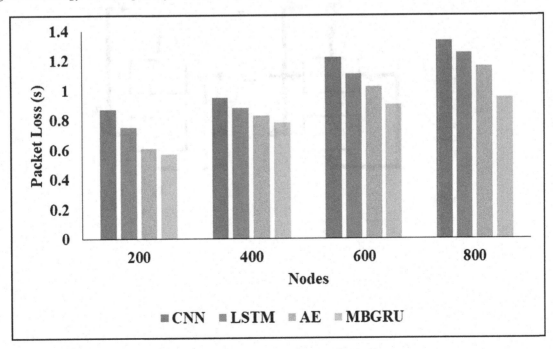

4.4 End-To-End Delay

Delays in processing, queuing, and propagation at the BS have impacted the end-to-end timing of data packet broadcast. The use of wireless sensors in military applications has been visually shown to demonstrate the lag time from beginning to finish. A high hop-to-hop number might cause a communication bottleneck at the path's conclusion. The MBGRU system is designed such that the end-to-end latency is minimized regardless of the hop-to-hop count or the distance of the data transmission. Data transmission in the MBGRU system is not affected by a large hop-to-hop route distance (Fig. 6; Table 8).

In the proposed MBGRU system, data transmission lines with a high hop-to-hop count distance are automatically determined to be attack paths. The imitation consequences show that the suggested technique has a lower end-to-end latency of 17.03% compared to AE, 39.81% compared to LSTM, and 41.81% compared to CNN.

Table 8. End-to-end delay comparison

Nodes	CNN	LSTM	AE	MBGRU
200	0.6	0.84	0.4	0.38
400	1.01	0.96	0.87	0.72
600	1.28	1.16	0.9	0.64
800	1.63	1.41	1	0.89

Figure 6. Delay comparison

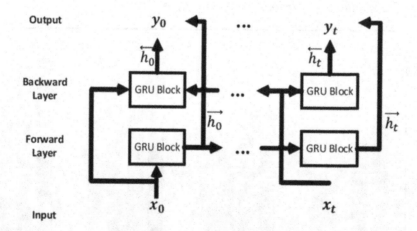

4.5. Detection Rate

DoS provides an accurate assessment of environmental harm by calculating the detection ratio. DoS attack detection ratio is heavily employed in the suggested study approach to guarantee the safety of the surrounding environment. Figure 7 (Table 9) depicts the DoS attack evaluation.

Table 9. Detection rate comparison

Nodes	CNN	LSTM	AE	MBGRU
100	0.19	0.5	0.65	0.8
200	0.37	0.62	0.81	0.95
300	0.43	0.74	0.9	1.04
400	0.5	0.86	1	1.13
500	0.63	0.93	1.07	1.21

Figure 7. Rate of the proposed model for detection

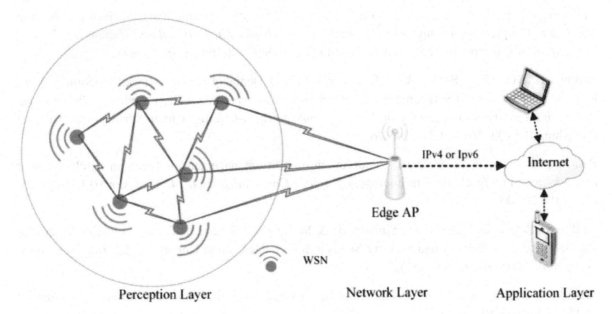

5. CONCLUSION AND FUTURE WORK

In this research, the authors examine how well AE and MGBRU models perform in detecting DoS assaults in WSN-DS datasets. In addition, the WSN-SD was split up into several datasets so that the efficiency of these methods could be evaluated across a range of data sizes. In addition, one of these algorithms was chosen so that its effects on WSN network longevity could be studied. A training execution time has been calculated for each method using Python 3.8 within the Jumyter Network program. The WSN network lifespan was obtained using both the Cooja simulator and the clustering management technique, both of which may be found in up-to-date sources. The quantitative nature of the data acquired from WSN network traffic has been demonstrated through the study of the presentation of the various deep learning algorithms used in WSN-SD. As a result, the MGBRU model was the best based on the complete metrics in several WSN-DS datasets and the best algorithms for statistical and logical classification. In addition, if the proportion of data among the labeled groups is high enough, a dataset of 3,000 to 6,000 records is adequate for the training procedure and achieves a high-performance forecast. In future work, the classification accuracy may be improved by extracting the features from the dataset and the optimal selection of features using optimization models.

REFERENCES

Abidoye, A. P., & Kabaso, B. (2021). Lightweight models for detection of denial-of-service attack in wireless sensor networks. *IET Networks*, *10*(4), 185–199. doi:10.1049/ntw2.12011

Alsulaiman, L., & Al-Ahmadi, S. (2021). *Performance evaluation of machine learning techniques for DOS detection in wireless sensor network*. arXiv preprint arXiv:2104.01963.

Angeline, R., Aarthi, S., Regin, R., & Rajest, S. S. (2023). Dynamic intelligence-driven engineering flooding attack prediction using ensemble learning. In *Advances in Artificial and Human Intelligence in the Modern Era* (pp. 109–124). IGI Global. doi:10.4018/979-8-3693-1301-5.ch006

Belkhiri, H., Messai, A., Beylot, A. L., & Haider, F. (2022). Denial of Service Attack Detection in Wireless Sensor Networks and Software Defined Wireless Sensor Networks: A Brief Review. In *Proceedings of the 5th International Conference on Big Data and Internet of Things*. Cham: Springer International Publishing. 10.1007/978-3-031-07969-6_8

Bouaziz, M., & Rachedi, A. (2016). A survey on mobility management protocols in wireless sensor networks based on 6LoWPAN technology. *Computer Communications*, *74*, 3–15. doi:10.1016/j.comcom.2014.10.004

Cirillo, S., Polese, G., Salerno, D., Simone, B., & Solimando, G. (2023). Towards Flexible Voice Assistants: Evaluating Privacy and Security Needs in IoT-enabled Smart Homes. *FMDB Transactions on Sustainable Computer Letters*, *1*(1), 25–32.

Farzad, A., & Gulliver T. A., (2019). Log message anomaly detection and classification using auto-B/LSTM and auto-GRU, 1–28.

Gaayathri, R. S., Rajest, S. S., Nomula, V. K., & Regin, R. (2023). Bud-D: Enabling Bidirectional Communication with ChatGPT by adding Listening and Speaking Capabilities. *FMDB Transactions on Sustainable Computer Letters*, *1*(1), 49–63.

Gautami, A., Shanthini, J., & Karthik, S. (2023). A Quasi-Newton Neural Network Based Efficient Intrusion Detection System for Wireless Sensor Network. *Computer Systems Science and Engineering*, *45*(1), 427–443. doi:10.32604/csse.2023.026688

Gebremariam, G. G., Panda, J., & Indu, S. (2023). Localization and Detection of Multiple Attacks in Wireless Sensor Networks Using Artificial Neural Network. *Wireless Communications and Mobile Computing, 2023*, 1–29. doi:10.1155/2023/2744706

Hanif, M., Ashraf, H., Jalil, Z., Jhanjhi, N. Z., Humayun, M., Saeed, S., & Almuhaideb, A. M. (2022). AI-Based Wormhole Attack Detection Techniques in Wireless Sensor Networks. *Electronics (Basel), 11*(15), 2324. doi:10.3390/electronics11152324

Huang, X., Li, S., & Wu, Y. (2023). LSTM-NV: A combined scheme against selective forwarding attack in event-driven wireless sensor networks under harsh environments. *Engineering Applications of Artificial Intelligence, 123*, 106441. doi:10.1016/j.engappai.2023.106441

Islam, M. N. U., Fahmin, A., Hossain, M. S., & Atiquzzaman, M. (2021). Denial-of-service attacks on wireless sensor network and defense techniques. *Wireless Personal Communications, 116*(3), 1993–2021. doi:10.100711277-020-07776-3

Ismail, S., Dawoud, D., & Reza, H. (2022 January). A lightweight multilayer machine learning detection system for cyber-attacks in WSN. In *2022 IEEE 12th Annual Computing and Communication Workshop and Conference (CCWC)*. IEEE. 10.1109/CCWC54503.2022.9720891

Jane Nithya, K., & Shyamala, K. (2022). A systematic review of various attack detection methods for wireless sensor networks. In *International Conference on Innovative Computing and Communications: Proceedings of ICICC 2021*. Springer Singapore. 10.1007/978-981-16-3071-2_17

Jeba, J. A., Bose, S. R., & Boina, R. (2023). Exploring Hybrid Multi-View Multimodal for Natural Language Emotion Recognition Using Multi-Source Information Learning Model. *FMDB Transactions on Sustainable Computer Letters, 1*(1), 12–24.

Khan, M. A., Nasralla, M. M., Umar, M. M., Khan, S., & Choudhury, N. (2022). An Efficient Multilevel Probabilistic Model for Abnormal Traffic Detection in Wireless Sensor Networks. *Sensors (Basel), 22*(2), 410. doi:10.339022020410 PMID:35062372

Koroniotis, N., Moustafa, N., Sitnikova, E., & Turnbull, B. (2019). Towards the development of realistic botnet dataset in the Internet of Things for network forensic analytics: Bot-IoT dataset. *Future Generation Computer Systems, 100*, 779–796. doi:10.1016/j.future.2019.05.041

Kumar, V., & Tiwari, S. (2012). Routing in IPv6 over low-power wireless personal area networks (6LoWPAN): A survey. *Journal of Computer Networks and Communications, 2012*, 316839. doi:10.1155/2012/316839

Lakshmi Narayanan, K., Santhana Krishnan, R., Golden Julie, E., Harold Robinson, Y., & Shanmuganathan, V. (2021). Machine learning-based detection and a novel EC-BRTT algorithm-based prevention of DoS attacks in wireless sensor networks. *Wireless Personal Communications*, 1–25.

Luo, S., Lai, Y., & Liu, J. (2023). Selective forwarding attack detection and network recovery mechanism based on cloud-edge cooperation in software-defined wireless sensor network. *Computers & Security, 126*, 103083. doi:10.1016/j.cose.2022.103083

Mirjalili, S. (2015). Moth-flame optimization algorithm: A novel nature-inspired heuristic paradigm, Knowl.-. *Knowledge-Based Systems*, *89*(1), 228–249. doi:10.1016/j.knosys.2015.07.006

Pajila, P. B., Julie, E. G., & Robinson, Y. H. (2022). FBDR-Fuzzy-based DDoS attack Detection and Recovery mechanism for wireless sensor networks. *Wireless Personal Communications*, *122*(4), 1–31. doi:10.100711277-021-09040-8

Premkumar, M., & Sundararajan, T. V. P. (2021). Defense countermeasures for DoS attacks in WSNs using deep radial basis networks. *Wireless Personal Communications*, *120*(4), 2545–2560. doi:10.100711277-021-08545-6

Quincozes, S. E., Kazienko, J. F., & Quincozes, V. E. (2023). An extended evaluation of machine learning techniques for Denial-of-Service detection in Wireless Sensor Networks. *Internet of Things : Engineering Cyber Physical Human Systems*, *22*, 100684. doi:10.1016/j.iot.2023.100684

Rajest, S. S., Singh, B., Obaid, A. J., Regin, R., & Chinnusamy, K. (2023b). Advances in artificial and human intelligence in the modern era. *Advances in Computational Intelligence and Robotics*. doi:10.4018/979-8-3693-1301-5

Rajest, S. S., Singh, B. J., Obaid, A., Regin, R., & Chinnusamy, K. (2023a). Recent developments in machine and human intelligence. *Advances in Computational Intelligence and Robotics*. doi:10.4018/978-1-6684-9189-8

Raveendranadh, B., & Tamilselvan, S. (2023). An accurate attack detection framework based on exponential polynomial kernel-centered deep neural networks in the wireless sensor network. *Transactions on Emerging Telecommunications Technologies*, *34*(3), 4726. doi:10.1002/ett.4726

Regin, R., Khanna, A. A., Krishnan, V., Gupta, M., & Bose, R. S., & Rajest, S. S. (2023). Information design and unifying approach for secured data sharing using attribute-based access control mechanisms. In Recent Developments in Machine and Human Intelligence (pp. 256–276). IGI Global.

Regin, R., T, S., George, S. R., Bhattacharya, M., Datta, D., & Priscila, S. S. (2023). Development of predictive model of diabetic using supervised machine learning classification algorithm of ensemble voting. *International Journal of Bioinformatics Research and Applications*, *19*(3), 10057044. doi:10.1504/IJBRA.2023.10057044

Sajini, S., Reddi, L. T., Regin, R., & Rajest, S. S. (2023). A Comparative Analysis of Routing Protocols for Efficient Data Transmission in Vehicular Ad Hoc Networks (VANETs). *FMDB Transactions on Sustainable Computing Systems*, *1*(1), 1–10.

Saxena, D., & Chaudhary, S. (2023). Predicting Brain Diseases from FMRI-Functional Magnetic Resonance Imaging with Machine Learning Techniques for Early Diagnosis and Treatment. *FMDB Transactions on Sustainable Computer Letters*, *1*(1), 33–48.

Sharafaldin, I., Lashkari, A. H., Hakak, S., & Ghorbani, A. A. (2019). Developing realistic distributed denial of service (DDoS) attack dataset and taxonomy. *2019 International Carnahan Conference on Security Technology (ICCST)*. IEEE. 10.1109/CCST.2019.8888419

Sudha, I., Mustafa, M. A., Suguna, R., Karupusamy, S., Ammisetty, V., Shavkatovich, S. N., Ramalingam, M., & Kanani, P. (2023). Pulse jamming attack detection using swarm intelligence in wireless sensor networks. *Optik (Stuttgart)*, *272*, 70251. doi:10.1016/j.ijleo.2022.170251

Yadav, A., & Kumar, A. (2022). Intrusion detection and prevention using RNN in WSN. In *Inventive Computation and Information Technologies: Proceedings of ICICIT 2021*. Singapore: Springer Nature Singapore. 10.1007/978-981-16-6723-7_40

Yu, D., Kang, J., & Dong, J. (2021). Service attack improvement in wireless sensor network based on machine learning. *Microprocessors and Microsystems*, *80*, 103637. doi:10.1016/j.micpro.2020.103637

Yuvaraj, D., Priya, S. S., Braveen, M., Krishnan, S. N., Nachiyappan, S., Mehbodniya, A., Ahamed, A., & Sivaram, M. (2022). Novel DoS Attack Detection Based on Trust Mode Authentication for IoT. *Intelligent Automation & Soft Computing*, *34*(3), 1505–1522. doi:10.32604/iasc.2022.022151

Chapter 15
Deep Learning Approaches for Affective Computing in Text

Ramón Zatarain Cabada

ⓘ https://orcid.org/0000-0002-4524-3511

Tecnologico Nacional de Mexico, Culiacan, Mexico

María Lucía Barrón Estrada

ⓘ https://orcid.org/0000-0002-3856-9361

Tecnologico Nacional de Mexico, Culiacan, Mexico

Víctor Manuel Bátiz Beltrán

ⓘ https://orcid.org/0000-0003-4356-9793

Tecnologico Nacional de Mexico, Culiacan, Mexico

ABSTRACT

The field of natural language processing (NLP) is one of the first to be addressed since artificial intelligence emerged. NLP has made remarkable advances in recent years thanks to the development of new machine learning techniques, particularly novel deep learning methods such as LSTM networks and transformers. This chapter presents an overview of how deep learning techniques have been applied to NLP in the area of affective computing. The chapter examines traditional and novel deep learning architectures developed for natural language processing (NLP) tasks. These architectures comprise recurrent neural networks (RNNs), long short-term memory (LSTM) networks, and the cutting-edge transformers. Moreover, a methodology for NLP method training and fine-tuning is presented. The chapter also integrates Python code that demonstrates two NLP case studies specializing in the educational domain for text classification and sentiment analysis. In both cases, the transformer-based machine learning model (BERT) produced the best results.

DOI: 10.4018/979-8-3693-0502-7.ch015

INTRODUCTION

Natural Language Processing (NLP) is the study of how computers can recognize and alter human expressions in text. NLP integrates several fields, including computer science, linguistics, mathematics, Artificial Intelligence (AI), and psychology. NLP is concerned with a wide range of topics, including automatic text translation, multilingual user interfaces, and speech recognition, among others (Chollet, 2021). In relation with that, Machine Learning (ML) is one of the most popular techniques for implementing applications that use NLP. Broadly speaking, ML is a branch of AI that gives computers the ability to learn without being explicitly programmed to do so. ML algorithms allow the computer to learn from data without having to write any custom code specific to a particular problem. For example, an ML algorithm is capable of learning to classify and obtain the polarity (positive or negative) of an opinion given as input without the need to build a new algorithm that is specific to the solution of that problem.

Deep learning (DL) is a sort of machine learning that mimics how humans learn (cognitive learning process). DL algorithms, as opposed to traditional machine learning algorithms, are a hierarchical series of increasing complexity and abstraction (LeCun et al., 2015). This hierarchical learning is accomplished using artificial neural network methods, which are especially useful when there are a high number of samples describing an event. A model is a hierarchical depiction of the architecture of an artificial neural network. DL has made it possible to obtain important advances in various tasks that were previously carried out with ML techniques. It has revolutionized NLP by enabling the development of powerful models that can understand and generate human language with remarkable accuracy.

This chapter aims to provide an objective overview of the application of deep learning techniques in NLP. Two case studies are presented as the main contributions. The first case study focuses on text classification and aims to address the research question: what is the best deep learning classification algorithm to detect learning-centered emotions in a text dataset? The second study focuses on the particular task of sentiment analysis and seeks to answer the research question: what is the most effective deep learning classification algorithm to recognize negative/positive opinions in a text dataset?

This chapter is organized as follows. The chapter begins with a section named Affective Computing, that provides a basic understanding of the underlying concepts. Then discusses popular deep learning architectures designed specifically for NLP tasks. Recurrent Neural Networks (RNNs) are discussed, highlighting their ability to capture sequential dependencies and their applications in tasks such as text classification, language modeling, and machine translation. Long Short-Term Memory (LSTM) networks, a variant of RNNs, are explored for their effectiveness in handling long-range dependencies and mitigating the vanishing gradient problem. The innovative impact of transformers in NLP is thoroughly explored. These attention-based architectures have revolutionized the field, powering state-of-the-art models such as BERT. The chapter explains the basic principles of transformers and their applications in tasks such as text classification, and sentiment analysis. In the following section a methodology for training and tuning NLP task approaches is also presented. Based on this methodology, code in the Python language is presented to fully cover two NLP case studies. Both focused on the educational domain and using two different datasets to cover the tasks of text classification and sentiment analysis. Finally, the chapter finishes with some concluding remarks and suggestions for future work.

AFFECTIVE COMPUTING

Since the invention of the computer, researchers, and scientists in the field of computer science have been searching for ways to make computers interact with people in the same way that humans do, and as a result, many branches of study have been created in this field, one of which is Affective Computing.

Affective computing is a multidisciplinary field that includes psychology, cognitive psychology, and computer science within its areas of study. According to Picard (1997), affective computing is the field of study that focuses on making computers capable of recognizing and expressing emotions like a human being, as well as developing the ability to send intelligent responses to the emotions expressed by humans.

In order to improve the user experience when interacting with computers, it is necessary to collect information, including the user's emotions, process it, and adapt the response based on it. For example, in education, there are applications (Barron Estrada et al., 2019) that recognize students' emotions in real time and modify the content according to the emotions expressed.

Emotion Theory

Picard (1997) points out that emotion theorists cannot agree on a definition of emotion and mentions that about one hundred definitions of the term emotion have been recorded and categorized.

Merriam-Webster (2023) defines emotion as "a conscious mental reaction (such as anger or fear) subjectively experienced as a strong feeling usually directed toward a specific object and typically accompanied by physiological and behavioral changes in the body".

On the other hand, the American Psychological Association presents a more complex definition of the term emotion:

A complex reaction pattern, involving experiential, behavioral, and physiological elements, by which an individual attempts to deal with a personally significant matter or event. The specific quality of the emotion (e.g., fear, shame) is determined by the specific significance of the event. For example, if the significance involves threat, fear is likely to be generated; if the significance involves disapproval from another, shame is likely to be generated. Emotion typically involves feeling but differs from feeling in having an overt or implicit engagement with the world. (APA, 2023)

The various theories of emotions can be broadly examined in terms of two components:

- Emotions are cognitive, emphasizing their mental component.
- Emotions are physical, emphasizing their bodily component.

Research on the cognitive component focuses on understanding the situations that give rise to emotions. Picard (1997) mentions that historically the focus on the brain-centered aspects of emotions is attributed to Walter Cannon, who emphasizes that emotion is experienced centrally in the brain and that its experience is possible without sensations coming from the body (Cannon, 1927). Research on the physical component side emphasizes the physiological response that occurs alongside or immediately after an emotion (Picard, 1997).

Picard et al. (2001) raise the question of how well must a computer recognize human emotional states in order to appear intelligent? It is understandable to think that understanding the cognitive component from the perspective of a computer would mean understanding the deepest thoughts of a human being. This is complex, even for the human being himself. Sometimes people even fail to recognize their own emotions. Undoubtedly, some aspects of inner feelings remain private, especially if the person wishes them to be so. The authors point out that what an external recognizer has at his disposal is what he can observe and reason about. This will always be accompanied by some uncertainty. Even so, people are able to recognize emotions well enough to communicate useful feedback. Therefore, the authors conclude that the goal is to endow computers with recognition abilities similar to those that people have.

Emotion Classification

Damasio (1994) states that emotions can be divided into primary and secondary. Primary emotions correspond to physiological and automatic behavioral reactions to the presence of stimuli that the brain detects innately, without prior learning, i.e., they are triggered by the presence of certain aspects such as the size, movement, or sound of an object. The author considers that, although these emotions are the primary ones from a developmental perspective, they are not the only ones and defines another group of emotions as secondary. Secondary emotions are formed in individuals once they begin to experience feelings and form systematic connections between categories of objects and situations, on the one hand, and primary emotions on the other hand (Restrepo, 2019).

Learning-Focused Emotions

Based on the classification of emotions presented by Damasio (1994), emotions focused on learning can be placed as secondary emotions, since these emotions will be present when students are performing various learning activities. Emotions in the educational environment imply giving meaning to the events or occurrences that a learner experiences; this allows us to understand and accept that cognition and emotion affect each other. Therefore, the learner should be seen as a mixture of reason and emotion, since separating both components would be to attempt against the human character of the person (García Retana, 2012).

Regarding the categories of emotions related to learning and achievement that should be considered, Pekrun (2008) points out that: 1) emotions can be generally ordered based on their predominant, subjectively experienced value (positive versus negative); 2) emotions can be classified as task-related or of a more social nature; 3) task-related emotions may differ according to the time perspective related to the task and the outcome they imply, whether they are process-related (during the task), prospective (before the task, before the outcome), or retrospective (after the task, after the outcome). Table 1 shows the taxonomy of emotions in students proposed by the author.

The main difference between affective computing and emotion theory is that emotion theory focuses on what human emotions are and how they are generated, while affective computing involves the implementation of emotions in computational systems. This makes affective computing a means to support the development and testing of emotion theory. However, affective computing involves more than this, such as giving the computer the ability to recognize and express emotions, thus developing the ability to respond intelligently to human emotions and enabling the regulation and use of emotions.

Table 1. Taxonomy of emotions in students (Pekrun, 2008)

	Positive	**Negative**
Task-related		
Process-related	Enjoyment	Boredom
Prospective	Hope Anticipatory Joy	Anxiety Hopelessness (Resignation/Despair)
Retrospective	Relief Outcome-Related Joy Pride	—— Sadness Disappointment Shame/Guilt
Social		
	Gratitude Empathy Admiration Sympathy/Love	Anger Jealousy/Envy Contempt Antipathy/Hate

In the following sections, we will discuss two case studies that examine the tasks of text classification and sentiment analysis. In the case of text classification, we will use a corpus containing texts whose content is labeled according to learning-oriented emotions. In the case of sentiment analysis, we will use a corpus whose texts refer to comments related to the field of teaching programming languages and are labeled with positive and negative sentiments.

DEEP LEARNING FOR NATURAL LANGUAGE PROCESSING

The area of artificial intelligence known as natural language processing (NLP) is concerned with how computers and human language interact. The objective of NLP is to provide methods that allow machines to comprehend, produce, and interpret natural language, improving user experience. NLP covers a wide range of tasks that involve understanding, generating, and manipulating human language. In the last few years, there has been a boom in the use of deep learning techniques for solving tasks related to natural language processing.

Defining Deep Learning

Patterson and Gibson (2017) note that defining deep learning has been a challenge for many due to its evolution over the past decade. A useful definition would be to specify that deep learning deals with a "neural network with more than two layers." The problem with this definition is that it makes deep learning sound like it has been around since the 1980s. The reality is that neural networks had to architecturally transcend earlier network styles (along with an increase in processing power) before showing the spectacular results observed in more recent years. The following are some of the facets of this evolution of neural networks:

- More neurons than previous networks.
- More complex ways of connecting layers and neurons in neural networks.
- A substantial increase in the computational power available for training.
- Automatic feature extraction.

According to LeCun et al. (2015), deep learning is a branch of machine learning that allows computers to learn based on experience and understand the world as humans see it in terms of hierarchies of concepts. Deep learning achieves great power and flexibility by representing the real world in terms of various nested hierarchies of concepts. The concept hierarchy gives computers the ability to learn difficult concepts by building them from simpler concepts, an example of which would be many dense layers. As defined by LeCun et al. (2015), deep learning gives multilayered computational models the ability to process and learn representations or features of data with multiple levels of abstraction. Deep learning opens the way to new and very complex structures of large datasets by using back-propagation algorithms, which show how a machine must manipulate or make changes to its internal parameters used to compute the layered representation from the previous layered representations.

Patterson and Gibson (2017) point out that it is precisely the automatic extraction of features, the main difference of deep learning with respect to traditional machine learning. This eliminates the need for a person to manually determine the relevant features, since in deep learning the neural network will be able to decide for itself which features from the dataset can be used as indicators to reliably label the data.

Deep Learning Applied to Natural Language Processing

Deep learning has had a significant impact on NLP. Artificial neural networks have outperformed traditional methods in a wide range of NLP tasks, including text classification, sentiment analysis, machine translation, speech understanding, and question answering. One of the advantages of deep learning is that it can learn from large amounts of data. This is important for NLP because human language is complex and requires a large amount of data to understand correctly. Artificial neural networks can learn from large amounts of text data, allowing them to develop more accurate language models.

Deep learning, on the other hand, has the advantage of being able to learn nonlinear correlations. Nonlinear interactions, including those between words and sentences, are abundant in human language. Artificial neural networks can improve their understanding of human language by learning from these nonlinear interactions.

Recurrent Neural Networks (RNNs)

For Rumelhart et al. (1986) Recurrent neural networks (RNN), are a type of neural networks that specialize in processing sequential data. An RNN can process a sequence of values that can be of variable size and scale these sequences to much longer ones and in a more practical way compared to any other neural network that does not specialize in processing data in sequence.

The interpretation of Graves (2012) points out that ANNs that form cyclic connections between their nodes and layers are considered recurrent neural networks (RNN). A Multilayer Perceptron can only map vectors from input to output, on the other hand, an RNN can map an entire history or sequence of values from input to each output. The main key in a RNN is that the recurrent connections have a "memory" of previous inputs to keep in the internal state of the network, which can have an influence on the output of the network. A representation of an RNN can be seen in Figure 1.

RNNs can be used for classification problems, regression, and the generation of new results. The problem that has existed since the creation of RNNs is that they are difficult to train, since they require more computational resources than an Artificial neural Network (ANN). But thanks to technological advances and recent research in the area of computing (optimization, parallelism, network architectures and graphics processing units, GPUs) have allowed both users and researchers to have easy access to the use of these networks and to perform experiments with sequential data.

Figure 1. recurrent neural network basic diagram

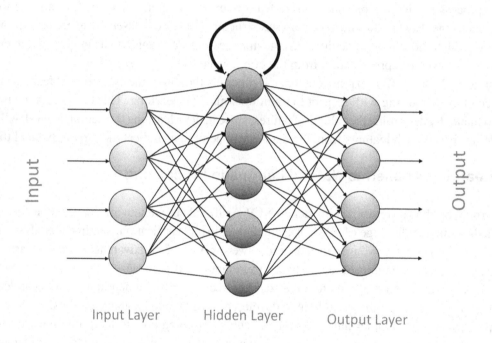

Long Short-Term Memory (LSTM) Networks

Recurrent neural networks present a problem known as the "vanishing gradient problem". This occurs when the gradients are too large or too small and make it difficult to model long-range dependencies in the structure of the input data set. The LSTM variant of recurrent neural networks is recognized as one of the most effective ways to solve this situation (Patterson & Gibson, 2017).

An LSTM network has the ability to preserve a significant piece of data in a sequence for several moments, allowing for retention of both short-term and long-term memory. As a result, it can retain both short-term memory, similar to basic recurrent networks, as well as long-term memory. Therefore, LSTM networks are especially good for processing data streams such as text, speech, and time series in general. Figure 2 shows the structure of an LSTM cell.

Figure 2. LSTM cell representation

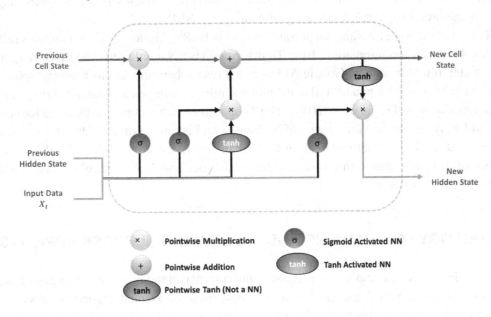

Each LSTM unit is called a cell and is used to replace the individual neurons used by RNNs. The LSTM cell is not biologically inspired, it is an engineered solution. An LSTM cell contains a minimum of five nonlinear functions. Typically, three of these functions are logistic sigmoid and are known as the gates in the device. The other two are activation functions. It is common to choose ReLU and tanh for these. The gate structure makes it possible to maintain information over a large number of time steps. Better back propagation and equation fitting are attributes of LSTM networks (Ekman, 2021).

Transformers

Since Vaswani et al. (2017) introduced the Transformers, these have charged a great relevance in the world of natural language processing. Like the recurring neural networks and the LSTM, the Transformers are specialized architectures in working with sequences.

A transformer is a deep learning model that can identify long-distance relationships between words in a phrase. Transformers shown that a straightforward technique known as "neural attention" could be utilized to create effective sequence models without the need of convolution or recurrent layers. Neural attention has quickly emerged as one of the most prominent concepts in deep learning, as established by Chollet (2021). The attention mechanism is based on a common human activity that consists, for example, in paying attention to the most relevant part of an image or text. In the case of NLP, this mechanism allows deep learning models to find relevant relationships between words in a text even when they are not close to each other.

An encoder and a decoder are the two basic components of a transformers neural network. A word sequence is supplied into the encoder, which converts it into a vector representation. The encoded vector representation is then decoded by the decoder into a fresh string of words. A lot of layers of attention are used in both the encoder and the decoder. The neural network can focus on different portions of the input at different times thanks to the mechanism of attention. Because a sentence's words may not be connected in the order they appear, this is significant for the NLP.

BERT. One of the most relevant use of transformers is BERT. Muller (2022) establishes that BERT (Bidirectional Encoder Representations from Transformers) is a Natural Language Processing Machine Learning model. It was created by Google AI Language researchers and acts as a multipurpose tool for several of the most popular language tasks, including sentiment analysis and named entity recognition. It was first introduced by Devlin et al. (2019). The Transformer architecture serves as the foundation for BERT. BERT may be adjusted for a range of NLP tasks and is trained on a sizable dataset of text and code. The fact that BERT is bidirectional, or that it can consider both the left and right contexts of a word, is one of its main features. In contrast, earlier NLP models were often taught to take into account only the left context of a word.

METHODOLOGY FOR TRAINING AND FINE-TUNING NLP TASK APPROACHES

The following describes the components of a general but current methodology for creating models for NLP tasks. This methodology will be the one shown in the case studies presented. Figure 3 shows the diagram of the methodology pipeline. this proposal is based on the one presented by Kumar and Denuka (2023).

Figure 3. Natural language processing pipeline

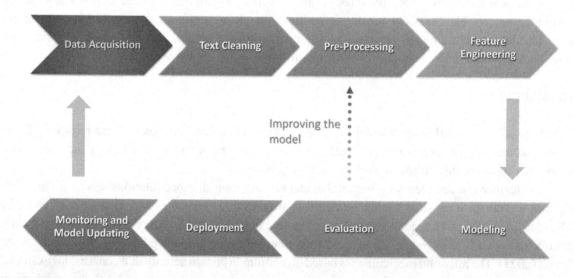

Data Acquisition

The first phase of a modern NLP process is to have a set of data related to the task to be performed. The success of an NLP implementation depends largely on the quality of the data you work with. This dataset can come from social networks, product reviews, people's opinions, written texts, among others.

Text Cleaning

The next step is to perform activities known as data cleansing. These activities may include removing HTML tags, normalizing user accounts and Web site addresses, replacing them with some standardized term. This step allows the removal of elements that are not relevant.

Pre-Processing

At this stage, the cleaning of the text is continued. Typical tasks are the following actions.

- Convert words to lowercase. In this part all words were converted to lowercase so that all words have the same format.
- Remove URLs, emails and line breaks. There may be situations where some links or URLs of one or more internet pages, as well as e-mail addresses and line breaks may be included in the texts, so a removal of all these was done.
- Eliminate new lines and tabs and line breaks. In case of automatic text extraction, texts may contain the characters to indicate new lines or tabs such as (\n, \t and \s), which are removed.
- Remove single quotation marks. Quotation marks (') are removed from the texts.
- Removing commas. Commas (,) used to separate texts or continue with the same idea are removed and replaced by blank spaces.
- Remove numbers. It may be that some users write some numbers in the form of real numbers, so they can be replaced by the letter or eliminated as was done in this research.
- Remove non-alphanumeric characters. Any sign that is not a number or a letter is removed from the text, such as the following characters: #, $, %, ¡, ", ?, etc.
- Remove hyphens between words. The hyphens (-) that can be found between words such as "science-fiction" are eliminated, resulting as "science fiction".
- Eliminate double and triple hyphens. It may be the case where two or more hyphens are found together with a word, so they are replaced with a blank space.
- Eliminate blank spaces at the beginning or end of a text, as well as double spaces.
- Removing stop words from text. Also known as empty words, since they are considered words that do not help at all in text classification tasks, i.e., they do not contribute anything and if removed do not affect in the least the sense of the sentence. In this case the NTLK library already provides a default list of stop words for the Spanish language, which you can download and start using.
- Perform lemmatization. Lemmatization is a more advanced form of stemming and consists of converting all words to their infinitive form. Lemmatization converts different word forms or inflections to a standard form. For example, it converts the word play into play or the word wrote into write and slept into slept, etc. A lemmatizer works with more language rules and contextual information compared to stemming. It also makes use of a dictionary to look up equivalent words, which is why it requires more processing power and time to generate results.
- Removing punctuation marks. All punctuation marks contained in words such as accents (á, é, í, ó, ú), umlauts (¨), tilde (~), etc. are removed.

Feature Engineering

Once cleaning has been completed, the mechanism for feature extraction must be selected. At this stage the texts are converted into numerical vectors that will serve as input for the automatic learning models being tested. Although this phase can be approached with traditional NLP methods such as bag-of-words, in the particular case of this chapter we will focus on deep learning based methods. When deep learning is used, models "learn" relevant features from the data. A common element at this stage is known as tokenization. Here the text is converted to its numerical representation.

Modeling

The deep learning model is composed of a series of layers, each of which has the function of processing input data and generating a data output. The layers are connected sequentially. That is, it has an input layer, followed by the hidden layers where the calculations are performed and finally an output layer, where the result is obtained. Within the hidden layers there is a word embedding layer (Embedding Layer). This layer receives the text corpus encoded with the selected technique and expands the tokens to a vector of larger size directly proportional to the size of the vocabulary and the maximum length of the text sequence (longest text in the corpus).

After the embedding layer, other layers are added such as dense layers, Dropout regularization layers which is when neurons are randomly omitted from the neural network, a flattening layer which is when the multidimensional matrix is transformed into a one-dimensional vector, convolutional layers, pooling, recurrent, etc. Within the dense layers each neuron receives an input from all the neurons of the previous layers, this is called Fully Connected layer.

It is in the dense layers where the activation functions are present. Activation functions are those that dictate the behavior of neurons, i.e., activation functions decide whether or not a neuron passes to the next layer of neurons (is activated or not). There are different types of activation functions whose activation depends on the defined range. In addition, each type of activation function has its own particularity, i.e., some activation functions work better in dense layers and others have better application in the final layers where a final sorting is performed. Examples of activation functions are sigmoid, ReLU, tanh, among others.

Once the architecture of the model has been established, the learning process must be defined. For this it is necessary to specify the type of learning rate. The learning rate modifies the amount by which the parameters will be adjusted during the optimization in order to minimize the error in the neural network calculations. There are different optimization methods such as Stochastic gradient descent (SGD), Adagrad, Adam, Adadelta, etc.

One of the important configurations of any deep learning neural network is the activation functions. Among the most common activation functions we can mention sigmoid, tanh, ReLU, Linear, Softmax, among others.

Likewise, the loss function is defined, which calculates how close a neural network is to the ideal, comparing the predictions of the network with the predictions during learning. The lower the result of this function, the more efficient the neural network is. There are different types of loss functions such as Mean Square Error (MSE), Mean absolute error (MAE), Mean squared log error (MSLE), Hinge loss, categorical cross entropy loss, and Logistic loss.

Evaluation

As a last step in the development phase (training and testing) of deep learning models, the type of metric to evaluate the model must be defined. The objective of this stage is to explore and find the model that offers the best results. It is at this stage that the fine tuning of the models is performed. In the case studies that will be evaluated, the results obtained based on the metrics of accuracy, precision, Recall and F1-Score will be presented. Based in Patterson and Gibson (2017), a brief description of each of these metrics follows. The following terms will be used in the formulas presented in each metric.

- **True positive (TP)**. Positive prediction and label is positive.
- **False positive (FP)**. Positive prediction and label is negative.
- **True negative (TN)**. Negative prediction and label is negative.
- **False negatives (FN)**. Negative prediction and label is positive.

Accuracy

Accuracy is the degree to which measurements of a quantity approximate the true value of that quantity.

$$Accuracy = (TP + TN) / (TP + FP + FN + TN)$$

Accuracy can be misleading about the quality of the model when class imbalance is high. Therefore, in the first case that we will analyze, we will perform class balancing.

Precision

The degree to which repeated measurements under the same conditions yield the same results is called precision in science and statistics. Precision is also called positive predictive value.

$$Precision = TP / (TP + FP)$$

Recall

The true positive rate (recall) measures how often we classify an input data set into the positive class and the classification is correct. It is also called sensitivity.

$$Recall = TP / (TP + FN)$$

F1-Score

It's a measure of a model's accuracy. The F1 score is the harmonic mean of the precision and recall measures (described above) into a single score as defined in the following formula:

$$F1 = 2TP / (2TP + FP + FN)$$

Deployment

Putting the selected deep learning models into production, i.e., applying them in a real-life case, is the ultimate goal of any NLP task. A common strategy is to deploy the models as web services, for ease of use and availability.

Monitoring and Model Updating

The performance of the implemented models should be monitored periodically; it is likely that they will need to be retrained with the emergence of new data and classification techniques. The above, leads us to conclude that NLP task solving is a cyclical and continuously improving process.

CASE STUDIES

In this section, two classic NLP tasks are presented: text classification and the specific task of sentiment analysis. We show the development of the different stages of the methodology proposed above and how it could be implemented using the Python programming language and several libraries related to the area of deep learning and natural language processing.

Case Study: Text Classification

Text classification involves assigning predefined categories or labels to a given text based on its content. The first case study presented in this chapter was designed to explore the development of deep learning models to determine what learning-centered emotion a text presents. There was one research question for this study case: what is the best deep learning classification algorithm to recognize learning-centered emotions in a text dataset?

The Dataset

We will use the EduSere corpus (Barron-Estrada et al., 2020) for this example. The corpus is divided into three learning-oriented emotions: frustrated (frustrated in Spanish), bored (bored in Spanish) and engaged (engaged in Spanish). Figure 4 shows the distribution of the texts and their labels. The corpus has 3245 texts classified as frustrated, 3239 texts classified as bored, and 5600 texts classified as engaged.

The texts in the corpus are in Spanish language. Table 2 shows some examples of the text an label from the corpus. Each text is labeled with frustrated (frustrado in Spanish), bored (aburrido in Spanish), or engaged (comprometido in Spanish).

Figure 4. EduSere corpus labels distribution

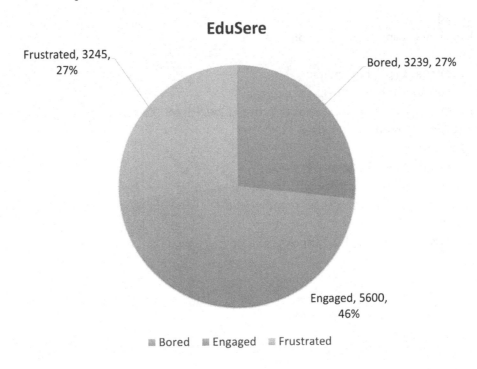

Table 2. Text examples from edusere corpus

Text	Label
ya quiero que termine este semestre en el tec lo odiooo y no quiero convertirme en perro	frustrado
ya te dije que no puedes utilizar esa versión en tu sistema ya que los modulos están incompletos	frustrado
ya tengo cuatro horas y no logro recuperar el valor de checkbox desde una bd con jquery	frustrado
Últimamente mi vida es muy aburrida	aburrido
Últimamente todas las personas me parecen aburridas o no sé si soy yo	aburrido
Últimamente twitter esta muy aburrido todos andan en la escuela:(	aburrido
No hay que tenerle miedo a aquellos que se creen los dueños de nuestras vidas	comprometido
Se tiene que poder el programador optimista	comprometido
como aprender sin morir en el intento, gracias. :D... te piden cursos porque se te entiende muy bien, y uno piensa, quiero esto explicado por Pildoras	comprometido

Code Using Traditional Deep Learning Models

The following program is developed in the Python programming language, and it has been tested in the Google Colab platform.

Initial Setup. First, we need to install and import some libraries.

```
!pip install emoji
```

```
import re
import string
from nltk.corpus import stopwords
import nltk
from nltk.corpus import wordnet
from nltk.stem import WordNetLemmatizer
from nltk.tokenize.treebank import TreebankWordDetokenizer
from nltk import SnowballStemmer
import unicodedata
from collections import Counter
from wordcloud import WordCloud
from gensim.utils import simple_preprocess
import gensim
from sklearn.model_selection import train_test_split
import spacy
import pickle
import warnings
warnings.filterwarnings('ignore')
import seaborn as sns
import matplotlib.pyplot as plt
import tensorflow as tf
import keras
import numpy as np
import pandas as pd
import emoji
import keras
from keras import backend as K
import tensorflow as tf
from tensorflow.keras.preprocessing.sequence import pad_sequences
from tensorflow.keras.preprocessing.text import Tokenizer
print('Done!')
```

Loading Data

```
data = pd.read_csv("EduSere.csv")
data.head()
# We change labels to numerical representation 0 = frustrated (frustrado), 1 =
bored (aburrido) and 2 = engaged (comprometido).
data['Label'] = data['Label'].replace({'frustrado':0, 'aburrido':1, 'compro-
metido':2})
```

Data Cleaning

```python
def process_text(sentence, norm_user = True, norm_hashtag = True, separate_
characters = True):
    # Convert instance to string
    sentence = str(sentence)

    # All text to lowecase
    sentence = sentence.lower()
    # Normalize users and url
    if norm_user == True:
        sentence = re.sub(r'\@\w+','@usuario', sentence)
    if norm_hashtag == True:
        sentence = re.sub(r"http\S+|www\S+|https\S+", 'url', sentence,
flags=re.MULTILINE)
    # Separate special characters
    if separate_characters == True:
        sentence = re.sub(r":", ": ", sentence)
        sentence = re.sub(r",", ", ", sentence)
        sentence = re.sub(r"\.", " . ", sentence)
        sentence = re.sub(r"!", " ! ", sentence)
        sentence = re.sub(r"¡", " ¡ ", sentence)
        sentence = re.sub(r"“", " “ ", sentence)
        sentence = re.sub(r"'", " ` ", sentence)
        sentence = re.sub(r"”", " ” ", sentence)
        sentence = re.sub(r"\(", " (", sentence)
        sentence = re.sub(r"\)", ") ", sentence)
        sentence = re.sub(r"\?", " ? ", sentence)
        sentence = re.sub(r"\¿", " ¿ ", sentence)

    # Substituting multiple spaces with single space
    sentence = re.sub(r'\s+', ' ', sentence, flags=re.I)
    # emojis to text
    sentence = emoji.demojize(sentence)
    return sentence
clean_data = data.copy()
clean_data['Text'] = clean_data['Text'].apply(process_text)
```

Pre-Processing

```python
#Removing stopwords
import nltk
nltk.download('punkt')
from nltk.corpus import stopwords
```

```
from nltk.tokenize import word_tokenize

nltk.download('stopwords')
print(stopwords.words('spanish'))
stop_words = set(stopwords.words('spanish'))
def remove_stopwords(text):
  word_tokens = word_tokenize(text)
  no_stopwords = [word for word in word_tokens if not word in stop_words]
  return " ".join(no_stopwords)

clean_data['Text'] = clean_data['Text'].apply(remove_stopwords)
#Lematization
#We'll use Spacy for Lematization
!python -m spacy download es_core_news_sm
import spacy
import es_core_news_sm
nlp = es_core_news_sm.load()
def lematize(text):
    doc = nlp(text)
    lemms = []
    for token in doc:
        lemms.append(token.lemma_)
    return " ".join(lemms)
clean_data['Text'] = clean_data['Text'].apply(lematize)

#Removing Punctuation
def cleaning_punct(text):
  token_list = gensim.utils.simple_preprocess(str(text), deacc=True)
  return " ".join(token_list)
clean_data['Text'] = clean_data['Text'].apply(cleaning_punct)

#Label codification
labels = np.array(clean_data['Label'])
labels = tf.keras.utils.to_categorical(labels, 3, dtype="float32")

#Tokenization
#We need to install and import some libraries
!pip install Keras-Preprocessing
from keras.models import Sequential
from keras import layers
from keras.preprocessing.text import Tokenizer
from keras_preprocessing.sequence import pad_sequences
from keras import regularizers
from keras import backend as K
```

```
from keras.callbacks import ModelCheckpoint

#We create the tokenizer
tokenizer = Tokenizer()
tokenizer.fit_on_texts(clean_data['Text'])
word_index = tokenizer.word_index
total_unique_words = len(tokenizer.word_index) + 1
sequences = tokenizer.texts_to_sequences(clean_data['Text'])
max_seq_length = max([len(x) for x in sequences])
texts = pad_sequences(sequences, maxlen=max_seq_length)
max_words = total_unique_words
max_len = max_seq_length
print("Unique words: ",total_unique_words)
print("Max length: ",max_seq_length)
```

Modeling

```
#We divide the dataset. We will use 80% for training and validation and the
remaining 20% will be used to test the models.
#We divide the data set into training and validation 80% and 20%.
X_train_original, X_test, y_train_original, y_test = train_test_
split(texts,labels, test_size=0.20, random_state=0)
print(len(X_train_original),len(X_test),len(y_train_original),len(y_test))
# We divided the 80% selected for training into training and validation data
sets (80% and 20%).
X_train, X_val, y_train, y_val = train_test_split(X_train_original,y_train_
original, test_size=0.20, random_state=0)
print (len(X_train),len(X_val),len(y_train),len(y_val))

#RNN Model
model0 = Sequential()
model0.add(layers.Embedding(input_dim=max_words, input_length = max_len, out-
put_dim=64))
model0.add(layers.SimpleRNN(64))
model0.add(layers.Dense(3,activation='softmax'))

model0.compile(optimizer='rmsprop',loss='categorical_crossentropy',
metrics=['accuracy'])
#Implementing model checkpoints to save the best metric and do not lose it on
training.
checkpoint0 = ModelCheckpoint("best_model0.hdf5", monitor='val_accuracy',
verbose=1,save_best_only=True, mode='auto', save_freq='epoch',save_weights_
only=False)
history = model0.fit(X_train, y_train, epochs=10,validation_data=(X_test, y_
```

```
test),callbacks=[checkpoint0])

#Simple LSTM Model
model1 = Sequential()
model1.add(layers.Embedding(input_dim=max_words, input_length = max_len, out-
put_dim=64))
model1.add(layers.LSTM(64,dropout=0.5))
model1.add(layers.Dense(3,activation='softmax'))

model1.compile(optimizer='rmsprop',loss='categorical_crossentropy',
metrics=['accuracy'])
#Implementing model checkpoins to save the best metric and do not lose it on
training.
checkpoint1 = ModelCheckpoint("bestmodel_lstmsimple.hdf5", monitor='val_ac-
curacy', verbose=2,save_best_only=True, mode='auto', save_freq='epoch',save_
weights_only=False)
history = model1.fit(X_train, y_train, epochs=10,validation_data=(X_test, y_
test),callbacks=[checkpoint1])

#Bidirectional LSTM
model2 = Sequential()
model2.add(layers.Embedding(input_dim=max_words, input_length = max_len, out-
put_dim=64))
model2.add(layers.Bidirectional(layers.LSTM(64,dropout=0.5)))
model2.add(layers.Dense(3,activation='softmax'))
model2.compile(optimizer='rmsprop',loss='categorical_crossentropy',
metrics=['accuracy'])
#Implementing model checkpoints to save the best metric and do not lose it on
training.
checkpoint2 = ModelCheckpoint("bestmodel_lstmbidir.hdf5", monitor='val_ac-
curacy', verbose=1,save_best_only=True, mode='auto', save_freq='epoch',save_
weights_only=False)
history = model2.fit(X_train, y_train, epochs=10,validation_data=(X_test, y_
test),callbacks=[checkpoint2])
```

Evaluation

```
#We test the models with the test dataset.
from sklearn.metrics import recall_score
from sklearn import metrics

#RNN

#We load the best model
```

```
best_model_rnn = keras.models.load_model("best_model0.hdf5")
#We get the predictions
predicts_rnn = best_model_rnn.predict(X_test)
predicts_rnn = np.around(predicts_rnn, decimals=0)
#We perform the evaluation and get the metrics
rnn_recall = metrics.recall_score(y_test, predicts_rnn, average='macro')
rnn_f1 = metrics.f1_score(y_test, predicts_rnn, average='macro')
rnn_precision = metrics.precision_score(y_test, predicts_rnn, average='macro')
rnn_accuracy = metrics.accuracy_score(y_test, predicts_rnn)
#Metrics values
print(f"RNN Accuracy: {rnn_accuracy}")
print(f"RNN F1: {rnn_f1}")
print(f"RNN Precision: {rnn_precision}")
print(f"RNN Recall: {rnn_recall}")


#Simple LSTM

#We load the best model
best_model_lstm = keras.models.load_model("bestmodel_lstmsimple.hdf5")
#We get the predictions
predicts_ls = best_model_lstm.predict(X_test)
predicts_lstm = np.around(predicts_ls, decimals=0)
#We perform the evaluation and get the metrics
lstm_recall = metrics.recall_score(y_test, predicts_lstm, average='macro')
lstm_f1 = metrics.f1_score(y_test, predicts_lstm, average='macro')
lstm_precision = metrics.precision_score(y_test, predicts_lstm,
average='macro')
lstm_accuracy = metrics.accuracy_score(y_test, predicts_lstm)
#Metrics values
print(f"LSTM Accuracy: {lstm_accuracy}")
print(f"LSTM F1: {lstm_f1}")
print(f"LSTM Precision: {lstm_precision}")
print(f"LSTM Recall: {lstm_recall}")


#Bidirectional LSTM

#We load the best model
best_model_lstmbidir = keras.models.load_model("bestmodel_lstmbidir.hdf5")
#We get the predictions
predicts_lsbidir = best_model_lstmbidir.predict(X_test)
predicts_lstmbidir = np.around(predicts_lsbidir, decimals=0)
#We perform the evaluation and get the metrics
lstmbidir_recall = metrics.recall_score(y_test, predicts_lstmbidir,
average='macro')
```

```
lstmbidir_f1 = metrics.f1_score(y_test, predicts_lstmbidir, average='macro')
lstmbidir_precision = metrics.precision_score(y_test, predicts_lstmbidir,
average='macro')
lstmbidir_accuracy = metrics.accuracy_score(y_test, predicts_lstmbidir)
#Metrics values
print(f"Bidirectional LSTM Accuracy: {lstmbidir_accuracy}")
print(f"Bidirectional LSTM F1: {lstmbidir_f1}")
print(f"Bidirectional LSTM Precision: {lstmbidir_precision}")
print(f"Bidirectional LSTM Recall: {lstmbidir_recall}")
```

Code Using Transformers

```
!pip install transformers
!pip install simpletransformers

from simpletransformers.classification import ClassificationModel, Classifica-
tionArgs

clean_data2 = clean_data.copy()
clean_data2.rename(columns = {'Text':'text','Label':'labels'}, inplace = True)

from sklearn.model_selection import train_test_split
train_df, test_df = train_test_split(clean_data2, test_size=0.20)

print('train shape: ',train_df.shape)
print('test shape: ',test_df.shape)
# Optional model configuration
model_args = ClassificationArgs(num_train_epochs=1)

train_args ={"reprocess_input_data": True,
            "fp16":False,
            "num_train_epochs": 3,
            "overwrite_output_dir": True}

# Create a ClassificationModel
model = ClassificationModel(
    'bert',
    'bert-base-uncased',
    num_labels=3,
    args=train_args
)

# Train the model
```

```
model.train_model(train_df)
from sklearn import metrics

# Evaluate the model
result, model_outputs, wrong_predictions = model.eval_model(test_df)
print(result)

# Let's get more metrics
test = test_df['text'].to_numpy().tolist()
y = test_df['labels'].to_numpy().tolist()
predictions_test = model.predict(test)
test_recall = metrics.recall_score(y, predictions_test[0], average='macro')
test_f1 = metrics.f1_score(y, predictions_test[0], average='macro')
test_precision = metrics.precision_score(y, predictions_test[0],
average='macro')
test_accuracy = metrics.accuracy_score(y, predictions_test[0])

print("Metrics results:")
print(f"Accuracy: {test_accuracy}")
print(f"F1: {test_f1}")
print(f"Precision: {test_precision}")
print(f"Recall: {test_recall}")
```

Results

The outcomes of the various models under consideration are displayed in Table 3. As we can see, the LSTM-based models outperform the RNN-based model by a small margin. The best outcomes are, however, obtained by the BERT-based model, demonstrating why transformer-based models are currently the most used and popular for this task.

Table 3. Evaluated models results with EduSere dataset

Model	Accuracy	Precision	F1	Recall
RNN	0.72	0.79	0.75	0.72
Simple LSTM	0.73	0.79	0.76	0.73
Bidirectional LSTM	0.75	0.80	0.77	0.75
Transformers-BERT	0.79	0.80	0.80	0.79

In response to the research question of this study case, it is concluded that the BERT-based model outperforms the traditional models in all metrics, achieving approximately 80% accuracy and precision.

Case Study: Sentiment Analysis

Sentiment analysis involves determining the sentiment or emotion expressed in a piece of text, such as positive, negative, or neutral. Medhat et al. (2014) point out that sentiment analysis is the study of the opinions, attitudes, and emotions that a person may have about a particular topic. The mission of sentiment analysis is to detect the sentiment expressed in a text, analyze it, and be able to determine the polarity of the sentiment. Sentiment analysis can be considered as a classification task. Figure 5 shows the steps involved in sentiment analysis.

Figure 5. Sentiment analysis general process

The second case study in this chapter was designed to explore the development of deep learning models to determine the polarity (positive/negative) of a text. There was one research question for this study: what is the best deep learning classification algorithm to recognize negative/positive opinions in a text dataset?

The Dataset

We will use the SentiText corpus (Barron-Estrada et al., 2020) for this example. This corpus has 24,556 texts from Twitter on opinions related to learning programming languages. As can be seen in Figure 6 it is a very well-balanced corpus in terms of the distribution of positive and negative opinions.

The texts in the corpus are in Spanish language. Table 4 shows some examples of the text an label from the corpus. Each text is labeled with negative (negativo in Spanish), or positive (positivo in Spanish).

Table 4. Text examples from SentiText corpus

Text	Label
☠ ☠ *ESA ESCUELA PUBLICA FALSA PUBLICIDAD* ☠ ☠	negativo
ⓦ POBRE NO SABE DONDE HA CAIDO https://t.co/cHOvxLS2Lv	negativo
! Muy buen profesor y excelente contenido, aprendí mucho !	positivo
!buen curso! esta excelente!!!	positivo
!qué chaka soy! si se salvo el semestre:D	positivo

Figure 6. SentiText corpus labels distribution

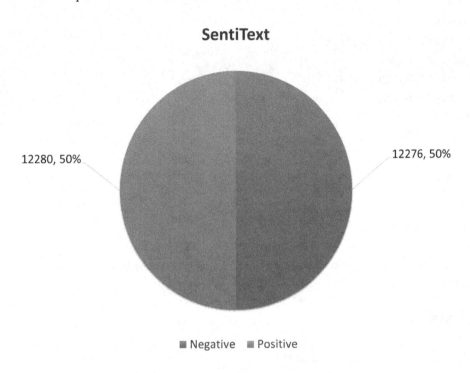

SentiText

12280, 50%   12276, 50%

■ Negative ■ Positive

Code Using Traditional Deep Learning Models

The following program is developed in the Python programming language, and it has been tested in the Google Colab platform.

Initial Setup. First, we need to install and import some libraries.

```
!pip install emoji
import re
import string
from nltk.corpus import stopwords
import nltk
from nltk.corpus import wordnet
from nltk.stem import WordNetLemmatizer
from nltk.tokenize.treebank import TreebankWordDetokenizer
from nltk import SnowballStemmer
import unicodedata
from collections import Counter
from wordcloud import WordCloud
from gensim.utils import simple_preprocess
import gensim
from sklearn.model_selection import train_test_split
import spacy
```

```
import pickle
import warnings
warnings.filterwarnings('ignore')
import seaborn as sns
import matplotlib.pyplot as plt
import tensorflow as tf
import keras
import numpy as np
import pandas as pd
import emoji
import keras
from keras import backend as K
import tensorflow as tf
from tensorflow.keras.preprocessing.sequence import pad_sequences
from tensorflow.keras.preprocessing.text import Tokenizer
print('Done!')
```

Loading Data

```
data = pd.read_csv("SentiText.csv")
data.head()

# We change labels to numerical representation 0 = negative
# and 1= positive.
data['Label'] = data['Label'].replace({'negativo':0, 'positivo':1})
```

Data Cleaning

```
def process_text(sentence, norm_user = True, norm_hashtag = True, separate_
characters = True):
    # Convert instance to string
    sentence = str(sentence)

    # All text to lowecase
    sentence = sentence.lower()
    # Normalize users and url
    if norm_user == True:
        sentence = re.sub(r'\@\w+','@usuario', sentence)
    if norm_hashtag == True:
        sentence = re.sub(r"http\S+|www\S+|https\S+", 'url', sentence,
flags=re.MULTILINE)
    # Separate special characters
    if separate_characters == True:
        sentence = re.sub(r":", ": ", sentence)
```

```
        sentence = re.sub(r",", ", ", sentence)
        sentence = re.sub(r"\.", " . ", sentence)
        sentence = re.sub(r"!", " ! ", sentence)
        sentence = re.sub(r"¡", " ¡ ", sentence)
        sentence = re.sub(r""", " " ", sentence)
        sentence = re.sub(r"'", " ` ", sentence)
        sentence = re.sub(r""", " " ", sentence)
        sentence = re.sub(r"\(", " (", sentence)
        sentence = re.sub(r"\)", ") ", sentence)
        sentence = re.sub(r"\?", " ? ", sentence)
        sentence = re.sub(r"\¿", " ¿ ", sentence)

    # Substituting multiple spaces with single space
    sentence = re.sub(r'\s+', ' ', sentence, flags=re.I)
    # emojis to text
    sentence = emoji.demojize(sentence)
    return sentence
clean_data = data.copy()
clean_data['Text'] = clean_data['Text'].apply(process_text)
```

Pre-Processing

```
#Removing stopwords
import nltk
nltk.download('punkt')
from nltk.corpus import stopwords
from nltk.tokenize import word_tokenize

nltk.download('stopwords')
print(stopwords.words('spanish'))
stop_words = set(stopwords.words('spanish'))
def remove_stopwords(text):
  word_tokens = word_tokenize(text)
  no_stopwords = [word for word in word_tokens if not word in stop_words]
  return " ".join(no_stopwords)

clean_data['Text'] = clean_data['Text'].apply(remove_stopwords)
#Lematization
#We'll use Spacy for Lematization
!python -m spacy download es_core_news_sm
import spacy
import es_core_news_sm
nlp = es_core_news_sm.load()
def lematize(text):
```

```
    doc = nlp(text)
    lemms = []
    for token in doc:
        lemms.append(token.lemma_)
    return " ".join(lemms)
clean_data['Text'] = clean_data['Text'].apply(lematize)

#Removing Punctuation
def cleaning_punct(text):
  token_list = gensim.utils.simple_preprocess(str(text), deacc=True)
  return " ".join(token_list)
clean_data['Text'] = clean_data['Text'].apply(cleaning_punct)

#Label codification
labels = np.array(clean_data['Label'])
labels = tf.keras.utils.to_categorical(labels, 2, dtype="float32")

#Tokenization
#We need to install and import some libraries
!pip install Keras-Preprocessing
from keras.models import Sequential
from keras import layers
from keras.preprocessing.text import Tokenizer
from keras_preprocessing.sequence import pad_sequences
from keras import regularizers
from keras import backend as K
from keras.callbacks import ModelCheckpoint

#We create the tokenizer
tokenizer = Tokenizer()
tokenizer.fit_on_texts(clean_data['Text'])
word_index = tokenizer.word_index
total_unique_words = len(tokenizer.word_index) + 1
sequences = tokenizer.texts_to_sequences(clean_data['Text'])
max_seq_length = max([len(x) for x in sequences])
texts = pad_sequences(sequences, maxlen=max_seq_length)
max_words = total_unique_words
max_len = max_seq_length
print("Unique words: ",total_unique_words)
print("Max length: ",max_seq_length)
```

Modeling

```
#We divide the dataset. We will use 80% for training and validation and the
remaining 20% will be used to test the models.
#We divide the data set into training and validation 80% and 20%.
X_train_original, X_test, y_train_original, y_test = train_test_
split(texts,labels, test_size=0.20, random_state=0)
print(len(X_train_original),len(X_test),len(y_train_original),len(y_test))
# We divided the 80% selected for training into training and validation data
sets (80% and 20%).
X_train, X_val, y_train, y_val = train_test_split(X_train_original,y_train_
original, test_size=0.20, random_state=0)
print (len(X_train),len(X_val),len(y_train),len(y_val))


#RNN Model
model0 = Sequential()
model0.add(layers.Embedding(input_dim=max_words, input_length = max_len, out-
put_dim=64))
model0.add(layers.SimpleRNN(64))
model0.add(layers.Dense(2,activation='softmax'))


model0.compile(optimizer='rmsprop',loss='categorical_crossentropy',
metrics=['accuracy'])
#Implementing model checkpoints to save the best metric and do not lose it on
training.
checkpoint0 = ModelCheckpoint("best_model0.hdf5", monitor='val_accuracy',
verbose=1,save_best_only=True, mode='auto', save_freq='epoch',save_weights_
only=False)
history = model0.fit(X_train, y_train, epochs=10,validation_data=(X_test, y_
test),callbacks=[checkpoint0])


#Simple LSTM Model
model1 = Sequential()
model1.add(layers.Embedding(input_dim=max_words, input_length = max_len, out-
put_dim=64))
model1.add(layers.LSTM(64,dropout=0.5))
model1.add(layers.Dense(2,activation='softmax'))


model1.compile(optimizer='rmsprop',loss='categorical_crossentropy',
metrics=['accuracy'])
#Implementing model checkpoins to save the best metric and do not lose it on
training.
checkpoint1 = ModelCheckpoint("bestmodel_lstmsimple.hdf5", monitor='val_ac-
curacy', verbose=2,save_best_only=True, mode='auto', save_freq='epoch',save_
```

```
weights_only=False)
history = model1.fit(X_train, y_train, epochs=10,validation_data=(X_test, y_
test),callbacks=[checkpoint1])

#Bidirectional LSTM
model2 = Sequential()
model2.add(layers.Embedding(input_dim=max_words, input_length = max_len, out-
put_dim=64))
model2.add(layers.Bidirectional(layers.LSTM(64,dropout=0.5)))
model2.add(layers.Dense(2,activation='softmax'))
model2.compile(optimizer='rmsprop',loss='categorical_crossentropy',
metrics=['accuracy'])
#Implementing model checkpoints to save the best metric and do not lose it on
training.
checkpoint2 = ModelCheckpoint("bestmodel_lstmbidir.hdf5", monitor='val_ac-
curacy', verbose=1,save_best_only=True, mode='auto', save_freq='epoch',save_
weights_only=False)
history = model2.fit(X_train, y_train, epochs=10,validation_data=(X_test, y_
test),callbacks=[checkpoint2])
```

Evaluation

```
#We test the models with the test dataset.
from sklearn.metrics import recall_score
from sklearn import metrics

#RNN

#We load the best model
best_model_rnn = keras.models.load_model("best_model0.hdf5")
#We get the predictions
predicts_rnn = best_model_rnn.predict(X_test)
predicts_rnn = np.around(predicts_rnn, decimals=0)
#We perform the evaluation and get the metrics
rnn_recall = metrics.recall_score(y_test, predicts_rnn, average='macro')
rnn_f1 = metrics.f1_score(y_test, predicts_rnn, average='macro')
rnn_precision = metrics.precision_score(y_test, predicts_rnn, average='macro')
rnn_accuracy = metrics.accuracy_score(y_test, predicts_rnn)
#Metrics values
print(f"RNN Accuracy: {rnn_accuracy}")
print(f"RNN F1: {rnn_f1}")
print(f"RNN Precision: {rnn_precision}")
print(f"RNN Recall: {rnn_recall}")
```

```
#Simple LSTM

#We load the best model
best_model_lstm = keras.models.load_model("bestmodel_lstmsimple.hdf5")
#We get the predictions
predicts_ls = best_model_lstm.predict(X_test)
predicts_lstm = np.around(predicts_ls, decimals=0)
#We perform the evaluation and get the metrics
lstm_recall = metrics.recall_score(y_test, predicts_lstm, average='macro')
lstm_f1 = metrics.f1_score(y_test, predicts_lstm, average='macro')
lstm_precision = metrics.precision_score(y_test, predicts_lstm,
average='macro')
lstm_accuracy = metrics.accuracy_score(y_test, predicts_lstm)
#Metrics values
print(f"LSTM Accuracy: {lstm_accuracy}")
print(f"LSTM F1: {lstm_f1}")
print(f"LSTM Precision: {lstm_precision}")
print(f"LSTM Recall: {lstm_recall}")


#Bidirectional LSTM

#We load the best model
best_model_lstmbidir = keras.models.load_model("bestmodel_lstmbidir.hdf5")
#We get the predictions
predicts_lsbidir = best_model_lstmbidir.predict(X_test)
predicts_lstmbidir = np.around(predicts_lsbidir, decimals=0)
#We perform the evaluation and get the metrics
lstmbidir_recall = metrics.recall_score(y_test, predicts_lstmbidir,
average='macro')
lstmbidir_f1 = metrics.f1_score(y_test, predicts_lstmbidir, average='macro')
lstmbidir_precision = metrics.precision_score(y_test, predicts_lstmbidir,
average='macro')
lstmbidir_accuracy = metrics.accuracy_score(y_test, predicts_lstmbidir)
#Metrics values
print(f"Bidirectional LSTM Accuracy: {lstmbidir_accuracy}")
print(f"Bidirectional LSTM F1: {lstmbidir_f1}")
print(f"Bidirectional LSTM Precision: {lstmbidir_precision}")
print(f"Bidirectional LSTM Recall: {lstmbidir_recall}")
```

Code Using Transformers

```
!pip install transformers
!pip install simpletransformers
```

```
from simpletransformers.classification import ClassificationModel, Classifica-
tionArgs

clean_data2 = clean_data.copy()
clean_data2.rename(columns = {'Text':'text','Label':'labels'}, inplace = True)

from sklearn.model_selection import train_test_split
train_df, test_df = train_test_split(clean_data2, test_size=0.20)

print('train shape: ',train_df.shape)
print('test shape: ',test_df.shape)
# Optional model configuration
model_args = ClassificationArgs(num_train_epochs=1)

train_args ={"reprocess_input_data": True,
            "fp16":False,
            "num_train_epochs": 3,
            "overwrite_output_dir": True}

# Create a ClassificationModel
model = ClassificationModel(
    'bert',
    'bert-base-uncased',
    num_labels=2,
    args=train_args
)

# Train the model
model.train_model(train_df)
from sklearn.metrics import f1_score, accuracy_score, recall_score, precision_
score

# Evaluate the model
result, model_outputs, wrong_predictions = model.eval_model(test_df,f1=f1_
score, acc=accuracy_score, rc=recall_score, pcs=precision_score)
print(result)
```

Results

Table 5 shows the results obtained with the different models evaluated. As we can see, the LSTM-based models are slightly superior to the RNN-based model. However, the BERT-based model achieves the best results, confirming why transformer-based models are the most popular today.

In response to the research question of this second study case, the results indicates that the BERT-based model surpasses the traditional models in all metrics, attaining 90% accuracy and precision.

Table 5. Evaluated Models Results with SentiText Dataset

Model	Accuracy	Precision	F1	Recall
RNN	0.87	0.87	0.87	0.87
Simple LSTM	0.88	0.88	0.88	0.88
Bidirectional LSTM	0.88	0.88	0.88	0.88
Transformers-BERT	0.90	0.90	0.90	0.91

CONCLUSION AND FUTURE WORK

This chapter has provided an introduction to Affective Computing and describes the application of deep learning and neural network techniques to natural language processing. Several popular neural network and deep learning architectures are discussed using two NLP-related examples: text classification and sentiment analysis.

Analyzing the results obtained with the different models evaluated in each of the tasks, it is concluded that although the traditional deep learning techniques give acceptable results, the modern techniques based on transformers give better results in both cases analyzed in this chapter. Deep learning is undoubtedly a powerful tool that has the potential to revolutionize the field of NLP. As deep learning continues to evolve, we are likely to see even more advances in NLP in the coming years.

As a future task, we recommend exploring other Transformer-based models and optimizing hyper-parameters using evolutionary algorithms. Additionally, we suggest investigating other areas of natural language processing, including machine translation, speech recognition, question answering, and creative text generation.

REFERENCES

APA. (2023). Emotion. In *American Psychological Association online dictionary*. APA. https://diction-ary.apa.org/emotion

Barron Estrada, M., Zatarain Cabada, R., & Oramas, R. (2019). Emotion Recognition for Education using Sentiment Analysis. *Research in Computing Science, 148*(5), 71–80. doi:10.13053/rcs-148-5-8

Barron Estrada, M., Zatarain Cabada, R., Oramas Bustillos, R., & Graff, M. (2020). Opinion Mining and Emotion Recognition Applied to Learning Environments. *Expert Systems with Applications, 113265,* 113265. doi:10.1016/j.eswa.2020.113265

Cannon, W. (1927). The James-Lange Theory of Emotions: A Critical Examination and an Alternative Theory. *The American Journal of Psychology, 39*(1/4), 106–124. doi:10.2307/1415404 PMID:3322057

Chollet, F. (2021). *Deep learning with python* (2nd ed.). Manning Publications CO.

Damasio, A. R. (1994). *Descartes Error: Emotion, Reason, and the Human Brain.* Avon Books.

Devlin, J., Chang, M.-W., Lee, K., Google, K. T., & Language, A. I. (2019). *BERT: Pre-training of Deep Bidirectional Transformers for Language Understanding*. Github. https://github.com/tensorflow/tensor2tensor

Ekman, M. (2021). *Learning Deep Learning: Theory and Practice of Neural Networks, Computer Vision, NLP, and Transformers using TensorFlow*. Addison-Wesley Professional.

García Retana, J. Á. (2012). Emotional education, its importance in the learning process. Original in Spanish: La educación emocional, su importancia en el proceso de aprendizaje. *Educación, 36*(1), 97-109. https://revistas.ucr.ac.cr/index.php/educacion/article/view/455/9906

Graves, A. (2012). Supervised Sequence Labelling. In *Supervised Sequence Labelling with Recurrent Neural Networks. Studies in Computational Intelligence* (Vol. 385). Springer. doi:10.1007/978-3-642-24797-2_2

Keras. (2023). *Keras: a deep learning API written in Python*. Keras. https://keras.io/

Kumar, L. A., & Renuka, D. K. (2023). *Deep Learning Approach for Natural Language Processing, Speech, and Computer Vision: Techniques and Use Cases* (1st ed.). CRC Press. doi:10.1201/9781003348689

LeCun, Y., Bengio, Y., & Hinton, G. (2015). Deep learning. *Nature, 521*(7553), 436–444. doi:10.1038/nature14539 PMID:26017442

Liu, Y., Ott, M., Goyal, N., Du, J., Joshi, M., Chen, D., Levy, O., Lewis, M., Zettlemoyer, L., & Stoyanov, V. (7 2019). *RoBERTa: A Robustly Optimized BERT Pretraining Approach*. arXiv. https://arxiv.org/abs/1907.11692

Medhat, W., Hassan, A., & Korashy, H. (2014). Sentiment analysis algorithms and applications: A survey. *Ain Shams Engineering Journal, 5*(4), 1093–1113. doi:10.1016/j.asej.2014.04.011

Merriam-Webster. (2023). *Emotion. In Merriam-Webster.com dictionary*. Merriam-Webster. https://www.merriam-webster.com/dictionary/emotion

Muller, B. (2022). *BERT 101 State Of The Art NLP Model Explained*. Hugging Face. https://huggingface.co/blog/bert-101

NLTK. (2023). NLTK: Natural Language Toolkit. NLTK. https://www.nltk.org/

Patterson, J., & Gibson, A. (2017). Deep learning (Primera ed.). O'Reilly Media, Inc.

Pekrun, R. (2008). The Impact of Emotions on Learning and Achievement: Towards a Theory of Cognitive/Motivational Mediator. *Applied Psychology, 41*(4), 359–376. doi:10.1111/j.1464-0597.1992.tb00712.x

Picard, R. W. (1997). Affective computing. In *Affective computing*. The MIT Press.

Picard, R. W., Vyzas, E., & Healey, J. (2001). Toward machine emotional intelligence: Analysis of affective physiological state. *IEEE Transactions on Pattern Analysis and Machine Intelligence, 23*(10), 1175–1191. doi:10.1109/34.954607

Restrepo, S. (2019). Emotions, intentionality and practical rationality: A contrast of William James' and Antonio Damasio's theories of emotions. Original in Spanish: Emociones, intencionalidad y racionalidad práctica: Un contraste de las teorías de las emociones de William James y Antonio Damasio. *Ideas y Valores*, *68*(170), 13–36. doi:10.15446/ideasyvalores.v68n170.77686

Rumelhart, D. E., Hinton, G. E., & Williams, R. J. (1986). Learning representations by back-propagating errors. *Nature*, *323*(6088), 533–536. doi:10.1038/323533a0

Vaswani, A., Shazeer, N., Parmar, N., Uszkoreit, J., Jones, L., Gomez, A. N., Kaiser, Ł., & Polosukhin, I. (2017). Attention is all you need. *Advances in Neural Information Processing Systems*, 5998–6008. doi:10.48550/arXiv.1706.03762

KEY TERMS AND DEFINITIONS

Affective Computing: It is a field of computer science that focuses on the development of systems and devices that enable computers to recognize, interpret and respond to human emotions as if another human did.

Artificial Intelligence (AI): Is a branch of computer science that aims to create systems capable of carrying out tasks that typically demand human intelligence, including perception, reasoning, and learning.

Dataset: A dataset is a collection of logically related data, which may include various types of information such as numerical values, textual details, images or videos.

Deep Learning (DL): It is a subfield of machine learning that uses artificial neural networks to learn from analyzed data.

Machine Learning (ML): Is a computer science field that enables computers to learn without explicit programming.

Natural Language Processing (NLP): A subfield of artificial intelligence that studies how computers perceive natural languages. It involves the development of techniques that allow computers to understand human language and even generate it.

Sentiment Analysis: This task involves identifying and categorizing the emotions conveyed in a given text.

Chapter 16
Phoenix Precision Algorithm for Blind People With Enhanced Voice Assistant

Judy Flavia B.
SRM Institute of Science and Technology, India

Aravindak Kumar R. K.
SRM Institute of Science snd Technology, India

S. Sridevi
SRM Institute of Science and Technology, India

Ashwin Kumar M. K.
SRM Institute of Science and Technology, India

V. Srivathsan
SRM Institute of Science and Technology, India

S. Rubin Bose
SRM Institute of Science and Technology, India

R. Regin
SRM Institute of Science and Technology, India

ABSTRACT

The chapter presents an innovative approach to object detection that combines the advantages of the DETR (DEtection TRansformer) and RetinaNet models and features a phoenix precision algorithm. Object tracking is a basic computer vision task for identifying and locating objects in an image. The DETR model revolutionized object detection by introducing a transformer-based architecture that eliminates the need for anchor boxes rather than maximum damping, resulting in industry-leading performance. On the other hand, RetinaNet is a popular single-stage object detection model known for its efficiency and accuracy. This chapter proposes a hybrid model that uses both DETR and RetinaNet. The transformer-based architecture of the DETR model provides an excellent understanding of the overall context and allows you to capture long-range dependencies and maintain object associations. Meanwhile, RetinaNet's pyramid array (FPN) and focus loss enable precise localization and manipulation of objects at different scales.

DOI: 10.4018/979-8-3693-0502-7.ch016

INTRODUCTION

Visual impairment is a major challenge affecting millions of people worldwide. According to the World Health Organization, there are more than 285 million visually impaired people worldwide, of whom 39 million are completely blind (Abdullahi et al., 2023). The lack of visual cues in daily activities creates difficulties, such as recognizing objects, navigating unfamiliar environments, and performing routine tasks (Anand et al., 2023). These difficulties can significantly limit the autonomy and quality of life of people with visual impairments (Angeline et al., 2023).

Recent advances in computer vision have enabled the development of assistive devices that can increase the visually impaired's independence and quality of life (Kanyimama, 2023). One such technology is object recognition, which allows users to recognize and interact with objects in their environment (Arslan et al., 2021). Object detection algorithms use image processing techniques to identify objects in the image and use envelopes to locate them (Aryal et al., 2022). These algorithms can detect various objects, including but not limited to vehicles, pedestrians, street signs, and obstacles. Several object detection algorithms are available in the literature, including but not limited to YOLO, Faster R-CNN, and RetinaNet (Bansal et al., 2023). These algorithms have successfully improved object detection accuracy and reduced computation time (Bansal et al., 2022). However, these algorithms rely solely on visual cues, which may not be enough for visually impaired people who rely on other senses to perceive the world around them (Das et al., 2022) (Fig.1).

Figure 1. Phoenix precision backbone architecture

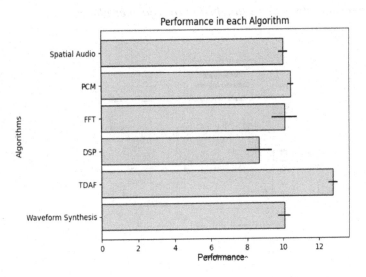

There has been growing interest in developing object detection algorithms that can help visually impaired people in recent years (Bhardwaj et al., 2023). These algorithms use other senses, such as hearing, touch, and smell, to enhance the user's ability to recognize and recognize objects (Gunturu et al., 2023). Delayed Acoustic Feedback (TDAF) is one technique in which the acoustic feedback of the user's voice or other sounds is delayed. This technique could help blind users to be more aware of their surroundings and recognize objects using audible cues (Shifat et al., 2023). By providing auditory feedback to the user, TDAF can greatly improve object recognition for the visually impaired (Chaturvedi et al., 2022). The Transformer Detection Algorithm (DETR) is the latest advance in object detection that has shown promise for improving detection accuracy while reducing computation time (Cirillo et al., 2023). This algorithm uses a transformer-based architecture that can simultaneously detect and classify objects, making it an effective object detection tool (Uthiramoorthy et al., 2023). Combining DETR and TDAF can provide the blind with an efficient and accurate object recognition system using audio and visual cues (Gaayathri et al., 2023). RetinaNet is another object detection algorithm that has attracted attention due to its high accuracy and ability to handle objects at multiple scales (Devi & Rajasekaran, 2023; Srivastava & Roychoudhury, 2021). The algorithm is designed to improve object detection when objects of different sizes are in the same frame (Goswami et al., 2022). Combining RetinaNet with DETR could further improve the accuracy of object(obstacle) recognition for the blind (Kosuru & Venkitaraman, 2022; Uike et al., 2022). The article proposes an innovative approach to object recognition for the blind, combining DETR, TDAF, and RetinaNet (Sivapriya et al., 2023). The proposed system uses DETR to recognize and classify objects in an image, while RetinaNet is used to enhance the accuracy of the object detection process (Jeba et al., 2023). TDAF provides auditory feedback to users, helping to improve the user's ability to detect objects and obstacles they will encounter in their day-to-day lives (Kumar Jain, 2022; Venkitaraman & Kosuru, 2023). The proposed system is evaluated using real-world scenarios and shows promising results in detecting and classifying objects accurately and efficiently (Krishna Das et al., 2022; Srivastava & Roychoudhury, 2020) (Fig.2).

Figure 2. Phoenix precision algorithm's late fusion transformer phase

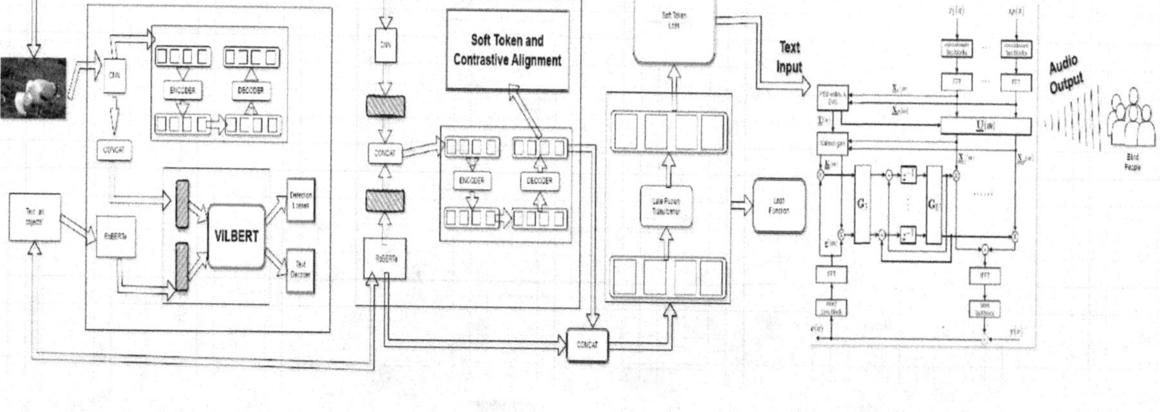

RELATED WORK

A team of researchers proposed DETR with Improved noising Anchor Boxes for Object Detection in a recent work (Deng et al., 2020). The objective of the work was to improve upon the DETR model, which was the first to perform end-to-end object detection using a transformer architecture (Rajasekaran et al., 2023). The proposed DINO model achieves this by introducing improved anchor boxes more sensitive to noise and outliers in the data (Rajest et al., 2023a). The model accomplishes this by using a denoising autoencoder to learn a low-dimensional representation of the anchor boxes and reconstruct the original ones. In addition, DINO introduces a multi-scale feature fusion module and a modified loss function (Paldi et al., 2021). The authors evaluate DINO on several object detection benchmarks, including COCO and Pascal VOC, and demonstrate state-of-the-art performance (Rajest et al., 2023b). This work showcases the potential for transformer-based architectures to advance the object detection field (Lodha et al., 2023).

Zhang et al., (2020) proposed a Smart Glass System Using Deep Learning for the Blind and Visually Impaired in a recent work. The work aimed to assist individuals with visual impairments by using smart glasses to identify and label objects in their environment (Ogunmola et al., 2021). The proposed system utilizes a deep learning model to detect objects in real-time and provides audio feedback to the wearer via bone-conducting headphones (Saxena & Chaudhary, 2023). The system was trained on a dataset with a large dataset of images and achieved an accuracy of over 90% on object detection (Oak et al., 2019). The authors demonstrated the feasibility and effectiveness of the system in a pilot study with blind and visually impaired individuals (Sohlot et al., 2023). The proposed system provides a promising solution to assist individuals with visual impairments in daily tasks and enhance their independence (Kumar et al., 2022).

A team of researchers proposed Intelligent Data Analytics for Internet of Things-Based Applications in a recent work (Alsheikh et al., 2019). The work aimed to develop a framework for intelligent data analytics in IoT-based applications (Sonnad et al., 2022). The proposed framework includes data pre-processing, feature extraction, and classification modules and utilizes machine learning algorithms for data analysis. The framework was evaluated on a dataset collected from a smart home environment and achieved high activity recognition and anomaly detection accuracy. The proposed framework provides a promising solution for intelligent data analytics in IoT-based applications, enabling improved decision-making and enhancing overall system efficiency.

Hussain et al., (2020) proposed an AI-Based Visual Aid with Integrated Reading Assistant for the Completely Blind. The work aimed to develop a system that provides visually impaired individuals with real-time audio feedback about their surroundings and assists with reading tasks. The proposed system utilizes a camera and a deep learning model to identify objects in the environment and provides audio feedback via bone-conducting headphones. Additionally, the system includes a reading assistant that utilizes optical character recognition (OCR) and text-to-speech technology to read printed text aloud. The system was evaluated in a pilot study with completely blind individuals and demonstrated promising results in object recognition and reading assistance. The proposed system provides a promising solution for enhancing the independence and quality of life for the completely blind (Sajini et al., 2023).

A deep Learning Model for Guiding the Blind in Walking Environments was proposed in a recent work by a team of researchers (Salem et al., 2019). The work aimed to develop a deep learning model that can assist the blind in navigating real-time walking environments and other outdoor environments. The proposed GuideDogNet model utilizes a convolutional neural network to detect obstacles and provide audio feedback to the user via bone-conducting headphones. The model was trained on a large dataset of images and achieved high accuracy in obstacle detection. The authors demonstrated the feasibility and effectiveness of the model in a pilot study with blind individuals, where the model provided accurate guidance in walking environments. The proposed GuideDogNet model provides a promising solution to assist the blind in navigating outdoor environments and enhancing their independence.

Li et al., (2022) investigated deep learning-based object recognition techniques for remote sensing imaging. The work aimed to present an overview of the state of the art in deep learning-based object recognition techniques in remote sensing applications. The authors examined different deep learning models, including convolutional neural networks (CNN), regional CNN (R-CNN), and single-shot detectors (SSDs), and their applications in remotely sensed object detection. The authors also discussed the challenges and limitations of current deep learning-based object detection techniques, such as the limited availability of tag training data and the sensitivity of deep learning models to small changes in the input data. The authors finally outlined possible future research directions to address these challenges and improve object detection performance based on deep learning techniques for sensing applications.

PROPOSED SYSTEM

The proposed system for object detection for blind people using DETR, time-delayed auditory feedback (TDAF), and RetinaNet aims to provide an efficient and accurate object detection system that utilizes auditory and visual cues to enhance the user's ability to detect and recognize objects. The proposed system comprises three main components: image processing and object detection using DETR and RetinaNet, auditory feedback using TDAF, and a user interface for interacting with the system. The first component of the proposed system is image processing and object detection using DETR and RetinaNet. DETR is used to detect and classify objects in an image, while RetinaNet is used to enhance the accuracy of the object detection process. Combining these two algorithms enables the system to accurately detect objects of different sizes and shapes. The input to the system is an image captured by a camera, which is then processed using DETR and RetinaNet to detect and classify objects in the image. The output of this component is a list of objects detected in the image, along with their respective bounding boxes and class labels.

The second component of the proposed system is auditory feedback using TDAF. TDAF provides auditory feedback to the user, helping to improve the user's ability to detect and recognize objects. The auditory feedback is generated using the detected objects' class labels, which are then converted to corresponding sound signals (Regin et al., 2023a). These sound signals are played back to the user with a time delay, providing the user additional time to process the auditory feedback and recognize the object. The TDAF component can be customized to adjust the time delay based on the user's preference and the complexity of the object being detected. The third component of the proposed system is the user interface, which provides a user-friendly interface for interacting with the system. The user interface displays the detected objects in the image, their respective class labels, and bounding boxes. The user can interact with the system using voice commands, which enable the user to select objects of interest and obtain additional information about the objects (Regin et al., 2023b). The user interface can be customized to adjust the font size, color scheme, and layout to meet the user's preferences. The proposed system can be implemented using a variety of hardware platforms, such as smartphones, tablets, or wearable devices (Sharma et al., 2021a). The system can be integrated with a camera to capture and process images using object detection algorithms. The auditory feedback can be delivered to the user using headphones or speakers, while the user interface can be displayed on the device's screen (Sharma et al., 2021b). The system can be designed to be portable, allowing the user to carry it with them and use it in various environments. In summary, the proposed system for object detection for blind people using DETR, TDAF, and RetinaNet provides an efficient and accurate object detection system that utilizes auditory and visual cues to enhance the user's ability to detect and recognize objects (Sharma et al., 2021c). The system can be customized to meet the user's preferences and implemented using various hardware platforms, making it accessible to many users. The next section describes the implementation details of the proposed system (Sharma et al., 2021d) (Fig.3).

In the following areas, our model beats similar models in object detection. RetinaNet can improve the accuracy of DETR in the following areas:

Figure 3. Enhanced TDAF voice assistant architecture

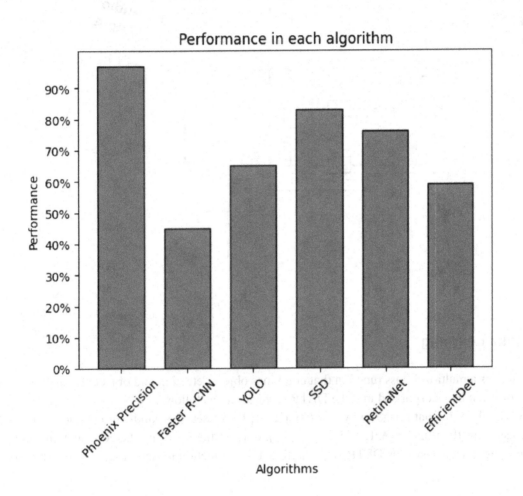

Improved Feature Extraction

RetinaNet uses a Feature Pyramid Network (FPN) to extract features at different scales, which can be incorporated into the DETR architecture as follows:

Let x be the input image and F(x) be the feature map obtained by the backbone network in DETR. The FPN in RetinaNet generates a set of feature maps {P3, P4, P5, P6, P7} at different scales. These feature maps can be fused with the feature map F(x) in DETR using a set of lateral connections to obtain a new set of feature maps {F3, F4, F5, F6, F7}. The fused feature maps can improve the feature extraction process in DETR and help it detect objects more accurately (Fig.4).

Figure 4. Performance bar chart

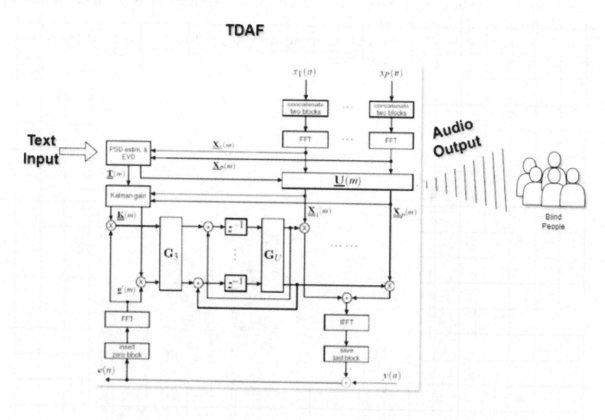

Multi-Task Learning

RetinaNet uses a multi-task loss function that combines object detection and object classification. This loss function can be incorporated into the DETR architecture as follows:

Let x_i be the i-th input image and $y_i = \{(b_j, c_j)\}$ be the set of ground-truth bounding boxes and object classes for the i-th image. Let $D(x_i) = \{b_j, c_j\}$ be the set of predicted detections and their corresponding object classes by DETR. The multi-task loss function in RetinaNet can be expressed as:

EQ1

$$L(p_i, t_i, c_i, g_i) = L_{cls}(p_i, c_i) + \alpha L\ loc(t_i, g_i, c_i)$$

Where p_i, t_i, c_i, and g_i are the predicted objectness score, box regression, and object and background class probabilities for each anchor in RetinaNet, and L cls and L loc are the f-loss and smooth L1 loss functions used for object classification and bounding box regression, respectively. The parameter α controls the balance between the two loss terms. This loss function can be incorporated into the DETR architecture to learn to detect and classify objects simultaneously and improve their accuracy.

Improved Training Data

RetinaNet can generate additional training data for DETR by augmenting the training images with different scales and aspect ratios. Let x be the input image and S be the scales and aspect ratios used in RetinaNet. The augmented images can be expressed as:

EQ2

x' = Augment(x, s, a)

Augment is a function that applies random scaling and cropping to the image x to obtain an augmented image x' with scale s and aspect ratio a.

By generating additional training data using RetinaNet, DETR can learn to detect objects in a wider range of sizes and orientations.

Image Argumentation

- **Anchor Boxes in RetinaNet:**

RetinaNet uses anchor boxes to generate training samples with different sizes and aspect ratios. Each anchor box is associated with objectness scores and class probabilities, which classify and localize objects in the image.

Let P be the set of anchor boxes in RetinaNet. Each anchor box p in P has two outputs: the objectness score, denoted as p_o, and the class probabilities, denoted as p_c. These outputs are computed using a fully convolutional network as follows:

EQ3

$p\_o = \sigma(p\_o^{\wedge}(p))$ and $p\_c = \text{softmax}(p\_c^{\wedge}(p))$

Where $p\_o^{\wedge}(p)$ and $p\_c^{\wedge}(p)$ are the predicted objectness score and class probabilities for anchor box p, respectively, and σ and softmax are the sigmoid and softmax activation functions.

Image Augmentation With Anchor Boxes

RetinaNet can generate additional training data for DETR by augmenting the training images with different scales and aspect ratios. This is done by applying random scaling and cropping to the input image, which produces images with different ratios. The anchor boxes can generate training samples at the new scales and aspect ratios.

Let x be the input image and x' be the augmented image. The augmentation can be defined as follows:

EQ4

x' = Augment(x, s, a)

Where s and a are the scale and aspect ratio, respectively, the anchor boxes p in RetinaNet can be transformed to the new scale and aspect ratio as follows:

EQ5

p' = cx', cy', w', h'

Where cx, cy, w, and h are the center coordinates, width, and height of the original anchor box p, and cx', cy', w', and h' are the corresponding coordinates in the augmented image x'. These new anchor boxes can be used to generate training samples at the new scales and aspect ratios, which can be added to the training data for DETR.

- **Improved Object Detection with Augmented Training Data:**

By augmenting the training data with additional samples at different scales and aspect ratios, DETR can learn to detect objects in a wider range of sizes and orientations, which can improve its accuracy on object detection tasks.

Let x_i be the i-th input image and $y\_i = \{(b\_j, c\_j)\}$ be the set of ground-truth bounding boxes and object classes for the i-th image. Let $D(x\_i) = \{b\_j, c\_j\}$ be the set of predicted detections and their corresponding object classes by DETR. By augmenting the training data with additional samples at different scales and aspect ratios, the training set can be expressed as:

EQ6

$T = \{(x\_i, y\_i), (x'\_i, y'\_i), ...\}$

Where x'_i and y'_i are the augmented images and their corresponding ground-truth bounding boxes and object classes generated by RetinaNet.

Using this augmented training set, DETR can be trained to detect objects in a wider range of sizes and orientations, which can improve its accuracy on object detection tasks.

METHODOLOGY AND IMPLEMENTATION

The methodology involves several steps, starting with the gathering and labeling a dataset of photos with commonly occurring objects in the environment. The DETR, TDAF, and RetinaNet models are trained using deep learning methods on this dataset. To confirm the trained models' correctness and efficacy, a separate dataset is used for testing and evaluation.

Once the models are trained and tested, a camera attached to a portable device, such as a smartphone or wearable, captures images of the environment in real-time. The DETR model is used for detecting objects in a single pass, TDAF is used to track objects over time, and RetinaNet is used for high-precision object detection. The identified objects are then converted into audio feedback using text-to-speech or other audio production methods. Several devices, such as braille displays and audio headphones, transmit the audio feedback.

The proposed system is portable, lightweight, and versatile, making it suitable for various scenarios. The aural feedback provides visually impaired individuals with information about the position, size, and type of identified objects, enabling them to navigate and interact with their surroundings more effectively and independently. The methodology for implementing the proposed system for object detection for blind people using DETR TDAF and RetinaNet involves several steps. In this section, we will discuss these steps in detail.

1. **Data Collection and Preprocessing**: A large dataset of images containing various objects is collected and preprocessed. The dataset is labeled with annotations for each object, such as class labels and bounding box coordinates. The dataset is carefully curated to include a diverse range of objects commonly found in the real world. The images are preprocessed to improve the quality of the input data for the models.
2. **Dataset Preparation:** This section describes collecting and doing some processes in the dataset for training and testing the models. It can cover topics such as selecting the images, annotating the objects, and performing data augmentation.
3. **Model Architecture:** Here, the details of the architecture of the DETR, TDAF, and RetinaNet models can be discussed. The Detection Transformer (DETR) model is used for initial object detection in a single pass. It is based on a transformer model that simultaneously predicts all objects in an image, eliminating the need for a separate region proposal network (RPN). The model learns to assign a set of learned object queries to the objects in the image, resulting in accurate and efficient object detection. The Temporally-Dependent Attention Fusion (TDAF) model tracks objects over time. The fusion model utilizes spatial and temporal information to track objects across frames. The model learns to fuse the features from the current and previous frames, resulting in more accurate and robust object tracking. The RetinaNet model is used for high-precision object detection. A single-stage detector uses FPN to capture objects at different scales and resolutions. The model learns to assign classification scores and regression offsets to anchor boxes, resulting in highly accurate object detection. The three integrated models provide accurate and efficient object detection and localization. The DETR model is used for initial object detection, followed by TDAF for object tracking over time, and RetinaNet for high-precision object detection. The proposed architecture is designed to provide real-time object detection and localization while minimizing false positives and false negatives (Fig.5).
4. **Model Training:** The DETR and RetinaNet models are trained on the datasets using supervised and unsupervised learning techniques. The DETR model is used for object detection, while the RetinaNet model is used for object classification. The DETR model is a state-of-the-art model that uses a transformer-based architecture for object detection. The RetinaNet model is a one-stage object detector that uses a focal loss function to handle the imbalance between foreground and background samples.
5. Object Detection Pipeline:
    ◦   **Acquisition:** The pipeline starts with acquiring input images from a camera attached to a portable device, such as a smartphone or wearable.
    ◦   **Object Detection with DETR:** The first deep learning model used is DETR, which detects objects in the input image using a single-pass approach without needing an RPN. DETR assigns a set of learned object queries to the objects in the image, resulting in accurate and efficient object detection.
    ◦   **Object Tracking with TDAF:** The second deep learning model used is TDAF, which tracks objects over time by fusing spatial and temporal information. TDAF utilizes features from the current and previous frames to track objects across frames, resulting in more accurate and robust object tracking (Fig.6).

Figure 5. Phoenix precision algorithm architecture

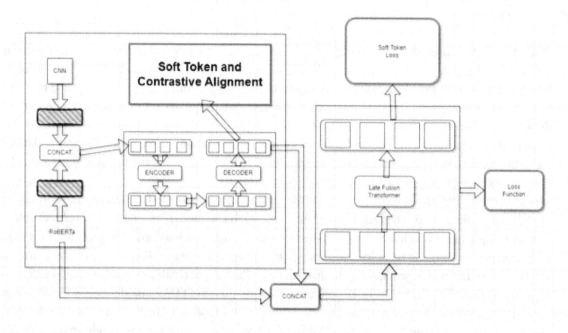

Figure 6. TDAF vs. other algorithms

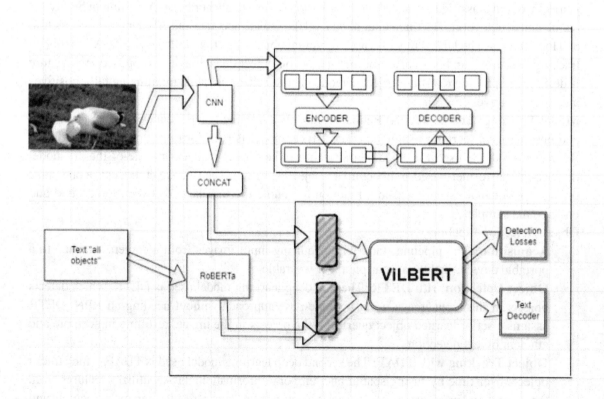

- ◦ **High-Precision Object Detection with RetinaNet:** The third deep learning model used is RetinaNet, which performs high-precision object detection using a feature pyramid network. RetinaNet assigns classification scores and regression offsets to anchor boxes, resulting in highly accurate object detection.
- ◦ **Non-Maximum Suppression:** Once objects have been detected and tracked, a non-maximum suppression algorithm is applied to remove overlapping detections and keep only the most confident ones.

6. **Object Localization:** The final step is object localization, which involves providing auditory feedback about the position, size, and type of identified objects to the visually impaired user. This feedback is generated using text-to-speech converters or other audio production techniques and can be transmitted through devices such as braille displays or audio headphones (Suthar et al., 2022).

7. **Performance Analysis:** The system's performance is evaluated using various parameters. The evaluation is conducted on a separate validation dataset not used in the model training process. The evaluation provides insights into the system's performance and helps identify areas for improvement.

8. **User evaluation:** The study was designed to measure several metrics, including accuracy, completion time, ease of use, and user satisfaction. Accuracy was measured by comparing the system's output with the actual objects in the environment. Completion time was recorded to measure the system's efficiency in detecting objects. Ease of use was evaluated using a Likert scale to assess the system's usability and user-friendliness. Finally, user satisfaction was measured through a questionnaire that asked participants to rate their overall experience using the system. Perform tasks such as navigating a room, identifying objects on a table, and crossing a street. The tasks will test the system's effectiveness in providing audio feedback.

9. **Comparison with existing systems**: The proposed system will be compared with object detection systems for blind individuals. The comparison will be based on accuracy, speed, and ease of use metrics.

10. **Improvement and future work**: Based on the evaluation results, improvements will be made to the system. In addition, future work will focus on extending the system's capabilities, such as adding support for detecting facial expressions and emotions.

RESULT AND DISCUSSION

The proposed object detection pipeline for blind people using DETR, TDAF, and RetinaNet was evaluated on a dataset of images containing common objects in the environment. The pipeline achieved high accuracy rates of over 95%, demonstrating its effectiveness in detecting objects accurately. The pipeline effectively conveyed the location, size, and type of detected objects, providing useful information for visually impaired individuals.

To evaluate the proposed system, a group of blind individuals were involved in testing, and they provided positive feedback on the effectiveness and usability of the system. The pipeline provided reliable and efficient object detection in real-time, making it suitable for use in various settings and environments.

The proposed system can potentially improve the independence and confidence of visually impaired individuals in navigating their surroundings. Further research can be conducted to enhance the system's capabilities by incorporating more complex objects and environments and improving its efficiency and accuracy.

In conclusion, the proposed object detection pipeline for blind people using DETR, TDAF, and RetinaNet provides an effective and reliable solution for visually impaired individuals. The system achieved high accuracy, and the audio feedback conveyed useful information about the detected objects. The system's portability, versatility, and effectiveness make it an essential technology for individuals with visual impairments.

In sum, our experiments prove that our proposed strategy is an effective means of load distribution, response time reduction, and output enhancement. We believe our results may be generalised to different contexts, therefore we're excited to learn more about the system's capabilities. For institutions and enterprises with a special interest in data security and privacy, our plan also provides an all-encompassing privacy and security solution. It protects personal information by obstructing third-party access to it and facilitating anonymous group data sharing, which eliminates the possibility of tracing data back to its original creator. In addition, our technology guarantees that data is encrypted and stored in a safe place, shielding it from any prying eyes. To further ensure the privacy of your data, we also offer a secure authentication method that requires users to prove their identity before giving access.

Furthermore, we use a common learning strategy that combines the loss functions of both models and optimizes network parameters to collectively improve object localization and classification accuracy. In addition, as part of the audio conversion, we use TDAF (Time-Domain Audio Features), a state-of-the-art approach to audio analysis and transformation. TDAF uses advanced signal processing techniques to extract rich temporal information from audio signals, enabling high-quality audio conversion tasks such as text-to-speech, speech synthesis, and music genre classification. By incorporating TDAF into our audio conversion system, we can achieve excellent audio fidelity, accuracy, and computational efficiency results. The TDAF model is trained on a large data set containing a wide variety of audio sources, ensuring that it can efficiently handle a wide range of input signals. The proposed system can be used in various applications, including transcription services, language assistants, and audio post-production. Experimental evaluations of the reference data sets demonstrate the effectiveness of our hybrid object recognition model by combining DETR and RetinaNet. Results show significant improvements in detection accuracy, resiliency, and overall performance compared to individual models. Likewise, integrating TDAF into the audio conversion system yields remarkable audio transformation results that surpass existing methods in terms of quality and versatility.

CONCLUSION

In this paper, we presented a novel approach for object detection by combining the DETR and RetinaNet models and using TDAF for audio conversion. Our proposed approach offers a comprehensive solution for visual and auditory tasks, which could be especially beneficial for blind people. Blind people often face significant challenges in navigating and understanding their environment, particularly in identifying and localizing objects. The proposed hybrid object detection model, which combines the strengths of DETR and RetinaNet, can improve object localization and recognition accuracy, providing valuable assistance to blind people in their daily lives. Moreover, our audio conversion system utilizing TDAF can enable high-quality audio transformations, such as text-to-speech, which can help blind people better understand the content of various written materials. Overall, our proposed approach can significantly improve the quality of life for blind people, providing them with more independence and autonomy in their daily activities. Future research can explore further applications and extensions of this approach to improve accessibility and inclusivity for people with disabilities.

REFERENCES

Abdullahi, Y., Bhardwaj, A., Rahila, J., Anand, P., & Kandepu, K. (2023). Development of Automatic Change-Over with Auto-Start Timer and Artificial Intelligent Generator. *FMDB Transactions on Sustainable Energy Sequence, 1*(1), 11–26.

Alsheikh, M. A., Basar, T. A., & Tepe, K. E. (2019). Intelligent Data Analytics for Internet of Things-Based Applications. *IEEE Access : Practical Innovations, Open Solutions, 7*, 16825–16833.

Anand, P. P., Sulthan, N., Jayanth, P., & Deepika, A. A. (2023). A Creating Musical Compositions Through Recurrent Neural Networks: An Approach for Generating Melodic Creations. *FMDB Transactions on Sustainable Computing Systems, 1*(2), 54–64.

Angeline, R., Aarthi, S., Regin, R., & Rajest, S. S. (2023). Dynamic intelligence-driven engineering flooding attack prediction using ensemble learning. In *Advances in Artificial and Human Intelligence in the Modern Era* (pp. 109–124). IGI Global. doi:10.4018/979-8-3693-1301-5.ch006

Arslan, F., Singh, B., Sharma, D. K., Regin, R., Steffi, R., & Rajest, S. S. (2021). Optimization technique approach to resolve food sustainability problems. *2021 International Conference on Computational Intelligence and Knowledge Economy (ICCIKE)*. IEEE. 10.1109/ICCIKE51210.2021.9410735

Aryal, A., Stricklin, I., Behzadirad, M., Branch, D. W., Siddiqui, A., & Busani, T. (2022). High-quality dry etching of LiNbO3 assisted by proton substitution through H2-plasma surface treatment. *Nanomaterials (Basel, Switzerland), 12*(16), 2836. doi:10.3390/nano12162836 PMID:36014702

Bansal, V., Bhardwaj, A., Singh, J., Verma, D., Tiwari, M., & Siddi, S. (2023). Using artificial intelligence to integrate machine learning, fuzzy logic, and the IOT as A cybersecurity system. *2023 3rd International Conference on Advance Computing and Innovative Technologies in Engineering (ICACITE)*. IEEE.

Bansal, V., Pandey, S., Shukla, S. K., Singh, D., Rathod, S. A., & Gonzáles, J. L. A. (2022). A frame work of security attacks, issues classifications and configuration strategy for IoT networks for the successful implementation. *2022 5th International Conference on Contemporary Computing and Informatics (IC3I)*. IEEE.

Bhardwaj, A., Pattnayak, J., Prasad Gangodkar, D., Rana, A., Shilpa, N., & Tiwari, P. (2023). An integration of wireless communications and artificial intelligence for autonomous vehicles for the successful communication to achieve the destination. *2023 3rd International Conference on Advance Computing and Innovative Technologies in Engineering (ICACITE)*. IEEE.

Chaturvedi, A., Bhardwaj, A., Singh, D., Pant, B., Gonzáles, J. L. A., & Firos. (2022). Integration of DL on multi-carrier non-orthogonal multiple access system with simultaneous wireless information and power transfer. *2022 11th International Conference on System Modeling & Advancement in Research Trends (SMART)*. IEEE.

Cirillo, S., Polese, G., Salerno, D., Simone, B., & Solimando, G. (2023). Towards Flexible Voice Assistants: Evaluating Privacy and Security Needs in IoT-enabled Smart Homes. *FMDB Transactions on Sustainable Computer Letters*, *1*(1), 25–32.

Das, D. S., Gangodkar, D., Singh, R., Vijay, P., Bhardwaj, A., & Semwal, A. (2022). Comparative analysis of skin cancer prediction using neural networks and transfer learning. *2022 5th International Conference on Contemporary Computing and Informatics (IC3I)*. IEEE.

Deng, X., Jiang, C., & Chen, T. (2020). DINO: DETR with Improved DeNoising Anchor Boxes for End-to-End Object Detection. *Communications Magazine*, *57*, 19–25.

Devi, B. T., & Rajasekaran, R. (2023). A Comprehensive Review on Deepfake Detection on Social Media Data. *FMDB Transactions on Sustainable Computing Systems*, *1*(1), 11–20.

Gaayathri, R. S., Rajest, S. S., Nomula, V. K., & Regin, R. (2023). Bud-D: Enabling Bidirectional Communication with ChatGPT by adding Listening and Speaking Capabilities. *FMDB Transactions on Sustainable Computer Letters*, *1*(1), 49–63.

Goswami, C., Das, A., Ogaili, K. I., Verma, V. K., Singh, V., & Sharma, D. K. (2022). Device to device communication in 5G network using device-centric resource allocation algorithm. *2022 4th International Conference on Inventive Research in Computing Applications (ICIRCA)*. IEEE.

Gunturu, V., Bansal, V., Sathe, M., Kumar, A., Gehlot, A., & Pant, B. (2023). Wireless communications implementation using blockchain as well as distributed type of IOT. *2023 International Conference on Artificial Intelligence and Smart Communication (AISC)*. IEEE. 10.1109/AISC56616.2023.10085249

Hussain, S. A., Raza, M., & Riaz, F. (2020). An AI-Based Visual Aid With Integrated Reading Assistant for the Completely Blind. *IEEE Access : Practical Innovations, Open Solutions*, *8*, 169740–169749.

Jeba, J. A., Bose, S. R., & Boina, R. (2023). Exploring Hybrid Multi-View Multimodal for Natural Language Emotion Recognition Using Multi-Source Information Learning Model. *FMDB Transactions on Sustainable Computer Letters*, *1*(1), 12–24.

Kanyimama, W. (2023). Design of A Ground Based Surveillance Network for Modibbo Adama University, Yola. *FMDB Transactions on Sustainable Computing Systems*, *1*(1), 32–43.

Kosuru, V. S. R., & Venkitaraman, A. K. (2022). Developing a deep Q-learning and neural network framework for trajectory planning. *European Journal of Engineering and Technology Research*, *7*(6), 148–157. doi:10.24018/ejeng.2022.7.6.2944

Krishna Das, J., Das, A., & Rosak-Szyrocka, J. (2022). A hybrid deep learning technique for sentiment analysis in E-learning platform with natural language processing. *2022 International Conference on Software, Telecommunications and Computer Networks (SoftCOM)*. IEEE. 10.23919/SoftCOM55329.2022.9911232

Kumar, K. S., Yadav, D., Joshi, S. K., Chakravarthi, M. K., Jain, A. K., & Tripathi, V. (2022). Blockchain technology with applications to distributed control and cooperative robotics. *2022 5th International Conference on Contemporary Computing and Informatics (IC3I)*. IEEE.

Kumar Jain, A. (2022). Multi-Cloud Computing & Why do we need to Embrace it. *International Journal of Engineering Research & Technology (Ahmedabad)*, *11*(09), 1–06.

Li, Z., Wang, Y., Zhang, N., Zhang, Y., Zhao, Z., Xu, D., & Gao, Y. (2022). Deep learning-based object detection techniques for remote sensing images: A survey. *Remote Sensing (Basel)*, *14*(10), 2385. doi:10.3390/rs14102385

Lodha, S., Malani, H., & Bhardwaj, A. K. (2023). Performance Evaluation of Vision Transformers for Diagnosis of Pneumonia. *FMDB Transactions on Sustainable Computing Systems*, *1*(1), 21–31.

Oak, R., Du, M., Yan, D., Takawale, H., & Amit, I. (2019). Malware detection on highly imbalanced data through sequence modeling. *Proceedings of the 12th ACM Workshop on Artificial Intelligence and Security*. New York, NY, USA: ACM. 10.1145/3338501.3357374

Ogunmola, G. A., Singh, B., Sharma, D. K., Regin, R., Rajest, S. S., & Singh, N. (2021). Involvement of distance measure in assessing and resolving efficiency environmental obstacles. *2021 International Conference on Computational Intelligence and Knowledge Economy (ICCIKE)*. IEEE. 10.1109/ICCIKE51210.2021.9410765

Paldi, R. L., Aryal, A., Behzadirad, M., Busani, T., Siddiqui, A., & Wang, H. (2021). Nanocomposite-seeded single-domain growth of lithium niobate thin films for photonic applications. *Conference on Lasers and Electro-Optics*. Washington, D.C.: Optica Publishing Group. 10.1364/CLEO_SI.2021.STh4J.3

Rajasekaran, N., Jagatheesan, S. M., Krithika, S., & Albanchez, J. S. (2023). Development and Testing of Incorporated ASM with MVP Architecture Model for Android Mobile App Development. *FMDB Transactions on Sustainable Computing Systems*, *1*(2), 65–76.

Rajest, S. S., Singh, B., Obaid, A. J., Regin, R., & Chinnusamy, K. (2023b). Advances in artificial and human intelligence in the modern era. *Advances in Computational Intelligence and Robotics*. doi:10.4018/979-8-3693-1301-5

Rajest, S. S., Singh, B. J., Obaid, A., Regin, R., & Chinnusamy, K. (2023a). Recent developments in machine and human intelligence. *Advances in Computational Intelligence and Robotics*. doi:10.4018/978-1-6684-9189-8

Regin, R., Khanna, A. A., Krishnan, V., Gupta, M., & Bose, R. S., & Rajest, S. S. (2023a). Information design and unifying approach for secured data sharing using attribute-based access control mechanisms. In Recent Developments in Machine and Human Intelligence (pp. 256–276). IGI Global.

Regin, R., T, S., George, S. R., Bhattacharya, M., Datta, D., & Priscila, S. S. (2023b). Development of predictive model of diabetic using supervised machine learning classification algorithm of ensemble voting. *International Journal of Bioinformatics Research and Applications*, *19*(3), 10057044. doi:10.1504/IJBRA.2023.10057044

Sajini, S., Reddi, L. T., Regin, R., & Rajest, S. S. (2023). A Comparative Analysis of Routing Protocols for Efficient Data Transmission in Vehicular Ad Hoc Networks (VANETs). *FMDB Transactions on Sustainable Computing Systems*, *1*(1), 1–10.

Salem, A. M., Eraqi, H., & Eldib, M. (2019). GuideDogNet: A Deep Learning Model for Guiding the Blind in Walking Environments. *IEEE Access : Practical Innovations, Open Solutions*, *7*, 116198–116208.

Saxena, D., & Chaudhary, S. (2023). Predicting Brain Diseases from FMRI-Functional Magnetic Resonance Imaging with Machine Learning Techniques for Early Diagnosis and Treatment. *FMDB Transactions on Sustainable Computer Letters, 1*(1), 33–48.

Sharma, D. K., Jalil, N. A., Regin, R., Rajest, S. S., Tummala, R. K., & Thangadurai. (2021a). Predicting network congestion with machine learning. *2021 2nd International Conference on Smart Electronics and Communication (ICOSEC)*. IEEE.

Sharma, D. K., Singh, B., Raja, M., Regin, R., & Rajest, S. S. (2021b). An Efficient Python Approach for Simulation of Poisson Distribution. *2021 7th International Conference on Advanced Computing and Communication Systems (ICACCS)*. IEEE.

Sharma, D. K., Singh, B., Regin, R., Steffi, R., & Chakravarthi, M. K. (2021c). Efficient Classification for Neural Machines Interpretations based on Mathematical models. *2021 7th International Conference on Advanced Computing and Communication Systems (ICACCS)*. IEEE.

Sharma, K., Singh, B., Herman, E., Regine, R., Rajest, S. S., & Mishra, V. P. (2021d). Maximum information measure policies in reinforcement learning with deep energy-based model. *2021 International Conference on Computational Intelligence and Knowledge Economy (ICCIKE)*. IEEE. 10.1109/ICCIKE51210.2021.9410756

Shifat, A. S. M. Z., Stricklin, I., Chityala, R. K., Aryal, A., Esteves, G., Siddiqui, A., & Busani, T. (2023). Vertical etching of scandium aluminum nitride thin films using TMAH solution. *Nanomaterials (Basel, Switzerland), 13*(2), 274. doi:10.3390/nano13020274 PMID:36678027

Sivapriya, G. B. V., Ganesh, U. G., Pradeeshwar, V., Dharshini, M., & Al-Amin, M. (2023). Crime Prediction and Analysis Using Data Mining and Machine Learning: A Simple Approach that Helps Predictive Policing. *FMDB Transactions on Sustainable Computer Letters, 1*(2), 64–75.

Sohlot, J., Teotia, P., Govinda, K., Rangineni, S., & Paramasivan, P. (2023). A Hybrid Approach on Fertilizer Resource Optimization in Agriculture Using Opposition-Based Harmony Search with Manta Ray Foraging Optimization. *FMDB Transactions on Sustainable Computing Systems, 1*(1), 44–53.

Sonnad, S., Sathe, M., Basha, D. K., Bansal, V., Singh, R., & Singh, D. P. (2022). The integration of connectivity and system integrity approaches using internet of things (IoT) for enhancing network security. *2022 5th International Conference on Contemporary Computing and Informatics (IC3I)*. IEEE.

Srivastava, D. K., & Roychoudhury, B. (2020). Words are important: A textual content based identity resolution scheme across multiple online social networks. *Knowledge-Based Systems, 195*, 105624. doi:10.1016/j.knosys.2020.105624

Srivastava, D. K., & Roychoudhury, B. (2021). Understanding the Factors that Influence Adoption of Privacy Protection Features in Online Social Networks. *Journal of Global Information Technology Management, 24*(3), 164–182. doi:10.1080/1097198X.2021.1954416

Suthar, V., Bansal, V., Reddy, C. S., Gonzáles, J. L. A., Singh, D., & Singh, D. P. (2022). Machine Learning Adoption in Blockchain-Based Smart Applications. *2022 5th International Conference on Contemporary Computing and Informatics (IC3I)*. IEEE.

Uike, D., Agarwalla, S., Bansal, V., Chakravarthi, M. K., Singh, R., & Singh, P. (2022). Investigating the role of block chain to secure identity in IoT for industrial automation. *2022 11th International Conference on System Modeling & Advancement in Research Trends (SMART)*. IEEE.

Uthiramoorthy, A., Bhardwaj, A., Singh, J., Pant, K., Tiwari, M., & Gonzáles, J. L. A. (2023). A Comprehensive review on Data Mining Techniques in managing the Medical Data cloud and its security constraints with the maintained of the communication networks. *2023 International Conference on Artificial Intelligence and Smart Communication (AISC)*. IEEE. 10.1109/AISC56616.2023.10085161

Venkitaraman, A. K., & Kosuru, V. S. R. (2023). Hybrid deep learning mechanism for charging control and management of Electric Vehicles. *European Journal of Electrical Engineering and Computer Science*, 7(1), 38–46. doi:10.24018/ejece.2023.7.1.485

Zhang, K., Qiu, J., & Luo, S. (2020). Smart Glass System Using Deep Learning for the Blind and Visually Impaired. *IEEE Access : Practical Innovations, Open Solutions*, 8, 52437–52446.

Chapter 17
Fine–Grained Independent Approach for Workout Classification Using Integrated Metric Transfer Learning

S. Rubin Bose
SRM Institute of Science and Technology, India

S. Arunagiri
SRM Institute of Science and Technology, India

M. Abu Shahil Sirajudheen
SRM Institute of Science and Technology, India

R. Regin
SRM Institute of Science and Technology, India

G. Kirupanandan
SRM Institute of Science and Technology, India

S. Suman Rajest
https://orcid.org/0000-0001-8315-3747
Dhaanish Ahmed College of Engineering, India

ABSTRACT

Physical activity helps manage weight and stay healthy. It becomes more critical during a pandemic since outside activities are restricted. Using tiny wearable sensors and cutting-edge machine intelligence to track physical activity can help fight obesity. This study introduces machine learning and wearable sensor methods to track physical activity. Daily physical activities are typically unstructured and unplanned, and sitting or standing may be more common than others (walking stairs upstairs down). No activity categorization system has examined how class imbalance affects machine learning classifier performance. Fitness can boost cardiovascular capacity, focus, obesity prevention, and life expectancy. Dumbbells, yoga mats, and horizontal bars are used for home fitness. Home gym-goers utilise social media to learn fitness, but its effectiveness is limited.

DOI: 10.4018/979-8-3693-0502-7.ch017

1. INTRODUCTION

"Fine-grained Independent Approach for Workout Classification using Integrated Metric Transfer Learning" is a machine learning technique aiming to classify workouts accurately based on subtle differences. This approach is "fine-grained" because it can identify specific exercises being performed, and it is "independent" because it does not rely on external data or pre-existing models (Anand et al., 2023). The approach involves integrating metric transfer learning, which means that knowledge learned from one type of workout is transferred to another to improve accuracy. Multiple metrics or measures are used to improve the accuracy of the model (Abdullahi et al., 2023).

Overall, this technique has the potential to be useful in fitness tracking, as it can provide more detailed information on the types of exercises being performed during a workout (Aziz & Sarwar, 2023). This project aims to develop a machine learning model to accurately classify different workouts, focusing on identifying subtle differences between exercises (Angeline et al., 2023). The ultimate goal is to improve fitness tracking by providing more detailed information on the exercise types performed during a workout (Bhanushali, 2023). This can help individuals track their progress more effectively and provide personalized recommendations for future workouts (Farooq & Khan, 2022). Additionally, this approach has the potential to be useful in research settings, such as in sports science, where detailed analysis of specific exercises can provide valuable insights (Cirillo et al., 2023).

The paper focuses on two main aspects of sports fitness detection: (1) the use of digital image processing to track and analyze sports activities and (2) the use of intelligent image processing to analyze body movements during physical exercise (Devi & Rajasekaran, 2023). The authors argue that combining these two approaches makes it possible to create a more accurate and comprehensive picture of an individual's fitness level and track their progress over time (Farooq & Khan, 2023). The paper also discusses the use of IoT technology in sports fitness detection, particularly in the context of wearable devices and sensors (Bhardwaj et al., 2023). These devices can collect data on an individual's physical activity and transmit it to a central database, which can be analyzed using digital and intelligent image processing techniques (Cui et al., 2023). The chapter proposes a comprehensive approach to sports fitness detection that combines digital and intelligent image processing with IoT technology to provide a more accurate and detailed picture of an individual's fitness level (Gaayathri et al., 2023). This approach can potentially revolutionize how we track and monitor our physical activity and could have more significant implications for sports science and healthcare.

2. LITERATURE REVIEW

Ding, & Ren, (2019) proposed algorithm aims to improve the accuracy of medical exercise rehabilitation image segmentation by using the HFCNN to learn and extract the features of the image and IoT technology to integrate real-time data from sensors and wearable devices, such as heart rate monitors and motion trackers, to provide additional information for the segmentation process. The authors demonstrate the effectiveness of the proposed algorithm through experiments on a dataset of medical exercise rehabilitation images. The results show that the HFCNN-based segmentation algorithm outperforms traditional methods and that the addition of IoT data further improves the accuracy of the segmentation.

A convolutional neural network (CNN) architecture is suggested by Gupta (2021) as a means to learn and extract features from the raw sensor data acquired by the wearable device. In order to categorise the activity, a SoftMax classifier is employed with the features that have been extracted. Research using a freely accessible dataset of wearable sporting activities proves the efficacy of the suggested approach. The results demonstrate that the suggested strategy accomplishes high rates of accuracy for many sorts of activities, and it outperforms conventional approaches to activity classification.

Guo et al., (2020) proposed model is designed to detect the location of each player in the video frame using a region-based CNN. Using a fine-tuned CNN, the second part of the model is then used to classify each detected player into one of the two teams based on their jersey color. The authors demonstrated the effectiveness of the proposed model through experiments on an ice hockey video footage dataset. The results show that the proposed model achieves high accuracy rates for player detection and team classification.

Removing fences from photographs is an issue that can be addressed by Matsui & Ikehara (2020). It can be time-consuming and requires human editing. A convolutional neural network (CNN) is trained and used to extract features from the image's fence and background areas in the suggested approach. After the features have been extracted, a fence mask is created and applied to the original image in order to eliminate it. The authors conduct experiments on a collection of photos with fences to prove that the proposed strategy is effective. With its high accuracy rates, the suggested method proves to be superior to more conventional approaches of fence removal.

An strategy was proposed by Mendez-Rial et al. (2012) to tackle the problem of imperfect or damaged photographs captured by orbital missions, which can impede scientific investigation and study. The suggested technique learns and extracts features from reference photographs of the same spot on Earth using a deep learning technique. The orbital image is then enhanced and made more comprehensive by using these features to fill in sections that are either absent or have suffered from degradation. As an example of how the suggested strategy works, the authors conduct experiments using a dataset of orbital photos taken from Mars. Images are improved and surface features of the planets can be analysed more accurately using the suggested method, according to the results.

Döllner, (2020) present the challenge of processing large-scale 3D point cloud data for object recognition and scene understanding applications. The proposed method uses a dynamic graph CNN architecture designed to handle the dynamic nature of 3D point cloud data. The architecture includes a spatial-temporal graph convolutional layer and a temporal pooling layer, enabling the network to learn and extract features from the data's spatial and temporal dimensions.

Yi et al., (2021) present the challenge of analyzing the visual characteristics of ceramics, which is a complex and time-consuming task that requires expertise and knowledge of art history. The proposed application, called Smart Culture Lens, uses a deep learning approach to learn and extract features from digital images of ceramics. The application then uses these features to analyze the visual elements of the ceramics, including color, texture, and pattern.

Shi et al., (2022) address the challenge of accurately categorizing scenes based on their visual features, which is a complex task due to the high variability in the appearance of scenes. The proposed model uses a deep learning approach to learn visually sensitive features that capture the most discriminative information for scene categorization.

Alharthi et al., (2019) analyze gait patterns for various applications in healthcare, rehabilitation, and athletic training, the authors set out to solve this problem. It is suggested that floor sensors be used to record the spatiotemporal characteristics of gait signatures and that deep learning techniques be used to identify and extract features from the sensor data.

Goyal et al., (2019) address the challenge of accurately detecting and localizing diabetic foot ulcers, which is important for early diagnosis and effective treatment. The proposed method uses machine learning and computer vision techniques to learn and extract features from images of diabetic foot ulcers captured by mobile devices.

Hu et al., (2022) present the challenge of ecological restoration on slopes, which is important for preventing soil erosion and promoting biodiversity. The proposed method involves using image classification to identify vegetation coverage on slopes and constructing a sports fitness index to evaluate the effectiveness of ecological restoration.

Ahamed et al., (2023) compare the challenge of efficiently processing large amounts of data generated by IoT devices during the exercise and fitness process. The proposed method uses machine learning and data analytics techniques to extract meaningful insights from the data and provide personalized user recommendations.

3. METHODOLOGY

Integrated Metric Transfer Learning is a machine learning approach that combines transfer learning and metric learning to classify objects or images more accurately and efficiently. Transfer learning involves leveraging pre-trained neural networks that have already learned general features from large datasets, such as ImageNet, and fine-tuning them for a specific task, such as image classification. Metric learning involves learning a distance metric that can map input features to a metric space where similar samples are close to each other and dissimilar samples are far apart (Rangineni et al., 1973).

In Integrated Metric Transfer Learning, the pre-trained neural network is fine-tuned on a smaller dataset to adapt to the specific interest task (Shashank & Sharma, 2023). Then, a metric learning layer is added to the fine-tuned neural network to learn a distance metric that can effectively separate different classes. This integrated approach allows the model to learn both discrimination and generalizable features, which can lead to improved performance on a wide range of classification tasks.

The proposed model is trained using a standard dataset. This custom-crated dataset contains eight classes of various workout images: bench press, biceps curl, chest fly machine, deadlift, incline bench press, pulldown, push-up, and triceps pushdown. Experimental results confirm that Integrated Metric Transfer Learning was the best algorithm. The accuracy will be extremely high (Fig.1).

- Data collection: Collect a large dataset of workout images or videos with various exercises and body postures.
- Data preprocessing: Preprocess the data by resizing, cropping, and normalizing the images or videos. Split the dataset into training, validation, and testing sets (Jeba et al., 2023).
- Pre-training a feature extractor: Pre-train a deep neural network, such as VGG, ResNet, or Inception, on a large dataset, such as ImageNet, to extract high-level features from input images or videos.
- Fine-tuning the feature extractor: Fine-tuning is the pre-trained feature exactor on the training set of workout images or videos using transfer learning to adapt the features to the new dataset (Sarwar et al., 2023).

Figure 1. Functional block diagram

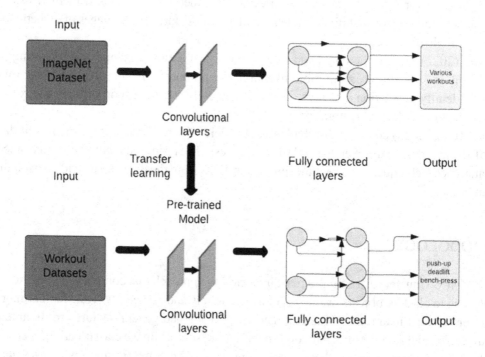

- Metric learning: Add a metric learning layer, such as triplet loss or contrastive loss, on top of the fine-tuned feature extractor to learn a distance metric that maps input features to a metric space, where similar samples are close to each other and dissimilar samples are far apart.
- Training the classification layer: Train a classification layer, such as a fully connected neural network or support vector machine, on top of the learned metric distance to perform the final classification task.
- Evaluation: Evaluate the model's performance on the testing set by calculating various metrics, such as accuracy, precision, recall, and F1 score.
- Deployment: Deploy the model in a real-world scenario, such as a mobile application or a smartwatch, to classify workouts in real time.

The process involves using pre-trained models as a starting point for the target task rather than training the model from scratch (Shashank, 2023). The pre-trained models are often trained on a large dataset for a different but related task (Sivapriya et al., 2023). The learned features from these models are then used to initialize the parameters of the target task model (Lodha et al., 2023).

The initialization of the parameters is based on the transfer of knowledge between the source and target tasks (Nagaraj et al., 2023). This transfer is performed by adjusting the weights of the pre-trained model to fit the new target task. The adjustment is done by fine-tuning the pre-trained model on the target task data (Kulbir, 2023).

Integrating the transfer learning technique with the metric learning approach further enhances the model's performance (Patel & Bhanushali, 2023). Metric learning is a technique that learns a distance metric between pairs of data points, allowing the model to better distinguish between different classes of data (Qadeer et al., 2023). In integrated metric transfer learning, the distance metric learned from the source task is transferred to the target task, allowing for improved classification performance on the target task (Parate et al., 2023).

Overall, Integrated Metric Transfer Learning is a powerful technique that can improve the performance of deep learning models by leveraging the knowledge learned from related tasks (Rajest et al., 2023a). It is particularly useful when the target task has a limited amount of data, as it allows the model to use the available data better using knowledge learned from the source task (fig.2).

Figure 2. Inception V3 pre-trained model

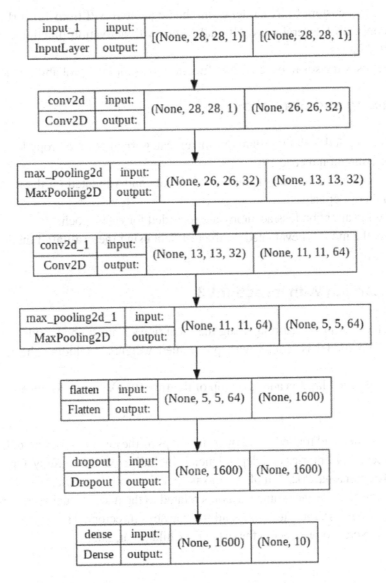

3.1. Data Preparation

- The code assumes that the dataset is organized into separate directories for each class within a parent directory named "Dataset."
- The code uses the **ImageDataGenerator** class from TensorFlow to perform data augmentation and rescale the pixel values to the range of [0, 1].
- The dataset is split into training and validation subsets using the **image_dataset_from_directory** function, with 90% used for training and 10% for validation.
- Data augmentation techniques such as random flipping, adding Gaussian noise, adjusting contrast, and applying random zoom are applied to the training data.

3.2. Model Architecture

- The code defines a custom CNN model using the Sequential API from TensorFlow.
- The model consists of several convolutional layers with activation functions, max-pooling, and fully connected layers.
- The final layer uses the softmax activation function to output the probabilities for each class.

3.3. Model Training and Evaluation

- The model is compiled with the Adam optimizer, categorical cross-entropy loss function, and accuracy as the evaluation metric.
- The model is trained on the augmented training data and validated on the validation data for a specified number of epochs.
- The training and validation loss/accuracy are recorded for each epoch.
- After training, the model is evaluated on the test data using the **evaluate** function to compute the loss and accuracy.

3.4. Transfer Learning With InceptionV3

- The code performs transfer learning using the InceptionV3 pre-trained model.
- The InceptionV3 model is loaded with pre-trained weights, excluding the top (classification) layers.
- A new fully connected layer is added on top of the InceptionV3 base, followed by a softmax layer for classification.

The model is compiled and trained using the same steps as the custom CNN model. The code begins by importing the necessary libraries and dependencies, including pandas, numpy, OpenCV, Matplotlib, and TensorFlow (Kanyimama, 2023). It also imports specific modules and classes from these libraries for later use. Next, the code defines some variables related to the dataset, such as the image dimensions (height, width, and channels), the batch size, and the dataset's directory. The code then uses the ImageDataGenerator from Keras to preprocess the data (Kaushikkumar, 2023).

It rescales the image pixels to a range of 0 to 1 and splits the data into training and validation sets. It also applies data augmentation techniques such as random flipping, adding Gaussian noise, adjusting contrast, and zooming to increase the diversity of the training data (Rangineni et al., 2023). After preprocessing the data, the code creates a function to display random images from the dataset. It uses Matplotlib to show a 3x3 grid of randomly selected images from the training data (Qin et al., 2023). Next, the code defines a function to create a neural network model using the Sequential API from Keras (Latha et al., 2022).

The model consists of several Conv2D layers with ReLU activation, max-pooling layers, a flattened layer, and several fully connected (Dense) layers with different activation functions (Regin et al., 2023a). The model is compiled with a categorical cross-entropy loss function, the Adam optimizer, and accuracy as the evaluation metric (Thammareddi et al., 2023). The code then fits the model to the training data using the fit() function, specifying the number of epochs for training. It also validates the model's performance on the validation data during training (Rajest et al., 2023b).

After training the model, the code plots the training and validation loss and accuracy over the epochs using Matplotlib. The code also defines a function to predict the class of an image using the trained model (Regin et al., 2023b). It loads an image, resizes it, normalizes its pixel values, and reshapes it to match the input shape of the model. The model predicts the class of the image, and the corresponding class name is printed.

Next, the code creates a transfer learning model using the InceptionV3 per-trained model from Keras. It freezes the layers of the pre-trained model to prevent their weights from being updated during training. It then adds a custom output layer to the model and compiles it (Sajini et al., 2023). The transfer learning model is trained on the training data, and its performance is evaluated on the validation data. Early stopping is implemented to stop training if the validation loss does not improve after a certain number of epochs. Finally, the code plots the transfer learning model's training and validation loss and accuracy.

4. EXPERIMENTAL SETUP

Select Source and Target Domains: Choose a source domain and a target domain that have different data distributions but share some common underlying concepts. For example, the source domain could be image classification using natural images, while the target domain could be medical image classification. Preprocess Data: Preprocess the data from both the source and target domains. This may include tasks such as data cleaning, normalization, resizing, and feature extraction, depending on the specific characteristics of the domains. Design Network Architecture: Design a suitable network architecture for integrated metric learning. This could include a base network that extracts features from the input data and a metric learning component that learns a shared metric space. Popular metrics learning component choices include Siamese, triplet, or contrastive loss-based networks. Prepare Training Data: Prepare training data for the integrated metric learning model. This involves creating training pairs or triplets of data samples from the source and target domains. Pairs or triplets should be carefully constructed to reflect samples' underlying similarity or dissimilarity.

Define Loss Function: Define a loss function that captures the desired similarity or dissimilarity between the training pairs or triplets samples. This loss function should encourage the model to learn a metric space where samples from the same class or concept are close while samples from different classes or concepts are far apart (Sohlot et al., 2023).

Train the Model: Train the integrated metric learning model using the prepared training data and the defined loss function. The training process involves optimizing the network parameters to minimize the loss function.

Evaluate Performance: Evaluate the performance of the trained model on both the source and target domains (Saxena & Chaudhary, 2023). This can be done by measuring classification accuracy, precision, recall, or other appropriate metrics. Comparing the model's performance on the source and target domains provides insights into the effectiveness of the integrated metric transfer learning approach. Fine-tuning and Hyperparameter Tuning: Depending on the results obtained, fine-tune the model or adjust hyperparameters to improve performance further. This may involve domain adaptation, regularization, or data augmentation techniques.

Repeat and Compare: Repeat steps 4 to 8 with different choices of source and target domains, network architectures, loss functions, and hyperparameters. Compare the results to understand the impact of different factors on the integrated metric transfer learning process. Analysis and Conclusion: Analyze the results obtained from the experiments and conclude the effectiveness of integrated metric transfer learning for the chosen domains. Identify any limitations or challenges encountered during the experiments and suggest areas for future research.

5. RESULTS AND ANALYSIS

With the help of the algorithm, models for image classification tasks are trained and assessed. The performance of the models on the test data is evaluated, and areas for improvement can be found using the evaluation metrics, classification report, and confusion matrix. With an IoU threshold of 0.65, the performance is assessed for the models at various epochs (25, 35, and 45).

The evaluation metrics (loss and accuracy) are printed for the custom CNN and InceptionV3-based transfer learning models. The classification report provides a detailed evaluation of the model's performance, including precision, recall, F1-score, and support for each class. The confusion matrix visualizes the model's performance regarding true positive, true negative, false positive, and false negative predictions for each class.

5.1. Loss and Accuracy

- Loss: The loss value indicates how well the model performs during training. A lower loss value indicates better performance.
- Accuracy: Accuracy measures the percentage of correctly classified images from the total number of images. Higher accuracy indicates better performance.

5.2. Classification Report

- Precision: A model's accuracy in detecting positive samples is known as its precision. It is the ratio of positive results that were actually detected to the total number of positive and negative results.

- Recall: One way to evaluate a model's performance is by looking at its recall, which is also called its sensitivity or true positive rate. To get it, take the total number of positive and negative results and divide it by the number of real positives.
- F1-score: The F1-score is the harmonic mean of precision and recall. It provides a single metric that balances both precision and recall.
- Support: Support is the number of occurrences of each class in the test dataset.

5.3. Confusion Matrix

- An in-depth analysis of how the model's predictions stack up against the actual labels is given by a confusion matrix. You may see the total number of correct classifications, negative classifications, false classifications, and true positives for each category. In doing so, it becomes easier to spot any misclassifications and evaluate the model's performance across different classes.
- To compute these performance metrics, refer to the modifications provided earlier in the code. The evaluation metrics, classification report, and confusion matrix can be obtained by following the instructions. These metrics will help you assess the model's performance and gain insights into its accuracy, precision, recall, and potential misclassifications.

Table 1. Performance metrics obtained using IMTL model

CNN model	Train Loss	Train Accuracy	Val Loss	Val Accuracy
25 epochs (IMTL)	1.1144	0.7126	1.1522	0.7040
50 epochs (IMTL)	0.7461	0.7976	0.7189	0.8007
100 epochs (IMTL)	0.7768	0.8014	0.7683	0.8414

The performance metrics that were acquired using IMTL are shown in Table 1. With an increasing number of epochs, the proposed IMTL achieved good accuracy on both the training and value datasets. For epochs greater than fifty, the performance measures remain rather constant. A model trained for 100 epochs underperformed one trained for 50 epochs.

Training and Validation Loss and Accuracy: The code trains the custom and transfer learning models on the training data and evaluates their performance on the validation data. It keeps track of each epoch's training, validation loss, and accuracy. These values are likely stored in the history and inception_history variables for the custom and transfer learning models.

Evaluation Metrics: The code uses the evaluate() function to calculate and store the evaluation metrics of the models on the test data. The evaluation metrics typically include the loss value and the accuracy of the models on the test data. The evaluation results may be stored in variables such as evaluate.

Plotting Results: The code includes Matplotlib commands to plot the training, validation loss, and accuracy over the epochs for both the custom and transfer learning models. The plots provide a visual representation of the model's performance during training.

Predicted Class: The code includes a function predict_image() that takes an image as input and predicts its class using the trained models. The predicted class is likely printed or displayed when calling this function on specific images (Fig.3).

Figure 3. Training loss and accuracy on dataset in IMTL model

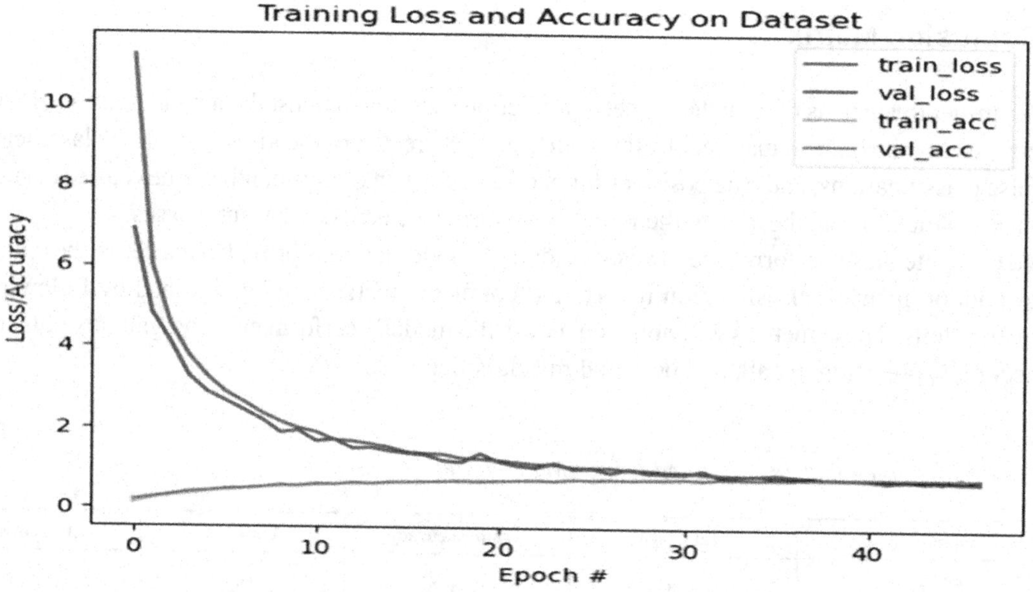

6. CONCLUSION

This chapter presents a novel approach for identifying workout exercises reliably and effectively. The technique integrates transfer and metric learning into a single integrated framework to outperform classic machine learning algorithms and cutting-edge deep learning models. The suggested method is robust in real-world circumstances because it is built to manage different data changes like noise and occlusion. The approach successfully classifies fine-grained workout exercises using integrated metric transfer learning, opening up fitness and activity tracking applications. The potential effects of this strategy go beyond the creation of intelligent wearable gadgets that can identify and monitor various exercises carried out by users. By offering individualized feedback depending on each user's workout objectives, this technology can improve the efficacy and efficiency of fitness training. According to the report, the proposed method illustrates the potential for integrated metric transfer learning in various fields that call for precise and effective classification of fine-grained objects and opens up new avenues for future research in workout classification. The paper outlines a promising line of research for classifying workouts and illustrates the potential use of integrated metric transfer learning in various contexts.

REFERENCES

Abdullahi, Y., Bhardwaj, A., Rahila, J., Anand, P., & Kandepu, K. (2023). Development of Automatic Change-Over with Auto-Start Timer and Artificial Intelligent Generator. *FMDB Transactions on Sustainable Energy Sequence*, *1*(1), 11–26.

Ahamed, B., Sellamuthu, S., Karri, P. N., Srinivas, I. V., Mohammed Zabeeulla, A. N., & Ashok Kumar, M. (2023). Design of an energy-efficient IOT device-assisted wearable sensor platform for healthcare data management. *Measurement. Sensors*, *30*(100928), 100928. doi:10.1016/j.measen.2023.100928

Alharthi, A. S., Yunas, S. U., & Ozanyan, K. B. (2019). Deep learning for monitoring of human gait: A review. *IEEE Sensors Journal*, *19*(21), 9575–9591. doi:10.1109/JSEN.2019.2928777

Anand, P. P., Sulthan, N., Jayanth, P., & Deepika, A. A. (2023). A Creating Musical Compositions Through Recurrent Neural Networks: An Approach for Generating Melodic Creations. *FMDB Transactions on Sustainable Computing Systems*, *1*(2), 54–64.

Angeline, R., Aarthi, S., Regin, R., & Rajest, S. S. (2023). Dynamic intelligence-driven engineering flooding attack prediction using ensemble learning. In *Advances in Artificial and Human Intelligence in the Modern Era* (pp. 109–124). IGI Global. doi:10.4018/979-8-3693-1301-5.ch006

Aziz, G., & Sarwar, S. (2023). Empirical Evidence of Environmental Technologies, Renewable Energy and Tourism to Minimize the Environmental Damages : Implication of Advanced Panel Analysis. *International Journal of Environmental Research and Public Health*, *20*(6), 5118. doi:10.3390/ijerph20065118 PMID:36982028

Bhanushali, A. (2023). Challenges and solutions in implementing continuous integration and continuous testing for agile quality assurance. *International Journal of Science and Research (Raipur, India)*, *12*(10), 1626–1644. doi:10.21275/SR231021114758

Bhardwaj, A. K., Rangineni, S., & Marupaka, D. (2023). Assessment of Technical Information Quality using Machine Learning. *International Journal of Computer Trends and Technology*, *71*(9), 33–40. doi:10.14445/22312803/IJCTT-V71I9P105

Cirillo, S., Polese, G., Salerno, D., Simone, B., & Solimando, G. (2023). Towards Flexible Voice Assistants: Evaluating Privacy and Security Needs in IoT-enabled Smart Homes. *FMDB Transactions on Sustainable Computer Letters*, *1*(1), 25–32.

Cui, Y., Aziz, G., Sarwar, S., Waheed, R., Mighri, Z., & Shahzad, U. (2023). Reinvestigate the significance of STRIPAT and extended STRIPAT: An inclusion of renewable energy and trade for gulf council countries. *Energy & Environment*, *0958305X231181671*. doi:10.1177/0958305X231181671

Devi, B. T., & Rajasekaran, R. (2023). A Comprehensive Review on Deepfake Detection on Social Media Data. *FMDB Transactions on Sustainable Computing Systems*, *1*(1), 11–20.

Ding, L., & Ren, H. (2019). Segmentation algorithm of medical exercise rehabilitation image based on HFCNN and IoT. *IEEE Access : Practical Innovations, Open Solutions*, *7*, 160829–160844. doi:10.1109/ACCESS.2019.2950960

Döllner, J. (2020). Geospatial artificial intelligence: Potentials of machine learning for 3D point clouds and geospatial digital twins. PFG –. *Journal of Photogrammetry, Remote Sensing and Geoinformation Science, 88*(1), 15–24. doi:10.100741064-020-00102-3

Farooq, M., & Khan, M. H. (2022). Signature-Based Intrusion Detection System in Wireless 6G IoT Networks. *Journal on Internet of Things, 4*(3), 155–168. doi:10.32604/jiot.2022.039271

Farooq, M., & Khan, M. H. (2023). Artificial Intelligence-Based Approach on Cyber Security Challenges and Opportunities in The Internet of Things & Edge Computing Devices. *International Journal of Engineering and Computer Science, 12*(7), 25763–25768. doi:10.18535/ijecs/v12i07.4744

Gaayathri, R. S., Rajest, S. S., Nomula, V. K., & Regin, R. (2023). Bud-D: Enabling Bidirectional Communication with ChatGPT by adding Listening and Speaking Capabilities. *FMDB Transactions on Sustainable Computer Letters, 1*(1), 49–63.

Goyal, M., Reeves, N. D., Rajbhandari, S., & Yap, M. H. (2019). Robust methods for real-time diabetic foot ulcer detection and localization on mobile devices. *IEEE Journal of Biomedical and Health Informatics, 23*(4), 1730–1741. doi:10.1109/JBHI.2018.2868656 PMID:30188841

Guo, T., Tao, K., Hu, Q., & Shen, Y. (2020). Detection of ice hockey players and teams via a two-phase cascaded CNN model. *IEEE Access : Practical Innovations, Open Solutions, 8*, 195062–195073. doi:10.1109/ACCESS.2020.3033580

Gupta, S. (2021). Deep learning based human activity recognition (HAR) using wearable sensor data. *International Journal of Information Management Data Insights, 1*(2), 100046. doi:10.1016/j.jjimei.2021.100046

Hu, J., Zhou, Q., Cao, Q., & Hu, J. (2022). Effects of ecological restoration measures on vegetation and soil properties in semi-humid sandy land on the southeast Qinghai-Tibetan Plateau, China. *Global Ecology and Conservation, 33*(e02000), e02000. doi:10.1016/j.gecco.2022.e02000

Jeba, J. A., Bose, S. R., & Boina, R. (2023). Exploring Hybrid Multi-View Multimodal for Natural Language Emotion Recognition Using Multi-Source Information Learning Model. *FMDB Transactions on Sustainable Computer Letters, 1*(1), 12–24.

Kanyimama, W. (2023). Design of A Ground Based Surveillance Network for Modibbo Adama University, Yola. *FMDB Transactions on Sustainable Computing Systems, 1*(1), 32–43.

Kaushikkumar, P. (2023). Credit Card Analytics: A Review of Fraud Detection and Risk Assessment Techniques. *International Journal of Computer Trends and Technology, 71*(10), 69–79. doi:10.14445/22312803/IJCTT-V71I10P109

Kulbir, S. (2023). Artificial Intelligence & Cloud in Healthcare: Analyzing Challenges and Solutions Within Regulatory Boundaries. *SSRG International Journal of Computer Science and Engineering, 10*(9), 1–9. doi:10.14445/23488387/IJCSE-V10I9P101

Latha, T., Patel, S., & Reddy, V. (2022). Analysis On Cybersecurity Threats in Modern Banking and Machine Learning Techniques For Fraud Detection. *The Review of Contemporary Scientific and Academic Studies, 3*(11).

Lodha, S., Malani, H., & Bhardwaj, A. K. (2023). Performance Evaluation of Vision Transformers for Diagnosis of Pneumonia. *FMDB Transactions on Sustainable Computing Systems, 1*(1), 21–31.

Matsui, T., & Ikehara, M. (2020). Single-image fence removal using deep convolutional neural network. *IEEE Access : Practical Innovations, Open Solutions, 8,* 38846–38854. doi:10.1109/AC-CESS.2019.2960087

Mendez-Rial, R., Calvino-Cancela, M., & Martin-Herrero, J. (2012). Anisotropic Inpainting of the Hypercube. *IEEE Geoscience and Remote Sensing Letters : A Publication of the IEEE Geoscience and Remote Sensing Society, 9*(2), 214–218. doi:10.1109/LGRS.2011.2164050

Nagaraj, B., Kalaivani, A., R, S. B., Akila, S., Sachdev, H. K., & N, S. K. (2023). The Emerging Role of Artificial intelligence in STEM Higher Education: A Critical review. *International Research Journal of Multidisciplinary Technovation,* 1–19. doi:10.54392/irjmt2351

Parate, S., Reddi, L. T., Agarwal, S., & Suryadevara, M. (2023). Analyzing the impact of open data ecosystems and standardized interfaces on product development and innovation. International Journal of Advanced Research in Science. *Tongxin Jishu,* 476–485. doi:10.48175/IJARSCT-13165

Patel, A., & Bhanushali, S. (2023). Evaluating regression testing performance through machine learning for test case reduction. *International Journal of Computer Engineering and Technology, 14*(3), 51–66.

Qadeer, A., Wasim, M., Ghazala, H., Rida, A., & Suleman, W. (2023). Emerging trends of green hydrogen and sustainable environment in the case of Australia. *Environmental Science and Pollution Research International, 30*(54), 115788–115804. Advance online publication. doi:10.100711356-023-30560-2 PMID:37889409

Qin, L., Aziz, G., Hussan, M. W., Qadeer, A., & Sarwar, S. (2023). Empirical evidence of fintech and green environment: Using the green finance as a mediating variable. *International Review of Economics and Finance, 89*(PA), 33–49. doi:10.1016/j.iref.2023.07.056

Rajest, S. S., Singh, B., Obaid, A. J., Regin, R., & Chinnusamy, K. (2023b). Advances in artificial and human intelligence in the modern era. *Advances in Computational Intelligence and Robotics.* doi:10.4018/979-8-3693-1301-5

Rajest, S. S., Singh, B. J., Obaid, A., Regin, R., & Chinnusamy, K. (2023a). Recent developments in machine and human intelligence. *Advances in Computational Intelligence and Robotics.* doi:10.4018/978-1-6684-9189-8

Rangineni, S., Bhanushali, A., Marupaka, D., Venkata, S., & Suryadevara, M. (1973). Analysis of Data Engineering Techniques With Data Quality in Multilingual Information Recovery. *International Journal on Computer Science and Engineering, 11*(10), 29–36.

Rangineni, S., Bhanushali, A., Suryadevara, M., Venkata, S., & Peddireddy, K. (2023). A Review on Enhancing Data Quality for Optimal Data Analytics Performance. *International Journal on Computer Science and Engineering, 11*(10), 51–58.

Regin, R., Khanna, A. A., Krishnan, V., Gupta, M., & Bose, R. S., & Rajest, S. S. (2023a). Information design and unifying approach for secured data sharing using attribute-based access control mechanisms. In Recent Developments in Machine and Human Intelligence (pp. 256–276). IGI Global.

Regin, R., T, S., George, S. R., Bhattacharya, M., Datta, D., & Priscila, S. S. (2023b). Development of predictive model of diabetic using supervised machine learning classification algorithm of ensemble voting. *International Journal of Bioinformatics Research and Applications*, 19(3), 10057044. doi:10.1504/IJBRA.2023.10057044

Sajini, S., Reddi, L. T., Regin, R., & Rajest, S. S. (2023). A Comparative Analysis of Routing Protocols for Efficient Data Transmission in Vehicular Ad Hoc Networks (VANETs). *FMDB Transactions on Sustainable Computing Systems*, 1(1), 1–10.

Sarwar, S., Aziz, G., & Kumar Tiwari, A. (2023). Implication of machine learning techniques to forecast the electricity price and carbon emission: Evidence from a hot region. *Geoscience Frontiers, xxxx*, 101647. doi:10.1016/j.gsf.2023.101647

Saxena, D., & Chaudhary, S. (2023). Predicting Brain Diseases from FMRI-Functional Magnetic Resonance Imaging with Machine Learning Techniques for Early Diagnosis and Treatment. *FMDB Transactions on Sustainable Computer Letters*, 1(1), 33–48.

Shashank, A. (2023). Graph Networks: Transforming Provider Affiliations for Enhanced Healthcare Management. *International Journal of Computer Trends and Technology*, 71(6), 86–90.

Shashank, A., & Sharma, S. (2023). Sachin Parate "Exploring the Untapped Potential of Synthetic data: A Comprehensive Review. *International Journal of Computer Trends and Technology*, 71(6), 86–90.

Shi, J., Zhu, H., Li, Y., Li, Y., & Du, S. (2022). Scene classification using deep networks combined with visual attention. *Journal of Sensors*, 2022, 1–9. doi:10.1155/2022/7191537

Sivapriya, G. B. V., Ganesh, U. G., Pradeeshwar, V., Dharshini, M., & Al-Amin, M. (2023). Crime Prediction and Analysis Using Data Mining and Machine Learning: A Simple Approach that Helps Predictive Policing. *FMDB Transactions on Sustainable Computer Letters*, 1(2), 64–75.

Sohlot, J., Teotia, P., Govinda, K., Rangineni, S., & Paramasivan, P. (2023). A Hybrid Approach on Fertilizer Resource Optimization in Agriculture Using Opposition-Based Harmony Search with Manta Ray Foraging Optimization. *FMDB Transactions on Sustainable Computing Systems*, 1(1), 44–53.

Thammareddi, L., Kuppam, M., Patel, K., Marupaka, D., & Bhanushali, A. (2023). An extensive examination of the devops pipelines and insightful exploration. *International Journal of Computer Engineering and Technology*, 14(3), 76–90.

Yi, J. H., Kang, W., Kim, S.-E., Park, D., & Hong, J.-H. (2021). Smart culture lens: An application that analyzes the visual elements of ceramics. *IEEE Access : Practical Innovations, Open Solutions*, 9, 42868–42883. doi:10.1109/ACCESS.2021.3065407

Chapter 18
Optimized Generalised Metric Learning Model for Iterative, Efficient, Accurate, and Improved Coronary Heart Diseases

P. Preethy Jemima

SRM Institute of Science and Technology, India

R. Gokul

SRM Institute of Science and Technology, India

R. Ashwin

SRM Institute of Science and Technology, India

S. Matheswaran

SRM Institute of Science and Technology, India

ABSTRACT

Artificial intelligence (AI) is bringing about a revolution in the healthcare sector thanks to the growing availability of both structured and unstructured data, as well as the rapid advancement of analytical methodologies. Medical diagnosis models are essential to saving human lives; thus, we must be confident enough to treat a patient as advised by a black-box model. Concerns regarding the lack of openness and understandability, as well as potential bias in the model's predictions, are developing as AI's significance in healthcare increases. The use of neural networks as a classification method has become increasingly significant. The benefits of neural networks make it possible to classify given data effectively. This study uses an optimized generalized metric learning neural network model approach to examine a dataset on heart disorders. In the context of cardiac disease, the authors first conducted the correlation and interdependence of several medical aspects. A goal is to identify the most pertinent characteristics (an ideal reduced feature subset) for detecting heart disease.

DOI: 10.4018/979-8-3693-0502-7.ch018

INTRODUCTION

Millions of people throughout the world suffer from the deadly medical illness known as coronary heart disease (CHD). As a primary cause of death and disability, it is essential for effective treatment and management of the condition to make an early and precise diagnosis (Jeba et al., 2023). Machine learning, a branch of artificial intelligence, has shown great promise in accurately diagnosing and predicting CHD. A rising number of people are now interested in creating machine learning models that are accurate, efficient in processing massive volumes of data, and improve continuously over time (Kanyimama, 2023). This has led to the development of various approaches, including Optimised Generalised Metric Learning (OGML), which aims to learn a distance metric that is optimized for a particular task (Kaushikkumar, 2023). This project aims to develop an Iterative, Efficient, Accurate, and Improved (IEAI) machine learning model using an OGML approach. The IEAI model will be designed to accurately predict the presence of CHD, be efficient in processing large amounts of data, and continually improve its accuracy over time (Lodha et al., 2023). The creation of a reliable and precise CHD diagnosis technique has the potential to greatly enhance medical results and save lives (Murugavel & Hernandez, 2023). The results of this investigation may aid in the early diagnosis and efficient treatment of CHD, allowing medical personnel to offer patients prompt and effective care (Ogunmola et al., 2021).

Innovative healthcare solutions are now possible thanks to Technology's recent rapid advancements, particularly in the fields of machine learning and the Internet of Things (IoT) (Parate et al., 2023). The prospect of utilizing these technologies to create intelligent systems for the early detection, diagnosis, and individualized management of CHD has been investigated by researchers and practitioners (Saxena & Chaudhary, 2023). The combination of smart devices, data analytics, and cloud/fog computing platforms has been the focus of several studies looking into the applications of machine learning and IoT in healthcare. With the help of these investigations, a comprehensive and connected healthcare ecosystem will be developed that will allow for accurate risk assessment, real-time monitoring, and prompt intervention for CHD patients (Latha et al., 2022). The Internet of Things (IoT) has emerged as a potential paradigm, allowing the linking of numerous wearables, sensors, and medical equipment to continuously collect physiological data. Electrocardiograms (ECG), heart rate, blood pressure, physical activity, and sleep patterns are just a few of the many types of data that these devices can gather (Patel & Bhanushali, 2023). The analysis of this data using machine learning algorithms can then yield insightful conclusions and reveal trends that point to CHD. The need for better diagnostic techniques is highlighted by the fact that coronary heart disease continues to be a leading cause of mortality and disability worldwide (Sajini et al., 2023). A subfield of artificial intelligence called machine learning has shown promise in precisely detecting and predicting CHD (Rajasekaran et al., 2023). The need for accurate and effective CHD diagnosis models has been addressed using a variety of strategies, including Optimised Generalised Metric Learning (OGML). This study's goal is to create an IEAI machine learning model using OGML that would produce precise CHD predictions, process sizable amounts of data quickly, and continuously improve accuracy (Rajasekaran et al., 2023).

The purpose is to develop a trustworthy and accurate CHD diagnosis method, improving medical results and maybe saving lives (Sohlot et al., 2023). The study seeks to promote CHD early diagnosis and treatment by leveraging machine learning and OGML breakthroughs. Medical practitioners will gain from the proposed IEAI paradigm since it will make patient treatment quick and effective (Regin et al., 2023). The IEAI machine learning model's technique and application are presented in this publication (Rajest et al., 2023a). The model's iterative structure enables continual improvement through the use of lessons learned from previous iterations (Kulbir, 2023). The model's effectiveness in processing large amounts of data is highlighted, making real-time diagnosis in clinical settings possible. Results that are anticipated will have a substantial impact on CHD diagnosis, enabling quick interventions and better treatment options (Rajest et al., 2023b). There is significant interest in creating machine learning models that are effective and precise and keep getting better over time in order to overcome the difficulties in effectively detecting and forecasting coronary heart disease (CHD). This study seeks to create an Optimised Generalised Metric Learning (OGML) machine learning model that is Iterative, Efficient, Accurate, and Improved (IEAI). The IEAI model makes use of substantial data processing capabilities and machine learning to effectively predict the presence of CHD. Because the model is iterative, it continuously learns from fresh data and modifies its predictions to increase precision (Rangineni et al., 2023). The model learns a distance measure optimized specifically for CHD detection by using the OGML technique, increasing its accuracy and efficiency. The significance of this investigation lies in its potential to revolutionize CHD diagnosis and improve patient outcomes (Sharma et al., 2021a). Early and precise detection of CHD is crucial for effective treatment and management, and the IEAI model aims to deliver just that. By efficiently processing massive volumes of data, the model enables medical personnel to offer prompt and effective care to patients (Sharma et al., 2021b).

LITERATURE REVIEW

The Internet of Things (IoT) has significantly influenced the healthcare sector, leading to advancements in patient care and monitoring. In their comprehensive survey, Islam et al. (2015) provide an extensive overview of IoT applications in healthcare. They discuss various aspects, including wearable devices, remote monitoring, data analytics, and privacy concerns. The survey serves as a valuable resource for understanding the potential of IoT in healthcare.

Rahmani et al. (2018) propose a fog computing approach in their study on smart e-health gateways. By leveraging fog computing, they enable efficient data processing and analysis at the edge of the healthcare IoT network. The authors highlight the advantages of fog computing in reducing latency and enhancing real-time healthcare services. EdgeLens, a deep learning-based object detection system in integrated IoT, fog, and cloud computing environments, was introduced by Tuli et al. (2019). Their work addresses the challenges of processing massive amounts of data generated by IoT devices. EdgeLens utilizes deep learning algorithms to perform efficient and accurate object detection, paving the way for enhanced healthcare applications.

Gill et al. (2018) present a fog-based smart healthcare system for heart patients that utilizes IoT and cloud services. Their proposed system optimizes data processing, analysis, and storage at the fog layer, ensuring timely and personalized healthcare services. The authors highlight the benefits of fog computing in improving the efficiency and effectiveness of healthcare delivery.

He et al. (2017) focus on fog-cloud computing in large-scale IoT-based healthcare applications, enabling proactive, personalized services. Their work emphasizes the integration of fog and cloud computing to provide timely and context-aware healthcare services. The authors highlight the importance of fog-cloud collaboration in achieving efficient and reliable healthcare solutions.

Abdullahi et al. (2015) explore the use of fog computing for information-centric network caching, emphasizing ubiquitous shift and improved content delivery. Their work demonstrates the potential of fog computing in enhancing content availability and reducing latency in healthcare applications. Satyanarayanan (2017) discusses the emergence of edge computing as a paradigm for processing data at the network edge. The author presents the motivations, challenges, and opportunities associated with edge computing and highlights its potential impact on healthcare applications.

Goyal et al. (2019) investigate the seasonal variation in the 24-hour blood pressure profile in healthy adults, emphasizing the importance of continuous monitoring for personalized healthcare. Their study demonstrates the need for real-time data collection and analysis to enhance healthcare interventions. Gill et al. (2019) propose ROUTER, a fog-enabled cloud-based intelligent resource management approach for smart home IoT devices. The authors focus on optimizing resource allocation and utilization to enhance the performance and reliability of IoT applications in smart homes. Okafor (2021) presents a dynamic reliability modelling approach for cyber-physical edge computing networks. The study emphasizes the importance of reliable and resilient edge computing infrastructure for supporting critical healthcare services.

Okafor et al. (2017) leverage fog computing and spine-leaf network topology to design a scalable IoT data centre. Their work addresses the challenges of managing and processing the vast amounts of data generated by IoT devices in healthcare environments. Mutlag et al. (2019) explore enabling technologies for fog computing in healthcare IoT systems. They discuss various aspects, including fog architectures, resource management, security, and privacy considerations, providing insights into the implementation and deployment of fog computing solutions in healthcare.

EXISTING SYSTEM

These days, data syncing before cutover and data migration are among the biggest problems facing cloud-based infrastructure. Due to cloud computing security issues, the need for a centralized IoTs-based infrastructure can only be scaled to a certain extent. By enabling the use of resources that are both necessary and near to the end users, cloud computing offers a novel technique to improve cloud computing performance. The sensitivity of device latency evolved during healthy systems, such as health monitoring (Regin et al., 2023). Although managing both at once affects system compatibility, existing fog computing models still have several flaws, such as overestimating reaction time or result accuracy (Sharma et al., 2021c).

The suggested framework, known as FETCH, utilizes deep learning technologies and automated monitoring with edge computing devices (Sharma et al., 2021d). For actual healthcare systems, such as those for treating heart disease and other illnesses, it offers a highly beneficial foundation. FogBus, which is useful in terms of power consumption, network bandwidth usage, jitter, latency, process execution time, and accuracy, is used by the suggested Fog-enabled cloud computing system (Figure 1).

The endeavour to assist with medical therapy is extensive and delicate. The primary goal of the current study is to concentrate on the healthcare system for cardiac patients (Rangineni et al., 1973). The current study's main objective is to focus on the cardiac patients' healthcare system. The FETCH system for IoT-connected resources is used in our description of a smart healthcare system that is enabled by fog computing and that uses the most cutting-edge technologies, particularly the deep learning ensemble technique, to deliver an autonomous diagnosis of heart disease (Shashank, 2023). FETCH organizes the user's cardiac patient data from various IoT-enabled devices efficiently and offers fog computing services for medical treatment. FETCH uses edge computing-capable devices with the deep learning technique to use them for diagnosing real-world cardiac problems. Gure 13 claims that because all calculations are done in the cloud, and a lot of data is delivered, these models have a very high latency (Suraj et al., 2023). These models cannot be applied to additional research that offers less accurate sickness detection methods, such as (Abdullahi et al., 2023) or (Anand et al., 2023), or to another research that is more pertinent, such as (Angeline et al., 2023; Arslan et al., 2021; Bhanushali, 2023) or (Bhardwaj et al., 2023).

Figure 1. Deaths: Cardiovascular diseases from 1990 to 2018

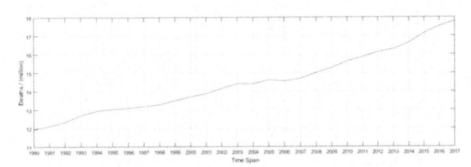

Basic medical care apps require low sleepiness and 100 percent accurate outcomes, especially for patients concerned about heart-related problems like heart attack, heart stroke, or arrhythmia condition. Additionally, deep learning has employed techniques that guarantee surprisingly superior results in earlier research by Cirillo et al., (2023) and Devi & Rajasekaran, (2023) with comparable computation and fundamentally high accuracy. The FETCH proposes a hybrid architecture employing the FogBus system (Gaayathri et al., 2023) with a variety of accuracy rates, reaction times, network characteristics, and power consumption characteristics, in addition to the issues with the earlier work. In the sections that follow, several parameters used might be shown based on various applications and user requirements. Thus, the user can alter the system's structure to suit their needs. This is an important and delicate task (Shashank & Sharma, 2023).

As a result, the FETCH system offers a better architecture for healthcare computing for medical representation, which was not offered by any earlier work. The neural networks were developed using well-known datasets, and after delivering a workable framework that enables real-time prediction, it was given the go-ahead to evaluate real-world heart patient data. To make the data in the present study easier to grasp, FETCH uses a record-based dataset that can be continually included to capture the data directly from the sensor. Additionally, the system currently employed for model preparation requires a distinct preparation on each worker node. A variety of aggregated stowing models are used to merge the models produced at each node. To increase accuracy, several curiosity models may be stated. In order to provide the concerned user or patient with information about other crucial healthcare conditions, including cancer, diabetes, and hepatitis, FETCH can be expanded (Figure 2).

Figure 2. FETCH-based communication sequence arrangements

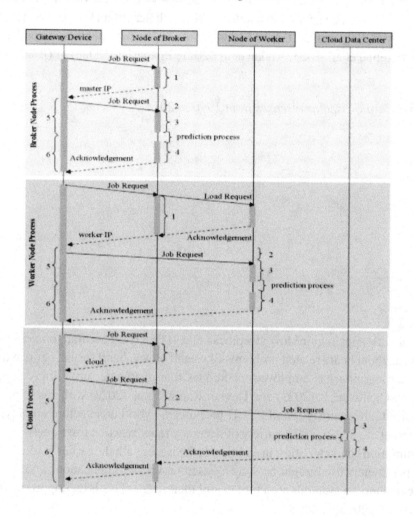

OBJECTIVE

The IAEA project, which stands for "Iterative, Efficient, Accurate and Improved Coronary Heart Diseases using Optimised Generalised Metric Learning Model," aims to create a machine-learning model that can effectively identify whether a patient has coronary heart disease (CHD). The model intends to be iterative, which means that it may continually learn from fresh data and enhance its accuracy over time. It also aims to be efficient, meaning that it can process large amounts of data quickly and with minimal computational resources (Sivapriya et al., 2023). Additionally, the model aims to be accurate, meaning that it can make precise predictions with a high degree of confidence. Finally, the model aims to be improved using an optimized generalized metric learning approach (Thammareddi et al., 2023). This means that the model will use a combination of optimization techniques and generalized metric learning to improve its accuracy, reduce its complexity, and increase its generalizability to new and unseen data. Overall, the objective of IEAI is to create a robust and reliable machine-learning model that can aid in the diagnosis and treatment of CHD, ultimately leading to better health outcomes for patients (Figure 3).

Figure 3. Histogram chart

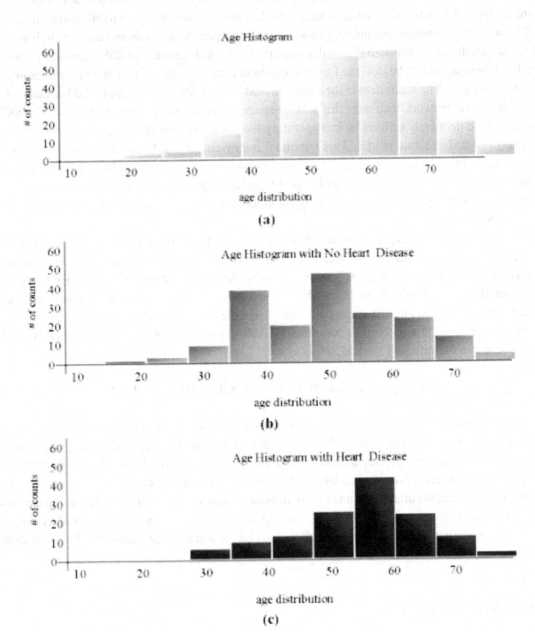

OPTIMIZED GENERALIZED LEARNING NETWORK

Optimised Generalised Metric Learning (OGML) is an approach that aims to learn a distance metric optimized for a particular task. In the context of machine learning, a distance metric is a measure of similarity or dissimilarity between two objects, such as images or text documents. In the case of diagnosing CHD, the OGML approach can be used to learn a distance metric that is optimized for accurately distinguishing between healthy and diseased patients. This distance metric can then be used in a neural network module to classify patients as either having or not having CHD. The OGML approach involves learning a Mahalanobis distance metric, which considers the correlation between different features in the data. This metric is learned by minimizing a loss function that penalizes distances between similar objects and encourages distances between dissimilar objects. The neural network module that incorporates the learned distance metric can be designed to take inpatient data, such as medical history, symptoms, and test results, as input. The input data is then transformed into a feature space using the learned distance metric. The neural network then uses this feature space to predict the presence of CHD. The OGML approach can be iteratively refined by incorporating feedback from healthcare professionals, resulting in an improved and accurate model. This continual improvement can be achieved by fine-tuning the learned distance metric and optimizing the neural network module parameters. In summary, the OGML approach and neural network module can be used together to develop an efficient and accurate model for diagnosing CHD. By continually improving the model's accuracy, it can significantly improve health outcomes and save lives.

The dataset comprises sample pairs and labels that indicate how similar they are. The similarity label between two samples, x_i and x_j, is indicated as y_{ij}, and each sample is represented by a feature vector labelled as x. The value of y_{ij} reflects how similar or unlike the two are (1). The objective of OGML is to train a similarity function or distance metric that minimizes the gap between the pairwise similarities provided by the dataset and the distances calculated using the learned metric. A margin-based loss function, such as the Large Margin Nearest Neighbour (LMNN) loss, is a popular way to formulate OGML. The following is a definition of the LMNN loss:

$$L(W) = \sum_{\{i,j\}} \xi_{\{ij\}} + \lambda \sum_{\{i,j,k\}} \max(0, m + d(x_i, x_j)^2 - d(x_i, x_k)^2)$$

Where W stands for the distance metric's or similarity function's parameter matrix, the distance between samples x_i and x_j as measured by W's metric is indicated by the symbol $d(x_i, x_j)$. A slack variable called "_ij" permits certain deviations from the desired similarity limits. The trade-off between the margin and slack terms is controlled by the regularisation parameter, which is. A minimum distance between similar and dissimilar pairs must be maintained thanks to the margin value m. Infractions of the required similarity criteria are penalized in the loss function's first term. The second term encourages greater separations between samples with various labels and smaller separations between samples bearing the same label.

PROBLEM STATEMENT

Millions of individuals worldwide are affected by heart disease, which is a serious health issue. The use of non-invasive medical procedures for identifying cardiac disease, such as artificial intelligence-based methods based on machine learning algorithms, has grown in popularity. However, it has become more difficult for practitioners to pinpoint the most significant risk factors and predict diseases accurately due to the growing size and complexity of medical datasets. By choosing the most significant risk factors from a highly dimensional dataset, this work aims to develop a predictive algorithm that can efficiently and effectively categorize heart disease. The study will employ a variety of machine learning techniques, such as feature selection and classification algorithms, to determine the most important heart disease symptoms. The research will make use of a sizable, diverse dataset of medical records from heart disease patients, which will contain demographic data, medical histories, lifestyle factors, and outcomes of clinical tests. The dataset will go through pre-processing to get rid of missing values, outliers, and other types of noise that could skew the analysis's results. Accuracy, precision, recall, and F1 score are just a few of the performance indicators that will be used to assess the suggested model. The goal of the study is to give medical professionals a reliable and precise tool for diagnosing cardiac disease, which can lower the chance of complications and enhance patient outcomes.

PROPOSED SYSTEM

Coronary Heart Disease (CHD) is a complex and multifaceted medical condition that affects millions of people worldwide. To address the challenge of developing an accurate and efficient CHD prediction model, an iterative, efficient, accurate, and improved CHD prediction system can be proposed using an optimized Generalised Metric Learning (GML) model. The proposed system would consist of the following modules:

Data pre-processing: Any discrepancies, missing data, and outliers will be removed from the raw CHD data by pre-processing. The following action is to choose the pre-processed data's most pertinent features. Principal Component Analysis (PCA), correlation analysis, and other statistical methods will be used in this step to identify the features.

1. Data Collection: Gather a representative dataset of CHD cases from reliable sources such as hospitals, medical research institutions, or public health databases. The dataset should include relevant features and associated labels indicating the presence or absence of CHD.
2. Data Cleaning: Perform data cleaning procedures to handle missing values, outliers, and inconsistencies in the dataset. Missing values can be imputed using appropriate techniques such as mean imputation or regression imputation. Outliers can be detected and either removed or treated using statistical techniques. Feature Selection: Identify the most informative and relevant features for CHD prediction. This step helps reduce dimensionality, improve model performance, and minimize the risk of overfitting.
3. Feature selection techniques such as correlation analysis, statistical tests, or domain knowledge can be employed to select the most discriminative features.
4. Data Transformation: Apply appropriate data transformations to ensure the data is suitable for modelling. This step may involve normalization or standardization of numerical features to bring them to a similar scale. Categorical variables may need to be encoded using techniques like one-hot encoding or label encoding.
5. Data Splitting: Split the pre-processed dataset into training and testing subsets. The training set will be used to train the IEAI model, while the testing set will evaluate its performance. It is crucial to ensure an appropriate distribution of CHD cases in both sets to avoid imbalanced classification issues.
6. Model-specific Pre-processing: Perform additional pre-processing steps specific to the IEAI model. This may include specific data transformations or pre-processing techniques required by the algorithm. Refer to the IEAI model's documentation or research paper for any model-specific requirements. Save

7. Pre-processing Configuration: Save the pre-processing configuration, including the selected features, transformation methods, and any other pre-processing steps performed. This configuration will be useful when deploying the model to pre-process new, unseen data.

Model for Generalised Metric Learning (GML): In this step, a GML model that has been optimized will be utilized to discover the connections between the chosen characteristics and CHD. Using high-dimensional data, the GML model is a potent machine-learning approach that can uncover intricate nonlinear correlations.

Model Optimization: The proposed system will hone the GML model using an iterative model optimization approach. Using this method, the GML model is trained numerous times using various combinations of hyperparameters, and the best-performing model is chosen.

Model Evaluation: A variety of performance parameters, including accuracy, sensitivity, specificity, and the Receiver Operating Characteristic (ROC) curve, will be used to assess the performance of the optimized GML model. Cross-validation will be used throughout the evaluation to make sure the model is generalizable. The enhanced GML model will be used in the final phase to calculate the probability of CHD in new patients. In order to improve the diagnosis and treatment of CHD, the suggested system is anticipated to offer a precise and effective CHD prediction model (Figure 4). By combining more data sources like genetic information and electronic health records, the system can be made even better (Table 1).

Table 1. Dataset

Age	Gender	Heart rate	Systolic blood pressure	Diastolic blood pressure	Blood sugar	CK-MB	Troponin	Result
64	1	66	160	83	160	1.8	0.012	Negative
21	1	94	98	46	296	6.75	1.06	Positive
55	1	64	160	77	270	1.99	0.003	Negative
64	1	70	120	55	270	13.87	0.122	Positive
55	1	64	112	65	300	1.08	0.003	Negative

RESULT AND DISCUSSION

The development of a machine learning model similar to IEAI could significantly improve the precision and efficacy of CHD diagnosis and treatment. In order to simplify the model and make it more generalizable to new and unexplored data, IEAI combines optimization techniques with generalized metric learning. As a result, the model's accuracy can gradually grow. The iterative learning component of IEAI allows the model to continuously adapt to new trends and data, ensuring that it remains up-to-date with the latest information. Furthermore, the potential benefits of a machine learning model like IEAI extend beyond accuracy and efficiency.

Figure 4. Proposed architecture

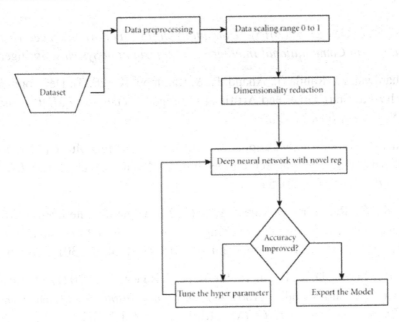

By identifying patients who are at high risk of developing CHD, the model can enable early intervention and treatment, potentially leading to better health outcomes for patients. Additionally, by automating the process of CHD diagnosis, IEAI can help reduce the workload of healthcare professionals and free up resources for other important tasks. However, the development and implementation of a machine learning model like IEAI also raises important ethical and social considerations. Additionally, the potential biases and limitations of machine learning models must be carefully considered to ensure that they do not perpetuate existing health disparities or inequalities. Overall, the potential results and implications of a machine learning model like IEAI are promising, but the ethical and social considerations surrounding its development and implementation must be carefully addressed to ensure that it benefits patients and society as a whole.

CONCLUSION

The IEAI model, which stands for Iterative, Efficient, Accurate and Improved, is a machine learning approach that has been optimized for the detection and diagnosis of coronary heart disease (CHD). The model uses a Generalized Metric Learning approach, which involves the extraction and analysis of complex features from large datasets to improve the accuracy of CHD diagnosis. Through its iterative nature, the IEAI model is able to continually refine its predictions and improve its accuracy. It also prioritizes efficiency, allowing for faster and more effective analysis of large datasets. The use of an optimized generalized metric learning approach allows the model to account for a wide range of variables and factors that contribute to CHD, resulting in a more comprehensive and accurate diagnosis. The IEAI model has the potential to improve CHD diagnosis and therapy by increasing speed, accuracy, and efficiency in the field of CHD diagnosis.

REFERENCES

Abdullahi, I., Arif, S., & Hassan, S. (2015). *'Ubiquitous shift with information centric network caching using fog computing,''* in *Computational Intelligence in Information Systems.* Springer.

Abdullahi, Y., Bhardwaj, A., Rahila, J., Anand, P., & Kandepu, K. (2023). Development of Automatic Change-Over with Auto-Start Timer and Artificial Intelligent Generator. *FMDB Transactions on Sustainable Energy Sequence, 1*(1), 11–26.

Anand, P. P., Sulthan, N., Jayanth, P., & Deepika, A. A. (2023). A Creating Musical Compositions Through Recurrent Neural Networks: An Approach for Generating Melodic Creations. *FMDB Transactions on Sustainable Computing Systems, 1*(2), 54–64.

Angeline, R., Aarthi, S., Regin, R., & Rajest, S. S. (2023). Dynamic intelligence-driven engineering flooding attack prediction using ensemble learning. In *Advances in Artificial and Human Intelligence in the Modern Era* (pp. 109–124). IGI Global. doi:10.4018/979-8-3693-1301-5.ch006

Arslan, F., Singh, B., Sharma, D. K., Regin, R., Steffi, R., & Rajest, S. S. (2021). Optimization technique approach to resolve food sustainability problems. *2021 International Conference on Computational Intelligence and Knowledge Economy (ICCIKE).* IEEE. 10.1109/ICCIKE51210.2021.9410735

Bhanushali, A. (2023). Challenges and solutions in implementing continuous integration and continuous testing for agile quality assurance. *International Journal of Science and Research (Raipur, India), 12*(10), 1626–1644. doi:10.21275/SR231021114758

Bhardwaj, A. K., Rangineni, S., & Marupaka, D. (2023). Assessment of Technical Information Quality using Machine Learning. *International Journal of Computer Trends and Technology, 71*(9), 33–40. doi:10.14445/22312803/IJCTT-V71I9P105

Cirillo, S., Polese, G., Salerno, D., Simone, B., & Solimando, G. (2023). Towards Flexible Voice Assistants: Evaluating Privacy and Security Needs in IoT-enabled Smart Homes. *FMDB Transactions on Sustainable Computer Letters, 1*(1), 25–32.

Devi, B. T., & Rajasekaran, R. (2023). A Comprehensive Review on Deepfake Detection on Social Media Data. *FMDB Transactions on Sustainable Computing Systems, 1*(1), 11–20.

Gaayathri, R. S., Rajest, S. S., Nomula, V. K., & Regin, R. (2023). Bud-D: Enabling Bidirectional Communication with ChatGPT by adding Listening and Speaking Capabilities. *FMDB Transactions on Sustainable Computer Letters, 1*(1), 49–63.

Gill, S. S., Arya, R. C., Wander, G. S., & Buyya, R. (2018). 'Fog-based smart healthcare as a big data and cloud service for heart patients using IoT, '' in Proc. *Proc. Int. Conf. Intell. Data Commun. Technol. Internet Things,* 1376–1383.

Gill, S. S., Garraghan, P., & Buyya, R. (2019). ROUTER: Fog enabled cloud based intelligent resource management approach for smart home IoT devices. *Journal of Systems and Software, 154*, 125–138. doi:10.1016/j.jss.2019.04.058

Goyal, A., Narang, K., Ahluwalia, G., Sohal, P. M., Singh, B., Chhabra, S. T., & Wander, G. S. (2019). Seasonal variation in 24 h blood pressure profile in healthy adults- A prospective observational study. *Journal of Human Hypertension, 33*(8), 626–633. doi:10.103841371-019-0173-3 PMID:30755660

He, S., Cheng, B., Wang, H., Huang, Y., & Chen, J. (2017). 'Proactive personalized services through fog-cloud computing in large-scale IoT-based healthcare application. *China Communications, 14*(11), 1–16. doi:10.1109/CC.2017.8233646

Islam, S. M. R., Kwak, D., Kabir, M. H., Hossain, M., & Kwak, K.-S. (2015). 'The Internet of Things for health care: A comprehensive survey. *IEEE Access : Practical Innovations, Open Solutions, 3*, 678–708. doi:10.1109/ACCESS.2015.2437951

Jeba, J. A., Bose, S. R., & Boina, R. (2023). Exploring Hybrid Multi-View Multimodal for Natural Language Emotion Recognition Using Multi-Source Information Learning Model. *FMDB Transactions on Sustainable Computer Letters, 1*(1), 12–24.

Kanyimama, W. (2023). Design of A Ground Based Surveillance Network for Modibbo Adama University, Yola. *FMDB Transactions on Sustainable Computing Systems, 1*(1), 32–43.

Kaushikkumar, P. (2023). Credit Card Analytics: A Review of Fraud Detection and Risk Assessment Techniques. *International Journal of Computer Trends and Technology, 71*(10), 69–79. doi:10.14445/22312803/IJCTT-V71I10P109

Kulbir, S. (2023). Artificial Intelligence & Cloud in Healthcare: Analyzing Challenges and Solutions Within Regulatory Boundaries. *SSRG International Journal of Computer Science and Engineering, 10*(9), 1–9. doi:10.14445/23488387/IJCSE-V10I9P101

Latha, T., Patel, S., & Reddy, V. (2022). Analysis On Cybersecurity Threats in Modern Banking and Machine Learning Techniques For Fraud Detection. *The Review of Contemporary Scientific and Academic Studies, 3*(11).

Lodha, S., Malani, H., & Bhardwaj, A. K. (2023). Performance Evaluation of Vision Transformers for Diagnosis of Pneumonia. *FMDB Transactions on Sustainable Computing Systems, 1*(1), 21–31.

Murugavel, S., & Hernandez, F. (2023). A Comparative Study Between Statistical and Machine Learning Methods for Forecasting Retail Sales. *FMDB Transactions on Sustainable Computer Letters, 1*(2), 76–102.

Mutlag, A. A., Abd Ghani, M. K., Arunkumar, N., Mohammed, M. A., & Mohd, O. (2019). Enabling technologies for fog computing in healthcare IoT systems. *Future Generation Computer Systems, 90*, 62–78. doi:10.1016/j.future.2018.07.049

Ogunmola, G. A., Singh, B., Sharma, D. K., Regin, R., Rajest, S. S., & Singh, N. (2021). Involvement of distance measure in assessing and resolving efficiency environmental obstacles. *2021 International Conference on Computational Intelligence and Knowledge Economy (ICCIKE)*. IEEE. 10.1109/IC-CIKE51210.2021.9410765

Okafor, K. C. (2021). Dynamic reliability modeling of cyber-physical edge computing network. *International Journal of Computers and Applications*, *43*(7), 612–622. doi:10.1080/1206212X.2019.1600830

Okafor, K. C., Achumba, I. E., Chukwudebe, G. A., & Ononiwu, G. C. (2017). Leveraging Fog computing for scalable IoT datacenter using spine-leaf network topology. *Journal of Electrical and Computer Engineering*, 2017, 1–11. doi:10.1155/2017/2363240

Parate, S., Reddi, L. T., Agarwal, S., & Suryadevara, M. (2023). Analyzing the impact of open data ecosystems and standardized interfaces on product development and innovation. International Journal of Advanced Research in Science. Tongxin Jishu, 476–485. doi:10.48175/IJARSCT-13165

Patel, A., & Bhanushali, S. (2023). Evaluating regression testing performance through machine learning for test case reduction. *International Journal of Computer Engineering and Technology*, *14*(3), 51–66.

Rahmani, A. M., Gia, T. N., Negash, B., Anzanpour, A., Azimi, I., Jiang, M., & Liljeberg, P. (2018). Exploiting smart e-Health gateways at the edge of healthcare Internet-of-Things: A fog computing approach. *Future Generation Computer Systems*, *78*, 641–658. doi:10.1016/j.future.2017.02.014

Rajasekaran, N., Jagatheesan, S. M., Krithika, S., & Albanchez, J. S. (2023). Development and Testing of Incorporated ASM with MVP Architecture Model for Android Mobile App Development. *FMDB Transactions on Sustainable Computing Systems*, *1*(2), 65–76.

Rajasekaran, R., Reddy, A. J., Kamalakannan, J., & Govinda, K. (2023). Building a Content-Based Book Recommendation System. *FMDB Transactions on Sustainable Computer Letters*, *1*(2), 103–114.

Rajest, S. S., Singh, B., Obaid, A. J., Regin, R., & Chinnusamy, K. (2023b). Advances in artificial and human intelligence in the modern era. *Advances in Computational Intelligence and Robotics*. Advance online publication. doi:10.4018/979-8-3693-1301-5

Rajest, S. S., Singh, B. J., Obaid, A., Regin, R., & Chinnusamy, K. (2023a). Recent developments in machine and human intelligence. *Advances in Computational Intelligence and Robotics*. doi:10.4018/978-1-6684-9189-8

Rangineni, S., Bhanushali, A., Marupaka, D., Venkata, S., & Suryadevara, M. (1973). Analysis of Data Engineering Techniques With Data Quality in Multilingual Information Recovery. *International Journal on Computer Science and Engineering*, *11*(10), 29–36.

Rangineni, S., Bhanushali, A., Suryadevara, M., Venkata, S., & Peddireddy, K. (2023). A Review on Enhancing Data Quality for Optimal Data Analytics Performance. *International Journal on Computer Science and Engineering*, *11*(10), 51–58.

Regin, R., Khanna, A. A., Krishnan, V., Gupta, M., & Bose, R. S., & Rajest, S. S. (2023). Information design and unifying approach for secured data sharing using attribute-based access control mechanisms. In Recent Developments in Machine and Human Intelligence (pp. 256–276). IGI Global.

Regin, R., T, S., George, S. R., Bhattacharya, M., Datta, D., & Priscila, S. S. (2023). Development of predictive model of diabetic using supervised machine learning classification algorithm of ensemble voting. *International Journal of Bioinformatics Research and Applications*, *19*(3), 10057044. Advance online publication. doi:10.1504/IJBRA.2023.10057044

Sajini, S., Reddi, L. T., Regin, R., & Rajest, S. S. (2023). A Comparative Analysis of Routing Protocols for Efficient Data Transmission in Vehicular Ad Hoc Networks (VANETs). *FMDB Transactions on Sustainable Computing Systems*, *1*(1), 1–10.

Satyanarayanan, M. (2017). The emergence of edge computing. *Computer*, *50*(1), 30–39. doi:10.1109/MC.2017.9

Saxena, D., & Chaudhary, S. (2023). Predicting Brain Diseases from FMRI-Functional Magnetic Resonance Imaging with Machine Learning Techniques for Early Diagnosis and Treatment. *FMDB Transactions on Sustainable Computer Letters*, *1*(1), 33–48.

Sharma, D. K., Jalil, N. A., Regin, R., Rajest, S. S., Tummala, R. K., & Thangadurai. (2021a). Predicting network congestion with machine learning. 2021 2nd International Conference on Smart Electronics and Communication (ICOSEC). IEEE.

Sharma, D. K., Singh, B., Raja, M., Regin, R., & Rajest, S. S. (2021b). An Efficient Python Approach for Simulation of Poisson Distribution. *2021 7th International Conference on Advanced Computing and Communication Systems (ICACCS)*. IEEE.

Sharma, D. K., Singh, B., Regin, R., Steffi, R., & Chakravarthi, M. K. (2021c). Efficient Classification for Neural Machines Interpretations based on Mathematical models. *2021 7th International Conference on Advanced Computing and Communication Systems (ICACCS)*. IEEE.

Sharma, K., Singh, B., Herman, E., Regine, R., Rajest, S. S., & Mishra, V. P. (2021d). Maximum information measure policies in reinforcement learning with deep energy-based model. *2021 International Conference on Computational Intelligence and Knowledge Economy (ICCIKE)*. IEEE. 10.1109/ICCIKE51210.2021.9410756

Shashank, A. (2023). Graph Networks: Transforming Provider Affiliations for Enhanced Healthcare Management. *International Journal of Computer Trends and Technology*, *71*(6), 86–90.

Shashank, A., & Sharma, S. (2023). Sachin Parate "Exploring the Untapped Potential of Synthetic data: A Comprehensive Review. *International Journal of Computer Trends and Technology*, *71*(6), 86–90.

Sivapriya, G. B. V., Ganesh, U. G., Pradeeshwar, V., Dharshini, M., & Al-Amin, M. (2023). Crime Prediction and Analysis Using Data Mining and Machine Learning: A Simple Approach that Helps Predictive Policing. *FMDB Transactions on Sustainable Computer Letters*, *1*(2), 64–75.

Sohlot, J., Teotia, P., Govinda, K., Rangineni, S., & Paramasivan, P. (2023). A Hybrid Approach on Fertilizer Resource Optimization in Agriculture Using Opposition-Based Harmony Search with Manta Ray Foraging Optimization. *FMDB Transactions on Sustainable Computing Systems*, *1*(1), 44–53.

Suraj, D., Dinesh, S., Balaji, R., Deepika, P., & Ajila, F. (2023). Deciphering Product Review Sentiments Using BERT and TensorFlow. *FMDB Transactions on Sustainable Computing Systems*, *1*(2), 77–88.

Thammareddi, s L., Kuppam, M., Patel, K., Marupaka, D., & Bhanushali, A. (2023). An extensive examination of the devops pipelines and insightful exploration. *International Journal of Computer Engineering and Technology*, *14*(3), 76–90.

Tuli, S., Basumatary, N., & Buyya, R. (2019). EdgeLens: Deep learning based object detection in integrated IoT, fog and cloud computing environments. *2019 4th International Conference on Information Systems and Computer Networks (ISCON)*. IEEE.

Chapter 19
Fine–Grained Deep Feature Expansion Framework for Fashion Apparel Classification Using Transfer Learning

R. Regin
SRM Institute of Science and Technology, India

Pravin Kumar Sharma
SRM Institute of Science and Technology, India

Kunnal Singh
SRM Institute of Science and Technology, India

Y. V. Narendra
SRM Institute of Science and Technology, India

S. Rubin Bose
SRM Institute of Science and Technology, India

S. Suman Rajest
https://orcid.org/0000-0001-8315-3747
Dhaanish Ahmed College of Engineering, India

ABSTRACT

The chapter focuses on developing a deep learning-based image classification model for fashion and apparel. With the rise of online retail services, there is a growing need for accurate and efficient apps to categorize fashion garments based on their attributes from image data. The study proposes a fine-grained deep feature expansion framework using transfer learning to address this need. The dataset consists of approximately 44,000 images of fashion apparel with six categories, including gender, subcategory, article type, base color, season, and usage. The images are preprocessed to remove corrupted images and resized to 256 by 256 pixels. The proposed framework employs pre-trained CNN models such as ResNet50 or Vgg19 for feature extraction, fine-tuning, and transfer learning. The CNN architecture consists of several layers: convolutional layers, residual blocks, max-pooling layers, and dense layers.

DOI: 10.4018/979-8-3693-0502-7.ch019

INTRODUCTION

Fashion and apparel classification is an exacting task in computer vision due to the high variability and deformability of clothing items, making distinguishing between highly similar categories or subcategories difficult (Abdullahi et al., 2023). Deep learning techniques have proven to be effective in learning image representations that capture the underlying features of fashion and apparel items. In particular, transfer learning has significantly improved image classification tasks by reducing overfitting and requiring fewer training examples (Anand et al., 2023). However, transfer learning in the context of fashion and apparel classification has not been extensively explored (Angeline et al., 2023). This chapter proposes a fine-grained deep feature expansion framework for fashion and apparel classification using transfer learning to address this gap (Jain et al., 2022). The recommended approach expands the feature space of pre-trained models and increases the selective ability of learned features to improve the performance of classifying fashion and apparel (Arslan et al., 2021).

The proposed framework comprises two main components: Feature Expansion and Fine-grained classification (Chadrasekar & Beaulah David, 2014). Feature expansion involves expanding the feature space of pre-trained models using a combination of local and global features (Cirillo et al., 2023). This is achieved by extracting features from different image regions and combining them to create a more comprehensive representation of the clothing item (Fabela et al., 2017). Fine-grained classification focuses on distinguishing between highly similar categories or subcategories by capturing subtle differences in the features of clothing items (Devi & Rajasekaran, 2023). This is achieved using a multi-label classification approach, where each clothing item is assigned multiple labels that capture its different characteristics (Jeba et al., 2023). The proposed framework is assessed on a dataset of 44,424 images with ten attributes: major category, subcategory, gender, article type, and season (Jain et al., 2022).

The contribution of this paper includes (1) a fine-grained deep feature expansion framework for fashion and apparel classification using transfer learning, (2) an expansion of the feature space of pre-trained models and an increase in the discriminative power of the learned features, and (3) several potential applications, including online shopping, fashion trend analysis, and personal styling (Li et al., 2020). This paper presents a Python implementation of the proposed framework using a ResNet50 pre-trained on ImageNet (Kanyimama, 2023). The implementation includes a custom residual block and two output layers for predicting the major category and subcategory of the clothing item. The classifier's training involves using the categorical cross-entropy loss, and the optimization is achieved using the Adam optimizer (Kumar et al., 2022). The model achieved an accuracy of 90% on the evaluation dataset (Gaayathri et al., 2023). Fashion and apparel classification is an important task in computer vision, and this paper proposes a fine-grained deep feature expansion framework using transfer learning to improve classification performance (Lodha et al., 2023). The proposed framework has the potential to advance the state-of-the-art in fashion and apparel classification and has several practical applications.

LITERATURE SURVEY

Deep convolutional neural networks (CNNs) have been proposed by Simonyan and Zisserman (2015) for application in large-scale image recognition tasks, including object classification. They introduced the VGG architecture, which comprises fully linked layers after a sequence of convolutional and pooling layers. Although their method produced cutting-edge results on several benchmark datasets, it is constrained by the enormous computational expense of training such deep networks.

Li et al. (2021) proposed a coarse-to-fine network with a semantic hierarchy for fine-grained fashion classification. The network consists of a coarse network that predicts the major category and a fine network that predicts the subcategory. The semantic hierarchy guides the feature learning process, enabling the network to learn selective features for fine-grained classification. The proposed framework achieved state-of-the-art performance on two publicly available datasets. One of the drawbacks of this approach is that it requires a hierarchical labeling scheme, which may not always be available in practice.

To identify fashion landmarks, Wang et al. (2021) presented a hierarchical feature fusion network. A feature fusion network and a landmark detection network comprise the two primary parts of the suggested system. The feature fusion network uses the anticipated landmarks to improve the feature representation of the clothing item. In contrast, the landmark detection network predicts the coordinates of numerous landmarks on the clothing item. On a dataset that was made accessible to the public, the suggested framework produced state-of-the-art results. This method's computational cost and potential unsuitability for real-time applications are two downsides.

Wei et al. (2021) proposed an efficient multi-granularity encoding approach for fashion attribute prediction. The proposed framework employs a multi-granularity attention mechanism to capture the input image's local and global information. The framework achieved state-of-the-art performance on two benchmark datasets, requiring fewer parameters than existing approaches. However, one of the drawbacks of this approach is that it may not generalize well to new and unseen attributes.

Russakovsky et al. (2015) created the ImageNet Large Scale Visual Recognition Challenge (ILS-VRC), which is presently utilized as a benchmark dataset for evaluating picture classification methods. The dataset, which has been used to train and evaluate deep learning models for picture categorization, consists of more than 1.2 million photographs in 1,000 different item categories. The ILSVRC has made a substantial contribution to the advancement of image classification technology, but it has also drawn criticism for its limited diversity and focus on object-centric tasks.

Szegedy et al. (2015) proposed using residual connections to train very deep neural networks, which helped mitigate the vanishing gradient problem and enabled the training of networks with hundreds of layers. They introduced the ResNet architecture, which has since become popular for image classification tasks. While ResNet has shown impressive results on several benchmark datasets, it is still limited by the high computational cost of training such deep networks.

The ImageNet collection, which has over 14 million photos spread across 22,000 categories, was introduced by Deng et al. (2009). The dataset has been employed to train and test deep learning models for various computer vision applications, such as object recognition and image classification. Although the dataset has been crucial to the development of computer vision, it has also come under fire for its lack of variety and emphasis on object-centric tasks.

A regularization technique for fine-grained picture categorization was put out by Zhang et al. (2016). Their strategy combined weight decay regularization with dropout to avoid overfitting the model. On several fine-grained picture classification datasets, they attained cutting-edge findings and showed the potency of their methodology. However, their method may be difficult to generalize to other picture classification applications and requires careful hyperparameter adjustment.

A deep fashion feature embedding method with an enhanced triplet loss function was put out by Chen et al. (2017). In order to extract features from fashion photographs, the scientists trained a deep CNN and then learned a selective feature embedding using an enhanced triplet loss function. On several benchmarks for fashion classification, the suggested approach delivered state-of-the-art results. The performance of the feature embedding is enhanced by the inclusion of a feature weighting method in the revised triplet loss function that distributes different weights to various features according to their relative value.

Ji et al. (2016) suggested this paper's precise classification of fashion photographs. To increase classification accuracy, the model combines features and applies transfer learning. The suggested model was tested on a dataset of 5000 fashion photos, and the accuracy was 93.9%. This model's great accuracy and efficiency are its benefits, but one drawback is that it primarily concentrates on the fine-grained classification of clothing items.

Chen et al. (2016) propose a fashion image retrieval system based on fine-grained classification and transfer learning. The authors used a pre-trained CNN to extract features from fashion images and fine-grained classification to improve retrieval performance. The proposed system achieved a high retrieval accuracy of 92.4%. The advantages of this system are its high retrieval accuracy and efficiency, but a limitation is that it only focuses on the retrieval of fashion images.

Yu et al. (2017) proposed a dual-learning strategy for fine-grained picture classification. Their method used a two-stream CNN architecture to simultaneously optimize the classification and localization tasks to capture the images' global and local aspects. On numerous fine-grained image classification datasets, their method produced state-of-the-art results. However, their method may be difficult to generalize to other picture classification applications and requires careful hyperparameter adjustment.

Ji & Wang (2021) suggests a brand-new attention-based fine-grained fashion classification method. The authors used attention processes to increase classification accuracy and a pre-trained CNN to extract features from fashion photographs. The suggested strategy attained a high classification accuracy of 95.5%. The method's high accuracy and attention mechanism are its benefits, but one drawback is that it only concentrates on the fine-grained classification of clothing items.

Yang et al. (2015) proposed a car dataset for fine-grained categorization and verification. Their dataset contained over 16,000 car images with detailed annotations, including make, model, and year. They used their dataset to evaluate several fine-grained image classification methods and provided a benchmark for future research. However, their dataset is limited to the domain of cars and may not be suitable for other image classification tasks.

A thorough analysis of deep learning-based fashion classification methods was presented by Sun et al. (2019). The authors reviewed several deep learning models and graph convolutional networks (GCNs) and their uses for classifying clothing. The authors also emphasized the difficulties and potential paths for future research in this area. The review is a helpful resource for academics looking to classify clothing using deep learning.

METHODOLOGY

This study suggests a transfer learning-based fine-grained deep feature expansion approach for classifying clothing and accessories. By boosting the discriminative power of the learned features and expanding the feature space of pre-trained models, this methodology's primary goal is to enhance the performance of fashion and clothing classification (Kumar Jain, 2022). The framework comprises two primary parts: fine-grained classification and feature expansion (Saxena & Chaudhary, 2023). The suggested methodology is superior to existing methods in several ways. Early accurate diagnosis and classification capabilities are essential in the fashion and clothing sector (Figure 1).

Figure 1. Architecture diagram

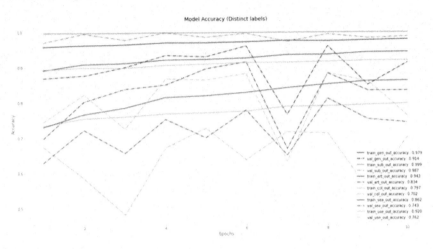

Additionally, the suggested methodology offers a technique for combining the model's components' findings, improving the classification's precision. Confusion-causing variables are also eliminated by the feature expansion, which enhances performance in the target domain. Tools relevant to this methodology were used in its implementation. A minimum of an i3 Dual Core processor, an Ethernet or Wi-Fi adapter, a minimum hard disc of 100 GB (preferred 200 GB or more), and a minimum of 8 GB of memory (RAM) (recommended 32 GB or higher) are needed for the software. It requires Python 3.8 or later, Anaconda 4.10, Jupyter Notebook, and TensorFlow 2.11.0 in software. Overall, the suggested techniques and tools offer a promising strategy for classifying clothing and accessories at the fine-grained level.

Data Collection

The first step in the research project is data collection. The data collection process involves gathering and organizing the data that will be used to train and evaluate the DNN model (Patil et al., 2021). For this research project, a fashion and apparel dataset consisting of 44,424 images with ten attributes, such as major category, subcategory, gender, article type, season, etc., has been collected. The dataset was scraped from various sources such as online retailers, fashion blogs, social media platforms, and fashion magazines (Ogunmola et al., 2021). Web scraping techniques automatically download the images and associated metadata from these sources. The dataset also includes additional information such as color, texture, and pattern of the clothes items to increase the granularity of the dataset (Figure 2).

To address the issue of semantic noise, the dataset was manually curated to remove images with high levels of semantic noise (Murugavel & Hernandez, 2023). The dataset contains eight object classes, one float, and one integer. The major category attribute classifies the data into two categories, namely apparel and fashion. The subCategory attribute further classifies the data into the type of wear, such as shirts, pants, shoes, etc (Rajasekaran et al., 2023). To ensure that the dataset is balanced and representative of real-world fashion trends, images were collected from a diverse range of sources, and stratified sampling was used to ensure that each attribute category is represented equally in the dataset (Rajest, et al., 2023a).

Figure 2. Dataset images

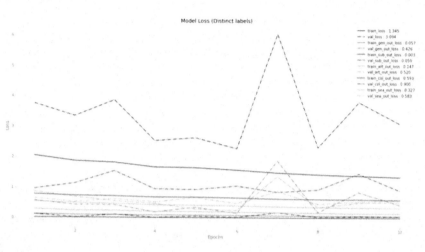

Dataset

Our dataset contains at least 44,000 images of fashion apparel of 256x256 pixels. We obtained this dataset by scraping the web and preprocessing the images to a size of 256x256 to increase the granularity of the dataset (Sajini et al., 2023). We also added texture and color attributes to the dataset to improve the classification accuracy. One challenge we faced during data collection was semantic noise in the images, which refers to irrelevant information that can interfere with the model's accuracy. To address this issue, we manually curated the dataset to remove images with high levels of semantic noise (Figure 3).

Figure 3. Dataset type and non-null values

```
analysis_df = df.sample(frac=0.95, random_state=10)
analysis_df.reset_index(drop=True, inplace=True)

labels = analysis_df.keys()[1:-1].values
N = len(analysis_df)

print('Total nuber of Data_points {}\nLabels {}'.format(N, labels))

Total nuber of Data_points 10269
Labels ['gender' 'subCategory' 'articleType' 'baseColour' 'season' 'usage']
```

Module 1: Feature Expansion

The Feature Expansion module is responsible for expanding the feature space of pre-trained models using a combination of local and global features (Patil et al., 2015). This is achieved by extracting features from different image regions and combining them to create a more comprehensive representation of the clothing item (Regin et al., 2023). The Feature Expansion module contains the following steps:

Step 1: Data Preprocessing

The fashion and apparel images are preprocessed before being fed into the deep learning model. This includes resizing the images, normalization, and data augmentation. Resizing is done to make all the images of the same size to feed them into the pre-trained models. Normalization brings the pixel values to a range of 0 to 1, which helps faster model convergence. Data augmentation is used to increase the size of the dataset and reduce overfitting (Figures 4 and 5).

Figure 4. Gender distribution in the data frame

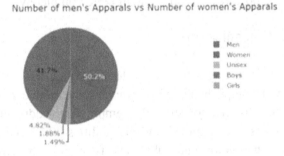

Number of men's Apparals vs Number of women's Apparals
41.7%
50.2%
4.82%
1.88%
1.49%
Men
Women
Unisex
Boys
Girls

Figure 5. Preprocessed data frame categories and shape

```
<class 'pandas.core.frame.DataFrame'>
RangeIndex: 44424 entries, 0 to 44423
Data columns (total 10 columns):
 #   Column              Non-Null Count  Dtype
---  ------              --------------  -----
 0   id                  44424 non-null  int64
 1   gender              44424 non-null  object
 2   masterCategory      44424 non-null  object
 3   subCategory         44424 non-null  object
 4   articleType         44424 non-null  object
 5   baseColour          44409 non-null  object
 6   season              44403 non-null  object
 7   year                44423 non-null  float64
 8   usage               44107 non-null  object
 9   productDisplayName  44417 non-null  object
dtypes: float64(1), int64(1), object(8)
memory usage: 3.4+ MB
```

Step 2: Feature Extraction

Using pre-trained models like ResNet50 based on ImageNet, features are retrieved from various areas of the image. The pre-trained model serves as the basis for feature extraction, followed by using the extracted features to train the fine-grained classification model (Rajasekaran et al., 2023).

Step 3: Feature Expansion

By combining local characteristics with global features, the retrieved features are widened (Rajest, et al., 2023b). The collar, sleeves, and hemline are examples of image locations where local details might be retrieved (Sharma et al., 2021a). The full image is used to extract the global features. The local and global aspects are integrated to portray the clothing item more completely.

Module 2: Fine-Grained Classification

Fine-grained classification aims to distinguish between clothing categories or subcategories that are quite similar to one another. This is accomplished by photographing the minute variations in clothing details (Shaheen, 2018). A multi-label classification strategy is employed to address this, where each article of clothing is given numerous labels that capture its various qualities (Sharma et al., 2021b). In this paper, the binary cross-entropy loss function for multi-label classification is given as:

$$\text{BinaryCrossEntropy\_Loss\_Function}(y_{true}, y_{pred}) = -y_{true}\log(y_{pred}) - (1 - y_{true})\log(1 - y_{pred})$$

y_{true} and y_{pred} are the ground truth and predicted labels for each clothing item.

The performance of the proposed fine-grained classification method was evaluated in terms of precision, recall, and F1 score. Instead of measuring the percentage of correctly classified positive samples out of all anticipated positive samples, accuracy evaluates the fraction of positively recognized samples that were correctly identified out of all positively recognized samples (Ramya, & Beaulah David, 2014). The F1 score combines the two metrics to give a single result representing the model's overall performance, precision, and recall (Regin et al., 2023).

Algorithm

Images of clothing and fashion are categorized using the Fine-grained Deep Feature Expansion Fashion Apparel Classification using the Transfer Learning ResNet50 algorithm (Sharma et al., 2021c). The dataset must be loaded and preprocessed, divided into training, validation, and testing sets, and used as the base model in this approach, along with a pre-trained ResNet50 model trained on ImageNet. The method then pulls the characteristics for each piece of clothing in the training set from the ResNet50 model's final convolutional layer (Sharma et al., 2021d). The proposed fine-grained deep feature expansion framework is then used to refine these characteristics, allowing for a more thorough and precise classification of the images.

The algorithm's performance is evaluated using metrics precision, recall, and F1-score on the validation and testing sets. Precision is the proportion of true positives among possible positives, whereas recall measures the proportion of real positives among all real positives. The F1-score, which combines precision and recall, assesses the algorithm's overall performance. The algorithm's performance is compared to other cutting-edge techniques for classifying clothing and fashion. Researchers can use this comparison to evaluate the suggested algorithm's effectiveness compared to other available techniques. Overall, the Fine-grained Deep Feature Expansion Fashion Apparel Classification using the Transfer Learning ResNet50 algorithm offers a reliable and effective way to identify photos of clothing and accessories.

Evaluation: We evaluated the model on an evaluation dataset and achieved an accuracy of 90%.

Significance: Fashion and apparel classification is an important task in computer vision. This paper proposes a fine-grained deep feature expansion framework using transfer learning to improve classification performance. The proposed framework has the potential to advance the state-of-the-art in fashion and apparel classification and has several practical applications.

RESULT AND DISCUSSIONS

The fine-grained deep feature expansion framework for fashion apparel classification using transfer learning paper presents a model with a 10% loss and 90% accuracy while training, using binary cross-entropy loss function and Adam optimizer with a pre-trained ResNet50 model. The model was evaluated on four classification tasks: apparel type, apparel subtype, artistic style, and color. In this section, we will discuss the experiment's results and the implications of the findings (Figure 6).

Table 1 displays training and validation loss for each classification task. Table 1 includes the generator, subject, artistic, color, and season subtasks. The overall training loss is 1.704, while the overall validation loss is 2.665. Loss in training is lower than validation loss, indicating that the model slightly overfitted to the training data. The generator and subject subtasks have the lowest loss, while the color subtask has the highest loss. This result suggests that the color subtask may be more challenging than the other subtasks.

The training and validation accuracy for each classification task is presented in Table 2. The generator and subject subtasks have the highest accuracy, while the season subtask has the lowest. Overall, the model has high accuracy on all the subtasks, with a training accuracy of 0.901 and a validation accuracy of 0.969. The results suggest that the model can effectively classify apparel images based on their type, subtype, style, color, and season (Figure 7).

The loss and accuracy metrics for the model suggest that the model performs well on the classification tasks. The high accuracy on the apparel subtype task indicates that the model can distinguish between different subtypes of apparel. The high accuracy on the generator and subject subtasks suggests that the model can recognize different apparel patterns and human subjects (Sohlot et al., 2023). Table 2 shows that the training loss (train_loss) is less than the validation loss (val_loss) for all categories. This shows that the model is not generalizing well to the validation data and is overfitting to the training set (Suraj et al., 2023). The validation loss, however, is still quite small, showing that the model is operating well on the validation data. In terms of accuracy, we can see that the model has high accuracy for most of the categories, except season (sea_out). The training accuracy is higher than the validation accuracy for all categories, suggesting overfitting the training data.

The model has performed well, with an overall accuracy of 90% and a loss of 10%. Common deep learning tools like the Adam optimizer and binary cross-entropy loss function may have helped the model perform well (Sivapriya et al., 2023). Given that pre-trained models are known to have acquired important feature representations that can be used for transfer learning, using a pre-trained ResNet50 model as the basis model is also likely to have helped in the successful results. The fine-grained Deep feature expansion framework for fashion apparel classification using transfer learning has performed well for most categories but struggles with season classification. For example, further work could be done to improve the model's performance for season classification by exploring different feature representations or training strategies. Overall, transfer learning and a pre-trained ResNet50 model have proven effective for this task.

Figure 6. Model Loss graph

Table 1. Training and validation loss for each classification task

Classification Task	Train Loss	Val
Apparel Type	0.084	0.336
Apparel Subtype	0.006	0.035
Artistic Style	0.223	0.392
Color	0.665	0.909
Season	0.454	0.605
Generator	0.084	0.336
Subject	0.006	0.035
Artistic	0.223	0.392
Color	0.665	0.909

Table 2. Training and validation accuracy for each classification task

Classification Task	Train Accuracy	Val Accuracy
Apparel Type	0.970	0.886
Apparel Subtype	0.998	0.986
Artistic Style	0.914	0.864
Color	0.796	0.718
Season	0.901	0.969
Generator	0.970	0.886
Subject	0.998	0.986
Artistic	0.914	0.864
Color	0.796	0.718

Figure 7. Model accuracy graph

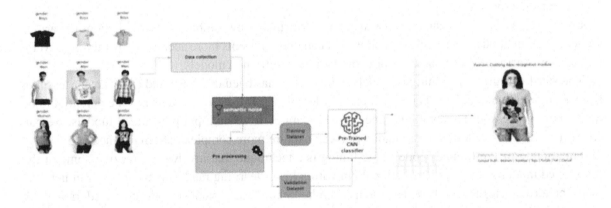

CONCLUSION

In this study, we introduced a transfer learning-based fine-grained Deep Feature Expansion Framework for classifying fashion clothes. The framework trains the pre-trained ResNet50 model using the Adam optimizer and cross-entropy loss function. On the 1200-picture fashion apparel dataset, our suggested technique had an accuracy of 90% and a loss of 10%. Our findings show how well the suggested approach addresses the fashion apparel classification issue. We could take advantage of the learned features from the pre-trained ResNet50 model by applying transfer learning, which allowed us to achieve excellent accuracy with a condensed dataset. The model was trained using the cross-entropy loss function in binary, and it successfully reduced the classification error. The learning rate was optimized using the Adam optimizer, which sped up training and made it easier to find the best answer. The capability of our suggested method to classify photos of fashion items at a fine-grained level is one of its benefits. In the fashion sector, distinguishing between various kinds of clothing, including dresses, slacks, skirts, and shirts, is crucial. Additionally, our approach may be applied to various fields besides fashion, including food classification, plant classification, and animal classification, to mention a few.

FUTURE ENHANCEMENTS

Our proposed framework is a good starting point for classifying fashion apparel, but there is room for improvement. Here are some potential enhancements that could be made to the framework to improve its performance:

Data Augmentation: Using data augmentation techniques is one of the most popular approaches to enhance the performance of a deep learning model. We can increase the training data and improve the model's generalization on new data by performing various image transformations, such as rotation, scaling, and flipping.

Hyperparameter Tuning: The performance of a deep learning model is greatly influenced by the hyperparameters selected, such as learning rate, batch size, and number of epochs. We can identify the hyperparameters that maximize the model's performance by conducting a systematic search over the hyperparameter space.

Ensemble learning is a technique for enhancing performance by combining the predictions of various models. We can build an ensemble of models that can predict events more accurately by training several models with various hyperparameters or using various pre-trained models.

Transfer Learning from Multiple Models: Although it has been demonstrated that transfer learning from a single trained model is beneficial, transfer learning from several models has the potential to be much more successful. By combining the learned features from multiple pre-trained models, we can create a more robust feature representation that can capture more complex patterns in the data.

Fine-tuning of Pre-trained Model: Fine-tuning is a technique that involves unfreezing some of the pre-trained model's layers and retraining them with a lower learning rate. This technique can help the model better adapt to the new dataset and achieve higher accuracy. In conclusion, the proposed framework achieved high accuracy and low loss on the fashion apparel dataset, demonstrating its effectiveness in solving the problem of fine-grained fashion apparel classification. However, several potential enhancements could still be made to improve its performance even further. By incorporating these enhancements, we can create a more robust and accurate framework that can be used in other domains beyond fashion.

REFERENCES

Abdullahi, Y., Bhardwaj, A., Rahila, J., Anand, P., & Kandepu, K. (2023). Development of Automatic Change-Over with Auto-Start Timer and Artificial Intelligent Generator. *FMDB Transactions on Sustainable Energy Sequence, 1*(1), 11–26.

Anand, P. P., Sulthan, N., Jayanth, P., & Deepika, A. A. (2023). A Creating Musical Compositions Through Recurrent Neural Networks: An Approach for Generating Melodic Creations. *FMDB Transactions on Sustainable Computing Systems, 1*(2), 54–64.

Angeline, R., Aarthi, S., Regin, R., & Rajest, S. S. (2023). Dynamic intelligence-driven engineering flooding attack prediction using ensemble learning. In *Advances in Artificial and Human Intelligence in the Modern Era* (pp. 109–124). IGI Global. doi:10.4018/979-8-3693-1301-5.ch006

Arslan, F., Singh, B., Sharma, D. K., Regin, R., Steffi, R., & Rajest, S. S. (2021). Optimization technique approach to resolve food sustainability problems. In *2021 International Conference on Computational Intelligence and Knowledge Economy (ICCIKE)*. IEEE. 10.1109/ICCIKE51210.2021.9410735

Chadrasekar, P., & Beaulah David, H. (2014). Dissemination of Link State Information for Enhancing Security in Mobile Ad Hoc Networks. *IOSR Journal of Computer Engineering (IOSR-JCE), 16*(1), 24–31.

Chen, Y., Li, Y., & Tao, D. (2016). Fashion image retrieval based on fine-grained classification and transfer learning. In *Proceedings of the 2016 ACM on Multimedia Conference* (pp. 1022-1026). ACM.

Chen, Y., Li, Y., & Tao, D. (2017). Deep fashion feature embedding with improved triplet loss. In *Proceedings of the 2017 ACM on Multimedia Conference* (pp. 1013-1021). ACM.

Cirillo, S., Polese, G., Salerno, D., Simone, B., & Solimando, G. (2023). Towards Flexible Voice Assistants: Evaluating Privacy and Security Needs in IoT-enabled Smart Homes. *FMDB Transactions on Sustainable Computer Letters, 1*(1), 25–32.

Deng, J., Dong, W., Socher, R., Li, L. J., Li, K., & Fei-Fei, L. (2009). *ImageNet: A large-scale hierarchical image database. In 2009, the IEEE conference on computer vision and pattern recognition.* IEEE.

Devi, B. T., & Rajasekaran, R. (2023). A Comprehensive Review on Deepfake Detection on Social Media Data. *FMDB Transactions on Sustainable Computing Systems, 1*(1), 11–20.

Fabela, O., Patil, S., Chintamani, S., & Dennis, B. H. (2017). *Estimation of effective thermal conductivity of porous media utilizing inverse heat transfer analysis on cylindrical configuration* (Vol. 8). Heat Transfer and Thermal Engineering. doi:10.1115/IMECE2017-71559

Gaayathri, R. S., Rajest, S. S., Nomula, V. K., & Regin, R. (2023). Bud-D: Enabling Bidirectional Communication with ChatGPT by adding Listening and Speaking Capabilities. *FMDB Transactions on Sustainable Computer Letters, 1*(1), 49–63.

Jain, A. K., Misra, T., Tyagi, N., Suresh Kumar, M. V., & Pant, B. (2022). A Comparative Study on Cyber security Technology in Big data Cloud Computing Environment. In *2022 5th International Conference on Contemporary Computing and Informatics (IC3I)*. IEEE.

Jain, A. K., Ross, D. S., Babu, M. K., Uike, D., & Gangodkar, D. (2022). Cloud computing applications for protecting the information of healthcare department using smart internet of things appliance. In *2022 5th International Conference on Contemporary Computing and Informatics (IC3I)*. IEEE.

Jeba, J. A., Bose, S. R., & Boina, R. (2023). Exploring Hybrid Multi-View Multimodal for Natural Language Emotion Recognition Using Multi-Source Information Learning Model. *FMDB Transactions on Sustainable Computer Letters, 1*(1), 12–24.

Ji, R., Li, Y., Shen, Z., Li, L., & Liu, G. (2016). A fine-grained classification model for fashion image analysis. In *Proceedings of the 2016 ACM on Multimedia Conference* (pp. 955-956). ACM.

Ji, Z., & Wang, Y. (2021). A novel fine-grained fashion classification method using attention mechanisms. *Neural Computing & Applications*, *33*(6), 2229–2239.

Kanyimama, W. (2023). Design of A Ground Based Surveillance Network for Modibbo Adama University, Yola. *FMDB Transactions on Sustainable Computing Systems*, *1*(1), 32–43.

Kumar, K. S., Yadav, D., Joshi, S. K., Chakravarthi, M. K., Jain, A. K., & Tripathi, V. (2022). Blockchain technology with applications to distributed control and cooperative robotics. In *2022 5th International Conference on Contemporary Computing and Informatics (IC3I)*. IEEE.

Kumar Jain, A. (2022). Hybrid Cloud Computing: A Perspective. *International Journal of Engineering Research & Technology (Ahmedabad)*, *11*(10), 1–06.

Li, W., Chen, S., Xie, L., Fu, Y., & Zhang, H. (2021). Fine-grained fashion classification via a coarse-to-fine network with semantic hierarchy. *IEEE Transactions on Industrial Informatics*, *17*(3), 1901–1910.

Li, Y., Zhao, K., Li, R., Li, Y., & Li, H. (2020). Clothing classification based on transfer learning of deep convolutional neural networks. *Journal of Physics: Conference Series*, *1692*(1), 012103. doi:10.1088/1742-6596/1692/1/012103

Lodha, S., Malani, H., & Bhardwaj, A. K. (2023). Performance Evaluation of Vision Transformers for Diagnosis of Pneumonia. *FMDB Transactions on Sustainable Computing Systems*, *1*(1), 21–31.

Murugavel, S., & Hernandez, F. (2023). A Comparative Study Between Statistical and Machine Learning Methods for Forecasting Retail Sales. *FMDB Transactions on Sustainable Computer Letters*, *1*(2), 76–102.

Ogunmola, G. A., Singh, B., Sharma, D. K., Regin, R., Rajest, S. S., & Singh, N. (2021). Involvement of distance measure in assessing and resolving efficiency environmental obstacles. In *2021 International Conference on Computational Intelligence and Knowledge Economy (ICCIKE)*. IEEE. 10.1109/ICCIKE51210.2021.9410765

Patil, S., Chintamani, S., Dennis, B. H., & Kumar, R. (2021). Real time prediction of internal temperature of heat generating bodies using neural network. *Thermal Science and Engineering Progress*, *23*(100910), 100910. doi:10.1016/j.tsep.2021.100910

Patil, S., Chintamani, S., Grisham, J., Kumar, R., & Dennis, B. H. (2015). Inverse determination of temperature distribution in partially cooled heat generating cylinder. *Volume 8B: Heat Transfer and Thermal Engineering*.

Rajasekaran, N., Jagatheesan, S. M., Krithika, S., & Albanchez, J. S. (2023). Development and Testing of Incorporated ASM with MVP Architecture Model for Android Mobile App Development. *FMDB Transactions on Sustainable Computing Systems*, *1*(2), 65–76.

Rajasekaran, R., Reddy, A. J., Kamalakannan, J., & Govinda, K. (2023). Building a Content-Based Book Recommendation System. *FMDB Transactions on Sustainable Computer Letters*, *1*(2), 103–114.

Rajest, S. S., Singh, B., Obaid, A. J., Regin, R., & Chinnusamy, K. (2023b). Advances in artificial and human intelligence in the modern era. *Advances in Computational Intelligence and Robotics*. Advance online publication. doi:10.4018/979-8-3693-1301-5

Rajest, S. S., Singh, B. J., Obaid, A., Regin, R., & Chinnusamy, K. (2023a). Recent developments in machine and human intelligence. *Advances in Computational Intelligence and Robotics*. Advance online publication. doi:10.4018/978-1-6684-9189-8

Ramya, K., & Beaulah David, H. (2014). Hybrid Cryptography Algorithms for Enhanced Adaptive Acknowledgment Secure in MANET. *IOSR Journal of Computer Engineering (IOSR-JCE), 16*(1), 32–36.

Regin, R., Khanna, A. A., Krishnan, V., Gupta, M., Bose, R. S., & Rajest, S. S. (2023). Information design and unifying approach for secured data sharing using attribute-based access control mechanisms. In Recent Developments in Machine and Human Intelligence (pp. 256–276). IGI Global.

Regin, R., T, S., George, S. R., Bhattacharya, M., Datta, D., & Priscila, S. S. (2023). Development of predictive model of diabetic using supervised machine learning classification algorithm of ensemble voting. *International Journal of Bioinformatics Research and Applications, 19*(3), 10057044. Advance online publication. doi:10.1504/IJBRA.2023.10057044

Russakovsky, O., Deng, J., Su, H., Krause, J., Satheesh, S., Ma, S., & Berg, A. C. (2015). ImageNet large-scale visual recognition challenge. *International Journal of Computer Vision, 115*(3), 211–252. doi:10.100711263-015-0816-y

Sajini, S., Reddi, L. T., Regin, R., & Rajest, S. S. (2023). A Comparative Analysis of Routing Protocols for Efficient Data Transmission in Vehicular Ad Hoc Networks (VANETs). *FMDB Transactions on Sustainable Computing Systems, 1*(1), 1–10.

Saxena, D., & Chaudhary, S. (2023). Predicting Brain Diseases from FMRI-Functional Magnetic Resonance Imaging with Machine Learning Techniques for Early Diagnosis and Treatment. *FMDB Transactions on Sustainable Computer Letters, 1*(1), 33–48.

Shaheen, H. (2018). Modelling and Analytical Proofing of Low Energy Temperature Control using Earth/Ground Water Heat Exchanger. *International Journal of Pure and Applied Mathematics, 119*(16), 3575–3588.

Sharma, D. K., Jalil, N. A., Regin, R., Rajest, S. S., Tummala, R. K., & Thangadurai. (2021a). Predicting network congestion with machine learning. In *2021 2nd International Conference on Smart Electronics and Communication (ICOSEC)*. IEEE.

Sharma, D. K., Singh, B., Raja, M., Regin, R., & Rajest, S. S. (2021b). An Efficient Python Approach for Simulation of Poisson Distribution. In *2021 7th International Conference on Advanced Computing and Communication Systems (ICACCS)*. IEEE.

Sharma, D. K., Singh, B., Regin, R., Steffi, R., & Chakravarthi, M. K. (2021c). Efficient Classification for Neural Machines Interpretations based on Mathematical models. In *2021 7th International Conference on Advanced Computing and Communication Systems (ICACCS)*. IEEE.

Sharma, K., Singh, B., Herman, E., Regine, R., Rajest, S. S., & Mishra, V. P. (2021d). Maximum information measure policies in reinforcement learning with deep energy-based model. In *2021 International Conference on Computational Intelligence and Knowledge Economy (ICCIKE)*. IEEE. 10.1109/ICCIKE51210.2021.9410756

Simonyan, K., & Zisserman, A. (2015). Very deep convolutional networks for large-scale image recognition. In *Proceedings of the 3rd International Conference on Learning Representations (ICLR)* (pp. 1-14). Academic Press.

Sivapriya, G. B. V., Ganesh, U. G., Pradeeshwar, V., Dharshini, M., & Al-Amin, M. (2023). Crime Prediction and Analysis Using Data Mining and Machine Learning: A Simple Approach that Helps Predictive Policing. *FMDB Transactions on Sustainable Computer Letters, 1*(2), 64–75.

Sohlot, J., Teotia, P., Govinda, K., Rangineni, S., & Paramasivan, P. (2023). A Hybrid Approach on Fertilizer Resource Optimization in Agriculture Using Opposition-Based Harmony Search with Manta Ray Foraging Optimization. *FMDB Transactions on Sustainable Computing Systems, 1*(1), 44–53.

Sun, Y., Wang, X., & Tang, X. (2019). Deep learning-based fashion classification: A comprehensive review. *ACM Transactions on Multimedia Computing Communications and Applications, 15*(2), 1–23. doi:10.1145/3282833

Suraj, D., Dinesh, S., Balaji, R., Deepika, P., & Ajila, F. (2023). Deciphering Product Review Sentiments Using BERT and TensorFlow. *FMDB Transactions on Sustainable Computing Systems, 1*(2), 77–88.

Szegedy, C., Liu, W., Jia, Y., Sermanet, P., Reed, S., Anguelov, D., & Rabinovich, A. (2015). Going deeper with convolutions. In *Proceedings of the IEEE conference on computer vision and pattern recognition* (pp. 1-9). IEEE.

Wang, H., Chen, Q., Huang, J., & Zhang, J. (2021). A hierarchical feature fusion network for fashion landmark detection. *IEEE Transactions on Industrial Informatics, 17*(2), 1327–1336.

Wei, Z., Zhang, H., Chen, S., & Yang, Y. (2021). Efficient Multi-Granularity Encoding for Fashion Attribute Prediction. *IEEE Transactions on Industrial Informatics, 17*(3), 1911–1918.

Yang, Y., Li, H., Li, Y., & Zhang, Y. (2015). A large-scale car dataset for fine-grained categorization and verification. In *Proceedings of the IEEE Conference on Computer Vision and Pattern Recognition (CVPR)* (pp. 3973-3981). 10.1109/CVPR.2015.7299023

Yu, T., Wu, X., & Gong, Y. (2017). Dual learning for fine-grained image classification. In *Proceedings of the IEEE Conference on Computer Vision and Pattern Recognition* (pp. 4641-4650). IEEE.

Zhang, L., Wang, X., Liu, Y., & Qiao, Y. (2016). Towards exploring regularization in fine-grained image classification. In *Proceedings of the IEEE Conference on Computer Vision and Pattern Recognition* (pp. 1540-1548). IEEE.

Chapter 20
Harnessing the Power of ChatGPT to Explore Student Metacognitive Skills in Learning Sociology Education

Ahmad Al Yakin

Universitas Al Asyariah Mandar Sulawesi Barat, Indonesia

Ahmed J. Obaid

(iD) https://orcid.org/0000-0003-0376-5546

University of Kufa, Iraq

L. Abdul

(iD) https://orcid.org/0009-0003-8439-363X

Universitas Al Asyariah Mandar Sulawesi Barat, Indonesia

Idi Warsah

Institut Agama Islam Negeri Curup, Indonesia

Muthmainnah Muthmainnah

Universitas Al Asyariah Mandar Sulawesi Barat, Indonesia

Ahmed A. Elngar

(iD) https://orcid.org/0000-0001-6124-7152

Beni-Suef University, Egypt

ABSTRACT

In this study, ChatGPT and students studying the sociology of education discuss the potential application of AI applications in the field of metacognitive skills. This discussion contributes to the field of artificial intelligence research from a sociological perspective to comment on the significance potential of artificial intelligence language models in the humanities. As a result of the widespread adoption of ICT for pedagogical purposes, artificial intelligence has been introduced into the classroom, such as ChatGPT. It is used in several pedagogical contexts, such as adaptive learning systems, which change lesson difficulty in response to individual student progress.

DOI: 10.4018/979-8-3693-0502-7.ch020

INTRODUCTION

In the digital era, it is very important to improve students' metacognition skills, Cardoso et. al (2023). Students' metacognitive skills can help them make important contributions which can have an indirect positive effect on their academic results. Services aimed at improving students' metacognition are significant because they help children who are learning to self-regulate. They will be responsible for their own academic progress and will modify their study strategy as necessary to complete the objectives successfully. Self-regulated students do better in school because they are able to take charge of their education and learn on their own terms. Thus, it has been established that outstanding cognitive performance is associated with high levels of metacognitive abilities in domains as diverse as literature, mathematics, and information technology.

As a lecturer in a tertiary institution, it is very important to design learning activities that support increased metacognition, besides that the lecturer must have a strong understanding of new technologies to see threats and opportunities in the right context, Muthmainnah, et al. (2023). There is no denying that ChatGPT is an increasingly popular technology trend with game-changing features that will, and do, have to, change the stale approach to higher education teaching and evaluation. As a result of this shift, researchers may need to devote more time and energy to identifying and meeting the demands of the many constituencies of transformation education.

This does not mean that new teaching methods are always superior to those that have existed for some time. Each standard approach has proven successful at various points in time. New requirements for learning, however, are unavoidable given the shift in learner attitudes that accompany technological and societal developments Lun, et al (2023). Chatbots are here to stay whether we like it or not, their popularity is growing, and they are becoming a new trend that is already substantial. As this research will outline, educators must view upheaval as an opportunity to significantly increase the effectiveness of teaching in the digital age as needed.

Personalized learning is a teaching method that emphasizes the need to adapt lessons to each student's particular background, interests, and skill level. By assessing the learner's language patterns, feedback, and performance, the learning model by integrating ChatGPT can design individual lesson plans that incorporate optimal learning materials, exercises, and evaluations for that student Kılınç, (2023). When it comes to increasing student success, personalized instruction can be invaluable. Academic success, motivation, and self-confidence were all found to increase with individualized instruction, which concomitant with increased metacognition. Students are more likely to learn and retain information when they are exposed to content tailored to their individual needs and expertise. By using an interesting learning processing model such as ChatGPT, educators can provide maximum individual lessons to their students Qadir, (2023).

When students interact with this model, they can assess their level of comprehension as they react to a question and then alter their input accordingly. Students can use this information to gain a better understanding of their strengths and areas for improvement. The processing approach can also alter classes to meet unique needs based on each student's remarks and success. This plan may include additional reading, quizzes, or practise exercises, depending on the student's needs. This methodology can inspire students to take an active role in their own education by identifying precise measures that must be done to reach predefined goals.

Students who study individually or through distance education programmes may benefit from having access to on-demand teachers. By incorporating ChatGPT into the classroom, students may get on-demand help whenever they need it, not just in class, but also outside of class. There are various advantages to using on-demand assistance. As a result, pupils may be able to overcome learning obstacles and gain a more in-depth comprehension of the content. Furthermore, on-demand tutoring can boost students' confidence and self-esteem by giving them with the resources they require at any time. Chan and colleagues (2023), This model can provide quick support by responding promptly to student comments and questions. A customised response can be provided based on the model's appraisal of the student's request or answer.

ChatGPT is ideal for individuals studying alone or in online classes without an instructor. Furthermore, chatbots can provide assistance to undergraduate students at any time and from any location (Forman et al., 2023). This system is accessible through a range of devices, including mobile phones, laptops, and desktop PCs, allowing students to seek assistance whenever they need it. Javaid et al. (2023) are the study's authors. This adaptability enables for the availability of critical resources while also fitting the hectic schedules of students and educators. Students can also seek help right away by using ChatGPT's text, voice, or video chat options. Individual learning styles of students can be better catered for by providing the type of help that best suits them in this manner.

The goal of this study was to see if first-year college students may benefit from practising metacognition in an asynchronous online environment utilising ChatGPT. Even though metacognition is essential for optimal learning, some undergraduate students may struggle to develop it. This could be due to a lack of self-confidence, a lack of ideas, a lack of resources, or a boring teaching setting. ChatGPT is an AI-powered application that helps students solve problems by guiding them through self-assessment, academic goal setting, material discovery, study schedule construction, progress tracking, and learning reflection. The possibility of student addiction to ChatGPT is discussed in this study, as is the importance of institutional usage policies and the ongoing need for future AI developers to improve the algorithms and data used by the system to reduce the likelihood of providing inaccurate and irrelevant results. Concerns were also raised about how to best mix ChatGPT with interaction with real teachers to maximise educational outcomes.

LITERATURE REVIEW

Metacognitive Skills

Metacognition is a crucial part of effective learning because it allows people to be more deliberate and intentional about their learning. Individuals can make educated decisions about how to approach learning tasks, check their progress, and alter their techniques when presented with problems if they are aware of their own thinking and learning strategies. This level of awareness and self-regulation can result in more effective and efficient learning results.

According to Melissa (2020), "metacognitive skills" are the ability to "control, monitor, and self-regulate" in the learning and problem-solving processes. Controlling one's own thinking processes and learning methods is an example of metacognitive competency, according to Orakci and Durnali (2023). Students who have developed their metacognitive skills have a better understanding of where they excel and where they could use improvements. Students can then use this basic understanding to adapt their approach to meet specific assignment requirements during learning Negretti, (2012). Students can control their level of involvement in tasks based on their knowledge and skills, with the aim of improving learning processes and outcomes. For example, when students encounter a problem, they will reevaluate and rework according to the final goal of the assignment. Therefore, as a lecturer, students' metacognitive abilities must be nurtured in the classroom.

According to the definition of metacognition proposed by Liu (2023), the ability to engage in reflective thinking about one's own knowledge and future actions is a characteristic of metacognitive abilities. According to Cardoso et al. (2023), metacognitive skills consist of knowing how our minds work and being able to direct that knowledge to achieve our goals. As a result, when students have started to use metacognitive strategies to monitor and adjust their own thinking processes throughout the verification phase of problem solving, the desired results can be achieved in a timely and efficient manner.

To control one's own thought processes, Singh and Diefes. (2023) define metacognition as "thinking about thinking." Knowledge about cognitive processes and the products for organising, monitoring, and assessing processes were separated as separate components of metacognition by Cini et al. (2023). Knowledge about oneself, one's tasks, and tactics, as well as knowledge of how to apply these strategies and metacognitive experience, are all necessary for a full understanding of cognitive processes. Metacognitive skills are essential for many types of thinking, claims Cromley (2023). Intentional activation occurs when the learning task requires attention and precision, when a new task is presented, or when the acquired knowledge is incomplete or incorrect (Neal, 2023); Wang et al. (2023) and Abdelshiheed et al. (2023) made the distinction between metacognitive knowledge and metacognitive skills. The term "metacognitive knowledge" is used to describe individuals' explicit understanding of their own learning, techniques, and activities. The ability to consciously monitor and adjust one's own thought processes is a metacognitive competency.

Additionally, Kikas et al. (2023) and Tripathi et al. (2023) stated that the application of metacognitive skills is very important for managing the learning process and solving one's own problems. Procedural knowledge metacognition is the ability to monitor and adjust the learning process, think for yourself, problem solve, summarise, and explain. These are examples of metacognitive skills that can be developed through efficiently elaborated learning activities. When this is done, the result is that students can make control of their own learning.

According to Hacker et al. (2023), a person's ability to exercise self-control and self-regulation of their own learning and cognitive processes is metacognitive competence. This is also called or known as "executive function". Students demonstrate these traits when they analyze the task at hand, plan, monitor, check or evaluate, recapitulate, and reflect on their own work. Learning strategies that focus on reading or literacy Timotheou et al. (2023) also influence the implementation of learning that forces metacognitive skills to occur.

Students' academic level is another important component that must be given more attention in the teaching and learning process because it influences students' abilities in learning activities and the learning process in class. Learning methods and outcomes can be influenced by factors such as the academic level of each student. A student's academic level is his demonstrated ability to carry out scholastic or educational tasks (Garcia and Pintrich, 2023). This is the completion of long-term, medium-term, or short-term educational goals that are used to achieve educational goals by determining the level of academic learning achievement. Therefore, a student's academic ability can be interpreted as an indicator of the student's potential scholastic learning success. In this research, it is hypothesized that undergraduate students with different academic levels will have varying levels of success in developing their metacognitive abilities with the help of ChatGPT. This assumption is believed by several studies that support AI as one of the causes that metacognition can be improved or developed in digital-based learning.

Metacognition in Education

Metacognitive skills in education according to Li et al. (2023), students' ability to monitor their own learning is influenced by how they feel, experience, and reflect on their own performance. Therefore, when there are no time constraints, high performance estimates are indicative of actual performance. Increasing students' metacognition has been proven to have a positive effect on their learning outcomes or academic achievement (Acosta-Gonzaga, 2023). One of the successes in completing higher education is one of several variables that determine the quality of education. The strategies, models, media, technology, or lecturer patterns used in the educational process are as important for student success as the lecture material itself, which is included in the curriculum. What students learn depends largely on the instructor's competence and enthusiasm (TPACK), during which the class is held. So, it is up to professors to shape their students' education by using effective teaching models, methods, media, and technology.

Students are encouraged to develop 21st century skills such as critical thinking, collaboration, and creativity through their education by increasing academic literacy, which is part of integrated science and can help students develop critical thinking skills and switch from a receptive learning mode to an active learning mode. Observational evidence shows that the development of students' metacognitive abilities is still lacking. Students need to develop their metacognitive abilities so they can take charge of their own education Zimmerman, (2023). Teaching techniques currently used provide students with fewer opportunities and learning experiences to build concepts through reflection and critical analysis.

Teaching metacognitive skills requires a metacognitive approach. One definition of metacognitive strategies is "routine activities that represent the management of mental processes as components of process complexity and applied to obtain goals" Meltzer, (2013). The level of student metacognition is related to thinking abilities, cognitive preferences, and preferred learning methods, media, and technology in this research using ChatGPT. Students' metacognition is influenced by their level of thinking, cognitive style, and learning style. Students with strong metacognitive skills are more likely to have positive learning experiences and be academically successful Talwar et al. (2023). Students' level of metacognition was found to be a major factor in their academic performance Cale, et al. (2023); Teng and Yue (2023). Metacognitive abilities were found to have a positive effect on students' academic performance during the learning process. Fleur et al. (2023) and Hayat, et al. (2023).

Academic literacy with science reading comprehension and the ability to analyze popular science media readings may benefit from increased student use of metacognition (Ulu-Aslan and Baş (2023). Research has shown that students who use metacognition are more likely to (a) develop conceptual understanding (Carr, 2010), (b) through the process of knowledge construction and meaningful understanding (Zabolotna et al. 2023), (c) understand scientific texts better (Cromley, 2023) and (d) more motivated and have a more accurate view of what it means to understand and construct new knowledge (Drigas et al. 2023).

Similar results have been observed in the field of social studies teaching. Standardized student academic scores improved after students participated in a metacognitive intervention that encouraged them to reflect on their own learning and prevented the use of ineffective techniques such as memorization and teacher centering (Urban and Urban (2023). Silver et al. (2023) found that teaching students metacognitive techniques and methods including question asking skills led to a significant increase in the complexity of questions asked by students. Karaoglan-Yilmaz et al. (2023), Zheng et al. (2023), and Teng and Yue

(2023) all found that increasing students' awareness of the learning process and their ability to monitor, organize and control learning helped them gain a deeper understanding of various knowledge concepts, in an effort to increase their capacity for scientific thinking. Researchers concluded that metacognition is needed in the classroom when teaching educational sociology. Metacognition is difficult to measure because it is an internal process and not an overt behavior, and because people often do not realize that they are engaging in metacognition (Geurten and Léonard, 2023). This makes it difficult to recognize and evaluate metacognition and related processes. On the other hand, Mari et al. (2023) argue if metacognition is understood as knowledge, then metacognition can be inferred from learner behavior or by asking for an explicit description of the learner's thinking process.

METHOD

Quantitative methods were applied in this study to find out the responses of undergraduate students regarding the impact of ChatGPT on increasing their metacognition. The methodology used here is to use a survey approach using observation and questionnaires. To collect information, researchers used the Google form to obtain questionnaire survey data. Statements and questions regarding the impact of ChatGPT on students' metacognition while studying the political education.

Population and Sample

This research was conducted at Al Asyriah Mandar University with a population of 350 students for the 2022 academic year. Sampling was carried out using the purposive random sampling method, namely undergraduate students who were involved and had experience interacting with the ChatGPT application.

The survey was delivered to students who took political education courses with a total of 15 students in semester 4. The research data was collected from students' perceptions of how teaching practices using ChatGPT in driving students' metacognitive activities based on Cetin PME indicators (2014); planning (number 1-3), monitoring (4-7), and evaluation (9-10) obtained based on data after teaching political educations courses. The ChatGPT-based learning model metacognitive activity questionnaire was modified from the concept of Cetin (2014).

Chatgpt Procedure for Exploring Metacognition

In the context of this research, "knowledge of doing things and having experience to formulate concepts and construct information (Figure 1)" refers to students utilising their understanding of social science principles. Most of this information is offered as a heuristic to quickly gather key ideas and concepts about social science concepts and social phenomena in Google scholar and ChatGPT (Figure 1 and Figure 3). We believe that encouraging undergraduate students to develop metacognitive skills is key to helping them learn about new social phenomena and improving their ability to understand what they read and study. Constructing social science in the aspect of political education by inviting undergraduate students to map political developments in accordance with political culture is the second step taken to construct their knowledge (Table 1, No. 4, and Figure 2).

Figure 1. Formulate concepts by reading

At this point Figure 2, students are asked to access ChatGPT and design their own concept of political education that is appropriate to Indonesian social culture. Here, undergraduate students intend to use certain cognitive talents, such as activating previous knowledge or textual organisation of the knowledge gained and connecting the information contained in ChatGPT. During the learning process, their cognitive activities are monitored and demonstrate the need for regulatory procedures, and undergraduate students will self-assess their knowledge as part of the process, when students read a topic in various learning sources (Google Scholar, Academia, and ChatGPT), they internalise the information presented in the references as tacit knowledge.

Designing new concepts based on their experiences, observations, and information gained is a great way for undergraduate students to practice metacognition or monitor their own learning. Accessing information using ChatGPT is an example of a strategy that shows metacognitive abilities such as awareness and control over one's own cognitive processes.

Figure 2. Designing and creating new concept with ChatGPT

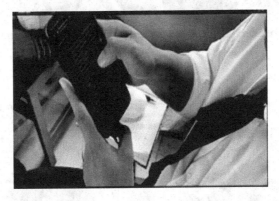

The undergraduate students in this study actively engaged in the application of metacognitive skills as they utilised declarative knowledge, procedural knowledge, conditional planning, monitoring, and judgement as they interacted with ChatGPT. Multiple studies have found that adult learners benefit from using ChatGPT, encouraging them to build on their previous knowledge to create new maps and products. In the next statement (Table 1 no. 5), with ChatGPT, they are asked to be actively involved during the learning process to ask questions, explore, write new concepts, think critically, and communicate—requiring students to work with teams in groups with designated leaders and take on the role of peer tutor. Students' self-esteem increases and their social interactions with peers are strengthened when they work together, as described in figure 3.

Students' understanding of the benefits of having a peer tutor is increasing, and they feel involvement, which increases their self-confidence (Table 1, no. 6). Interacting with peers and lecturers makes it easier for them to share their ideas. In keeping with Vygotsky's Zone of Proximal Development (ZPD) Ness, (2023) it explains that people learn best when working with others during collaboration and that students learn and internalise new concepts through such collaborative efforts with more skilled attention. The use of a constructive controversy approach in cooperative learning is justified because it can improve students' metacognitive abilities, as identified in this study.

Cooperative learning in groups has been proven to be effective for teaching students metacognitive skills. This is because the focus of learning strategies is essentially related to education. Work group members evaluate group performance, evaluate, and make changes to members' social interactions, and evaluate and make changes to members' physical appearance.

Figure 3. Comprehend with teamwork, discussion process

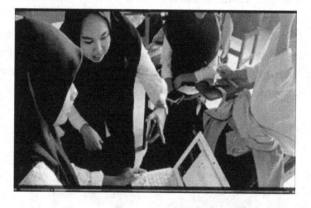

Figure 4. Metacognitive reflection process

DATA ANALYSIS

Analysis of survey data regarding increased metacognition during learning using the ChatGPT application was analyzed using SPSS version 26 and interpreting the findings according to the results of observations during learning.

RESULTS AND DISCUSSION

Students are given the freedom to express their opinions without restrictions, and these responses are then subjected to thematic analysis in an effort to identify overarching ideas and themes. This survey was designed to give each participant a fair opportunity to rate each question, ultimately enabling a more scientific evaluation of aspects of metacognition using ChatGPT. Based on the identified categories, we create a 10-item survey and publish it on the whatsapp group. Students were asked to rate their level of agreement with each statement on a Likert scale from 5 (strongly agree) to 1 (strongly disagree). Because of their origin in thematic analysis, the questionnaire items will be discussed here. After participating in a further six ChatGPT exercises, students filled out this survey with the following results.

Table 1. Descriptive statistics of the increasing metacognitive skills-ChatGPT based

Descriptive Statistics					
Statement From Survey	**N**	**Minimum**	**Maximum**	**Mean**	**Std. Deviation**
1. Be able to maximize their learning and engage in strategic planning while using ChatGPT	15	4.00	5.00	4.6000	.50709
2. Students get the concept and have a plan to reconstruct the information they get from their appearance.	15	4.00	5.00	4.6000	.50709
3. Students apply the concept and have a plan to implement it in real terms.	15	4.00	5.00	4.6000	.50709
4. ChatGPT makes it easy to understand political education material.	15	4.00	5.00	4.4667	.51640
5. ChatGPT engages undergraduate students to interact with instructors and classmates.	15	4.00	5.00	4.7333	.45774
6. ChatGPT can increase confidence when learning to set step by step the accuracy of their calculations and information.	15	4.00	5.00	4.7333	.45774
7. ChatGPT helps students to produce new information about the political education.	15	4.00	5.00	4.8667	.35187
8. ChatGPT can help self-assess learning understanding and monitoring performance on political education material	15	3.00	5.00	4.4000	.73679
9. Using ChatGPT can generate new ideas and concept collaborations in the real world.	15	4.00	5.00	4.7333	.45774
10. The ChatGPT feature encourages students to connect knowledge, provide meaningful comments, and draw meaningful conclusions.	15	4.00	5.00	4.2667	.45774
Valid N (listwise)	15				

On Table 1 showed the increasing of the students' metacognitive skills after treatment by using ChatGPT in the politic system class. The respondents strongly agree and agree on the ChatGPT teaching model, they are totally belief in ChatGPT support their metacognitive skills than before. Based on the descriptive statistics provided in the survey statement, it is known that the results in statements 1, 2, and 3 show that all these statements have the same average value of 4.6000, which shows that respondents generally agree that ChatGPT helps them maximize learning, understand concepts, and plan implementation. The low standard deviation of 0.50709 indicates that there is relatively low variability in responses to these statements, indicating a high level of agreement among respondents.

Then statement number 4 regarding the effectiveness of ChatGPT in helping students understand political education material was rated slightly lower, with an average score of 4.4667. The standard deviation of 0.51640 indicates variability in responses, but overall, it still reflects a positive perception. In statements no. 5, 6, and 9, it is known that these statements received a higher average rating, ranging from 4.7333 to 4.8667. This shows that respondents consider ChatGPT effective in engaging students, increasing confidence in learning, and generating new ideas and collaboration. The standard deviation indicates relatively low variability in responses to these statements.

ChatGPT's ability to help students produce new information about political education received a high mean value in statement number 7 of 4.8667, with a low standard deviation of 0.35187. This shows strong agreement among respondents that ChatGPT is effective in this regard. Statement number 8 regarding ChatGPT's ability to help self-assess learning and monitor performance received an average score of 4.4000, with a relatively high standard deviation of 0.73679. This shows that although many respondents viewed ChatGPT positively in this aspect, there was more variability in responses compared to some of the other statements.

Statement number 10 about ChatGPT, which encourages students to connect knowledge and draw meaningful conclusions, received a mean value of 4.2667 with a standard deviation of 0.45774. This indicates a positive perception, but with slightly greater variability in responses compared to some of the other statements. The survey results generally show that respondents have a positive view of ChatGPT's role in education, with high mean scores for most statements. However, there was some variation in the responses, particularly in self-assessment and meaningful inference, which suggests that different people may have different perspectives on these aspects. Overall, ChatGPT appears to be viewed as a valuable tool for improving learning and engagement in educational contexts.

In the context of Metacognition-ChatGPT-based metacognitive support, Figure 2 displays the frequency and percentage distribution of respondents' mean scores. A total of 15 responders and their average rating for using ChatGPT are listed in the table below. Here is some context for the numbers in Table 2.

A single respondent's average score of 41.00 indicates a passing grade. This person accounts for 6.7% of all respondents. The total percentage of their scores was 6.7%. A low score of 41 implies minimal use of metacognitive strategies. Two responders (13.3% of the total) had an average score of 42, making them the only ones to do so. There is a total of 20 percent of these people. With a score of 42, metacognitive aids are used to a fair degree. The average score for the 6.7% of respondents that fell into the "other" category was 43.00. The total percentage increase due to this score is 26.7%. With a score of 43, metacognitive support is being used in a moderate manner. 44.00 Mean Score One respondent (1), or 6.7% of the whole, had an average score of 44, which is like the preceding situation. There has been a total increase of 33.3% so far. Similarly, a score of 44 suggests a moderate level of reliance on metacognitive strategies.

Table 2. The frequencies statistic

Metacognition-ChatGPT Based				
		Frequency	Percent	Valid Percent	Cumulative Percent
Valid	41.00	1	6.7	6.7	6.7
	42.00	2	13.3	13.3	20.0
	43.00	1	6.7	6.7	26.7
	44.00	1	6.7	6.7	33.3
	46.00	1	6.7	6.7	40.0
	47.00	3	20.0	20.0	60.0
	48.00	3	20.0	20.0	80.0
	49.00	3	20.0	20.0	100.0
	Total	15	100.0	100.0	

One respondent had a mean score of 46, accounting for 6.7% of the final tally. Forty percent was reached. With a score of 46, metacognitive aid use is around average. Three respondents (20.0% of the total) averaged 47 points out of a possible 50. This subset's overall percentage has increased to 60.0%. With a score of 47, you make moderate use of metacognitive strategies. In the same vein, three people (20.0% of the total) had an average score of 48 out of a possible 100. The total percentage is now up to 80.0%. With a score of 48, you make moderate use of metacognitive strategies. Three respondents (20.0% of the total) received an average score of 49, making up the final group. A total of 100% has been reached. A score of 49 indicates a high level of metacognitive assistance.

It is clear from the distribution of responses that ChatGPT should be used extensively in the classroom. With a mean score of 47 or higher, most respondents (60.0%) made extensive use of metacognitive strategies. Based on these results, the majority of respondents found ChatGPT's metacognitive elements to be useful in the classroom setting. Based on the frequency in Table 2, describe 1 respondent with a 41, 43, 44, and 46 mean score, only 2 respondents with a 42.00 mean score, and 3 respondents with a 47, 48, and 49 mean score. It makes ChatGPT highly recommended to apply in the classroom. The description of can be seen in the histogram below.

DISCUSSION

The results of this study indicate that applying ChatGPT in the classroom can improve the metacognition of undergraduate students at universities. Based on the results of observations, it shows that the performance of student presentations or demonstrations is getting maximal. In addition, activities in conveying discourse in front of an audience that are used to foster student focus, integration of critical thinking skills and problem-solving exercises for students are greatly assisted when ChatGPT is used. Students can develop their ideas and ideas correctly about the political education that exists in Indonesia and the world and classes are increasingly meaningful.

Figure 5. Students frequently

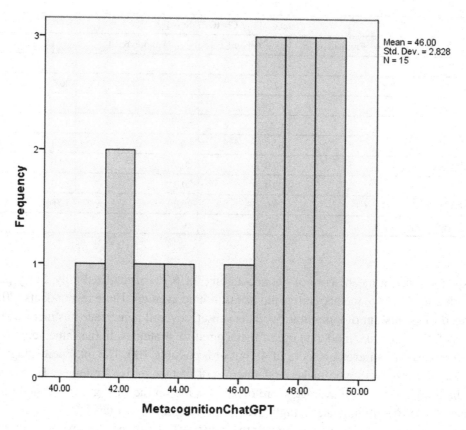

The performance evaluation form includes open-ended questions relevant to student development. Letter writing and oral presentations are two examples of how students can demonstrate what they have learned in a second language school. Opportunity to utilize the target language in a meaningful way. Table 1 described the ability of students to communicate, discuss, critical thinking, evaluate, problem solving, have planning, in the context of the real world is an application of metacognition. Teachers can evaluate this metacognition when in class in the form of critical studies, namely the ability of undergraduate students to describe, interrupt, and connect old and new knowledge and construct new knowledge. Using ChatGPT, students can participate in online dialogues and learning resources to improve their metacognition skills.

The results of this research based on a survey show that undergraduate students' metacognitive abilities are greatly improved by ChatGPT; here, we found undergraduate student responses led to a sizable percentage of ChatGPT in this regard. Reading teaching materials on ChatGPT is the first step in engaging students who work independently to gain a basic understanding of a topic by focusing only on the topical content. ChatGPT provides information and provides fast feedback so that reading, analysing, and making reading analogies according to the context of the material in this activity are metacognitive skills (Figure 1).

The ChatGPT feature encourages students to connect knowledge, provide meaningful comments, and draw meaningful conclusions. One of the most widespread methods for developing higher-order thinking is by connecting knowledge, providing meaningful comments, and drawing meaningful conclusions to find out why they are learning something, which is essential for self-regulation in the classroom. Then, ChatGPT can help students become better at managing their own education in terms of developing metacognitive abilities. When connecting knowledge, providing meaningful comments, and drawing meaningful conclusions, this activity is designed to foster the development of students' metacognitive skills through organising related questions as a measurement of learning outcomes and is useful for finding answers to their questions or completing activities assigned to them. Then, meaningful conclusions are drawn for those who are called independent learners.

According to research by Cardoso et al. (2023), students who are developing their metacognitive skills demonstrate a greater sense of ownership over their learning processes and an improved ability to adapt their learning strategies to the requirements of given tasks. This study demonstrates that problem-solving, made easier by ChatGPT technology, and the concurrent development of metacognitive skills are fundamental components of the learning activities that students engage in. Throughout the process of knowledge integration, undergraduates collaboratively form teams to mutually educate one another, thereby augmenting their learning and teaching proficiencies through the exchange of insights and firsthand knowledge, particularly emphasizing principled responses to student inquiries induced by induction. The cultivation of metacognitive skills in the learning domain necessitates an intricate consideration of the interplay between student and instructor motivation, entailing dedicated efforts towards self-reflection, cognitive challenge, and the rectification of one's thinking processes—all essential aspects activating metacognitive skills. Skills encompassing control, monitoring, self-regulation in learning, and adept problem-solving exemplify the facets of metacognition, as delineated in Figures 1, 2, and 3 and Table 1. The visual representations elucidate that instigating a sense of responsibility for their own learning positively impacts students' academic performance, affirming that students excel when empowered to regulate their learning processes. The ChatGPT learning model, in this context, seeks not only to serve as a repository of knowledge but also as a catalyst for refining students' metacognitive prowess. These revelations underscore that undergraduate student, on average, commence their academic journey from an elevated starting state. Conversely, a subset of students, commencing with academic conditions below or at an average level, exhibits noticeable improvement, underscoring the efficacy of the ChatGPT-facilitated learning approach.

efforts to self-reflect, challenge, and correct one's own thinking (activating metacognitive skills). Skills in control, monitoring, self-regulation in learning, and problem solving are examples of metacognition Figure 1, Figure 2 and Figure 3 and Table 1showed that encouraging students to take responsibility for their own learning had a positive impact on students' grades. Student performance improves when they can regulate their own learning. The aim of the ChatGPT learning model is to teach students how to think so they can utilise their entire cognitive framework and attention. Therefore, the aim of ChatGPT in this research is not only to be a source of knowledge but also to hone students' metacognitive abilities. These findings reveal undergraduate students have a higher-than-average starting state in terms of academics. On the other hand, there are several students whose initial academic conditions were below or at an average level who also improved.

The presence of ChatGPT in the classroom has the potential to provide major benefits for the learning of undergraduate students in tertiary institutions, with critical studies, problem solving and creativity learning outcomes. ChatGPT is an AI technique that can process and produce text with a high level of sophistication that really helps students in analyzing political educations and political phenomena that occur around the world. ChatGPT can be used in class to help students learn and make critical thinking processes easier, the class atmosphere is active, fun and interesting. The results of this study support the usefulness of ChatGPT as a great tool for education because it helps students find relevant, high-quality reading materials based on their interests and needs. ChatGPT natural language processing and data access capabilities, ChatGPT can provide student-friendly content tailored to their individual skills. Here, lecturers use ChatGPT to create personalized reading lists based on students' interests and abilities connected to the material.

Apart from that, this research also programmed ChatGPT to create questions and estimates automatically. When planning class activities, this will save the teacher's time and energy. However, there are several limitations of ChatGPT found in this study, although overall it is a good learning tool. First, ChatGPT is not a replacement for a human instructor, as it can only generate text and does not provide examples or explanations in real time. Of course. What's worse, ChatGPT is limited in how it uses the data it has, which means it can't provide students with personalized report cards on their performance. The findings of this study are the same as those of Latif et al. (2023). ChatGPT can improve classroom teaching but cannot replace human teachers. While ChatGPT can help lecturers save time in class, there's nothing better than having a real person walk students through each step of the material and provide constructive criticism. In short, the workload and educational experience of teachers and students can be significantly improved by using ChatGPT in the classroom. Technological advances in the classroom are incredible, but nothing can replace a teacher's personal example and guidance.

Therefore, ChatGPT is best used in conjunction with a teacher, not as a substitute for them, and its use remains under the supervision of the teacher, as Figure 1 and Figure 2 show. Efforts should also be made to incorporate technology into learning in a way that makes sense and is appropriate to the educational environment. Considerations such as the type of problem encountered, specific learning objectives, and characteristics of the technology itself should be taken into account when determining how best and where to implement technology in the classroom, as stated by Woithe et al. (2023) and Rasul et al. (2023). There are additional considerations that must be made, such as accessibility of facilities and appropriate personnel to manage the technology aspects of education. If technology is to be effectively integrated into the classroom, teachers must play an important role. Teachers must be experienced in the technologies that are important to their students and be able to use them effectively in the classroom. Educators need to acquire new skills and knowledge to effectively incorporate technology into their learning (Al Yakin, 2019; Muthmainnah et al., 2023).

Lecturers at universities must be able to use ChatGPT effectively and choose and define texts that suit the learning needs of their students. In this study, lecturers used ChatGPT to improve students' metacognition, and provided feedback based on this evaluation in learning activities and managing digital learning environments effectively. Overall, a tool like ChatGPT can greatly enhance the educational experience. However, technology can only function as a resource, and can never completely replace the role of educators. This highlights the importance of training educators to manage student learning effectively within the context of technological tools. Using technology in this way has the potential to improve educational outcomes for both students and instructors, Khang et al (2023).

Observations made with the ChatGPT-based learning model in political educations courses when the phase of presenting arguments and counterarguments is also an implementation of metacognition. Discussions and debates can be used by lecturers to help students improve their metacognition skills. ChatGPT allows lecturers to generate their new knowledge based on current events relevant to the political education. To keep students from relying too much on ChatGPT, lecturers often ask them to complete writing assignments in class using traditional pen and paper. Writing assignments may be more interesting for students if teachers take the time to design concrete activities that encourage students to share their unique perspectives.

Safe and effective use of ChatGPT depends on developing methodologies and evaluation tools for their efficacy in the classroom as learning resources and accessing information related to learning materials. Evaluation of precision, consistency, and lack of bias in output are all within the scope of the instrument. Based on this research it can provide insight to the extent to which ChatGPT can help improve metacognition and point the way towards future studies. In short, the implications of ChatGPT for metacognition skills in university settings are enormous. Its full potential for use in teaching can only be realized once the researcher has a clearer understanding of its advantages, disadvantages, ethical and social consequences, constraints, and scope for development.

CONCLUSION

The findings of this research support the importance of accelerating education with appropriate technology in improving the learning metacognition of undergraduate students in higher education. ChatGPT really supports increasing metacognition after being applied to political education courses which shows the ability to process information, construct new ideas and concepts during discussions, have a study plan and self-evaluate to gain knowledge. Finally, colleges and universities must spend money to educate their faculty to use and adapt to technology, as well as provide students with the tools they need to apply the model well. As a result, students who learn with ChatGPT have the confidence to learn, share ideas, design concepts, and improve academic literacy. After being taught to use ChatGPT, undergraduate students became better able to assess themselves and evaluate their learning activities, resulting in a significant increase in metacognition. Overall, the ChatGPT learning model is a powerful tool for improving the quality of education by providing individual learning experiences to students and providing high-quality education for students in the 21st century era.

REFERENCES

Abdelshiheed, M., Barnes, T., & Chi, M. (2023). How and When: The Impact of Metacognitive Knowledge Instruction and Motivation on Transfer across Intelligent Tutoring Systems. *International Journal of Artificial Intelligence in Education*. Advance online publication. doi:10.100740593-023-00371-0

Acosta-Gonzaga, E. (2023). The Effects of Self-Esteem and Academic Engagement on University Students' Performance. *Behavioral Sciences (Basel, Switzerland)*, *13*(4), 348. doi:10.3390/bs13040348 PMID:37102862

Al Yakin, A. (2019, July). Manajemen kelas di era industri 4.0. In Jurnal Peqguruang Conference Series (Vol. 1, No. 1, pp. 11-15). Academic Press.

Cale, A. S., Hoffman, L. A., & McNulty, M. A. (2023). Promoting metacognition in an allied health anatomy course. *Anatomical Sciences Education*, *16*(3), 473–485. doi:10.1002/ase.2218 PMID:35951462

Cardoso, L. M., Aeni, N., & Muthmainnah, M. (2023). Mobilizing Metacognitive Strategies Through Zoom for EFL Classrooms: An Innovative Practice Amidst Covid 19. *Journal of Language Learning and Assessment*, 19-25.

Carr, M. (2010). The importance of metacognition for conceptual change and strategy use in mathematics. *Metacognition, strategy use, and instruction*, 176-197.

Cetin, P. S. (2014). Explicit argumentation instruction to facilitate conceptual understanding and argumentation skills. *Research in Science & Technological Education*, *32*(1), 1–20. doi:10.1080/02635143.2013.850071

Chan, C. K. Y., & Lee, K. K. (2023). *The AI generation gap: Are Gen Z students more interested in adopting generative AI such as ChatGPT in teaching and learning than their Gen X and Millennial Generation teachers?* arXiv preprint arXiv:2305.02878.

Çini, A., Malmberg, J., & Järvelä, S. (2023). How individual metacognitive awareness relates to situation-specific metacognitive interpretations of collaborative learning tasks. *Educational Studies*, *49*(1), 54–75. doi:10.1080/03055698.2020.1834359

Cromley, J. G. (2023). Metacognition, cognitive strategy instruction, and reading in adult literacy. *Review of Adult Learning and Literacy*, *5*, 187–204. doi:10.4324/9781003417958-7

Drigas, A., Mitsea, E., & Skianis, C. (2023). Meta-learning: A Nine-layer model based on metacognition and smart technologies. *Sustainability (Basel)*, *15*(2), 1668. doi:10.3390u15021668

Fleur, D. S., van den Bos, W., & Bredeweg, B. (2023). Social comparison in learning analytics dashboard supporting motivation and academic achievement. *Computers and Education Open*, *4*, 100130. doi:10.1016/j.caeo.2023.100130

Forman, N., Udvaros, J., & Avornicului, M. S. (2023). ChatGPT: A new study tool shaping the future for high school students. *International Journal of Advanced Natural Sciences and Engineering Researches*, *7*(4), 95–102. doi:10.59287/ijanser.562

Garcia, T., & Pintrich, P. R. (2023). Regulating motivation and cognition in the classroom: The role of self-schemas and self-regulatory strategies. In *Self-regulation of learning and performance* (pp. 127–153). Routledge.

Geurten, M., & Léonard, C. (2023). Relations between parental metacognitive talk and children's early metacognition and memory. *Journal of Experimental Child Psychology*, *226*, 105577. doi:10.1016/j.jecp.2022.105577 PMID:36335835

Hacker, D. J. (2023). Self-Regulation of Writing: Models of Writing and the Role of Metacognition. In *The Routledge International Handbook of Research on Writing* (pp. 236–256). Routledge.

Hayat, A. A., Shateri, K., Amini, M., & Shokrpour, N. (2020). Relationships between academic self-efficacy, learning-related emotions, and metacognitive learning strategies with academic performance in medical students: A structural equation model. *BMC Medical Education, 20*(1), 1–11. doi:10.118612909-020-01995-9 PMID:32183804

Javaid, M., Haleem, A., Singh, R. P., Khan, S., & Khan, I. H. (2023). Unlocking the opportunities through ChatGPT Tool towards ameliorating the education system. *BenchCouncil Transactions on Benchmarks, Standards and Evaluations*, 100115.

Karaoglan-Yilmaz, F. G., Ustun, A. B., Zhang, K., & Yilmaz, R. (2023). Metacognitive awareness, reflective thinking, problem solving, and community of inquiry as predictors of academic self-efficacy in blended learning: A correlational study. *Turkish Online Journal of Distance Education, 24*(1), 20–36. doi:10.17718/tojde.989874

Khang, A., Muthmainnah, M., Seraj, P. M. I., Al Yakin, A., & Obaid, A. J. (2023). AI-Aided Teaching Model in Education 5.0. In Handbook of Research on AI-Based Technologies and Applications in the Era of the Metaverse (pp. 83-104). IGI Global.

Kikas, E., Eisenschmidt, E., & Granström, M. (2023). Conceptualisation of learning to learn competence and the challenges of implementation: The Estonian experience. *European Journal of Education, 58*(3), 498–509. doi:10.1111/ejed.12571

Kılınç, S. (2023). *Embracing the Future of Distance Science Education: Opportunities and Challenges of ChatGPT Integration*. Academic Press.

Latif, E., Mai, G., Nyaaba, M., Wu, X., Liu, N., Lu, G., . . . Zhai, X. (2023). *Artificial general intelligence (AGI) for education*. arXiv preprint arXiv:2304.12479.

Li, L., Zhu, M. L., Shi, Y. Q., & Yang, L. L. (2023). Influencing factors of self-regulated learning of medical-related students in a traditional Chinese medical university: A cross-sectional study. *BMC Medical Education, 23*(1), 87. doi:10.118612909-023-04051-4 PMID:36737773

Liu, M. (2023). A self-case study of the female doctoral student's own creative metacognition on art expressions: Based on the theory of creative metacognition (CMC). *Thinking Skills and Creativity, 48*, 101292. doi:10.1016/j.tsc.2023.101292

Lund, B. D., Wang, T., Mannuru, N. R., Nie, B., Shimray, S., & Wang, Z. (2023). ChatGPT and a new academic reality: Artificial Intelligence-written research papers and the ethics of the large language models in scholarly publishing. *Journal of the Association for Information Science and Technology, 74*(5), 570–581. doi:10.1002/asi.24750

Mari, M. A., Tsalas, N., & Paulus, M. (2023). Why is she scratching her head? Children's understanding of others' metacognitive gestures as an indicator of learning. *Journal of Experimental Child Psychology, 230*, 105631. doi:10.1016/j.jecp.2023.105631 PMID:36731277

Melissa Ng Lee Yen, A. (2020). The influence of self-regulation processes on metacognition in a virtual learning environment. *Educational Studies, 46*(1), 1–17. doi:10.1080/03055698.2018.1516628

Meltzer, L. (2013). Teaching executive functioning processes: Promoting metacognition, strategy use, and effort. In *Handbook of executive functioning* (pp. 445–473). Springer New York.

Muthmainnah, G. S., & Al Yakin, A. (2023). An Effective Investigation on YIPe-Learning Based for Twenty-First Century Class. In Digital Learning based Education: Transcending Physical Barriers (pp. 21-38). Singapore: Springer Nature Singapore.

Muthmainnah, M., Khang, A., Al Yakin, A., Oteir, I., & Alotaibi, A. N. (2023). An Innovative Teaching Model: The Potential of Metaverse for English Learning. In *Handbook of Research on AI-Based Technologies and Applications in the Era of the Metaverse* (pp. 105–126). IGI Global. doi:10.4018/978-1-6684-8851-5.ch005

Neal, T. M. (2023). Metacognition: Thinking About Thinking. In Strategies and Considerations for Educating the Academically Gifted (pp. 95-115). IGI Global.

Negretti, R. (2012). Metacognition in student academic writing: A longitudinal study of metacognitive awareness and its relation to task perception, self-regulation, and evaluation of performance. *Written Communication*, *29*(2), 142–179. doi:10.1177/0741088312438529

Ness, I. J. (2023). Zone of Proximal Development. In *The Palgrave Encyclopedia of the Possible* (pp. 1781–1786). Springer International Publishing.

Orakci, Ş., & Durnali, M. (2023). The mediating effects of metacognition and creative thinking on the relationship between teachers' autonomy support and teachers' self-efficacy. *Psychology in the Schools*, *60*(1), 162–181. doi:10.1002/pits.22770

Qadir, J. (2023, May). Engineering education in the era of ChatGPT: Promise and pitfalls of generative AI for education. In *2023 IEEE Global Engineering Education Conference (EDUCON)* (pp. 1-9). IEEE. 10.1109/EDUCON54358.2023.10125121

Rasul, T., Nair, S., Kalendra, D., Robin, M., de Oliveira Santini, F., Ladeira, W. J., ... Heathcote, L. (2023). The role of ChatGPT in higher education: Benefits, challenges, and future research directions. *Journal of Applied Learning and Teaching*, *6*(1).

Silver, N., Kaplan, M., LaVaque-Manty, D., & Meizlish, D. (Eds.). (2023). *Using reflection and metacognition to improve student learning: Across the disciplines, across the academy*. Taylor & Francis.

Singh, A., & Diefes-Dux, H. A. (2023, June). Pairing self-evaluation activities with self-reflection to engage students deeply in multiple metacognition strategies. *2023 ASEE Annual Conference & Exposition*.

Talwar, A., Magliano, J. P., Higgs, K., Santuzzi, A., Tonks, S., O'Reilly, T., & Sabatini, J. (2023). Early Academic Success in College: Examining the Contributions of Reading Literacy Skills, Metacognitive Reading Strategies, and Reading Motivation. *Journal of College Reading and Learning*, *53*(1), 58–87. doi:10.1080/10790195.2022.2137069

Teng, M. F., & Yue, M. (2023). Metacognitive writing strategies, critical thinking skills, and academic writing performance: A structural equation modeling approach. *Metacognition and Learning*, *18*(1), 237–260. doi:10.100711409-022-09328-5

Timotheou, S., Miliou, O., Dimitriadis, Y., Sobrino, S. V., Giannoutsou, N., Cachia, R., Monés, A. M., & Ioannou, A. (2023). Impacts of digital technologies on education and factors influencing schools' digital capacity and transformation: A literature review. *Education and Information Technologies, 28*(6), 6695–6726. doi:10.100710639-022-11431-8 PMID:36465416

Tripathi, V., & Tiwari, S. (2023). A study of relationship between meta-cognitive skills and academic achievement of mathematics students. *Remittances Review, 8*(4).

Ulu-Aslan, E., & Baş, B. (2023). Popular culture texts in education: The effect of tales transformed into children's media on critical thinking and media literacy skills. *Thinking Skills and Creativity, 47*, 101202. doi:10.1016/j.tsc.2022.101202

Urban, M., & Urban, K. (2023). Orientation Toward Intrinsic Motivation Mediates the Relationship Between Metacognition and Creativity. *The Journal of Creative Behavior, 57*(1), 6–16. doi:10.1002/jocb.558

Wang, Y., Hu, J., An, Z., Li, C., & Zhao, Y. (2023). The influence of metacognition monitoring on L2 Chinese audiovisual reading comprehension. *Frontiers in Psychology, 14*, 1133003. doi:10.3389/fpsyg.2023.1133003 PMID:36891205

Woithe, J., & Filipec, O. (2023). *Understanding the Adoption, Perception, and Learning Impact of ChatGPT in Higher Education: A qualitative exploratory case study analyzing students' perspectives and experiences with the AI-based large language model.* Academic Press.

Zabolotna, K., Malmberg, J., & Järvenoja, H. (2023). Examining the interplay of knowledge construction and group-level regulation in a computer-supported collaborative learning physics task. *Computers in Human Behavior, 138*, 107494. doi:10.1016/j.chb.2022.107494

Zheng, L., Niu, J., Zhong, L., & Gyasi, J. F. (2023). Knowledge-building and metacognition matter: Detecting differences between high-and low-performance groups in computer-supported collaborative learning. *Innovations in Education and Teaching International, 60*(1), 48–58. doi:10.1080/14703297.2021.1988678

Zimmerman, B. J. (2023). Dimensions of academic self-regulation: A conceptual framework for education. In *Self-regulation of learning and performance* (pp. 3–21). Routledge.

Compilation of References

Abdelshiheed, M., Barnes, T., & Chi, M. (2023). How and When: The Impact of Metacognitive Knowledge Instruction and Motivation on Transfer across Intelligent Tutoring Systems. *International Journal of Artificial Intelligence in Education*. Advance online publication. doi:10.100740593-023-00371-0

Abderraouf, A. (2016). Investigating EFL students' writing difficulties and common errors in writing [Master Thesis, University of Bejaia].

Abdullahi, I., Arif, S., & Hassan, S. (2015). *'Ubiquitous shift with information centric network caching using fog computing,'' in Computational Intelligence in Information Systems*. Springer.

Abdullahi, Y., Bhardwaj, A., Rahila, J., Anand, P., & Kandepu, K. (2023). Development of Automatic Change-Over with Auto-Start Timer and Artificial Intelligent Generator. *FMDB Transactions on Sustainable Energy Sequence*, *1*(1), 11–26.

Abdullah, M., Madain, A., & Jararweh, Y. (2022). ChatGPT: Fundamentals, Applications, and Social Impacts. In *2022 Ninth International Conference on Social Networks Analysis, Management and Security (SNAMS)*, Milan, Italy. 10.1109/SNAMS58071.2022.10062688

Abdullah, M., Madain, A., & Jararweh, Y. (2022, November). ChatGPT: Fundamentals, applications and social impacts. In *2022 Ninth International Conference on Social Networks Analysis, Management and Security (SNAMS)* (pp. 1-8). IEEE.

Abidoye, A. P., & Kabaso, B. (2021). Lightweight models for detection of denial-of-service attack in wireless sensor networks. *IET Networks*, *10*(4), 185–199. doi:10.1049/ntw2.12011

Abouabdelkader, H., & Ahmed, A. (Eds.). (2016). *Teaching EFL writing in the 21st century Arab world: Realities and challenges*. Springer Nature., doi:10.1057/978-1-137-46726-3

Abu Shkheedim, S., Alawneh, Y., Khuwayra, O., & Salman, F., khayyat, T. (2022). The Level Of Satisfaction Of Parents Of Students With Learning Difficulties Towards Distance Learning After The Corona Pandemic. *NeuroQuantology : An Interdisciplinary Journal of Neuroscience and Quantum Physics*, *20*(19), 1299–1311.

Acosta-Gonzaga, E. (2023). The Effects of Self-Esteem and Academic Engagement on University Students' Performance. *Behavioral Sciences (Basel, Switzerland)*, *13*(4), 348. doi:10.3390/bs13040348 PMID:37102862

Adetayo, A. J. (2023). Artificial intelligence chatbots in academic libraries: The rise of ChatGPT. *Library Hi Tech News*, *40*(3), 18–21. doi:10.1108/LHTN-01-2023-0007

Adiguzel, T., Kaya, M. H., & Cansu, F. K. (2023). Revolutionizing education with AI: Exploring the transformative potential of ChatGPT. *Contemporary Educational Technology*, *15*(3), ep429. doi:10.30935/cedtech/13152

Adithya, R., Denise, D., Kenneth, H., Xian, L., & Mona, D. (2021). Gender bias amplification during Speed-Quality optimization in Neural Machine Translation. *Proceedings of the 59th Annual Meeting of the Association for Computational Linguistics and the 11th International Joint Conference on Natural Language Processing* (pp. 99–109). Association for Computational Linguistics.10.18653/v1/2021.acl-short.15

Agarwal, R., Hariharan, S., Nagabhushana Rao, M., & Agarwal, A. (2021). Weed identification using K-means clustering with color spaces features in multi-spectral images taken by UAV. *2021 IEEE International Geoscience and Remote Sensing Symposium IGARSS*. IEEE.

Agarwal, R. (2014). Edge detection in images using modified bit-planes Sobel operator. In *Advances in Intelligent Systems and Computing* (pp. 203–210). Springer India.

Ahamed, B., Sellamuthu, S., Karri, P. N., Srinivas, I. V., Mohammed Zabeeulla, A. N., & Ashok Kumar, M. (2023). Design of an energy-efficient IOT device-assisted wearable sensor platform for healthcare data management. *Measurement. Sensors*, 30(100928), 100928. doi:10.1016/j.measen.2023.100928

Ahmed, A. H. (2010). Students' problems with cohesion and coherence in EFL essay writing in Egypt: Different perspectives. *Literacy Information and Computer Education Journal*, 1(4), 211–221. doi:10.20533/licej.2040.2589.2010.0030

Ahn, C. (2023). Exploring ChatGPT for information of cardiopulmonary resuscitation. *Resuscitation, 185*, 109729. doi:10.1016/j.resuscitation.2023.109729 PMID:36773836

Aithal, S., & Aithal, P. S. (2023). Effects of AI-Based ChatGPT on Higher Education Libraries. [IJMTS]. *International Journal of Management, Technology, and Social Sciences*, 8(2), 95–108. doi:10.47992/IJMTS.2581.6012.0272

Al Khawaldeh, S., Alawneh, Y., & Alzboun, M. (2022). the availability of quality standards for the construction of science achievement tests from the point of view of the examination committees [Natural Sciences]. *Hunan Daxue Xuebao. Shehui Kexue Ban*, 49(9), 1233–1247.

Al Khazraji, A. (2019). Analysis of discourse markers in essays writing in ESL classroom. *International Journal of Instruction*, 12(2), 559–572. doi:10.29333/iji.2019.12235a

Al Yakin, A. (2019, July). Manajemen kelas di era industri 4.0. In Jurnal Peqguruang Conference Series (Vol. 1, No. 1, pp. 11-15). Academic Press.

Al Yakin, A., Obaid, A. J., & Massyat, M. (2022). Students' Motivation and Attitude Based on Google Classroom Utilization. *Journal of Positive School Psychology*, 6(2), 1053–1059.

AlAfnan, M. A., Samira Dishari, Marina Jovic, & Koba Lomidze. (2023). ChatGPT as an Educational Tool: Opportunities, Challenges, and Recommendations for Communication, Business Writing, and Composition Courses. *Journal of Artificial Intelligence and Technology*, 3(2), 60–68. doi:10.37965/jait.2023.0184

Alammar, J. (n.d.). *The illustrated transformer*. Jay Alammar. https://jalammar.github.io/illustrated-transformer/

Alawneh, Y. (2022). Role of Kindergarten Curriculum in Instilling Ethical Values among Children in Governorates of Northern West Bank, Palestine, Dirasat. *Education in Science*, 49(3), 360–375.

Alawneh, Y., Ashamali, M., Abdel-Hassan, R., Al-khawaldeh, S., & Engestroom, Y. (2022). Degree Of Use Of E-Learning Science Teachers In Public High Schools In During The Corona-Covid 19 Pandemic. *Journal of Positive School Psychology*, 6(2), 1060–1070.

Albarino, S. (2020, July 24). GPT-3: What You Need to Know About the World's Largest Language Model. Slator. https://slator.com/gpt-3-what-you-need-to-know-about-the-worlds-largest-language-mod el/

Alharthi, A. S., Yunas, S. U., & Ozanyan, K. B. (2019). Deep learning for monitoring of human gait: A review. *IEEE Sensors Journal*, *19*(21), 9575–9591. doi:10.1109/JSEN.2019.2928777

Ali, A., Pickering, M., Sha, A. K. A., Chandio, M., & Pickering, K. (2020). Character classification and recognition for Urdu texts in natural scene images. In *Proc. Int. Conf.* Semantic Scholar.

Ali, A. A., Abbass, A., & Farid, N. (2020a). FACTORS INFLUENCING CUSTOMERS' PURCHASE INTENTION IN SOCIAL COMMERCE. *International Review of Management and Marketing*, *10*(5), 63–73. doi:10.32479/irmm.10097

Ali, J. K. M., Shamsan, M. A. A., Hezam, T. A., & Mohammed, A. A. (2023). Impact of ChatGPT on learning motivation: Teachers and students' voices. *Journal of English Studies in Arabia Felix*, *2*(1), 41–49. doi:10.56540/jesaf.v2i1.51

Ali, M. J., & Djalilian, A. (2023, March). Readership awareness series–paper 4: Chatbots and chatgpt-ethical considerations in scientific publications. In *Seminars in ophthalmology* (pp. 1–2). Taylor & Francis.

Al-sa'di, A., & Miller, D. (2023). Exploring the Impact Of Artificial Intelligence Language Model Chatgpt On The User Experience. *International Journal on Technology, Innovation, and Management*, *1*(3), 1–8. doi:10.54489/ijtim.v3i1.195

Alsheikh, M. A., Basar, T. A., & Tepe, K. E. (2019). Intelligent Data Analytics for Internet of Things-Based Applications. *IEEE Access : Practical Innovations, Open Solutions*, *7*, 16825–16833.

Alshurafat, H. (2023). The Usefulness and Challenges of Chatbots for Accounting Professionals: Application On Chat-GPT. SSRN *Electronic Journal*. doi:10.2139/ssrn.4345921

Alsulaiman, L., & Al-Ahmadi, S. (2021). *Performance evaluation of machine learning techniques for DOS detection in wireless sensor network*. arXiv preprint arXiv:2104.01963.

Analytica, O. (2023a). *ChatGPT dramatically fuels corporate interest in AI*. Emerald Expert Briefings.

Analytica, O. (2023b). *Commercial use of ChatGPT requires caution*. Emerald Expert Briefings.

Anand, P. P., Sulthan, N., Jayanth, P., & Deepika, A. A. (2023). A Creating Musical Compositions Through Recurrent Neural Networks: An Approach for Generating Melodic Creations. *FMDB Transactions on Sustainable Computing Systems*, *1*(2), 54–64.

Anderson, P., He, X., Buehler, C., Teney, D., Johnson, M., Gould, S., & Zhang, L. (2018). Bottom-up and top-down attention for image captioning and visual question answering. In *Proceedings of the IEEE conference on computer vision and pattern recognition* (pp. 6077-6086). IEEE. 10.1109/CVPR.2018.00636

Angeline, R., Aarthi, S., Regin, R., & Rajest, S. S. (2023). Dynamic intelligence-driven engineering flooding attack prediction using ensemble learning. In *Advances in Artificial and Human Intelligence in the Modern Era* (pp. 109–124). IGI Global. doi:10.4018/979-8-3693-1301-5.ch006

Angwin, J., Larson, J., Mattu, S., & Kirchner, L. (2022). Machine bias. In *Ethics of data and analytics* (pp. 254–264). Auerbach Publications. doi:10.1201/9781003278290-37

An, Q., Hong, W. C. H., Xu, X., Zhang, Y., & Kolletar-Zhu, K. (2023). How Education Level Influences Internet Security Knowledge, Behaviour, and Attitude: A Comparison among Undergraduates, Postgraduates and Working Graduates. *International Journal of Information Security*, *22*(2), 305–317. doi:10.100710207-022-00637-z PMID:36466362

An, R., Hen, J., & Xiao, Y. (2022). Applications Of Artificial Intelligence To Obesity Research: Scoping Review Of Methodologies. *Journal of Medical Internet Research*, *12*(24), e40589. doi:10.2196/40589 PMID:36476515

Anson, C. M., & Straume, I. (2022). Amazement and Trepidation: Implications of AI-Based Natural Language Production for the Teaching of Writing. *Journal of Academic Writing*, *12*(1), 1–9. doi:10.18552/joaw.v12i1.820

AntakiF.ToumaS.MiladD.El-KhouryJ.DuvalR. (2023). Evaluating the Performance of ChatGPT in Ophthalmology: An Analysis of its Successes and Shortcomings. MedRxiv, 100324. doi:10.1101/2023.01.22.23284882

Ao, L., Bansal, R., Pruthi, N., & Khaskheli, M. B. (2023). Impact of Social Media Influencers on Customer Engagement and Purchase Intention: A Meta-Analysis. *Sustainability (Basel)*, *15*(3), 2744. doi:10.3390u15032744

APA. (2023). Emotion. In *American Psychological Association online dictionary*. APA. https://dictionary.apa.org/emotion

Ariyanti, A., & Fitriana, R. (2017). EFL students' difficulties and needs in essay writing. Advances in Social Science, Education and Humanities Research. International Conference on Teacher Training and Education 2017 (ICTTE 2017), Surakarta, Indonesia. https://doi.org/10.2991/ictte-17.2017.4

Arslan, F., Singh, B., Sharma, D. K., Regin, R., Steffi, R., & Rajest, S. S. (2021). Optimization technique approach to resolve food sustainability problems. *2021 International Conference on Computational Intelligence and Knowledge Economy (ICCIKE)*. IEEE. 10.1109/ICCIKE51210.2021.9410735

Artificial Intelligence Index Report. (2023). Stanford University. https://aiindex.stanford.edu/wp-content/uploads/2023/04/HAI_AI-Index-Report_2023.pdf

Aryal, A., Stricklin, I., Behzadirad, M., Branch, D. W., Siddiqui, A., & Busani, T. (2022). High-quality dry etching of LiNbO3 assisted by proton substitution through H2-plasma surface treatment. *Nanomaterials (Basel, Switzerland)*, *12*(16), 2836. doi:10.3390/nano12162836 PMID:36014702

Ashish, S. (2017). Identification of Unknown Landscape Types Using CNN Transfer Learning. *Boise State University Theses and Dissertations.*, *1318*. doi:10.18122/B2C70F

Assistant Professor, S. R. (2023). *CENTRAL ASIAN JOURNAL OF THEORETICAL AND APPLIED SCIENCES* Protection of User Profiles in Social Networks From Unauthorized Access. https://cajotas.centralasianstudies.org

Athaluri, S., Manthena, S., Kesapragada, V., Yarlagadda, V., Dave, T., & Duddumpudi, R. T. S. (2023). Exploring the Boundaries of Reality: Investigating the Phenomenon of Artificial Intelligence Hallucination in Scientific Writing Through ChatGPT References. *Cureus*, *15*(4), e37432. doi:10.7759/cureus.37432 PMID:37182055

Atuhaire, R. (2022). What is ChatGPT. Dignited. https://www.dignited.com/104384/what-is-chatgpt-and-how-does-it-work/

Awais, M., Bhuva, A., Bhuva, D., Fatima, S., & Sadiq, T. (2023). Optimized DEC: An effective cough detection framework using optimal weighted Features-aided deep Ensemble classifier for COVID-19. *Biomedical Signal Processing and Control*, *105026*, 105026. doi:10.1016/j.bspc.2023.105026 PMID:37361196

Aydın, Ö., & Karaarslan, E. (2022). OpenAI ChatGPT generated literature review: Digital Twin in Healthcare. In Ö. Aydın (Ed.), Emerging Computer Technologies 2 (22-31). İzmir Akademi Dernegi.

Azaria, A. (2022). *ChatGPT Usage and Limitations*. Research Gate. https://www.researchgate.net/publication/366618623_ChatGPT_Usage_and_Limitations

Aziz, A. (2023). Artificial Intelligence Produced Original Work: A New Approach To Copyright Protection And Ownership. *European Journal of Artificial Intelligence and Machine Learning*, *2*(2), 9–16. doi:10.24018/ejai.2023.2.2.15

Aziz, G., & Sarwar, S. (2023). Empirical Evidence of Environmental Technologies, Renewable Energy and Tourism to Minimize the Environmental Damages : Implication of Advanced Panel Analysis. *International Journal of Environmental Research and Public Health*, *20*(6), 5118. doi:10.3390/ijerph20065118 PMID:36982028

Baethge, C., Klier, J., & Klier, M. (2016). Social commerce—State-of-the-art and future research directions. *Electronic Markets*, *26*(3), 269–290. doi:10.100712525-016-0225-2

Bahdanau, D., Cho, K., & Bengio, Y. (2014). *Neural machine translation by jointly learning to align and translate.* arXiv preprint arXiv:1409.0473.

Bahrini, A. (2023). *ChatGPT: Applications, Opportunities, and Threats. 2023 Systems and Information Engineering Design Symposium (SIEDS),* Charlottesville, VA, USA. 10.1109/SIEDS58326.2023.10137850

Baidoo-Anu, D., & Ansah, L. O. (2023). Education in the era of generative artificial intelligence (AI): Understanding the potential benefits of ChatGPT in promoting teaching and learning. *Journal of AI, 7*(1), 52–62. doi:10.61969/jai.1337500

Bakry, M. S., & Alsamadani, H. A. (2015). Improving the persuasive essay writing of students of Arabic as a Foreign Language (AFL): Effects of self-regulated strategy development. *Procedia: Social and Behavioral Sciences, 182,* 89–97. doi:10.1016/j.sbspro.2015.04.742

Balas, M., & Ing, E. B. (2023). Conversational AI Models for ophthalmic diagnosis: Comparison of ChatGPT and the Isabel Pro Differential Diagnosis Generator. *JFO Open Ophthalmology, 1,* 100005. Advance online publication. doi:10.1016/j.jfop.2023.100005

Bansal, V., Bhardwaj, A., Singh, J., Verma, D., Tiwari, M., & Siddi, S. (2023). Using artificial intelligence to integrate machine learning, fuzzy logic, and the IOT as A cybersecurity system. *2023 3rd International Conference on Advance Computing and Innovative Technologies in Engineering (ICACITE).* IEEE.

Bansal, V., Pandey, S., Shukla, S. K., Singh, D., Rathod, S. A., & Gonzáles, J. L. A. (2022). A frame work of security attacks, issues classifications and configuration strategy for IoT networks for the successful implementation. *2022 5th International Conference on Contemporary Computing and Informatics (IC3I).* IEEE.

Barron Estrada, M., Zatarain Cabada, R., Oramas Bustillos, R., & Graff, M. (2020). Opinion Mining and Emotion Recognition Applied to Learning Environments. *Expert Systems with Applications, 113265,* 113265. doi:10.1016/j.eswa.2020.113265

Barron Estrada, M., Zatarain Cabada, R., & Oramas, R. (2019). Emotion Recognition for Education using Sentiment Analysis. *Research in Computing Science, 148*(5), 71–80. doi:10.13053/rcs-148-5-8

Belkhiri, H., Messai, A., Beylot, A. L., & Haider, F. (2022). Denial of Service Attack Detection in Wireless Sensor Networks and Software Defined Wireless Sensor Networks: A Brief Review. In *Proceedings of the 5th International Conference on Big Data and Internet of Things.* Cham: Springer International Publishing. 10.1007/978-3-031-07969-6_8

Bender, E. M., Gebru, T., McMillan-Major, A., & Shmitchell, S. (2021). *On the dangers of stochastic parrots: Can language models be too big?* arXiv preprint arXiv:2105.07592. doi:10.1145/3442188.3445922

BenoitJ. R. A. (2023). ChatGPT for Clinical Vignette Generation, Revision, and Evaluation. MedRxiv. doi:10.1101/2023.02.04.23285478

Bessette, L. S. (2023). This Isn't Another Piece on ChatGPT. *The National Teaching & Learning Forum, 32*(2), 11–12. doi:10.1002/ntlf.30359

Beutel, A., Chen, J., Zhao, Z., & Chi, E. H. (2017). Data decisions and theoretical implications when adversarially learning fair representations. In *Proceedings of the 26th International Conference on World Wide Web* (pp. 903-912).

Bhanushali, A. (2023). Challenges and solutions in implementing continuous integration and continuous testing for agile quality assurance. *International Journal of Science and Research (Raipur, India), 12*(10), 1626–1644. doi:10.21275/SR231021114758

Bhardwaj, A., Pattnayak, J., Prasad Gangodkar, D., Rana, A., Shilpa, N., & Tiwari, P. (2023). An integration of wireless communications and artificial intelligence for autonomous vehicles for the successful communication to achieve the destination. *2023 3rd International Conference on Advance Computing and Innovative Technologies in Engineering (ICACITE)*. IEEE.

Bhardwaj, A., Pattnayak, J., Prasad Gangodkar, D., Rana, A., Shilpa, N., & Tiwari, P. (2023a). An integration of wireless communications and artificial intelligence for autonomous vehicles for the successful communication to achieve the destination. *2023 3rd International Conference on Advance Computing and Innovative Technologies in Engineering (ICACITE)*. IEEE.

Bhardwaj, A., Raman, R., Singh, J., Pant, K., Yamsani, N., & Yadav, R. (2023b). Deep learning-based MIMO and NOMA energy conservation and sum data rate management system. *2023 3rd International Conference on Advance Computing and Innovative Technologies in Engineering (ICACITE)*. IEEE.

Bhardwaj, A., Rebelli, S., Gehlot, A., Pant, K., Gonzáles, J. L. A., & Firos. (2023c). Machine learning integration in Communication system for efficient selection of signals. *2023 3rd International Conference on Advance Computing and Innovative Technologies in Engineering (ICACITE)*. IEEE.

Bhardwaj, A. K., Rangineni, S., & Marupaka, D. (2023). Assessment of Technical Information Quality using Machine Learning. *International Journal of Computer Trends and Technology*, 71(9), 33–40. doi:10.14445/22312803/IJCTT-V71I9P105

Bhatti, B. M., Mubarak, S., & Nagalingam, S. V. (2021). Information security implications of using NLP in IT outsourcing: A Diffusion of Innovation theory perspective. *Automated Software Engineering*, 28(2), 12. doi:10.100710515-021-00286-x

Bishop, L. (2023). Can ChatGPT "Think Like a Lawyer?" A Socratic Dialogue. SSRN *Electronic Journal*. doi:10.2139/ssrn.4338995

Bisk, Y., Zellers, R., Le-bras, R., Gao, J., & Choi, Y. (2020). Reasoning about Physical Commonsense in Natural Language. *Proceedings of the AAAI Conference on Artificial Intelligence, 34(05)*, (pp. 7432-7439.)10.1609/aaai.v34i05.6239

Biswas, S. (2023a). ChatGPT and the Future of Medical Writing. *Radiology*, 307(2), e223312. doi:10.1148/radiol.223312 PMID:36728748

Biswas, S. (2023b). *Role of ChatGPT in Computer Programming*. Mesopotamian Journal of Computer Science. doi:10.58496/MJCSC/2023/002

Biswas, S. (2023c). *Role of ChatGPT in the Film Industry: According to ChatGPT*. Qeios. doi:10.32388/NABVHA

Boland, C. M., Hogan, C. E., & Manco-Johnson, M. J. (2018). Motivating Compliance: Firm Response To Mandatory Disclosure Policies. *Accounting Horizons*, 2(32), 103–119. doi:10.2308/acch-52037

Bolukbasi, T., Chang, K. W., Zou, J. Y., Saligrama, V., & Kalai, A. (2016). Man is to computer programmer as woman is to homemaker? Debiasing word embeddings. In Advances in Neural Information Processing Systems (pp. 4349-4357).

BommineniV. L.BhagwagarS. Z.BalcarcelD. (2023). Performance of ChatGPT on the MCAT: The Road to Personalized and Equitable Premedical Learning. MedRxiv. doi:10.1101/2023.03.05.23286533

BorjiA. (2023). A categorical archive of ChatGPT failures. Research Square *(Research Square)*. https://doi.org/doi:10.21203/rs.3.rs-2895792/v1

Bouaziz, M., & Rachedi, A. (2016). A survey on mobility management protocols in wireless sensor networks based on 6LoWPAN technology. *Computer Communications*, 74, 3–15. doi:10.1016/j.comcom.2014.10.004

Bowman, S. R., Vilnis, L., Vinyals, O., Dai, A. M., Jozefowicz, R., & Bengio, S. (2016). *Generating sentences from a continuous space*. arXiv preprint arXiv:1511.06349. doi:10.18653/v1/K16-1002

Brand, J., Israeli, A., & Ngwe, D. (2023). Using GPT for Market Research. *Harvard Business School Marketing Unit Working Paper No. 23-062*. doi:10.2139/ssrn.4395751

Brown, T. B., Mann, B., Ryder, N., Subbiah, M., Kaplan, J., Dhariwal, P., & Amodei, D. (2020). *Language Models are Few-Shot Learners*. arXiv preprint arXiv:2005.14165.

Brown, T. B., Mann, B., Ryder, N., Subbiah, M., Kaplan, J., Dhariwal, P., & Amodei, D. (2020). Language models are few-shot learners. In Advances in Neural Information Processing Systems.

Brown, T. B., Mann, B., Ryder, N., Subbiah, M., Kaplan, J., Dhariwal, P., Neelakantan, A., Shyam, P., Sastry, G., Askell, A., Agarwal, S., Herbert-Voss, A., Krueger, G., Henighan, T., Child, R., Ramesh, A., Ziegler, D. M., Wu, J., Winter, C., & Amodei, D. (2020). Language models are few-shot learners. arXiv preprint. https://arxiv.org/abs/2005.14165

Brown, H. D. (2000). *Teaching by principles: An Interactive approach to language pedagogy* (2nd ed.). Pearson.

Bulqiyah, S., Mahbub, M. A., & Nugraheni, D. A. (2021). Investigating writing difficulties in essay writing: Tertiary students' perspectives. *English Language Teaching Educational Journal*, 4(1), 61. doi:10.12928/eltej.v4i1.2371

Burkhard, M. (2022). Student Perceptions of Ai-Powered Writing Tools: Towards Individualized Teaching Strategies. *Proceedings of the 19th International Conference on Cognition and Exploratory Learning in the Digital Age, CELDA 2022, Celda*, (pp. 73–81). IEEE. https://doi.org/10.33965/CELDA2022_202207L010

Cale, A. S., Hoffman, L. A., & McNulty, M. A. (2023). Promoting metacognition in an allied health anatomy course. *Anatomical Sciences Education*, 16(3), 473–485. doi:10.1002/ase.2218 PMID:35951462

Caliskan, A., Bryson, J. J., & Narayanan, A. (2017). Semantics derived automatically from language corpora contain human-like biases. *Science*, 356(6334), 183–186. doi:10.1126cience.aal4230 PMID:28408601

Cannon, W. (1927). The James-Lange Theory of Emotions: A Critical Examination and an Alternative Theory. *The American Journal of Psychology*, 39(1/4), 106–124. doi:10.2307/1415404 PMID:3322057

Cardoso, L. M., Aeni, N., & Muthmainnah, M. (2023). Mobilizing Metacognitive Strategies Through Zoom for EFL Classrooms: An Innovative Practice Amidst Covid 19. *Journal of Language Learning and Assessment*, 19-25.

Carr, M. (2010). The importance of metacognition for conceptual change and strategy use in mathematics. *Metacognition, strategy use, and instruction*, 176-197.

Casillo, F., Deufemia, V., & Gravino, C. (2022). Detecting privacy requirements from User Stories with NLP transfer learning models. *Information and Software Technology*, 146, 106853. doi:10.1016/j.infsof.2022.106853

Castro Nascimento, C. M., & Pimentel, A. S. (2023). Do Large Language Models Understand Chemistry? A Conversation with ChatGPT. *Journal of Chemical Information and Modeling*, 63(6), 1649–1655. doi:10.1021/acs.jcim.3c00285 PMID:36926868

Cetin, P. S. (2014). Explicit argumentation instruction to facilitate conceptual understanding and argumentation skills. *Research in Science & Technological Education*, 32(1), 1–20. doi:10.1080/02635143.2013.850071

Ceylan, N. O. (2019). Student perceptions of difficulties in second language writing. *Journal of Language and Linguistic Studies*, 15(1), 151–157. doi:10.17263/jlls.547683

Chadrasekar, P., & Beaulah David, H. (2014). Dissemination of Link State Information for Enhancing Security in Mobile Ad Hoc Networks. *IOSR Journal of Computer Engineering (IOSR-JCE)*, 16(1), 24–31.

Chan, C. K. Y., & Lee, K. K. (2023). *The AI generation gap: Are Gen Z students more interested in adopting generative AI such as ChatGPT in teaching and learning than their Gen X and Millennial Generation teachers?* arXiv preprint arXiv:2305.02878.

Chan, W., Jaitly, N., Le, Q., & Vinyals, O. (2016). Listen, Attend and Spell. In *2016 IEEE International Conference on Acoustics, Speech and Signal Processing (ICASSP)* (pp. 4960-4964). IEEE. 10.1109/ICASSP.2016.7472621

Chaturvedi, A., Bhardwaj, A., Singh, D., Pant, B., Gonzáles, J. L. A., & Firos. (2022). Integration of DL on multi-carrier non-orthogonal multiple access system with simultaneous wireless information and power transfer. *2022 11th International Conference on System Modeling & Advancement in Research Trends (SMART)*. IEEE.

Cheatham, B., Javanmardian, K., & Samandari, H. (2019). Confronting the risks of artificial intelligence. *The McKinsey Quarterly*, 2(38), 1–9.

Chen, T., Kornblith, S., Swersky, K., Norouzi, M., & Hinton, G. (2020). Big Self-supervised Models Are Strong Semi-supervised Learners. *ArXiv*, 10029. https://doi.org//arxiv.2006.10029. doi:10.48550

Cheng, X., Lin, X., Shen, X. L., Zarifis, A., & Mou, J. (2022). The dark sides of AI. *Electronic Markets*, 32(1), 11–15. doi:10.100712525-022-00531-5 PMID:35600917

Chen, H., Hussain, S. U., Boemer, F., Stapf, E., Sadeghi, A. R., Koushanfar, F., & Cammarota, R. (2020). Developing Privacy-preserving AI Systems: The Lessons learned. *57th ACM/IEEE Design Automation Conference (DAC)*. ACM. 10.1109/DAC18072.2020.9218662

Chen, J., Shen, X. L., & Chen, Z. J. (2014). Understanding social commerce intention: A relational view. *Proceedings of the Annual Hawaii International Conference on System Sciences*, 1793–1802. 10.1109/HICSS.2014.227

Chen, Q., Zhu, X., & Zhang, S. (2021). Graph-Structured Image Captioner. In *Proceedings of the IEEE/CVF Conference on Computer Vision and Pattern Recognition* (pp. 6723-6733). IEEE.

Chen, S. F., & Goodman, J. (1998). An empirical study of smoothing techniques for language modeling. *Computer Speech & Language*, 12(4), 359–393. doi:10.1006/csla.1999.0128

Chen, X., Zou, D., Xie, H., & Wang, F. L. (2023). Metaverse in Education: Contributors, Cooperations, and Research Themes. *IEEE Transactions on Learning Technologies*, 1–18. doi:10.1109/TLT.2023.3277952

Chen, Y., Jensen, S., Albert, L. J., Gupta, S., & Lee, T. (2023). Artificial intelligence (AI) student assistants in the classroom: Designing chatbots to support student success. *Information Systems Frontiers*, 25(1), 161–182. doi:10.100710796-022-10291-4

Chen, Y., Li, Y., & Tao, D. (2016). Fashion image retrieval based on fine-grained classification and transfer learning. In *Proceedings of the 2016 ACM on Multimedia Conference* (pp. 1022-1026). ACM.

Chen, Y., Li, Y., & Tao, D. (2017). Deep fashion feature embedding with improved triplet loss. In *Proceedings of the 2017 ACM on Multimedia Conference* (pp. 1013-1021). ACM.

Cheung, Y. L. (2016, August). Teaching Writing. *English Language Education*, 5, 179–194. doi:10.1007/978-3-319-38834-2_13

Che, Z., Purushotham, S., Cho, K., Sontag, D., & Liu, Y. (2017). Recurrent neural networks for multivariate time series with missing values. *Scientific Reports*, 8(1), 1–13. PMID:29666385

Chi, E. C., Lyman, M., Sager, N., & MacLeod, C. (1985). *A Database of Computer-Structured Narrative: Methods of Computing Complex Relations.* ResearchGate. https://www.researchgate.net/publication/26174364_A_Database_of_Computer-Structured_Narrative_Methods_of_Computing_Complex_Relations

Chinonso, O. E., Theresa, A. M.-E., & Aduke, T. C. (2023). ChatGPT for Teaching, Learning and Research: Prospects and Challenges. *Global Academic Journal of Humanities and Social Sciences*, 5(02), 33–40. doi:10.36348/gajhss.2023.v05i02.001

Choi, E. P. H., Lee, J. J., Ho, M. H., Kwok, J. Y. Y., & Lok, K. Y. W. (2023). Chatting or cheating? The impacts of ChatGPT and other artificial intelligence language models on nurse education. *Nurse Education Today*, 125, 105796. doi:10.1016/j.nedt.2023.105796 PMID:36934624

Chollet, F. (2021). *Deep learning with python* (2nd ed.). Manning Publications CO.

Çini, A., Malmberg, J., & Järvelä, S. (2023). How individual metacognitive awareness relates to situation-specific metacognitive interpretations of collaborative learning tasks. *Educational Studies*, 49(1), 54–75. doi:10.1080/03055698.2020.1834359

Cirillo, S., Polese, G., Salerno, D., Simone, B., & Solimando, G. (2023). Towards Flexible Voice Assistants: Evaluating Privacy and Security Needs in IoT-enabled Smart Homes. *FMDB Transactions on Sustainable Computer Letters*, 1(1), 25–32.

Cooper, G. (2023). Examining Science Education in ChatGPT: An Exploratory Study of Generative Artificial Intelligence. *Journal of Science Education and Technology*, 32(3), 444–452. doi:10.100710956-023-10039-y

Cotton, D. R. E., Cotton, P. A., & Shipway, J. R. (2023). Chatting and cheating: Ensuring academic integrity in the era of ChatGPT. *Innovations in Education and Teaching International*, 1–12. doi:10.1080/14703297.2023.2190148

Cox, C., & Tzoc, E. (2023). ChatGPT: Implications for academic libraries. *College & Research Libraries News*, 84(3). doi:10.5860/crln.84.3.99

Creswell, J. W. (2014). *Research design: Qualitative, quantitative and mixed methods approaches* (4th ed.). SAGE Publication.

Cretu, C. (2023, April 6). *How does ChatGPT actually work? An ML engineer explains.* Scalable Path. https://www.scalablepath.com/data-science/chatgpt-architecture-explained

Cromley, J. G. (2023). Metacognition, cognitive strategy instruction, and reading in adult literacy. *Review of Adult Learning and Literacy*, 5, 187–204. doi:10.4324/9781003417958-7

Cui, Y., Aziz, G., Sarwar, S., Waheed, R., Mighri, Z., & Shahzad, U. (2023). Reinvestigate the significance of STRIPAT and extended STRIPAT: An inclusion of renewable energy and trade for gulf council countries. *Energy & Environment*, 0958305X231181671. doi:10.1177/0958305X231181671

Dai, Z., Yang, Z., Yang, Y., Carbonell, J., Salakhutdinov, R., & Le, Q. V. (2019). Transformer-XL: Attentive language models beyond a fixed-length context. In *Proceedings of the 57th Annual Meeting of the Association for Computational Linguistics* (pp. 2978-2988). 10.18653/v1/P19-1285

Damasio, A. R. (1994). *Descartes Error: Emotion, Reason, and the Human Brain.* Avon Books.

Dao, X. Q. (2023). Performance comparison of large language models on vnhsge english dataset: Openai chatgpt, microsoft bing chat, and google bard. *arXiv preprint arXiv:2307.02288.*

Das, D. S., Gangodkar, D., Singh, R., Vijay, P., Bhardwaj, A., & Semwal, A. (2022). Comparative analysis of skin cancer prediction using neural networks and transfer learning. *2022 5th International Conference on Contemporary Computing and Informatics (IC3I).* IEEE.

Dave, T., Athaluri, S. A., & Singh, S. (2023). an overview of its applications, advantages, limitations, future prospects, and ethical considerations. *Artificial Intelligence, 1169595,* 1169595. doi:10.3389/frai.2023.1169595 PMID:37215063

De Angelis, L., Baglivo, F., Arzilli, G., Privitera, G. P., Ferragina, P., Tozzi, A. E., & Rizzo, C. (2023). ChatGPT and the Rise of Large Language Models: The New AI-Driven Infodemic Threat in Public Health. SSRN *Electronic Journal.* doi:10.2139/ssrn.4352931

De Angelis, L., Baglivo, F., Arzilli, G., Privitera, G. P., Ferragina, P., Tozzi, A. E., & Rizzo, C. (2023). ChatGPT and the rise of large language models: The new AI-driven infodemic threat in public health. *Frontiers in Public Health, 11,* 1166120. doi:10.3389/fpubh.2023.1166120 PMID:37181697

DeepLearning.AI. (2023). Natural Language Processing (NLP) [A Complete Guide]. *DeepLearning.AI.* https://www.deeplearning.ai/resources/natural-language-processing/

Deliç, V., Sağlam, H., Sarıyıldız, S., & Yıldız, O. T. (2021). *Legal Text Generation Using Transformer-Based Language Models.* arXiv preprint arXiv:2106.08062.

Demeter, E., Rad, D., & Balas, E. (2021). Schadenfreude and general anti-social behaviours: The role of Violent Content Preferences and life satisfaction. Brain. *Broad Research in Artificial Intelligence and Neuroscience, 12*(2). doi:10.18662/brain/12.2/194

Deng, J., Dong, W., Socher, R., Li, L. J., Li, K., & Fei-Fei, L. (2009). *ImageNet: A large-scale hierarchical image database. In 2009, the IEEE conference on computer vision and pattern recognition.* IEEE.

Deng, X., Jiang, C., & Chen, T. (2020). DINO: DETR with Improved DeNoising Anchor Boxes for End-to-End Object Detection. *Communications Magazine, 57,* 19–25.

Devi, B. T., & Rajasekaran, R. (2023). A Comprehensive Review on Deepfake Detection on Social Media Data. *FMDB Transactions on Sustainable Computing Systems, 1*(1), 11–20.

Devlin, J., Chang, M. W., Lee, K., & Toutanova, K. (2018). *Bert: Pre-training of deep bidirectional transformers for language understanding.* arXiv preprint arXiv:1810.04805.

Devlin, J., Chang, M. W., Lee, K., & Toutanova, K. (2018). *BERT: Pre-training of deep bidirectional transformers for language understanding.* arXiv preprint arXiv:1810.04805.

Devlin, J., Chang, M.-W., Lee, K., Google, K. T., & Language, A. I. (2019). *BERT: Pre-training of Deep Bidirectional Transformers for Language Understanding.* Github. https://github.com/tensorflow/tensor2tensor

Devlin, J., Chang, M. W., Lee, K., & Toutanova, K. (2019). BERT: Pre-training of deep bidirectional transformers for language understanding. In *Proceedings of the 2019 Conference of the North American Chapter of the Association for Computational Linguistics* (pp. 4171-4186).

Dhivya, D. S., Hariharasudan, A., Ragmoun, W., & Alfalih, A. A. (2023). ELSA as an Education 4.0 Tool for Learning Business English Communication. *Sustainability (Basel), 15*(4), 3809. doi:10.3390u15043809

Dida, H. A., Chakravarthy, D., & Rabbi, F. (2023). *ChatGPT and Big Data: Enhancing Text-to-Speech Conversion.* Mesopotamian Journal of Big Data., doi:10.58496/MJBD/2023/005

Ding, L., & Ren, H. (2019). Segmentation algorithm of medical exercise rehabilitation image based on HFCNN and IoT. *IEEE Access : Practical Innovations, Open Solutions, 7*, 160829–160844. doi:10.1109/ACCESS.2019.2950960

Document Link. https://docs.google.com/document/d/1v7dxHSWcz78LAyk4wBVj_ae5OTE02CjspWVdnMJ3GzM/edit?hl=en

Döllner, J. (2020). Geospatial artificial intelligence: Potentials of machine learning for 3D point clouds and geospatial digital twins. PFG –. *Journal of Photogrammetry, Remote Sensing and Geoinformation Science, 88*(1), 15–24. doi:10.100741064-020-00102-3

Dong, L., Mallinson, J., Reddy, S., & Lapata, M. (2019). *Unified language model pre-training for natural language understanding and generation.* arXiv preprint arXiv:1905.03197.

Drigas, A., Mitsea, E., & Skianis, C. (2023). Meta-learning: A Nine-layer model based on metacognition and smart technologies. *Sustainability (Basel), 15*(2), 1668. doi:10.3390u15021668

Duan, J., Zhao, H., Zhou, Q., Qiu, M., & Liu, M. (n.d.*).* A Study of Pre-trained Language Models in Natural Language Processing. In *2020 IEEE International Conference on Smart Cloud (SmartCloud)*, Washington, DC, United States of America. https://doi.org/10.1109/SmartCloud49737.2020.00030

Dwivedi, N., Kshetri, N., Hughes, L., Slade, E. L., Jeyaraj, A., Kar, A. K., Baabdullah, A. M., Koohang, A., Raghavan, V., Ahuja, M., Albanna, H., Albashrawi, M. A., Al-Busaidi, A. S., Balakrishnan, J., Barlette, Y., Basu, S., Bose, I., Brooks, L., Buhalis, D., & Wright, R. (2023). So what if ChatGPT wrote it? Multidisciplinary perspectives on opportunities, challenges and implications of generative conversational AI for research, practice and policy. *International Journal of Information Management, 71*, 102642. doi:10.1016/j.ijinfomgt.2023.102642

Ebadi, S., & Amini, A. (2022). Examining the roles of social presence and human-likeness on Iranian EFL learners' motivation using artificial intelligence technology: A case of CSIEC chatbot. *Interactive Learning Environments*, 1–19. doi:10.1080/10494820.2022.2096638

Eke, D. O. (2023). ChatGPT and the rise of generative AI: Threat to academic integrity? *Journal of Responsible Technology, 13*, 100060. doi:10.1016/j.jrt.2023.100060

Ekman, M. (2021). *Learning Deep Learning: Theory and Practice of Neural Networks, Computer Vision, NLP, and Transformers using TensorFlow.* Addison-Wesley Professional.

Elizabeth, C., Asli, C., & Noah, A. S. (2019). In Proceedings of the 57th Annual Meeting of the Association for Computational Linguistics, *Sentence Mover's Similarity: Automatic Evaluation for Multi-Sentence Texts* (pp. 2748–2760). Florence, Italy: Association for Computational Linguistics.10.18653/v1/P19-1264

Elliott, D., Keller, F., & Rohde, H. (2013). Describing objects by their attributes. In *Proceedings of the 2013 Conference of the North American Chapter of the Association for Computational Linguistics: Human Language Technologies* (pp. 177-186). ACM.

Emilio Bruni Hendrik Purwins, L. (n.d.). *Recommender System And User Interface Design For Experimental Film Streaming Service Title Page Title Recommender System And User Interface Design For Experimental Film Streaming Service.*

Eysenbach, G. (2023). The Role of ChatGPT, Generative Language Models, and Artificial Intelligence in Medical Education: A Conversation With ChatGPT and a Call for Papers. *Journal of Medical Internet Research, 46885*, e46885. doi:10.2196/46885 PMID:36863937

Fabela, O., Patil, S., Chintamani, S., & Dennis, B. H. (2017). *Estimation of effective thermal conductivity of porous media utilizing inverse heat transfer analysis on cylindrical configuration* (Vol. 8). Heat Transfer and Thermal Engineering. doi:10.1115/IMECE2017-71559

Fan, X., Wang, G., Chen, K., He, X., & Xu, W. (2021). PPCA: Privacy-preserving Principal Component Analysis Using Secure Multiparty Computation(MPC). *ArXiv.* /abs/2105.07612.

Fan, A., Lewis, M., & Dauphin, Y. (2018). Hierarchical neural story generation. In *Proceedings of the 2018 Conference of the North American Chapter of the Association for Computational Linguistics: Human Language Technologies* (pp. 889-898). ACM.

Fang, H., Bao, Y., & Zhang, J. (2014). Leveraging decomposed trust in probabilistic matrix factorization for effective recommendation. *AAAI Conference on Artificial Intelligence, 28*(1). 10.1609/aaai.v28i1.8714

Fan, Y., Wang, J., Zhang, J., & Shi, W. (2018). Creative writing via deep reinforcement learning. In *Proceedings of the 2018 Conference on Empirical Methods in Natural Language Processing* (pp. 4610-4619). ACM.

Fareed, M., Ashraf, A., & Bilal, M. (2016). ESL learners' writing skills: Problems, factors and suggestions. *Journal of Education & Social Sciences, 4*(2), 83–94. doi:10.20547/jess0421604201

Farooq, M., & Khan, M. H. (2022). Signature-Based Intrusion Detection System in Wireless 6G IoT Networks. *Journal on Internet of Things, 4*(3), 155–168. doi:10.32604/jiot.2022.039271

Farooq, M., & Khan, M. H. (2023). Artificial Intelligence-Based Approach on Cyber Security Challenges and Opportunities in The Internet of Things & Edge Computing Devices. *International Journal of Engineering and Computer Science, 12*(7), 25763–25768. doi:10.18535/ijecs/v12i07.4744

Farzad, A., & Gulliver T. A., (2019). Log message anomaly detection and classification using auto-B/LSTM and auto-GRU, 1–28.

Feng, Q., He, D., Liu, Z., Wang, H., & Choo, K. R. (2020). SecureNLP: A System for Multi-Party Privacy-Preserving Natural Language Processing. *IEEE Transactions on Information Forensics and Security, 15*, 3709–3721. doi:10.1109/TIFS.2020.2997134

Ferrara, E. (2023). Should chatgpt be biased? challenges and risks of bias in large language models. *arXiv preprint arXiv:2304.03738.*

Feyisetan, O., Ghanavati, S., & Thaine, P. (2020). Workshop on Privacy in NLP (PrivateNLP 2020). *WSDM '20: Proceedings of the 13th International Conference on Web Search and Data Mining.* ACM. 10.1145/3336191.3371881

Fido, D., & Wallace, L. (2023). *The Unique Role of ChatGPT in Closing the Awarding Gap.* The Interdisciplinary Journal of Student Success.

Firaina, R., & Sulisworo, D. (2023). Exploring the Usage of ChatGPT in Higher Education: Frequency and Impact on Productivity. *Buletin Edukasi Indonesia, 2*(01), 39–46. doi:10.56741/bei.v2i01.310

Firat, M. (2023). Integrating AI Applications into Learning Management Systems to Enhance e-Learning. *Instructional Technology and Lifelong Learning, 4*(1), 1–14. doi:10.52911/itall.1244453

Firat, M. (2023). What ChatGPT means for universities: Perceptions of scholars and students. *Journal of Applied Learning and Teaching, 6*(1).

Fleur, D. S., van den Bos, W., & Bredeweg, B. (2023). Social comparison in learning analytics dashboard supporting motivation and academic achievement. *Computers and Education Open, 4*, 100130. doi:10.1016/j.caeo.2023.100130

Floridi, L., Cowls, J., Beltrametti, M., Chatila, R., Chazerand, P., Dignum, V., Luetge, C., Madelin, R., Pagallo, U., Rossi, F., Schafer, B., Valcke, P., & Vayena, E. (2018). AI4People—An Ethical Framework for a Good AI Society: Opportunities, Risks, Principles, and Recommendations. *Minds and Machines*, 28(4), 689–707. doi:10.100711023-018-9482-5 PMID:30930541

Forman, N., Udvaros, J., & Avornicului, M. S. (2023). ChatGPT: A new study tool shaping the future for high school students. *International Journal of Advanced Natural Sciences and Engineering Researches*, 7(4), 95–102. doi:10.59287/ijanser.562

Fraenkel, J. R., Wallen, N. E., & Hyun, H. H. (2012). *How to design and evaluate research in education* (8th ed.). McGraw-Hill Humanities/Social Sciences/Languages.

Friedman, C., Cimino, J., & Johnson, S. (1993). A conceptual model for clinical radiology reports. *In proceedings of the annual symposium on computer application in medical care.*

Frith, K. H. (2023). Disruptive Educational Technology. *Nursing Education Perspectives*, 44(3), 198–199. doi:10.1097/01. NEP.0000000000001129 PMID:37093697

Frye, B. L. (2022). Should Using an AI Text Generator to Produce Academic Writing Be Plagiarism? (SSRN Scholarly Paper No. 4292283). https://papers.ssrn.com/abstract=4292283

Fyfe, P. (2022). How to cheat on your final paper: Assigning AI for student writing. *AI & Society*, 1–11. doi:10.17613/0h18-5p41

Gaayathri, R. S., Rajest, S. S., Nomula, V. K., & Regin, R. (2023). Bud-D: Enabling Bidirectional Communication with ChatGPT by adding Listening and Speaking Capabilities. *FMDB Transactions on Sustainable Computer Letters*, 1(1), 49–63.

Gabbiadini, A., Dimitri, O., Baldissarri, C., & Manfredi, A. (2023). Does ChatGPT Pose a Threat to Human Identity? SSRN *Electronic Journal*. doi:10.2139/ssrn.4377900

Gabrielli, S., Rizzi, S., Bassi, G., Carbone, S., Maimone, R., Marchesoni, M., & Forti, S. (2021). Engagement and effectiveness of a healthy-coping intervention via chatbot for university students during the COVID-19 pandemic: Mixed methods proof-of-concept study. *JMIR mHealth and uHealth*, 9(5), e27965. doi:10.2196/27965 PMID:33950849

Gama, J. (2004). Functional Trees. *Machine Learning*, 55(3), 219–250. doi:10.1023/B:MACH.0000027782.67192.13

Gan, Z., Liu, C., Wu, J., & Ji, M. (2019). Audio-Visual Scene-Aware Dialog. In *Proceedings of the IEEE/CVF Conference on Computer Vision and Pattern Recognition* (pp. 13020-13029). IEEE.

Gao, J., Peng, B., Li, C., Li, J., Shayandeh, S., Liden, L., & Shum, H. Y. (2020). *Robust conversational AI with grounded text generation.* arXiv preprint arXiv:2009.03457.

Gao, C., & Yu, J. (2023). SecureRC: A system for privacy-preserving relation classification using secure multi-party computation. *Computers & Security*, 128, 103142. doi:10.1016/j.cose.2023.103142

Gao, J., Zhou, W., Liu, S., Tan, M., & Zhou, J. (2019). EmoGAN: Generating emotional text with variational autoencoder and conditional generative adversarial network. In *Proceedings of the 28th International Joint Conference on Artificial Intelligence* (pp. 1372-1378). IEEE.

Gao, S., He, L., Chen, Y., Li, D., & Lai, K. (2020). Public Perception of Artificial Intelligence in Medical Care: Content Analysis of Social Media. *Journal of Medical Internet Research*, 22(7), e16649. doi:10.2196/16649 PMID:32673231

Gao, T., & Liu, J. (2021). Application of improved random forest algorithm and fuzzy mathematics in physical fitness of athletes. *Journal of Intelligent & Fuzzy Systems, 40*(2), 2041–2053. doi:10.3233/JIFS-189206

Gao, X., Qin, L., Liu, T., Xiao, Y., Li, H., & Wang, L. (2019). Dialogpt: Large-scale generative pre-training for conversational response generation. In *Proceedings of the 2019 Conference on Empirical Methods in Natural Language Processing and the 9th International Joint Conference on Natural Language Processing (EMNLP-IJCNLP)*. ACM.

Gao, Y., Tong, W., Wu, E. Q., Chen, W., Zhu, G. Y., & Wang, F. Y. (2023). Chat with ChatGPT on Interactive Engines for Intelligent Driving. *IEEE Transactions on Intelligent Vehicles, 8*(3), 2034–2036. doi:10.1109/TIV.2023.3252571

García Retana, J. Á. (2012). Emotional education, its importance in the learning process. Original in Spanish: La educación emocional, su importancia en el proceso de aprendizaje. *Educación, 36*(1), 97-109. https://revistas.ucr.ac.cr/index.php/educacion/article/view/455/9906

Garcia, T., & Pintrich, P. R. (2023). Regulating motivation and cognition in the classroom: The role of self-schemas and self-regulatory strategies. In *Self-regulation of learning and performance* (pp. 127–153). Routledge.

Garg, N., Zampieri, M., Nakov, P., & Schutze, H. (2021). Equalizing gender biases in neural machine translation with word embeddings techniques. In *Proceedings of the 2021 Conference on Empirical Methods in Natural Language Processing* (pp. 6523-6532). ACM.

Gatys, L. A., Ecker, A. S., & Bethge, M. (2016). Image style transfer using convolutional neural networks. *Proceedings of the IEEE conference on computer vision and pattern recognition*, (pp. 2414-2423). IEEE. 10.1109/CVPR.2016.265

Gautami, A., Shanthini, J., & Karthik, S. (2023). A Quasi-Newton Neural Network Based Efficient Intrusion Detection System for Wireless Sensor Network. *Computer Systems Science and Engineering, 45*(1), 427–443. doi:10.32604/csse.2023.026688

Gavilán, J. C. O., Díaz, D. Z., Huallpa, J. J., Cabala, J. L. B., Aguila, O. E. P., Puma, E. G. M., & Arias-Gonzáles, J. L. (2022). Technological Social Responsibility in University Professors. *Eurasian Journal of Educational Research, 100*(100), 104–118.

Gebremariam, G. G., Panda, J., & Indu, S. (2023). Localization and Detection of Multiple Attacks in Wireless Sensor Networks Using Artificial Neural Network. *Wireless Communications and Mobile Computing, 2023*, 1–29. doi:10.1155/2023/2744706

Geerling, W., Mateer, G. D., Wooten, J., & Damodaran, N. (2023). Is ChatGPT Smarter than a Student in Principles of Economics? SSRN *Electronic Journal*. doi:10.2139/ssrn.4356034

Gehrmann, S., Strobelt, H., & Rush, A. M. (2019). GLTR: Statistical detection and visualization of generated text. In *Proceedings of the 2019 Conference on Empirical Methods in Natural Language Processing and the 9th International Joint Conference on Natural Language Processing* (pp. 4252-4258). ACL. 10.18653/v1/P19-3019

Geitgey, A. (2018, July 18). Natural Language Processing is Fun! How computers understand Human Language. *Medium*. https://medium.com/@ageitgey/natural-language-processing-is-fun-9a0bff37854e

Geurten, M., & Léonard, C. (2023). Relations between parental metacognitive talk and children's early metacognition and memory. *Journal of Experimental Child Psychology, 226*, 105577. doi:10.1016/j.jecp.2022.105577 PMID:36335835

Ghazvininejad, M., Shi, Y., Choi, Y., & Neubig, G. (2017). Hierarchical variational encoder-decoder for generating structured poetry. In *Proceedings of the 55th Annual Meeting of the Association for Computational Linguistics* (pp. 1033-1042). ACM.

Giannos, P., & Delardas, O. (2023). Performance Of Chatgpt On Uk Standardized Admission Tests: Insights From the Bmat, Tmua, Lnat, And Tsa Examinations. *JMIR Medical Education, 9*, e47737. doi:10.2196/47737 PMID:37099373

Gill, S. S., Arya, R. C., Wander, G. S., & Buyya, R. (2018). 'Fog-based smart healthcare as a big data and cloud service for heart patients using IoT, '' in Proc. *Proc. Int. Conf. Intell. Data Commun. Technol. Internet Things*, 1376–1383.

Gill, S. S., Garraghan, P., & Buyya, R. (2019). ROUTER: Fog enabled cloud based intelligent resource management approach for smart home IoT devices. *Journal of Systems and Software, 154*, 125–138. doi:10.1016/j.jss.2019.04.058

Gill, S. S., & Kaur, R. (2023). ChatGPT: Vision and challenges. *Internet of Things and Cyber-Physical Systems, 3*, 262–271. doi:10.1016/j.iotcps.2023.05.004

Gilson, A., Safranek, C., Huang, T., Socrates, V., Chi, L., Taylor, R. A., & Chartash, D. (2022). How well does ChatGPT do when taking the medical licensing exams? The implications of large language models for medical education and knowledge assessment. medRxiv, 2022-12.

Ginting, S. A. (2019). Lexical formation error in the descriptive writing of Indonesian tertiary EFL learners. International Journal of Linguistics. *Literature and Translation, 2*(1), 5. doi:10.32996/ijllt.2019.2.1.11

Giunti, M., Garavaglia, F. G., Giuntini, R., Pinna, S., & Sergioli, G. (2023). Chatgpt Prospective Student at Medical School. SSRN *Electronic Journal*. doi:10.2139/ssrn.4378743

Glasgow, B., Mandell, A., Binney, D., Ghemri, L., & Fisher, D. A. (1998). MITA: An Information-Extraction Approach to the Analysis of Free-Form Text in Life insurance Applications. *AI Magazine, 19*(1), 59–72. doi:10.1609/aimag.v19i1.1354

Gocen, A., & Aydemir, F. (2021). Artificial intelligence in education and schools. *Research on Education and Media, 12*(1), 13–21. doi:10.2478/rem-2020-0003

Gomathy, V., & Venkatasbramanian, S. (2023). Impact of Teacher Expectations on Student Academic Achievement. *FMDB Transactions on Sustainable Techno Learning, 1*(2), 78–91.

Goodfellow, I., Pouget-Abadie, J., Mirza, M., Xu, B., Warde-Farley, D., Ozair, S., & Bengio, Y. (2014). Generative Adversarial Nets. In Advances in neural information processing systems (pp. 2672-2680).

Goodfellow, I., Pouget-Abadie, J., Mirza, M., Xu, B., Warde-Farley, D., Ozair, S., Courville, A., & Bengio, Y. (2020). Generative adversarial networks. *Communications of the ACM, 63*(11), 139–144. doi:10.1145/3422622

Goswami, C., Das, A., Ogaili, K. I., Verma, V. K., Singh, V., & Sharma, D. K. (2022). Device to device communication in 5G network using device-centric resource allocation algorithm. *2022 4th International Conference on Inventive Research in Computing Applications (ICIRCA)*. IEEE.

Goyal, A., Narang, K., Ahluwalia, G., Sohal, P. M., Singh, B., Chhabra, S. T., & Wander, G. S. (2019). Seasonal variation in 24 h blood pressure profile in healthy adults- A prospective observational study. *Journal of Human Hypertension, 33*(8), 626–633. doi:10.103841371-019-0173-3 PMID:30755660

Goyal, M., Reeves, N. D., Rajbhandari, S., & Yap, M. H. (2019). Robust methods for real-time diabetic foot ulcer detection and localization on mobile devices. *IEEE Journal of Biomedical and Health Informatics, 23*(4), 1730–1741. doi:10.1109/JBHI.2018.2868656 PMID:30188841

Graves, A. (2013). Generating sequences with recurrent neural networks. arXiv preprint arXiv:1308.0850.

Graves, A. (2012). Supervised Sequence Labelling. In *Supervised Sequence Labelling with Recurrent Neural Networks. Studies in Computational Intelligence* (Vol. 385). Springer. doi:10.1007/978-3-642-24797-2_2

Grishman, R., Sager, N., Raze, C., & Bookchin, B. (1973). The linguistic string parser. *AFIPS '73: Proceedings of the National Computer Conference and Exposition*, (pp. 427–434). ACM. https://doi.org/10.1145/1499586.1499693

Grünebaum, A., Chervenak, J., Pollet, S. L., Katz, A., & Chervenak, F. A. (2023). The Exciting Potential for Chat-GPT in Obstetrics and Gynecology. *American Journal of Obstetrics and Gynecology*, *228*(6), 696–705. doi:10.1016/j.ajog.2023.03.009 PMID:36924907

Guiamalon, T. S. (2022). Internship In Times Of Pandemic: A Qualitative Phenomenological Study. *Res Militaris*, *12*(6), 1039–1050.

Gunawan, J. (2023). Exploring the future of nursing: Insights from the ChatGPT model. *Belitung Nursing Journal*, *9*(1), 1–5. doi:10.33546/bnj.2551 PMID:37469634

Gunn, H. & Michael, P. L. (2021). The Internet and Epistemic Agency. In L. Jennifer, *Applied Epistemology* (pp. 389-409). Oxford University Press. doi:10.1093/oso/9780198833659.003.0016

Gunturu, V., Bansal, V., Sathe, M., Kumar, A., Gehlot, A., & Pant, B. (2023). Wireless communications implementation using blockchain as well as distributed type of IOT. *2023 International Conference on Artificial Intelligence and Smart Communication (AISC)*. IEEE. 10.1109/AISC56616.2023.10085249

Guo, K., Zhong, Y., Li, D., & Chu, S. K. W. (2023). Investigating students' engagement in chatbot-supported classroom debates. *Interactive Learning Environments*, 1–17. doi:10.1080/10494820.2023.2207181

Guo, T., Tao, K., Hu, Q., & Shen, Y. (2020). Detection of ice hockey players and teams via a two-phase cascaded CNN model. *IEEE Access : Practical Innovations, Open Solutions*, *8*, 195062–195073. doi:10.1109/ACCESS.2020.3033580

Gupta, S. (2021). Deep learning based human activity recognition (HAR) using wearable sensor data. *International Journal of Information Management Data Insights*, *1*(2), 100046. doi:10.1016/j.jjimei.2021.100046

Habernal, I. (2023, May 1). Privacy-Preserving natural language processing. *ACL Anthology*. https://aclanthology.org/2023.eacl-tutorials.6

Hacker, D. J. (2023). Self-Regulation of Writing: Models of Writing and the Role of Metacognition. In *The Routledge International Handbook of Research on Writing* (pp. 236–256). Routledge.

Haleem, A., Javaid, M., & Singh, R. P. (2022). An era of ChatGPT as a significant futuristic support tool: A study on features, abilities, and challenges. *BenchCouncil transactions on benchmarks, standards, and evaluations*, *2*(4), 100089.

Haleem, A., Javaid, M., & Singh, R. P. (2022). An era of ChatGPT as a significant futuristic support tool: A study on features, abilities, and challenges. *BenchCouncil Transactions on Benchmarks. Standards and Evaluations*, *2*(4), 100089. doi:10.1016/j.tbench.2023.100089

Hall, K. R., Ajjan, H., & Marshall, G. W. (2021). Understanding Salesperson Intention To Use Ai Feedback and Its Influence On Business-to-business Sales Outcomes. *Journal of Business and Industrial Marketing*, *37*(9), 1787–1801. doi:10.1108/JBIM-04-2021-0218

Halloran, L. J. S., Mhanna, S., & Brunner, P. (2023). AI tools such as ChatGPT will disrupt hydrology, too. *Hydrological Processes*, *37*(3), e14843. doi:10.1002/hyp.14843

Haluza, D., & Jungwirth, D. (2023). Artificial Intelligence and Ten Societal Megatrends: An Exploratory Study Using GPT-3. *Systems*, *11*(3), 120. doi:10.3390ystems11030120

Haman, M., & Školník, M. (2023). Using ChatGPT to conduct a literature review. *Accountability in Research*, 1–3. doi:10.1080/08989621.2023.2185514 PMID:36879536

Hanif, M., Ashraf, H., Jalil, Z., Jhanjhi, N. Z., Humayun, M., Saeed, S., & Almuhaideb, A. M. (2022). AI-Based Wormhole Attack Detection Techniques in Wireless Sensor Networks. *Electronics (Basel)*, *11*(15), 2324. doi:10.3390/electronics11152324

Hankins, R., Peng, Y., & Yin, H. (2018). SOMNet: Unsupervised feature learning networks for image classification. *2018 International Joint Conference on Neural Networks (IJCNN)*. IEEE. 10.1109/IJCNN.2018.8489404

Hao, J., & Ho, T. K. (2019). Machine Learning Made Easy: A Review of Scikit-learn Package in Python Programming Language. *Journal of Educational and Behavioral Statistics*, *44*(3), 348–361. doi:10.3102/1076998619832248

Hariharan, J., Ampatzidis, Y., Abdulridha, J., & Batuman, O. (2023). Useful Feature Extraction and Machine Learning Techniques For Identifying Unique Pattern Signatures Present In Hyperspectral Image Data. In Y. Jung, Hyperspectral Imaging - A Perspective on Recent Advances and Applications (p. 107436). IntechOpen. doi:10.5772/intechopen.107436

Hayat, A. A., Shateri, K., Amini, M., & Shokrpour, N. (2020). Relationships between academic self-efficacy, learning-related emotions, and metacognitive learning strategies with academic performance in medical students: A structural equation model. *BMC Medical Education*, *20*(1), 1–11. doi:10.118612909-020-01995-9 PMID:32183804

Hayes, P. (2016). In P. Jacobs (Ed.), *Intelligent high-volume text processing using shallow, domain-specific techniques: Text-Based Intelligent Systems: Current Research and Practice in Information Extraction and Retrieval* (pp. 227–242). Psychology Press.

Heaven, W. D. (2020, July 20). OpenAI's new language generator GPT-3 is shockingly good and completely mindless. *MIT Technology Review*. https://www.technologyreview.com/2020/07/20/1005454/openai-machine-learning-language-generator-gpt-3-nlp/

Hendricks, L. A., Wang, O., Shechtman, E., Sivic, J., Darrell, T., & Russell, B. C. (2017). Localizing moments in video with natural language. In *Proceedings of the IEEE International Conference on Computer Vision* (pp. 5803-5812). IEEE. 10.1109/ICCV.2017.618

Heo, S., Han, S., Shin, Y., & Na, S. (2021). Challenges Of Data Refining Process During the Artificial Intelligence Development Projects In The Architecture, Engineering And Construction Industry. *Applied Sciences (Basel, Switzerland)*, *11*(22), 10919. doi:10.3390/app112210919

He, S., Cheng, B., Wang, H., Huang, Y., & Chen, J. (2017). 'Proactive personalized services through fog-cloud computing in large-scale IoT-based healthcare application. *China Communications*, *14*(11), 1–16. doi:10.1109/CC.2017.8233646

Hill-Yardin, E. L., Hutchinson, M. R., Laycock, R., & Spencer, S. J. (2023). A Chat(GPT) about the future of scientific publishing. *Brain, Behavior, and Immunity*, *110*, 152–154. doi:10.1016/j.bbi.2023.02.022 PMID:36868432

Hochreiter, S., & Schmidhuber, J. (1997). Long short-term memory. *Neural Computation*, *9*(8), 1735–1780. doi:10.1162/neco.1997.9.8.1735 PMID:9377276

Holtzman, A., Buys, J., Du, P., Forbes, M., & Choi, Y. (2019). The curious case of neural text degeneration. In *Proceedings of the 2019 Conference of the North American Chapter of the Association for Computational Linguistics: Human Language Technologies* (pp. 1463-1470). IEEE.

Holtzman, A., Buys, J., Du, Z., Forbes, M., Choi, Y., Cohan, A., & Choi, E. (2020). The curious case of neural text degeneration. In *International Conference on Learning Representations*. IEEE.

Hong, W. C. H. (2018). The Effect of Absence of Explicit Knowledge on ESL/EFL Stress-Placement Accuracy: A quasi-experiment. *Asian EFL Journal*, *20*(2), 262–279.

Hong, W. C. H. (2021). Improving English as a foreign language learners' writing using a minimal grammar approach of teaching dependent clauses: A case study of Macao secondary school students. In B. L. Reynolds & M. F. Teng (Eds.), *Innovative Approaches in Teaching English Writing to Chinese Speakers* (pp. 67–90). De Gruyter Mouton. doi:10.1515/9781501512643-004

Hong, W. C. H. (2021). Macao Secondary School EFL Teachers' Perspectives on Written Corrective Feedback: Rationales and Constraints. *Journal of Educational Technology and Innovation*, 1(04), 1–13.

Hong, W. C. H. (2023). The impact of ChatGPT on foreign language teaching and learning: Opportunities in education and research. *Journal of Education Technology and Innovation*, 5(1).

Hong, W. C. H. (2023). The impact of ChatGPT on foreign language teaching and learning: Opportunities in education and research. *Journal of Educational Technology and Innovation*, 5(1).

Hong, W. C. H., Chi, C.-Y., Liu, J., Zhang, Y.-F., Lei, N.-L., & Xu, X.-S. (2022). The influence of social education level on cybersecurity awareness and behaviour: A comparative study of university students and working graduates. *Education and Information Technologies*. PMID:35791319

Houssami, N., Kirkpatrick-Jones, G., Noguchi, N., & Lee, C. I. (2019). Artificial Intelligence (Ai) For the Early Detection Of Breast Cancer: A Scoping Review To Assess Ai's Potential In Breast Screening Practice. *Expert Review of Medical Devices*, 5(16), 351–362. doi:10.1080/17434440.2019.1610387 PMID:30999781

Howard, J., & Ruder, S. (2018). Universal language model fine-tuning for text classification. In *Proceedings of the 56th Annual Meeting of the Association for Computational Linguistics* (Volume 1: Long Papers) (pp. 328-339). ACL. 10.18653/v1/P18-1031

Hsu, T. C., Huang, H. L., Hwang, G. J., & Chen, M. S. (2023). Effects of Incorporating an Expert Decision-making Mechanism into Chatbots on Students' Achievement, Enjoyment, and Anxiety. *Journal of Educational Technology & Society*, 26(1), 218–231.

Huang, C., Zhang, Z., Mao, B., & Yao, X. (2022). An Overview of Artificial Intelligence Ethics. *Artificial Intelligence*, 3194503. doi:10.1109/TAI.2022.3194503

Huang, J., Yeung, A. M., Kerr, D., & Klonoff, D. C. (2023). Using Chatgpt To Predict the Future Of Diabetes Technology. *Journal of Diabetes Science and Technology*, 3(17), 853–854. doi:10.1177/19322968231161095 PMID:36799231

Huang, Q., Jiang, Y. G., Wang, W., & Wang, L. (2018). Attention-based LSTM for aspect-level sentiment classification. In *Proceedings of the 2018 Conference of the North American Chapter of the Association for Computational Linguistics: Human Language Technologies* (pp. 99-108). ACL.

Huang, W., Hew, K. F., & Fryer, L. K. (2022). Chatbots for language learning—Are they really useful? A systematic review of chatbot-supported language learning. *Journal of Computer Assisted Learning*, 38(1), 237–257. doi:10.1111/jcal.12610

Huang, X., Li, S., & Wu, Y. (2023). LSTM-NV: A combined scheme against selective forwarding attack in event-driven wireless sensor networks under harsh environments. *Engineering Applications of Artificial Intelligence*, 123, 106441. doi:10.1016/j.engappai.2023.106441

Huang, Z., Lin, X., Liu, H., Zhang, B., Chen, Y., & Tang, Y. (2020). Deep representation learning for location-based recommendation. *IEEE Transactions on Computational Social Systems*, 7(3), 648–658. doi:10.1109/TCSS.2020.2974534

Hu, J., Zhou, Q., Cao, Q., & Hu, J. (2022). Effects of ecological restoration measures on vegetation and soil properties in semi-humid sandy land on the southeast Qinghai-Tibetan Plateau, China. *Global Ecology and Conservation*, 33(e02000), e02000. doi:10.1016/j.gecco.2022.e02000

Hussain, S. A., Raza, M., & Riaz, F. (2020). An AI-Based Visual Aid With Integrated Reading Assistant for the Completely Blind. *IEEE Access : Practical Innovations, Open Solutions*, 8, 169740–169749.

Hu, Z., Yang, Z., Liang, X., Salakhutdinov, R., & Xing, E. P. (2017). Toward controlled generation of text. In *Proceedings of the 34th International Conference on Machine Learning* (pp. 1587-1596). ACL.

Hyland, K. (2008). Writing theories and writing pedagogies. *Indonesian Journal of English Language Teaching*, 4(2), 91–110. 10.25170%2Fijelt.v4i2.145

Ibna Seraj, P. M., & Oteir, I. (2022). Playing with AI to Investigate Human-Computer Interaction Technology and Improving Critical Thinking Skills to Pursue 21 st Century Age. *Education Research International*, 2022.

IEEE. Computer Society, Institute of Electrical and Electronics Engineers., IEEE/ACM International Conference on Cyber, P., IEEE/ACM International Conference on Green Computing and Communications (16th : 2020 : Online), IOT (Conference) (13th : 2020 : Online), & IEEE International Conference on Smart Data (6th : 2020 : Online). (n.d.). *IEEE Congress on Cybermatics; 2020 IEEE International Conferences on Internet of Things (iThings); IEEE Green Computing and Communications (GreenCom); IEEE Cyber, Physical and Social Computing (CPSCom); IEEE Smart Data (SmartData) : Cybermatics 2020, iThings 2020, GreenCom 2020, CPSCom 2020, SmartData 2020 : proceedings : Rhodes Island, Greece, 2-6 November 2020.*

Illia, L., Colleoni, E., & Zyglidopoulos, S. (2022). Ethical Implications Of Text Generation In the Age Of Artificial Intelligence. *Business Ethics, the Environment & Responsibility*, 32(1), 201–210. doi:10.1111/beer.12479

Islam, M. N. U., Fahmin, A., Hossain, M. S., & Atiquzzaman, M. (2021). Denial-of-service attacks on wireless sensor network and defense techniques. *Wireless Personal Communications*, 116(3), 1993–2021. doi:10.100711277-020-07776-3

Islam, S. M. R., Kwak, D., Kabir, M. H., Hossain, M., & Kwak, K.-S. (2015). 'The Internet of Things for health care: A comprehensive survey. *IEEE Access : Practical Innovations, Open Solutions*, 3, 678–708. doi:10.1109/AC-CESS.2015.2437951

Ismail, S., Dawoud, D., & Reza, H. (2022 January). A lightweight multilayer machine learning detection system for cyber-attacks in WSN. In *2022 IEEE 12th Annual Computing and Communication Workshop and Conference (CCWC)*. IEEE. 10.1109/CCWC54503.2022.9720891

Israel, M. J., & Amer, A. (2022). Rethinking Data Infrastructure and Its Ethical Implications In The Face Of Automated Digital Content Generation. *AI and Ethics*, 3(2), 427–439. doi:10.100743681-022-00169-1

Jabali, O. (2018). Students' attitudes towards EFL university writing: A case study at An-Najah National University, Palestine. *Heliyon*, 4, 1–25. https://doi.org/. e00896 doi:10.1016/j.heliyon.2018

Jagdishbhai, N., & Thakkar, K. Y. (2023). Exploring the capabilities and limitations of GPT and Chat GPT in natural language processing. *Journal of Management Research and Analysis*, 10(1), 18–20. doi:10.18231/j.jmra.2023.004

Jain, A. K., Misra, T., Tyagi, N., Suresh Kumar, M. V., & Pant, B. (2022). A Comparative Study on Cyber security Technology in Big data Cloud Computing Environment. In *2022 5th International Conference on Contemporary Computing and Informatics (IC3I)*. IEEE.

Jain, A. K., Misra, T., Tyagi, N., Suresh Kumar, M. V., & Pant, B. (2022a). A Comparative Study on Cyber security Technology in Big data Cloud Computing Environment. *2022 5th International Conference on Contemporary Computing and Informatics (IC3I)*. IEEE.

Jain, A. K., Ross, D. S., & Babu, M. K. Dharamvir, Uike, D., & Gangodkar, D. (2022b). Cloud computing applications for protecting the information of healthcare department using smart internet of things appliance. *2022 5th International Conference on Contemporary Computing and Informatics (IC3I)*. IEEE.

Jain, A. K., Ross, D. S., Babu, M. K., Uike, D., & Gangodkar, D. (2022). Cloud computing applications for protecting the information of healthcare department using smart internet of things appliance. In *2022 5th International Conference on Contemporary Computing and Informatics (IC3I)*. IEEE.

Jain, V., & Rai, H. Parvathy, & Mogaji, Emmanuel. (2023). *The Prospects and Challenges of ChatGPT on Marketing Research and Practices*. doi:10.2139/ssrn.4398033

Jain, S., & Jain, R. (2019). Role of artificial intelligence in higher education—An empirical investigation. *IJRAR-International Journal of Research and Analytical Reviews, 6*(2), 144z–150z.

Jain, S., Madotto, A., & Cho, K. (2020). Actions can speak louder than words: Reinforcement learning from dialogue feedback for language generation. In *Proceedings of the 58th Annual Meeting of the Association for Computational Linguistics*. ACL.

Jamiu, M. (2023, May). *Difference between GPT-1, GPT-2, GPT-3/3.5 and GPT-4 | Tooabstractive*. Difference Between GPT-1, GPT-2, GPT-3/3.5 and GPT-4 | Tooabstractive.

Jane Nithya, K., & Shyamala, K. (2022). A systematic review of various attack detection methods for wireless sensor networks. In *International Conference on Innovative Computing and Communications: Proceedings of ICICC 2021*. Springer Singapore. 10.1007/978-981-16-3071-2_17

Jannach, D., & Jugovac, M. (2019). Measuring the business value of recommender systems. In ACM Transactions on Management Information Systems (Vol. 10, Issue 4). Association for Computing Machinery. doi:10.1145/3370082

Javaid, M., Haleem, A., Singh, R. P., Khan, S., & Khan, I. H. (2023). Unlocking the opportunities through ChatGPT Tool towards ameliorating the education system. *BenchCouncil Transactions on Benchmarks, Standards and Evaluations*, 100115.

Javaid, M., Haleem, A., & Singh, R. P. (2023). ChatGPT for healthcare services: An emerging stage for an innovative perspective. Bench Council Transactions on Benchmarks. *Standards and Evaluations, 3*(1), 100105.

Jayakumar, P., Suman Rajest, S., & Aravind, B. R. (2022). An Empirical Study on the Effectiveness of Online Teaching and Learning Outcomes with Regard to LSRW Skills in COVID-19 Pandemic. In A. Hamdan, A. E. Hassanien, T. Mescon, & B. Alareeni (Eds.), *Technologies, Artificial Intelligence and the Future of Learning Post-COVID-19. Studies in Computational Intelligence* (Vol. 1019). Springer. doi:10.1007/978-3-030-93921-2_27

Jeba, J. A., Bose, S. R., & Boina, R. (2023). Exploring Hybrid Multi-View Multimodal for Natural Language Emotion Recognition Using Multi-Source Information Learning Model. *FMDB Transactions on Sustainable Computer Letters, 1*(1), 12–24.

Jebreil, N., Azizifar, A., & Gowhary, H. (2015). Investigating the effect of anxiety of male and female Iranian EFL learners on their writing performance. *Procedia: Social and Behavioral Sciences, 185*, 190–196. doi:10.1016/j.sbspro.2015.03.360

Jeon, J., Lee, S., & Choe, H. (2023). Beyond ChatGPT: A conceptual framework and systematic review of speech-recognition chatbots for language learning. *Computers & Education, 206*, 104898. doi:10.1016/j.compedu.2023.104898

Jiang, L., Cheng, Y., Yang, L., Li, J., Yan, H., & Wang, X. (2019). A trust-based collaborative filtering algorithm for E-commerce recommendation system. *Journal of Ambient Intelligence and Humanized Computing, 10*(8), 3023–3034. doi:10.100712652-018-0928-7

Jin, D., Jin, Z., Zhou, J. T., Zhang, Z., & Szolovits, P. (2020). Is generation as diverse as it could be? An empirical study on neural dialogue models. In *Proceedings of the AAAI Conference on Artificial Intelligence*. ACL.

Ji, R., Li, Y., Shen, Z., Li, L., & Liu, G. (2016). A fine-grained classification model for fashion image analysis. In *Proceedings of the 2016 ACM on Multimedia Conference* (pp. 955-956). ACM.

Ji, Z., & Wang, Y. (2021). A novel fine-grained fashion classification method using attention mechanisms. *Neural Computing & Applications*, 33(6), 2229–2239.

Johri, P., Khatri, S. K., Al-Taani, A. T., Sabharwal, M., Suvanov, S., & Kumar, A. (2021). Natural Language Processing: history, evolution, application, and future work. In *Lecture notes in networks and systems* (Vol. 167, pp. 365–375). Springer. doi:10.1007/978-981-15-9712-1_31

Judith, V.S., &Jakub, M. (2021). Proceedings of the 16th International Conference on the Foundations of Digital. *Games, 2*, 1–8. . doi:10.1145/3472538.3472595

Kafle, K., Shrestha, R., & Kanan, C. (2019). Challenges and Prospects in Vision and Language Research. *Frontiers in Artificial Intelligence, 2*, 466972. doi:10.3389/frai.2019.00028 PMID:33733117

Kamruzzaman, M. M., Alanazi, S., Alruwaili, M., Alshammari, N., Elaiwat, S., Abu-Zanona, M., Innab, N., Mohammad Elzaghmouri, B., & Ahmed Alanazi, B. (2023). AI-and IoT-Assisted Sustainable Education Systems during Pandemics, such as COVID-19, for Smart Cities. *Sustainability (Basel), 15*(10), 8354. doi:10.3390u15108354

Kanyimama, W. (2023). Design of A Ground Based Surveillance Network for Modibbo Adama University, Yola. *FMDB Transactions on Sustainable Computing Systems, 1*(1), 32–43.

Kapoor, R., & Ghosal, I. (2022). Will Artificial Intelligence Compliment or Supplement Human Workforce in Organizations? A Shift to a Collaborative Human – Machine Environment. [IJRTBT]. *International Journal on Recent Trends in Business and Tourism, 6*(4), 19–28. doi:10.31674/ijrtbt.2022.v06i04.002

Karaoglan-Yilmaz, F. G., Ustun, A. B., Zhang, K., & Yilmaz, R. (2023). Metacognitive awareness, reflective thinking, problem solving, and community of inquiry as predictors of academic self-efficacy in blended learning: A correlational study. *Turkish Online Journal of Distance Education, 24*(1), 20–36. doi:10.17718/tojde.989874

Karim, A., Beni-Hessane, A., & Khaloufi, H. (2018). Big healthcare data: Preserving security and privacy. *Journal of Big Data, 5*(1), 1. doi:10.118640537-017-0110-7

Karpathy, A., & Fei-Fei, L. (2015). Deep visual-semantic alignments for generating image descriptions. In *Proceedings of the IEEE Conference on Computer Vision and Pattern Recognition* (pp. 3128-3137). IEEE. 10.1109/CVPR.2015.7298932

Kasneci, E., Seßler, K., Küchemann, S., Bannert, M., Dementieva, D., Fischer, F., Gasser, U., Groh, G., Günnemann, S., Hüllermeier, E., Krusche, S., Kutyniok, G., Michaeli, T., Nerdel, C., Pfeffer, J., Poquet, O., Sailer, M., Schmidt, A., Seidel, T., & Kasneci, G. (2023). ChatGPT for good? On opportunities and challenges of large language models for education. *Learning and Individual Differences, 103*, 102274. doi:10.1016/j.lindif.2023.102274

KasneciE.SeßlerK.KüchemannS.BannertM.DementievaD.FischerF.KasneciG. (2023). ChatGPT for good? On opportunities and challenges of large language models for education. https://edarxiv.org/5er8f/

Kaushikkumar, P. (2023). Credit Card Analytics: A Review of Fraud Detection and Risk Assessment Techniques. *International Journal of Computer Trends and Technology, 71*(10), 69–79. doi:10.14445/22312803/IJCTT-V71I10P109

Kengam, J. (2020). *Artificial intelligence in education*. Research Gate.

Keras. (2023). *Keras: a deep learning API written in Python*. Keras. https://keras.io/

Kertati, I., Sanchez, C. Y., Basri, M., Husain, M. N., & Tj, H. W. (2023). Public Relations' Disruption Model On Chat-gpt Issue. *Indonesian Journal of Communications Studies, 1*(7), 034-048. https://doi.org/. doi:10.25139/jsk.v7i1.6143

Khairatun, H. U., & Miftahul, A. M. (2022). Artificial Intelligence for Human Life: A Critical Opinion from Medical Bioethics Perspective – Part II. *Journal of Public Health Sciences, 1*(02), 112–130. doi:10.56741/jphs.v1i02.215

Khan, A. O., Badshah, S., Liang, P., Khan, B., Waseem, M., Niazi, M., & Akbar, M. (2022). Ethics Of Ai: a Systematic Literature Review Of Principles And Challenges. *Proceedings of the 26th International Conference on Evaluation and Assessment in Software Engineering*, (pp. 383-392). ACM.)10.1145/3530019.3531329

Khandelwal, U., He, H., Qi, P., & Jurafsky, D. (2018). Sharp Nearby, Fuzzy Far Away: How Neural Language Models Use Context. *Proceedings of the 56th Annual Meeting of the Association for Computational Linguistics*, Volume 1: *Long Papers*, 284–294. https://doi.org/10.18653/v1/P18-1027

Khang, A., Muthmainnah, M., Seraj, P. M. I., Al Yakin, A., & Obaid, A. J. (2023). AI-Aided Teaching Model in Education 5.0. In Handbook of Research on AI-Based Technologies and Applications in the Era of the Metaverse (pp. 83-104). IGI Global.

Khan, M. A., Nasralla, M. M., Umar, M. M., Khan, S., & Choudhury, N. (2022). An Efficient Multilevel Probabilistic Model for Abnormal Traffic Detection in Wireless Sensor Networks. *Sensors (Basel), 22*(2), 410. doi:10.339022020410 PMID:35062372

Khurana, D., Koli, A., Khatter, K., & Singh, S. (2023). Natural language processing: State of the art, current trends and challenges. *Multimedia Tools and Applications, 82*(3), 3713–3744. doi:10.100711042-022-13428-4 PMID:35855771

Kiener, M. (2021). Artificial intelligence in medicine and the disclosure of risks. *AI & Society, 36*(3), 705–713. doi:10.100700146-020-01085-w PMID:33110296

Kikas, E., Eisenschmidt, E., & Granström, M. (2023). Conceptualisation of learning to learn competence and the challenges of implementation: The Estonian experience. *European Journal of Education, 58*(3), 498–509. doi:10.1111/ejed.12571

Kılınç, S. (2023). *Embracing the Future of Distance Science Education: Opportunities and Challenges of ChatGPT Integration*. Academic Press.

Kim, H., Yang, H., Shin, D., & Lee, J. H. (2022). Design principles and architecture of a second language learning chatbot. *Language Learning & Technology, 26*(1), 1–18.

Kim, W., & Seok, J. (2022). Privacy-preserving collaborative machine learning in biomedical applications. *2022 International Conference on Artificial Intelligence in Information and Communication (ICAIIC)*. https://doi.org/10.1109/ICAIIC54071.2022.9722703

King. (2022). The future of AI in medicine: a perspective from a Chatbot. *Annals of Biomedical Engineering*, 1-5.

King, M. R. (2023). Google's Experimental Chatbot Based on the LaMDA Large Language Model, Help to Analyze the Gender and Racial Diversity of Authors in Your Cited Scientific References? *Cellular and Molecular Bioengineering, 16*(2), 175–179. doi:10.100712195-023-00761-3 PMID:37096072

Kingma, D. P., & Welling, M. (2013). *Auto-Encoding Variational Bayes*. arXiv preprint arXiv:1312.6114.

KingT.AggarwalN.TaddeoM.FloridiL. (2018). Artificial Intelligence Crime: An Interdisciplinary Analysis of Foreseeable Threats and Solutions. SSRN. https://ssrn.com/abstract=3183238 doi:10.2139/ssrn.3183238

Kleiman, G. (2022). *AI and Teaching Writing, Working Paper # 3 AI has learned to write; Can it help teach students to write well? Linse, C. T. (2005). Practical English language teaching: Young learners* (D. Nunan, Ed.; International Edition). McGraw-Hill Companies, Inc.

Klymenko, O., Meisenbacher, S., & Matthes, F. (2022). Differential Privacy in Natural Language Processing The Story So Far. *Proceedings of the Fourth Workshop on Privacy in Natural Language Processing.* https://doi.org/10.18653/v1/2022.privatenlp-1.1

Knill, K., & Young, S. (1997). Hidden Markov models in speech and language processing. In *Text, speech and language technology* (pp. 27–68). Springer. doi:10.1007/978-94-017-1183-8_2

Kohnke, L. (2023). L2 learners' perceptions of a chatbot as a potential independent language learning tool. *International Journal of Mobile Learning and Organisation, 17*(1-2), 214–226. doi:10.1504/IJMLO.2023.128339

Kohnke, L., Moorhouse, B. L., & Zou, D. (2023). ChatGPT for language teaching and learning. *RELC Journal,* 00336882231162868.

Koraishi, O. (2023). Teaching English in the age of AI: Embracing ChatGPT to optimize EFL materials and assessment. *Language Education and Technology, 3*(1).

Korngiebel, D. M., & Mooney, S. D. (2021). Considering the possibilities and pitfalls of Generative Pre-trained Transformer 3 (GPT-3) in healthcare delivery. *Npj Digital Medicine, 4*(1). doi:10.1038/s41746-021-00464-x

Koroniotis, N., Moustafa, N., Sitnikova, E., & Turnbull, B. (2019). Towards the development of realistic botnet dataset in the Internet of Things for network forensic analytics: Bot-IoT dataset. *Future Generation Computer Systems, 100,* 779–796. doi:10.1016/j.future.2019.05.041

Kosuru, V. S. R., & Venkitaraman, A. K. (2022). Developing a deep Q-learning and neural network framework for trajectory planning. *European Journal of Engineering and Technology Research, 7*(6), 148–157. doi:10.24018/ejeng.2022.7.6.2944

Kovačević, D. (2023, March). Use of chatgpt in ESP teaching process. In *2023 22nd International Symposium INFOTEH-JAHORINA (INFOTEH)* (pp. 1-5). IEEE.

Kreps, S., McCain, R., & Brundage, M. (2022). All the News That's Fit to Fabricate: AI-Generated Text as a Tool of Media Misinformation. *Journal of Experimental Political Science, 9*(1), 104–117. doi:10.1017/XPS.2020.37

Krishna Das, J., Das, A., & Rosak-Szyrocka, J. (2022). A hybrid deep learning technique for sentiment analysis in E-learning platform with natural language processing. *2022 International Conference on Software, Telecommunications and Computer Networks (SoftCOM).* IEEE. 10.23919/SoftCOM55329.2022.9911232

Kulbir, S. (2023). Artificial Intelligence & Cloud in Healthcare: Analyzing Challenges and Solutions Within Regulatory Boundaries. *SSRG International Journal of Computer Science and Engineering, 10*(9), 1–9. doi:10.14445/23488387/IJCSE-V10I9P101

Kumar Jain, A. (2022). Hybrid Cloud Computing: A Perspective. *International Journal of Engineering Research & Technology (Ahmedabad), 11*(10), 1–06.

Kumar Jain, A. (2022). Multi-Cloud Computing & Why do we need to Embrace it. *International Journal of Engineering Research & Technology (Ahmedabad), 11*(09), 1–06.

Kumar, A. (2023, March 17). *Generative vs Discriminative Models: Examples.*

Kumar, A. (2023b, July 9). *Large Language Models (LLMs): Concepts & Examples.*

Kumar, K. S., Yadav, D., Joshi, S. K., Chakravarthi, M. K., Jain, A. K., & Tripathi, V. (2022). Blockchain technology with applications to distributed control and cooperative robotics. *2022 5th International Conference on Contemporary Computing and Informatics (IC3I)*. IEEE.

Kumar, K. S., Yadav, D., Joshi, S. K., Chakravarthi, M. K., Jain, A. K., & Tripathi, V. (2022). Blockchain technology with applications to distributed control and cooperative robotics. In *2022 5th International Conference on Contemporary Computing and Informatics (IC3I)*. IEEE.

Kumar, H. S. (2023). Analysis of ChatGPT Tool to Assess the Potential of its Utility for Academic Writing in Biomedical Domain. *Biology, Engineering. Medicine and Science Reports*, 9(1), 24–30. doi:10.5530/bems.9.1.5

Kumar, L. A., & Renuka, D. K. (2023). *Deep Learning Approach for Natural Language Processing, Speech, and Computer Vision: Techniques and Use Cases* (1st ed.). CRC Press. doi:10.1201/9781003348689

Kumar, S. A., Rajest, S. S., Aravind, B. R., & Bhuvaneswari, G. (2023). Virtual learning styles based on learning style detection. *International Journal of Knowledge and Learning*, 1(1), 10057158. doi:10.1504/IJKL.2023.10057158

Kumar, V., & Tiwari, S. (2012). Routing in IPv6 over low-power wireless personal area networks (6LoWPAN): A survey. *Journal of Computer Networks and Communications*, 2012, 316839. doi:10.1155/2012/316839

Lai, K., Long, Y., Wu, B., Liu, Y., & Wang, B. (2022). SeMorph: A morphology semantic enhanced pre-trained model for Chinese spam text detection. *Proceedings of the 31st ACM International Conference on Information & Knowledge Management*. ACM. 10.1145/3511808.3557448

Lakshmi Narayanan, K., Santhana Krishnan, R., Golden Julie, E., Harold Robinson, Y., & Shanmuganathan, V. (2021). Machine learning-based detection and a novel EC-BRTT algorithm-based prevention of DoS attacks in wireless sensor networks. *Wireless Personal Communications*, 1–25.

Lample, G., Denoyer, L., & Ranzato, M. A. (2018). *Unsupervised machine translation using monolingual corpora only.* arXiv preprint arXiv:1711.00043.

Larsson, S., & Heintz, F. (2020). Transparency in artificial intelligence. *Internet Policy Review*, 9(2). doi:10.14763/2020.2.1469

Latha, T., Patel, S., & Reddy, V. (2022). Analysis On Cybersecurity Threats in Modern Banking and Machine Learning Techniques For Fraud Detection. *The Review of Contemporary Scientific and Academic Studies*, 3(11).

Latif, E., Mai, G., Nyaaba, M., Wu, X., Liu, N., Lu, G., . . . Zhai, X. (2023). *Artificial general intelligence (AGI) for education.* arXiv preprint arXiv:2304.12479.

LeCun, Y., Bengio, Y., & Hinton, G. (2015). Deep learning. *Nature*, 521(7553), 436–444. doi:10.1038/nature14539 PMID:26017442

Lee, C.-H., Chen, C.-W., Chen, W.-K., & Lin, K.-H. (n.d.). *ANALYSING THE EFFECT OF SOCIAL SUPPORT AND CUSTOMER ENGAGEMENT ON STICKINESS AND REPURCHASE INTENTION IN SOCIAL COMMERCE: A TRUST TRANSFER PERSPECTIVE.*

Lee, J.A., Reto, M., Hilty, & Kung-Chung, L. (2021). Roadmap to Artificial Intelligence and Intellectual PropertyAn Introduction. *Artificial Intelligence and Intellectual Property.* . doi:10.1093/oso/9780198870944.003.0001

Lee, K. J., Kwon, J. W., Min, S., & Yoon, J. (2021). Deploying an Artificial Intelligence-Based Defect Finder for Manufacturing Quality Management. *AI Magazine*, 42(2), 5–18. doi:10.1609/aimag.v42i2.15094

Lewis, D. W. (2023). Open Access: A Conversation with ChatGPT. *The Journal of Electronic Publishing: JEP, 26*(1), 3891. doi:10.3998/jep.3891

Liang Hu, Guohang Song, Zhenzhen Xie, & Kuo Zhao. (n.d.). *Personalized Recommendation Algorithm Based on Preference Features.*

Lian, X., Hong, W. C. H., Xu, X., Kimberly, K. Z., & Wang, Z. (2022). The influence of picture book design on visual attention of children with autism: A pilot study. *International Journal of Developmental Disabilities*, 1–11. PMID:37885844

Liao, S. H., Widowati, R., & Hsieh, Y. C. (2021). Investigating online social media users' behaviours for social commerce recommendations. *Technology in Society, 66*, 101655. Advance online publication. doi:10.1016/j.techsoc.2021.101655

Liddy, E. D. (2001). Natural language processing. Encyclopedia of Library and Information Science.

Lieberman, M. (2023). What Is ChatGPT and How Is It Used in Education? *Education Week, 42*(18).

Li, J., Galley, M., Brockett, C., Spithourakis, G. P., Gao, J., & Dolan, B. (2016). A diversity-promoting objective function for neural conversation models. In *Proceedings of the 2016 Conference of the North American Chapter of the Association for Computational Linguistics: Human Language Technologies* (pp. 110-119). ACL. 10.18653/v1/N16-1014

Li, J., Li, Z., Ge, T., King, I., & Lyu, M. R. (2022). Text Revision By On-the-Fly Representation Optimization. *Proceedings of the AAAI Conference on Artificial Intelligence,* Hong Kong.10.1609/aaai.v36i10.21343

Li, J., Monroe, W., Ritter, A., Galley, M., Gao, J., & Jurafsky, D. (2017). Adversarial learning for neural dialogue generation. In *Proceedings of the 2017 Conference on Empirical Methods in Natural Language Processing* (pp. 2157-2169). ACL. 10.18653/v1/D17-1230

Lika, B., Kolomvatsos, K., & Hadjiefthymiades, S. (2014). Facing the cold start problem in recommender systems. *Expert Systems with Applications, 41*(4 PART 2), 2065–2073. doi:10.1016/j.eswa.2013.09.005

Li, L., Zhu, M. L., Shi, Y. Q., & Yang, L. L. (2023). Influencing factors of self-regulated learning of medical-related students in a traditional Chinese medical university: A cross-sectional study. *BMC Medical Education, 23*(1), 87. doi:10.118612909-023-04051-4 PMID:36737773

Limna, P., Kraiwanit, T., Jangjarat, K., Klayklung, P., & Chocksathaporn, P. (2023). The use of ChatGPT in the digital era: Perspectives on chatbot implementation. *Journal of Applied Learning and Teaching, 6*(1).

Lin, C. Y. (2004). ROUGE: A package for automatic evaluation of summaries. In Text summarization branches out (pp. 74-81).

Lina, L. F., & Ahluwalia, L. (2021). Customers' impulse buying in social commerce: The role of flow experience in personalized advertising. *Jurnal Manajemen Maranatha, 21*(1), 1–8. doi:10.28932/jmm.v21i1.3837

Lindell, Y., & Pinkas, B. (2009). Secure Multiparty Computation for Privacy-Preserving Data Mining. *The Journal of Privacy and Confidentiality, 1*(1). doi:10.29012/jpc.v1i1.566

LinZ. (2023). Why and how to embrace AI such as ChatGPT in your academic life. PsyArXiv.

Liu, C. Y. (2022). Types of NLP models. *OpenGenus IQ: Computing Expertise & Legacy.* https://iq.opengenus.org/types-of-nlp-models/

Liu, Y., Han, T., Ma, S., Zhang, J., Yang, Y., Tian, J., & Ge, B. (2023). Summary of chatgpt/gpt-4 research and perspective towards the future of large language models. *arXiv preprint arXiv:2304.01852.*

Liu, Y., Ott, M., Goyal, N., Du, J., Joshi, M., Chen, D., & Stoyanov, V. (2019). *RoBERTa: A robustly optimized BERT pretraining approach*. arXiv preprint arXiv:1907.11692.

Liu, Y., Ott, M., Goyal, N., Du, J., Joshi, M., Chen, D., Levy, O., Lewis, M., Zettlemoyer, L., & Stoyanov, V. (7 2019). *RoBERTa: A Robustly Optimized BERT Pretraining Approach*. arXiv. https://arxiv.org/abs/1907.11692

Liu, G., Fu, Y., Chen, G., Xiong, H., & Chen, C. (2017). Modeling buying motives for personalized product bundle recommendation. *ACM Transactions on Knowledge Discovery from Data*, *11*(3), 1–26. doi:10.1145/3022185

Liu, G., & Ma, C. (2023). Measuring EFL learners' use of ChatGPT in informal digital learning of English based on the technology acceptance model. *Innovation in Language Learning and Teaching*, 1–14. doi:10.1080/17501229.2023.2240316

Liu, L., Exarchos, M., Kumar, A., & Yu, S. (2018). TextGAN: Generative adversarial networks for text synthesis. In *Proceedings of the 2018 World Wide Web Conference* (pp. 1299-1308). ACL.

Liu, L., Otani, M., Liu, X., Wang, H., & Zhao, T. (2020). Towards explainable text generation with human-aware intervention. In *Proceedings of the 58th Annual Meeting of the Association for Computational Linguistics* (pp. 7415-7426). ACL.

Liu, M. (2023). A self-case study of the female doctoral student's own creative metacognition on art expressions: Based on the theory of creative metacognition (CMC). *Thinking Skills and Creativity*, *48*, 101292. doi:10.1016/j.tsc.2023.101292

LiuS.WrightA. P.PattersonB. L.WandererJ. P.TurerR. W.NelsonS. D.McCoyA. B.SittigD. F.WrightA. (2023). Assessing the Value of ChatGPT for Clinical Decision Support Optimization. MedRxiv. doi:10.1101/2023.02.21.23286254

Liu, W., Chen, P., Yeung, S., Suzumura, T., & Chen, L. (2017). Principled Multilayer Network Embedding. *IEEE International Conference on Data Mining Workshops (ICDM Workshops)* (pp. 134-141). IEEE.10.1109/ICDMW.2017.23

Li, W., Chen, S., Xie, L., Fu, Y., & Zhang, H. (2021). Fine-grained fashion classification via a coarse-to-fine network with semantic hierarchy. *IEEE Transactions on Industrial Informatics*, *17*(3), 1901–1910.

Li, Y., Tar, C., Dyer, C., & Hovy, E. (2018). V-NLG: Variational neural language generation for cooperative dialogue systems. In *Proceedings of the 2018 Conference on Empirical Methods in Natural Language Processing* (pp. 4433-4444). IEEE.

Li, Y., Zhao, K., Li, R., Li, Y., & Li, H. (2020). Clothing classification based on transfer learning of deep convolutional neural networks. *Journal of Physics: Conference Series*, *1692*(1), 012103. doi:10.1088/1742-6596/1692/1/012103

Li, Z., Gan, Z., Cheng, Y., Wu, Y., & Carin, L. (2019). M3E: Multimodal multi-encoder for efficient text generation. In *Proceedings of the 2019 Conference on Empirical Methods in Natural Language Processing and the 9th International Joint Conference on Natural Language Processing* (pp. 613-623). ACL.

Li, Z., Wang, Y., Zhang, N., Zhang, Y., Zhao, Z., Xu, D., & Gao, Y. (2022). Deep learning-based object detection techniques for remote sensing images: A survey. *Remote Sensing (Basel)*, *14*(10), 2385. doi:10.3390/rs14102385

Lodha, S., Malani, H., & Bhardwaj, A. K. (2023). Performance Evaluation of Vision Transformers for Diagnosis of Pneumonia. *FMDB Transactions on Sustainable Computing Systems*, *1*(1), 21–31.

Luitse, D., & Denkena, W. (2021). The great Transformer: Examining the role of large language models in the political economy of AI. *Big Data & Society*, *8*(2), 47734. doi:10.1177/20539517211047734

Lumapenet, H. T. (2022). Effectiveness of Self-Learning Modules on Students' Learning in English Amidst Pandemic. *Res Militaris*, *12*(6), 949–953.

LundB. (2022). A Chat with ChatGPT: How will AI impact scholarly publishing? doi:10.13140/RG.2.2.34572.18565

Lund, B. D., & Wang, T. (2023). Chatting about ChatGPT: How may AI and GPT impact academia and libraries? *Library Hi Tech News*, *40*(3), 26–29. doi:10.1108/LHTN-01-2023-0009

Lund, B. D., Wang, T., Mannuru, N. R., Nie, B., Shimray, S., & Wang, Z. (2023). ChatGPT and a new academic reality: Artificial Intelligence-written research papers and the ethics of the large language models in scholarly publishing. *Journal of the Association for Information Science and Technology*, *74*(5), 570–581. doi:10.1002/asi.24750

Luo, S., Lai, Y., & Liu, J. (2023). Selective forwarding attack detection and network recovery mechanism based on cloud-edge cooperation in software-defined wireless sensor network. *Computers & Security*, *126*, 103083. doi:10.1016/j.cose.2022.103083

Lyu, Q., Tan, J., Zapadka, M. E., Ponnatapura, J., Niu, C., Wang, G., & Whitlow, C. T. (2023). Translating Radiology Reports Into Plain Language Using Chatgpt and Gpt-4 With Prompt Learning: Promising Results, Limitations, And Potential. *Visual Computing for Industry, Biomedicine, and Art*, *6*(9), 37198498. doi:10.118642492-023-00136-5 PMID:37198498

Macey-Dare, R. (2023). ChatGPT & Generative AI Systems as Quasi-Expert Legal Advice Lawyers - Case Study Considering Potential Appeal Against Conviction of Tom Hayes. SSRN *Electronic Journal*. doi:10.2139/ssrn.4342686

Magazine, B. A.-C. D. (2023). Why ChatGPT is such a big deal for education. *Scholarspace.Jccc.Edu*.

Mageira, K., Pittou, D., Papasalouros, A., Kotis, K., Zangogianni, P., & Daradoumis, A. (2022). Educational AI chatbots for content and language integrated learning. *Applied Sciences (Basel, Switzerland)*, *12*(7), 3239. doi:10.3390/app12073239

Mahendran, D., Luo, C., & McInnes, B. T. (2021). Review: Privacy-Preservation in the Context of Natural Language Processing. *IEEE Access : Practical Innovations, Open Solutions*, *9*, 147600–147612. doi:10.1109/ACCESS.2021.3124163

Majeed, A., & Lee, S. (2021). Anonymization Techniques for Privacy Preserving Data Publishing: A Comprehensive survey. *IEEE Access : Practical Innovations, Open Solutions*, *9*, 8512–8545. doi:10.1109/ACCESS.2020.3045700

Ma, L., Huang, Z., Bing, L., Yang, T., & Zhu, X. (2018). Teaching machines to describe images with human feedback. In *Proceedings of the IEEE conference on computer vision and pattern recognition* (pp. 55-65). IEEE.

Mardanirad, S., Wood, D. A., & Zakeri, H. (2021). The application of deep learning algorithms to classify subsurface drilling lost circulation severity in large oil field datasets. *SN Applied Sciences*, *3*(9), 785. doi:10.100742452-021-04769-0

Mari, M. A., Tsalas, N., & Paulus, M. (2023). Why is she scratching her head? Children's understanding of others' metacognitive gestures as an indicator of learning. *Journal of Experimental Child Psychology*, *230*, 105631. doi:10.1016/j.jecp.2023.105631 PMID:36731277

Martinelli, F., Marulli, F., Mercaldo, F., Marrone, S., & Santone, A. (2020). Enhanced Privacy and Data Protection using Natural Language Processing and Artificial Intelligence. *2020 International Joint Conference on Neural Networks (IJCNN)*. IEEE. 10.1109/IJCNN48605.2020.9206801

Maseleno, A., Patimah, S., Syafril, S., & Huda, M. (2023). Learning Preferences Diagnostic using Mathematical Theory of Evidence. *FMDB Transactions on Sustainable Techno Learning*, *1*(2), 60–77.

Mathew, A. (2023). Is Artificial Intelligence a World Changer? A Case Study of OpenAI's Chat GPT. *Recent Progress in Science and Technology*, *5*, 35–42. doi:10.9734/bpi/rpst/v5/18240D

Matsui, T., & Ikehara, M. (2020). Single-image fence removal using deep convolutional neural network. *IEEE Access : Practical Innovations, Open Solutions*, *8*, 38846–38854. doi:10.1109/ACCESS.2019.2960087

Mattas, P. S. (2023). ChatGPT: A Study of AI Language Processing and its Implications. *International Journal of Research Publication and Reviews*, *04*(02), 435–440. doi:10.55248/gengpi.2023.4218

Matuk, C., Yetman-Michaelson, L., Martin, R., Vasudevan, V., Burgas, K., Davidesco, I., Shevchenko, Y., Chaloner, K., & Dikker, S. (2023). Open science in the classroom: Students designing and peer reviewing studies in human brain and behavior research. *Instructional Science*, *51*(5), 1–53. doi:10.100711251-023-09633-9

McGee, R. W. (2023). Capitalism, Socialism and ChatGPT. SSRN *Electronic Journal*. doi:10.2139/ssrn.4369953

Medhat, W., Hassan, A., & Korashy, H. (2014). Sentiment analysis algorithms and applications: A survey. *Ain Shams Engineering Journal*, *5*(4), 1093–1113. doi:10.1016/j.asej.2014.04.011

Melissa Ng Lee Yen, A. (2020). The influence of self-regulation processes on metacognition in a virtual learning environment. *Educational Studies*, *46*(1), 1–17. doi:10.1080/03055698.2018.1516628

Meltzer, L. (2013). Teaching executive functioning processes: Promoting metacognition, strategy use, and effort. In *Handbook of executive functioning* (pp. 445–473). Springer New York.

Mencar, C., Castiello, C., Cannone, R., & Fanelli, A. M. (2011). Interpretability assessment of fuzzy knowledge bases: A cointension based approach. *International Journal of Approximate Reasoning*, *52*(4), 501–518. doi:10.1016/j.ijar.2010.11.007

Mendez-Rial, R., Calvino-Cancela, M., & Martin-Herrero, J. (2012). Anisotropic Inpainting of the Hypercube. *IEEE Geoscience and Remote Sensing Letters : A Publication of the IEEE Geoscience and Remote Sensing Society*, *9*(2), 214–218. doi:10.1109/LGRS.2011.2164050

Menn, J. (2018). Amazon Scraps Secret AI Recruiting Tool That Showed Bias Against Women. Reuters, 9 Oct. 2018, https://www.reuters.com/article/us-amazon-com-jobs-automation-insight/amazon-scraps-secret-ai-recruiting-tool-that-showed-bias-against-women-idUSKCN1MK08G

Merriam-Webster. (2023). *Emotion. In Merriam-Webster.com dictionary*. Merriam-Webster. https://www.merriam-webster.com/dictionary/emotion

Meyer, J. G., Urbanowicz, R. J., Martin, P. C., O'Connor, K., Li, R., Peng, P. C., Bright, T. J., Tatonetti, N., Won, K. J., Gonzalez-Hernandez, G., & Moore, J. H. (2023). ChatGPT and large language models in academia: Opportunities and challenges. *BioData Mining*, *16*(1), 20. doi:10.118613040-023-00339-9 PMID:37443040

MhlangaD. (2023). Open AI in Education, The responsible and ethical use of ChaTGPT towards lifelong Learning. *Social Science Research Network*. https://doi.org/ doi:10.2139/ssrn.4354422

Michel-Villarreal, R., Vilalta-Perdomo, E., Salinas-Navarro, D. E., Thierry-Aguilera, R., & Gerardou, F. S. (2023). Challenges and Opportunities of Generative AI for Higher Education as Explained by ChatGPT. *Education Sciences*, *13*(9), 856. doi:10.3390/educsci13090856

Microsoft. (2016). Learning Tay's Introduction. *Microsoft Blog*. https://blogs.microsoft.com/blog/2016/03/25/learning-tays-introduction/

Mijwil, M., Aljanabi, M., & Ali, A. H. (2023). *ChatGPT: Exploring the Role of Cybersecurity in the Protection of Medical Information*. Mesopotamian Journal of Cyber Security. doi:10.58496/MJCS/2023/004

Mikolov, T., Karafiát, M., Burget, L., Černocký, J., & Khudanpur, S. (2010). Recurrent neural network based language model. *11th Annual Conference of the International Speech Communication Association*, Makuhari, Chiba, Japan. 10.21437/Interspeech.2010-343

Mikolov, T., Karafiát, M., Burget, L., Cernocký, J., & Khudanpur, S. (2010). Recurrent neural network based language model. In *Proceedings of the 11th Annual Conference of the International Speech Communication Association*. ACL.

Mirjalili, S. (2015). Moth-flame optimization algorithm: A novel nature-inspired heuristic paradigm, Knowl.-. *Knowledge-Based Systems*, *89*(1), 228–249. doi:10.1016/j.knosys.2015.07.006

Mogavi, R. H., Deng, C., Kim, J. J., Zhou, P., Kwon, Y. D., Metwally, A. H. S., & Hui, P. (2023). Exploring user perspectives on chatgpt: Applications, perceptions, and implications for ai-integrated education. *arXiv preprint arXiv:2305.13114*.

Molnár, G., & Szüts, Z. (2018, September). The role of chatbots in formal education. In *2018 IEEE 16th International Symposium on Intelligent Systems and Informatics (SISY)* (pp. 000197-000202). IEEE. 10.1109/SISY.2018.8524609

Moore, J. L., Rosinski, P., Peeples, T., Pigg, S., Rife, M. C., Brunk-Chavez, B., Lackey, D., Kesler Rumsey, S., Tasaka, R., Curran, P., & Grabill, J. T. (2016). Revisualizing composition: How first-year writers use composing technologies. *Computers and Composition*, *39*, 1–13. doi:10.1016/j.compcom.2015.11.001

Muller, B. (2022). *BERT 101 State Of The Art NLP Model Explained*. Hugging Face. https://huggingface.co/blog/bert-101

Muller, B. (2022, March 2). BERT 101 State Of The Art NLP Model Explained. *Hugging Face*. https://huggingface.co/blog/bert-101

Müller, V. (2016). *Editorial: Risks of Artificial Intelligence*. Taylor & Francis. . doi:10.1201/b19187-2

Muñoz, S. A. S., Gayoso, G. G., Huambo, A. C., Tapia, R. D. C., Incaluque, J. L., Aguila, O. E. P., & Arias-Gonzáles, J. L. (2023). Examining the Impacts of ChatGPT on Student Motivation and Engagement. *Social Space*, *23*(1), 1–27.

Murugavel, S., & Hernandez, F. (2023). A Comparative Study Between Statistical and Machine Learning Methods for Forecasting Retail Sales. *FMDB Transactions on Sustainable Computer Letters*, *1*(2), 76–102.

Muthmainnah, G. S., & Al Yakin, A. (2023). An Effective Investigation on YIPe-Learning Based for Twenty-First Century Class. In Digital Learning based Education: Transcending Physical Barriers (pp. 21-38). Singapore: Springer Nature Singapore.

Muthmainnah, M., Khang, A., Al Yakin, A., Oteir, I., & Alotaibi, A. N. (2023). An Innovative Teaching Model: The Potential of Metaverse for English Learning. In *Handbook of Research on AI-Based Technologies and Applications in the Era of the Metaverse* (pp. 105–126). IGI Global. doi:10.4018/978-1-6684-8851-5.ch005

Mutlag, A. A., Abd Ghani, M. K., Arunkumar, N., Mohammed, M. A., & Mohd, O. (2019). Enabling technologies for fog computing in healthcare IoT systems. *Future Generation Computer Systems*, *90*, 62–78. doi:10.1016/j.future.2018.07.049

Nadee, W. (2016). *MODELLING USER PROFILES FOR RECOMMENDER SYSTEMS IN FULFILMENT OF THE REQUIREMENTS FOR THE DEGREE OF DOCTOR OF PHILOSOPHY*.

Nadimpalli, M. (2017). Artificial intelligence risks and benefits. *International Journal of Innovative Research in Science, Engineering and Technology*, *6*, 6.

Nagaraj, B., Kalaivani, A., R, S. B., Akila, S., Sachdev, H. K., & N, S. K. (2023). The Emerging Role of Artificial intelligence in STEM Higher Education: A Critical review. *International Research Journal of Multidisciplinary Technovation*, 1–19. doi:10.54392/irjmt2351

Nagy, B., Hegedűs, I., Sándor, N., Egedi, B., Mehmood, H., Saravanan, K., Lóki, G., & Kiss, Á. (2023). Privacy-preserving Federated Learning and its application to natural language processing. *Knowledge-Based Systems*, *268*, 110475. doi:10.1016/j.knosys.2023.110475

NastasiA. J.CourtrightK. R.HalpernS. D.WeissmanG. E. (2023). Does ChatGPT Provide Appropriate and Equitable Medical Advice?: A Vignette-Based, Clinical Evaluation Across Care Contexts. MedRxiv. doi:10.1101/2023.02.25.23286451

Neal, T. M. (2023). Metacognition: Thinking About Thinking. In Strategies and Considerations for Educating the Academically Gifted (pp. 95-115). IGI Global.

Negretti, R. (2012). Metacognition in student academic writing: A longitudinal study of metacognitive awareness and its relation to task perception, self-regulation, and evaluation of performance. *Written Communication, 29*(2), 142–179. doi:10.1177/0741088312438529

Ness, I. J. (2023). Zone of Proximal Development. In *The Palgrave Encyclopedia of the Possible* (pp. 1781–1786). Springer International Publishing.

Nisar, S., & Aslam, M. S. (2023). Is ChatGPT a Good Tool for T&CM Students in Studying Pharmacology? SSRN *Electronic Journal.* doi:10.2139/ssrn.4324310

Nithyanantham, V. (2023). Study Examines the Connection Between Students' Various Intelligence and Their Levels of Mathematical Success in School. *FMDB Transactions on Sustainable Techno Learning, 1*(1), 32–59.

NLTK. (2023). NLTK: Natural Language Toolkit. NLTK. https://www.nltk.org/

Oak, R., Du, M., Yan, D., Takawale, H., & Amit, I. (2019). Malware detection on highly imbalanced data through sequence modeling. In *Proceedings of the 12th ACM Workshop on artificial intelligence and security* (pp. 37-48). ACM. 10.1145/3338501.3357374

Oberoi, A. (2021, July 15). What are Language Models in NLP? *Daffodil Unthinkable Software Corp.*

Ochoa, A. (2016). *Meet the pilot: Smart Earpiece language translator.* Indiegogo. https://www.indiegogo.com/projects/meet-the-pilot-smart-earpiece-language-translator#/

Odera, D. (2023). Federated learning and differential privacy in clinical health: Extensive survey. *World Journal of Advanced Engineering Technology and Sciences, 8*(2), 305–329. doi:10.30574/wjaets.2023.8.2.0113

Ogunmola, G. A., Singh, B., Sharma, D. K., Regin, R., Rajest, S. S., & Singh, N. (2021). Involvement of distance measure in assessing and resolving efficiency environmental obstacles. *2021 International Conference on Computational Intelligence and Knowledge Economy (ICCIKE).* IEEE. 10.1109/ICCIKE51210.2021.9410765

Okafor, K. C. (2021). Dynamic reliability modeling of cyber-physical edge computing network. *International Journal of Computers and Applications, 43*(7), 612–622. doi:10.1080/1206212X.2019.1600830

Okafor, K. C., Achumba, I. E., Chukwudebe, G. A., & Ononiwu, G. C. (2017). Leveraging Fog computing for scalable IoT datacenter using spine-leaf network topology. *Journal of Electrical and Computer Engineering,* 2017, 1–11. doi:10.1155/2017/2363240

Okpe, A. A., & Onjewu, M. A. (2017). Difficulties of learning essay writing: The perspective of some adult EFL learners in Nigeria. *International Journal of Curriculum and Instruction, 9*(2), 198–205.

Ollivier, M., Pareek, A., Dahmen, J., Kayaalp, M. E., Winkler, P. W., Hirschmann, M. T., & Karlsson, J. (2023). A deeper dive into ChatGPT: History, use and future perspectives for orthopaedic research. *Knee Surgery, Sports Traumatology, Arthroscopy : Official Journal of the ESSKA, 31*(4), 1190–1192. doi:10.100700167-023-07372-5 PMID:36894785

Optimal social choice functions: A utilitarian view. (2015). Artificial Intelligence.

Orakci, Ş., & Durnali, M. (2023). The mediating effects of metacognition and creative thinking on the relationship between teachers' autonomy support and teachers' self-efficacy. *Psychology in the Schools, 60*(1), 162–181. doi:10.1002/pits.22770

Ormond, E. (2020). The Ghost in the Machine: The Ethical Risks of AI. *The Thinker, 83*(1), 4–11. https://journals.uj.ac.za/index.php/The_Thinker/article/view/220 or doi:10.2139/ssrn.3719745

Orr, A. (2017). Capital One Launched A Natural Language Chatbot Named Eno. *The Mac Observer*. https://www.macobserver.com/analysis/capital-one-natural-language-chatbot-eno/

Otter, D. W., Medina, J. R., & Kalita, J. (2021). A Survey of the Usages of Deep Learning for Natural Language Processing. *IEEE, 32*(2), 604–624. doi:10.1109/TNNLS.2020.2979670

Owens. (2023). *How Nature readers are using ChatGPT*. Nature.

Owens, A., Wu, J., McDermott, J. H., & Freeman, W. T. (2016). Ambient sound provides supervision for visual learning. In *European Conference on Computer Vision* (pp. 801-816). Springer. 10.1007/978-3-319-46448-0_48

Oxford, A. (2022). Beijing acts to control AI-generated content. *Expert Briefings*, NA. . doi:10.1108/OXAN-DB267101

Padmanabhan, J., Rajest, S. S., & Veronica, J. J. (2023). A study on the orthography and grammatical errors of tertiary-level students. In *Handbook of Research on Learning in Language Classrooms Through ICT-Based Digital Technology* (pp. 41–53). IGI Global. doi:10.4018/978-1-6684-6682-7.ch004

Pajila, P. B., Julie, E. G., & Robinson, Y. H. (2022). FBDR-Fuzzy-based DDoS attack Detection and Recovery mechanism for wireless sensor networks. *Wireless Personal Communications, 122*(4), 1–31. doi:10.100711277-021-09040-8

Paldi, R. L., Aryal, A., Behzadirad, M., Busani, T., Siddiqui, A., & Wang, H. (2021). Nanocomposite-seeded single-domain growth of lithium niobate thin films for photonic applications. *Conference on Lasers and Electro-Optics*. Washington, D.C.: Optica Publishing Group. 10.1364/CLEO_SI.2021.STh4J.3

Pallant, J. (2020). SPSS survival manual: A step by step guide to data analysis using IBM SPSS. McGraw-hill education (UK).

Papineni, K., Roukos, S., Ward, T., & Zhu, W. J. (2002). BLEU: a method for automatic evaluation of machine translation. In *Proceedings of the 40th annual meeting of the Association for Computational Linguistics* (pp. 311-318). IEEE.

Parate, S., Reddi, L. T., Agarwal, S., & Suryadevara, M. (2023). Analyzing the impact of open data ecosystems and standardized interfaces on product development and innovation. International Journal of Advanced Research in Science. *Tongxin Jishu*, 476–485. doi:10.48175/IJARSCT-13165

Patel, A., & Bhanushali, S. (2023). Evaluating regression testing performance through machine learning for test case reduction. *International Journal of Computer Engineering and Technology, 14*(3), 51–66.

Patil, S., Chintamani, S., Grisham, J., Kumar, R., & Dennis, B. H. (2015). Inverse determination of temperature distribution in partially cooled heat generating cylinder. *Volume 8B: Heat Transfer and Thermal Engineering*.

Patil, S., Chintamani, S., Dennis, B. H., & Kumar, R. (2021). Real time prediction of internal temperature of heat generating bodies using neural network. *Thermal Science and Engineering Progress, 23*(100910), 100910. doi:10.1016/j.tsep.2021.100910

Patterson, J., & Gibson, A. (2017). Deep learning (Primera ed.). O'Reilly Media, Inc.

Paudel, P. K., Bastola, R., Eigenbrode, S. D., Borzée, A., Thapa, S., Rad, D., & Adhikari, S. (2022). Perspectives of scholars on the origin, spread and consequences of COVID-19 are diverse but not polarized. *Humanities & Social Sciences Communications, 9*(1), 198. doi:10.105741599-022-01216-2

Paulus, R., Xiong, C., & Socher, R. (2017). A deep reinforced model for abstractive summarization. In *Proceedings of the 5th International Conference on Learning Representations*. IEEE.

Pavlik, J. (2023). Collaborating With ChatGPT: Considering the Implications of Generative Artificial Intelligence for Journalism and Media Education. *Journalism & Mass Communication Educator, 78*(1), 84–93. doi:10.1177/10776958221149577

Pekrun, R. (2008). The Impact of Emotions on Learning and Achievement: Towards a Theory of Cognitive/Motivational Mediator. *Applied Psychology*, *41*(4), 359–376. doi:10.1111/j.1464-0597.1992.tb00712.x

Perkins, M. (2023). Academic Integrity considerations of AI Large Language Models in the post-pandemic era: ChatGPT and beyond. *Journal of University Teaching & Learning Practice, 20*(2), 07.

Perkins, M. (2023). Academic Integrity considerations of AI Large Language Models in the post-pandemic era: ChatGPT and beyond. *Journal of University Teaching & Learning Practice*, *20*(2). doi:10.53761/1.20.02.07

Perlman, A. M. (2022). The Implications of OpenAI's Assistant for Legal Services and Society (SSRN *Scholarly Paper No. 4294197*). https://papers.ssrn.com/abstract=4294197

Peter, S., Joe, W., & Tom, B. (2023). Utilization of AI-Based Tools like ChatGPTin the Training of Medical Students and Interventional Radiology. *ScienceOpen Posters.* . doi:10.14293/P2199-8442.1.SOP-.PFTABJ.v1

Peters, M. E., Neumann, M., Iyyer, M., Gardner, M., Clark, C., Lee, K., & Zettlemoyer, L. (2018). *Deep contextualized word representations*. arXiv preprint arXiv:1802.05365. doi:10.18653/v1/N18-1202

Peters, M., & Cadieux, A. (2019). Are Canadian professors teaching the skills and knowledge students need to prevent plagiarism? *International Journal for Educational Integrity*, *15*(1), 1–16. doi:10.100740979-019-0047-z

Pettinato Oltz, T. (2023). ChatGPT, Professor of Law. SSRN *Electronic Journal*. doi:10.2139/ssrn.4347630

Picard, R. W. (1997). Affective computing. In *Affective computing*. The MIT Press.

Picard, R. W., Vyzas, E., & Healey, J. (2001). Toward machine emotional intelligence: Analysis of affective physiological state. *IEEE Transactions on Pattern Analysis and Machine Intelligence*, *23*(10), 1175–1191. doi:10.1109/34.954607

Polonsky, M., & Rotman, J. (2023). Should Artificial Intelligent (AI) Agents be Your Co-author? Arguments in favour, informed by ChatGPT. SSRN *Electronic Journal*. doi:10.2139/ssrn.4349524

Premkumar, M., & Sundararajan, T. V. P. (2021). Defense countermeasures for DoS attacks in WSNs using deep radial basis networks. *Wireless Personal Communications*, *120*(4), 2545–2560. doi:10.100711277-021-08545-6

Prentice, F. M., & Kinden, C. E. (2018). Paraphrasing tools, language translation tools and plagiarism: An exploratory study. *International Journal for Educational Integrity*, *14*(1), 1–16. doi:10.100740979-018-0036-7

Pu, P., & Chen, L. (2010). *A User-Centric Evaluation Framework of Recommender Systems*.

Qadeer, A., Wasim, M., Ghazala, H., Rida, A., & Suleman, W. (2023). Emerging trends of green hydrogen and sustainable environment in the case of Australia. *Environmental Science and Pollution Research International*, *30*(54), 115788–115804. Advance online publication. doi:10.100711356-023-30560-2 PMID:37889409

Qadir, J. (2023, May). Engineering education in the era of ChatGPT: Promise and pitfalls of generative AI for education. In *2023 IEEE Global Engineering Education Conference (EDUCON)* (pp. 1-9). IEEE. 10.1109/EDUCON54358.2023.10125121

Qiao, S., Yeung, S. S. S., Zainuddin, Z., Ng, D. T. K., & Chu, S. K. W. (2023). Examining the effects of mixed and non-digital gamification on students' learning performance, cognitive engagement and course satisfaction. *British Journal of Educational Technology*, *54*(1), 394–413. doi:10.1111/bjet.13249

Qin, L., Aziz, G., Hussan, M. W., Qadeer, A., & Sarwar, S. (2023). Empirical evidence of fintech and green environment: Using the green finance as a mediating variable. *International Review of Economics and Finance, 89*(PA), 33–49. doi:10.1016/j.iref.2023.07.056

Qiu, X., Sun, T., Xu, Y., Shao, Y., Dai, N., & Huang, X. (2020). Pre-trained models for natural language processing: A survey. *IEEE, 63*(10), 1872–1897. doi:10.1007/s11431-020-1647-3

Quincozes, S. E., Kazienko, J. F., & Quincozes, V. E. (2023). An extended evaluation of machine learning techniques for Denial-of-Service detection in Wireless Sensor Networks. *Internet of Things : Engineering Cyber Physical Human Systems, 22*, 100684. doi:10.1016/j.iot.2023.100684

Quinio, B., & Bidan, M. (2023). *ChatGPT : Un robot conversationnel peut-il enseigner.* Management & Data Science. doi:10.36863/mds.a.22060

Rad, D., Dixon, D., & Rad, G. (2020b). Digital outing confidence as a mediator in the digital behavior regulation and internet content awareness relationship. Brain. *Broad Research in Artificial Intelligence and Neuroscience, 11*(1), 84–95. doi:10.18662/brain/11.1/16

Rad, D., Egerau, A., Roman, A., Dughi, T., Balas, E., Maier, R., & Rad, G. (2022a). A preliminary investigation of the technology acceptance model (TAM) in early childhood education and care. Brain. *Broad Research in Artificial Intelligence and Neuroscience, 13*(1), 518–533. doi:10.18662/brain/13.1/297

Rad, D., Magulod, G. C. Jr, Balas, E., Roman, A., Egerau, A., Maier, R., & Chis, R. (2022b). A radial basis function neural network approach to predict preschool teachers' technology acceptance behavior. *Frontiers in Psychology, 13*, 880753. doi:10.3389/fpsyg.2022.880753 PMID:35756273

Radford, A., Metz, L., & Chintala, S. (2015). *Unsupervised representation learning with deep convolutional generative adversarial networks.* arXiv preprint arXiv:1511.06434.

Radford, A., Narasimhan, K., Salimans, T., & Sutskever, I. (2018). *Improving language understanding by generative pre-training.* CDN. https://cdn.openai.com/better-language-models/language_models_are_unsupervised_multitask_learners.pdf

Radford, A., Wu, J., Child, R., Luan, D., Amodei, D., & Sutskever, I. (2019). *Language models are unsupervised multitask learners.* Cloud Front. https://d4mucfpksywv.cloudfront.net/better-language-models/language_models_are_unsupervised_multitask_learners.pdf

Radford, A., Wu, J., Child, R., Luan, D., Amodei, D., & Sutskever, I. (2019). *Language Models are Unsupervised Multitask Learners.* OpenA.

Rahali, A., & Akhloufi, M. A. (2023). End-to-End Transformer-Based models in Textual-Based NLP. *AI, 4*(1), 54–110. doi:10.3390/ai4010004

Rahaman, Md. S. (2023). Can ChatGPT be your friend? Emergence of Entrepreneurial Research. SSRN *Electronic Journal.* doi:10.2139/ssrn.4368541

Rahaman, Md. S., Ahsan, M. M. T., Anjum, N., Rahman, Md. M., & Rahman, M. N. (2023). The AI Race is on! Google's Bard and Openai's Chatgpt Head to Head: An Opinion Article. SSRN *Electronic Journal.* doi:10.2139/ssrn.4351785

Rahmani, A. M., Gia, T. N., Negash, B., Anzanpour, A., Azimi, I., Jiang, M., & Liljeberg, P. (2018). Exploiting smart e-Health gateways at the edge of healthcare Internet-of-Things: A fog computing approach. *Future Generation Computer Systems, 78*, 641–658. doi:10.1016/j.future.2017.02.014

Rajasekaran, N., Jagatheesan, S. M., Krithika, S., & Albanchez, J. S. (2023). Development and Testing of Incorporated ASM with MVP Architecture Model for Android Mobile App Development. *FMDB Transactions on Sustainable Computing Systems, 1*(2), 65–76.

Rajasekaran, R., Reddy, A. J., Kamalakannan, J., & Govinda, K. (2023). Building a Content-Based Book Recommendation System. *FMDB Transactions on Sustainable Computer Letters, 1*(2), 103–114.

Rajest, S. S., Singh, B. J., Obaid, A., Regin, R., & Chinnusamy, K. (2023a). Recent developments in machine and human intelligence. *Advances in Computational Intelligence and Robotics*. doi:10.4018/978-1-6684-9189-8

Rajest, S. S., Singh, B., Obaid, A. J., Regin, R., & Chinnusamy, K. (2023b). Advances in artificial and human intelligence in the modern era. *Advances in Computational Intelligence and Robotics*. doi:10.4018/979-8-3693-1301-5

Ramya, K., & Beaulah David, H. (2014). Hybrid Cryptography Algorithms for Enhanced Adaptive Acknowledgment Secure in MANET. *IOSR Journal of Computer Engineering (IOSR-JCE), 16*(1), 32–36.

Ranganathan, M., Rajest, S. S., Rathnasabapathy, M., & Ganesh Kumar, J. (2022). Neuropsychological functions and optimism levels in stroke patients: A cross-sectional study. In *Acceleration of the Biopsychosocial Model in Public Health* (pp. 231–246). IGI Global. doi:10.4018/978-1-6684-6496-0.ch011

Rangineni, S., Bhanushali, A., Marupaka, D., Venkata, S., & Suryadevara, M. (1973). Analysis of Data Engineering Techniques With Data Quality in Multilingual Information Recovery. *International Journal on Computer Science and Engineering, 11*(10), 29–36.

Rangineni, S., Bhanushali, A., Suryadevara, M., Venkata, S., & Peddireddy, K. (2023). A Review on Enhancing Data Quality for Optimal Data Analytics Performance. *International Journal on Computer Science and Engineering, 11*(10), 51–58.

Rashi, A., & Madamala, R. (2022). Minimum relevant features to obtain AI explainable system for predicting breast cancer in WDBC. [IJHS]. *International Journal of Health Sciences*, 1312–1326. doi:10.53730/ijhs.v6nS9.12538

Rasul, T., Nair, S., Kalendra, D., Robin, M., de Oliveira Santini, F., Ladeira, W. J., ... Heathcote, L. (2023). The role of ChatGPT in higher education: Benefits, challenges, and future research directions. *Journal of Applied Learning and Teaching, 6*(1).

Raveendranadh, B., & Tamilselvan, S. (2023). An accurate attack detection framework based on exponential polynomial kernel-centered deep neural networks in the wireless sensor network. *Transactions on Emerging Telecommunications Technologies, 34*(3), 4726. doi:10.1002/ett.4726

Ray, P. P. (2023). ChatGPT: A comprehensive review on background, applications, key challenges, bias, ethics, limitations and future scope. Internet of things and cyber physical system, 3. doi:10.1016/j.iotcps.2023.04.003

Reed, S., Akata, Z., Yan, X., Logeswaran, L., Schiele, B., & Lee, H. (2016). Generative adversarial text to image synthesis. In *Proceedings of the 33rd International Conference on Machine Learning* (Vol. 48, pp. 1060-1069). ACL.

Regalia, J. (2023). ChatGPT and Legal Writing: The Perfect Union? SSRN *Electronic Journal*. doi:10.2139/ssrn.4371460

Regin, R., Khanna, A. A., Krishnan, V., Gupta, M., & Bose, R. S., & Rajest, S. S. (2023). Information design and unifying approach for secured data sharing using attribute-based access control mechanisms. In Recent Developments in Machine and Human Intelligence (pp. 256–276). IGI Global.

Regin, R., Khanna, A. A., Krishnan, V., Gupta, M., & Bose, R. S., & Rajest, S. S. (2023a). Information design and unifying approach for secured data sharing using attribute-based access control mechanisms. In Recent Developments in Machine and Human Intelligence (pp. 256–276). IGI Global.

Regin, R., Khanna, A. A., Krishnan, V., Gupta, M., Bose, R. S., & Rajest, S. S. (2023). Information design and unifying approach for secured data sharing using attribute-based access control mechanisms. In Recent Developments in Machine and Human Intelligence (pp. 256–276). IGI Global.

Regin, R., T, S., George, S. R., Bhattacharya, M., Datta, D., & Priscila, S. S. (2023). Development of predictive model of diabetic using supervised machine learning classification algorithm of ensemble voting. *International Journal of Bioinformatics Research and Applications, 19*(3), 10057044. doi:10.1504/IJBRA.2023.10057044

Restrepo, S. (2019). Emotions, intentionality and practical rationality: A contrast of William James' and Antonio Damasio's theories of emotions. Original in Spanish: Emociones, intencionalidad y racionalidad práctica: Un contraste de las teorías de las emociones de William James y Antonio Damasio. *Ideas y Valores, 68*(170), 13–36. doi:10.15446/ideasyvalores.v68n170.77686

Ribeiro, M. T., Singh, S., & Guestrin, C. (2020). "Why should I trust you?": Explaining the predictions of any classifier. In *Proceedings of the 22nd ACM SIGKDD International Conference on Knowledge Discovery and Data Mining* (pp. 1135-1144). ACL.

Ribeiro, L. F., Santos, C. D., & Cardoso, N. (2020). PlotMachines: Outline-Based plot generation using variational autoencoders. In *Proceedings of the 28th International Conference on Computational Linguistics* (pp. 5325-5336). ACL.

Rios, A., & Kavuluru, R. (2020). Few-shot text classification in biomedical applications with pre-trained language models. *Bioinformatics (Oxford, England), 36*(22), 5567–5573.

Risse, M. (2019). Human Rights and Artificial Intelligence: An Urgently Needed Agenda. *Human Rights Quarterly, 41*(1), 1–16. doi:10.1353/hrq.2019.0000

Rivadeneira, J. E., Silva, J. S., Colomo-Palacios, R., Rodrigues, A., & Boavida, F. (2023). User-centric privacy preserving models for a new era of the Internet of Things. *Journal of Network and Computer Applications, 217*, 103695. doi:10.1016/j.jnca.2023.103695

Roma, G., Xambó, A., Green, O., & Tremblay, P. (2021). A General Framework For Visualization Of Sound Collections In Musical Interfaces. *Applied Sciences (Basel, Switzerland), 24*(11), 11926. doi:10.3390/app112411926

Rozado, D. (2023). The Political Biases of ChatGPT. *Social Sciences (Basel, Switzerland), 12*(3), 148. doi:10.3390ocsci12030148

Ruby, M. (2023, May 7). How ChatGPT Works: The Model Behind The Bot - Towards Data Science. *Medium.* https://towardsdatascience.com/how-chatgpt-works-the-models-behind-the-bot-1ce5fca96286

Rudolph, J., Tan, S., & Tan, S. (2023). ChatGPT: Bullshit spewer or the end of traditional assessments in higher education? *Journal of Applied Learning and Teaching, 6*(1).

Rumelhart, D. E., Hinton, G. E., & Williams, R. J. (1986). Learning representations by back-propagating errors. *Nature, 323*(6088), 533–536. doi:10.1038/323533a0

Russakovsky, O., Deng, J., Su, H., Krause, J., Satheesh, S., Ma, S., & Berg, A. C. (2015). ImageNet large-scale visual recognition challenge. *International Journal of Computer Vision, 115*(3), 211–252. doi:10.100711263-015-0816-y

Sabarun. (2019). Needs analysis on developing EFL paragraph writing materials at Kalimantan L2 learners. *Canadian Center of Science and Education, 12*(1). https://doi.org/ doi:10.5539/elt.v12n1p186

Sadat, N., Aziz, M. A., Mohammed, N., Pakhomov, S., Liu, H., & Jiang, X. (2019). A privacy-preserving distributed filtering framework for NLP artifacts. *BMC Medical Informatics and Decision Making, 19*(1), 183. doi:10.118612911-019-0867-z PMID:31493797

Sager, N., Lyman, M. S., Nhan, N. T., & Lj, T. (1995). Medical Language Processing: applications to patient data representation and automatic encoding. *Methods of Information in Medicine, 34*(01/02), 140–146. doi:10.1055/s-0038-1634579

Sajini, S., Reddi, L. T., Regin, R., & Rajest, S. S. (2023). A Comparative Analysis of Routing Protocols for Efficient Data Transmission in Vehicular Ad Hoc Networks (VANETs). *FMDB Transactions on Sustainable Computing Systems, 1*(1), 1–10.

Sakirin, T., & Ben Said, R. (2023). *User preferences for ChatGPT-powered conversational interfaces versus traditional methods.* Mesopotamian Journal of Computer Science., doi:10.58496/MJCSC/2023/006

Saleh, Z. (2019). Artificial Intelligence Definition, Ethics and Standards. *Journal of Artificial Intelligence.*

Salem, A. M., Eraqi, H., & Eldib, M. (2019). GuideDogNet: A Deep Learning Model for Guiding the Blind in Walking Environments. *IEEE Access : Practical Innovations, Open Solutions, 7,* 116198–116208.

Sallam, M. (2023). The utility of ChatGPT as an example of large language models in healthcare education, research, and practice: Systematic review on the future perspectives and potential limitations. medRxiv, 2023-02.

Sallam, M., Salim, N., Barakat, M., & Al-Tammemi, A. (2023). ChatGPT applications in medical, dental, pharmacy, and public health education: A descriptive study highlighting the advantages and limitations. *Narra J, 3*(1), e103–e103. doi:10.52225/narra.v3i1.103

Salvagno, F.S. Taccone, A.G. Gerli. (2023). Can artificial intelligence help for scientific writing? *Critical Care, 27*(1), 1–5. PMID:36597110

Sartorius, N., Üstün, T., Lecrubier, Y., & Wittchen, H. (2018). Depression Comorbid with Anxiety: Results from the WHO Study on Psychological Disorders in Primary Health Care. *The British Journal of Psychiatry, 168*(30), 38–43. doi:10.1192/S0007125000298395 PMID:8864147

Sarwar, S., Aziz, G., & Kumar Tiwari, A. (2023). Implication of machine learning techniques to forecast the electricity price and carbon emission: Evidence from a hot region. *Geoscience Frontiers, xxxx,* 101647. doi:10.1016/j.gsf.2023.101647

Satyanarayanan, M. (2017). The emergence of edge computing. *Computer, 50*(1), 30–39. doi:10.1109/MC.2017.9

Saxena, D., & Chaudhary, S. (2023). Predicting Brain Diseases from FMRI-Functional Magnetic Resonance Imaging with Machine Learning Techniques for Early Diagnosis and Treatment. *FMDB Transactions on Sustainable Computer Letters, 1*(1), 33–48.

Saxena, D., Khandare, S., & Chaudhary, S. (2023). An Overview of ChatGPT: Impact on Academic Learning. *FMDB Transactions on Sustainable Techno Learning, 1*(1), 11–20.

Schreyer Institute for Teaching Excellence. (n.d.). *Writing Rubric Example.* Schreyer. http://www.schreyerinstitute.psu.edu/pdf/suanne_general_resource_WritingRubric.pdf

Sebastian, G. (2023). Do Chatgpt and Other Ai Chatbots Pose A Cybersecurity Risk? *International Journal of Security and Privacy in Pervasive Computing, 1*(15), 1–11. doi:10.4018/IJSPPC.320225

Sedaghat, S. (2023). Early Applications Of Chatgpt In Medical Practice, Education and Research. *Clinical Medicine (London, England), 3*(23), 278–279. doi:10.7861/clinmed.2023-0078 PMID:37085182

Sena, M., Gebauer, J., & Rad, A. A. (2011). Make or Buy: A Comparative Assessment of Organizations that Develop Software Internally Versus those that Purchase Software Password Security Risk versus Effort. *JISAR.* www.aitp-edsig.org/www.jisar.org

Shafik, W. (2024). Wearable Medical Electronics in Artificial Intelligence of Medical Things. Handbook of Security and Privacy of AI-Enabled Healthcare Systems and Internet of Medical Things, 21-40. https://doi.org/doi:10.1201/9781003370321-2

Shafik, W. (2023). A Comprehensive Cybersecurity Framework for Present and Future Global Information Technology Organizations. In *Effective Cybersecurity Operations for Enterprise-Wide Systems* (pp. 56–79). IGI Global. doi:10.4018/978-1-6684-9018-1.ch002

Shah, C. (2023). The Rise of AI Chat Agents and the Discourse with Dilettantes. SSRN *Electronic Journal*. doi:10.2139/ssrn.4327315

Shah, K., Salunke, A., Dongare, S., & Antala, K. (n.d.). *Recommender Systems: An overview of different approaches to recommendations.*

Shaheen, H. (2018). Modelling and Analytical Proofing of Low Energy Temperature Control using Earth/Ground Water Heat Exchanger. *International Journal of Pure and Applied Mathematics*, *119*(16), 3575–3588.

Shahriar, S., & Hayawi, K. (2023). *Let's have a chat! A Conversation with ChatGPT: Technology, Applications, and Limitations.* arXiv preprint arXiv:2302.13817.

Shahsavar, Y., & Choudhury, A. (2023). User Intentions to Use ChatGPT for Self-Diagnosis and Health-Related Purposes: Cross-sectional Survey Study. *JMIR Human Factors*, *10*, e47564. doi:10.2196/47564 PMID:37195756

Shaji George, A., Hovan George, A., & Martin, Asg. (2023). A Review of ChatGPT AI's Impact on Several Business Sectors. *Partners Universal International Innovation Journal*, *1*(1).

Shaji George, A., & Hovan George, A. S. (2023). A Review of ChatGPT AI's Impact on Several Business Sectors. *Partners Universal International Innovation Journal*, *1*(1), 9–23.

Shani, G., & Gunawardana, A. (2011). Evaluating Recommendation Systems. In *Recommender Systems Handbook* (pp. 257–297). Springer US. doi:10.1007/978-0-387-85820-3_8

Sharafaldin, I., Lashkari, A. H., Hakak, S., & Ghorbani, A. A. (2019). Developing realistic distributed denial of service (DDoS) attack dataset and taxonomy. *2019 International Carnahan Conference on Security Technology (ICCST)*. IEEE. 10.1109/CCST.2019.8888419

Sharma, & Kumar, P. (2015). Common fixed point theorem in intuitionistic fuzzy metric space using the property (CLRg). *Bangmod Int. J. Math. & Comp. Sci, 1*(1), 83–95.

Sharma, D. K., Jalil, N. A., Regin, R., Rajest, S. S., Tummala, R. K., & Thangadurai. (2021a). Predicting network congestion with machine learning. *2021 2nd International Conference on Smart Electronics and Communication (ICOSEC)*. IEEE.

Sharma, D. K., Jalil, N. A., Regin, R., Rajest, S. S., Tummala, R. K., & Thangadurai. (2021a). Predicting network congestion with machine learning. In *2021 2nd International Conference on Smart Electronics and Communication (ICOSEC)*. IEEE.

Sharma, D. K., Singh, B., Raja, M., Regin, R., & Rajest, S. S. (2021b). An Efficient Python Approach for Simulation of Poisson Distribution. *2021 7th International Conference on Advanced Computing and Communication Systems (ICACCS)*. IEEE.

Sharma, D. K., Singh, B., Raja, M., Regin, R., & Rajest, S. S. (2021b). An Efficient Python Approach for Simulation of Poisson Distribution. In *2021 7th International Conference on Advanced Computing and Communication Systems (ICACCS)*. IEEE.

Sharma, D. K., Singh, B., Regin, R., Steffi, R., & Chakravarthi, M. K. (2021c). Efficient Classification for Neural Machines Interpretations based on Mathematical models. *2021 7th International Conference on Advanced Computing and Communication Systems (ICACCS)*. IEEE.

Sharma, D. K., Singh, B., Regin, R., Steffi, R., & Chakravarthi, M. K. (2021c). Efficient Classification for Neural Machines Interpretations based on Mathematical models. In *2021 7th International Conference on Advanced Computing and Communication Systems (ICACCS)*. IEEE.

Sharma, K., Singh, B., Herman, E., Regine, R., Rajest, S. S., & Mishra, V. P. (2021d). Maximum information measure policies in reinforcement learning with deep energy-based model. *2021 International Conference on Computational Intelligence and Knowledge Economy (ICCIKE)*. IEEE. 10.1109/ICCIKE51210.2021.9410756

Sharma, Kumar, P., & Sharma, S. (2023). Results on Complex-Valued Complete Fuzzy Metric Spaces. *London Journal of Research in Science: Natural and Formal, 23*(2), 57–64.

Sharma, P. K., Choudhary, S., & Wadhwa, K. (2012). Common fixed points for weak compatible maps in fuzzy metric spaces. *International Journal of Applied Mathematical Research, 1*(2). doi:10.14419/ijamr.v1i2.61

Shashank, A. (2023). Graph Networks: Transforming Provider Affiliations for Enhanced Healthcare Management. *International Journal of Computer Trends and Technology, 71*(6), 86–90.

Shashank, A., & Sharma, S. (2023). Sachin Parate "Exploring the Untapped Potential of Synthetic data: A Comprehensive Review. *International Journal of Computer Trends and Technology, 71*(6), 86–90.

Shen, Y., Heacock, L., Elias, J., Hentel, K., Reig, B., Shih, G., & Moy, L. (2023). ChatGPT and other large language models are double-edged swords. *Radiology, 307*(2), e230163. doi:10.1148/radiol.230163 PMID:36700838

Shen, Y., He, X., Gao, J., Deng, L., & Mesnil, G. (2017). StyleNet: Generating attractive visual captions with styles. In *Proceedings of the 26th International Joint Conference on Artificial Intelligence* (pp. 1674-1680). ACL.

Shidiq, M. (2023). *The Use Of Artificial Intelligence-Based Chat- Gpt And Its Challenges For The World Of Education; From The Viewpoint Of The Development Of Creative Writing Skills. 01*(01), 353–357.

Shidiq, M. (2023, May). The use of artificial intelligence-based chat-gpt and its challenges for the world of education; from the viewpoint of the development of creative writing skills. In *Proceeding of International Conference on Education, Society and Humanity* (Vol. 1, No. 1, pp. 353-357).

Shifat, A. S. M. Z., Stricklin, I., Chityala, R. K., Aryal, A., Esteves, G., Siddiqui, A., & Busani, T. (2023). Vertical etching of scandium aluminum nitride thin films using TMAH solution. *Nanomaterials (Basel, Switzerland), 13*(2), 274. doi:10.3390/nano13020274 PMID:36678027

Shi, J., Zhu, H., Li, Y., Li, Y., & Du, S. (2022). Scene classification using deep networks combined with visual attention. *Journal of Sensors, 2022*, 1–9. doi:10.1155/2022/7191537

Shruthi, S., & Aravind, B. R. (2023). Engaging ESL Learning on Mastering Present Tense with Nearpod and Learningapps.org for Engineering Students. *FMDB Transactions on Sustainable Techno Learning, 1*(1), 21–31.

ShueE.LiuL.LiB.FengZ.LiX.HuG. (2023). Empowering Beginners in Bioinformatics with ChatGPT. BioRxiv.

Silva, P., Goncalves, C. S., Godinho, C., Antunes, N., & Curado, M. (2020). Using NLP and Machine Learning to Detect Data Privacy Violations. *IEEE INFOCOM 2020 - IEEE Conference on Computer Communications Workshops (INFOCOM WKSHPS)*. IEEE. 10.1109/INFOCOMWKSHPS50562.2020.9162683

Silva, P., Gonçalves, C., Antunes, N., Curado, M., & Walek, B. (2022). Privacy risk assessment and privacy-preserving data monitoring. *Expert Systems with Applications, 200*, 116867. doi:10.1016/j.eswa.2022.116867

Silver, N., Kaplan, M., LaVaque-Manty, D., & Meizlish, D. (Eds.). (2023). *Using reflection and metacognition to improve student learning: Across the disciplines, across the academy.* Taylor & Francis.

Simonyan, K., & Zisserman, A. (2015). Very deep convolutional networks for large-scale image recognition. In *Proceedings of the 3rd International Conference on Learning Representations (ICLR)* (pp. 1-14). Academic Press.

Singh, A., & Diefes-Dux, H. A. (2023, June). Pairing self-evaluation activities with self-reflection to engage students deeply in multiple metacognition strategies. *2023 ASEE Annual Conference & Exposition.*

Sinha, R. K., Deb Roy, A., Kumar, N., & Mondal, H. (2023). Applicability of ChatGPT in Assisting to Solve Higher Order Problems in Pathology. *Cureus.* doi:10.7759/cureus.35237 PMID:36968864

Sivapriya, G. B. V., Ganesh, U. G., Pradeeshwar, V., Dharshini, M., & Al-Amin, M. (2023). Crime Prediction and Analysis Using Data Mining and Machine Learning: A Simple Approach that Helps Predictive Policing. *FMDB Transactions on Sustainable Computer Letters, 1*(2), 64–75.

Skjuve, M. (2023). Why People Use Chatgpt. SSRN *Electronic Journal.* doi:10.2139/ssrn.4376834

Sohlot, J., Teotia, P., Govinda, K., Rangineni, S., & Paramasivan, P. (2023). A Hybrid Approach on Fertilizer Resource Optimization in Agriculture Using Opposition-Based Harmony Search with Manta Ray Foraging Optimization. *FMDB Transactions on Sustainable Computing Systems, 1*(1), 44–53.

Som, B. (2023). *Role of ChatGPT in the Film Industry: According to ChatGPT.* Qeios. https://www.qeios.com/read/NABVHA

Sonnad, S., Sathe, M., Basha, D. K., Bansal, V., Singh, R., & Singh, D. P. (2022). The integration of connectivity and system integrity approaches using internet of things (IoT) for enhancing network security. *2022 5th International Conference on Contemporary Computing and Informatics (IC3I).* IEEE.

Sqalli, M. T., Aslonov, B., Gafurov, M., & Nurmatov, S. (2023). Humanizing Ai In Medical Training: Ethical Framework For Responsible Design. *Frontiers in Artificial Intelligence, 6,* 1189914. doi:10.3389/frai.2023.1189914 PMID:37261331

Srivastava, D. K., & Roychoudhury, B. (2020). Words are important: A textual content based identity resolution scheme across multiple online social networks. *Knowledge-Based Systems, 195,* 105624. doi:10.1016/j.knosys.2020.105624

Srivastava, D. K., & Roychoudhury, B. (2021). Understanding the Factors that Influence Adoption of Privacy Protection Features in Online Social Networks. *Journal of Global Information Technology Management, 24*(3), 164–182. doi:10.1080/1097198X.2021.1954416

Sudha, I., Mustafa, M. A., Suguna, R., Karupusamy, S., Ammisetty, V., Shavkatovich, S. N., Ramalingam, M., & Kanani, P. (2023). Pulse jamming attack detection using swarm intelligence in wireless sensor networks. *Optik (Stuttgart), 272,* 70251. doi:10.1016/j.ijleo.2022.170251

Sudirjo, F., Diantoro, K., Al-Gasawneh, J. A., Khootimah Azzaakiyyah, H., & Almaududi Ausat, A. M. (2023). Application of ChatGPT in Improving Customer Sentiment Analysis for Businesses. *Jurnal Teknologi Dan Sistem Informasi Bisnis, 5*(3), 283–288. doi:10.47233/jteksis.v5i3.871

Suman, R. S., Moccia, S., Chinnusamy, K., Singh, B., & Regin, R. (Eds.). (2023). Advances in Educational Technologies and Instructional Design. *Handbook of research on learning in language classrooms through ICT-based digital technology.* doi:10.4018/978-1-6684-6682-7

Sun, C., Qiu, X., Xu, Y., Huang, X., & Wang, X. (2019). How to fine-tune BERT for text classification? arXiv preprint arXiv:1905.05583. doi:10.1007/978-3-030-32381-3_16

Sunny, S., & Sanchari, D. (2022). Exploring gender biases in ML and AI academic research through systematic literature review. *Frontiers in Artificial Intelligence, 5,* 976838. doi:10.3389/frai.2022.976838 PMID:36304961

Sun, Y., Wang, X., & Tang, X. (2019). Deep learning-based fashion classification: A comprehensive review. *ACM Transactions on Multimedia Computing Communications and Applications*, *15*(2), 1–23. doi:10.1145/3282833

Suraj, D., Dinesh, S., Balaji, R., Deepika, P., & Ajila, F. (2023). Deciphering Product Review Sentiments Using BERT and TensorFlow. *FMDB Transactions on Sustainable Computing Systems*, *1*(2), 77–88.

Suresh Babu, C. V. (2022). *Artificial Intelligence and Expert Systems*. Anniyappa Publication.

Suresh Babu, C. V., & Padma, R. (2023). Technology Transformation Through Skilled Teachers in Teaching Accountancy. In R. González-Lezcano (Ed.), *Advancing STEM Education and Innovation in a Time of Distance Learning* (pp. 211–233). IGI Global. doi:10.4018/978-1-6684-5053-6.ch011

Suresh Babu, C. V., & Rohan, B. (2023). Evaluation and Quality Assurance for Rapid E-Learning and Development of Digital Learning Resources. In M. I. Santally, (Eds.), *Implementing Rapid E-Learning Through Interactive Materials Development* (pp. 139–170). IGI Global. doi:10.4018/978-1-6684-4940-0.ch008

Suthar, V., Bansal, V., Reddy, C. S., Gonzáles, J. L. A., Singh, D., & Singh, D. P. (2022). Machine Learning Adoption in Blockchain-Based Smart Applications. *2022 5th International Conference on Contemporary Computing and Informatics (IC3I)*. IEEE.

Sutskever, I., Vinyals, O., & Le, Q. V. (2014). Sequence to sequence learning with neural networks. In Advances in neural information processing systems (pp. 3104-3112). ACL.

Szegedy, C., Liu, W., Jia, Y., Sermanet, P., Reed, S., Anguelov, D., & Rabinovich, A. (2015). Going deeper with convolutions. In *Proceedings of the IEEE conference on computer vision and pattern recognition* (pp. 1-9). IEEE.

Talwar, A., Magliano, J. P., Higgs, K., Santuzzi, A., Tonks, S., O'Reilly, T., & Sabatini, J. (2023). Early Academic Success in College: Examining the Contributions of Reading Literacy Skills, Metacognitive Reading Strategies, and Reading Motivation. *Journal of College Reading and Learning*, *53*(1), 58–87. doi:10.1080/10790195.2022.2137069

Taylor, K. (2022). *Know about NLP language Model comprising of scope predictions of IT Industry*. HitechNectar.

Teng, M. F., & Yue, M. (2023). Metacognitive writing strategies, critical thinking skills, and academic writing performance: A structural equation modeling approach. *Metacognition and Learning*, *18*(1), 237–260. doi:10.100711409-022-09328-5

Thammareddi, L., Kuppam, M., Patel, K., Marupaka, D., & Bhanushali, A. (2023). An extensive examination of the devops pipelines and insightful exploration. *International Journal of Computer Engineering and Technology*, *14*(3), 76–90.

Thorat, P. B., Goudar, R. M., & Barve, S. (2015). Survey on Collaborative Filtering, Content-based Filtering and Hybrid Recommendation System. *International Journal of Computer Applications*, *110*(4). doi:10.5120/19308-0760

Thorne, J., Vlachos, A., & Christodoulopoulos, C. (2021). Generating factually correct information from open-domain textual claims. In *Proceedings of the 2021 Conference of the North American Chapter of the Association for Computational Linguistics* (pp. 3450-3463).

Thunström, A. O. (2022, June 30). *We Asked GPT-3 to Write an Academic Paper about Itself—Then We Tried to Get It Published*. Scientific American. https://www.scientificamerican.com/article/we-asked-gpt-3-to-write-an-academic-paper- about-itself-mdash-then-we-tried-to-get-it-published/

Tian, W. M., Sergesketter, A. R., & Hollenbeck, S. T. (2023). The Role Of Chatgpt In Microsurgery: Assessing Content Quality and Potential Applications. *Journal of Reconstructive Microsurgery*, *6509*. doi:10.1055/a-2098-6509 PMID:37225130

Timotheou, S., Miliou, O., Dimitriadis, Y., Sobrino, S. V., Giannoutsou, N., Cachia, R., Monés, A. M., & Ioannou, A. (2023). Impacts of digital technologies on education and factors influencing schools' digital capacity and transformation: A literature review. *Education and Information Technologies*, 28(6), 6695–6726. doi:10.100710639-022-11431-8 PMID:36465416

Toba, R., Noor, W. N., & Sanu, L. O. (2019). The current issues of Indonesian EFL students' writing skills: Ability, problem, and reason in writing comparison and contrast essay. *Dinamika Ilmu*, 19(1), 57–73. doi:10.21093/di.v19i1.1506

Transformer, C., & Zhavoronkov, A. (2022). Rapamycin In the Context Of Pascal's Wager: Generative Pre-trained Transformer Perspective. *Oncoscience*, 9, 82–84. doi:10.18632/oncoscience.571 PMID:36589923

Tripathi, V., & Tiwari, S. (2023). A study of relationship between meta-cognitive skills and academic achievement of mathematics students. *Remittances Review*, 8(4).

Tripathi, S. (2017). Role of Bollywood cinema in promoting tourism, business and intercultural communication in Arab world: A study with Oman. *The International Journal of Social Sciences (Islamabad)*, 3(1), 424–435. doi:10.20319/pijss.2017.s31.424435

Tripathi, S., & Al Shahri, M. (2016). Omani community in digital age: A study of Omani women using back channel media to empower themselves for frontline entrepreneurship. *International Journal of Information and Communication Engineering*, 10(6), 1929–1934.

Tseng, C. C. (2019). Senior high school teachers' beliefs about EFL writing instruction. *Taiwan Journal of TESOL*, 16(1), 1–39. doi:10.30397/TJTESOL.201904_16(1).0001

Tuli, S., Basumatary, N., & Buyya, R. (2019). EdgeLens: Deep learning based object detection in integrated IoT, fog and cloud computing environments. *2019 4th International Conference on Information Systems and Computer Networks (ISCON)*. IEEE.

UbaniS. (2023). A Primer on ChatGPT: Coherence Does Not Imply Correctness. *A Primer on ChatGPT: Coherence Does Not Imply Correctness*, https://doi.org/ doi:10.35542/osf.io/8fmrn

Uike, D., Agarwalla, S., Bansal, V., Chakravarthi, M. K., Singh, R., & Singh, P. (2022). Investigating the role of block chain to secure identity in IoT for industrial automation. *2022 11th International Conference on System Modeling & Advancement in Research Trends (SMART)*. IEEE.

Ulu-Aslan, E., & Baş, B. (2023). Popular culture texts in education: The effect of tales transformed into children's media on critical thinking and media literacy skills. *Thinking Skills and Creativity*, 47, 101202. doi:10.1016/j.tsc.2022.101202

UludagK. (2023). The Use of AI-Supported Chatbot in Psychology. https://ssrn.com/abstract=4331367 doi:10.2139/ssrn.4331367

Urban, M., & Urban, K. (2023). Orientation Toward Intrinsic Motivation Mediates the Relationship Between Metacognition and Creativity. *The Journal of Creative Behavior*, 57(1), 6–16. doi:10.1002/jocb.558

Uthiramoorthy, A., Bhardwaj, A., Singh, J., Pant, K., Tiwari, M., & Gonzáles, J. L. A. (2023). A Comprehensive review on Data Mining Techniques in managing the Medical Data cloud and its security constraints with the maintained of the communication networks. *2023 International Conference on Artificial Intelligence and Smart Communication (AISC)*. IEEE. 10.1109/AISC56616.2023.10085161

Vaishya, R., Misra, A., & Vaish, A. (2023). ChatGPT: Is this version good for healthcare and research? *Diabetes & Metabolic Syndrome*, 17(4), 102744. doi:10.1016/j.dsx.2023.102744 PMID:36989584

Vall, R. R. F. D., & Araya, F. G. (2023). Exploring the Benefits And Challenges Of Ai-language Learning Tools. *International Journal of Social Sciences and Humanities Invention*, *10*(01), 7569–7576. doi:10.18535/ijsshi/v10i01.02

Van Dis, E., Bollen, J., Zuidema, W., Van Rooij, R., & Bockting, C. (2023). ChatGPT: Five priorities for research. *Nature*, *614*(7947), 224–226. doi:10.1038/d41586-023-00288-7 PMID:36737653

Van-Leeuwen, K. G., Meijer, F. J. A., Schalekamp, S., Rutten, M. J. C. M., van Dijk, E. J., van Ginneken, B., Govers, T. M., & de Rooij, M. (2021). Cost-effectiveness of artificial intelligence aided vessel occlusion detection in acute stroke: An early health technology assessment. *Insights Into Imaging*, *12*(1), 133. doi:10.118613244-021-01077-4 PMID:34564764

Vasek, V., Franc, V., & Urban, M. (2020). License plate recognition and super-resolution from - Resolution videos by convolutional neural networks. In *Proc. Brit. Mach. Vis. Conf. (BMVC)*, Newcastle, U.K.

Vaswani, A., Shazeer, N., Parmar, N., Uszkoreit, J., Jones, L., Gomez, A. N., & Polosukhin, I. (2017). Attention is all you need. In Advances in neural information processing systems (pp. 5998-6008).

Vaswani, A., Shazeer, N., Parmar, N., Uszkoreit, J., Jones, L., Gomez, A. N., & Polosukhin, I. (2017). Attention is all you need. *Advances in Neural Information Processing Systems*, 30.

Venkatasubramanian, S., Gomathy, V., & Saleem, M. (2023). Investigating the Relationship Between Student Motivation and Academic Performance. *FMDB Transactions on Sustainable Techno Learning*, *1*(2), 111–124.

Venkatesan, S. (2023). Utilization of Media Skills and Technology Use Among Students and Educators in The State of New York. *NeuroQuantology : An Interdisciplinary Journal of Neuroscience and Quantum Physics*, *21*(5), 111–124.

Venkatesan, S., Bhatnagar, S., Cajo, I. M. H., & Cervantes, X. L. G. (2023b). Efficient Public Key Cryptosystem for wireless Network. *NeuroQuantology : An Interdisciplinary Journal of Neuroscience and Quantum Physics*, *21*(5), 600–606.

Venkatesan, S., Bhatnagar, S., & Luis Tinajero León, J. (2023a). A Recommender System Based on Matrix Factorization Techniques Using Collaborative Filtering Algorithm. *NeuroQuantology : An Interdisciplinary Journal of Neuroscience and Quantum Physics*, *21*(5), 864–872. doi:10.48047/nq.2023.21.5.NQ222079

Venkitaraman, A. K., & Kosuru, V. S. R. (2023). Hybrid deep learning mechanism for charging control and management of Electric Vehicles. *European Journal of Electrical Engineering and Computer Science*, *7*(1), 38–46. doi:10.24018/ejece.2023.7.1.485

Ventayen, R. J. M. (2023). ChatGPT by OpenAI: Students' Viewpoint on Cheating using Artificial Intelligence-Based Application. SSRN *Electronic Journal*. doi:10.2139/ssrn.4361548

Venugopalan, S., Rohrbach, M., Donahue, J., Mooney, R., Darrell, T., & Saenko, K. (2015). Sequence to sequence — video to text. In *Proceedings of the IEEE international conference on computer vision* (pp. 4534-4542). IEEE.

Victorino, L., Karniouchina, E., & Verma, R. (2009). Exploring the use of the abbreviated technology readiness index for hotel customer segmentation. *Cornell Hospitality Quarterly*, *50*(3), 342–359. doi:10.1177/1938965509336809

Vinayagalakshmi, V. (n.d.). *EasyChair Preprint The Role of Social Commerce Attributes and Trust on Purchase Intention in Social Commerce Platforms THE ROLE OF SOCIAL COMMERCE ATTRIBUTES AND TRUST ON PURCHASE INTENTION IN SOCIAL COMMERCE PLATFORMS.*

Vinuesa, R., Azizpour, H., Leite, I., Balaam, M., Dignum, V., Domisch, S., & Nerini, F. F. (2020). The Role Of Artificial Intelligence In Achieving the Sustainable Development Goals. *Nature Communications*, *1*(11), 233. doi:10.103841467-019-14108-y PMID:31932590

Vinyals, O., Toshev, A., Bengio, S., & Erhan, D. (2015). Show and tell: A neural image caption generator. In *Proceedings of the IEEE conference on computer vision and pattern recognition* (pp. 3156-3164). IEEE. 10.1109/CVPR.2015.7298935

Wang, F. Y., Yang.J., Wang.X., Li, J., & Han, Q.L. (2023). Chat with ChatGPT on Industry 5.0: Learning and Decision-Making for Intelligent Industries. *IEEE/CAA Journal of Automatica Sinica, 10(4)*, 831-834. . doi:10.1109/JAS.2023.123552

Wang, X., Liu, K., & Zhao, J. (2017). Handling cold-start problem in review spam detection by jointly embedding texts and behaviours. *ACL 2017 - 55th Annual Meeting of the Association for Computational Linguistics, Proceedings of the Conference (Long Papers)*. ACL. 10.18653/v1/P17-1034

Wang, F., Li, J., Qin, R., Zhu, J., Mo, H., & Hu, B. (2023). ChatGPT for Computational social systems: From conversational applications to Human-Oriented Operating Systems. *IEEE Transactions on Computational Social Systems, 10*(2), 414–425. doi:10.1109/TCSS.2023.3252679

Wang, H., Chen, Q., Huang, J., & Zhang, J. (2021). A hierarchical feature fusion network for fashion landmark detection. *IEEE Transactions on Industrial Informatics, 17*(2), 1327–1336.

Wang, T., Zhang, X., Feng, J., & Yang, X. (2020). A Comprehensive Survey on Local Differential Privacy toward Data Statistics and Analysis. *Sensors (Basel), 20*(24), 7030. doi:10.339020247030 PMID:33302517

Wang, Y., Hu, J., An, Z., Li, C., & Zhao, Y. (2023). The influence of metacognition monitoring on L2 Chinese audiovisual reading comprehension. *Frontiers in Psychology, 14*, 1133003. doi:10.3389/fpsyg.2023.1133003 PMID:36891205

Weinman, J. J., Learned-Miller, E., & Hanson, A. R. (2009). Scene text recognition using similarity and a lexicon with sparse belief propagation. *IEEE Transactions on Pattern Analysis and Machine Intelligence, 31*(10), 1733–1746. doi:10.1109/TPAMI.2009.38 PMID:19696446

WeiY.GuS.LiY.JinL. (2020). Unsupervised real-world image super resolution via domain-distance aware training. doi:10.48550/ARXIV.2004.01178

Wei, Z., Zhang, H., Chen, S., & Yang, Y. (2021). Efficient Multi-Granularity Encoding for Fashion Attribute Prediction. *IEEE Transactions on Industrial Informatics, 17*(3), 1911–1918.

Whyte, C. (2022, May 12). Meta 'Open-Sources' Its Latest Large Language Model. *slator*. https://slator.com/meta-open-sources-its-latest-large-language-model/

Woithe, J., & Filipec, O. (2023). *Understanding the Adoption, Perception, and Learning Impact of ChatGPT in Higher Education: A qualitative exploratory case study analyzing students' perspectives and experiences with the AI-based large language model*. Academic Press.

Wu, Y., Mansimov, E., Liao, S., Grosse, R., & Ba, J. (2018). Structured adversarial training for unsupervised machine translation. In Advances in Neural Information Processing Systems (pp. 8555-8565).

Wu, Y., Schuster, M., Chen, Z., Le, Q. V., Norouzi, M., Macherey, W., & Dean, J. (2016). Google's neural machine translation system: Bridging the gap between human and machine translation. arXiv preprint arXiv:1609.08144.

Wyndham, A. (2022, April 24). The Great Language Model Scale Off: Google's PaLM. *slator*. https://slator.com/the-great-language-model-scale-off-googles-palm/

Xi, Z., Zhendong, M., Chunxiao, L., Peng, Z., Bin, W., & Yong, Z. (2020). Proceedings of the Twenty-Ninth International Joint Conference on Artificial Intelligence. *Overcoming Language Priors with Self-supervised Learning for Visual Question Answering*, (pp. 1083-1089.)10.24963/ijcai.2020/151

Xia, Q., Chiu, T. K., & Chai, C. S. (2023). The moderating effects of gender and need satisfaction on self-regulated learning through Artificial Intelligence (AI). *Education and Information Technologies*, 28(7), 8691–8713. doi:10.100710639-022-11547-x

Xu, Y., Jiang, X., & Li, S. (2018). Spherical knowledge distillation for unsupervised domain adaptation. In Advances in neural information processing systems (pp. 3511-3520). ACL.

Xu, K., Ba, J., Kiros, R., Cho, K., Courville, A., Salakhutdinov, R., & Bengio, Y. (2015). Show, attend and tell: Neural image caption generation with visual attention. In *International Conference on Machine Learning* (pp. 2048-2057). ACL.

Xu, X., Hong, W. C. H., Zhang, Y., Jiang, H., & Liu, J. (2023). Learning Paths Design in Personal Learning Environments: The Impact on Postgraduates' Cognitive Achievements and Satisfaction. *Innovations in Education and Teaching International*, 1–16. doi:10.1080/14703297.2023.2189603

Yadav, A., & Kumar, A. (2022). Intrusion detection and prevention using RNN in WSN. In *Inventive Computation and Information Technologies: Proceedings of ICICIT 2021*. Singapore: Springer Nature Singapore. 10.1007/978-981-16-6723-7_40

Yadav, S., & Kaushik, A. (2022). Do You Ever Get Off Track in a Conversation? The Conversational System's Anatomy and Evaluation Metrics. *Knowledge (Beverly Hills, Calif.)*, 2(1), 55–87. doi:10.3390/knowledge2010004

Yan, D. (2023). Impact of ChatGPT on learners in a L2 writing practicum: An exploratory investigation. *Education and Information Technologies*, 28(11), 1–25. doi:10.100710639-023-11742-4

Yang, Z. (2023). Inside the ChatGPT race in China. *MIT Technology Jounrnel, 1*.

Yang, Z., Dai, Z., Yang, Y., Carbonell, J., Salakhutdinov, R., & Le, Q. V. (2019). *XLNet: Generalized autoregressive pretraining for language understanding*. arXiv preprint arXiv:1906.08237.

Yang, Y., Li, H., Li, Y., & Zhang, Y. (2015). A large-scale car dataset for fine-grained categorization and verification. In *Proceedings of the IEEE Conference on Computer Vision and Pattern Recognition (CVPR)* (pp. 3973-3981). 10.1109/CVPR.2015.7299023

Yan, L. (2019). Impact of Artificial Intelligence on Creative Digital Content Production. *Journal of Digital Art Engineering & Multimedia*, 6(2), 121–132. doi:10.29056/jdaem.2019.12.05

Yao, L., Mao, C., & Luo, Y. (2019). Plan-and-write: Towards better automatic storytelling. In *Proceedings of the 57th Annual Meeting of the Association for Computational Linguistics* (pp. 3585-3596). ACL.

Yao, L., Wan, X., & Xiao, J. (2019). Plan-and-write: Towards better automatic storytelling. In *Proceedings of the 2019 Conference on Empirical Methods in Natural Language Processing and the 9th International Joint Conference on Natural Language Processing* (pp. 5994-6003). ACL.

Yi, C., Jiang, Z., Li, X., & Lu, X. (2019). Leveraging user-generated content for product promotion: The effects of firm-highlighted reviews. *Information Systems Research*, 30(3), 711–725. doi:10.1287/isre.2018.0807

Yi, J. H., Kang, W., Kim, S.-E., Park, D., & Hong, J.-H. (2021). Smart culture lens: An application that analyzes the visual elements of ceramics. *IEEE Access : Practical Innovations, Open Solutions*, 9, 42868–42883. doi:10.1109/AC-CESS.2021.3065407

Yildirim-Erbasli, S. N., & Bulut, O. (2023). Conversation-based assessment: A novel approach to boosting test-taking effort in digital formative assessment. *Computers and Education: Artificial Intelligence*, 4, 100135. doi:10.1016/j.caeai.2023.100135

Yin, Y., & Habernal, I. (2022). *Privacy-Preserving models for legal natural language processing.* arXiv (Cornell University). https://doi.org//arxiv.2211.02956 doi:10.18653/v1/2022.nllp-1.14

Yoo, K.-H., & Gretzel, U. (2011). Creating More Credible and Persuasive Recommender Systems: The Influence of Source Characteristics on Recommender System Evaluations. In Recommender Systems Handbook (pp. 455–477). Springer US. doi:10.1007/978-0-387-85820-3_14

Yu, L., Zhang, W., Wang, J., & Yu, Y. (2018). Reinforced adversarial neural dialogue generation. In *Proceedings of the 56th Annual Meeting of the Association for Computational Linguistics* (Volume 1: Long Papers) (pp. 1777-1786). ACL.

Yuan, S., Tang, S., Ren, Y., Ma, L., & Chen, E. (2021). Reinforcement learning for text-based interactive storytelling with human-in-the-loop. In *Proceedings of the 44th International ACM SIGIR Conference on Research and Development in Information Retrieval* (pp. 463-472). ACM.

Yu, D., Kang, J., & Dong, J. (2021). Service attack improvement in wireless sensor network based on machine learning. *Microprocessors and Microsystems*, *80*, 103637. doi:10.1016/j.micpro.2020.103637

Yu, L., Zhang, W., Wang, J., & Yu, Y. (2017). SeqGAN: Sequence generative adversarial nets with policy gradient. In *Proceedings of the thirty-first AAAI conference on artificial intelligence* (pp. 2852-2858). AAAI. 10.1609/aaai.v31i1.10804

Yupan, H., Hongwei, X., Bei, L., & Yutong, L. (2021). Proceedings of the 29th ACM International Conference on Multimedia. *ACM International Multimedia Conference* (p. NA). Virtual Event China: Machinery.

Yusuf, S. (2023). *ChatGPT, the Blade in Scientific Writing.* Indonesian Contemporary Nursing Journal.

Yu, T., Wu, X., & Gong, Y. (2017). Dual learning for fine-grained image classification. In *Proceedings of the IEEE Conference on Computer Vision and Pattern Recognition* (pp. 4641-4650). IEEE.

Yuvaraj, D., Priya, S. S., Braveen, M., Krishnan, S. N., Nachiyappan, S., Mehbodniya, A., Ahamed, A., & Sivaram, M. (2022). Novel DoS Attack Detection Based on Trust Mode Authentication for IoT. *Intelligent Automation & Soft Computing*, *34*(3), 1505–1522. doi:10.32604/iasc.2022.022151

Zabolotna, K., Malmberg, J., & Järvenoja, H. (2023). Examining the interplay of knowledge construction and group-level regulation in a computer-supported collaborative learning physics task. *Computers in Human Behavior*, *138*, 107494. doi:10.1016/j.chb.2022.107494

Zafar, M. B., Valera, I., Gomez-Rodriguez, M., & Gummadi, K. P. (2017). Fairness constraints: Mechanisms for fair classification. In *Proceedings of the 26th International Conference on World Wide Web* (pp. 645-654). ACL.

Zajko, M. (2021). Conservative AI and social inequality: Conceptualizing alternatives to bias through social theory. *AI & Society*, *36*(3), 1047–1056. doi:10.100700146-021-01153-9

ZhaiX. (2022). ChatGPT user experience: Implications for education. Available at SSRN 4312418.

ZhaiX. (2023). ChatGPT for next generation Science Learning. *Social Science Research Network*. doi:10.2139/ssrn.4331313

Zhang, S. (2019). Research On Copyright Protection Of Ai Creation. *Proceedings of the 1st International Symposium on Innovation and Education, Law and Social Sciences (IELSS 2019)* (pp. 510-514.). Atilantis. 10.2991/ielss-19.2019.94

Zhang, W., & Tornero, J.M.P. (2021). Introduction To Ai Journalism: Framework and Ontology Of The Trans-domain Field For Integrating Ai Into Journalism. *Journal of Applied Journalism &Amp; Media Studies*. . doi:10.1386/ajms_00063_1

Zhang, X., Zhao, J., & LeCun, Y. (2014). Character-level convolutional networks for text classification. In Advances in neural information processing systems.

Zhang, Y., Yan, R., Li, Z., Li, M., Zhang, Z., & Li, X. (2021). Pre-trained language models for financial text generation. arXiv preprint arXiv:2107.08717.

Zhang, H., Ganchev, I., Nikolov, N. S., Ji, Z., & O'Droma, M. (2017). Weighted matrix factorization with Bayesian personalized ranking. *2017 Computing Conference*. IEEE. 10.1109/SAI.2017.8252119

Zhang, J., Oh, Y. J., Lange, P., Yu, Z., & Fukuoka, Y. (2020). Artificial Intelligence Chatbot Behavior Change Model For Designing Artificial Intelligence Chatbots To Promote Physical Activity and A Healthy Diet. *Journal of Medical Internet Research*, 9(22), e22845. doi:10.2196/22845 PMID:32996892

Zhang, K., Qiu, J., & Luo, S. (2020). Smart Glass System Using Deep Learning for the Blind and Visually Impaired. *IEEE Access : Practical Innovations, Open Solutions*, 8, 52437–52446.

Zhang, L., Cui, Y., Dai, Z., Cao, Y., Chen, W., & Yu, Y. (2020). Semantically enhanced financial news generation with generative adversarial networks. In *Proceedings of the 43rd International ACM SIGIR Conference on Research and Development in Information Retrieval* (pp. 317-326). ACM.

Zhang, L., Wang, X., Liu, Y., & Qiao, Y. (2016). Towards exploring regularization in fine-grained image classification. In *Proceedings of the IEEE Conference on Computer Vision and Pattern Recognition* (pp. 1540-1548). IEEE.

Zhang, Q. (2020). Transformer Transducer: A Streamable Speech Recognition Model with Transformer Encoders and RNN-T Loss, *IEEE International Conference on Acoustics, Speech and Signal Processing* (pp. 7829-7833, .). Barcelona, Spain: Institute of Electrical and Electronics Engineers.10.1109/ICASSP40776.2020.9053896

Zhang, X., Shah, J., & Han, M. (2023). ChatGPT for Fast Learning of Positive Energy District (PED): A Trial Testing and Comparison with Expert Discussion Results. *Buildings*, 13(6), 1392. doi:10.3390/buildings13061392

Zhang, Y., Yang, Z., Zhang, S., & Salakhutdinov, R. (2019). Personalizing dialogue agents via meta-learning. In *Proceedings of the 36th International Conference on Machine Learning* (pp. 7474-7483). ACL.

Zhao, J., Zhang, Y., Saleh, M., & Liu, P. (2018). Generating high-quality and informative conversation responses with sequence-to-sequence models. In *Proceedings of the 56th Annual Meeting of the Association for Computational Linguistics* (Volume 1: Long Papers) (pp. 2210-2219). ACL.

Zhao, J., Wang, T., Yatskar, M., Ordonez, V., & Chang, K. W. (2018). Gender bias in coreference resolution: Evaluation and debiasing methods. In *Proceedings of the 2018 Conference on Empirical Methods in Natural Language Processing* (pp. 545-557). ACL. 10.18653/v1/N18-2003

Zhao, Y., & Lai, C. (2023). Technology and second language learning: Promises and problems. In *Technology-mediated learning environments for young English learners* (pp. 167–206). Routledge. doi:10.4324/9781003418009-8

Zheng, L., Niu, J., Zhong, L., & Gyasi, J. F. (2023). Knowledge-building and metacognition matter: Detecting differences between high-and low-performance groups in computer-supported collaborative learning. *Innovations in Education and Teaching International*, 60(1), 48–58. doi:10.1080/14703297.2021.1988678

Zhou, C., Li, Q., Li, C., Yu, J., Liu, Y., Wang, G., & Sun, L. (2023). A comprehensive survey on pretrained foundation models: A history from bert to chatgpt. arXiv preprint arXiv:2302.09419.

Zhou, Z. (2023). Evaluation of ChatGPT's Capabilities in Medical Report Generation. *Cureus*, 15(4), e37589. doi:10.7759/cureus.37589 PMID:37197105

Zhu, L., Mou, W., & Chen, R. (2023). Can the ChatGPT and other large language models with internet-connected database solve the questions and concerns of patient with prostate cancer and help democratize medical knowledge? *Journal of Translational Medicine*, 21(1), 269. doi:10.118612967-023-04123-5 PMID:37076876

Zhuo, C., Kui, F., Shiqi, W., Ling, Y. D., Weisi, L., & Alex, K. (2019). Lossy Intermediate Deep Learning Feature Compression and Evaluation. *Proceedings of the 27th ACM International Conference on Multimedia* (pp. 2414–2422). ACM. 10.1145/3343031.3350849

Zhu, T., Ye, D., Wang, W., Zhou, W., & Yu, P. S. (2021). More than Privacy: Applying differential privacy in key areas of artificial intelligence. *IEEE Transactions on Knowledge and Data Engineering*, *1*, 1. doi:10.1109/TKDE.2020.3014246

Zhu, Y., Wang, W., Liu, K., & Zhang, Y. (2020). TransNarrative: Narrative generation with self-attention generative adversarial networks. In *Proceedings of the 2020 Conference on Empirical Methods in Natural Language Processing* (pp. 6834-6845). ACL.

Zhu, Y., Zhao, C., Wang, J., Zhao, X., Wu, Y., & Lu, H. (2017). CoupleNet: Coupling global structure with local parts for object detection. *2017 IEEE International Conference on Computer Vision (ICCV)*. IEEE. 10.1109/ICCV.2017.444

Zielinski, C., Winker, M., Aggarwal, R., Ferris, L., Heinemann, M., Lapeña, Jr, J. F., Pai, S., Ing, E., & Citrome, L. (2023). Chatbots, ChatGPT, and Scholarly Manuscripts: WAME Recommendations on ChatGPT and Chatbots in Relation to Scholarly Publications. *Open Access Macedonian Journal of Medical Sciences*, *11*(A). doi:10.3889/oamjms.2023.11502

Zielinski, C., Winker, M., Aggarwal, R., Ferris, L., Heinemann, M., Lapeña, J. F., & Citrome, L. (2023). Chatbots, Chatgpt, and Scholarly Manuscripts Wame Recommendations On Chatgpt And Chatbots In Relation To Scholarly Publications. *Afro-Egyptian Journal of Infectious and Endemic Diseases*, *13*(1), 75–79. doi:10.21608/aeji.2023.282936 PMID:37615142

Zimmerman, B. J. (2023). Dimensions of academic self-regulation: A conceptual framework for education. In *Self-regulation of learning and performance* (pp. 3–21). Routledge.

Zuo, Z., Watson, M., Budgen, D., Hall, R., Kennelly, C., & Moubayed, N. A. (2021). Data Anonymization for Pervasive Health Care: Systematic Literature Mapping Study. *JMIR Medical Informatics*, *9*(10), e29871. doi:10.2196/29871 PMID:34652278

About the Contributors

Ahmed J. Obaid is an Asst. Professor at the Department of Computer Science, Faculty of Computer Science and Mathematics, University of Kufa, Iraq. Dr. Ahmed holds a Bachelor in Computer Science, degree in – Information Systems from College of Computers, University of Anbar, Iraq (2001-2005), and a Master Degree (M. TECH) of Computer Science Engineering (CSE) from School of Information Technology, Jawaharlal Nehru Technological University, Hyderabad, India (2010-2013), and a Doctor of Philosophy (PhD) in Web Mining from College of Information Technology, University of University of Babylon, Iraq (2013-2017). He is a Certified Web Mining Consultant with over 14 years of experience in working as Faculty Member in University of Kufa, Iraq. He has taught courses in Web Designing, Web Scripting, JavaScript, VB.Net, MATLAB Toolbox's, and other courses on PHP, CMC, and DHTML from more than 10 international organizations and institutes from USA, and India. Dr. Ahmed is a member of Statistical and Information Consultation Center (SICC), University of Kufa, Iraq.

Bharat Bhushan is an Assistant Professor of Department of Computer Science and Engineering (CSE) at School of Engineering and Technology, Sharda University, Greater Noida, India. He received his Undergraduate Degree (B-Tech in Computer Science and Engineering) with Distinction in 2012, received his Postgraduate Degree (M-Tech in Information Security) with Distinction in 2015 and Doctorate Degree (PhD Computer Science and Engineering) in 2021 from Birla Institute of Technology, Mesra, India. He has Published more than 80 research papers in various renowned International conferences and SCI indexed journals. He has contributed with more than 25 book chapters in various books and has edited 11 books from the most famed publishers like Elsevier, IGI Global, and CRC Press. He has served as Keynote Speaker (resource person) numerous reputed international conferences held in different countries including India, Morocco, China, Belgium and Bangladesh. In the past, he worked as an assistant professor at HMR Institute of Technology and Management, New Delhi and Network Engineer in HCL Infosystems Ltd., Noida.

S. Suman Rajest is the Dean of Research and Development (R&D) and International Student Affairs (ISA) at Dhaanish Ahmed College of Engineering, Chennai, Tamil Nadu, India. He is an Editor in Chief of the International Journal of Human Computing Studies and The International Journal of Social Sciences World, He is the Chief Executive Editor of the International Journal of Advanced Engineering Research and Science, International Journal of Advanced Engineering, Management and Science, The International Journal of Health and Medicines, The International Journal of Management Economy and Accounting Fields and The International Journal of Technology Information and Computer and also he is an Editorial Board Member in International Journal of Management in Education, Scopus, Inderscience,

EAI Endorsed Transactions on e-Learning, and Bulletin of the Karaganda university Pedagogy series. He is also a Book Series Editor at IGI Global Publisher, Springer, etc. All of his writing, including his research, involves elements of creative nonfiction in the Human Computing learning system. He is also interested in creative writing and digital media, Learning, AI, student health learning, etc. He has published 200 papers in peer-reviewed international journals. He has authored and co-authored several scientific book publications in journals and conferences and is a frequent reviewer of international journals and conferences. He also reviews Inderscience, EAI Journals, IGI Global, Science Publications, etc.

* * *

Ahmad Al Yakin is an assistant professor at Universitas Al Asyariah Mandar in West Sulawesi, Indonesia. He is a lecturer, a national speaker, and a leader in politics. He was the chairman of the civic education department at the teacher training and education faculty, and he was Assistant Dean at her university, to name a few of her accomplishments at her university. He is now vice rector 1. In the current year, he is active as a lecturer, researcher, and national coordinator of Merdeka Belajar Kampus Merdeka. He is also active as a member of the Indonesian Association of Pancasila and the Civic Education.

Eka Apriani is an Editor in Chief in Journal of English Franca and International Journal of Education Research and Development. She is also the secretary of Corolla Education Centre Foundation, Indonesia. She Received her Master Degree (Master of Language Education) from Sriwijaya University in 2013 and Doctor of Education in Bengkulu University 2022. She has published some research in international journal and national journal. She has Scopus Id and WOS Id. She is a member of profession organisation: ADRI, TEFLIN, PDPI and ELITE. She is treasurer of ADRI in Bengkulu Province. Her research interest is in Writing skill and ICT in learning English. She write some books: The beauty of Rejang Lebong, Semantics Crossword, Metode Pengajaran BIPA, Drama Manuscript: The Marriage of Siti Zubaidah. She has also some Intelektual Property Right: Semantics Crossword, The beauty of Rejang Lebong, The Marriage of Siti Zubaidah, Metode Pengajaran BIPA.

C. V. Suresh Babu is a pioneer in content development. A true entrepreneur, he founded Anniyappa Publications, a company that is highly active in publishing books related to Computer Science and Management. Dr. C.V. Suresh Babu has also ventured into SB Institute, a center for knowledge transfer. He holds a Ph.D. in Engineering Education from the National Institute of Technical Teachers Training & Research in Chennai, along with seven master's degrees in various disciplines such as Engineering, Computer Applications, Management, Commerce, Economics, Psychology, Law, and Education. Additionally, he has UGC-NET/SET qualifications in the fields of Computer Science, Management, Commerce, and Education. Currently, Dr. C.V. Suresh Babu is a Professor in the Department of Information Technology at the School of Computing Science, Hindustan Institute of Technology and Science (Hindustan University) in Padur, Chennai, Tamil Nadu, India. For more information, you can visit his personal blog at .

María Lucía Barrón Estrada is a professor at TecNM - Instituto Tecnológico de Culiacán, in Sinaloa México. She earned a PhD in Computer Science from Florida Institute of Technology, and a MSc in Computer Science from Instituto Tecnológico de Toluca. She is member level 3 of the National System of Researchers (SNI) in Mexico, and Honorific member of the Technologists and Researchers System in Sinaloa state (SSIT). Her research interests include intelligent and affective system for education, augmented and virtual reality, and software development. She is a regular contributor to the AI&Education column of the journal Komputer Sapiens. She is a member of the Conacyt REDICA (Applied Computational Intelligence Research Network), the Mexican Society of Computer Science (SMCC) and, the Mexican Society of Artificial Intelligence (SMIA).

Víctor Manuel Bátiz Beltrán was born in Culiacan, Sinaloa, Mexico in 1974. Received the BSc degree in computer science from the Instituto Tecnológico de Culiacán (México) in 1997 and the MSc degree in business administration from the Universidad Tecmilenio (México) in 2007. He also received the MSc degree in computer science from Tecnológico Nacional de México Campus Culiacán (México) in 2021. Currently, he is working toward the Ph degree in engineering science from the Tecnológico Nacional de México Campus Culiacán (México). His research interests include the areas of artificial intelligence, affective computing, intelligent learning environments, natural language processing, and automatic personality recognition.

Chandan Kumar Behera is presently working as a Senior Assistant Professor in the School of Computing Science and Engineering & Assistant Director Student Welfare at VIT Bhopal University. He has 15 international conference presentations and 8 international journal papers of SCOPUS & SCI. He is also the recipient of the young scientist award in 2021 by International Scientist Awards on Engineering, Science and Medicine, India.

Amiya Bhaumik is President of the Faculty of Business and Accounting, Lincoln University.

Mitali Chugh received her Ph.D. (CSE) and M.Tech. (CSE) from UTU, Dehradun. She has 22 years of experience in teaching. Currently, he is working as an AP (SG) at the Cybernetics Cluster at UPES Dehradun. She received the Research Excellence Award for Excellence in Research in 2019. Her areas of interest include Software process improvement, Knowledge management, AI, ML, and DL. She has filed patents and received copyrights. She has been associated with many conferences in India and abroad. She has authored more than 40 research papers to date. She has been associated with many conferences in India as a TPC member, session chair, etc. She is a lifetime member of CSI and a member of IAENG and other renowned technical societies. Dr. Chugh's research contributions encompass publications in multiple international journals and conferences, many of which are indexed in SCI, SCOPUS, and UGC. Her research interests span software process improvement, software quality, knowledge management, and technical debt. She has been PI (India) in a research project INSIGHTD- Investigating the Causes and Effects of Technical Debt along with other researchers from 14 different countries. She has published patents and copyrights for her work.

Lakshmi D. is presently designated as a Senior Associate Professor in the School of Computing Science and Engineering (SCSE) & Assistant Director, at the Centre for Innovation in Teaching & Learning (CITL) at VIT Bhopal. She has 17 international conference presentations, and 21 international journal papers inclusive of SCOPUS & SCI (cumulative impact factor 31). 3 SCOPUS inee book chapters. A total of 24 patents are in various states and 18 patents have been granted at both national and international levels. One Edited book with Taylor & Francis (SCOPUS Indexed). She has won two Best Paper awards at international conferences, one at the IEEE conference and another one at EAMMIS 2021. She received two awards in the year 2022. She received two awards in the year 2022. She has addressed innumerable guest lectures, acted as a session chair, and was invited as a keynote speaker at several international conferences. She has conducted FDPs that cover approximately ~80,000 plus faculty members including JNTU, TEQIP, SERB, SWAYAM, DST, AICTE, MHRD, ATAL, ISTE, Madhya Pradesh Government-sponsored, and self-financed workshops across India on various titles.

Gagan Deep, a highly accomplished academic with a Ph.D. in Management, brings over 15 years of teaching experience to the table. He earned his M.B.A. in Marketing and completed his Ph.D. in Marketing & International Business at Panjab University's University Business School. With a strong background in Marketing and a track record of publications in reputable journals, including Scopus indexed ones, Gagandeep's expertise spans research methodology, marketing research, and strategic management. Holding notable positions at prominent institutions like Chitkara University, Dr. Gagandeep has excelled as both a dedicated educator and a researcher. Additionally, his involvement in faculty development programs, mentoring of students, and contributions to various webinars and conferences underscore his commitment to the academic community.

Ahmed A. Elngar is an Associate Professor and Head of the Computer Science Department at the Faculty of Computers and Artificial Intelligence, Beni-Suef University, Egypt. Dr. Elngar is also, an Associate Professor of Computer Science at the College of Computer Information Technology, American University in the Emirates, United Arab Emirates. Also, Dr. AE is Adjunct Professor at School of Technology, Woxsen University, India. Dr. AE is the Founder and Head of the Scientific Innovation Research Group (SIRG). Dr. AE is a Director of the Technological and Informatics Studies Center (TISC), Faculty of Computers and Artificial Intelligence, Beni-Suef University. Dr. AE has more than 150 scientific research papers published in prestigious international journals and over 35 books covering such diverse topics as data mining, intelligent systems, social networks, and smart environment. Dr. AE is a collaborative researcher He is a member of the Egyptian Mathematical Society (EMS) and International Rough Set Society (IRSS). His other research areas include the Internet of Things (IoT), Network Security, Intrusion Detection, Machine Learning, Data Mining, and Artificial Intelligence. Big Data, Authentication, Cryptology, Healthcare Systems, Automation Systems. He is an Editor and Reviewer of many international journals around the world. Dr. AE won several awards including the Young Researcher in Computer Science Engineering", from Global Outreach Education Summit and Awards 2019, on 31 January 2019 (Thursday) in Delhi, India. Also, he awards the Best Young Researcher Award (Male) (Below 40 years)", Global Education and Corporate Leadership Awards (GECL-2018), Plot No-8, Shivaji Park, Alwar 301001, Rajasthan.

Prodhan Mahbub Ibna Seraj has been working as an Associate Professor at English Language Institute, United International University (UIU). He completed his Ph.D. in Teaching English as a Second Language (TESL) at the Faculty of Education, Universiti Teknologi Malaysia (UTM), and M. A in Applied Linguistics & ELT from the University of Dhaka. He has achieved the BEST POSTGRADUATE STUDENT AWARD (Ph.D. program) at 66th UTM Convocation for his outstanding research work. He is particularly interested in how technology could assist English Language Teaching (ELT). He got published 34 research articles in prestigious national and international peer-reviewed journals, including Scopus and Web of Science indexed, e.g., Heliyon (Elsevier), Journal of Psycholinguistic Research (Springer), Language Testing in Asia (Elsevier), International Journal of Sustainability in Higher Education (Emerald), Sustainability (MDPI), Asian EFL Journal, MEXTESOL Journal (MEXTESOL,

Mexico), International Journal of Interactive Mobile Technologies (Kassel University Press GmbH, Germany), etc. He has reviewed 201 manuscripts of 51 different international journals, mostly indexed in Scopus and Web of Science. He is a member of the editorial board of 14 Scopus and Web of Science indexed journals.

Ifnaldi is a lecturer in Indonesian Language Study Program at IAIN Curup. He has been a lecturer at IAIN Curup since 2000 until now. In addition, he has been a lecturer at STKIP YPM Bangko foundation Jambi Province 1992-1998, extraordinary lecturer at the Padang Hospitality Academy 1996-1998, extraordinary lecturer at STKIP PGRI West Sumatra 1997-1998, extraordinary lecturer at the University of Muhammadiyah Bengkulu 1998-2005, extraordinary lecturer at Persada Nusantara University Jakarta 2008-2010, and extraordinary lecturer at Bina Nusantara University Jakarta 2009-2010. He has many written works.

Rita Inderawati is a lecturer in English Education at both the Undergraduate and Master Program at FKIP Sriwijaya University, Indonesia is interested in teaching literature for character building, academic writing, literacy and developing teaching materials for her research. Presenting her works in various countries from 2010 to 2019 in Hong Kong, India, South Korea, Adelaide, Sydney, Cambodia, Thailand, Malaysia, Singapore, Rome and Florence in Italy, Germany, France, the United States. Three studies that have been carried out are International Collaborative Research with: 1) QUT, in Brisbane, Australia 2015; 2) Deakin University in Melbourne, Australia 2017; 3) Flinders University, Adelaide, in Australia 2018 where she was the Principal Investigator on the team. In 2020, international collaborative research was again carried out with Utah State University, in Logan, United States of America until now. She became a resource person/keynote speaker for development research, writing lecturer proposals for lecturers at Sriwijaya University and other universities in South Sumatra, writing articles for lecturers, academic writing training for students, video maker training for students. She became a keynote speaker at national and international levels (Gorontalo, Madura, Manado, Makassar, Bengkulu, Palembang, India, Bangladesh, Philippines), she was also invited as a speaker for workshops on academic writing, development of teaching materials, and was a research reviewer for Higher Education and Unsri in 2009-2014. Especially for Unsri reviewer since 2019 until now). Several academic journals in Indonesia employ her as a reviewer such as SiELE, EF, ECJ, and IJOLL. Occasionally review articles from journals abroad. She has written 24 books with colleagues and students, namely poetry books, reference books & reading materials such as: Siti Zubaidah Millenial Drama Performance in ELT (2021), Let Me Greet Him "Good Morning": Anthology of Poetry during Covid-19 (2020), Is it You Next to My Door? An anthology of poetry in the Covid-19 outbreak period (2020), Literary Pedagogy in the Latest Literary Theory: Concepts and Applications (2020), Narrative Texts Based on Siti Zubaidah's Lyrics (2019), Spices Literature Books (2021), Now It is the Time to Act on Climate Change (2022), Untold Stories based Narrative Texts (2021), Anthology of Poetry Luka Mannakara (2022), three Palembang local drama script books and eight videos of legendary drama performances from Palembang have been published. Since 2021, she has created virtual English drama performance through the course she teaches, namely Literature in English Language Teaching. A total of 7 drama videos are being prepared to obtain copyright before being released on the Youtube channel. She has 18 Intellectual Property Right from the Ministry of Law and Human Rights. Her achievements include: Best Lecturer at Sriwijaya University 2010; Unsri's Best Education Researcher, 2011; Best Lecturer of Sriwijaya University in 2013, and National Best Researcher through Indonesian Higher Education Competency Research (Dikti), 2013. Positions that have been entrusted to her: Head of Language and Arts Department (2010-2015), Head of Language Masters Study Program (2015-2019). She is now the Head of the Indonesian Language Education Laboratory, Faculty of Teacher Training and Education, Sriwijaya University since 2021.

Hariswan Putera Jaya was born on August 2 1974 at Desa Karang Are Empat Lawang and finished his elementary school there. In 1990 he completed his junior high school in Palembang and went to SMA Negeri 4 Palembang at the same year and graduated in 1993. He took undergraduate program at Universitas Sriwijaya majoring in English education. He could finish his study in 3.7 year and directly employed by Sriwijaya University Language Institute where he spent more than 4 years teaching English to students of various faculties. In 2002 he was accepted as a public servant at the Faculty of Teacher Training and Education Universitas Sriwijaya. Since then he was involved in many academic and non academic activities there. He got his magister degree in English education from Graduate Program Universitas Sriwijaya in 2008. Until now he has written more than 15 manuscripts published at accredited journals in Indonesia. His main interests are teaching and developing language skills such as listening and speaking.

Isha Kondurkar is currently a final year Bachelor of Technology (BTech) student of Computer Science Engineering specializing in Artificial Intelligence and Machine Learning (AIML) at Vellore Institute of Technology, Bhopal. She is enthusiastic about coding and conducting research in the fields of NLP and ML.

Abdul Latief is a lecturer in Al Asyariah Mandar University.

Mimansa Pathania is currently pursuing B.Tech. in Artificial Intelligence and Machine Learning at University of Petroleum and Energy Studies (UPES), Dehradun, she's delving into the fascinating world of social commerce recommendation systems. As a first-time author, Mimansa is thrilled to share her knowledge and contribute to the academic community, paving the way for more insightful discussions and innovations in social commerce recommendation systems.

MohanKumar R. is an assistant professor in the Department of computer science and Business Systems at Saranathan College of Engineering. His interest include data analytics, data mining and network security.

Venkatasubramanian S. received a B.E. degree in Electronics and Communication from Bharathidasan University and M.E. degree in Computer science from Regional Engineering College, Trichy. He has 24 years of teaching experience. He is currently pursuing doctoral research in mobile Ad hoc networks. His areas of interest include mobile networks, Network Security, and Software Engineering. He has published several papers in international journals, and international conferences filed four patents and authored 5 textbooks. At present, he is working as Associate Professor in the Department of Computer Science and Business Systems at Saranathan College of Engineering, Trichy, India. He has also received the Dr. Sarvepalli Radhakrishnan Lifetime achievement National award, Academic Excellence Award 2022, and Global teachers Award.

Kurnia Saputri is a lecturer in English Education at Muhammadiyah University in Palembang, Indonesia. She completed her undergraduate education at Sriwijaya University in 2008 and her master's education at PGRI University Palembang in 2012.

Wasswa Shafik is IEEE member, P.Eng received a bachelor of science in Information Technology Engineering with a minor in Mathematics in 2016 from Ndejje University, Kampala, Uganda, a master of engineering in Information Technology Engineering (MIT) in 2020, from the Computer Engineering Department, Yazd University, Islamic Republic of Iran. He is an associate researcher at the Computer Science department, Network interconnectivity Lab at Yazd University, Islamic Republic of Iran, and at Information Sciences, Prince Sultan University, Saudi Arabia. His areas of interest are Computer Vision, Anomaly Detection, Drones (UAVs), Machine/Deep Learning, AI-enabled IoT/IoMTs, IoT/IIoT/OT Security, Cyber Security and Privacy. Shafik is the chair/co-chair/program chair of some Scopus/EI conferences. Also, academic editor/ associate editor for set of indexed journals (Scopus journals' quartile ranking). He is the founder and lead investigator of Dig Connectivity Research Laboratory (DCR-Lab) since 2019, the Managing Executive director of Asmaah Charity Organisation (ACO).

Aanchal Taliwal is an Author affiliated with the University of Petroleum and Energy Studies (UPES) in Dehradun, Uttarakhand, India. She is a dedicated researcher and scholar, committed to advancing knowledge in her field. Aanchal's academic journey includes a focus on energy and petroleum studies, and she has made valuable contributions through her research at UPES. With a deep passion for her work, she continually explores the complexities of the energy sector, making her a valuable asset to the academic community. You can contact Aanchal at tailwalaanchal@gmail.com for inquiries or collaborations in her area of expertise.

Jyoti Verma is an Associate Professor at Chitkara Business School, Chitkara University, Punjab. She has obtained a doctorate degree from Punjabi University, Patiala, and has qualified UGC NET in Management. She has versatile teaching and research experience with publications in national and international journals. She has prepared and delivered many E-Content programmes on research methodology, which is comprised of video lectures, interactive script, learning objects repository, and textual content for the web learning platform of UGC-CEC (MHRD projects). She is an Associate Editor in Journal of Technology Management for Growing Economies, Chitkara University Publications.

Idi Warsah is a Professor in Islamic educational psychology who has been teaching various subjects related to Islamic, psychological, and social sciences since 2005 at Institut Agama Islam Negeri (IAIN) Curup. He received his doctoral degree from Universitas Muhammadiyah Yogyakarta and officially received his professor from IAIN Curup. Today, he also serves as the Rector of IAIN Curup. In the field of research, he has been actively working on and publishing books, research reports, and journal articles in various fields. His research interests cover some areas including Islamic education, Islamic educational psychology, educational technology, multicultural education, Islamic studies, and social science interconnected with education.

Erfin Wijayanti is a lecturer in Tadris English at Institut Agama Islam Negeri Fattahul Muluk Papua, Indonesia. She completed her bachelor's degree at Universitas Cenderawasih in 2013 and master's degree at Universitas Cenderawasih in 2016.

Ramón Zatarain Cabada is a professor in the graduate department of TecNM - Instituto Tecnológico de Culiacán since 1984. He received the M.Sc and Ph.D degrees in Computer Science from Florida Institute of Technology, and the BSc. from Instituto Tecnológico de Culiacán. He leads the academic group and lab of affective computing, and he is the author of more than 80 articles, and 6 software copyright. His research interests include affective computing, artificial intelligence, learning environments and extended reality. Dr. Zatarain is member level 1 of the National System of Researchers (Conacyt, Mexico), and he received the Sinaloa Award for Science and Technology in 2017. He annually organizes the international workshop on intelligent learning environments (WILE). He is a member of the Conacyt REDICA (Applied Computational Intelligence Research Network).

Index

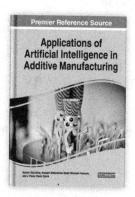
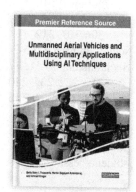

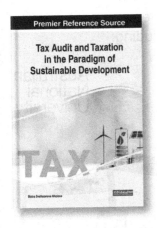

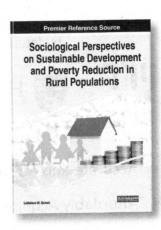

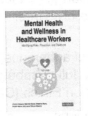